Inhabitants of Harford County Maryland

1791–1800

Henry C. Peden, Jr.

HERITAGE BOOKS
2012

HERITAGE BOOKS
AN IMPRINT OF HERITAGE BOOKS, INC.

Books, CDs, and more—Worldwide

For our listing of thousands of titles see our website
at
www.HeritageBooks.com

Published 2012 by
HERITAGE BOOKS, INC.
Publishing Division
100 Railroad Ave. #104
Westminster, Maryland 21157

Copyright © 1999 Henry C. Peden, Jr.

All rights reserved. No part of this book may be reproduced or transmitted in any form or by any means, electronic or mechanical, including photocopying, recording or by any information storage and retrieval system without written permission from the author, except for the inclusion of brief quotations in a review.

International Standard Book Numbers
Paperbound: 978-1-58549-067-7
Clothbound: 978-0-7884-8998-3

FOREWORD

In 1993 I compiled and published a voluminous book that contained over 30,000 entries about people living in Harford County between 1773 and 1790. In 1999 the original *Early Harford Countians* was reprinted in two volumes with a supplemental third volume that contained information omitted from the initial publication. I then continued with the compilation of records about early inhabitants of Harford County with this volume that covers the ensuing decade, thereby bringing the 18th century to completion.

This book contains information gleaned from miscellaneous and obscure records (spanning the years 1791 through 1800) that most researchers rarely consult or perhaps don't know where to find them. It includes genealogical information gleaned from tax lists, insolvent lists, store accounts, medical ledger entries, county court minutes, criminal court dockets, field survey books, Bible records, and cemetery records and inscriptions. In addition, there are some commonly known records, i. e., the 1800 census index and various vital records (births, baptisms, marriages, deaths, and burials) that have been previously published, but contained errors, some of which have been corrected herein. With the exception of a few land tracts and their owners cited in some field survey books, county land records (grantors and grantees) have not been included in this book due to time and space constraints. Such records, of course, would be a worthwhile publication unto themselves.

It should be noted that some records between 1791 and 1800 have been previously published by myself and others. It was not my intent to duplicate their work in this book; therefore, one should consult the following books for additional data: *Harford County, Maryland, Marriage Licenses, 1777-1865*, by Helene Maynard Davis and Jon Harlan Livezey (1993); *Maryland Marriages, 1778-1800*, by Robert W. Barnes (1978); *Abstracts of the Orphans Court of Harford County, 1778-1800*, by Henry C. Peden, Jr. (1990); *St. John's and St. George's Parish Registers, 1696-1851*, by Henry C. Peden, Jr. (1987); *Heirs and Legatees of Harford County, 1774-1802*, by Henry C. Peden, Jr. (1989; *St. George's Parish Register, 1689-1793*, by Bill and Martha Reamy (1988); *Quaker Records of Northern Maryland, 1716-1800*, by Henry C. Peden, Jr. (1993); *Harford County Wills, 1774-1800*, by Ralph H. Morgan, Jr. (1990); *Hunter Sutherland's Slave Manumissions and Sales in Harford County, 1775-1865*, by Carolyn Greenfield Adams (1999); and, *Bible and Family Records of Harford County and Environs* (a series of special publications available from the Harford County Genealogical Society, P. O. Box 15, Aberdeen, Maryland 21001).

Each entry in this volume has a two-digit reference code assigned to it which is intended to direct the researcher to the original records, or copies thereof, which are maintained either at the Historical Society of Harford County in Bel Air, the Maryland Historical Society in Baltimore, or the Maryland State Archives in Annapolis. The codes and a description of the records follow.

AH = Aquila Hall's Bush River Store Account Book, 1771-1805, in the Archives Section of the Historical Society of Harford County.

BC = Cemetery card files are maintained by Bethel Presbyterian Church near Madonna. In 1987 copies of these cards were obtained from the church through Evelyn M. Best, keeper of the cards (now deceased), and I donated a copy to the Family History Section of the Historical Society of Harford County.

CB = Survey field book of David and William Clark, 1770-1812, on microfilm (COAGSERM 1243) at the Maryland State Archives and a paper copy (DC & WC III) is held by the Circuit Court of Harford County.

CC = County Court Minute Books, 1795 and 1797, in the Court Records Section of the Historical Society of Harford County.

CD = Criminal Court Dockets, 1795 and 1797, in the Court Records Section of the Historical Society of Harford County.

CI = *The 1800 Census of Harford County* was published in 1972 by Raymond B. Clark, Jr. (now deceased), by Ronald Vern Jackson (Accelerated Indexing Systems) in 1973, and by F. Edward Wright (Family Line Publications) in 1986. Although accurate for the most part, they contained a number of misspelled names which I have corrected. In my book I have mentioned only the head of family and district of residence since it was not my intent to reprint the entire census again.

CM = County Court Minute Book, 1798-1800, is in the Court Records Section of the Historical Society of Harford County.

HB = Gleanings from the *Harford Historical Bulletin* (as cited).

HW = Index to Harford County wills probated between 1791 and 1800 (libers AJ-R and AJ-2). For a complete abstract, see *Harford County Wills, 1774-1800*, by Ralph H. Morgan, Jr. (1990).

IL = Insolvent lists, 1791-1793, were kept by the county court to indicate who had not paid the county taxes and road taxes levied against them. The original lists (file folders that begin with accession number 31) are maintained in the Court Records

Section of the Historical Society of Harford County.

JA = Dr. John Archer's Medical Ledger F, 1786-1796, in the Manuscripts Division (MS.1502) of the Maryland Historical Society. Abstracts from the ledger were published by the Harford County Genealogical Society in 1992.

JS = Survey field book of James Steele concerned survey work he performed by order of the court in 1799 and 1800 with regards to the chancery case of David West vs. Jesse Jarrett over a land dispute near the Pennsylvania line. A photocopy of the book is in the Archives Section (file SP-24-RF) of the Historical Society of Harford County.

PR = Parish registers of St. John's and St. George's Episcopal Churches have been published (by Peden and Reamy, as noted above) and some of that information has been corrected herein. A copy of the register is on microfilm (M416) at the Maryland State Archives.

SB = Survey field book of Daniel Scott, 1792-1796, in the Archives Section of the Historical Society of Harford County.

TI = Tombstone inscriptions in Harford County have been copied over the past 40 years and the information (now being computerized) is on file cards in the Family History Section of the Historical Society of Harford County. Many of the transcriptions contain errors and should be used with caution. Nevertheless, those who died between 1791 and 1800 (or were born during that time and died later and have a marker at their gravesite) are included herein with the place of burial.

TL = The General Tax Lists for the 13th Collection District of Maryland, 1798-1800, have been microfilmed and are available at the Maryland State Archives (SM56 M864, "Maryland State Papers, Federal Direct Tax, Harford County, 1798"). Information herein has been gleaned from the General Tax Assessment List and the Supplementary Tax List for Non-Residents only. It should be noted that this is not the Particular Assessment List which is a separate schedule that describes the buildings and oftentimes names the land tracts. They are quite difficult if not impossible to read, but would still make a worthwhile publication unto themselves. Paper copies are on file in the Historical Society of Harford County. As for the 1798 General Tax Assessment Lists, they have five major headings with sub-headings as follows: (1) NAMES OF PERSONS BY WHOM PAYABLE; (2) DWELLING HOUSES SUBJECT, AS SUCH, TO THE TAX: Number of dwellings; Number of inferior houses included in the valuation; Quantity of ground included in the valuation (acres, perches, square feet); Where situated in the collection district; How distinguished; Amount of valuation (dollars and cents); In what class rated; Rate per centum payable on the valuation; Amount of tax (dollars and cents); (3) LANDS SUBJECT, AS SUCH, TO THE TAX: Number of tracts or lots; Quantity in acres, perches, square feet; Number of buildings included in the valuation; Where situated in the collection district; By what name, etc., known or distinguished; Amount of valuation (dollars and cents); Rate per centum affected on the valuation; Amount of tax (dollars and cents); (4) SLAVES SUBJECT TO THE TAX: Number of slaves; Tax (50 cents on each taxable); Total amount of tax (dollars and cents); and, (5) WHOLE AMOUNT OF TAXES PAYABLE BY EACH PERSON (dollars and cents). The Supplementary List contains names of non-residents who owned land in Harford County between 1798 and 1800. Most of them lived in Baltimore Town and Baltimore County, but several lived in other counties and in other states. At the end of the list is this statement by the tax collector: "I do hereby acknowledge to have this day received from William Wilson, Surveyor of the Revenue for the Thirteenth Assessment District of Maryland, a verified Supplementary List of Taxes payable on Dwelling Houses, Lands, and Slaves, within the 13th Collection District of Maryland (the foregoing list being a true duplicate thereof of the amount of taxes exhibited in said list amounting to three hundred and twenty-five dollars and eleven cents. Witness my hand this 7th day of August, 1800, Thomas Jeffery, Collector of the 13th Collection District, Maryland." Information of significance to genealogists has been gleaned from the General Tax Assessment Lists and the Supplementary List of Non-Residents as follows: owners (taxpayers), occupants, numbers of buildings (dwellings and inferior houses), acreage of tracts and lots, property locations (hundreds), valuation amounts, and number of slaves. Essentially everything except the rates and amounts of taxes have been included herein. It appears, however, that the property was classed and taxed at either 2 or 3 per centum of the assessed value, and slaves between the ages of 12 and 45 were taxed at the flat rate of 50 cents each.

WH = William R. Hall's Store Account Ledger, 1788-1793, in the Manuscripts Division (MS.1516, Box 9, Vol. XXIII) of the Maryland Historical Society.

I trust that this information will be useful to those who are researching their early Harford County ancestors. I wish to extend my sincere appreciation to Mary Herbert in the Manuscripts Division of the Maryland Historical Society and to Alice Williams, Margaret Bishop, and Marlene Magness, dedicated volunteers at the Historical Society of Harford County, for their assistance during the compilation of this book.

Henry C. Peden, Jr.
Bel Air, Maryland
July 4, 1999

HARFORD COUNTY, MARYLAND
Hundreds, 1776-1800
Districts, 1800

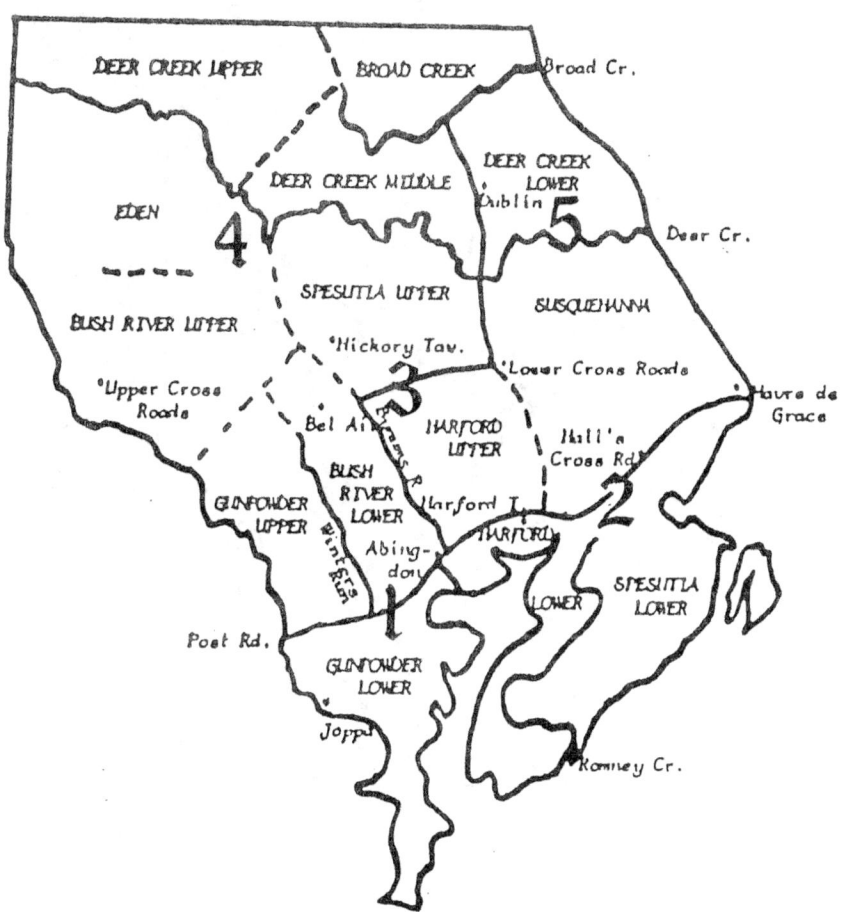

Hundreds postulated by Jon Harlan Livezey
Districts generalized by Henry C. Peden, Jr.

HARFORD COUNTY, MARYLAND AND ENVIRONS CIRCA 1795

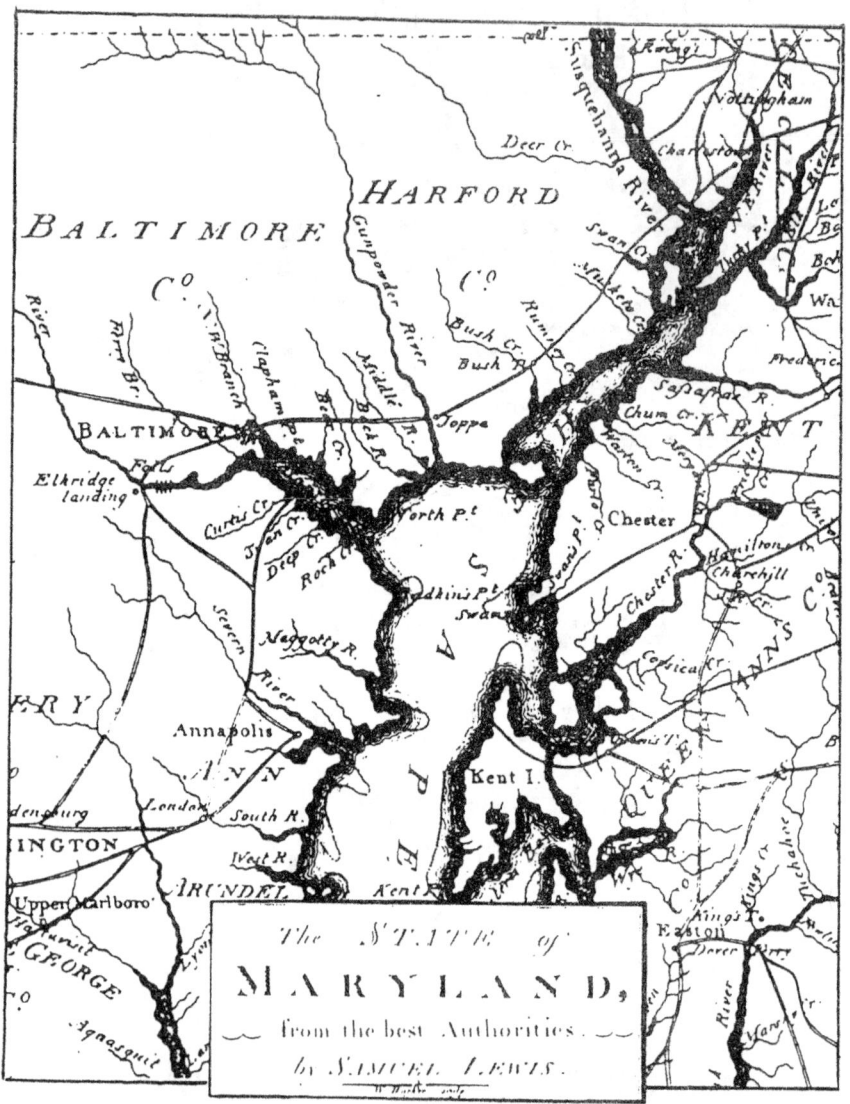

From a map by Samuel Lewis (c1754-1822), of Philadelphia, 1795
(Source: On the Map, Washington College, Chestertown MD, 1983)

INHABITANTS OF HARFORD COUNTY, MARYLAND, 1791-1800

ACRES, THOMAS, head of family in 1800 (3rd District). {Ref: CI}

ADAIR (O'DAIR), WILLIAM, charged for assaulting Samuel Kenley (Kingsley) in 1797. {Ref: CD, August Term, 1797}. Also see "Barney Barclay" and "Paul Chamberlain" and "Philip Chamberlain" and "William O'Dair," q.v.

ADAMS, ELIZABETH, see "John Little," q.v.

ADAMS, JAMES, bur. Feb 4, 1798. {Ref: PR}

ADAMS, JOHN, see "William Ashmore," q.v.

ADAMS, JOHN, head of family in 1800 (2nd District). {Ref: CI}

ADAMS, JOHN, head of family in 1800 (4th District). {Ref: CI}

ADAMS, JOHN, head of family in 1800 (5th District). {Ref: CI}

ADAMS, JOHN JR., head of family in 1800 (5th District). {Ref: CI}

ADAMSON, MARY, see "William Devlin Smith" and "John Devlin" and "Robert Stein Smith," q.v.

ADKINSON, ANN, b. Aug 23, 1796, d. Feb 3, 1828, bur. in the Amos Jones Family Graveyard in Fallston. {Ref: TI}. Also see "Ann Atkinson," q.v.

ADLUM & HUGHES, taxpayers, 1798, Susquehanna Hd., 1 dwelling house, 1 inferior house, 1 acre (Josias Bailey, occupant), $150 valuation; 6 tracts (1221 acres, 120 perches) and 1 building (Josias Bailey, Robert Jeffery, and William Evatt, occupants), $2793.94 valuation; taxpayers, Susquehanna Hd., 1 dwelling house, 3 inferior houses, 2 acres (R. Jeffry, occupant), $125 valuation, no slaves. "Robert Jeffery" was listed three times as "R. Jeffry" and "R. Jeffery" and "Robt. Jeffery" on two different lists. {Ref: TL}

ADLUM & MARPLE, see "Marple & Adlum," q.v.

ADLUM, JOHN, taxpayer, 1798, Spesutia Lower Hd., 1 dwelling house, 7 inferior houses, 2 acres, $700 valuation; 3 tracts (558 acres) in Spesutia Lower Hd., $4854.94 valuation, 6 slaves. {Ref: TL}

ADLUM, JOHN (major), head of family in 1800 (2nd District). {Ref: CI}

ADLUM, JOSEPH, m. Ann McPhail on Nov 8, 1798. {Ref: PR}

ADLUM, THOMAS, m. Sarah McCaskey on Apr 7, 1799. {Ref: PR}

ADLUM, THOMAS, head of family in 1800 (Havre de Grace). {Ref: CI}

ADY (EADY), JAMES, head of family in 1800 (3rd District). {Ref: CI}

ADY, JONATHAN, taxpayer, 1798, Gunpowder Upper Hd., 1 dwelling house, 5 inferior houses, 2 acres, $120 valuation, no slaves. {Ref: TL}

ADY, JONATHAN JR., insolvent on list returned for the road tax due for 1791 by John Bull. {Ref: IL 31.14}

ADY (EADY), JOSHUA, head of family in 1800 (3rd District). {Ref: CI}

ADY, MARY, consort of Samuel, b. 1793, d. Oct 9, 1845, in her 52nd year, bur. in Christ Episcopal (Rock Spring) Church Cemetery. {Ref: TI}

ADY, SAMUEL, see "Mary Ady," q.v.

ADY, WILLIAM, taxpayer, 1798, Bush River Lower Hd., 1 dwelling house, 3 inferior houses, 1 acre, $180 valuation; 2 tracts (384 acres) in Bush River Lower Hd., $1125 valuation, 1 slave. {Ref: TL}

ADY (EADY), WILLIAM, head of family in 1800 (3rd District). {Ref: CI}

AFRICAN LADY, see "Corbin Bond," q.v.

AIKEN (AKIN), SAMUEL, insolvent on lists of taxes due in 1791 and 1792 in Broad Creek Hd., as returned by Robert Amos, Jr. in 1791 and Benjamin Preston in 1792. {Ref: IL 31.03, 31.12, 31.22}

AIKEN (AKIN), WILLIAM, insolvent on lists of taxes due in 1791 and 1792 in Broad Creek Hd., as returned by Robert Amos, Jr. in 1791 and Benjamin Preston in 1792, but his name was then crossed off the 1792 list. {Ref: IL 31.03, 31.12, 31.22}

AIKISON, MICAM(?), insolvent on a list for county taxes due in 1792 as returned by Benjamin Preston. {Ref: IL 31.00}

AILES, ISAAC, son of Stephen and Sarah, b. 17th of 2nd month, 1797. {Ref: Ailes-Phillips Bible}

AILES, ESTHER, dau. of Stephen and Sarah, b. 17th of 11th month, 1798. {Ref: Ailes-Phillips Bible}

AILES, SARAH, dau. of Stephen and Sarah, b. 10th of 9th month, 1800. {Ref: Ailes-Phillips Bible}

AILES, STEPHEN SR., d. 7th of 4th month, 1793, "about 2 o'clock on Firstday morning, aged 43 years, all to 1 month & 2 days." {Ref: Ailes-Phillips Bible}

AITKEN, SARAH, m. James Taylor on Feb 6, 1800. {Ref: PR}. Also see "William Taylor," q.v.

AKERLY, FINCH, taxpayer, 1798, Harford Upper Hd., no dwelling house listed in this part of the tax schedule, 1 tract (10 acres), $67.50 valuation, no slaves. {Ref: TL}

AKERLY (AKALY), FINCH, head of family in 1800 (3rd District). {Ref: CI}

AKIN, JAMES, charged for assaulting Thomas Heaps in 1794. {Ref: CD, March Term, 1795}

AKINS, THOMAS, head of family in 1800 (2nd District). {Ref: CI}

ALBERT, EDWARD, son of Philip and Rachel, b. Jan 15, 1798, bapt. Apr 10, 1798. {Ref: PR}

ALBERT, PHILIP, taxpayer, 1798, Deer Creek Middle Hd., 1 dwelling house, 3 inferior houses, 2 acres, $180 valuation; 4 tracts (272 acres, 40 perches) in Deer Creek Middle Hd., $333.47 valuation, no slaves. In another part of the tax schedule the occupant is listed as Samuel Norris. {Ref: TL}

ALBERT, PHILLIP, head of family in 1800 (5th District). {Ref: CI}

ALBERT, RACHEL, see "Edward Albert," q.v.

ALDERSON, ABEL, see "Richard Mechem," q.v.

ALDREDG, JACOB, insolvent, Harford Lower and Spesutia Lower Hundreds, on a tax list returned by George Lyttle on Sep 21, 1791. {Ref: IL 31.20, 31.21}

ALDRIDG, JACOB, insolvent, Harford Lower and Spesutia Lower Hundreds (listed as a single man), on a tax list returned by George Lyttle on Sep 21, 1791. {Ref: IL 31.20, 31.21}

ALDRIDGE, JACOB, insolvent on a list for the road tax due for 1791 in Harford Upper, Harford Lower, and Spesutia Upper as returned by Robert Amos, Jr. on

Sep 18, 1793. {Ref: IL 31.18}

ALDRIDGE, JACOB, insolvent on a list for the road tax due for 1791 in Harford Upper, Harford Lower, and Spesutia Upper as returned by Robert Amos, Jr. on Sep 18, 1793. {Ref: IL 31.18}

ALDRIDGE(?), SARAH, head of family in 1800 (Belle Air). {Ref: CI}

ALEXANDER, ANDREW, taxpayer, 1798, Broad Creek Hd., no dwelling house listed in this part of the tax schedule, 1 tract (96 acres), $196.95 valuation, no slaves. {Ref: TL}

ALEXANDER, ANDREW, insolvent on lists in Broad Creek Hd. in 1791, as returned by Robert Amos, Jr., but his name was then crossed off both lists. {Ref: IL 31.12, 31.22}

ALEXANDER, ANDREW, head of family in 1800 (5th District). {Ref: CI}

ALEXANDER, ISABEL, tract *Alexander's Dependance* surveyed in 1796. {Ref: CB, SB}

ALEXANDER, ISABELLA, head of family in 1800 (5th District). {Ref: CI}

ALEXANDER, ISSABELLA, taxpayer, 1798, Deer Creek Middle Hd., no dwelling house listed in this part of the tax schedule, 3 tracts (244 acres, 80 perches), $331.94 valuation, no slaves. {Ref: TL}

ALEXANDER, JAMES, insolvent on lists in Broad Creek Hd. in 1791, as returned by Robert Amos, Jr., but his name was then crossed off both lists. {Ref: IL 31.12, 31.22}

ALEXANDER, JAMES, taxpayer, 1798, Broad Creek Hd., no dwelling house listed in this part of the tax schedule, 1 tract (75 acres), $146.25 valuation, no slaves. {Ref: TL}

ALEXANDER, JAMES (York County), insolvent on lists of taxes due in 1791 and 1792 in Broad Creek Hd., as returned by Robert Amos, Jr. in 1791 and Benjamin Preston in 1792. {Ref: IL 31.03, 31.12, 31.22}

ALEXANDER, JOHN, head of family in 1800 (5th District). {Ref: CI}

ALLEN, BRASSEYA, see "John Allen" and "Richard Nun Allen" and "Matthew Johnson Allen," q.v.

ALLEN (ALLIN) & HAMBLETON, taxpayers, 1798, Bush River Lower Hd., 1 dwelling house, 1 inferior house, 40 perches of land, $700 valuation, no slaves. {Ref: TL}

ALLEN, CATHERINE HANNAH, dau. of William and Hannah, b. Sep 1, 1799. {Ref: Allen-Raymond Bible}

ALLEN, EBEN N., see "Elecia M. Allen" and "Elizabeth Allen," q.v.

ALLEN, ELECIA M., second wife of Eben N., b. 1795, d. Jan 13, 1823, in her 28th year, bur. in St. George's Episcopal Church Cemetery at Perryman. {Ref: TI}

ALLEN, ELIZABETH, first wife of Eben N., b. 1792, d. Jun 14, 1816, in her 24th year, bur. in St. George's Episcopal Church Cemetery at Perryman. {Ref: TI}

ALLEN, HANNAH, see "Catherine Hannah Allen" and "William Allen," q.v.

ALLEN, ISAAC, m. Mary Herring on Dec 24, 1800. {Ref: PR}

ALLEN, ISAAC, head of family in 1800 (2nd District). {Ref: CI}

ALLEN, JAMES, head of family in 1800 (5th District). {Ref: CI}. Also see "Lesley Curtis," q.v.

ALLEN, JOHN, see "Richard Nun Allen" and "Matthew Johnson Allen" and "Walter Billingsley, Sr." and "Dr. Jacob Hall," q.v.

ALLEN, JOHN, son of Rev. John and Brasseya, b. Feb 18, 1796, bapt. Mar 27, 1796, d. Nov 12, 1810, aged 16 [sic], bur. in St. George's Episcopal Church Cemetery at Perryman. {Ref: TI, PR}.

ALLEN, JOHN, taxpayer, 1798, Susquehanna Hd., no dwelling house listed in this part of the tax schedule, 1 tract (2 acres), $53.44 valuation, no slaves. {Ref: TL}

ALLEN (ALLIN), JOHN, insolvent on a list for the county tax due for 1793 in Susquehanna Hd. as returned to the levy court by Thomas Taylor on May 28, 1794, who noted "put in my hands last fall." {Ref: IL 31.12}

ALLEN, JOHN, head of family in 1800 (3rd District). {Ref: CI}

ALLEN, JOHN (reverend), head of family in 1800 (1st District). {Ref: CI}

ALLEN, JOHN ("ship"), head of family in 1800 (2nd District). {Ref: CI}

ALLEN, JOHN ("tayler"), charged for assaulting John Madden in 1795. {Ref: CD, March and August Terms, 1795}

ALLEN, MATTHEW JOHNSON (doctor), son of Rev. John and Brasseya, b. Jul 16, 1800, bapt. Aug 1, 1800, d. in Tallahassee, Florida on Dec 27, 1851, in his 51st year, bur. in St. George's Episcopal Church Cemetery at Perryman. {Ref: TI, PR}

ALLEN (ALLIN), MOSES, insolvent on list returned for the road tax due for 1791 by John Bull. {Ref: IL 31.14}

ALLEN, MOSES, insolvent on a list for county taxes due in 1792 as returned by Benjamin Preston. {Ref: IL 31.00}

ALLEN, REBECCA, taxpayer, 1798, Bush River Lower Hd., no dwelling house listed in this part of the tax schedule, 1 tract (57 acres, 120 perches), $174.66 valuation, no slaves. {Ref: TL}

ALLEN, REBECCA, head of family in 1800 (3rd District). {Ref: CI}

ALLEN, RICHARD NUN, son of Rev. John and Brasseya, b. Dec 11, 1797, bapt. Jan 7, 1798. {Ref: PR}

ALLEN, ROBERT (doctor), b. 1792, d. May 5, 1855, in his 63rd year, bur. in Deer Creek Friends Cemetery in Darlington. {Ref: TI}. Also see "William Allen," q.v.

ALLEN, WILLIAM, see "Mary Husband," q.v.

ALLEN, WILLIAM, son of Robert and Hannah, b. Nov 3, 1769 in Wexford, Ireland, sailed from Cork on Aug 23, 1794, landed in Philadelphia on Oct 19th following, married Hannah Bond, dau. of Thomas and Catherine, of Harford County, on Apr 12, 1798, and d. Aug 16, 1860. {Ref: Allen-Raymond Bible}

ALLEN, WILLIAM, served on a Petit Jury in March, 1799 and March, 1800. {Ref: CM}

ALLEN, WILLIAM, head of family in 1800 (1st District). {Ref: CI}

ALLEN, WILLIAM, head of family in 1800 (2nd District). {Ref: CI}

ALLEN (ALLEIN), WILLIAM, will probated Sep 6, 1791. {Ref: HW}

ALLENDER, ELIASE, head of family in 1800 (1st District). {Ref: CI}

ALLENDER, ELIZABETH, bur. Dec 6, 1798. {Ref: PR}. Also see "Joshua Allender" and "Mary Allender" and Elizabeth Ellender," q.v.

ALLENDER (ALLINDER), JAMES, insolvent on lists of taxes due in 1791 and 1792 in Broad Creek Hd., as returned by Robert Amos, Jr. in 1791 and Benjamin Preston in 1792. {Ref: IL 31.03, 31.12, 31.22}

ALLENDER (ALLINDER), JAMES ("run"), insolvent on a list of the county tax due William Osborn, sheriff, for 1791, as returned by Edward Prigg on Sep 20, 1791. {Ref: IL 31.17}

ALLENDER (ALLINDER), JANE, insolvent on lists returned for the county and road taxes due for 1791 by John Bull in Gunpowder Lower Hundred. {Ref IL 31.14, 31.15}

ALLENDER (ALLINDER), JOHN ("run"), insolvent on a list of the county tax due William Osborn, sheriff, for 1791, as returned by Edward Prigg on Sep 20, 1791. {Ref: IL 31.17}

ALLENDER (ALLINDER), JOHN, insolvent on lists of taxes due in 1791 and 1792 in Broad Creek Hd., as returned by Robert Amos, Jr. in 1791 and Benjamin Preston in 1792. {Ref: IL 31.03, 31.12, 31.22}

ALLENDER, JOHN, taxpayer, 1798, Gunpowder Lower Hd., no dwelling house listed in this part of the tax schedule, 1 tract (10 acres), $157.50 valuation, no slaves. {Ref: TL}

ALLENDER, JOHN, head of family in 1800 (1st District). {Ref: CI}

ALLENDER, JOHN (Baltimore County), insolvent on list returned for the county tax for 1791 by William Osburn in Gunpowder Lower Hd. (which listed him as a single man). {Ref: IL 31.15}

ALLENDER, JOHN WANE, son of William and Sophia, b. May 5, 1796. {Ref: PR}

ALLENDER, JOSHUA, son of Nicholas and Elizabeth, b. Mar 11, 1788, bapt. Oct 24, 1795. {Ref: PR}

ALLENDER, MARY, dau. of Nicholas and Elizabeth, b. Apr 1, 1786, bapt. Oct 24, 1795. {Ref: PR}

ALLENDER, NICHOLAS, see "Joshua Allender" and "Mary Allender," q.v.

ALLENDER, NICHOLAS, taxpayer, 1798, Harford Upper Hd., no dwelling house listed in this part of the tax schedule, 1 tract (170 acres), $410.63 valuation, no slaves. {Ref: TL}

ALLENDER, NICHOLAS, had an account at Hall's Store in February, 1791. {Ref: WH}

ALLENDER, NICHOLAS, taxpayer, 1798, Bush River Lower Hd., no dwelling house listed in this part of the tax schedule, no land listed, 1 slave. {Ref: TL}

ALLENDER, NICHOLAS, m. Sarah Bradford on Jun 19, 1797. {Ref: PR}

ALLENDER, NICHOLAS, head of family in 1800 (Abingdon). {Ref: CI}

ALLENDER, NICHOLAS, head of family in 1800 (3rd District). {Ref: CI}

ALLENDER, SOPHIA, see "John Wane Allender," q.v.

ALLENDER, WILLIAM, insolvent on a list in 1792 in Broad Creek Hd., as returned by Benjamin Preston. {Ref: IL 31.03}. Also see "John Wane Allender," q.v.

ALLENDER (ALLINDER), WILLIAM (Baltimore County), insolvent on lists returned for the county and road taxes due for 1791 by John Bull in Gunpowder

Lower Hundred. {Ref: IL 31.14, 31;15}

ALLINDER (ALLINDER), WILLIAM'S HEIRS, insolvents on list returned for the road tax due for 1791 by John Bull. {Ref: IL 31.14}

ALMOND, JACOB, head of family in 1800 (4th District). {Ref: CI}

ALMONEY, JOHN, insolvent on list returned by Robert Carlile for taxes due for the year 1791. {Ref: IL 31.16}

ALMONEY, JOHN, taxpayer, 1798, Bush River Upper & Eden Hd., 1 dwelling house, 1 inferior house, 2 acres, $110 valuation; 1 tract (90 acres) in Bush River Upper & Eden Hd., $202.50 valuation, 1 slave. {Ref: TL}

ALMONY, JOHN, head of family in 1800 (4th District). {Ref: CI}

AMBY, JOHN, see "John Hamby," q.v.

AMMONDS, ISAAC, charged with assaulting James Bradley in 1797. {Ref: CD, March and August Terms, 1797}

AMMONDS, ISAAC, JOHN, JOSHUA, AND WILLIAM JR., charged for assaulting John Daugherty in 1797. {Ref: CD, March and August Terms, 1797}

AMMONDS (AMMONS), THOMAS, insolvent on lists for the county tax and road tax due for 1791 (which spelled the name "Ammonds") and 1792 in Deer Creek Lower Hd., as returned by Thomas Taylor on Sep 17, 1792. {Ref: IL 31.12, 31.03}

AMMONDS (AMMONS), THOMAS, charged with assaulting James Bradley in 1797. {Ref: CD, March and August Terms, 1797}

AMMONS, WILLIAM ("poor"), insolvent on a list of the county tax due William Osborn, sheriff, for 1791, as returned by Edward Prigg on Sep 20, 1791. {Ref: IL 31.17}

AMMONS, WILLIAM, insolvent on lists of taxes due in 1791 and 1792 in Broad Creek Hd., as returned by Robert Amos, Jr. in 1791 and Benjamin Preston in 1792. {Ref: IL 31.03, 31.12, 31.22}

AMMONS (AMONS), WILLIAM, head of family in 1800 (5th District). {Ref: CI}

AMOS, ANN, dau. of Daniel and Sarah Amos, b. 1798, d. Sep 20, 1886, aged 88, bur. in Harford (Old Brick) Baptist Church Cemetery. {Ref: TI}. Also see "Daniel Cunningham," q.v.

AMOS, AQUILA, insolvent on lists returned by Robert Carlile and John Guyton (the latter listed him as a single man and spelled the name as "Aqul. Amoss") for taxes due for the year 1791. {Ref: IL 31.16, 31.19}

AMOS, AQUILA, insolvent on lists returned by Robert Carlile and John Guyton (the latter spelled the name as "Aqul. Amoss") for taxes due for the year 1791. {Ref: IL 31.16, 31.19}

AMOS, BENJAMIN, see "Hugh Whiteford (tanner)," q.v.

AMOS, BENJAMIN (OF JAMES), insolvent on a list for the road tax for 1792, as returned for Robert Amoss, tax collector. {Ref: IL 13.12}

AMOS, BENJAMIN (OF JAMES), taxpayer, 1798, Gunpowder Upper Hd., 1 dwelling house, 4 inferior houses, 2 acres, $200 valuation; 12 tracts (463 acres) in Gunpowder Upper Hd., $1711.13 valuation, 2 slaves. {Ref: TL}

AMOS, DANIEL, taxpayer, 1798, Bush River Upper & Eden Hd., 1 dwelling house, 3 inferior houses, 2 acres, $175 valuation; 4 tracts (198 acres) in Bush River Upper & Eden Hd., $445.50 valuation, 5 slaves. {Ref: TL}

AMOS, ELIAS ELLICOT, son of James Amos and Hannah Lee, b. on 13th of 10th month, 1799, d. on 30th of 6th month, 1821, in his 22nd year, bur. in family graveyard at "Mt. Soma" and reinterred in Little Falls Quaker Cemetery at Fallston in 1915. {Ref: TI, and Little Falls Cemetery Records}

AMOS, ELIJAH, insolvent on list returned by Robert Carlile for taxes due for the year 1791. {Ref: IL 31.16}

AMOS, ELIZABETH, insolvent on lists returned by Robert Carlile and John Guyton (the latter spelled the name as "Eliz. Amoss") for taxes due for the year 1791. {Ref: IL 31.16, 31.19}

AMOS, ISAAC, see "Julia A. Amos," q.v.

AMOS, JAMES, see "Benjamin Amos (of James)" and "James Amos, Jr. (of James)" and "William Amos (of William)" and "Elias Ellicot Amos," q.v.

AMOS (AMOSS), JAMES, tract *James's Care* surveyed in 1799 and tract *Chock's Neighbour* surveyed in 1800. {Ref: CB}

AMOS, JAMES SR., taxpayer, 1798, Bush River Upper & Eden Hd., 1 dwelling house, 4 inferior houses, 2 acres, $200 valuation; 1 tract (298 acres) in Bush River Upper & Eden Hd., $670.50 valuation, 6 slaves. {Ref: TL}

AMOS, JAMES JR. (OF JAMES), taxpayer, 1798, Gunpowder Upper Hd., 1 dwelling house, 7 inferior houses, 2 acres, $450 valuation; taxpayer, 1798, Gunpowder Upper Hd., 1 dwelling house, 5 inferior houses, 2 acres, $200 valuation; 1 dwelling house, 1 inferior house, 1 acre, $105 valuation; 8 tracts (1020 acres, 80 perches) in Gunpowder Upper Hd., $3375.84 valuation, 6 slaves. {Ref: TL}

AMOS, JAMES (OF ROBERT), taxpayer, 1798, Bush River Upper & Eden Hd., 1 dwelling house, 2 inferior houses, 2 acres, $105 valuation, no slaves. {Ref: TL}

AMOS, JAMES (OF WILLIAM), taxpayer, 1798, Gunpowder Upper Hd., 1 dwelling house, 3 inferior houses, 2 acres, $200 valuation; 4 tracts (158 acres) in Gunpowder Upper Hd., $533.25 valuation, no slaves. {Ref: TL}

AMOS, JOHN A.(?), b. 1791, d. 1854, aged 63, bur. in Fellowship Cemetery near Harkins. {Ref: TI}

AMOS, JOSHUA, taxpayer, 1798, Bush River Upper & Eden Hd., 1 dwelling house, no inferior houses, 2 acres, $120 valuation; 2 tracts (158 acres) in Bush River Upper & Eden Hd., $805.50 valuation, no slaves. {Ref: TL}

AMOS, JULIA A., wife of Isaac, b. 1800, d. Oct 3, 1872, bur. in Bethel Presbyterian Church Cemetery at Madonna. {Ref: BC}

AMOS, LUKE, taxpayer, 1798, Gunpowder Upper Hd., no dwelling house listed in this part of the tax schedule, 2 tracts (60 acres), $203.62, no slaves. {Ref: TL}

AMOS, MARY, taxpayer, 1798, Bush River Upper & Eden Hd., 1 dwelling house, 4 inferior houses, 2 acres, $110 valuation; 2 tracts (78 acres) in Bush River Upper & Eden Hd., $175.50 valuation, 1 slave. {Ref: TL}. Also see "James Watt,"

q.v.

AMOS, MAULDEN ("gone to George I."), insolvent on list returned by Robert Carlile for taxes due for the year 1791. {Ref: IL 31.16}

AMOS (AMOSS), MORDECAI, mentioned in a survey deposition on Sep 23, 1799. {Ref: JS}

AMOS, MORDECAI SR., insolvent on list returned by Robert Carlile for taxes due for the year 1791. {Ref: IL 31.16}

AMOS, MORDECAI JR., insolvent on list returned by Robert Carlile for taxes due for the year 1791. {Ref: IL 31.16}

AMOS, MORDICA SR., taxpayer, 1798, Bush River Upper & Eden Hd., 1 dwelling house, 2 inferior houses, 2 acres, $150 valuation; 1 tract (33 acres) in Bush River Upper & Eden Hd., $74.25 valuation, 1 slave. {Ref: TL}

AMOS, MORDICA JR., taxpayer, 1798, Gunpowder Upper Hd., 1 dwelling house, 5 inferior houses, 2 acres, $120 valuation; 6 tracts (176 acres, 80 perches), $643.50 valuation, 2 slaves. {Ref: TL}

AMOS, NICHOLAS, insolvent on lists returned by Robert Carlile and John Guyton (the latter spelled the name as "Nich. Amoss") for taxes due for the year 1791. {Ref: IL 31.16, 31.19}

AMOS, PRISCILLA, b. Oct 26, 1797, d. Feb 26, 1857, aged 59 years and 4 months, bur. in Union Chapel Methodist Church Cemetery at Wilna. {Ref: TI}

AMOS, RACHEL, b. 1799 or 1800, d. Dec 4, 1861, in her 62nd year, bur. in Union Chapel Methodist Church Cemetery at Wilna. {Ref: TI}

AMOS, ROBERT, see "James Amos (of Robert)," q.v.

AMOS, ROBERT, taxpayer, 1798, Bush River Upper & Eden Hd., 1 dwelling house, 8 inferior houses, 2 acres, $500 valuation; 12 tracts (1216 acres, 40 perches) in Bush River Upper & Eden Hd., $1972.69 valuation, 3 slaves. {Ref: TL}

AMOS (AMOSS), ROBERT, tract *Robertson's Chance* surveyed between 1792 and 1796, and tract *The Improvement* surveyed in 1797. {Ref: CB, SB}

AMOS (AMOSS), ROBERT, mentioned in a survey deposition on Sep 27, 1799. {Ref: JS}

AMOS, ROBERT, tax collector, who compiled and returned lists of insolvents, 1791-1793; also listed as "Robert Amoss" and "Robert Amos, Jr." {Ref: IL 31.12, 31.14, 31.16}

AMOS, ROBERT JR., had an account at Hall's Store in March, 1791. {Ref: WH}

AMOS, ROBERT JR., taxpayer, 1798, Bush River Upper & Eden Hd., 1 dwelling house, 4 inferior houses, 2 acres, $220 valuation; 6 tracts (435 acres, 120 perches) in Bush River Upper & Eden Hd., $980.44 valuation, 4 slaves. {Ref: TL}

AMOS, ROBERT C., b. Sep 25, 1800, d. Dec 14, 1865, bur. in Harford (Old Brick) Baptist Church Cemetery. {Ref: TI}

AMOS, SALLY, bur. Nov 25, 1795, aged 3 years. {Ref: PR}

AMOS, SARAH, b. 1792, d. Oct 7, 1869, aged 77, bur. in Harford (Old Brick) Baptist Church Cemetery. {Ref: TI}

AMOS, THOMAS, taxpayer, 1798, Bush River Upper & Eden Hd., 1 dwelling house, 3 inferior houses, 2 acres, $300 valuation; 3 tracts (354 acres, 40 perches) in Bush River Upper & Eden Hd., $927.74 valuation, 2 slaves. {Ref: TL}

AMOS, THOMAS (Baltimore County), insolvent on list returned by Robert Carlile for taxes due for the year 1791. {Ref: IL 31.16}

AMOS, WILLIAM, see "James Amos (of William)" and "William Amos (of William)" and "William Amos (of James)," q.v.

AMOS, WILLIAM JR., treated by Dr. John Archer on Aug 25, 1793; also mentioned his wife and child (no names given). {Ref: JA}

AMOS, WILLIAM SR., taxpayer, 1798, Gunpowder Upper Hd., 1 dwelling house, 4 inferior houses, 2 acres, $200 valuation; 1 tract (100 acres) in Gunpowder Upper Hd., $337.50 valuation, no slaves. {Ref: TL}

AMOS, WILLIAM (OF JAMES), taxpayer, 1798, Bush River Upper & Eden Hd., 1 dwelling house, 6 inferior houses, 2 acres, $475 valuation; 5 tracts (475 acres, 120 perches) in Bush River Upper & Eden Hd., $1074.94 valuation, 2 slaves. {Ref: TL}

AMOS, WILLIAM (OF WILLIAM), taxpayer, 1798, Gunpowder Upper Hd., 1 dwelling house, 6 inferior houses, 2 acres, $300 valuation; 1 tract (180 acres) in Gunpowder Upper Hd., $675 valuation, no slaves. {Ref: TL}

AMOS, ZACHERIAH, taxpayer, 1798, Bush River Upper & Eden Hd., 1 dwelling house, 3 inferior houses, 2 acres, $175 valuation; 1 tract (98 acres) in Bush River Upper & Eden Hd., $220.50 valuation, no slaves. {Ref: TL}

AMOSS, AQUILLA (OF M.), head of family in 1800 (4th District). {Ref: CI}

AMOSS, AQUILLA (OF W.), head of family in 1800 (4th District). {Ref: CI}

AMOSS, BENJAMIN, tracts *Small* and *Not So Small* surveyed between 1792 and 1796. {Ref: SB}

AMOSS, BENJAMIN, tract *Mount Pleasant* surveyed in 1796, tract *Patty's Inheritance* surveyed in 1796 and granted in 1797, tract *The Enlargement* surveyed in 1798, and tract *Wood Lot* surveyed in 1796 and granted in 1798. {Ref: CB}

AMOSS, BENJAMIN, served on a Grand Jury in August, 1798 and August, 1799 and August, 1800. {Ref: CM}

AMOSS, BENJAMIN, head of family in 1800 (4th District). {Ref: CI}

AMOSS, BENJAMIN (OF B.), head of family in 1800 (4th District). {Ref: CI}

AMOSS, DANIEL (OF R.), head of family in 1800 (4th District). {Ref: CI}

AMOSS, FREDERICK, head of family in 1800 (4th District). {Ref: CI}

AMOSS, GEORGE, head of family in 1800 (4th District). {Ref: CI}

AMOSS, GEORGE, served on a Grand Jury in March, 1798, on a Petit Jury in March, 1799, and on a Grand Jury in March, 1800. {Ref: CM}

AMOSS, JAMES, see "William Amoss" and "Mordocai Amoss," q.v.

AMOSS, JAMES JR., head of family in 1800 (3rd District). {Ref: CI}

AMOSS, JAMES JR., head of family in 1800 (4th District). {Ref: CI}

AMOSS, JAMES (OF JAMES), appointed a Judge of Elections in the 3rd District following resignation of Jacob Norris on Jul 28, 1800. {Ref: CM}

AMOSS, JAMES (OF JOS.), head of family in 1800 (4th District). {Ref: CI}
AMOSS, JAMES (OF M.), head of family in 1800 (4th District). {Ref: CI}
AMOSS, JAMES (OF RB.), head of family in 1800 (4th District). {Ref: CI}
AMOSS, JAMES (OF ROBERT), served on a Grand Jury in August, 1799 and August, 1800. {Ref: CM}
AMOSS, JAMES (OF W.), head of family in 1800 (3rd District). {Ref: CI}
AMOSS, JONES(?), head of family in 1800 (4th District). {Ref: CI}
AMOSS, LEMUEL HOWARD, b. 1792, d. on 23rd of 4th month, 1883, in his 91st year, bur. in Little Falls Quaker Cemetery in Fallston. {Ref: TI}. Also see "Rachel Pearson Amoss," q.v.
AMOSS, MARY, head of family in 1800 (4th District). {Ref: CI}
AMOSS, MAULDEN ("gone out of state"), insolvent on a list for 1791 in Gunpowder Upper and Bush River Lower Hundreds, as filed by John Bond, Deputy Sheriff, on Sep 20, 1791. {Ref: IL 31.24}
AMOSS, MORDECAI JR., served on a Petit Jury in August, 1799 and on a Grand Jury in August, 1800. {Ref: CM}
AMOSS, MORDICA, head of family in 1800 (4th District). {Ref: CI}
AMOSS, MORDICA, JR., head of family in 1800 (4th District). {Ref: CI}
AMOSS, MORDICA (OF J.), head of family in 1800 (3rd District). {Ref: CI}
AMOSS, MORDOCAI (OF JAMES), served on a Petit Jury in August, 1798. {Ref: CM}
AMOSS, RACHEL PEARSON, wife of Lemuel H., b. in 1798, d. on 15th of 3rd month, 1881, in her 83rd year, bur. in Little Falls Quaker Cemetery in Fallston. {Ref: TI}
AMOSS, ROBERT, see "James Amoss," q.v.
AMOSS, ROBERT, tract *Good Hope* surveyed between 1792 and 1796. {Ref: SB}
AMOSS, ROBERT JR., tract *Amoss' Plains* surveyed in 1799. {Ref: CB}
AMOSS, ROBERT, served on a Grand Jury in March, 1799 and March, 1800. {Ref: CM}
AMOSS, ROBERT, head of family in 1800 (4th District). {Ref: CI}
AMOSS, ROBERT JR., head of family in 1800 (4th District). {Ref: CI}
AMOSS, ROBERT JR., tract *Lancelot's Fortune* surveyed between 1792 and 1796. {Ref: SB}
AMOSS, SUSAN, see "James Benton McComas," q.v.
AMOSS, THOMAS ("gone"), insolvent on a list for 1791 in Gunpowder Upper and Bush River Lower Hundreds, as filed by John Bond, Deputy Sheriff, on Sep 20, 1791. {Ref: IL 31.24}
AMOSS, THOMAS, head of family in 1800 (4th District). {Ref: CI}
AMOSS, THOMAS JR., head of family in 1800 (4th District). {Ref: CI}
AMOSS, WILLIAM, b. 1799 or 1800, d. Dec 18, 1872, in his 73rd year, bur. in Union Chapel Methodist Church Cemetery at Wilna. {Ref: TI}
AMOSS, WILLIAM, head of family in 1800 (3rd District). {Ref: CI}
AMOSS, WILLIAM JR., head of family in 1800 (3rd District). {Ref: CI}
AMOSS, WILLIAM (OF J.), head of family in 1800 (4th District). {Ref: CI}

AMOSS, WILLIAM (OF JAMES), tract *Saint Omer* surveyed between 1792 and 1796. {Ref: SB}

AMOSS, WILLIAM LEE, b. 1795, d. on 28th of 10th month, 1870, in his 75th year, bur. in Little Falls Quaker Cemetery in Fallston. {Ref: TI}

AMOSS, ZACHARIAS, head of family in 1800 (4th District). {Ref: CI}

ANDERSON, AMOS, son of Daniel and Rachel, b. Oct 18, 1793. {Ref: PR}

ANDERSON, CASSANDRA, see "John Clark," q.v.

ANDERSON, CATHERINE, will probated Jan 23, 1798. {Ref: HW}

ANDERSON, DANIEL, see "Amos Anderson" and "Susanna Anderson," q.v.

ANDERSON, DANIEL, taxpayer, 1798, Susquehanna Hd., 1 dwelling house, 4 inferior houses, 2 acres, $235 valuation; 2 tracts (162 acres) in Susquehanna Hd., $290.25 valuation, 2 slaves. {Ref: TL}

ANDERSON, DANIEL, treated by Dr. John Archer on May 23, 1791; also mentioned a child (no name given). {Ref: JA}

ANDERSON, HUGH, taxpayer, 1798, Bush River Upper & Eden Hd., 1 dwelling house, 2 inferior houses, 2 acres, $120 valuation; $120 valuation; 2 tracts (343 acres, 120 perches) in Bush River Upper & Eden Hd., $583.87 valuation, 1 slave. {Ref: TL}

ANDERSON, HUGH, head of family in 1800 (4th District). {Ref: CI}

ANDERSON, JAMES, head of family in 1800 (4th District). {Ref: CI}

ANDERSON, JAMES, head of family in 1800 (5th District); two men by this name in this district. {Ref: CI}

ANDERSON, JAMES, taxpayer, 1798, Bush River Upper & Eden Hd., 1 dwelling house, 4 inferior houses, 2 acres, $300 valuation; 1 tract (494 acres) in Bush River Upper & Eden Hd., $1296 valuation, 2 slaves. {Ref: TL}

ANDERSON, JAMES, taxpayer, 1798, Deer Creek Middle Hd., no dwelling house listed in this part of the tax schedule, 1 tract (100 acres), $254.99 valuation, no slaves. {Ref: TL}

ANDERSON, JAMES ("charge with property"), insolvent on lists in 1791 due county taxes and road taxes in "Deer Creek Upper, Middle, and Broad Creek Hundreds" as returned by Robert Amos, Jr. {Ref: IL 31.12, 31.22}

ANDERSON, JAMES (free negro), taxpayer, 1798, Gunpowder Upper Hd., no dwelling house listed in this part of the tax schedule, 1 tract (20 acres), $56.25 valuation. {Ref: TL}

ANDERSON, JAMES JR., taxpayer, 1798, Broad Creek Hd., no dwelling house listed in this part of the tax schedule, 3 tracts (109 acres), $143.50 valuation, no slaves. {Ref: TL}

ANDERSON, JOSEPH, mentioned in a survey deposition on May 24, 1799. {Ref: JS}

ANDERSON, PEGGY, head of family in 1800 (2nd District). {Ref: CI}

ANDERSON, RACHEL, head of family in 1800 (2nd District). {Ref: CI}. Also see "Amos Anderson" and "Susanna Anderson," q.v.

ANDERSON, SUSANNA, dau. of Daniel and Rachel, b. Oct 6, 1795. {Ref: PR}

ANDERSON, THOMAS ("gone"), insolvent on lists due for 1790 and 1791 "fund taxes" and county taxes in Susquehanna Hd., as returned by Thomas Taylor. {Ref: IL 31.12, 31.02}

ANDERSON, WILLIAM, insolvent on lists returned by Robert Carlile and John Guyton for taxes due for the year 1791. {Ref: IL 31.16, 31.19}

ANDERSON, WILLIAM, insolvent on a list for 1791 in Gunpowder Upper and Bush River Lower Hundreds, as filed by John Bond, Deputy Sheriff, on Sep 20, 1791. {Ref: IL 31.24}

ANDERSON, WILLIAM, head of family in 1800 (4th District). {Ref: CI}

ANDERSON, WILLIAM (blacksmith), insolvent on list returned by Robert Carlile for taxes due for the year 1791. {Ref: IL 31.16}

ANDREW, NANCY, wife of William G., b. May 20, 1791, d. Dec 25, 1858, bur. in Cokesbury Methodist Cemetery in Abingdon. {Ref: TI}

ANDREW, WILLIAM G., see "Nancy Andrew," q.v.

ANDREWS, ABRAHAM, son of Abraham and Mary, b. Jan 5, 1795. {Ref: PR}

ANDREWS, ABRAHAM, taxpayer, 1798, Harford Upper Hd., no dwelling house listed in this part of the tax schedule, 1 tract (60 acres), $118.13 valuation, 1 slave. {Ref: TL}

ANDREWS, ABRAHAM, head of family in 1800 (3rd District). {Ref: CI}

ANDREWS, MARY, see "Abraham Andrews," q.v.

ANGLE, MRS., see "Havre de Grace Company," q.v.

ANNAN, WILLIAM, will probated May 5, 1791. {Ref: HW}

ANNIS, THOMAS, m. Mary Dunn on Sep 7, 1797. {Ref: PR}

ANTHONY, PHELIX, see "Felix Anthony Mathew," q.v.

APPAL, JOHN, b. 1800, d. Oct 21, 1888, in his 88th year, bur. in Old Salem Evangelical Cemetery near Madonna. {Ref: TI}

ARCHER, CALEB G., b. 1799, d. Oct 12, 1881, aged 82, bur. in Union Chapel Methodist Church Cemetery at Wilna. {Ref: TI}

ARCHER, JOHN (doctor), consulted with Dr. Arnet of York County in 1792. {Ref: JA}

ARCHER, JOHN (doctor), taxpayer, 1798, Spesutia Upper Hd., 1 dwelling house, 4 inferior houses, 2 acres, $510 valuation; 3 tracts (648 acres) in Spesutia Upper Hd., $1884.37 valuation, 3 slaves. {Ref: TL}

ARCHER, JOHN (doctor), head of family in 1800 (3rd District). {Ref: CI}

ARCHER, THOMAS, purchased oats on Nov 29, 1795 at Bush River Store. {Ref: AH}

ARCHER, THOMAS (doctor), head of family in 1800 (2nd District). {Ref: CI}

ARMITAGE, JAMES, taxpayer, 1798, Gunpowder Upper Hd., 1 dwelling house, 4 inferior houses, 2 acres, $120 valuation; 1 tract (68 acres) in Gunpowder Upper Hd., $186.75 valuation, no slaves. In another part of the tax schedule the occupant is listed as Mary Dutton. {Ref: TL}

ARMITAGE (ARMYTORGE), JAMES, head of family in 1800 (1st District). {Ref: CI}

ARMITAGE, JOHN, charged for assaulting William McComas in 1797. {Ref: CD, March Term, 1797}

ARMSTRONG, CASSANDRA, see "Harriot Armstrong," q.v.

ARMSTRONG, FORD, see "John Murphy," q.v.

ARMSTRONG, FORD ("charge twice"), insolvent on a list for the road tax due for 1791 in Harford Upper, Harford Lower, and Spesutia Upper as returned by Robert Amos, Jr. on Sep 18, 1793. {Ref: IL 31.18}

ARMSTRONG, FORD (FORDE), head of family in 1800 (2nd District). {Ref: CI}

ARMSTRONG, HARRIOT, dau. of Solomon and Cassandra, b. Jan 15, 1797, bapt. Dec 17, 1797. {Ref: PR}

ARMSTRONG, JAMES, insolvent on a list for the road tax due for 1791 in Harford Upper, Harford Lower, and Spesutia Upper as returned by Robert Amos, Jr. on Sep 18, 1793. {Ref: IL 31.18}

ARMSTRONG, JOSHUA ("dead"), insolvent on lists due for 1790 and 1791 "fund taxes" and county taxes in Susquehanna Hd., as returned by Thomas Taylor. {Ref: IL 31.12, 31.02}

ARMSTRONG, LEVINA, taxpayer, 1798, Harford Upper Hd., no dwelling house listed in this part of the tax schedule, 1 tract (119 acres), $221.24 valuation, no slaves. {Ref: TL}

ARMSTRONG, LEVINA, head of family in 1800 (2nd District). {Ref: CI}

ARMSTRONG, MARGARET, m. Charles McLaughlin on Feb 6, 1799. {Ref: PR}

ARMSTRONG, NEAMIAH, head of family in 1800 (4th District). {Ref: CI}

ARMSTRONG, NEHEMIAH, mentioned in a survey deposition on Jan 28, 1800 as "said place was where Nehemiah Armstrong formerly lived." {Ref: JS}

ARMSTRONG, ROBERT, head of family in 1800 (3rd District). {Ref: CI}. Also see "Joshua Day," q.v.

ARMSTRONG, SOLOMON, see "Harriot Armstrong" and "Benjamin Everest," q.v.

ARMSTRONG, SOLOMON, insolvent on a list for the road tax due for 1791 in Harford Upper, Harford Lower, and Spesutia Upper as returned by Robert Amos, Jr. on Sep 18, 1793. {Ref: IL 31.18}

ARMSTRONG, SOLOMON, taxpayer, 1798, Susquehanna Hd., no dwelling house listed in this part of the tax schedule, no land listed, 1 slave. {Ref: TL}

ARMSTRONG, SOLOMON, head of family in 1800 (2nd District). {Ref: CI}

ARNET, DOCTOR, see "Dr. John Archer," q.v.

ARNOLD, ELIZABETH, see "William Smith," q.v.

ARNOLD, EPHERIM, head of family in 1800 (2nd District). {Ref: CI}

ARNOLD, EPHRAIM, taxpayer, 1798, Susquehanna Hd., no dwelling house listed in this part of the tax schedule, 2 tracts (100 acres), $315 valuation, no slaves. In another part of the tax schedule the occupant of one tract is listed as William Arnold. {Ref: TL}

ARNOLD, HARRIOTT SUSAN, dau. of William and Susan, b. Feb 19, 1796. {Ref: PR}

ARNOLD, HENRY FIELDING, son of William and Susan (Susanna), b. Aug 27, 1797. {Ref: PR}

ARNOLD, MARY, dau. of William and Susan (Susanna), b. Aug 7, 1799. {Ref: PR}
ARNOLD, SUSAN (SUSANNA), see "Harriott Susan Arnold" and "Henry Fielding Arnold" and "Mary Arnold," q.v.
ARNOLD, WILLIAM, see "Ephraim Arnold" and "Harriott Susan Arnold" and "Henry Fielding Arnold" and "Mary Arnold," q.v.
ARNOLD, WILLIAM, taxpayer, 1798, Susquehanna Hd., no dwelling house listed in this part of the tax schedule, no land listed, 1 slave. {Ref: TL}
ARNOLD, WILLIAM, head of family in 1800 (2nd District). {Ref: CI}
ARNOLD, WILLIAM, head of family in 1800 (5th District). {Ref: CI}
ASBURY, JOHN, head of family in 1800 (3rd District). {Ref: CI}
ASHMEAD, JOHN, taxpayer, 1798, Bush River Upper & Eden Hd., 1 dwelling house, 1 inferior house, 2 acres, $150 valuation; 1 tract (181 acres, 80 perches) in Bush River Upper & Eden Hd., $345.37 valuation, no slaves. {Ref: TL}
ASHMEAD, JOHN, served on a Grand Jury in August, 1798 and August, 1799. {Ref: CM}
ASHMEAD, JOHN, charged in 1794 (nature of the case not stated). {Ref: CD, March Term, 1795}
ASHMORE, JOHN, taxpayer, 1798, Deer Creek Middle Hd., no dwelling house listed in this part of the tax schedule, no land listed, 1 slave. {Ref: TL}
ASHMORE, JOHN, served on a Grand Jury in March, 1798, on a Petit Jury in March, 1799, and on a Grand Jury in March, 1800. {Ref: CM}
ASHMORE, JOHN, head of family in 1800 (4th District). {Ref: CI}
ASHMORE, WILLIAM, see "James Barnet," q.v.
ASHMORE, WILLIAM, taxpayer, 1798, Deer Creek Middle Hd., 1 dwelling house, 9 inferior houses, 2 acres, $450 valuation; 6 tracts (1206 acres, 120 perches) in Deer Creek Middle Hd., $2940.45 valuation, 9 slaves. In another part of the tax schedule the occupants are listed as Nathaniel Roach, John Adams, Frank Barnhouse, William Moore, and Patrick Donnell. {Ref: TL}
ASHMORE, WILLIAM, tracts *Is It Mine* surveyed in 1794 (corrected survey in 1796) and tract *John's Adventure* surveyed in 1796. {Ref: CB, SB}
ASHMORE, WILLIAM, head of family in 1800 (5th District). {Ref: CI}
ASHTON, JOHN, head of family in 1800 (3rd District). {Ref: CI}
ASHTON, JOSEPH, head of family in 1800 (3rd District). {Ref: CI}
ASHTON (ASTON), JOSEPH, taxpayer, 1798, Bush River Lower Hd., no dwelling house listed in this part of the tax schedule, 1 tract (191 acres), $376.30 valuation, no slaves. {Ref: TL}. Also see "John S. Whittaker," q.v.
ASKEW, WILLIAM, m. Sarah Calwell on Dec 10, 1794. {Ref: PR}
ASKUE, WILLIAM, head of family in 1800 (3rd District). {Ref: CI}
ATKINSON, ANN, consort of David Atkinson and dau. of Amos and Ann Jones, b. 1793, d. Feb 2, 1823, aged 28, bur. in the Amos Jones Family Graveyard in Fallston. {Ref: TI}. Also see "Ann Adkinson," q.v.
ATKINSON, DAVID, b. 1792, d. on 16th of 5th month, 1875, in his 83rd year, bur. in Little Falls Quaker Cemetery in Fallston. {Ref: TI}. Also see "Ann

Atkinson," q.v.
ATKINSON, ISAAC, taxpayer, 1798, Gunpowder Upper Hd., no dwelling house listed in this part of the tax schedule, 1 tract (51 acres), $238.50 valuation, no slaves. {Ref: TL}
ATKINSON, ISAAC, head of family in 1800 (3rd District). {Ref: CI}
ATKINSON, MICHAEL, insolvent, Harford Lower and Spesutia Lower Hundreds, on a tax list returned by George Lyttle on Sep 21, 1791. {Ref: IL 31.20, 31.21}
ATKISON, GREENBURY, insolvent on a list for the county tax due for 1793 in Harford Upper, Harford Lower, and Spesutia Lower Hundreds returned to the levy court by Thomas Taylor on May 28, 1794. {Ref: IL 31.12}
ATTKINSON, MICHAEL, insolvent on a list for the road tax due for 1791 in Harford Upper, Harford Lower, and Spesutia Upper as returned by Robert Amos, Jr. on Sep 18, 1793. {Ref: IL 31.18}. Also see "Micam Aikison," q.v.
ATWILL, WILLIAM, head of family in 1800 (3rd District). {Ref: CI}
AUSTIN, JOHN, see "John Brinton," q.v.
AUSTIN, JOHN, taxpayer, 1798, Deer Creek Lower Hd., 1 dwelling house, 2 inferior houses, 2 acres, $700 valuation; 2 tracts (450 acres) in Deer Creek Lower Hd., $1543.50 valuation, no slaves. {Ref: TL}
AUSTIN, JOHN, head of family in 1800 (5th District). {Ref: CI}
AUSTIN, JOHN JR., head of family in 1800 (5th District). {Ref: CI}
AUZE & TERME, see "Terme & Auze," q.v.
AYRES (AYERS), THOMAS, see "Joseph Robinson" and "William Robinson" and "Mary Robinson" and "James Robinson" and "Matthew Cook," q.v.
AYRES (AYERS), THOMAS, tract *Angle* surveyed between 1792 and 1796. {Ref: SB}
AYRES (AYERS), THOMAS, licensed retailer in March, 1795 and August, 1797. {Ref: CC}
AYRES (AYERS), THOMAS (esquire), head of family in 1800 (4th District). {Ref: CI}
AYRES (AYERS), THOMAS JR., licensed ordinary (tavern) in March, 1795 and August, 1797, and a retailer's license in August, 1797. {Ref: CC}
AYRES (AYERS), THOMAS JR., taxpayer, 1798, Bush River Upper & Eden Hd., 1 dwelling house, 2 inferior houses, 1 acre, $200 valuation; 1 tract (29 acres) in Bush River Upper & Eden Hd., $65.25 valuation, 2 slaves. {Ref: TL}
AYRES (AYERS), THOMAS SR., taxpayer, 1798, Bush River Upper & Eden Hd., 1 dwelling house, 5 inferior houses, 2 acres, $300 valuation; 12 tracts (682 acres, 80 perches) in Bush River Upper & Eden Hd., $1618.87 valuation, 2 slaves. {Ref: TL}
AYRES (AYERS), THOMAS SR., called to serve on a Petit Jury in March, 1800 (but the number of days served was blank). {Ref: CM}
AYRES (AYERS), THOMAS W., served on a Petit Jury in August, 1800. {Ref: CM}
AYRES (AYERS), THOMAS W., head of family in 1800 (4th District). {Ref: CI}
BACKWOOD, JAMES, son of Samuel and Mary, b. Sep 14, 1790, bapt. Oct 6, 1795. {Ref: PR}

BACKWOOD, JOHN, son of Samuel and Mary, b. Feb 12, 1788, bapt. Oct 6, 1795. {Ref: PR}

BACKWOOD, MARY, see "John Backwood" and "James Backwood," q.v.

BACKWOOD, SAMUEL, see "John Backwood" and "James Backwood," q.v.

BACTER (BAXTER?), JACOB, head of family in 1800 (1st District). {Ref: CI}

BAGELEY, SAMUEL H. b. 1792, d. Apr 17, 1851, in his 59th year, bur. in Stump Family Graveyard near Craig's Corner. {Ref: TI}

BAGLEY, J. ORRICK, b. 1799 or 1800, d. Jan 5, 1877, aged 77, bur. in Union Chapel Methodist Church Cemetery at Wilna. {Ref: TI}

BAGLEY, WILLIAM, taxpayer, 1798, Deer Creek Lower Hd., 1 dwelling house, 2 inferior houses, 2 acres, $130 valuation; 2 tracts (165 acres) in Deer Creek Lower Hd., $919.69 valuation, no slaves. {Ref: TL}

BAGLEY, WILLIAM, head of family in 1800 (5th District). {Ref: CI}

BAGNET, MARGARET, see "Sarah Turner," q.v.

BAILES, ELIZABETH, taxpayer, 1798, Gunpowder Lower Hd., 1 dwelling house, 2 inferior houses, 2 acres, $170 valuation; 3 tracts (305 acres, 80 perches) in Gunpowder Lower Hd., $1408.50 valuation, 2 slaves. {Ref: TL}

BAILEY, AQUILA, see "John Wood," q.v.

BAILEY, AVARILLA, see "Charles Bailey," q.v.

BAILEY, BENEDICT, insolvent on list returned for the road tax due for 1791 by John Bull. {Ref: IL 31.14}

BAILEY, BENEDICT, insolvent on a list for county taxes due in 1792 as returned by Benjamin Preston. {Ref: IL 31.00}

BAILEY, BENEDICT, see "Mary Barnes," q.v.

BAILEY, CHARLES, son of Josias and Avarilla, b. Jan 7, 1797. {Ref: PR}

BAILEY, HARRIET, wife of John, b. Dec 24, 1796, d. Dec 30, 1870, aged 74 years and 6 days, bur. in Rock Run Cemetery at Craig's Corner. {Ref: TI}

BAILEY, JOHN, see "Harriet Bailey," q.v.

BAILEY, JOSIAS, see "Charles Bailey" and "Adlum & Hughes," q.v.

BAILEY, MARTHA, b. 1793, d. Feb 1, 1869, in her 76th year, bur. in Deer Creek Harmony Presbyterian Church Cemetery near Darlington. {Ref: TI}

BAILEY, MRS., wife of Thomas, Esq., bur. Oct --, 1791, aged 60. {Ref: PR}

BAILEY, THOMAS, see "Mrs. Bailey," q.v.

BAILEY, WILLIAM, insolvent on list returned for the road tax due for 1791 by John Bull. {Ref: IL 31.14}

BAILY, JOSEPH, insolvent on a list for the county tax due for 1791 in Susquehanna Hd., as returned by Thomas Taylor on Sep 17, 1792. {Ref: IL 31.12, 31.02}

BAILY, JOSIAH, insolvent on a list for the county tax due for 1791 in Susquehanna Hd., as returned by Thomas Taylor on Sep 17, 1792. {Ref: IL 31.12, 31.02}

BAILY, MARY, insolvent on a list for the county tax due for 1793 in Susquehanna Hd. as returned to the levy court by Thomas Taylor on May 28, 1794, who noted "put in my hands last fall." {Ref: IL 31.12}

BAKER, ABRAHAM, head of family in 1800 (4th District). {Ref: CI}

BAKER, CHARLES, licensed tavernkeeper in March, 1795 and March, 1797. {Ref: CC}

BAKER, CHARLES, served on a Petit Jury in August, 1797 and Augutst, 1798 and on a Grand Jury in March, 1800. {Ref: CC, CM}

BAKER, CHARLES, head of family in 1800 (3rd District). {Ref: CI}

BAKER, CHARLES (OF THEO), insolvent on list returned for the road tax due for 1791 by John Bull. {Ref: IL 31.14}

BAKER, CHRISTIAN, will probated Jan 15, 1793. {Ref: HW}

BAKER, CORDELIA, see "Morgan Jones," q.v.

BAKER, ELIZABETH, wife of James P., b. 1800, d. Sep 20, 1879, aged 79, bur. in McKendree Cemetery near Black Horse. {Ref: TI}

BAKER, FRANCIS, insolvent on a list for the road tax due for 1791 in Harford Upper, Harford Lower, and Spesutia Upper as returned by Robert Amos, Jr. on Sep 18, 1793. {Ref: IL 31.18}

BAKER, GEDION, head of family in 1800 (1st District). {Ref: CI}

BAKER, GEDON, insolvent on list returned by Robert Carlile for taxes due for the year 1791. {Ref: IL 31.16}

BAKER, GIDEON, taxpayer, 1798, Gunpowder Upper Hd., no dwelling house listed in this part of the tax schedule, 1 tract (40 acres) in Gunpowder Upper Hd., $67.50 valuation, no slaves. {Ref: TL}

BAKER, GIDIEON, insolvent on a list for 1791 in Gunpowder Upper and Bush River Lower Hundreds, as filed by John Bond, Deputy Sheriff, on Sep 20, 1791. {Ref: IL 31.24}

BAKER, HENRY, taxpayer, 1798, Spesutia Lower Hd., no dwelling house listed in this part of the tax schedule, 1 tract (44 perches, 21 sq. ft.), $13.50 valuation, no slaves. {Ref: TL}

BAKER, JAMES, see "Mrs. Baker," q.v.

BAKER, JAMES, taxpayer, 1798, Gunpowder Upper Hd., no dwelling house listed in this part of the tax schedule, 1 tract (9 acres) in Gunpowder Upper Hd., $131.63 valuation, no slaves. {Ref: TL}

BAKER, JAMES, insolvent on list returned by Robert Carlile for taxes due for the year 1791. {Ref: IL 31.16}

BAKER, JAMES, insolvent on a list for 1791 in Gunpowder Upper and Bush River Lower Hundreds, as filed by John Bond, Deputy Sheriff, on Sep 20, 1791. {Ref: IL 31.24}

BAKER, JAMES, head of family in 1800 (3rd District). {Ref: CI}

BAKER, JAMES P., b. 1794, d. May 30, 1871, aged 77, bur. in McKendree Cemetery near Black Horse. {Ref: TI}. Also see "Elizabeth Baker," q.v.

BAKER, JOHN, insolvent on a list for the road tax due for 1791 in Harford Upper, Harford Lower, and Spesutia Upper as returned by Robert Amos, Jr. on Sep 18, 1793. {Ref: IL 31.18}

BAKER, JOHN, "twist chargd" (meaning "charged twice"), insolvent on a list of the county tax due William Osborn, sheriff, for 1791, as returned by Edward Prigg on Sep 20, 1791. {Ref: IL 31.17}

BAKER, JOHN, insolvent on lists in 1791 due county taxes and road taxes in "Deer Creek Upper, Middle, and Broad Creek Hundreds" as returned by Robert Amos, Jr. {Ref: IL 31.12, 31.22}

BAKER, MRS., wife of James, bur. Nov 18, 1793, and at the same time a child was interred in the same grave with the mother. {Ref: PR}

BAKER, NICHOLAS, head of family in 1800 (2nd District). {Ref: CI}

BAKER, WILLIAM, see "David Ross" and "William Barton" and "James Rampley," q.v.

BAKER, WILLIAM, taxpayer, 1798, Gunpowder Lower Hd., no dwelling house listed in this part of the tax schedule, no land listed, 1 slave. {Ref: TL}

BAKER, WILLIAM, mentioned in a survey deposition on Jan 14, 1800 as "to Wm. Baker's house where he now lives [and] to Wm. Baker's spring." {Ref: JS}

BAKER, WILLIAM, head of family in 1800 (1st District). {Ref: CI}

BAKER, WILLIAM, head of family in 1800 (4th District). {Ref: CI}

BALDERSON, ISAIAH (Baltimore Town), or NICHOLAS COOPER, taxpayer, 1798, Broad Creek Hd., 1 dwelling house, 2 inferior houses, 2 acres, $170 valuation; 5 tracts (263 acres) in Broad Creek Hd. (Nicholas Cooper, occupant), $548.16 valuation, no slaves. {Ref: TL}

BALDERSON, JACOB, taxpayer, 1798, Deer Creek Middle Hd., no dwelling house listed in this part of the tax schedule, no land listed, 1 tract (86 acres), $169.31 valuation, no slaves. {Ref: TL}

BALDERSON, JACOB, head of family in 1800 (5th District). {Ref: CI}

BALDWIN, CHARLOTTE, wife of Silas, b. 1793, d. Mar 16, 1868, in her 75th year, bur. in Harford (Old Brick) Baptist Church Cemetery. {Ref: TI}

BALDWIN, JAMES, b. 1791, d. Jun 4, 1869, in his 78th year, bur. in Harford (Old Brick) Baptist Church Cemetery. {Ref: TI}

BALDWIN, JEMIMA, head of family in 1800 (3rd District). {Ref: CI}

BALDWIN, JOHN, head of family in 1800 (2nd District). {Ref: CI}

BALDWIN, SILAS, taxpayer, 1798, Bush River Lower Hd., 1 dwelling house, 1 inferior house, 1 acre and 80 perches, $100.50 valuation; 1 tract (105 acres, 80 perches) in Bush River Lower Hd., $307.97 valuation, no slaves. {Ref: TL}. Also see "Charlotte Baldwin," q.v.

BALDWIN, WILLIAM, taxpayer, 1798, Gunpowder Upper Hd., 1 dwelling house, 6 inferior houses, 2 acres, $500 valuation; 1 tract (298 acres) in Gunpowder Upper Hd., $1005.75 valuation, 4 slaves. {Ref: TL}

BALDWIN, WILLIAM, head of family in 1800 (4th District). {Ref: CI}

BALEY, WILLIAM, insolvent on a list for 1791 in Gunpowder Upper and Bush River Lower Hundreds, as filed by John Bond, Deputy Sheriff, on Sep 20, 1791. {Ref: IL 31.24}

BANE, WILLIAM, charged for keeping an ordinary (tavern) without a license and for selling liquors in 1797. {Ref: CD, March Term, 1797}
BANKHEAD, HUGH, taxpayer, 1798, Deer Creek Upper Hd., 1 dwelling house, 2 acres, $101 valuation; 2 tracts (128 acres) in Deer Creek Upper Hd., $165.30 valuation, no slaves. {Ref: TL}
BANKHEAD, HUGH, insolvent on lists in 1791 in Deer Creek Upper Hd., as returned by Robert Amos, Jr. {Ref: IL 31.12, 31.22}
BANKHEAD, HUGH, head of family in 1800 (4th District). {Ref: CI}
BANKHEAD, JOHN, husband of Elizabeth Robinson, b. 1793, d. Mar 29, 1858, bur. in Bethel Presbyterian Church Cemetery at Madonna. {Ref: BC}
BANKHEAD, WILLIAM, taxpayer, 1798, Bush River Upper & Eden Hd., 1 dwelling house, 1 inferior house, 2 acres, $120 valuation; 2 tracts (365 acres, 80 perches) in Bush River Upper & Eden Hd., $411.19 valuation, 1 slave. {Ref: TL}
BANKHEAD, WILLIAM, head of family in 1800 (4th District). {Ref: CI}
BARCKLEY, ELIZABETH, head of family in 1800 (5th District). {Ref: CI}
BARCLAY, BARNET, charged for assaulting Joshua Bennett in 1794. {Ref: CD, March Term, 1795}
BARCLAY, BARNEY, charged with assaulting William Adair in 1797. {Ref: CD, March and August Terms, 1797}
BARCLAY, JOHN, served on a Petit Jury in March, 1798 and August, 1799. {Ref: CM}
BARCLAY, JOHN, taxpayer, 1798, Broad Creek Hd., 1 dwelling house, 4 inferior houses, 2 acres, $200 valuation; 2 tracts (422 acres) and 1 other building in Broad Creek Hd., $842.62 valuation, 2 slaves. In another part of the tax schedule the occupant is listed as Henry Ellis. {Ref: TL}
BARCROFT, JOHN, taxpayer, 1798, Gunpowder Upper Hd., no dwelling house listed in this part of the tax schedule, 1 tract (156 acres) in Gunpowder Upper Hd., $474.75 valuation, no slaves. {Ref: TL}
BARCROFT, JOHN, head of family in 1800 (4th District). {Ref: CI}
BARCROFT, JONAS, taxpayer, 1798, Bush River Upper & Eden Hd., 1 dwelling house, 2 inferior houses, 2 acres, $105 valuation; 1 tract (123 acres) in Bush River Upper & Eden Hd., $241.88 valuation, no slaves. {Ref: TL}
BARCROFT, JONAS, head of family in 1800 (4th District). {Ref: CI}
BARE, BARBARY (BARBARA ANN), see "Henry Bare" and "Joseph Bare" and "Elizabeth Bare" and "Samuel Bare," q.v.
BARE, ELIZABETH, dau. of John and Barbara Ann, b. Dec 31, 1785, bapt. Sep 7, 1800. {Ref: PR}
BARE, HENRY, son of John and Barbary, b. Sep 12, 1796, bapt. Sep 16, 1796. {Ref: PR}
BARE, JOHN, see "Henry Bare" and "Joseph Bare" and "Elizabeth Bare" and "Samuel Bare," q.v.
BARE, JOSEPH, son of John and Barbara Ann, b. Jun 18, 1790, bapt. Sep 7, 1800. {Ref: PR}
BARE, SAMUEL, son of John and Barbara Ann, b. Nov 18, 1787, bapt. Sep 7,

1800. {Ref: PR}
BARLEY, MATHIAS, insolvent, Harford Lower and Spesutia Lower Hundreds, on a tax list returned by George Lyttle on Sep 21, 1791. {Ref: IL 31.20, 31.21}
BARNABY, RICHARD, insolvent on list returned for the county tax for 1791 by William Osburn in Gunpowder Lower Hd. (which listed him as a single man). {Ref: IL 31.15}
BARNABY, WILLIAM, insolvent on list returned for the road tax due for 1791 by John Bull. {Ref: IL 31.14}
BARNES (BARNS), AMOS ("for John Wood's heirs"), appeared on "a list of insolvents it being for personal property for the road taxs [sic] for 1791" filed by Robert Amoss, tax collector. {Ref: IL 31.12}
BARNES, AMOS, had an account at Hall's Store in October, 1791. {Ref: WH}
BARNES, AMOS, will probated Oct 21, 1797. {Ref: HW}
BARNES, AMOS' HEIRS, or BENNET BARNES, taxpayers, 1798, Susquehanna Hd., 1 dwelling house, 1 acre and 80 perches (Bennet Barnes, occupant), $150 valuation, no slaves; also, taxpayers, Spesutia Lower Hd., no dwelling house listed in this part of the tax schedule, no land listed, 2 slaves (Bennet Barnes, superintendent). {Ref: TL}
BARNES, AMOSS, head of family in 1800 (2nd District). {Ref: CI}
BARNES, BENJAMIN, insolvent on a list for the county tax due for 1791 in Susquehanna Hd., as returned by Thomas Taylor on Sep 17, 1792. {Ref: IL 31.12, 31.02}
BARNES, BENNET, see "Amos Barnes' heirs," q.v.
BARNES, BENNET, taxpayer, 1798, Spesutia Lower Hd., 1 dwelling house, 1 inferior house, 44 perches and 21 sq. ft. of land, $475 valuation, 1 slave. {Ref: TL}
BARNES (BARNS), BENNET, served on a Grand Jury in August, 1798. {Ref: CM}
BARNES, BENNETT, had an account at Hall's Store in December, 1791. {Ref: WH}
BARNES, BENNETT, head of family in 1800 (2nd District). {Ref: CI}
BARNES, ELIZABETH, see "Harriot Barnes" and "Richard Barnes," q.v.
BARNES, ELIZABETH, taxpayer, 1798, Deer Creek Lower Hd., no dwelling house listed in this part of the tax schedule, no land listed, 2 slaves. {Ref: TL}
BARNES, ELIZABETH, head of family in 1800 (5th District). {Ref: CI}
BARNES (BARNS), ELIZABETH, dau. of Richard and Sarah, b. Jun 16, 1795. {Ref: Richard Barnes Bible}
BARNES, FORD, see "Sarah Barnes," q.v.
BARNES, FORD, served as constable in Susquehanna Hd., 1799. {Ref: CM}
BARNES, FORD, taxpayer, 1798, Susquehanna Hd., 1 dwelling house, 1 inferior house, 1 acre and 80 perches, $250 valuation, no slaves. {Ref: TL}
BARNES (BARNS), FORD, bur. Sep 9, 1800. {Ref: PR}
BARNS, FORD, d. Feb 5, 1798. {Ref: Richard Barnes Bible}
BARNES (BARNS), GREGORY, see "Harriot Barnes" and "Richard Barnes," q.v.
BARNES, GREGORY, head of family in 1800 (2nd District). {Ref: CI}
BARNES, GREGORY JR., head of family in 1800 (2nd District). {Ref: CI}
BARNES, GREGORY JR., taxpayer, 1798, Susquehanna Hd., no dwelling house

listed in this part of the tax schedule, 2 tracts (94 acres, 120 perches), $238.63 valuation, no slaves. {Ref: TL}

BARNES, GREGORY SR., taxpayer, 1798, Susquehanna Hd., no dwelling house listed in this part of the tax schedule, 1 tract (75 acres), $326.25 valuation, no slaves. {Ref: TL}

BARNES (BARNS), HARRIOT, dau. of Gregory and Elizabeth, b. Dec 24, 1796. {Ref: PR}

BARNES, HARRIOTT, dau. of Myer and Margaret Barnes, b. Oct 27, 1799, bapt. 24, 1800. {Ref: PR}

BARNES, HENRY, b. Jan 7, 1792, d. Mar 3, 1858, aged 66 years, 1 month, and 24 days [sic], bur. in Angel Hill Cemetery in Havre de Grace. {Ref: TI}. Also see "Sarah B. Barnes," q.v.

BARNES, HOSEA, had an account at Hall's Store in October, 1791. {Ref: WH}

BARNES, HOSEA, taxpayer, 1798, Spesutia Lower Hd., no dwelling house listed in this part of the tax schedule, no land listed, 1 slave. {Ref: TL}

BARNES, HOSHEA, see "John Lisbey Barnes," q.v.

BARNES, JAMES, had an account at Hall's Store in April, 1791. {Ref: WH}

BARNES, JAMES, subpoenaed to the Grand Jury in August, 1797. {Ref: CC}

BARNES, JAMES, taxpayer, 1798, Susquehanna Hd., no dwelling house listed in this part of the tax schedule, 2 tracts (172 acres), $349.88 valuation, no slaves. {Ref: TL}

BARNES, JAMES, head of family in 1800 (2nd District); two men by this name in this district. {Ref: CI}

BARNES, JOB ("Redstone"), insolvent on lists due for 1790 and 1791 "fund taxes" and county taxes in Susquehanna Hd., as returned by Thomas Taylor. {Ref: IL 31.12, 31.02}

BARNES, JOB, taxpayer, 1798, Deer Creek Lower Hd., no dwelling house listed in this part of the tax schedule, 3 tracts (150 acres) and 3 other buildings (Elisha Day and Elizabeth Barney or Barny, occupants), $682.88 valuation, no slaves. {Ref: TL}

BARNES, JOHN, see "Joseph Barnes" and "Joseph, William, and John Barnes," q.v.

BARNES, JOHN, insolvent on a list for the road tax due in 1791 in Susquehanna Hd., as returned by Thomas Taylor. {Ref: IL 31.02}

BARNES, JOHN LISBEY (LUSBY?), son of Hoshea and Mary, b. Dec 17, 1797, bapt. Jul 1, 1798. {Ref: PR}

BARNES, JOSEPH, head of family in 1800 (3rd District). {Ref: CI}

BARNES (BARNS), JOSEPH, treated by Dr. John Archer on Nov 26, 1793; also mentioned his wife (no name given). {Ref: JA}

BARNES, JOSEPH, WILLIAM, AND JOHN, taxpayers, 1798, Spesutia Upper Hd., no dwelling house listed in this part of the tax schedule, 2 tracts (134 acres) in Spesutia Upper Hd., $618.75 valuation, no slaves. {Ref: TL}. In another part of the tax schedule the occupants are listed as Joseph Barnes, Mary McMath, John Ellis, Jr., and John and William Barnes.

BARNES, MARGARET (MARGARITE), head of family in 1800 (1st District). {Ref: CI}. Also see "Harriott Barnes," q.v.

BARNES, MARY, see "John Lisbey Barnes" and "Joseph, William, and John Barnes," q.v.

BARNES, MARY, dau. of Nehemiah and Margaret, b. Oct 29, 1795. {Ref: PR}

BARNES, MARY, taxpayer, 1798, Susquehanna Hd., no dwelling house listed in this part of the tax schedule, 1 tract (50 acres), $185.62 valuation, no slaves. {Ref: TL}. In another part of the tax schedule the occupant is listed as Benedict Bailey.

BARNES (BARNS), MORDECAI G., son of Richard and Sarah, b. Aug 13, 1791, d. Apr 30, 1866, aged 75, bur. in Barnes Family Cemetery near Earlton. {Ref: TI, and Richard Barnes Bible}. Also see "Sarah Barnes," q.v.

BARNES, MYER, see "Harriott Barnes," q.v.

BARNES, NEHEMIAH, see "Mary Barnes," q.v.

BARNES (BARNS), NEHEMIAH, insolvent, Harford Lower and Spesutia Lower Hundreds (listed as a single man), on a tax list returned by George Lyttle on Sep 21, 1791. {Ref: IL 31.20, 31.21}

BARNES (BARNS), NEHEMIAH, insolvent on a list for the road tax due for 1791 in Harford Upper, Harford Lower, and Spesutia Upper as returned by Robert Amos, Jr. on Sep 18, 1793. {Ref: IL 31.18}

BARNES, RICHARD, see "Mordecai G. Barnes" and "Elizabeth Barnes" and "Ford Barnes," q.v.

BARNES, RICHARD, taxpayer, 1798, Susquehanna Hd., no dwelling house listed in this part of the tax schedule, 3 tracts (120 acres), $416.25 valuation, 1 slave. {Ref: TL}

BARNES, RICHARD, head of family in 1800 (2nd District). {Ref: CI}

BARNES (BARNS), RICHARD, son of Gregory and Elizabeth, b. Mar 26, 1799. {Ref: PR}

BARNES, RUTH, insolvent on a list for the county tax due for 1791 in Susquehanna Hd., as returned by Thomas Taylor on Sep 17, 1792. {Ref: IL 31.12, 31.02}

BARNES, SARAH, see "Mary Barnes" and "Elizabeth Barnes" and "Mordecai G. Barnes," q.v.

BARNES, SARAH, dau. of Ford Barnes and Mary Gilbert, b. Jan 24, 1796. {Ref: PR}

BARNES, SARAH, wife of Mordecai G., b. 1792, d. Aug 23, 1873, aged 81, bur. in Barnes Family Cemetery near Earlton. {Ref: TI}

BARNES, SARAH B., wife of Henry, b. Oct 26, 1793, d. Jun 5, 1811, aged 18 years, 2 months and 5 days [sic], bur. in Angel Hill Cemetery in Havre de Grace. {Ref: TI}

BARNES, THOMAS, insolvent on a list for county taxes due in 1792 as returned by Benjamin Preston. {Ref: IL 31.00}

BARNES (BARNS), THOMAS, insolvent on list returned for the road tax due for 1791 by John Bull. {Ref: IL 31.14}

BARNES, WILLIAM, see "Joseph Barnes" and "Joseph, William, and John Barnes," q.v.

BARNES, WILLIAM, insolvent on a list for the county tax due for 1793 in Susquehanna Hd. as returned to the levy court by Thomas Taylor on May 28, 1794, who noted "put in my hands last fall." {Ref: IL 31.12}

BARNES, WILLIAM, taxpayer, 1798, Susquehanna Hd., no dwelling house listed in this part of the tax schedule, 1 tract (50 acres), $172.50 valuation, no slaves. {Ref: TL}. In another part of the tax schedule the occupant is listed as Crispin Cuningham.

BARNES, WILLIAM, head of family in 1800 (2nd District). {Ref: CI}

BARNES, WILLIAM, head of family in 1800 (3rd District). {Ref: CI}

BARNETT (BARNET), JAMES, treated by Dr. John Archer on Apr 7, 1791; noted he lived near William Ashmore. {Ref: JA}

BARNETT (BARNET), JAMES JR., served on a Grand Jury in March, 1798 and on a Petit Jury in March, 1800. {Ref: CM}

BARNETT (BARNET), JAMES JR., taxpayer, 1798, Deer Creek Middle Hd., no dwelling house listed in this part of the tax schedule, 3 tracts (186 acres), $366.19 valuation, no slaves. {Ref: TL}

BARNETT (BARNET), JAMES JR., tract *Variation* surveyed in 1789 and granted in 1801. {Ref: CB}

BARNETT (BARNET), JAMES SR., served on a Grand Jury in August, 1798 and August, 1799, and on a Petit Jury in 1800. {Ref: CM}

BARNETT (BARNET), JAMES SR., taxpayer, 1798, Deer Creek Middle Hd., 1 dwelling house, 4 inferior houses, 2 acres, $200 valuation; 5 tracts (208 acres, 120 perches) in Deer Creek Middle Hd., $309.58 valuation, no slaves. {Ref: TL}. In another part of the tax schedule the occupant is listed as Thomas Montgomery.

BARNETT, JAMES SR., head of family in 1800 (5th District). {Ref: CI}

BARNETT, JAMES (OF M.), head of family in 1800 (5th District). {Ref: CI}

BARNETT, JANE, insolvent on lists due for 1790 and 1791 "fund taxes" and county taxes in Susquehanna Hd., as returned by Thomas Taylor. {Ref: IL 31.12, 31.02}

BARNETT, JOSEPH, charged for felony (nature of case not stated) in 1792. {Ref: CD, March Term, 1795}

BARNETT (BARNET), MARK, taxpayer, 1798, Broad Creek Hd., 1 dwelling house, 1 inferior house, 2 acres, $101 valuation; 1 tract (185 acres) in Broad Creek Hd., $166.87 valuation, no slaves. {Ref: TL}

BARNETT, MARK, head of family in 1800 (5th District). {Ref: CI}

BARNETT, THOMAS, head of family in 1800 (5th District). {Ref: CI}

BARNETT, WILLIAM, head of family in 1800 (5th District). {Ref: CI}

BARNETT (BARNET), WILLIAM, taxpayer, 1798, Broad Creek Hd., no dwelling house listed in this part of the tax schedule, 1 tract (127 acres), $188.62 valuation, no slaves. {Ref: TL}. In another part of the tax schedule the occupant is listed as William James.

BARNEY (BARNY), ELIZABETH, see "Job Barnes," q.v.

BARNEY, JOHN H., taxpayer, 1798, Harford Upper Hd., 1 dwelling house, 6 inferior houses, 1 acre, $2000 valuation, 3 slaves; taxpayer, 1798, Harford Upper Hd., 1 dwelling house, 4 inferior houses, 1 acre, $500 valuation, no slaves. {Ref: TL}

BARNEY, JOHN H., subpoenaed to the Grand Jury in August, 1797. {Ref: CC}

BARNEY, JOHN H., served as foreman on a Grand Jury in August, 1798, and on a Petit Jury in March, 1800. {Ref: CM}

BARNEY, JOHN H., licensed ordinary (tavern) and ferry operator in March, 1795, and August, 1797. {Ref: CC}

BARNEY, JOHN HOLLAND, appointed a Judge of Elections in the 2nd District on Jul 28, 1800. {Ref: CM}

BARNHOUSE, FRANCIS, head of family in 1800 (5th District). {Ref: CI}

BARNHOUSE, FRANK, see "William Ashmore," q.v.

BARNHOUSE, JOHN, insolvent on list returned for the road tax due for 1791 by John Bull. {Ref: IL 31.14}

BARNHOUSE, JOHN, insolvent on a list for county taxes due in 1792 as returned by Benjamin Preston. {Ref: IL 31.00}

BARREN, MARIA (Mrs.), b. 1799, d. Sep 15, 1884, aged 85, bur. in Grove Presbyterian Church Cemetery in Aberdeen. {Ref: TI}

BARRETT (BARRET), ELIZABETH, taxpayer, 1798, Bush River Upper & Eden Hd., 1 dwelling house, 2 inferior houses, 2 acres, $150 valuation; 1 tract (261 acres) in Bush River Upper & Eden Hd., $587.25 valuation, no slaves. {Ref: TL}

BARRETT, ELIZABETH, head of family in 1800 (4th District). {Ref: CI}

BARRETT, JAMES, head of family in 1800 (5th District). {Ref: CI}

BARRETT, JOHN, see "Ralph McCreary," q.v.

BARRETT, JOHN, insolvent on list returned by Robert Carlile for taxes due for the year 1791. {Ref: IL 31.16}

BARRETT, JOHN, head of family in 1800 (3rd District). {Ref: CI}

BARROW, JOHN, insolvent on lists returned by Robert Carlile and John Guyton for taxes due for the year 1791. {Ref: IL 31.16, 31.19}

BARRY, EDWARD, head of family in 1800 (5th District). {Ref: CI}

BARTHEY, MATHIAS, insolvent on a list for the road tax due for 1791 in Harford Upper, Harford Lower, and Spesutia Upper as returned by Robert Amos, Jr. on Sep 18, 1793. {Ref: IL 31.18}

BARTLE, BARNEY, subpoenaed to the Grand Jury in August, 1797. {Ref: CC}

BARTLE, BERNARD, charged for assaulting Thomas Coffield in 1797. {Ref: CD, August Term, 1797}

BARTLETT, BARNARD, head of family in 1800 (Havre de Grace). {Ref: CI}

BARTLEY, BARNABAS, see "Mary Ann Bartley," q.v.

BARTLEY, BARNEY, taxpayer, 1798, Spesutia Lower Hd., 1 dwelling house, 44 perches, 21 sq. ft., $320 valuation, no slaves. {Ref: TL}. Also see "John Kentlemyre and B. Bartley" and "Elizabeth Bartley," q.v.

BARTLEY, BERNARD, see "Elizabeth Bartley," q.v.

BARTLEY, ELIZABETH, dau. of Barney and Elizabeth, b. Apr 26, 1799, bapt.

May 6, 1799. {Ref: PR}

BARTLEY, ELIZABETH, dau. of Bernard and Elizabeth, b. Oct 20, 1795, bapt. Sep 11, 1796. {Ref: PR}

BARTLEY, ELIZABETH, see "Elizabeth Bartley," q.v.

BARTLEY, MARY, insolvent on a list for the county tax due for 1793 in Harford Upper, Harford Lower, and Spesutia Lower Hundreds returned to the levy court by Thomas Taylor on May 28, 1794, but a line was drawn through her name. {Ref: IL 31.12}

BARTLEY, MARY ANN, dau. of Barnabas and Nancy, b. Sep 28, 1800, bapt. Dec 26, 1800. {Ref: PR}

BARTLEY, NANCY, see "Mary Ann Bartley," q.v.

BARTON, ANN, dau. of Asael and Susanna, b. Dec 15, 1794. {Ref: PR}

BARTON, ASAEL, see "Margarett Wooden Barton" and "Ann Barton," q.v.

BARTON, JAMES, taxpayer, 1798, Deer Creek Upper Hd., no dwelling house listed in this part of the tax schedule, 2 tracts (200 acres), $281.25 valuation, no slaves. {Ref: TL}

BARTON, JAMES, insolvent on a list for the road tax for 1792, as returned for Robert Amoss, tax collector (James Barton's name appeared on the same list twice). {Ref: IL 13.12}

BARTON, JAMES, granted a tavern permit on June 26, 1797. {Ref: CC}

BARTON, JAMES ("goaler"), charged for selling liquors in 1797 and fined 600 lbs. of tobacco. {Ref: CD, March Term, 1797}

BARTON, JAMES (major), head of family in 1800 (4th District). {Ref: CI}

BARTON, JAMES JR., head of family in 1800 (5th District). {Ref: CI}

BARTON, JOSHUA, insolvent on lists returned by Robert Carlile and John Guyton for taxes due for the year 1791. {Ref: IL 31.16, 31.19}

BARTON, MARGARETT WOODEN, dau. of Asael and Susanna, b. Mar 4, 1793, bapt. Jul 14, 1793. {Ref: PR}

BARTON, PHEBE, had an account at Hall's Store in March, 1791; also noted that she was the wife of Thomas Barton. {Ref: WH}

BARTON, RUTH, see "Ralph Yarley," q.v.

BARTON, SUSANNA, see "Margarett Wooden Barton" and "Ann Barton," q.v.

BARTON, THOMAS, had an account at Hall's Store in June, 1791. {Ref: WH}. See "Phebe Barton," q.v.

BARTON, THOMAS, AND ROBERTS, ARCHIBALD, tract *Barton's Chance in the Risen* surveyed between 1792 and 1796. {Ref: SB}

BARTON, WILLIAM, see "James Rampley," q.v.

BARTON, WILLIAM, taxpayer, 1798, Deer Creek Upper Hd., no dwelling house listed in this part of the tax schedule, 1 tract (200 acres), $281.25 valuation, no slaves. {Ref: TL}. In another part of the tax schedule the occupant is listed as William Baker.

BARTON, WILLIAM, mentioned in a survey deposition on Jan 14, 1800 as "into Wm. Barton's field where said [James] Rampley proves he cleared." {Ref: JS}

BARTON, WILLIAM H., head of family in 1800 (4th District). {Ref: CI}
BARTON, WILLIAM (OF J.), head of family in 1800 (4th District). {Ref: CI}
BATEMAN, WILLIAM, insolvent on a list for the county tax due for 1793 in Susquehanna Hd. as returned to the levy court by Thomas Taylor on May 28, 1794, who noted "put in my hands last fall." {Ref: IL 31.12}
BATEMAN, WILLIAM, head of family in 1800 (3rd District). {Ref: CI}
BAUGHMAN, MARGARET, m. George Webb on Nov 8, 1798. {Ref: PR}
BAUGHMAN, MITHIAS, head of family in 1800 (2nd District). {Ref: CI}
BAXTER, JACOB, see "Thomas Bond (of Thomas)" and "Jacob Bacter," q.v.
BAXTER, JOHN, insolvent on a list for 1791 in Gunpowder Upper and Bush River Lower Hundreds, as filed by John Bond, Deputy Sheriff, on Sep 20, 1791. {Ref: IL 31.24}
BAXTER, JOHN, head of family in 1800 (Havre de Grace). {Ref: CI}
BAXTER(?), JOHN, head of family in 1800 (3rd District). {Ref: CI}
BAXTER, REBECCA, dau. of William and Sarah, b. Jan 23, 1784, bapt. Aug 13, 1795. {Ref: PR}
BAXTER, SARAH, bur. Jul 14, 1793, aged 40. {Ref: PR}. Also see "Thomas Stocksdale" and "Rebecca Baxter," q.v.
BAXTER, WILLIAM, see "Rebecca Baxter," q.v.
BAY, HUGH, taxpayer, 1798, Deer Creek Upper Hd., no dwelling house listed in this part of the tax schedule, 1 tract (179 acres, 80 perches), $350.30 valuation, no slaves. {Ref: TL}
BAY, HUGH, taxpayer, 1798, Bush River Upper & Eden Hd., 1 dwelling house, 2 inferior houses, 2 acres, $200 valuation; 1 tract (145 acres) in Bush River Upper & Eden Hd., $285.47 valuation, 2 slaves. {Ref: TL}
BAY, HUGH, head of family in 1800 (4th District). {Ref: CI}
BAY, HUGH, head of family in 1800 (5th District). {Ref: CI}
BAY, ISABEL, see "Samuel Street," q.v.
BAY, JOHN, see "Thomas Bay," q.v.
BAY, JOHN, insolvent on lists returned by Robert Carlile and John Guyton (who listed him as a single man) for taxes due for the year 1791. {Ref: IL 31.16, 31.19}
BAY, JOHN, husband of Jemima Street, b. Mar 2, 1796, d. Nov 22, 1850, bur. in Bethel Presbyterian Church Cemetery at Madonna. {Ref: BC}
BAY, JOHN, granted a tavern license in March and August, 1797. {Ref: CC}
BAY, JOHN, head of family in 1800 (4th District). {Ref: CI}
BAY, NATHAN, head of family in 1800 (3rd District). {Ref: CI}
BAY, THOMAS, son of John Bay and Arabella Turner, and husband of Asenath Ann McClure, b. Jul 13, 1792, d. Novembe 25, 1876, bur. in Bethel Presbyterian Church Cemetery at Madonna. {Ref: BC}
BAY, WILLIAM, insolvent on a list for the road tax for 1792, as returned for Robert Amoss, tax collector. {Ref: IL 13.12}
BAY, WILLIAM, taxpayer, 1798, Bush River Lower Hd., no dwelling house listed in this part of the tax schedule, 2 tracts (106 acres) in Bush River Lower Hd.,

$235.13 valuation, no slaves. {Ref: TL}
BAY, WILLIAM, insolvent on a list for the road tax for 1792, as returned for Robert Amoss, tax collector. {Ref: IL 13.12}
BAY, WILLIAM, head of family in 1800 (3rd District). {Ref: CI}
BAYARD, SAMUEL, had an account at Hall's Store in January, 1791. {Ref: WH}
BAYLAFF (BAYLASS?), ELIZABETH, dau. of Thomas and Ann, b. Aug 10, 1755, bapt. Mar 20, 1796. {Ref: PR}
BAYLES, BENJAMIN, see "Samuel Bayles (of Benjamin)," q.v.
BAYLES, ELIZABETH (widow), taxpayer, 1798, Susquehanna Hd., 1 dwelling house, 1 inferior house, 2 acres, $100.50 valuation; 1 tract (198 acres) in Susquehanna Hd., $816.75 valuation, no slaves. {Ref: TL}. In another part of the tax schedule her name is listed without the "widow" and the occupant is listed as William Carroll.
BAYLES, NATHANIEL, see "Samuel Bayles (of Nathaniel)," q.v.
BAYLES, SAMUEL, taxpayer, 1798, Susquehanna Hd., 1 dwelling house, 2 inferior houses, 2 acres, $250 valuation; 1 tract (168 acres) in Susquehanna Hd., $504 valuation, no slaves. {Ref: TL}
BAYLES, SAMUEL, served on a Petit Jury in March, 1799. {Ref: CM}
BAYLES, SAMUEL (OF BENJAMIN), taxpayer, 1798, no dwelling house listed in this part of the tax schedule, 1 tract (61 acres) in Susquehanna Hd., $199.12 valuation, no slaves. {Ref: TL}
BAYLES, SAMUEL (OF NATHANIEL), taxpayer, 1798, Susquehanna Hd., no dwelling house listed in this part of the tax schedule, 1 tract (80 acres), $466.88 valuation, no slaves. {Ref: TL}
BAYLEY, BENEDICT, see "Ezekiel Bayley" and "Edwin Bayley," q.v.
BAYLEY, EDWIN, son of Benedict and Mary, b. May 20, 1797, bapt. Jun 20, 1797. {Ref: PR}
BAYLEY, EZEKIEL, son of Benedict and Mary, b. Mar 12, 1799. {Ref: PR}
BAYLEY, MARY, see "Ezekiel Bayley" and "Edwin Bayley," q.v.
BAYLEY, NEHEMIAH ("dead"), insolvent on lists due for 1790 and 1791 "fund taxes" and county taxes in Susquehanna Hd., as returned by Thomas Taylor (name spelled twice as "Bayley" and once as "Baily"). {Ref: IL 31.12, 3102}
BAYLIS, AQUILLA, head of family in 1800 (2nd District). {Ref: CI}
BAYLIS, BENEDICT, head of family in 1800 (2nd District). {Ref: CI}
BAYLIS (BAYLISS), DANIEL, insolvent on a list for the county tax due for 1793 in Susquehanna Hd. as returned to the levy court by Thomas Taylor on May 28, 1794, who noted "put in my hands last fall." {Ref: IL 31.12}
BAYLIS, DANIEL, head of family in 1800 (5th District). {Ref: CI}
BAYLIS, JOSIAS, head of family in 1800 (2nd District). {Ref: CI}
BAYLIS, MARY, head of family in 1800 (2nd District). {Ref: CI}
BAYLIS, SAMUEL, served on a Petit Jury in August, 1797. {Ref: CC}
BAYLIS, SAMUEL, head of family in 1800 (2nd District). {Ref: CI}

BAYLIS, SAMUEL JR., head of family in 1800 (2nd District). {Ref: CI}
BAYNE, ANN, m. Joshua Hartley on Feb 13, 1798. {Ref: PR}
BEAN, EDMOND, head of family in 1800 (Havre de Grace). {Ref: CI}
BEAN, EDWARD (EDMOND?), m. Elizabeth Wood on May 23, 1797. {Ref: PR}. Also see "Sarah Bean," q.v.
BEAN, ELIZABETH, see "Sarah Bean," q.v.
BEAN, SARAH, dau. of Edward (Edmond?) and Elizabeth, b. Aug 11, 1799. {Ref: PR}
BEANS, JONATHAN, b. on 19th of 12th month, 1791, d. on 19th of 3rd month, 1873, in his 83rd [sic] year, bur. in Little Falls Quaker Cemetery in Fallston. {Ref: TI}
BEANS, ELIZABETH W., b. 1793, d. on 26th of 8th month, 1881, in her 88th year, bur. in Little Falls Quaker Cemetery in Fallston. {Ref: TI}
BEAR, JOHN, taxpayer, 1798, Spesutia Lower Hd., 1 dwelling house, 44 perches and 21 sq. ft. of land, $250 valuation; 1 tract (132 perches, 63 sq. ft.) in Spesutia Lower Hd., $67.50 valuation, no slaves. {Ref: TL}
BEAST, PAUL, insolvent on a list for 1791 in Gunpowder Upper and Bush River Lower Hundreds, as filed by John Bond, Deputy Sheriff, on Sep 20, 1791 (who listed him as a single man). {Ref: IL 31.24}
BEATTY, ELEANOR, see "Eli Turner," q.v.
BEATTY, JEMIMA, see "James Benton McComas," q.v.u
BEATTY, JOHN, see "Eleanor Turner," q.v.
BEATY, ANN, consort of Samuel, b. 1792, d. Oct 5, 1837, bur. in Bethel Presbyterian Church Cemetery at Madonna. {Ref: BC}
BEATY, ARCHIBALD, see "James Phillips, Sr.," q.v.
BEATY, ARCHIBALD, taxpayer, 1798, Harford Lower Hd., 1 dwelling house, 6 inferior houses, 2 acres, $115 valuation; 4 tracts (412 acres, 120 perches) in Harford Lower Hd., $1628.89 valuation, 14 slaves. {Ref: TL}
BEATY, ARCHIBALD, head of family in 1800 (2nd District). {Ref: CI}
BEATY, JOHN, head of family in 1800 (4th District). {Ref: CI}. Also see "James Rampley" and "Mary Montgomery," q.v.
BEATY, SAMUEL, see "Ann Beaty," q.v.
BEATY, THOMAS, head of family in 1800 (1st District). {Ref: CI}
BEATY, WILLIAM, taxpayer, 1798, Bush River Upper & Eden Hd., 1 dwelling house, 2 inferior houses, 2 acres, $105 valuation; 1 tract (98 acres) in Bush River Upper & Eden Hd., $165.38 valuation, 2 slaves. {Ref: TL}
BEATY, WILLIAM, head of family in 1800 (4th District). {Ref: CI}
BEAUMONT, MARY, wife of Mifflin, b. 1797 or 1798, d. Oct 28, 1877, in her 80th year, bur. in Union Chapel Methodist Church Cemetery at Wilna. {Ref: TI}
BEAUMONT, MIFFLIN, b. 1799 or 1800, d. Nov 1, 1884, in his 85th year, bur. in Union Chapel Methodist Church Cemetery at Wilna. {Ref: TI}
BEAVEN, CHARLES, head of family in 1800 (5th District). {Ref: CI}
BEAVEN (BEAVER?), CHARLES, taxpayer, 1798, Deer Creek Middle Hd., 1

dwelling house, 3 inferior houses, 2 acres, $110 valuation; 1 tract (97 acres, 80 perches) in Deer Creek Middle Hd., $124.31 valuation, no slaves. {Ref: TL}. In another part of the tax schedule the occupant is listed as George McCausland. Also see "James Garrett," q.v.

BEAVEN, RICHARD, head of family in 1800 (5th District). {Ref: CI}

BEEMAN, JOSEPH, b. Aug 7, 1799, d. Jan 1, 1889, bur. in Churchville Presbyterian Church Cemetery. {Ref: TI}

BELL, ---- [blank space], (schoolmaster), insolvent on lists in 1791 due county taxes and road taxes in "Deer Creek Upper, Middle, and Broad Creek Hundreds" as returned by Robert Amos, Jr. (who wrote it as if the name was "Bill Schoolmaster") and yet another list prepared by Edward Prigg in 1791 listed it as "Bell School (Master), run." {Ref: IL 31.12, 31.22, 31.17}

BELL, DAVID, taxpayer, 1798, Bush River Upper & Eden Hd., 1 dwelling house, 3 inferior houses, 2 acres, $300 valuation; 1 tract (263 acres, 80 perches) in Bush River Upper & Eden Hd., $592.88 valuation, 1 slave. {Ref: TL}

BELL, DAVID, served on a Grand Jury in March, 1798. {Ref: CM}

BELL, DAVID, head of family in 1800 (4th District). {Ref: CI}

BELL, JAMES, taxpayer, 1798, Susquehanna Hd., 1 dwelling house, 2 inferior houses, 2 acres, $350 valuation, 3 tracts (213 acres, 120 perches) in Susquehanna Hundred; taxpayer, 1798, Susquehanna Hd., 1 dwelling house, 2 inferior houses, 2 acres, $225 valuation (J. McClaskey, occupant), 1 other building (Dennis Lendrigan, occupant), and 1 other building (Charles Yoakam or Yoakum, occupant), $590.62 valuation altogether, plus 2 slaves; taxpayer, 1798, Susquehanna Hd., 1 tract (13 acres), $126 valuation, no slaves. {Ref: TL}

BELL, JOHN, taxpayer, 1798, Bush River Upper & Eden Hd., 1 dwelling house, 2 inferior houses, 2 acres, $300 valuation; 2 tracts (221 acres, 80 perches) in Bush River Upper & Eden Hd., $622.12 valuation, no slaves. {Ref: TL}

BELL, JOHN, head of family in 1800 (4th District). {Ref: CI}

BELL, LETHE, see "Jesse Bell Johnson," q.v.

BELL, MARY, head of family in 1800 (3rd District). {Ref: CI}

BELL, REBECCA, see "Robert Kirkwood," q.v.

BELL, ROBERT, head of family in 1800 (2nd District). {Ref: CI}

BENNETT (BENNET), CASSEY, child of Philip and Sarah, b. Jan 26, 1798, bapt. Jun 15, 1800. {Ref: PR}

BENNETT, JAMES, head of family in 1800 (1st District). {Ref: CI}

BENNETT, JOSHUA, see "Barnet Barclay," q.v.

BENNETT (BENNET), PHILIP, see "Josias Carvil Hall" and "Cassey Bennett," q.v.

BENNETT, PHILIP, insolvent on a list for the road tax due for 1791 in Harford Upper, Harford Lower, and Spesutia Upper as returned by Robert Amos, Jr. on Sep 18, 1793. {Ref: IL 31.18}

BENNETT, PHILLIP, purchased a quarter beef and 10 pair of shoes on Nov 9,

1797 at Bush River Store. {Ref: AH}
BENNETT, PHILLIP, insolvent, Harford Lower and Spesutia Lower Hundreds, on a tax list returned by George Lyttle on Sep 21, 1791. {Ref: IL 31.20, 31.21}
BENNETT, PHILLIP, head of family in 1800 (2nd District). {Ref: CI}
BENNETT, SARAH, see "Cassey Bennett," q.v.
BENNETT (BENNET), WILLIAM, see "Asa Taylor," q.v.
BENNETT, WILLIAM, head of family in 1800 (2nd District). {Ref: CI}
BENNINGTON (BENINGTON), JEREMIAH, head of family in 1800 (5th District). {Ref: CI}. Also see "Isaac Henry," q.v.
BENNINGTON (BENINGTON), WILLIAM ("poor"), insolvent on a list of the county tax due William Osborn, sheriff, for 1791, as returned by Edward Prigg on Sep 20, 1791. {Ref: IL 31.17}
BENNINGTON (BENINGTON), WILLIAM, head of family in 1800 (5th District). {Ref: CI}
BENNINGTON, WILLIAM, insolvent on lists of taxes due in 1791 and 1792 in Broad Creek Hd., as returned by Robert Amos, Jr. in 1791 and Benjamin Preston in 1792. {Ref: IL 31.03}
BENTLEY, JOSHUA, insolvent on list returned by Robert Carlile for taxes due for the year 1791. {Ref: IL 31.16}
BENTLEY, WILLIAM, insolvent on list returned for the road tax due for 1791 by John Bull. {Ref: IL 31.14}
BENTLEY, WILLIAM, insolvent on a list for 1791 in Gunpowder Upper and Bush River Lower Hundreds, as filed by John Bond, Deputy Sheriff, on Sep 20, 1791 (who listed him as a single man). {Ref: IL 31.24}
BERKIN (BERKINS), CHARLES, insolvent on lists of taxes due in 1791 and 1792 in Broad Creek Hd., as returned by Robert Amos, Jr. in 1791 and Benjamin Preston in 1792. {Ref: IL 31.03, 31.12, 31.22}
BERRY, EDWARD, see "James Rampley," q.v.
BESHONG, JOHN, head of family in 1800 (5th District). {Ref: CI}
BESHONG (BOSONG), JOHN, insolvent on lists in 1791 due county taxes and road taxes in "Deer Creek Upper, Middle, and Broad Creek Hundreds" as returned by Robert Amos, Jr. {Ref: IL 31.12, 31.22}
BEVARD, ANNE AMOS, dau. of William and Rebecca, b. Nov 11, 1799. {Ref: PR}
BEVARD, CHARLES, taxpayer, 1798, Deer Creek Lower Hd., no dwelling house listed in this part of the tax schedule, 1 tract (80 acres), $157.50 valuation, no slaves. {Ref: TL}
BEVARD, GEORGE, b. Jan 4, 1796, d. Feb 14, 1869, bur. in Deer Creek Friends Cemetery in Darlington. {Ref: TI}. Also see "Mary Wallis Bevard," q.v.
BEVARD, JAMES, m. Amelia Chance on Feb 4, 1798. {Ref: PR}
BEVARD, MARY WALLIS, wife of George, b. Sep 6, 1797, d. Mar 9, 1860, bur. in Deer Creek Friends Cemetery in Darlington. {Ref: TI}
BEVARD, REBECCA, see "Anne Amos Bevard," q.v.
BEVARD, WILLIAM, see "Anne Amos Bevard," q.v.

BEVEN (BEVIN), CHARLES, taxpayer, 1798, Broad Creek Hd., no dwelling house listed in this part of the tax schedule, no land listed, 4 slaves. {Ref: TL}. Also see "Peggy Steel," q.v.

BEVEN (BEVIN), RICHARD, taxpayer, 1798, Broad Creek Hd., no dwelling house listed in this part of the tax schedule, no land listed, 1 slave. {Ref: TL}

BEVIN, CHARLES, treated by Dr. John Archer on Dec 27, 1795; also mentioned his wife (no name given). {Ref: JA}

BIAYS, RACHEL, dau. of Joseph and Elizabeth Biays, was b. in 1797, m. Capt. John A. Webster, d. Oct 3, 1868, aged 72, bur. in the Dallam-Webster Family Cemetery near Creswell. {Ref: TI}

BIDDISON, ANN, dau. of Mesheck and Kerenhappuck, b. Mar 11, 1798. {Ref: PR}

BIDDISON (BIDDESON), DANIEL, son of Mesheck and Karenhappock, b. Nov 26, 1793. {Ref: PR}

BIDDISON, KERENHAPPUCK (KARENHAPPOCK), see "Salem Biddison" and "Daniel Biddison" and "Shadrick Biddison" and "Mesheck Biddison," q.v.

BIDDISON, MESHECK, see "Salem Biddison" and "Daniel Biddison" and "Shadrick Biddison" and "Ann Biddison," q.v.

BIDDISON, SALEM, son of Mesheck and Kerenhappuck, b. Mar 30, 1791. {Ref: PR}

BIDDISON, SHADRICK (SHADRACK), son of Mesheck and Kerenhappuck, b. Nov 17, 1795. {Ref: PR}

BIDDLE, AUGUSTA, see "Elizabeth Nelson," q.v.

BIDDLE, BENJAMIN F., b. 1799, d. Jan 18, 1883, aged 84, bur. in Harford (Old Brick) Baptist Church Cemetery. {Ref: TI}

BIDDLE (BIDDEL), JOHN, head of family in 1800 (4th District). {Ref: CI}

BIDDLE, JOHN B., taxpayer, 1798, Bush River Upper & Eden Hd., 1 dwelling house, 2 inferior houses, 2 acres, $105 valuation; 6 tracts (218 acres, 120 perches) in Bush River Upper & Eden Hd., $492.19, no slaves. {Ref: TL}

BIDDLE, JOHN B., served on a Grand Jury in March, 1798 and on a Petit Jury in March, 1800. {Ref: CM}

BIDDLE, RICHARD, insolvent on list returned by Robert Carlile for taxes due for the year 1791. {Ref: IL 31.16}

BIDDLE, RICHARD, taxpayer, 1798, Bush River Upper & Eden Hd., no dwelling house listed in this part of the tax schedule, no land listed, 2 slaves. {Ref: TL}

BIDDLE (BIDDEL), RICHARD, head of family in 1800 (4th District). {Ref: CI}

BILLINGSLEA, CLEMENCY, will probated Sep 2, 1794. {Ref: HW}

BILLINGSLEA, ELIZABETH FREEBORN, b. Aug 27, 1794, d. Dec 18, 1858, bur. in Cokesbury Methodist Cemetery in Abingdon. {Ref: TI}

BILLINGSLEA, JAMES, served on a Grand Jury in March, 1799 and March, 1800. {Ref: CM}

BILLINGSLEA, JAMES, m. Elizabeth Matthews on Sep 14, 1797. {Ref: PR}

BILLINGSLEA, JOSIAS, treated by Dr. John Archer on Oct 4, 1799; also mentioned his wife (no name given) and son William. {Ref: JA}

BILLINGSLEA, WILLIAM, served on a Petit Jury in August, 1799 and on a Grand Jury in August, 1800. {Ref: CM}. Also see "Josias Billingslea," q.v.
BILLINGSLEY, FRANCIS, insolvent on a list for 1791 in Gunpowder Upper and Bush River Lower Hundreds, as filed by John Bond, Deputy Sheriff, on Sep 20, 1791. {Ref: IL 31.24}
BILLINGSLEY, JAMES, taxpayer, 1798, Bush River Lower Hd., 1 dwelling house, 2 inferior houses, 1 acre, $500 valuation; 1 tract (5 acres) in Bush River Lower Hd., $73.12 valuation, 3 slaves. {Ref: TL}
BILLINGSLEY, JAMES, licensed retailer in March, 1795. {Ref: CC}
BILLINGSLEY, JAMES, head of family in 1800 (Abingdon). {Ref: CI}
BILLINGSLEY, RUTH, taxpayer, 1798, Harford Upper Hd., 1 dwelling house, 5 inferior houses, 2 acres, $175 valuation; 1 tract (236 acres) in Harford Upper Hd., $531 valuation, 2 slaves. {Ref: TL}
BILLINGSLEY, RUTH, head of family in 1800 (1st District). {Ref: CI}
BILLINGSLEY, WALTER, tract *Mentz* surveyed between 1792 and 1796. {Ref: SB}
BILLINGSLEY, WALTER, head of family in 1800 (3rd District). {Ref: CI}
BILLINGSLEY, WALTER, head of family in 1800 (4th District). {Ref: CI}
BILLINGSLEY, WALTER JR., taxpayer, 1798, Bush River Upper & Eden Hd., 1 dwelling house, 2 inferior houses, 2 acres, $110 valuation; 1 tract (121 acres) in Bush River Upper & Eden Hd., $212.25 valuation, no slaves. {Ref: TL}
BILLINGSLEY, WALTER SR., taxpayer, 1798, Spesutia Upper Hd., 1 dwelling house, 9 inferior houses, 2 acres, $325 valuation; 1 tract (797 acres) in Spesutia Upper Hd., $2561.63 valuation, 2 slaves. {Ref: TL}. In another part of the tax schedule the occupants are listed as John Allen, Philip Renshaw, and John Wakeland.
BILLINGSLEY, WILLIAM, served on a Petit Jury in August, 1797. {Ref: CC}
BIRD, MORTEN (MARTIN?), subpoenaed to the Grand Jury in August, 1797. {Ref: CC}
BIRKHEAD, MATTHEW, taxpayer, 1798, Gunpowder Lower Hd., 1 dwelling house, 2 inferior houses, 2 acres, $120 valuation; 1 tract (398 acres) in Gunpowder Lower Hd., $895.50 valuation, 7 slaves. {Ref: TL}
BIRKHEAD, THOMAS, m. Elizabeth Waters on Dec 7, 1797. {Ref: PR}
BIRKHEAD, THOMAS H., taxpayer, 1798, Gunpowder Lower Hd., 1 dwelling house, 5 inferior houses, 2 acres, $300 valuation; 1 tract (298 acres) on Gunpowder Upper Hd., $1386 valuation, 4 slaves. {Ref: TL}
BIRMINGHAM, REBECCA, taxpayer, 1798, Bush River Upper & Eden Hd., 1 dwelling house, 2 inferior houses, 2 acres, $120 valuation; 2 tracts (216 acres, 120 perches) in Bush River Upper & Eden Hd., $365.60 valuation, 1 slave. {Ref: TL}
BIRMINGHAM (BURMINGHAM), REBECCA, head of family in 1800 (4th District). {Ref: CI}
BISHOP, CATHERINE, wife of John Pennington, b. Feb 7, 1800. {Ref: John Pennington Bible}. Also see "Elizabeth Bishop," q.v.

BISHOP, ELIZABETH, dau. of William and Catherine, b. Feb 1, 1800, bapt. Jun 12, 1800. {Ref: PR}

BISHOP, WILLIAM, see "Elizabeth Bishop," q.v.

BLACK, JOHN, taxpayer, 1798, Bush River Upper & Eden Hd., 1 dwelling house, 2 acres, $120 valuation; 1 tract (133 acres) in Bush River Upper & Eden Hd., $299.25 valuation, no slaves. {Ref: TL}

BLACK, JOHN, head of family in 1800 (4th District). {Ref: CI}

BLAIR, HUGH HOWARD, b. 1796 in the Parish of Deserteraught, County Tyrone, Ireland, d. Feb 28, 1869, aged 73, bur. in St. Mary's Episcopal Church Cemetery. {Ref: TI}

BLAKE, ISAAC, see "Rachel Blake" and "Jinny Jones," q.v.

BLAKE, MARGARET, see "Rachel Blake," q.v.

BLAKE, RACHEL, dau. of Isaac and Margaret, b. about fall in 1780, bapt. May 5, 1799. {Ref: PR}

BLAKE, RACHEL, m. Marshall Lee on Jan 13, 1799. {Ref: PR}

BLAKE, SARAH, m. Thomas Brooks on Jul 17, 1798. {Ref: PR}

BLAKEY, EDWARD, head of family in 1800 (4th District). {Ref: CI}

BLANEY, EDWARD, see "Patrick Doran," q.v.

BLANEY, JOHN, b. 1791, d. Jul 2, 1866, in his 75th year, bur. in Angel Hill Cemetery in Havre de Grace. {Ref: TI}

BLANEY, MARY, taxpayer, 1798, Bush River Upper & Eden Hd., 1 dwelling house, 2 inferior houses, 2 acres, $300 valuation; 3 tracts (180 acres, 80 perches) in Bush River Upper & Eden Hd., $394.87, 3 slaves. {Ref: TL}

BLANEY, MARY, head of family in 1800 (4th District). {Ref: CI}

BLANEY, THOMAS, charged in 1794 (nature of the case not stated). {Ref: CD, March Term, 1795}

BLAXTON, ELIJAH, insolvent on lists returned for the county and road taxes due for 1791 by John Bull in Gunpowder Lower Hd. (name spelled as "Blacstone" on one list). {Ref: IL 31.14, 31.15}

BLOODGOOD, JOHN, head of family in 1800 (4th District). {Ref: CI}

BOARMAN, BENJAMIN W., b. 1800, d. Sep 21, 1869, in his 69th year, bur. in St. Ignatius Catholic Church Cemetery in Hickory. {Ref: TI}

BOARMAN, LOUISA, see "Louisa M. Scott," q.v.

BODKIN, THOMAS ("run"), insolvent on a list of the county tax due William Osborn, sheriff, for 1791, as returned by Edward Prigg on Sep 20, 1791. {Ref: IL 31.17}

BODKIN, WILLIAM, insolvent on a list in 1792 in Broad Creek Hd., as returned by Benjamin Preston. {Ref: IL 31.03}

BODKIN, WILLIAM ("run"), insolvent on a list of the county tax due William Osborn, sheriff, for 1791, as returned by Edward Prigg on Sep 20, 1791. {Ref: IL 31.17}

BODY, PETER, son of Benjamin and Jane, b. Nov 25, 1794. {Ref: PR}

BODY, SARAH, head of family in 1800 (2nd District). {Ref: CI}

BOIL, ANN, see "Hugh Boil," q.v.

BOIL, HUGH, son of Hugh and Ann, b. Mar 11, 1796, bapt. Apr 3, 1796. {Ref: PR}
BOLAND, JUDITH, dau. of Peter and Rachel, b. in January, 1793. {Ref: PR}
BOLSTER, WILLIAM, taxpayer, 1798, Gunpowder Lower Hd., no dwelling house listed in this part of the tax schedule, no land listed, 3 slaves. {Ref: TL}
BOLSTER, WILLIAM, head of family in 1800 (1st District). {Ref: CI}
BONAR, JOHN, licensed retailer in March, 1795. {Ref: CC}
BOND, BUCKLAR, treated by Dr. John Archer on Aug 16, 1793. {Ref: JA}
BOND, BUCKLER, served on a Petit Jury in August, 1798 and August, 1800, and on a Grand Jury in August, 1799. {Ref: CM}
BOND, BUCKLER, taxpayer, 1798, Bush River Lower Hd., 1 dwelling house, 3 inferior houses, 1 acre and 80 perches, $320 valuation; 2 tracts (532 acres) in Bush River Lower Hd., $3142.12 valuation, 2 slaves; taxpayer, 1798, Bush River Lower Hd., 1 dwelling house, 2 inferior houses, 80 perches of land, $135 valuation, no slaves. {Ref: TL}
BOND, BUCKLER, insolvent on a list for the road tax for 1792, as returned for Robert Amoss, tax collector. {Ref: IL 13.12}
BOND, BUCKLER, head of family in 1800 (3rd District). {Ref: CI}
BOND, CATHERINE, see "William Allen," q.v.
BOND, CORBIN (negro), b. c1795, probably the son of Indian Will and "The African Lady" (name not given), slaves owned by Dennis Bond. Corbin was only 4 ft. 5 in. tall and was known as the "Little Black Guinea Man." {Ref: HB 36:30-31 (1988)}
BOND, DENNIS, see "Corbin Bond," q.v.
BOND, DENNIS, served on a Petit Jury in August, 1798 and August, 1799 and August, 1800. {Ref: CM}
BOND, DENNIS, taxpayer, 1798, Bush River Lower Hd., 1 dwelling house, 7 inferior houses, 2 acres, $255 valuation; 4 tracts (541 acres) in Bush River Lower Hd., $1825.88 valuation, 9 slaves. {Ref: TL}
BOND, DENNIS, head of family in 1800 (3rd District). {Ref: CI}
BOND, DENNIS (esquire), treated by Dr. John Archer on Dec 26, 1795; also mentioned inoculation of children Harriott, Jimmy, and Fanny Bond. {Ref: JA}
BOND, EDWARD (OF WILLIAM), taxpayer, 1798, Gunpowder Upper Hd., no dwelling house listed in this part of the tax schedule, 1 tract (28 acres) in Gunpowder Upper Hd., $96.75 valuation, no slaves. {Ref: TL}
BOND, FANNY, see "Dennis Bond, Esq.," q.v.
BOND, FELL, served on a Petit Jury in March, 1798. {Ref: CM}
BOND, GEORGE, head of family in 1800 (4th District). {Ref: CI}
BOND, HARRIOTT, see "Dennis Bond, Esq.," q.v.
BOND, J., insolvent on a list for the road tax due for 1791 in Harford Upper, Harford Lower, and Spesutia Upper as returned by Robert Amos, Jr. on Sep 18, 1793. {Ref: IL 31.18}
BOND, JACOB, tract *Muskratt Hall* surveyed between 1792 and 1796. {Ref: SB}
BOND, JACOB, insolvent on a list for the road tax for 1792, as returned for Robert

Amoss, tax collector. {Ref: IL 13.12}

BOND, JACOB, taxpayer, 1798, Gunpowder Lower Hd., 1 dwelling house, 8 inferior houses, 2 acres, $500 valuation; 2 tracts (420 acres) in Gunpowder Lower Hd., $1522.12 valuation, 6 slaves. {Ref: TL}

BOND, JACOB, head of family in 1800 (1st District). {Ref: CI}

BOND, JAMES, see "Lambert Wilmer Bond," q.v.

BOND, JAMES, served on a Petit Jury in March, 1799. {Ref: CM}

BOND, JAMES, taxpayer, 1798, Bush River Lower Hd., 1 dwelling house, 5 inferior houses, 2 acres, $380 valuation; 5 tracts (455 acres) in Bush River Lower Hd., $1591.88 valuation, no slaves; taxpayer, 1798, Bush River Lower Hd., 1 dwelling house, 80 perches of land, $280 valuation; 1 tract (200 acres) in Gunpowder Upper Hd., $315 valuation, no slaves; taxpayer, 1798, Bush River Lower Hd., 1 dwelling house, 80 perches of land, $120 valuation, no slaves. {Ref: TL}. His name was listed once as "James Bon, Esqr."

BOND, JAMES (esquire). treated by Dr. John Archer on Jul 22, 1794. {Ref: JA}

BOND, JAMES (esquire), head of family in 1800 (Belle Air). {Ref: CI}

BOND, JIMMY, see "Dennis Bond, Esq.," q.v.

BOND, JOHN, see "Thomas Bond" and "Thomas Bond (of John)" and "Richard Ruff: and "William Bond," q.v.

BOND, JOHN, will probated Dec 23, 1791. {Ref: HW}

BOND, JOHN, deputy sheriff, 1791. {Ref: IL 31.24}

BOND, JOHN, head of family in 1800 (1st District). {Ref: CI}

BOND, JOHN, of Joppa, bur. Mar 10, 1793, aged 27. {Ref: PR}

BOND, JOHN (carpenter), insolvent on list returned for the road tax due for 1791 by John Bull. {Ref: IL 31.14}

BOND, JOHN (doctor), head of family in 1800 (3rd District). {Ref: CI}

BOND, JOHN (sheriff), head of family in 1800 (Belle Air). {Ref: CI}

BOND, JOHN C., subpoenaed to the Grand Jury in August, 1797. {Ref: CC}

BOND, JOHN (OF JOHN), taxpayer, 1798, Gunpowder Upper Hd., 1 dwelling house, 6 inferior houses, 2 acres, $250 valuation; 6 tracts (385 acres, 40 perches) in Gunpowder Upper Hd., $909.56 valuation, 1 slave. {Ref: TL}

BOND, JOHN (OF W.), head of family in 1800 (3rd District). {Ref: CI}

BOND, JOHN (OF WILLIAM), taxpayer, 1798, Gunpowder Upper Hd., no dwelling house listed in this part of the tax schedule, 1 tract (128 acres) in Gunpowder Upper Hd., $488.25 valuation, no slaves. {Ref: TL}

BOND, LAMBERT WILMER, son of James and Martha, b. Aug 29, 1795. {Ref: PR}

BOND, MARTHA, see "Lambert Wilmer Bond," q.v.

BOND, MORDICA, head of family in 1800 (4th District). {Ref: CI}

BOND, NICHOLAS M., b. May 23, 1797, d. Apr 15, 1866, bur. in the Bond Family Graveyard which was on Tollgate Road near Bel Air. {Ref: TI}

BOND, PEGGY, see "John Hambleton," q.v.

BOND, RALPH, served on a Petit Jury in March, 1798 and on a Grand Jury in

March, 1799. {Ref: CM}

BOND, RALPH, taxpayer, 1798, Bush River Lower Hd., 1 dwelling house, 5 inferior houses, 1 acre and 80 perches, $200 valuation; 5 tracts (455 acres) in Bush River Lower Hd., $1324.69 valuation, 2 slaves. {Ref: TL}

BOND, RICHARD, see "Jesse Jarrett," q.v.

BOND, SALLY CHARITY, see "Moses Maxwell," q.v.

BOND, SAMUEL, head of family in 1800 (Belle Air). {Ref: CI}. Also see "Thomas Bond," q.v.

BOND, SARAH (Mrs.), b. Jan --, 1793, in County Wicklow, Ireland, d. Oct 31, 1868, at Cheltonham, Pennsylvania, in her 75th year, bur. in St. George's Episcopal Church Cemetery at Perryman, Maryland. {Ref: TI}

BOND, THOMAS, see "William Allen," q.v.

BOND, THOMAS, bur. Sep 3 or 5, 1800. {Ref: PR}.

BOND, THOMAS (esquire), subpoenaed to the Grand Jury in August, 1797. {Ref: CC}

BOND, THOMAS (OF DANIEL), insolvent on a list for the road tax for 1792, as returned for Robert Amoss, tax collector. {Ref: II. 13.12}

BOND, THOMAS (OF DANIEL), subpoenaed to the Grand Jury in August, 1797. {Ref: CC}

BOND, THOMAS (OF JOHN), taxpayer, 1798, Gunpowder Upper Hd., 1 dwelling house, 5 inferior houses, 2 acres, $350 valuation; 3 tracts (482 acres, 80 perches) in Gunpowder Upper Hd., $1412.44 valuation, 2 slaves. {Ref: TL}

BOND, THOMAS (OF JOHN), served on a Petit Jury in March, 1798, as a Grand Jury foreman in March, 1799, and on a Grand Jury in March, 1800. {Ref: CM}

BOND, THOMAS (OF JOHN), head of family in 1800 (3rd District). {Ref: CI}

BOND, THOMAS (OF SAMUEL), served on a Petit Jury in March, 1798. {Ref: CM}

BOND, THOMAS (OF THOMAS), subpoenaed to the Grand Jury in August, 1797. {Ref: CC}

BOND, THOMAS (OF THOMAS), taxpayer, 1798, Bush River Lower Hd., 1 dwelling house, 8 inferior houses, 2 acres, $300 valuation; 5 tracts (683 acres) in Bush River Lower Hd., $2493.28 valuation, 8 slaves. In another part of the tax schedule the occupants are listed as Charles Gordon, William Saunders, Jacob Baxter, Nicholas Moales, and Isaac Kennard. Also, taxpayer, 1 tract (130 acres) in Eden Hd., $658.13 valuation, no slaves. {Ref: TL}

BOND, THOMAS (OF THOMAS), appointed a Judge of Elections in the 1st District following the resignation of John Rumsey filed on Dec 31, 1800. {Ref: CM}

BOND, THOMAS S., taxpayer, 1798, Bush River Upper & Eden Hd., 1 dwelling house, 3 inferior houses, 2 acres, $105 valuation; 1 tract (254 acres) in Bush River Upper & Eden Hd., $1285.87 valuation, 2 slaves. {Ref: TL}

BOND, THOMAS S. (esquire), head of family in 1800 (4th District). {Ref: CI}

BOND, TREGO, had an account at Hall's Store in February, 1791; also noted in account "paid his father on May 25, 1790." {Ref: WH}

BOND, WILLIAM, see "John Bond (of William)" and "Edward Bond (of

William)," q.v.

BOND, WILLIAM (OF JOHN), insolvent on a list for 1791 in Gunpowder Upper and Bush River Lower Hundreds, as filed by John Bond, Deputy Sheriff, on Sep 20, 1791. {Ref: IL 31.24}

BOND, WILLIAM (OF SAMUEL), treated by Dr. John Archer on May 1, 1793. {Ref: JA}

BOND, ZACHEUS, taxpayer, 1798, Deer Creek Middle Hd., 1 dwelling house, 4 inferior houses, 2 acres; $230 valuation; 2 tracts (300 acres) in Deer Creek Middle Hd., including 2 other buildings (Samuel Rogers and John McLaughlen, occupants), $787.50 valuation, 1 slave. {Ref: TL}

BOND, ZACHEUS O., head of family in 1800 (5th District). {Ref: CI}

BONDS, HARRY (negro), insolvent on a list for 1791 in Gunpowder Upper and Bush River Lower Hundreds, as filed by John Bond, Deputy Sheriff, on Sep 20, 1791. {Ref: IL 31.24}

BONER, JAMES, taxpayer, 1798, Susquehanna Hd., no dwelling house listed in this part of the tax schedule, 2 tracts (150 acres), $416.25 valuation, no slaves. {Ref: TL}

BONER, JAMES, head of family in 1800 (2nd District). {Ref: CI}

BONER, JOHN, treated by Dr. John Archer on Sep 3, 1791; also mentioned his wife (no name given). {Ref: JA}

BONER, JOHN ("out back"), insolvent on lists due for 1790 and 1791 "fund taxes" and county taxes in Susquehanna Hd., as returned by Thomas Taylor. {Ref: IL 31.12, 31.02}

BOOLER, JOHN, head of family in 1800 (4th District). {Ref: CI}

BONNELL, HANNAH, see "John Bowers, " q.v.

BOOTHE, RICHARD, head of family in 1800 (3rd District). {Ref: CI}

BOOTS, SAMUEL, subpoenaed to the Grand Jury in August, 1797. {Ref: CC}

BOOTS, SAMUEL, appeared on list of "recognizances" of the court for appearance of William O'Dair in 1797. {Ref: CD, August Term, 1797}

BOSLEY, ELIJAH, tract *Hand in Hand* surveyed between 1792 and 1796. {Ref: SB}

BOSLEY, ELIJAH (Baltimore County), taxpayer, 1798, Bush River Upper & Eden Hd., 3 tracts (485 acres), $1636.87 valuation, no slaves. {Ref: TL}

BOSLEY, EZEKIEL (Baltimore County), taxpayer, 1798, Deer Creek Middle Hd., 1 tract (291 acres), $654.75 valuation, no slaves. {Ref: TL}

BOSLEY, VINCENT, tracts *Jones's Mistake* and *Peter* surveyed between 1792 and 1796. {Ref: SB}

BOSLEY, VINCENT, taxpayer, 1798, Deer Creek Upper Hd., 1 dwelling house, 1 inferior house, 2 acres, $104 valuation; 3 tracts (499 acres) in Deer Creek Upper Hd., $599.62 valuation, 2 slaves. {Ref: TL}

BOSLEY, VINCENT, head of family in 1800 (4th District). {Ref: CI}

BOTTS, BETSY, see "Sarah Botts," q.v.

BOTTS, ELIZA, see "Sarah Botts," q.v.

BOTTS, ISAAC, taxpayer, 1798, Susquehanna Hd., no dwelling house listed in this part of the tax schedule, 1 tract (119 acres, 80 perches), $627.76 valuation,

no slaves. {Ref: TL}
BOTTS, ISAAC, head of family in 1800 (2nd District). {Ref: CI}
BOTTS, JOHN, taxpayer, 1798, Susquehanna Hd., no dwelling house listed in this part of the tax schedule, 1 tract (53 acres), $267 valuation, 3 slaves. {Ref: TL}
BOTTS, JOHN, head of family in 1800 (2nd District). {Ref: CI}
BOTTS, SARAH, treated by Dr. John Archer on Jan 12, 1791, mentioned dau. Betsy, and treated on Jan 24, 1791, mentioned dau. Eliza. {Ref: JA}
BOULDIN, CHARLES D., b. 1796, d. Sep 26, 1882, in his 86th year, bur. in Christ Episcopal (Rock Spring) Church Cemetery. {Ref: TI}
BOULDIN, MARY GOVER WILSON, wife of Charles D., b. 1799, d. Mar 24, 1877, in her 78th year, bur. in Christ Episcopal (Rock Spring) Church Cemetery. {Ref: TI}
BOWEN, ELISHA, insolvent on a list in 1792 in Deer Creek Lower Hd., as returned by Benjamin Preston. {Ref: IL 31.03}. Also see "William Mitchell," q.v.
BOWEN, ELISHA ("can't be found"), insolvent on lists due for 1790 and 1791 "fund taxes" and was crossed off the 1791 road tax list in Deer Creek Lower Hd., as returned by Thomas Taylor. {Ref: IL 31.12}
BOWEN, ELISHA, head of family in 1800 (2nd District). {Ref: CI}
BOWERS, JOHN, m. Hannah Bronwell (Bonnell?) on Nov 3, 1793. {Ref: PR}
BOWLES (BOWLS), THOMAS ("out back" and "gone back"), insolvent on lists due for 1790 and 1791 "fund taxes" and county taxes in Susquehanna Hd., as returned by Thomas Taylor. {Ref: IL 31.12, 31.02}
BOWLEY, DANIEL (Baltimore Town), or MAHLON THOMPSON, taxpayer, 1798, Susquehanna Hd., 1 tract (434 acres) and 1 building (Mahlon Thompson, occupant), $1254.37 valuation, no slaves. {Ref: TL}
BOWLIN, PETER, head of family in 1800 (2nd District). {Ref: CI}
BOWMAN, HENRY, taxpayer, 1798, Susquehanna Hd., no dwelling house listed in this part of the tax schedule, 1 tract (26 acres), $218.25 valuation, no slaves. {Ref: TL}
BOWMAN, HENRY, treated by Dr. John Archer on Sep 3, 1795. {Ref: JA}
BOWMAN, HENRY, b. 1796 or 1797, d. Jan --, 1872, in his 75th year, bur. in Rock Run Cemetery at Craig's Corner. {Ref: TI}
BOWMAN, HENRY, head of family in 1800 (Havre de Grace). {Ref: CI}
BOWMAN, HENRY JR., head of family in 1800 (2nd District). {Ref: CI}
BOWMAN, ISRAEL, head of family in 1800 (Belle Air). {Ref: CI}. Also see "John Brown," q.v.
BOWMAN, JOHN, b. 1793, d. 1857, bur. in Rock Run Cemetery at Craig's Corner. {Ref: TI}
BOWMAN, JOHN ("Redstone"), insolvent on lists due for 1790 and 1791 "fund taxes" and county taxes in Susquehanna Hd., as returned by Thomas Taylor. {Ref: IL 31.12, 31.02}
BOWMAN, ROBERT, see "Sylvester Bowman," q.v.
BOWMAN, ROBERT, taxpayer, 1798, Deer Creek Middle Hd., no dwelling house listed in this part of the tax schedule, no land listed, 3 slaves. {Ref: TL}

BOWMAN, ROBERT, head of family in 1800 (5th District). {Ref: CI}
BOWMAN, SYLVESTER (SILVESTER), taxpayer, 1798, Deer Creek Middle Hd., 1 dwelling house, 5 inferior houses, 2 acres, $160 valuation; 1 tract (300 acres) in Deer Creek Middle Hd., $410.63 valuation, 3 slaves. {Ref: TL}. In another part of the tax schedule the occupant is listed as Robert Bowman.
BOWMAN, SYLVESTER (reverend), treated by Dr. John Archer on Feb 1, 1791. {Ref: JA}
BOWNE, SAMUEL, b. on 18th of 6th month, 1797, d. on 20th of 1st month, 1879, bur. in Little Falls Quaker Cemetery in Fallston. {Ref: TI}
BOWSER, BENJAMIN, insolvent on a list for the road tax due for 1791 in Harford Upper, Harford Lower, and Spesutia Upper as returned by Robert Amos, Jr. on Sep 18, 1793. {Ref: IL 31.18}
BOXT, PETER, taxpayer, 1798, Spesutia Lower Hd., no dwelling house listed in this part of the tax schedule, 1 tract (88 perches, 42 sq. ft.), $27 valuation, no slaves. {Ref: TL}
BOYCE, CAPTAIN, had an account at Hall's Store in January, 1791. {Ref: WH}
BOYCE, R. (captain), had an account at Hall's Store in September, 1791. {Ref: WH}
BOYCE, ROGER, vestryman, 1796-1797, St. George's Episcopal Church. {Ref: PR}
BOYCE, ROGER, subpoenaed to the Grand Jury in August, 1797. {Ref: CC}
BOYCE, ROGER, taxpayer, 1798, Spesutia Lower Hd., 1 dwelling house, 2 inferior houses, 44 perches and 21 sq. ft. of land, $1000 valuation; 1 tract (1 acre, 16 perches, 84 sq. ft.) in Spesutia Lower Hd., $90 valuation, 9 slaves. {Ref: TL}
BOYCE, ROGER, m. Hannah Day on Dec 3, 1797. {Ref: PR}
BOYCE, ROGER, head of family in 1800 (Havre de Grace). {Ref: CI}
BOYD, ANNA, dau. of John and Avarilla, b. Jan 29, 1800. {Ref: PR}
BOYD, AVARILLA, see "Isabella Boyd" and "Anna Boyd," q.v.
BOYD, COOPER, taxpayer, 1798, Broad Creek Hd., no dwelling house listed in this part of the tax schedule, 2 tracts (60 acres), $251.25 valuation, no slaves. {Ref: TL}
BOYD, COOPER, insolvent on lists in Broad Creek Hd. in 1791, as returned by Robert Amos, Jr., but his name was then crossed off both lists. {Ref: IL 31.12, 31.22}
BOYD, COOPER, head of family in 1800 (5th District). {Ref: CI}
BOYD, COOPER S., b. Jun 5, 1792, d. May 3, 1850, aged 57 years, 10 months and 29 days [sic], bur. in Darlington Cemetery. {Ref: TI}
BOYD, ISABELLA, dau. of John and Avarilla, b. Aug 15, 1798. {Ref: PR}
BOYD, JOHN, see "Isabella Boyd" and "Anna Boyd," q.v.
BOYD, JOHN, taxpayer, 1798, Spesutia Lower Hd., 1 dwelling house, 1 inferior house, 44 perches and 21 sq. ft. of land, $540 valuation, no slaves. {Ref: TL}
BOYD, JOHN, head of family in 1800 (Havre de Grace). {Ref: CI}
BOYD, JOHN, head of family in 1800 (5th District). {Ref: CI}
BOYD, JOHN (York County), insolvent on a list of the county tax due William Osborn, sheriff, for 1791, as returned by Edward Prigg on Sep 20, 1791. {Ref: IL 31.17}

BOYD, JOHN (York County), insolvent on lists in 1792 in Broad Creek Hd., as returned by Benjamin Preston; also appeared in the 1791 list as "Jno. Boyd," but his name was then crossed off the list. {Ref: IL 31.03, 31.12, 31.22}

BOYD, SARAH, m. Mathew Molton on Jun 17, 1798. {Ref: PR}

BOYD, STEPHEN, b. in York County on Feb 15, 1794, d. in Harford County on Feb 18, 1854, bur. in Deer Creek Harmony Presbyterian Church Cemetery near Darlington. {Ref: TI}

BOYER, AUGUSTIN, non-resident (place of residence not stated, probably Cecil County), or JAMES DEAVER, taxpayer, 1798, Spesutia Lower Hd., no dwelling house listed in this part of the tax schedule, no land listed, 1 slave (James Deaver, superintendent).

BOYER, DAVID, head of family in 1800 (1st District). {Ref: CI}

BOYER, WILLIAM, insolvent, Harford Lower and Spesutia Lower Hundreds (listed as a single man), on a tax list returned by George Lyttle on Sep 21, 1791. {Ref: IL 31.20, 31.21}

BRADENBAUGH, MARGARET, b. 1796, d. Dec 2, 1872, in her 76th year, bur. in McKendree Cemetery near Black Horse. {Ref: TI}

BRADFORD, GEORGE, see "William Bradford," q.v.

BRADFORD, GEORGE, bur. May 19, 1800. {Ref: PR}

BRADFORD, GEORGE JR., served on a Petit Jury in August, 1797. {Ref: CC}

BRADFORD, GEORGE JR., taxpayer, 1798, Bush River Lower Hd., 1 dwelling house, 5 inferior houses, 2 acres, $200 valuation; 1 tract (300 acres) in Bush River Lower Hd., $900 valuation, 2 slaves. {Ref: TL}

BRADFORD, GEORGE SR., taxpayer, 1798, Harford Upper Hd., 1 dwelling house, 3 inferior houses, 2 acres, $100.50 valuation; 2 tracts (129 acres) in Harford Upper Hd., $290.25 valuation, 4 slaves. {Ref: TL}

BRADFORD, SARAH, m. Nicholas Allender on Jun 19, 1797. {Ref: PR}. Also see "James Fullerton," q.v.

BRADFORD, SARAH, head of family in 1800 (1st District). {Ref: CI}

BRADFORD, WILLIAM, bur. Feb 12, 1794, aged 55. {Ref: PR}

BRADFORD, WILLIAM JR., insolvent on a list for the road tax due for 1791 in Harford Upper, Harford Lower, and Spesutia Upper as returned by Robert Amos, Jr. on Sep 18, 1793. {Ref: IL 31.18}

BRADFORD, WILLIAM (OF GEORGE), subpoenaed to the Grand Jury in August, 1797. {Ref: CC}

BRADIN (BREDIN), ENOCH, will probated Jul 19, 1791. {Ref: HW}

BRADLEY, BRIDGET, wife of Patrick, native of the Parish of Maghera, County Derry, Ireland, b. 1793, d. Jul 7, 1863, aged 70, bur. in St. Ignatius Catholic Church Cemetery in Hickory. {Ref: TI}

BRADLEY, EDWARD, head of family in 1800 (4th District). {Ref: CI}

BRADLEY, JAMES, see "Thomas Ammonds" and "Isaac Ammonds," q.v.

BRADLEY, JOHN, see "Sarah Bradley," q.v.

BRADLEY, MARY, dau. of John and Mary, b. Sep 9, 1795, bapt. Sep 17, 1794.

{Ref: PR}. Also see "Sarah Bradley," q.v.
BRADLEY, PATRICK, see "Bridget Bradley," q.v.
BRADLEY, SARAH, dau. of John and Mary, b. Aug 16, 1793, bapt. Sep 17, 1794. {Ref: PR}
BRADY, JOHN (Baltimore County), taxpayer, 1798, Bush River Upper & Eden Hd., 1 tract (70 acres, 80 perches), $59.48 valuation, no slaves. {Ref: TL}
BRADY, NORRY(?), m. John Wilson on Apr 20, 1797. {Ref: PR}
BRADY, SYLVESTER, taxpayer, 1798, no dwelling house listed in this part of the tax schedule, 1 tract (20 acres) in Deer Creek Upper Hd., $30 valuation, no slaves. {Ref: TL}
BRAZIER, ROBERT, head of family in 1800 (1st District). {Ref: CI}
BRAZIER, THOMAS, head of family in 1800 (1st District). {Ref: CI}
BRAIZER, WILLIAM, head of family in 1800 (1st District). {Ref: CI}
BRANIAN, JOHN, m. Sarah George on Jun 23, 1791. {Ref: PR}
BRANION, THOMAS, see "Thomas Brannon, Jr.," q.v.
BRANNON, THOMAS JR., charged for assaulting Alexander Osborn in 1794. {Ref: CD, March and August Terms, 1795}. His name was listed as "Thomas Branion" and "Thomas Brannon, Jr."
BRANNON, JOHN, head of family in 1800 (5th District). {Ref: CI}
BRANNON, PATRICK ("gone" and "run away"), insolvent on lists due for 1790 and 1791 "fund taxes" and county taxes in Susquehanna Hd., as returned by Thomas Taylor. {Ref: IL 31.12, 31.02}
BRANNON, WILLIAM, treated by Dr. John Archer on Oct 7, 1796. {Ref: JA}. Also see "Robert Colegate," q.v.
BRANNON, WILLIAM, head of family in 1800 (2nd District). {Ref: CI}
BRAVOE(?), JOHN, head of family in 1800 (2nd District). {Ref: CI}
BRAY, WILLIAM, insolvent, Harford Lower and Spesutia Lower Hundreds (listed as a single man), on a tax list returned by George Lyttle on Sep 21, 1791. {Ref: IL 31.20, 31.21}
BRAY, WILLIAM, insolvent on a list for the road tax due for 1791 in Harford Upper, Harford Lower, and Spesutia Upper as returned by Robert Amos, Jr. on Sep 18, 1793. {Ref: IL 31.18}
BRAZIER, FRANCES, see "Hannah Ritter Gallion Brazier," q.v.
BRAZIER, HANNAH RITTER GALLION, dau. of Robert and Frances, b. Nov 27, 1780, bapt. Jul 28, 1796. {Ref: PR}
BRAZIER, MARTHA, m. John McGill on Nov 10, 1796. {Ref: PR}
BRAZIER, ROBERT, served as constable in Gunpowder Lower Hd., 1800. {Ref: CM}. Also see "Hannah Ritter Gallion Brazier," q.v.
BREVARD, CHARLES, head of family in 1800 (5th District). {Ref: CI}
BREVARD, JAMES, purchased 312 ft. of plank on Mar 2, 1794 at Bush River Store. {Ref: AH}
BREVARD, WILLIAM, head of family in 1800 (5th District). {Ref: CI}
BREW, JAMES, insolvent on a list for the road tax due for 1791 in Harford Upper,

Harford Lower, and Spesutia Upper as returned by Robert Amos, Jr. on Sep 18, 1793. {Ref: IL 31.18}

BREWER, JAMES, see "Thomas Courtney," q.v.

BREWER, JAMES, m. Margaret Young on Aug 31, 1797. {Ref: PR}

BREWER, JAMES, head of family in 1800 (2nd District). {Ref: CI}

BRICE, JAMES E., head of family in 1800 (5th District). {Ref: CI}

BRIARLY, NATHANIEL, see "Nathaniel Bryarly," q.v.

BRIERLY, HUGH, taxpayer, 1798, Bush River Upper & Eden Hd., 1 dwelling house, 3 inferior houses, 2 acres, $110 valuation; 2 tracts (223 acres, 40 perches) in Bush River Upper & Eden Hd., $502.30 valuation, 1 slave. {Ref: TL}

BRIERLY, JOHN, see "Robert Brierly (of John)," q.v.

BRIERLY, MARGARET, taxpayer, 1798, Deer Creek Middle Hd., no dwelling house listed in this part of the tax schedule, no land listed, 1 slave. {Ref: TL}. Also see "John Forwood (of William)," q.v.

BRIERLY, ROBERT, taxpayer, 1798, Bush River Upper & Eden Hd., 1 dwelling house, 7 inferior houses, 2 acres, $800 valuation; 2 tracts (318 acres) in Bush River Upper & Eden Hd., $783 valuation, 5 slaves. {Ref: TL}

BRIERLY, ROBERT (OF JOHN), taxpayer, 1798, Bush River Upper & Eden Hd., 1 dwelling house, 1 inferior house, 2 acres, $150 valuation; 2 tracts (212 acres) in Bush River Upper & Eden Hd., $477 valuation, no slaves. {Ref: TL}. In another part of the tax schedule the occupant is listed as Thomas Brierly.

BRIERLY, THOMAS, taxpayer, 1798, Bush River Upper & Eden Hd., 1 dwelling house, 2 acres, $110 valuation; 1 tract (158 acres) in Bush River Upper & Eden Hd., $355.50 valuation, no slaves. {Ref: TL}. Also see "Robert Brierly (of John)," q.v.

BRINDLE, NATHANIEL, b. Feb 3, 1794, d. Sep 26, 1880, aged 86 years, 7 months, and 23 days, bur. in the Heaps Cemetery in northern Harford County. {Ref: TI}

BRINDLE, SARAH, b. Dec 24, 1793, d. Jan 29, 1879, aged 85 years, 1 month, and 5 days, bur. in the Heaps Cemetery in northern Harford County. {Ref: TI}

BRINDLEY, BENJAMIN, head of family in 1800 (4th District). {Ref: CI}

BRINDLEY, JAMES, or NICHOLAS SUDER, taxpayer, 1798, Spesutia Lower Hd., no dwelling house listed in this part of the tax schedule, 1 tract (44 perches, 21 sq. ft.), $22.50 valuation (Nicholas Suder, occupant), no slaves. {Ref: TL}

BRINDLY, HENRY, insolvent on lists in 1791 due county taxes and road taxes in "Deer Creek Upper, Middle, and Broad Creek Hundreds" as returned by Robert Amos, Jr. {Ref: IL 31.12, 31.22}

BRINEY, JOHN H. (esquire), head of family in 1800 (Havre de Grace). {Ref: CI}

BRINTON, JOHN, or JOHN AUSTIN, taxpayers, 1798, Deer Creek Lower Hd., no dwelling house listed in this part of the tax schedule, 1 tract (50 acres) in possession of John Austin, $1781.24 valuation, no slaves. {Ref: TL}

BRISCOE, ANN, see "Samuel Briscoe," q.v.

BRISCOE, JOSEPH, head of family in 1800 (2nd District). {Ref: CI}. Also see "Samuel Briscoe," q.v.
BRISCOE, SAMUEL, son of Joseph and Ann, b. Apr 16, 1797, bapt. Jul 3, 1798. {Ref: PR}
BRITCHFIELD, ADAM, insolvent on a list for the road tax due for 1791 in Harford Upper, Harford Lower, and Spesutia Upper as returned by Robert Amos, Jr. on Sep 18, 1793. {Ref: IL 31.18}
BRONWELL, HANNAH, see "John Bowers," q.v.
BROOK, CLEMENT (Baltimore County), taxpayer, 1798, Spesutia Lower Hd., 1 tract (1 acre, 16 perches, 84 sq. ft.), $67.50 valuation, no slaves. {Ref: TL}
BROOK, JOHN, head of family in 1800 (1st District). {Ref: CI}
BROOK, THOMAS, head of family in 1800 (3rd District). {Ref: CI}
BROOK, WILLIAM, head of family in 1800 (2nd District). {Ref: CI}
BROOKE, ANN, b. Jun 29, 1792, d. Mar 3, 1856, aged 65 years, 8 months, and 4 days, bur. in Churchville Presbyterian Church Cemetery. {Ref: TI}
BROOKE, CASSANDRA, bur. Jun 6, 1797. {Ref: PR}
BROOKE, JOHN, insolvent on a list for 1791 in Gunpowder Upper and Bush River Lower Hundreds, as filed by John Bond, Deputy Sheriff, on Sep 20, 1791. {Ref: IL 31.24}
BROOKE, RICHARD, m. Cassandra Prigg on Dec 29, 1795. {Ref: PR}
BROOKS, JOHN, son of Thomas and Sarah, b. Jun 12, 1799, bapt. Jul 21, 1800. {Ref: PR}. Also see "Robert Brooks" and "Sarah Brooks" and "Martha Brooks," q.v.
BROOKS, JOHN, insolvent on a list for the road tax due for 1791 in Harford Upper, Harford Lower, and Spesutia Upper as returned by Robert Amos, Jr. on Sep 18, 1793. {Ref: IL 31.18}
BROOKS, KITTY (Miss), treated by Dr. John Archer on Jan 28, 1791 and Nov 21, 1792 (spelled name "Ketty"). {Ref: JA}
BROOKS, MARGARET, see "Robert Brooks" and "Sarah Brooks" and "Martha Brooks," q.v.
BROOKS, MARTHA, dau. of John and Margaret, b. Dec 27, 1786, bapt. Jul 21, 1800. {Ref: PR}
BROOKS, MARY, m. Bowyer Grace on Apr 26, 1798. {Ref: PR}
BROOKS, ROBERT, son of John and Margaret, b. Jul 13, 1791, bapt. Jul 21, 1800. {Ref: PR}
BROOKS, SARAH, dau. of John and Margaret, b. Apr 25, 1785, bapt. Jul 21, 1800. {Ref: PR}. Also see "John Brooks," q.v.
BROOKS, THOMAS, m. Sarah Blake on Jul 17, 1798. {Ref: PR}. Also see "John Brooks," q.v.
BROOME, JAMES, head of family in 1800 (2nd District). {Ref: CI}
BROOKS, WILLIAM, taxpayer, 1798, Spesutia Lower Hd., no dwelling house listed in this part of the tax schedule, no land listed, 2 slaves. {Ref: TL}
BROWN, AQUILA, son of John and Susanna, b. Apr 12, 1792, bapt. Dec 22,

1795. {Ref: PR}

BROWN, AVARILLA, dau. of Thomas and Elinor, b. Sep 9, 1796, bapt. Apr 27, 1800. {Ref: PR}

BROWN, DAVID, insolvent on lists returned by Robert Carlile and John Guyton for taxes due for the year 1791. {Ref: IL 31.16, 31.19}

BROWN, EDWARD, see "Mary Brown," q.v.

BROWN, EDWARD, insolvent on list returned for the road tax due for 1791 by John Bull. {Ref: IL 31.14}

BROWN, EDWARD, insolvent on a list for 1791 in Gunpowder Upper and Bush River Lower Hundreds, as filed by John Bond, Deputy Sheriff, on Sep 20, 1791 (who listed him as a single man). {Ref: IL 31.24}

BROWN, EDWARD, head of family in 1800 (3rd District). {Ref: CI}

BROWN, ELINOR, see "Garret Brown" and "Avarilla Brown" and "William Brown," q.v.

BROWN, FREEBORN, see "Catherine Smith," q.v.

BROWN, FREEBORN, taxpayer, 1798, Spesutia Lower Hd., 1 dwelling house, 1 inferior house, 88 perches and 42 sq. ft. of land, $1000 valuation; 1 tract (88 perches, 42 sq. ft.) in Spesutia Lower Hd., $45 valuation, no slaves; taxpayer, 1798, Susquehanna Hd., 1 dwelling house, 3 inferior houses, 2 acres, $275 valuation; 3 tracts (668 acres) in Susquehanna Hd., $3006 valuation, 5 slaves. {Ref: TL}

BROWN, FREEBORN, charged for neglecting his duty in 1790 as overseer of the roads, and for staking a road in 1794. {Ref: CD, March Term, 1795}

BROWN, FREEBORN, head of family in 1800 (3rd District). {Ref: CI}

BROWN, GARRET, son of Thomas and Elinor, b. Jun 11, 1794, bapt. Apr 27, 1800. {Ref: PR}

BROWN, GARRETT (captain), insolvent, Harford Lower and Spesutia Lower Hundreds, on a tax list returned by George Lyttle on Sep 21, 1791. {Ref: IL 31.20, 31.21}

BROWN, GARRETT (captain), "dead and the property insolvent," insolvent on a list for the road tax due for 1791 in Harford Upper, Harford Lower, and Spesutia Upper as returned by Robert Amos, Jr. on Sep 18, 1793. {Ref: IL 31.18}

BROWN, GEORGE, head of family in 1800 (3rd District). {Ref: CI}

BROWN, JACOB, head of family in 1800 (2nd District). {Ref: CI}

BROWN, JAMES, insolvent on a list for the road tax due for 1791 in Harford Upper, Harford Lower, and Spesutia Upper as returned by Robert Amos, Jr. on Sep 18, 1793. {Ref: IL 31.18}

BROWN, JAMES, insolvent, Harford Lower and Spesutia Lower Hundreds (listed as a single man), on a tax list returned by George Lyttle on Sep 21, 1791. {Ref: IL 31.20, 31.21}

BROWN, JAMES ("can't be found"), insolvent on lists due for 1790 and 1791 "fund taxes" and county taxes in Susquehanna Hd., as returned by Thomas Taylor. {Ref: IL 31.12, 31.02}

BROWN, JAMES JR., head of family in 1800 (2nd District). {Ref: CI}

45

BROWN, JOHN, see "Susanna Brown" and "William Brown" and "Aquila Brown," q.v.

BROWN, JOHN, insolvent, Harford Lower and Spesutia Lower Hundreds (listed as a single man), on a tax list returned by George Lyttle on Sep 21, 1791. {Ref: IL 31.20, 31.21}

BROWN, JOHN, bur. Apr 1, 1796. {Ref: PR}

BROWN, JOHN, bur. Sep 9, 1798. {Ref: PR}

BROWN, JOHN, insolvent on a list for the road tax due for 1791 in Harford Upper, Harford Lower, and Spesutia Upper as returned by Robert Amos, Jr. on Sep 18, 1793. {Ref: IL 31.18}

BROWN, JOHN ("can't be found"), insolvent on lists due for 1790 and 1791 "fund taxes" in Deer Creek Lower and Susquehanna Hundreds, as returned by Thomas Taylor. {Ref: IL 31.12, 31.02}

BROWN, JOHN, head of family in 1800 (2nd District). {Ref: CI}

BROWN, JOHN, or ISRAEL BOWMAN, taxpayer, 1798, Bush River Lower Hd., 1 dwelling house, 40 perches of land (Israel Bowman, occupant), $120 valuation; 1 tract (40 perches) in Bush River Lower Hd., $78.75 valuation, no slaves. {Ref: TL}

BROWN, JOHN, or MATHEW KENNARD, taxpayer, 1798, Bush River Lower Hd., 1 dwelling, 120 perches of land (Mathew Kennard, occupant), $180 valuation, no slaves. {Ref: TL}

BROWN, JOHN THOMAS, bur. Mar 2, 1794, aged 22. {Ref: PR}

BROWN, JOHN THOMAS, will probated Mar 21, 1794. {Ref: HW}

BROWN, JOSHUA, on "a list of insolvents it being for personal property for the road taxs [sic] for 1791" filed by Robert Amoss. {Ref: IL 31.12}

BROWN, JOSHUA, insolvent on a list for the road tax due for 1791 in Harford Upper, Harford Lower, and Spesutia Upper as returned by Robert Amos, Jr. on Sep 18, 1793 (his name was crossed off the list). {Ref: IL 31.18}

BROWN, MARY, taxpayer, 1798, Gunpowder Lower Hd., 1 dwelling house, 4 inferior houses, 2 acres, $300 valuation; 1 tract (198 acres) in Gunpowder Lower Hd., $668.25 valuation, 7 slaves. {Ref: TL}

BROWN, MARY (executrix of Edward), insolvent on a list for the road tax due for 1791 in Harford Upper, Harford Lower, and Spesutia Upper as returned by Robert Amos, Jr. on Sep 18, 1793. {Ref: IL 31.18}

BROWN, SARAH, insolvent on list returned for the road tax due for 1791 by John Bull. {Ref: IL 31.14}

BROWN, SOLOMON, taxpayer, 1798, Bush River Upper & Eden Hd., 1 dwelling house, 1 inferior house, 2 acres, $105 valuation; 3 tracts (92 acres) in Bush River Upper & Eden Hd., $181.12 valuation, no slaves. {Ref: TL}

BROWN, SOLOMON, head of family in 1800 (4th District). {Ref: CI}

BROWN, SUSANNA, see "William Brown" and "Aquila Brown" and "George Copeland's heirs," q.v.

BROWN, SUSANNA, taxpayer, 1798, Harford Lower Hd., no dwelling house

listed in this part of the tax schedule, no land listed, 4 slaves. {Ref: TL}
BROWN, SUSANNA, dau. of John and Susanna, b. Jan 30, 1795, bapt. Mar 19, 1795. {Ref: PR}
BROWN, SUSANNA, head of family in 1800 (2nd District). {Ref: CI}
BROWN, THOMAS, see "Garret Brown" and "Avarilla Brown" and "William Brown" and "Norris Lester" and "James Lee," q.v.
BROWN, THOMAS, insolvent on a list for the county tax for 1792 returned by Thomas Taylor on May 28, 1794, "it being an additional list." {Ref: IL 31.12}
BROWN, THOMAS, insolvent on a list for the county tax due for 1793 in Susquehanna Hd. as returned to the levy court by Thomas Taylor on May 28, 1794, who noted "put in my hands last fall." {Ref: IL 31.12}
BROWN, THOMAS, insolvent on a list of the county tax due William Osborn, sheriff, for 1791, as returned by Edward Prigg on Sep 20, 1791. {Ref: IL 31.17}
BROWN, THOMAS, insolvent on a list for the road tax due for 1791 in Harford Upper, Harford Lower, and Spesutia Upper as returned by Robert Amos, Jr. on Sep 18, 1793. {Ref: IL 31.18}
BROWN, THOMAS, insolvent on lists of taxes due in 1791 and 1792 in Broad Creek Hd., as returned by Robert Amos, Jr. in 1791 and Benjamin Preston in 1792. {Ref: IL 31.03, 31.12, 31.22}
BROWN, THOMAS, b. 1798, d. Apr 4, 1816, bur. in Bethel Presbyterian Church Cemetery at Madonna. {Ref: BC}
BROWN, THOMAS, head of family in 1800 (2nd District). {Ref: CI}
BROWN, THOMAS, head of family in 1800 (5th District). {Ref: CI}
BROWN, THOMAS SR., head of family in 1800 (5th District). {Ref: CI}
BROWN, WILLIAM, son of Thomas and Elinor, b. Apr 26, 1798, bapt. Apr 27, 1800. {Ref: PR}
BROWN, WILLIAM, insolvent on lists for the county tax and road tax due for 1791 in Deer Creek Lower Hd., as returned by Thomas Taylor on Sep 17, 1792. {Ref: IL 31.12}
BROWN, WILLIAM, son of John and Susanna, b. Feb 6, 1791, bapt. Dec 22, 1795. {Ref: PR}
BROWNING, PEREGRINE, "capias on presentment for Joseph Robinson" [assault case?] in 1797. {Ref: CD, March Term, 1797}
BROWNING, PEREGRINE (Baltimore Town), or HERMAN COX, taxpayer, 1798, Bush River Lower Hd., 1 dwelling house, 80 perches of land (Herman Cox, occupant), $100.50 valuation, no slaves. {Ref: TL}
BROWNING (BRONING), MARY, head of family in 1800 (1st District). {Ref: CI}
BROWNING, WILLIAM, will probated Dec 14, 1798. {Ref: HW}
BROWNLEY, ARTHUR, head of family in 1800 (1st District). {Ref: CI}
BROWNLEY, CATHERINE, taxpayer, 1798, Spesutia Upper Hd., 1 dwelling house, 5 inferior houses, 1 acre and 80 perches, $325 valuation; 1 tract (188 acres, 80 perches) in Spesutia Upper Hd., $492.30 valuation, 4 slaves. {Ref: TL}
BROWNLEY, JOSEPH, served on a Grand Jury in March, 1799 and on a Petit

Jury in March, 1800. {Ref: CM}
BROWNLEY, JOSEPH, head of family in 1800 (3rd District). {Ref: CI}
BRUCEBANKS, BENJAMIN'S HEIRS, or JAMES MICHAEL, taxpayers, 1798, Spesutia Lower Hd., no dwelling house listed in this part of the tax schedule, 2 tracts (87 acres), $381.49 valuation (James Michael, occupant), no slaves. {Ref: TL}
BRUCEBANKS, BLANCH, insolvent on a list for the road tax due for 1791 in Harford Upper, Harford Lower, and Spesutia Upper as returned by Robert Amos, Jr. on Sep 18, 1793. {Ref: IL 31.18}
BRUSHBANKS, BLANCH, insolvent, Harford Lower and Spesutia Lower Hundreds, on a tax list returned by George Lyttle on Sep 21, 1791. {Ref: IL 31.20, 31.21}
BRYAN, THOMAS, see "Thomas B. Onion," q.v.
BRYANT, THOMAS, head of family in 1800 (3rd District). {Ref: CI}
BRYARLY, DAVID, see "Robert Bryarly," q.v.
BRYARLY, HUGH, will probated Oct 8, 1799. {Ref: HW}
BRYARLY, JAMES, see "Robert Bryarly," q.v.
BRYARLY, JOHN ("run"), insolvent on lists due for 1790 and 1791 "fund taxes" and county taxes in Susquehanna Hd., as returned by Thomas Taylor. {Ref: IL 31.12, 31.02}
BRYARLY, MARY ANN (Miss), b. 1796, d. Seotember 13, 1865, in her 69th year, bur. in Christ Episcopal (Rock Spring) Church Cemetery. {Ref: TI}
BRYARLY (BRIARLY), NATHANIEL, will probated Aug 12, 1794. {Ref: HW}
BRYARLY, ROBERT, insolvent on a list for the road tax for 1792, as returned for Robert Amoss, tax collector. {Ref: IL 13.12}
BRYARLY, ROBERT, treated by Dr. Archer on Feb 7, 1795; mentioned the inoculation of his family: Wakeman, David, Thomas, James, and Sally. {Ref: JA}. Name also spelled "Bryerly" and "Briarly" in this ledger.
BRYARLY, ROBERT, head of family in 1800 (4th District). {Ref: CI}
BRYARLY, ROBERT (OF THOMAS), tract *Deserted Lot Corrected* surveyed between 1792 and 1796. {Ref: SB}
BRYARLY, SALLY, see "Robert Bryarly," q.v.
BRYARLY, THOMAS, see "Robert Bryarly," q.v.
BRYARLY, WAKEMAN, see "Robert Bryarly," q.v.
BRYERLY, JOHN, insolvent, Harford Lower and Spesutia Lower Hundreds, on a tax list returned by George Lyttle on Sep 21, 1791. {Ref: IL 31.20, 31.21}
BRYERLY, JOHN, insolvent on a list for the road tax due for 1791 in Harford Upper, Harford Lower, and Spesutia Upper as returned by Robert Amos, Jr. on Sep 18, 1793. {Ref: IL 31.18}
BRYERLY, ROBERT, see "Negro Cass" and "Negro Dinah" and "Negro Hagar," q.v.
BUCHANAN & YOUNG (Baltimore Town), or JOSEPH MILES, taxpayer, 1798, Broad Creek Hd., 1 tract (265 acres, 80 perches) and 1 building (Joseph Miles, occupant), $298.69 valuation, no slaves. {Ref: TL}

BUCK, BENJAMIN, son of Christopher and Keziah, b. Dec 13 or 18, 1795. {Ref: PR}
BUCK, BENJAMIN MERRYMAN, son of John and Catherine, b. Jun 18, 1797. {Ref: PR}
BUCK, CATHERINE, bur. Aug 20 or 26, 1799, aged 30. {Ref: PR}. Also see "Benjamin Merryman Buck," q.v.
BUCK, CHRISTOPHER, see "Benjamin Buck," q.v.
BUCK, JAMES, son of Joshua and Sarah, b. Nov 17, 1793. {Ref: PR}
BUCK, JOHN, see "Benjamin Merryman Buck," q.v.
BUCK, JOHN, bur. Oct 8, 1793, aged 72. {Ref: PR}. Also see "Mrs. Buck," q.v.
BUCK, JOHN, bur. Mar 10, 1798, aged 15. {Ref: PR}
BUCK, JOSHUA, see "James Buck" and "Sarah Buck," q.v.
BUCK, KEZIAH, see "Benjamin Buck," q.v.
BUCK, MRS., relict of John Buck, bur. Oct 30, 1793, aged 70. {Ref: PR}
BUCK, SARAH, dau. of Joshua and Sarah, b. Mar 3, 1798. {Ref: PR}. Also see "James Buck," q.v.
BUCKINGHAM, BASIL, head of family in 1800 (3rd District). {Ref: CI}
BUCKINGHAM, THOMAS, insolvent on a list for 1791 in Gunpowder Upper and Bush River Lower Hundreds, as filed by John Bond, Deputy Sheriff, on Sep 20, 1791. {Ref: IL 31.24}
BUCKINGHAM, WILLIAM, b. 1795, d. May 17, 1861, aged 66, bur. in Union Chapel Methodist Church Cemetery at Wilna. {Ref: TI}
BUCKINGTON, THOMAS, insolvent on list returned by Robert Carlile for taxes due for the year 1791. {Ref: IL 31.16}
BUDD, GEORGE'S HEIRS, or JAMES HOLLIS, taxpayers, 1798, Spesutia Lower Hd., 1 dwelling house, 3 inferior houses, 2 acres (James Hollis, occupant), $110 valuation; 1 tract (318 acres) in Spesutia Lower Hd., $2449.58 valuation, no slaves. {Ref: TL}
BUDD, SAL., insolvent, Harford Lower and Spesutia Lower Hundreds (listed as a single man), on a tax list returned by George Lyttle on Sep 21, 1791. {Ref: IL 31.20, 31.21}
BUDD, SAMUEL, insolvent on a list for the road tax due for 1791 in Harford Upper, Harford Lower, and Spesutia Upper as returned by Robert Amos, Jr. on Sep 18, 1793. {Ref: IL 31.18}
BUDD, SARAH, see "Daniel Moores," q.v.
BUDD(?), THOMAS, head of family in 1800 (1st District). {Ref: CI}
BULL, ABRAHAM, taxpayer, 1798, Gunpowder Upper Hd., no dwelling house listed in this part of the tax schedule, 1 tract (32 acres) in Gunpowder Upper Hd., $164.25 valuation, no slaves. {Ref: TL}
BULL, ABRAM, see "Walter Bull," q.v.
BULL, BEN (negro), insolvent on a list for the road tax for 1792, as returned for Robert Amoss, tax collector. {Ref: IL 13.12}
BULL, BILLINGSLEA, served on a Petit Jury in March, 1798. {Ref: CM}
BULL, BILLINGSLEY, head of family in 1800 (3rd District). {Ref: CI}

BULL, ELENOR, head of family in 1800 (3rd District). {Ref: CI}
BULL, ELIONER, taxpayer, 1798, Gunpowder Upper Hd., no dwelling house listed in this part of the tax schedule, 1 tract (73 acres) in Gunpowder Upper Hd., $265.50 valuation, no slaves. {Ref: TL}
BULL, ELIZA R., wife of John L., b. Jan 12, 1799, d. Jan 13, 1862, bur. in Deer Creek Methodist Church Cemetery at Chestnut Hill. {Ref: TI}
BULL, ISAAC, see "Josias S. and Isaac Bull," q.v.
BULL, JACOB, see "Margarett Bull," q.v.
BULL, JACOB, taxpayer, 1798, Spesutia Upper Hd., no dwelling house listed in this part of the tax schedule, 5 tracts (211 acres) in Spesutia Upper Hd., $593.15 valuation, 1 slave. {Ref: TL}. In another part of the tax schedule one of the occupants is listed as Negro Aquila.
BULL, JACOB, mentioned in a survey in 1799. {Ref: JS}
BULL, JACOB, head of family in 1800 (3rd District). {Ref: CI}
BULL, JACOB JR., insolvent on a list for 1791 in Gunpowder Upper and Bush River Lower Hundreds, as filed by John Bond, Deputy Sheriff, on Sep 20, 1791. {Ref: IL 31.24}
BULL, JACOB SR., insolvent on a list for 1791 in Gunpowder Upper and Bush River Lower Hundreds, as filed by John Bond, Deputy Sheriff, on Sep 20, 1791. {Ref: IL 31.24}
BULL, JOHN, see "John Pritchard" and "Leslie Curtis," q.v.
BULL, JOHN, compiled and returned a list of insolvents for the road tax due for 1791 for Robert Amoss, tax collector. {Ref: IL 31.14}
BULL, JOHN, served as constable in Eden Hd., 1797-1800. {Ref: CC, CM}
BULL, JOHN, licensed tavernkeeper in March, 1795. {Ref: CC}
BULL, JOHN, charged for selling liquors in 1794. {Ref: CD, March and August Terms, 1795}
BULL, JOHN, compiled and returned a list of tax insolvents in 1791. {Ref: IL 31.14}
BULL, JOHN, head of family in 1800 (Belle Air). {Ref: CI}
BULL, JOHN (innkeeper), taxpayer, 1798, Bush River Lower Hd., no dwelling house listed in this part of the tax schedule, no land listed, 1 slave. {Ref: TL}
BULL, JOHN (Baltimore County), insolvent on a list for 1791 in Gunpowder Upper and Bush River Lower Hundreds, as filed by John Bond, Deputy Sheriff, on Sep 20, 1791. {Ref: IL 31.24}
BULL, JOHN (OF JOHN), taxpayer, 1798, Spesutia Upper Hd., 1 dwelling house, 80 perches of land, $110 valuation; 1 tract (38 acres, 80 perches) in Spesutia Upper Hd., $274.50 valuation, no slaves. {Ref: TL}
BULL, JOHN (OF JOHN), head of family in 1800 (3rd District). {Ref: CI}
BULL, JOHN L., see "Eliza R. Bull," q.v.
BULL, JOSIAS S., head of family in 1800 (4th District). {Ref: CI}
BULL, JOSIAS S. AND ISAAC, taxpayers, 1798, no dwelling house listed in this part of the tax schedule, 2 tracts (98 acres) in Bush River Upper & Eden Hd., $783 valuation, no slaves. {Ref: TL}

BULL, MARGARETT, dau. of Jacob and Sarah, b. Mar 14, 1791. {Ref: PR}
BULL, RICHARD, granted a tavern license in March, 1797. {Ref: CC}
BULL, RICHARD, taxpayer, 1798, Gunpowder Lower Hd., 1 dwelling house, 2 inferior houses, 40 perches of land, $200 valuation, no slaves. {Ref: TL}
BULL, SARAH, taxpayer, 1798, Gunpowder Upper Hd., 1 dwelling house, 6 inferior houses, 2 acres, $350 valuation; 4 tracts (256 acres) in Gunpowder Upper Hd., $909 valuation, no slaves. {Ref: TL}. ALso see "Margarett Bull," q.v.
BULL, SUSANNAH, will probated Nov 13, 1792. {Ref: HW}
BULL, TOM (negro), insolvent on a list for the road tax for 1792, as returned for Robert Amoss, tax collector. {Ref: IL 13.12}
BULL, WALTER, served on a Petit Jury in August, 1797. {Ref: CC}
BULL, WALTER, taxpayer, 1798, Spesutia Upper Hd., 1 dwelling house, 2 inferior houses, 1 acre, $145 valuation; 1 tract (214 acres) in Spesutia Upper Hd., $452.25 valuation, 1 slave. {Ref: TL}
BULL, WALTER, served on a Grand Jury in March, 1800. {Ref: CM}
BULL, WALTER, head of family in 1800 (3rd District). {Ref: CI}
BULL, WALTER (OF WILLIAM), treated by Dr. Archer on Nov 27, 1792; also mentioned wife and child (no names given). {Ref: JA}
BULL, WILLIAM, tract *Bull's Care* surveyed between 1792 and 1796. {Ref: SB}
BULL, WILLIAM, granted a tavern license in March, 1797, retailer's permit in July, 1797, and a tavern license in August, 1797. {Ref: CC}
BULL, WILLIAM, taxpayer, 1798, Spesutia Upper Hd., 1 dwelling house, 5 inferior houses, 1 acre and 80 perches, $205 valuation; 2 tracts (128 acres, 80 perches) in Spesutia Upper Hd., $640.13 valuation, no slaves. {Ref: TL}
BULL, WILLIAM, balance due on Oct 24, 1797 at Bush River Store. {Ref: AH}
BULL, WILLIAM, insolvent on lists returned by Robert Carlile and John Guyton for taxes due for the year 1791. {Ref: IL 31.16, 31.19}
BULL, WILLIAM, will probated Jan 4, 1791. {Ref: HW}
BULL, WILLIAM (OF ABRAM), treated by Dr. Archer on Dec 8, 1792. {Ref: JA}. Also see "Walter Bull," q.v.
BULL, WILLIAM LOVE, b. Jan 20, 1797, d. Oct 3, 1876, bur. in Deer Creek Methodist Church Cemetery at Chestnut Hill. {Ref: TI}
BUNTIN, BILLY D., head of family in 1800 (3rd District). {Ref: CI}
BUNTING, BILLY DREW, taxpayer, 1798, Bush River Lower Hd., 1 dwelling house, 1 inferior house, 80 perches of land, $160 valuation, 5 slaves. {Ref: TL}
BURCHFIELD, ADAM, insolvent, Harford Lower and Spesutia Lower Hundreds (listed as a single man), on a tax list returned by George Lyttle on Sep 21, 1791. {Ref: IL 31.20, 31.21}
BURGES, JOSEPH, taxpayer, 1798, Gunpowder Lower Hd., 1 dwelling house, 1 acre, $150 valuation, no slaves. {Ref: TL}
BURGESS, JOSEPH, insolvent on a list for 1791 in Gunpowder Upper and Bush River Lower Hundreds, as filed by John Bond, Deputy Sheriff, on Sep 20, 1791. {Ref: IL 31.24}

BURGESS, JOSEPH, head of family in 1800 (Abingdon). {Ref: CI}
BURGESS, MICHAEL, insolvent on a list for 1791 in Gunpowder Upper and Bush River Lower Hundreds, as filed by John Bond, Deputy Sheriff, on Sep 20, 1791. {Ref: IL 31.24}
BURK, JAMES, head of family in 1800 (5th District). {Ref: CI}
BURK, JOHN, head of family in 1800 (Havre de Grace). {Ref: CI}
BURK, PETER, insolvent, Harford Lower and Spesutia Lower Hundreds (listed as a single man), on a tax list returned by George Lyttle on Sep 21, 1791. {Ref: IL 31.20, 31.21}
BURK, PETER, insolvent on a list for the road tax due for 1791 in Harford Upper, Harford Lower, and Spesutia Upper as returned by Robert Amos, Jr. on Sep 18, 1793. {Ref: IL 31.18}
BURKE, JOHN, see "William Goldsmith Burke," q.v.
BURKE, JOHN, m. Susanna Templeton on May 25, 1797. {Ref: PR}.
BURKE, JOHN, subpoenaed to the Grand Jury in August, 1797. {Ref: CC}
BURKE, SUSANNA, see "William Goldsmith Burke," q.v.
BURKE, WILLIAM GOLDSMITH, son of John and Susanna, b. May 19, 1798, bapt. May 5, 1799. {Ref: PR}
BURKHEAD, MATHEW, head of family in 1800 (1st District). {Ref: CI}
BURKHEAD, THOMAS (doctor), head of family in 1800 (1st District). {Ref: CI}
BURKINS, ELENOR, head of family in 1800 (3rd District). {Ref: CI}
BURMINGHAM, REBECCA, see "Rebecca Birmingham," q.v.
BURNETT, SARAH, b. on 11th of 6th month 1797(?), d. on 20th of 12th month, 1850, bur. in Little Falls Quaker Cemetery in Fallston. {Ref: TI}
BURNS (BURNES), ANDREW, head of family in 1800 (2nd District). {Ref: CI}. Also see "William Mitchell," q.v.
BURNS, MARY, m. Thomas Rand on May 5, 1799. {Ref: PR}
BURNSIDE, JOSEPH, had an account at Hall's Store in July, 1791. {Ref: WH}
BURNSIDES, JOSEPH, had an account at Hall's Store in January, 1791. {Ref: WH}
BURTON, JANE, insolvent on a list for the county tax due for 1793 in Susquehanna Hd. as returned to the levy court by Thomas Taylor on May 28, 1794, who noted "put in my hands last fall." {Ref: IL 31.12}
BURTON, JANE, taxpayer, 1798, Susquehanna Hd., no dwelling house listed in this part of the tax schedule, 2 tracts (110 acres), $185.63 valuation, no slaves. {Ref: TL}
BUSH, ARNOLD, head of family in 1800 (3rd District). {Ref: CI}
BUSSEY, BENNET, taxpayer, 1798, Spesutia Upper Hd., 1 dwelling house, 7 inferior houses, 1 acre, $305 valuation; 5 tracts (861 acres) in Spesutia Upper Hd., $3024 valuation, 5 slaves; taxpayer, 1798, Spesutia Upper Hd., 1 dwelling house, 80 perches of land, $185 valuation, no slaves; taxpayer, 1798, Spesutia Upper Hd., 1 dwelling house, 1 inferior house, 80 perches of land, $145 valuation, no slaves. {Ref: TL}
BUSSEY, BENNET, served as a Grand Jury foreman in March, 1798, as a Grand

Jury member in March, 1799, and as a Grand Jury foreman in March, 1800. {Ref: CM}

BUSSEY, BENNET, appointed a Judge of Elections in the 3rd District on Jul 28, 1800. {Ref: CM}

BUSSEY, BENNET (esquire), treated by Dr. Archer on Sep 21, 1797; also mentioned his son Clement. {Ref: JA}

BUSSEY, BENNETT (esquire), head of family in 1800 (3rd District). {Ref: CI}

BUSSEY, CLEMENT, see "Bennet Bussey," q.v.

BUSSEY, EDWARD, head of family in 1800 (Belle Air). {Ref: CI}

BUSSEY, EDWARD (Baltimore County), insolvent on list returned by Robert Carlile for taxes due for the year 1791. {Ref: IL 31.16}

BUSSEY, EDWARD B., taxpayer, 1798, Bush River Upper & Eden Hd., 1 dwelling house, 2 inferior houses, 2 acres, $110 valuation; 1 tract (148 acres) in Bush River Upper & Eden Hd., $333 valuation, 1 slave. {Ref: TL}

BUSSEY, JESSE (esquire), treated by Dr. Archer on Sep 20, 1791. {Ref: JA}

BUSSEY, RUTH (widow), treated by Dr. Archer on Oct 3, 1793; also mentioned she lived near "C. Town" [Cooptown]. {Ref: JA}

BUTLER, CLEMENT, b. May 9, 1796. {Ref: Butler-Roberts Bible}. Also see "Isabella Butler," q.v.

BUTLER, ISABELLA (neé Streett), wife of Clement, b. Dec 28, 1793. {Ref: Butler-Roberts Bible}

BUTLER, JOHN, insolvent on list returned for the road tax due for 1791 by John Bull. {Ref: IL 31.14}

BUTLER, JOHN, b. 1794, d. Sep 2, 1847, bur. in a cemetery now on Aberdeen Proving Grounds. {Ref: TI}

BUTLER, RICHARD, insolvent on a list for the road tax due for 1791 in Harford Upper, Harford Lower, and Spesutia Upper as returned by Robert Amos, Jr. on Sep 18, 1793. {Ref: IL 31.18}

BUTLER, RICHARD, m. Sarah Potts on Dec 29, 1792. {Ref: PR}

BUTLER, THOMAS, head of family in 1800 (5th District). {Ref: CI}. Also see "Henrietta Wheeler," q.v.

BYARD, JAMES, head of family in 1800 (Abingdon). {Ref: CI}. Also see "William Wilson (silversmith)," q.v.

BYARD, SAMUEL, insolvent on a list for the county tax due for 1793 in Susquehanna Hd. as returned to the levy court by Thomas Taylor on May 28, 1794, who noted "put in my hands last fall." {Ref: IL 31.12}

CAHALL, JAMES, insolvent on a list for the road tax due for 1791 in Harford Upper, Harford Lower, and Spesutia Upper as returned by Robert Amos, Jr. on Sep 18, 1793. {Ref: IL 31.18}

CAHELE, JAMES, insolvent, Harford Lower and Spesutia Lower Hundreds (listed as a single man), on a tax list returned by George Lyttle on Sep 21, 1791. {Ref: IL 31.20, 31.21}

CAHIEL, ELENOR, head of family in 1800 (5th District). {Ref: CI}

CAIN, AQUILLA, head of family in 1800 (2nd District). {Ref: CI}

CAIN, DENNIS, see "Dennis Cane," q.v.
CAIN, EDWARD, head of family in 1800 (5th District). {Ref: CI}. Also see "Henrietta Wheeler," q.v.
CAIN, ELIZABETH, taxpayer, 1798, Spesutia Upper Hd., 1 dwelling house, 3 inferior houses, 1 acre, $255 valuation; 2 tracts (452 acres) in Spesutia Upper Hd., $1738.87 valuation, 3 slaves; taxpayer, 1798, Bush River Lower Hd., 1 dwelling house, 2 inferior houses, 1 acre, $180 valuation, no slaves. {Ref: TL}
CAIN, ELIZABETH, head of family in 1800 (3rd District). {Ref: CI}
CAIN, TIMOTHY, head of family in 1800 (2nd District). {Ref: CI}
CAIRNES, MARGARET, see "Richard Hope Kirkwood," q.v.
CALDER, JAMES, insolvent on list returned by John Guyton for taxes due for the year 1791. {Ref: IL 31.19}
CALDER, JOHN (captain), insolvent on list returned by Robert Carlile for taxes due for the year 1791. {Ref: IL 31.16}. Also see "Sarah Turner," q.v.
CALDER, JOHN, taxpayer, 1798, Bush River Upper & Eden Hd., 1 dwelling house, 4 inferior houses, 2 acres, $150 valuation; 3 tracts (102 acres) in Bush River Upper & Eden Hd., $229.50 valuation, no slaves. {Ref: TL}
CALDWELL, JOHN, see "John Hopkins," q.v.
CALDWELL, SAMUEL, taxpayer, 1798, Gunpowder Upper Hd., 1 dwelling house, 4 inferior houses, 2 acres, $220 valuation; 1 tract (123 acres) in Gunpowder Upper Hd., $415.25 valuation, 2 slaves. {Ref: TL}
CALDWELL, WILLIAM, taxpayer, 1798, Bush River Lower Hd., 1 dwelling house, 1 inferior house, 80 perches of land, $280 valuation; 1 tract in Bush River Lower Hd. (no description), $33.75 valuation, 1 slave. {Ref: TL}
CALHOUN, JAMES (Baltimore Town), taxpayer, 1798, Deer Creek Lower Hd., 2 tracts (300 acres), $765 valuation, no slaves. {Ref: TL}
CALHOUN, JAMES (Baltimore Town), insolvent on lists in 1791 due county taxes and road taxes in "Deer Creek Upper, Middle, and Broad Creek Hundreds" as returned by Robert Amos, Jr. {Ref: IL 31.12, 31.22}
CALHOUN, WILLIAM ("poor"), insolvent on lists due for 1790 and 1791 "fund taxes" and county taxes in Susquehanna Hd., as returned by Thomas Taylor. {Ref: IL 31.12, 31.02}
CALWELL, ----, see "Gallion & Calwell," q.v.
CALWELL (COLWELL), ANN, head of family in 1800 (3rd District). {Ref: CI}
CALWELL, DAVID, head of family in 1800 (4th District). {Ref: CI}
CALWELL (CALWILL), JOHN, head of family in 1800 (5th District). {Ref: CI}
CALWELL, MARY T., b. 1791, d. Dec 31, 1862, aged 71, bur. in Little Falls Quaker Cemetery in Fallston. {Ref: TI}
CALWELL, SAMUEL, served on a Grand Jury in August, 1798 and on a Petit Jury in August, 1799. {Ref: CM}
CALWELL, SARAH, see "William Askew," q.v.
CAMBEL, JOHN, insolvent, Harford Lower and Spesutia Lower Hundreds (listed as a single man), on a tax list returned by George Lyttle on Sep 21, 1791. {Ref

IL 31.20, 31.21}

CAMBELL, JOHN, head of family in 1800 (3rd District). {Ref: CI}

CAMBELL, THOMAS, head of family in 1800 (5th District). {Ref: CI}

CAMERON, WILLIAM, see "William Comrun," q.v.

CAMPBELL (CAMPBLE), MARGARET, insolvent on lists of taxes due in 1791 and 1792 in Broad Creek Hd., as returned by Robert Amos, Jr. in 1791 and Benjamin Preston in 1792, but her name was then crossed off both lists. {Ref: IL 31.03, 31.12, 31.22}

CAMPBELL, SAMUEL, taxpayer, 1798, Deer Creek Upper Hd., no dwelling house listed in this part of the tax schedule, 1 tract (14 acres), $31.50 valuation, no slaves. {Ref: TL}

CAMPBELL, THOMAS, taxpayer, 1798, Deer Creek Middle Hd., 1 tract (64 acres) and 1 building, $108 valuation, no slaves. {Ref: TL}

CAMPBLE, HANNAH, insolvent on list returned by Robert Carlile for taxes due for the year 1791. {Ref: IL 31.16}

CAMPBLE, JOHN, insolvent on a list for the road tax due for 1791 in Harford Upper, Harford Lower, and Spesutia Upper as returned by Robert Amos, Jr. on Sep 18, 1793. {Ref: IL 31.18}

CAN, JOHN, insolvent on list returned by Robert Carlile for taxes due for the year 1791. {Ref: IL 31.16}

CAN, ROBERT, insolvent on lists in 1791 due county taxes and road taxes in "Deer Creek Upper, Middle, and Broad Creek Hundreds" as returned by Robert Amos, Jr., but his name was then crossed off both lists. {Ref: IL 31.12, 31.22}

CANE, DENNIS (weaver), will probated Aug 2, 1796. {Ref: HW}

CANEAR, JOSEPH, see "Michael Kelly," q.v.

CANEY, HUGH, charged for assaulting Thomas Simmons in 1795. {Ref: CD, August Term, 1795}

CANEY, HUGH, charged for assaulting Daniel Scott and Thomas Simmons in 1797. {Ref: CD, March Term, 1797}

CANNON (CANNER?), HENRY, purchased bar iron on Jun 13, 1797 at Bush River Store. {Ref: AH}

CANNON, ERASMUS, see "Christian Hoofman," q.v.

CANNON, MOSES, head of family in 1800 (2nd District). {Ref: CI}. Also see "Benedict Edward Hall," q.v.

CANNON, ROSS, head of family in 1800 (2nd District). {Ref: CI}

CANNON, SAMUEL, insolvent on a list for the road tax due for 1791 in Harford Upper, Harford Lower, and Spesutia Upper as returned by Robert Amos, Jr. on Sep 18, 1793. {Ref: IL 31.18}

CANNON, SAMUEL, insolvent on lists for the county tax and road tax due for 1791 and 1792 in Deer Creek Lower Hd., as returned by Thomas Taylor on Sep 17, 1792. {Ref: IL 31.12, 31.03}

CANNON, SAMUEL, see "James Phillips, Sr.," q.v.

CANON, JOHN, b. 1793, d. May 2, 1855, aged 62, bur. in St. George's Episcopal Church Cemetery at Perryman. {Ref: TI}

CANVOSS (CANOOSS?), THOMAS, head of family in 1800 (3rd District). {Ref: CI}

CAPENS, THOMAS, mentioned in a survey deposition on Jan 18, 1800 as "to where Thos. Capens house formerly stood as proved by Michael Laru." {Ref: JS}

CAREY, JOHN, head of family in 1800 (4th District). {Ref: CI}

CARLILE & GILBERT, licensed retailers in March, 1795. {Ref: CC}

CARLILE, HARRIOT, bur. Nov 4, 1796. {Ref: PR}

CARLILE, JOHN, taxpayer, 1798, Harford Lower Hd., 1 dwelling house, 6 inferior houses, 2 acres, $275 valuation; 1 tract (324 acres) in Harford Lower Hd., $1230.98 valuation, 6 slaves. {Ref: TL}

CARLILE, JOHN, served on a Petit Jury in August, 1798. {Ref: CM}

CARLILE, JOHN (major), vestryman, 1792, 1794-1797, 1799, St. George's Episcopal Church. {Ref: PR}

CARLILE, JOHN (general), head of family in 1800 (1st District). {Ref: CI}

CARLILE, LANSLETT, head of family in 1800 (4th District). {Ref: CI}

CARLILE, LANSLOT, insolvent on a list for 1791 in Gunpowder Upper and Bush River Lower Hundreds, as filed by John Bond, Deputy Sheriff, on Sep 20, 1791. {Ref: IL 31.24}

CARLILE, LANT., insolvent on list returned by Robert Carlile for taxes due for the year 1791. {Ref: IL 31.16}

CARLILE, ROBERT, served as constable in Eden Hd., 1797. {Ref: CC, CM}

CARLILE, ROBERT, compiled and returned a list of tax insolvents in 1791. {Ref: IL 31.16}

CARLILE, ROBERT, head of family in 1800 (4th District). {Ref: CI}

CARLIN, GEORGE, head of family in 1800 (5th District). {Ref: CI}. Also see "Henrietta Wheeler," q.v.

CARLIN, JAMES, taxpayer, 1798, Bush River Upper & Eden Hd., 1 dwelling house, 4 inferior houses, 2 acres, $250 valuation; 3 tracts (170 acres) in Bush River Upper & Eden Hd., $446.24 valuation, 2 slaves. {Ref: TL}

CARLIN, JAMES, head of family in 1800 (4th District). {Ref: CI}

CARLIN, JOHN, head of family in 1800 (3rd District). {Ref: CI}

CARLIN, JOSEPH, head of family in 1800 (5th District). {Ref: CI}. Also see "John Evatt," q.v.

CARLISLE, JOHN, vestryman, 1798, St. George's Episcopal Church. {Ref: PR}

CARLON, GEORGE, insolvent on lists in 1791 due county taxes and road taxes in "Deer Creek Upper, Middle, and Broad Creek Hundreds" as returned by Robert Amos, Jr., but his name was then crossed off both lists. {Ref: IL 31.12, 31.22}

CARLON, JAMES, served on a Petit Jury in August, 1797, on a Grand Jury in August, 1798 and August, 1799, and on a Petit Jury in August, 1800. {Ref: CC, CM}

CARLON, JAMES, insolvent on a list for the road tax for 1792, as returned for Robert Amoss, tax collector (James Carlon's name appeared on the same list twice). {Ref: IL 13.12}

CARMAN, AMELIA, m. John Dutton on Jun 26, 1800. {Ref: PR}

CARMAN, NANCY, see "Robert Whiteford," q.v.
CARMON, ANDREW, head of family in 1800 (4th District). {Ref: CI}
CARR, JESSE (father), b. Jun 1, 1796, d. Apr 6, 1890, bur. in Emory Methodist Church Cemetery at Mill Green. {Ref: TI}
CARR, MARGARETT, see "Peter Long," q.v.
CARR, ROBERT, head of family in 1800 (5th District). {Ref: CI}
CARR, WILLIAM, taxpayer, 1798, Gunpowder Upper Hd., 1 dwelling house, 2 inferior houses, 2 acres, $150 valuation; 1 tract (42 acres) in Gunpowder Upper Hd., $141.75 valuation, no slaves. {Ref: TL}
CARR, WILLIAM, served as constable in Gunpowder Upper Hd., 1797-1799. {Ref: CC, CM}
CARR, WILLIAM, insolvent on a list for county taxes due in 1792 as returned by Benjamin Preston. {Ref: IL 31.00}
CARR, WILLIAM, insolvent on list returned for the road tax due for 1791 by John Bull. {Ref: IL 31.14}
CARROL, BENJAMIN, head of family in 1800 (1st District). {Ref: CI}
CARROL, JAMES, head of family in 1800 (1st District). {Ref: CI}
CARROL, JAMES JR., treated by Dr. Archer on Apr 6, 1796. {Ref: JA}
CARROL, MARY, m. William Fox on Aug 15, 1797. {Ref: PR}
CARROL, PETER, head of family in 1800 (4th District). {Ref: CI}
CARROL, ROBERT, head of family in 1800 (5th District). {Ref: CI}
CARROL, WILLIAM, head of family in 1800 (2nd District). {Ref: CI}
CARROLL, AQUILA, see "Peter Carroll," q.v.
CARROLL, BENJAMIN, taxpayer, 1798, Gunpowder Upper Hd., 1 dwelling house, 4 inferior houses, 2 acres, $150 valuation; 2 tracts (269 acres) in Gunpowder Upper Hd., $563.60 valuation, 2 slaves. {Ref: TL}
CARROLL, BENJAMIN, m. Milly Preston on Dec 25, 1792. {Ref: PR}
CARROLL, BENJAMIN, subpoenaed to the Grand Jury in August, 1797. {Ref: CC}
CARROLL, BENJAMIN, served as constable in Gunpowder Lower Hd., 1797-1799, and court bailiff, 1799-1800. {Ref: CC, CM}
CARROLL, BENJAMIN, see "Peter Carroll," q.v.
CARROLL, CHARLES, OF CARROLLTON, had an account at Hall's Store in May, 1791 (but it should be noted that this famous Maryland Signer was not a resident of Harford County). {Ref: WH}
CARROLL, DELIA, see "Nathan Horner," q.v.
CARROLL, ELIZABETH, insolvent on list returned for the road tax due for 1791 by John Bull. {Ref: IL 31.14}
CARROLL, ELIZABETH, will probated Jun 23, 1792. {Ref: HW}
CARROLL, JAMES, will probated Jun 12, 1792. {Ref: HW}
CARROLL, JAMES, taxpayer, 1798, Bush River Lower Hd., 1 dwelling house, 3 inferior houses, 1 acre and 80 perches, $150 valuation; 1 tract (98 acres, 80 perches) in Bush River Lower Hd., $221.62 valuation, 2 slaves. {Ref: TL}
CARROLL, JOHN, insolvent on lists in 1791 due county taxes and road taxes in

"Deer Creek Upper, Middle, and Broad Creek Hundreds" as returned by Robert Amos, Jr. {Ref: IL 31.12, 31.22}

CARROLL, PETER, charged for perjury in 1794 and several people were summoned to court in 1795, including Aquila Carroll, James Carroll and Benjamin Carroll. {Ref: CD, March and August Terms, 1795, and March Term, 1797}

CARROLL, WILLIAM, see "Elizabeth Bayles," q.v.

CARRYGIN, HUGH(?), head of family in 1800 (5th District). {Ref: CI}

CARRYGIN, MANSSON (MANASON), head of family in 1800 (5th District). {Ref: CI}

CARSINS, ANN, wife of John, b. Feb 16, 1798, d. Jan 25, 1879, aged 80 years, 11 months, and 9 days, bur. in the Barnes Family Cemetery near Earlton. {Ref: TI}

CARSINS, JOHN, b. Feb 18, 1795, d. Oct 20, 1838, bur. in the Barnes Family Cemetery near Earlton. {Ref: TI}

CARSON, JOHN, insolvent on a list for 1791 in Gunpowder Upper and Bush River Lower Hundreds, as filed by John Bond, Deputy Sheriff, on Sep 20, 1791. {Ref: IL 31.24}

CARSON, JOHN, insolvent on list returned by Robert Carlile for taxes due for the year 1791. {Ref: IL 31.16}

CARTER, ARABELLA, m. Peter Ross on Aug 14, 1800. {Ref: PR}

CARTER, DANIEL ("gone to the back woods"), insolvent on lists in 1791 due county taxes and road taxes in "Deer Creek Upper, Middle, and Broad Creek Hundreds" as returned by Robert Amos, Jr. {Ref: IL 31.12, 31.22}

CARTER, DARBY, insolvent on list returned by Robert Carlile for taxes due for the year 1791. {Ref: IL 31.16}

CARTER, JACOB, insolvent on lists for the county tax and road tax due for 1791 in Deer Creek Lower Hd., as returned by Thomas Taylor on Sep 17, 1792. {Ref: IL 31.12, 31.03}

CARTER, JOHN, see "John Stump," q.v.

CARTER, JOHN, head of family in 1800 (2nd District). {Ref: CI}

CARTER, JOHN, head of family in 1800 (4th District). {Ref: CI}

CARTER, JOSIAS, served on a Grand Jury in August, 1798 and August, 1799. {Ref: CM}

CARTER, JOSIAS, taxpayer, 1798, Bush River Upper & Eden Hd., 1 dwelling house, 4 inferior houses, 2 acres, $105 valuation; 3 tracts (304 acres, 80 perches) in Bush River Upper & Eden Hd., $856.97 valuation, 2 slaves. {Ref: TL}

CARTER, JOSIAS, tract *Mary's Delight* surveyed in 1793. {Ref: CB}

CARTER, JOSIAS, head of family in 1800 (4th District). {Ref: CI}

CARTER, SAMUEL (at Stafford Mills), treated by Dr. Archer on Sep 13, 1793. {Ref: JA}

CARTIE, DARBY, insolvent on a list for 1791 in Gunpowder Upper and Bush River Lower Hundreds, as filed by John Bond, Deputy Sheriff, on Sep 20, 1791 (who listed him as a single man). {Ref: IL 31.24}

CARTON, ELIZABETH, see "George Carton" and "Jane Carton" and "William Carton" and "Mary Carton," q.v.

CARTON, GEORGE, son of Joseph and Elizabeth, b. Jul 12, 1794, bapt. Sep 25, 1796. {Ref: PR}

CARTON, JANE, dau. of Joseph and Elizabeth, b. Jul 4, 1796, bapt. Sep 25, 1796. {Ref: PR}

CARTON, JOSEPH, see "George Carton" and "Jane Carton" and "William Carton" and "Mary Carton," q.v.

CARTON, MARY, dau. of Joseph and Elizabeth, b. Sep 5, 1800. {Ref: PR}

CARTON, WILLIAM, son of Joseph and Elizabeth, b. in October, 1798. {Ref: PR}

CARTWRIGHT, JAMES McKELVEY, son of John Cartwright and Sarah Hamme, b. Jan 3, 1798, bapt. Apr 9, 1798. {Ref: PR}

CARTWRIGHT, JOHN, see "James McKelvey Cartwright," q.v.

CARTY, FRANCIS, m. Magdalen Juel on Oct 1, 1792. {Ref: PR}

CARTY, HANNAH, m. Joseph Thomas on Oct 29, 1799. {Ref: PR}

CARVER, ELIZABETH, see "William Carver," q.v.

CARVER, HENRY, see "William Carver" and "Margaret Severson," q.v.

CARVER, HENRY, insolvent on a list for the road tax due for 1791 in Harford Upper, Harford Lower, and Spesutia Upper as returned by Robert Amos, Jr. on Sep 18, 1793. {Ref: IL 31.18}

CARVER, HENRY, subpoenaed to the Grand Jury in August, 1797. {Ref: CC}

CARVER, HENRY, taxpayer, 1798, Spesutia Lower Hd., 1 dwelling house, 2 inferior houses, 44 perches, 21 sq. ft., $460 valuation; 1 tract (44 perches, 21 sq. ft.) in Spesutia Lower Hd., $90 valuation, no slaves. {Ref: TL}

CARVER, HENRY, head of family in 1800 (Havre de Grace). {Ref: CI}

CARVER, HENRY (blacksmith in Havre de Grace), treated by Dr. Archer on Aug 17, 1791; also mentioned a child (no name given). {Ref: JA}

CARVER, JOSEPH C., b. 1797, d. Jul 22, 1860, bur. in Angel Hill Cemetery in Havre de Grace. {Ref: TI}. Also see "Mary Carver," q.v.

CARVER, MARY, wife of Joseph C., b. 1797, d. Jun 22, 1873, aged 76 years, bur. in Angel Hill Cemetery in Havre de Grace. {Ref: TI}

CARVER, WILLIAM, son of Henry and Elizabeth, b. Jun 24, 1798, bapt. Nov 8, 1798. {Ref: PR}

CASHMAN, CORNELIUS' EXECUTORS, insolvent on list returned for the road tax due for 1791 by John Bull. {Ref: IL 31.14}

CASSON (CARSON?), JAMES, head of family in 1800 (3rd District). {Ref: CI}

CATHERWOOD, JOHN, see "John Chanthanwood" and "Dixon Gorsuch," q.v.

CATHERWOOD, JOHN, insolvent on a list of the county tax due William Osborn, sheriff, for 1791, as returned by Edward Prigg on Sep 20, 1791. {Ref: IL 31.17}

CATHERWOOD, JOHN, insolvent on lists in 1791 due county taxes and road taxes in "Deer Creek Upper, Middle, and Broad Creek Hundreds" as returned by Robert Amos, Jr. {Ref: IL 31.12, 31.22}

CAUFIELD, THOMAS, licensed retailer in March, 1795. {Ref: CC}

CAULFIELD, CHARLOTTE, dau. of Thomas and Martha, b. Jul 9, 1795, bapt. Jun 12, 1796. {Ref: PR}

CAULFIELD, MARTHA, see "Charlotte Caulfield," q.v.
CAULFIELD, THOMAS, see "Thomas Coffield" and "Charlotte Caulfield," q.v.
CAVINER, JOHN, insolvent on a list for the road tax due for 1791 in Deer Creek Lower Hd., as returned by Thomas Taylor on Sep 17, 1792, and on the 1792 county tax list which spelled the name "Cavenner." {Ref: IL 31.12, 31.03}
CEARNS, WILLIAM, taxpayer, 1798, Bush River Upper & Eden Hd., 1 dwelling house, 2 inferior houses, 2 acres, $150 valuation; 1 tract (98 acres, 80 perches) in Bush River Upper & Eden Hd., $138.37 valuation, no slaves. {Ref: TL}. Also see "William Kearn" and "William Kerns," q.v.
CENY (CURY?), ROBERT, insolvent on list returned by Robert Carlile for taxes due for the year 1791. {Ref: IL 31.16}
CHACKTON, MONSIEUR, taxpayer, 1798, Gunpowder Lower Hd., 1 dwelling house, 1 inferior house, 80 perches of land, $250 valuation; no slaves. {Ref: TL}
CHALK, BENJAMIN, head of family in 1800 (4th District). {Ref: CI}
CHALK, GEORGE, taxpayer, 1798, Bush River Upper & Eden Hd., 1 dwelling house, 1 inferior house, 2 acres, $105 valuation; 3 tracts (136 acres) in Bush River Upper & Eden Hd., $306 valuation, no slaves. {Ref: TL}
CHALK, GEORGE, head of family in 1800 (4th District). {Ref: CI}
CHALK, JOHN, taxpayer, 1798, Bush River Upper & Eden Hd., 1 dwelling house, 3 inferior houses, 2 acres, $105 valuation; 6 tracts (286 acres) in Bush River Upper & Eden Hd., $643.50 valuation, no slaves. {Ref: TL}
CHALK, JOHN, head of family in 1800 (4th District). {Ref: CI}
CHALK, TUDOR, head of family in 1800 (4th District). {Ref: CI}
CHAMBERLAIN, ELIZABETH, see "Maria Chamberlain" and "Philip Chamberlain," q.v.
CHAMBERLAIN, JOHN, treated by Dr. Archer on Aug 13, 1792; also mentioned he lived near Griffith Gittings' Mill. {Ref: JA}
CHAMBERLAIN, MARIA, dau. of Philip and Elizabeth, b. May 24, 1799, bapt. Jul 12, 1799. {Ref: PR}
CHAMBERLAIN, PAUL, charged for assaulting William Adair in 1797. {Ref: CD, March and August Terms, 1797}
CHAMBERLAIN, PAUL, subpoenaed to the Grand Jury in August, 1797. {Ref: CC}
CHAMBERLAIN, PHILIP, see "Maria Chamberlain" and "William O'Dair," q.v.
CHAMBERLAIN, PHILIP, granted a retailer's permit on July 26, 1797. {Ref: CC}
CHAMBERLAIN, PHILIP, charged for assaulting William Adair and found guilty by verdict in 1797; Paul Chamberlain was security for fine and fees; subsequently charged for assaulting and "snaping a pistol" on Thomas Coffield. {Ref: CD, March and August Terms, 1797}
CHAMBERLAIN, PHILIP, subpoenaed to the Grand Jury in August, 1797. {Ref: CC}
CHAMBERLAIN, PHILIP, taxpayer, 1798, Spesutia Lower Hd., 1 dwelling house, 1 inferior house, 44 perches, 21 sq. ft., $250 valuation; 1 tract (44 perches, 21 sq. ft.) in Spesutia Lower Hd., $78.74 valuation, no slaves. {Ref: TL}
CHAMBERLAIN, PHILIP, son of Philip and Elizabeth, b. Jan 25, 1797, bapt. Sep

7, 1797. {Ref: PR}
CHAMBERLAIN (CHAMBALIN), PHILLIP, head of family in 1800 (Havre de Grace). {Ref: CI}
CHAMBERS, ELIZABETH, head of family in 1800 (2nd District). {Ref: CI}
CHAMBERS, MARY, bur. Nov 21, 1796, aged 56. {Ref: PR}
CHAMBERS, WILLIAM, m. Elizabeth Doyle on Nov 7, 1799. {Ref: PR}
CHAMBERS, WILLIAM, head of family in 1800 (1st District). {Ref: CI}
CHANCE, AMELIA, m. James Bevard on Feb 4, 1798. {Ref: PR}
CHANCEY, BENJAMIN, see "James Phillips, Sr.," q.v.
CHANCEY, BENJAMIN, taxpayer, 1798, Spesutia Lower Hd., no dwelling house listed in this part of the tax schedule, no land listed, 5 slaves. {Ref: TL}
CHANCEY (CHANCY), BENJAMIN, head of family in 1800 (2nd District). {Ref: CI}
CHANCEY, GEORGE, taxpayer, 1798, Harford Lower Hd., 1 dwelling house, 8 inferior houses, 2 acres, $400 valuation; 6 tracts (392 acres) in Harford Lower Hd., $2158.65 valuation, 4 slaves. {Ref: TL}
CHANCEY, GEORGE, head of family in 1800 (2nd District). {Ref: CI}
CHANCEY, GEORGE JR., taxpayer, 1798, Harford Lower Hd., no dwelling house listed in this part of the tax schedule, no land listed, 4 slaves. {Ref: TL}. Also see "George Copeland," q.v.
CHANCEY, JOHN, taxpayer, 1798, Spesutia Lower Hd., 1 dwelling house, 5 inferior houses, 2 acres, $215 valuation; 1 tract (254 acres) in Spesutia Lower Hd., $1416.60 valuation, 5 slaves. {Ref: TL}
CHANCEY, JOHN, head of family in 1800 (2nd District). {Ref: CI}
CHANDLEY, ANN, m. Patrick McLaughlin on Nov 8, 1798. {Ref: PR}
CHANDLEY, BENJAMIN, taxpayer, 1798, Spesutia Lower Hd., 1 dwelling house, 1 inferior house, 44 perches, 21 sq. ft., $200 valuation, no slaves. {Ref: TL}
CHANEY, MARGARET, insolvent on a list for the road tax due for 1791 in Harford Upper, Harford Lower, and Spesutia Upper as returned by Robert Amos, Jr. on Sep 18, 1793. {Ref: IL 31.18}
CHANEY, THOMAS, insolvent, Harford Lower and Spesutia Lower Hundreds, on a tax list returned by George Lyttle on Sep 21, 1791. {Ref: IL 31.20, 31.21}
CHANEY, THOMAS, insolvent on a list for the road tax due for 1791 in Harford Upper, Harford Lower, and Spesutia Upper as returned by Robert Amos, Jr. on Sep 18, 1793. {Ref: IL 31.18}
CHANEY, THOMAS, head of family in 1800 (2nd District). {Ref: CI}
CHANLEY, BENJAMIN, head of family in 1800 (Havre de Grace). {Ref: CI}
CHANLEY, WILLIAM, head of family in 1800 (Havre de Grace). {Ref: CI}
CHANTHANWOOD (CATHERWOOD?), JOHN, head of family in 1800 (4th District). {Ref: CI}
CHAPEN, PERRY, head of family in 1800 (1st District). {Ref: CI}
CHAPMAN, NANCY, head of family in 1800 (3rd District). {Ref: CI}
CHARLETON, JOHN, head of family in 1800 (4th District). {Ref: CI}

CHAUNCEY, ANN, m. John Dougherty on Apr 3, 1800. {Ref: PR}
CHAUNCEY, ANN ELIZA, dau. of Benjamin and Elizabeth, b. Aug 15, 1799, bapt. Sep 8, 1800. {Ref: PR}
CHAUNCEY, BENJAMIN, son of Benjamin and Elizabeth, b. Apr 3, 1797, bapt. Sep 8, 1800. {Ref: PR}. Also see "Mary Chauncey" and "Ann Eliza Chauncey," q.v.
CHAUNCEY, BENJAMIN, bur. Apr 24, 1797. {Ref: PR}
CHAUNCEY, ELIZABETH, see "Mary Chauncey" and "Benjamin Chauncey" and "Ann Eliza Chauncey" and "John Chauncey" and "Nestor Chauncey," q.v.
CHAUNCEY, FRANCES, see "George Chauncey," q.v.
CHAUNCEY, GEORGE, son of George and Frances, b. Apr 27, 1798, bapt. Jul 28, 1798. {Ref: PR}
CHAUNCEY, GEORGE, vestryman, 1794, 1799, St. George's Episcopal Church. {Ref: PR}
CHAUNCEY, JOHN, son of John and Elizabeth, b. Oct 22, 1790, bapt. Feb 9, 1797. {Ref: PR}
CHAUNCEY, JOHN, vestryman, 1796-1797, 1799, and warden, 1798, St. George's Episcopal Church. {Ref: PR}
CHAUNCEY, MARY, b. 1747, d. Jul 1, 1798, bur. in a cemetery now on Aberdeen Proving Grounds. {Ref: TI}
CHAUNCEY, MARY, dau. of Benjamin and Elizabeth, b. Nov 18, 1793, bapt. Sep 8, 1800. {Ref: PR}
CHAUNCEY, MARY, bur. Jul 3, 1798. {Ref: PR}
CHAUNCEY, NESTOR, son of John and Elizabeth, b. Mar 21, 1793, bapt. Feb 9, 1797. {Ref: PR}
CHENEY, EDITH, b. 1800, d. in 7th month, 1871, bur. in Forest Hill Quaker Cemetery. {Ref: TI}
CHENEY, THOMAS, see "David Craif," q.v.
CHERRY, JAMES, insolvent on a list for 1791 in Gunpowder Upper and Bush River Lower Hundreds, as filed by John Bond, Deputy Sheriff, on Sep 20, 1791. {Ref: IL 31.24}
CHERRY, ROBERT, insolvent on a list for 1791 in Gunpowder Upper and Bush River Lower Hundreds, as filed by John Bond, Deputy Sheriff, on Sep 20, 1791 (who listed him as a single man). {Ref: IL 31.24}
CHERRY, ROBERT, head of family in 1800 (5th District). {Ref: CI}
CHESHOLM, THOMAS, m. Sarah Rigdon on Jan 28, 1796. {Ref: PR}
CHESNEY, BENJAMIN, insolvent on a list for county taxes due in 1792 as returned by Benjamin Preston. {Ref: IL 31.00}
CHESNEY, MARY, wife of William, Jr., b. May 26, 1797, d. Nov 26, 1874, bur. in Rock Run Cemetery at Craig's Corner. {Ref: TI}
CHESNEY, THOMAS, had an account at Hall's Store in September, 1791, which noted payment "by his wife and for his daughter." {Ref: WH}
CHESNEY, WILLIAM, taxpayer, 1798, Susquehanna Hd., 2 tracts (108 acres) and

1 building, $312.75 valuation, no slaves. {Ref: TL}
CHESNEY, WILLIAM, head of family in 1800 (2nd District). {Ref: CI}
CHESNEY, WILLIAM JR., see "Mary Chesney," q.v.
CHESOLM, JOHN, see "Stephen Chesolm," q.v.
CHESOLM, STEPHEN, son of John Chesolm and Sarah Dawney, b. Feb 18, 1800, bapt. Jun 10, 1800. {Ref: PR}
CHEW, CAROLINE F., wife of Edward M., b. Aug 7, 1797, d. May 16, 1852, aged 55 years and 9 days, bur. in Trappe Church Cemetery. {Ref: TI}
CHEW, CASSANDRA MORGAN, dau. of Thomas Sheredine and Elizabeth, b. Nov 12, 1796. {Ref: PR}
CHEW, EDWARD M., b. Mar 16, 1800, d. May 16, 1878, aged 78 years and 2 months, bur. in Trappe Church Cemetery. {Ref: TI}. Also see "Caroline F. Chew," q.v.
CHEW, ELIZABETH, see "Cassandra Morgan Chew" and "William Morgan Chew," q.v.
CHEW, NATHAN, insolvent, Harford Lower and Spesutia Lower Hundreds (listed as a single man), on a tax list returned by George Lyttle on Sep 21, 1791. {Ref: IL 31.20, 31.21}
CHEW, RICHARD, insolvent on lists returned for the county and road taxes due for 1791 by John Bull in Gunpowder Lower Hundred. {Ref: IL 31.14, 31.15}
CHEW, RICHARD ("gone"), insolvent on lists due for 1790 and 1791 "fund taxes" and county taxes in Susquehanna Hd., as returned by Thomas Taylor. {Ref: IL 31.12, 31.02}
CHEW, THOMAS, see "James Lee Morgan," q.v.
CHEW, THOMAS, taxpayer, 1798, Deer Creek Lower Hd., 1 dwelling house, 4 inferior houses, 2 acres, $600 valuation; 3 tract (400 acres) in Deer Creek Lower Hd., $1442.25 valuation, 2 slaves. {Ref: TL}
CHEW, THOMAS, head of family in 1800 (5th District). {Ref: CI}
CHEW, THOMAS SHEREDINE, see "Cassandra Morgan Chew" and "William Morgan Chew," q.v.
CHEW, WILLIAM MORGAN, son of Thomas Sheredine and Elizabeth, b. Jul 14, 1791. {Ref: PR}
CHILSON, WALTER, head of family in 1800 (1st District). {Ref: CI}
CHINWITH (CHINOITH), THOMAS, head of family in 1800 (4th District). {Ref: CI}
CHINWITH, WILLIAM, insolvent on a list for 1791 in Gunpowder Upper and Bush River Lower Hundreds, as filed by John Bond, Deputy Sheriff, on Sep 20, 1791 (who listed him as a single man). {Ref: IL 31.24}
CHINWORTH, THOMAS, insolvent on list returned for the road tax due for 1791 by John Bull. {Ref: IL 31.14}
CHINWORTH, WILLIAM, insolvent on list returned for the road tax due for 1791 by John Bull. {Ref: IL 31.14}
CHISHOLM, THOMAS, taxpayer, 1798, Harford Upper Hd., no dwelling house listed in this part of the tax schedule, no land listed, 1 slave. {Ref: TL}

CHISHOLM, THOMAS, head of family in 1800 (1st District). {Ref: CI}
CHISNEY, BENJAMIN, insolvent on list returned for the road tax due for 1791 by John Bull. {Ref: IL 31.14}
CHOCK, GEORGE AND JOHN, tract *Salisbury* surveyed in 1798. {Ref: CB}
CHRISTIE, CHARLES, treated by Dr. Archer on Oct 24, 1791; also mentioned his wife (no name given). {Ref: JA}. Also see "Gabriel Christie," q.v.
CHRISTIE, GABRIEL, had an account at Hall's Store in January, 1791. {Ref: WH}
CHRISTIE, GABRIEL, subpoenaed to the Grand Jury in August, 1797. {Ref: CC}
CHRISTIE, GABRIEL, taxpayer, 1798, Spesutia Lower Hd., 1 dwelling house, 4 inferior houses, 88 perches, 42 sq. ft., $600 valuation; 5 tracts (96 acres, 60 perches, 105 sq. ft.) in Spesutia Lower Hd., $2154.38 valuation; 5 slaves. {Ref: TL}
CHRISTIE, GABRIEL (esquire), treated by Dr. Archer on Oct 16, 1797; also mentioned his son Charles in 1790. {Ref: JA}
CHRISTIE, GABRIEL (esquire), head of family in 1800 (Havre de Grace). {Ref: CI}
CHRISTOPHER, JAMES, head of family in 1800 (1st District). {Ref: CI}
CHURCHMAN, ENOCK, tract *Octagon* surveyed between 1792 and 1796. {Ref: SB}
CLARK, ABRAHAM, insolvent on list returned by Robert Carlile for taxes due for the year 1791. {Ref: IL 31.16}
CLARK, BARNETT, head of family in 1800 (5th District). {Ref: CI}
CLARK, DAVID, treated by Dr. Archer on Oct 20, 1792; also mentioned his wife and dau. (no names given). {Ref: JA}
CLARK, DAVID, taxpayer, 1798, Spesutia Upper Hd., 1 dwelling house, 3 inferior houses, 1 acre, $200 valuation; 2 tracts (442 acres) in Spesutia Upper Hd., $936 valuation, 1 slave. {Ref: TL}
CLARK, DAVID, head of family in 1800 (3rd District). {Ref: CI}
CLARK, GEORGE, head of family in 1800 (3rd District). {Ref: CI}
CLARK, JAMES, see "Jennet Hutchinson," q.v.
CLARK, JAMES, taxpayer, 1798, Deer Creek Middle Hd., 1 tract (188 acres, 40 perches) and 1 building, $367.90 valuation, 1 slave. {Ref: TL}. In another part of the tax schedule the occupant is listed as Thomas Mitchell.
CLARK, JAMES ("charge twice"), insolvent on lists in 1791 due county taxes and road taxes in "Deer Creek Upper, Middle, and Broad Creek Hundreds" as returned by Robert Amos, Jr. {Ref: IL 31.12, 31.22}
CLARK, JAMES ("Scoch"), "twist chargd" (meaning "Scotchman, twice charged"), insolvent on a list of the county tax due William Osborn, sheriff, for 1791, as returned by Edward Prigg on Sep 20, 1791. {Ref: IL 31.17}
CLARK, JOHN, see "Maria Clark" and "William McMath," q.v.
CLARK, JOHN, served as constable in Spesutia Upper Hd., 1798-1800. {Ref: CM}
CLARK, JOHN, m. Cassandra Anderson on Nov 15, 1794. {Ref: PR}
CLARK, JOHN, head of family in 1800 (3rd District). {Ref: CI}
CLARK, MARIA, dau. of John and Nancy, b. Mar 23, 1797. {Ref: PR}
CLARK, NANCY, see "Maria Clark," q.v.

CLARK, RUTH, see "Ruth Quinlan," q.v.
CLARK, THOMAS ("gone"), insolvent on lists due for 1790 and 1791 "fund taxes" and county taxes in Susquehanna Hd., as returned by Thomas Taylor. {Ref: IL 31.12, 31.02}
CLARK, THOMAS, taxpayer, 1798, Bush River Upper & Eden Hd., 1 dwelling house, 3 inferior houses, 2 acres, $150 valuation; 1 tract (227 acres) in Bush River Upper & Eden Hd., $446.91 valuation, no slaves. {Ref: TL}. [The tax list showed the name as "Thoma Clark"].
CLARK, THOMAS, head of family in 1800 (4th District). {Ref: CI}
CLARK, WILLIAM, treated by Dr. Archer on Aug 10, 1794. {Ref: JA}
CLARK, WILLIAM, insolvent on a list for the road tax for 1792, as returned for Robert Amoss, tax collector. {Ref: IL 13.12}
CLARK, WILLIAM, mentioned in a survey deposition on Sep 26, 1799. {Ref: JS}
CLARK, WILLIAM, head of family in 1800 (3rd District). {Ref: CI}
CLARK, WILLIAM SR., taxpayer, 1798, Spesutia Upper Hd., 1 dwelling house, 3 inferior houses, 1 acre, $165 valuation; 3 tracts (366 acres) in Spesutia Upper Hd., $1235.25 valuation, 1 slave. {Ref: TL}
CLARK, WILLIAM JR., served on a Petit Jury in March, 1798 and March, 1799 and August, 1800. {Ref: CM}
CLARK, WILLIAM JR., taxpayer, 1798, Spesutia Upper Hd., 1 tract (80 acres) and 1 building, $376.88 valuation, 1 slave. {Ref: TL}
CLARK, WILLIAM JR., head of family in 1800 (3rd District). {Ref: CI}
CLARKE, DAVID, had an account at Hall's Store in August, 1791. {Ref: WH}
CLARKE, FRANCIS, head of family in 1800 (4th District). {Ref: CI}
CLAYTON, JOSEPH, m. Sarah Wills on Aug 18, 1796. {Ref: Clayton-Archer Bible}
CLEMENTS, THOMAS (Kent County), insolvent on a list for 1791 in Gunpowder Upper and Bush River Lower Hundreds, as filed by John Bond, Deputy Sheriff, on Sep 20, 1791. {Ref: IL 31.24}
CLEMENTS, THOMAS, insolvent on list returned by Robert Carlile for taxes due for the year 1791. {Ref: IL 31.16}
CLEMONS, CHRISTOPHER, insolvent on list returned for the road tax due for 1791 by John Bull. {Ref: IL 31.14}
CLENDENIN, ALPHA, dau. of John and Elizabeth, b. 1800, d. Jul 25, 1802, bur. in Bethel Presbyterian Church Cemetery at Madonna. {Ref: BC}
CLENDENIN, DAVID, head of family in 1800 (3rd District). {Ref: CI}
CLENDENIN, ELIZABETH, see "Alpha Clendenin" and "Robert Clendenin," q.v.
CLENDENIN, JOHN, head of family in 1800 (4th District). {Ref: CI}
CLENDENIN, ROBERT, son of John and Elizabeth, b. 1797, d. Aug 5, 1802, bur. in Bethel Presbyterian Church Cemetery at Madonna. {Ref: BC}
CLENDENING, DAVID, taxpayer, 1798, Spesutia Upper Hd., no dwelling house listed in this part of the tax schedule, no land listed, 3 slaves. {Ref: TL}. Also see "John and David Clendening," q.v.
CLENDENING, JOHN, taxpayer, 1798, Bush River Upper & Eden Hd., no

dwelling house listed in this part of the tax schedule, no land listed, 3 slaves. {Ref: TL}. Also see "John and David Clendening" and "Alpha Clendenin" and "Robert Clendenin," q.v.

CLENDENING, JOHN, appointed a Judge of Elections in the 4th District on Jul 28, 1800. {Ref: CM}

CLENDENING, JOHN AND DAVID, taxpayers, 1798, Bush River Upper & Eden Hd., 1 dwelling house, 5 inferior houses, 2 acres, $400 valuation; taxpayers, 1798, Bush River Upper & Eden Hd., 1 dwelling house, 3 inferior houses, 2 acres, $350 valuation; 2 tracts (672 acres, 120 perches) in Bush River Upper & Eden Hd., $1522.69 valuation, no slaves. {Ref: TL}

CLENDENNON (CLENDINEN), JAMES, will probated Dec 8, 1795. {Ref: HW}. Also see "Samuel Elliot" and "Richard Cooley," q.v.

CLINE, SARAH, m. Peter Night on Mar 5, 1798. {Ref: PR}

CLINEFILTER, JOHN, head of family in 1800 (4th District). {Ref: CI}

CLOMAN, FRANCIS, taxpayer, 1798, Susquehanna Hd., 2 tracts (43 acres, 124 perches, 21 sq. ft.) and 2 buildings, $168 valuation, no slaves. {Ref: TL}

CLOMAN (CLOWMAN), FRANCIS, head of family in 1800 (3rd District). {Ref: CI}

CLOUD, ABNER, insolvent on list returned for the road tax due for 1791 by John Bull. {Ref: IL 31.14}

CLOUD, ABNER'S HEIRS, taxpayers, 1798, Gunpowder Upper Hd., 3 tracts (534 acres, 120 perches), $1040.63 valuation; no buildings listed, no slaves. {Ref: TL}

COALE, ABRAHAM, taxpayer, 1798, Harford Lower Hd., 1 dwelling house, 3 inferior houses, 2 acres, $200 valuation; 1 tract (397 acres) in Harford Lower Hd., $2387.70 valuation, 2 slaves. {Ref: TL}

COALE, ANN, taxpayer, 1798, Bush River Upper & Eden Hd., 1 tract (34 acres) and 1 building, $144 valuation, no slaves. {Ref: TL}

COALE, EZEKIEL, taxpayer, 1798, Susquehanna Hd., 2 tracts (92 acres) and 1 building, $211.50 valuation, no slaves. {Ref: TL}

COALE, ISAAC, taxpayer, 1798, Susquehanna Hd., 3 tracts (110) and 1 building, $579.38 valuation, no slaves. {Ref: TL}

COALE, JAMES, taxpayer, 1798, Harford Lower Hd., no dwelling house listed in this part of the tax schedule, no land listed, 1 slave. {Ref: TL}

COALE, JOHN, taxpayer, 1798, Harford Lower Hd., 1 dwelling house, 6 inferior houses, 2 acres, $150 valuation; 1 tract (371 acres, 40 perches) in Harford Lower Hd., $2714.76 valuation, 7 slaves. {Ref: TL}

COALE, MARGUERITE, head of family in 1800 (3rd District). {Ref: CI}

COALE, PHILIP, treated by Dr. Archer on Apr 2, 1791. {Ref: JA}

COALE, PHILLIP, will probated Sep 14, 1791. {Ref: HW}

COALE, RICHARD, taxpayer, 1798, Deer Creek Lower Hd., 1 tract (89 acres) and 1 building, $445.50 valuation, no slaves. {Ref: TL}

COALE, SAMUEL, taxpayer, 1798, Susquehanna Hd., 1 dwelling house, 2 inferior houses, 2 acres, $100.50 valuation; 2 tracts (123 acres) in Susquehanna Hd.,

$415.12 valuation, no slaves. {Ref. TL}

COALE, SKIPWITH, treated by Dr. Archer on Mar 21, 1793; also mentioned his wife (no name given). {Ref. JA}. Also see "Negro Sam," q.v.

COALE, SKIPWITH SR., taxpayer, 1798, Deer Creek Lower Hd., 1 dwelling house, 6 inferior houses, 2 acres, $600 valuation; 1 tract (154 acres) in Deer Creek Lower Hd., $519.75 valuation, no slaves. {Ref. TL}

COALE, SKIPWITH JR., taxpayer, 1798, Deer Creek Lower Hd., 1 dwelling house, 3 inferior houses, 2 acres, $190 valuation; 1 tract (100 acres) in Deer Creek Lower Hd., $168.75 valuation, no slaves. {Ref. TL}

COALE, SUSAN, see "William Coale," q.v.

COALE, THOMAS, taxpayer, 1798, Susquehanna Hd., 2 tracts (90 acres) and 1 building, $185.63 valuation, no slaves. {Ref. TL}

COALE, WILLIAM, taxpayer, 1798, Deer Creek Lower Hd., 1 dwelling house, 2 inferior houses, 2 acres, $500 valuation; 1 tract (107 acres) in Deer Creek Lower Hd., $473.62 valuation, no slaves. {Ref. TL}. Also see "William Ellis," q.v.

COALE, WILLIAM, taxpayer, 1798, Spesutia Lower Hd., 1 dwelling house, 1 inferior house, 44 perches, 21 sq. ft., $600 valuation, no slaves. {Ref. TL}

COALE, WILLIAM (at Deer Creek), treated by Dr. Archer on Jul 11, 1791; also mentioned his dau. Susan. {Ref. JA}

COATNEY, JONAS, head of family in 1800 (2nd District). {Ref. CI}

COATNEY, THOMAS, head of family in 1800 (2nd District). {Ref. CI}

COCHRAN, PLEASANT LUCAS, wife of James, b. 1794, d. 1866, bur. in Cokesbury Methodist Cemetery in Abingdon. {Ref. TI}

COEN, ELIZABETH, wife of John, b. Nov 13, 1791, d. Mar 28, 1818, bur. in the Barnes Family Cemetery near Earlton. {Ref. TI}

COEN, JOHN, b. 1792, d. Feb 2, 1871, aged 79, bur. in the Barnes Family Cemetery near Earlton. {Ref. TI}. Also see "Elizabeth Coen," q.v.

COEN, NANCY (Mrs.), b. 1799, d. Jun 7, 1866, aged 67, bur. in the Barnes Family Cemetery near Earlton.{Ref. TI}

COFFIELD, THOMAS, see "William O'Dair" and "Negro Guy" and "Bernard Bartle" and "Samuel Nowry" and "Philip Chamberlain" and "Thomas Caulfield," q.v.

COFFIELD, THOMAS, subpoenaed to the Grand Jury in August, 1797. {Ref. CC}

COFFIELD, THOMAS, head of family in 1800 (Havre de Grace). {Ref. CI}

COFFIELD (COFIELD), THOMAS, taxpayer, 1798, Spesutia Lower Hd., no dwelling house listed in this part of the tax schedule, no land listed, 1 slave. {Ref. TL}

COIN, DOMINICK, head of family in 1800 (5th District). {Ref. CI}

COLDER, JOHN, head of family in 1800 (4th District). {Ref. CI}

COLDWELL, SAMUEL, insolvent on a list for the road tax for 1792, as returned for Robert Amoss, tax collector. {Ref. IL 13.12}

COLE, ABRAHAM, head of family in 1800 (2nd District). {Ref. CI}

COLE, ANN, daugter of Ezekiel and Sarah, b. Oct 22, 1798, d. Oct 22, 1819. {Ref

COLE, CAROLINE, dau. of Ezekiel and Sarah, b. Oct 22, 1798, d. Oct 22, 1819. {Ref: Ezekiel Cole Bible}
{Ref: Ezekiel Cole Bible}
COLE, CHARITY, m. George Henderson on Jun 19, 1800. {Ref: PR}
COLE, EPHRAIM, insolvent on a list for the county tax due for 1791 in Susquehanna Hd., as returned by Thomas Taylor on Sep 17, 1792. {Ref: IL 31.12}
COLE, EZEKIEL, see "Matilda Cole" and "Ann Cole" and "Sarah Cole" and "Caroline Cole," q.v.
COLE, EZEKIEL, son of James and Jane, m. Sarah Courtney on Aug 8, 1792, and d. Feb 24, 1813, aged 50 years, 11 months, and 24 days. {Ref: Ezekiel Cole Bible}
COLE, EZEKIEL, head of family in 1800 (2nd District). {Ref: CI}
COLE, HANNAH, dau. of John Beagle and Priscilla, b. Mar 4, 1799, bapt. Feb 10, 1800. {Ref: PR}
COLE, ISAAC, head of family in 1800 (2nd District). {Ref: CI}
COLE, JAMES, head of family in 1800 (2nd District). {Ref: CI}. Also see "Ezekiel Cole" and "John Hanson's heirs," q.v.
COLE, JAMES, b. 1792, d. Nov 17, 1851, bur. in a cemetery now on Aberdeen Proving Grounds. {Ref: TI}
COLE, JAMES, b. Jul 15, 1791, d. Jul 4, 1878, bur. in the Cole Family Graveyard in Aberdeen. {Ref: TI}
COLE, JAMES, m. Catherine Hollis (Holles) on Apr 4, 1797. {Ref: PR}
COLE, JANE, see "Ezekiel Cole," q.v.
COLE, JOHN B., head of family in 1800 (2nd District). {Ref: CI}. Also see "Hannah Cole," q.v.
COLE, MATILDA, dau. of Ezekiel and Sarah, b. Nov 13, 1793, d. Oct 14, 1804.
{Ref: Ezekiel Cole Bible}
COLE, PRISCILLA, see "Hannah Cole," q.v.
COLE, RICHARD, head of family in 1800 (5th District). {Ref: CI}
COLE, SAMUEL, head of family in 1800 (3rd District). {Ref: CI}
COLE, SARAH, dau. of Ezekiel and Sarah, b. Jun 19, 1795, d. Septe,ber 27, 1804. {Ref: Ezekiel Cole Bible}. Also see "Matilda Cole" and "Ann Cole" and "Caroline Cole" and "Ezekiel Cole," q.v.
COLE, SKIPWITH, m. Elizabeth Gilbert on Jan 22, 1797. {Ref: PR}
COLE, SKIPWITH, head of family in 1800 (5th District). {Ref: CI}
COLE, SKIPWORTH, head of family in 1800 (5th District). {Ref: CI}
COLE, SOPHIA, m. Jervis Gilbert on Nov 29, 1798. {Ref: PR}
COLE, THOMAS, head of family in 1800 (2nd District). {Ref: CI}
COLE, WILLIAM, subpoenaed to the Grand Jury in August, 1797. {Ref: CC}
COLE, WILLIAM, head of family in 1800 (1st District). {Ref: CI}
COLE, WILLIAM, head of family in 1800 (Havre de Grace). {Ref: CI}
COLE, WILLIAM, head of family in 1800 (5th District). {Ref: CI}
COLEBY, THOMAS, head of family in 1800 (2nd District). {Ref: CI}
COLEGATE, RICHARD, tract *Colegate's Fowling Ground* surveyed between 1792 and 1796. {Ref: SB}

COLEGATE, ROBERT (Baltimore Town), or WILLIAM BRANNON, taxpayer, 1798, Susquehanna Hd., 1 dwelling house, 3 inferior houses, 2 acres, $175 valuation; 2 tracts (433 acres, 120 perches) and 1 building (William Brannon, occupant) in Susquehanna Hd., $1288.12 valuation, no slaves. {Ref: TL}

COLEMAN, BECKY, see "Rev. John Coleman," q.v.

COLEMAN, CHARLES, m. Lydia Forwood on Mar 15 or 17, 1791. {Ref: PR}

COLEMAN, CHARLES RIDGELY, d. Aug 5, 1795. {Ref: PR}

COLEMAN, CUTHBERT WILLIAM, d. Oct 5, 1794. {Ref: PR}

COLEMAN, JOHN (reverend), of Baltimore County, or THOMAS JOHNSON, taxpayer, 1798, Bush River Lower Hd., 1 dwelling house, 2 inferior houses, 1 acre (Thomas Johnson, occupant), $180 valuation; 2 tracts (102 acres, 40 perches) in Bush River Lower Hd. (Thomas Johnson, occupant), $347.63 valuation, no slaves. {Ref: TL}

COLEMAN, JOHN (reverend), treated by Dr. Archer on Aug 4, 1795; also mentioned his dau. Becky. {Ref: JA}

COLEMAN, JOHN (reverend), Baltimore County, or EDWARD HAMBLETON, taxpayer, 1798, Bush River Lower Hd., 1 dwelling house, 5 inferior houses, 1 acre and 80 perches (Edward Hambleton, occupant), $300 valuation; 2 tracts (538 acres, 80 perches) in Bush River Lower Hd. (Edward Hambleton, occupant), $1860.75 valuation, no slaves. {Ref: TL}

COLEMAN, JOHN, son of John, d. Aug 8, 1795. {Ref: PR}

COLEMAN, SAMUEL JARRETT, d. Aug 17, 1791, aged 2 months. {Ref: PR}

COLEMAN, SAMUEL WILLIAMSON, d. Oct 24, 1793. {Ref: PR}

COLESON, WILLIAM, insolvent on a list for the road tax due for 1791 in Harford Upper, Harford Lower, and Spesutia Upper as returned by Robert Amos, Jr. on Sep 18, 1793. {Ref: IL 31.18}

COLLINS, ANN, head of family in 1800 (4th District). {Ref: CI}

COLLINS, CATY MARIA, dau. of George and Sarah, b. Mar 19, 1796. {Ref: PR}

COLLINS, CHARITY, head of family in 1800 (2nd District). {Ref: CI}

COLLINS (COLLINGS), EPHRAIM, had an account at Hall's Store in January, 1791. {Ref: WH}. Also see "Josias W. Dallam," q.v.

COLLINS, GEORGE, see "Caty Maria Collins," q.v.

COLLINS, HANNAH, see "Mary Collins," q.v.

COLLINS, ISAAC, insolvent, Harford Lower and Spesutia Lower Hundreds (listed as a single man), on a tax list returned by George Lyttle on Sep 21, 1791. {Ref: IL 31.20, 31.21}

COLLINS, ISAAC, insolvent on a list for the road tax due for 1791 in Harford Upper, Harford Lower, and Spesutia Upper as returned by Robert Amos, Jr. on Sep 18, 1793. {Ref: IL 31.18}

COLLINS, JACOB, see "Mary Collins" and "Josias W. Dallam," q.v.

COLLINS, JACOB, charged for assaulting Nathaniel Henderson in 1793. {Ref: CD. March and August Terms, 1795}

COLLINS, JACOB, head of family in 1800 (2nd District). {Ref: CI}

COLLINS, JOHN, insolvent on a list for the road tax due for 1791 in Harford Upper, Harford Lower, and Spesutia Upper as returned by Robert Amos, Jr. on Sep 18, 1793. {Ref: IL 31.18}
COLLINS (COLLINGS), JOHN, had an account at Hall's Store in August, 1791. {Ref: WH}
COLLINS, MARY, dau. of Jacob and Hannah, b. Mar 15, 1791. {Ref: PR}
COLLINS, SARAH, see "James Woodland" and "Caty Maria Collins," q.v.
COMBEST, JACOB, had an account at Hall's Store in December, 1791. {Ref: WH}
COMBEST, JACOB ("in Spesu"), insolvent on a list for the county tax due for 1793 in Susquehanna Hd. as returned to the levy court by Thomas Taylor on May 28, 1794, who noted "put in my hands last fall." {Ref: IL 31.12}
COMBEST, JACOB, insolvent on a list for the road tax due for 1791 in Harford Upper, Harford Lower, and Spesutia Upper as returned by Robert Amos, Jr. on Sep 18, 1793. {Ref: IL 31.18}
COMBEST, MARY, see "Susan Ann Hollis," q.v.
COMBEST, UTIE, insolvent on a list for the road tax due for 1791 in Harford Upper, Harford Lower, and Spesutia Upper as returned by Robert Amos, Jr. on Sep 18, 1793 (his name was crossed off the list). {Ref: IL 31.18}
COMBEST, UTY, had an account at Hall's Store in March, 1791; also showed an entry which "Uty Combest" signed as "Utey Combes" in the ledger. {Ref: WH}
COMLEY, JOHN, head of family in 1800 (Havre de Grace). {Ref: CI}
COMMINGS, JESSEES, see "Jesse Cumins," q.v.
COMPAGNON, MONSIEUR (Baltimore Town), or MR. DELMAS, taxpayer, 1798, Bush River Lower Hd., 1 dwelling house, 5 inferior houses, 1 acre and 80 perches (Mr. Delmas, occupant) $300 valuation; 2 tracts (228 acres, 80 perches) in Bush River Lower Hd. (Mr. Delmas, occupant), $1026 valuation, 2 slaves. {Ref: TL}. In another part of the tax schedule the occupant is listed as Francis Delmas.
COMRUN (COMREN), WILLIAM ("run"), insolvent on lists due for 1790 and 1791 "fund taxes" and county taxes in Susquehanna Hd., as returned by Thomas Taylor. {Ref: IL 31.12, 31.02}
CONCLIN, MATTHEW, insolvent on a list for the road tax due for 1791 in Harford Upper, Harford Lower, and Spesutia Upper as returned by Robert Amos, Jr. on Sep 18, 1793. {Ref: IL 31.18}
CONLEY, DONN, insolvent on list returned by Robert Carlile for taxes due for the year 1791. {Ref: IL 31.16}
CONN, ANN, se "Jesse Mathews," q.v.
CONN, ELIZABETH, taxpayer, 1798, Gunpowder Upper Hd., 1 dwelling house, 2 inferior houses, 2 acres. $150 valuation; 1 tract (43 acres) in Gunpowder Upper Hd., $96.75 valuation, no slaves. {Ref: TL}
CONN, ELIZABETH, head of family in 1800 (3rd District). {Ref: CI}
CONN, JANE (JANETT), see "Arnold Rush," q.v.
CONNELLEY, MARY, head of family in 1800 (4th District). {Ref: CI}

CONNELLY, MARY, head of family in 1800 (4th District). {Ref: CI}
CONNELLY (CONNOLY), MARY, insolvent on lists of taxes due in 1791 and 1792 in Broad Creek Hd., as returned by Robert Amos, Jr. in 1791 and Benjamin Preston in 1792. {Ref: IL 31.03, 31.12, 31.22}
CONNER, MICHAEL, insolvent on list returned by Robert Carlile for taxes due for the year 1791. {Ref: IL 31.16}
CONNOLLY, DONN, will probated Mar 25, 1800. {Ref: HW}
CONWAY, MICHAEL, insolvent on lists returned for the county and road taxes due for 1791 by John Bull in Gunpowder Lower Hd. (name spelled as "Conaway" on one list). {Ref: IL 31.14, 31.15}
COOK, JACOB, see "Mrs. Cook," q.v.
COOK, JANE, m. William Holmes on Dec 7, 1796. {Ref: PR}
COOK, JOHN, insolvent on a list in 1792 in Deer Creek Lower Hd., as returned by Benjamin Preston. {Ref: IL 31.03}
COOK, JOHN, subpoenaed to the Grand Jury in August, 1797. {Ref: CC}
COOK, JOHN, will probated May 22, 1798. {Ref: HW}
COOK, MATTHEW, charged for disturbing the peace towards Thomas Ayres in 1794 and ordered to keep the peace in 1795. {Ref: CD, March Term, 1795}
COOK, MRS. (widow of Robert), treated by Dr. Archer on Jan 8, 1791; also mentioned her son Jacob and that she lived near Bald Friar. {Ref: JA}
COOK, ROBERT, see "Mrs. Cook," q.v.
COOK, SAMUEL, charged (nature of case not stated) in 1797. {Ref: CD, March Term, 1797}
COOK, SARAH, insolvent on a list in 1792 in Deer Creek Lower Hd., as returned by Benjamin Preston. {Ref: IL 31.03}
COOK, SARAH, taxpayer, 1798, Deer Creek Lower Hd., 2 tracts (50 acres) and 1 building, $168.75 valuation, no slaves. {Ref: TL}
COOLEY (COOLY), JOHN, served on a Grand Jury in August, 1798 and August, 1799 and August, 1800. {Ref: CM}
COOLEY, JOHN, tracts *Quaker Bottom* and *Reavery* surveyed between 1792 and 1796. {Ref: SB}
COOLEY, JOHN, taxpayer, 1798, Susquehanna Hd., 1 dwelling house, 3 inferior houses, 2 acres, $250 valuation; 4 tracts (305 acres, 40 perches) and 1 building in Susquehanna Hd., $1053.76 valuation, 1 slave. {Ref: TL}
COOLEY, JOHN, appointed a Judge of Elections in the 2nd District on Jul 28, 1800. {Ref: CM}
COOLEY, JOHN, insolvent on a list for county taxes due in 1792 as returned by Benjamin Preston. {Ref: IL 31.00}
COOLEY, JOHN, insolvent on list returned for the road tax due for 1791 by John Bull. {Ref: IL 31.14}
COOLEY, JOHN (captain), head of family in 1800 (2nd District). {Ref: CI}
COOLEY, RICHARD, treated by Dr. Archer on Oct 9, 1791; also mentioned a child (no name given) and that he lived near James Clendenon's. {Ref: JA}

COOLEY, WILLIAM, see "Patrick Smith," q.v.

COOLEY, WILLIAM, insolvent on a list for county taxes due in 1792 as returned by Benjamin Preston. {Ref: IL 31.00}

COOLEY, WILLIAM, head of family in 1800 (4th District). {Ref: CI}

COOP, HANNAH, insolvent on lists returned by Robert Carlile and John Guyton for taxes due for the year 1791. {Ref: IL 31.16, 31.19}

COOP, JAMES, insolvent on a list for county taxes due in 1792 as returned by Benjamin Preston. {Ref: IL 31.00}

COOP, JOHN, insolvent, Harford Lower and Spesutia Lower Hundreds (listed as a single man), on a tax list returned by George Lyttle on Sep 21, 1791. {Ref: IL 31.20, 31.21}. Also see "Jno. Cop," q.v.

COOP, RICHARD, insolvent on lists returned by Robert Carlile and John Guyton (who listed him as a single man) for taxes due for the year 1791. {Ref: IL 31.16, 31.19}

COOP, ZACARIAH, insolvent, Harford Lower and Spesutia Lower Hundreds (listed as a single man), on a tax list returned by George Lyttle on Sep 21, 1791. {Ref: IL 31.20, 31.21}. Also see "Zac. Cop," q.v.

COOPER, ----, see "John Daugherty," q.v.

COOPER, ALEXANDER, taxpayer, 1798, Broad Creek Hd., no dwelling house listed in this part of the tax schedule, 2 tracts (109 acres), $236.25 valuation, no slaves. {Ref: TL}

COOPER, BENJAMIN, head of family in 1800 (1st District). {Ref: CI}

COOPER, CALVEN, insolvent on list returned by Robert Carlile for taxes due for the year 1791. {Ref: IL 31.16}

COOPER, HENRY, head of family in 1800 (3rd District). {Ref: CI}

COOPER, HENRY JR., head of family in 1800 (3rd District). {Ref: CI}

COOPER, HENRY JR., taxpayer, 1798, Spesutia Upper Hd., 1 dwelling house, 2 inferior houses, 1 acre, $150 valuation, 1 slave. {Ref: TL}

COOPER, HENRY SR., taxpayer, 1798, Spesutia Upper Hd., 1 dwelling house, 5 inferior houses, 1 acre, $200 valuation; 2 tracts (309 acres) and 1 other building (Philip Cooper, occupant), $577.69 valuation altogether, 2 slaves. {Ref: TL}

COOPER, ISABELLA, head of family in 1800 (4th District). {Ref: CI}

COOPER, ISSABELLA, taxpayer, 1798, Bush River Upper & Eden Hd., 1 dwelling house, 2 inferior houses, 2 acres, $105 valuation; 1 tract (181 acres, 80 perches) in Bush River Upper & Eden Hd., $255.66 valuation, no slaves. {Ref: TL}

COOPER, JAMES, taxpayer, 1798, Deer Creek Middle Hd., 1 tract (114 acres, 40 perches) and 1 building, $225.92 valuation, no slaves. {Ref: TL}

COOPER, JAMES, head of family in 1800 (5th District). {Ref: CI}

COOPER, JOHN, see "James Robinson" and "Leslie Curtis," q.v.

COOPER, JOHN, treated by Dr. Archer on Feb 13, 1791; also mentioned his wife (no name given) and that he lived near Peach Bottom. {Ref: JA}

COOPER, JOHN, insolvent on list returned by Robert Carlile for taxes due for the year 1791. {Ref: IL 31.16}

COOPER, NICHOLAS, see "Isaiah Balderson," q.v.
COOPER, NICHOLAS, treated by Dr. Archer on Feb 10, 1799. {Ref: JA}
COOPER, NICHOLAS, head of family in 1800 (5th District). {Ref: CI}
COOPER, PHILIP (PHILLIP), head of family in 1800 (3rd District). {Ref: CI}. Also see "Henry Cooper, Sr.," q.v.
COOPER, SARAH, see "William Everitt," q.v.
COOPER, STEPHEN, taxpayer, 1798, Broad Creek Hd., 3 tracts (310 acres, 120 perches) and 1 building, $632.22 valuation, no slaves. {Ref: TL}. In another part of the tax schedule the occupant is listed as David McKisson.
COOPER, THOMAS, tracts *Cooper's Addition* and *Cooper's Purchase* surveyed between 1792 and 1796. {Ref: SB}
COOPER, WILLIAM, b. 1795, d. 1859, aged 64, bur. in Mountain Christian Church Cemetery. {Ref: TI}
COOPER, WILLIAM, head of family in 1800 (3rd District). {Ref: CI}
COP, JNO., insolvent on a list for the road tax due for 1791 in Harford Upper, Harford Lower, and Spesutia Upper as returned by Robert Amos, Jr. on Sep 18, 1793. {Ref: IL 31.18}
COP, ZAC., insolvent on a list for the road tax due for 1791 in Harford Upper, Harford Lower, and Spesutia Upper as returned by Robert Amos, Jr. on Sep 18, 1793. {Ref: IL 31.18}
COPELAND, GEORGE'S HEIRS, or GEORGE CHANCEY JR. AND GEORGE PATTERSON, taxpayers, 1798, Harford Lower Hd., 1 dwelling house, 6 inferior houses, 2 acres, $200 valuation; 2 tracts (446 acres) in Harford Lower Hd., $2001.82 valuation (G. Patterson, occupant), no slaves; also, taxpayers, 1 dwelling house, 2 inferior houses, Harford Lower Hd. (Susanna Brown, occupant), $180 valuation, no slaves. {Ref: TL}
COPELAND, JAMES GALLION, son of John and Margaret, b. Sep 14, 1792, bapt. Oct 18, 1795. {Ref: PR}
COPELAND, JOHN, see "James Gallion Copeland" and "Margaret Copeland," q.v.
COPELAND, MARGARET, see "James Gallion Copeland" and "Margaret Copeland," q.v.
COPELAND, SARAH, m. Nathaniel Moreton on Mar 1, 1798. {Ref: PR}
COPELAND, WILLIAM PITT, son of John and Margaret, b. Jun 6, 1795, bapt. Oct 18, 1795. {Ref: PR}
CORBETT, JAMES, insolvent on list returned by Robert Carlile for taxes due for the year 1791. {Ref: IL 31.16}
CORBETT, JOHN, insolvent on list returned by Robert Carlile for taxes due for the year 1791. {Ref: IL 31.16}
CORBETT, SAM, insolvent on list returned by Robert Carlile for taxes due for the year 1791. {Ref: IL 31.16}
CORBIN, JOHN, insolvent on list returned by Robert Carlile for taxes due for the year 1791. {Ref: IL 31.16}

CORBIN, JOHN, insolvent on a list for 1791 in Gunpowder Upper and Bush River Lower Hundreds, as filed by John Bond, Deputy Sheriff, on Sep 20, 1791. {Ref: IL 31.24}
CORBIN, JOHN, head of family in 1800 (3rd District). {Ref: CI}
CORBIN, NATHAN, insolvent on a list for 1791 in Gunpowder Upper and Bush River Lower Hundreds, as filed by John Bond, Deputy Sheriff, on Sep 20, 1791. {Ref: IL 31.24}
CORBIN, NATHAN, head of family in 1800 (1st District). {Ref: CI}
CORBIN, NATHANIEL, insolvent on list returned by Robert Carlile for taxes due for the year 1791. {Ref: IL 31.16}
CORD, ----, see "Nathan Hughes," q.v.
CORD (CORDE), ABRAHAM, head of family in 1800 (1st District). {Ref: CI}
CORD, AMOS, taxpayer, 1798, Spesutia Lower Hd., 1 dwelling house, 4 inferior houses, 2 acres, $115 valuation; 1 tract (2 acres) in Spesutia Lower Hd., $51.75 valuation, no slaves. {Ref: TL}
CORD, AMOS, insolvent on a list for the road tax due for 1791 in Harford Upper, Harford Lower, and Spesutia Upper as returned by Robert Amos, Jr. on Sep 18, 1793. {Ref: IL 31.18}
CORD, AMOS, m. Elizabeth Swaine on Jan 23, 1798. {Ref: PR}
CORD (CORDE), AMOSS, head of family in 1800 (2nd District). {Ref: CI}
CORD (CORDE), AMOSS JR., head of family in 1800 (2nd District). {Ref: CI}
CORD, ELIZABETH, see "Thomas Johnson," q.v.
CORD, JOHN, taxpayer, 1798, Gunpowder Lower Hd., 1 dwelling house, 2 inferior houses, 2 acres, $150 valuation, no slaves. {Ref: TL}
CORD (CORDE), JOHN, head of family in 1800 (1st District). {Ref: CI}
CORK, JACOB, insolvent on a list in 1792 in Deer Creek Lower Hd., as returned by Benjamin Preston. {Ref: IL 31.03}
CORRIGAN, BARTHOLOMEW, b. 1792, County Sligo, Ireland, d. Feb 4, 1866, aged 74, bur. in St. Ignatius Catholic Church Cemetery in Hickory. {Ref: TI}
CORRIGAN, FANNIE, wife of Bartholomew, b. 1796, d. Mar 24, 1880, aged 84, bur. in St. Ignatius Catholic Church Cemetery in Hickory. {Ref: TI}
COSE (COX?), JOSEPH, head of family in 1800 (Abingdon). {Ref: CI}
COSKERY (COSKEY?), TORRENCE, head of family in 1800 (5th District). {Ref: CI}
COSTEN, ROSANNA, see "John Williams," q.v.
COT(?), JOHN, insolvent on a list for 1791 in Gunpowder Upper and Bush River Lower Hundreds, as filed by John Bond, Deputy Sheriff, on Sep 20, 1791 (who listed him as a single man). {Ref: IL 31.24}
COTTY, EDWARD, insolvent, Harford Lower and Spesutia Lower Hundreds, on a tax list returned by George Lyttle on Sep 21, 1791. {Ref: IL 31.20, 31.21}
COTTY, EDWARD, insolvent on a list for the road tax due for 1791 in Harford Upper, Harford Lower, and Spesutia Upper as returned by Robert Amos, Jr. on Sep 18, 1793. {Ref: IL 31.18}

COURTAULD, LOUISA S., b. Oct 7, 1800, d. Aug 27, 1866, bur. in Darlington Cemetery. {Ref: TI}
COURTNEY, AVARILLA, wife of Cyrus, b. Jun 20, 1791, d. Mar 321, 1871, bur. in Grove Presbyterian Church Cemetery in Aberdeen. {Ref: TI}
COURTNEY, CYRUS, see "Avarilla Courtney," q.v.
COURTNEY, ELEANOR, m. Richard Taylor on Dec 25, 1800. {Ref: PR}. Also see "John Courtney" and "Hollis Hanson Courtney" and "Thomas Courtney," q.v.
COURTNEY, HANSON, son of Thomas and Sarah, b. Dec 11, 1792. {Ref: John Hanson Bible}
COURTNEY, HOLLIS, b. Jul 22, 1797, d. Jan 19, 1886, aged 88 years, 5 months, and 28 days, bur. in Angel Hill Cemetery in Havre de Grace. {Ref: TI}. Also see "John Courtney" and "Hollis Hanson Courtney," q.v.
COURTNEY, HOLLIS HANSON, son of Hollis and Elinor, b. Jul 21, 1797, bapt. Jun 16, 1799. {Ref: PR}
COURTNEY, JOHN, son of Hollis and Elinor, b. Feb 8, 1796, bapt. Jun 16, 1799. {Ref: PR}
COURTNEY, JONAS, see "John Hanson's heirs" and "Jonas Coatney," q.v.
COURTNEY, MICHAEL, insolvent on a list for county taxes due in 1792 as returned by Benjamin Preston. {Ref: IL 31.00}
COURTNEY (CORTNEY), MICHAEL, insolvent on list returned for the road tax due for 1791 by John Bull. {Ref: IL 31.14}
COURTNEY, SARAH, wife of Hollis, b. Dec 16, 1794, d. Jul 29, 1878, bur. in Angel Hill Cemetery in Havre de Grace. {Ref: TI}. Also see "Hanson Courtney" and Ezekiel Cole," q.v.
COURTNEY, THOMAS, taxpayer, 1798, Susquehanna Hd., 1 dwelling house, 5 inferior houses, 2 acres, $250 valuation; 5 tracts (316 acres, 7 perches), 1 building, and 2 slaves; plus, 2 other buildings (Eleanor Courtney and James Brewer, occupants) in Susquehanna Hd., $1022.73 valuation altogether. {Ref: TL}. Also see "Hanson Courtney" and "Thomas Coatney," q.v.
COUSSINS, JOHN, head of family in 1800 (1st District). {Ref: CI}
COVENHOVEN, HANNAH, taxpayer, 1798, Gunpowder Upper Hd., 1 dwelling house, 4 inferior houses, 2 acres, $120 valuation; 1 tract (10 acres) in Gunpowder Upper Hd., $11.25 valuation, no slaves. {Ref: TL}
COVENHOVEN, JACOB, taxpayer, 1798, Gunpowder Upper Hd., 1 tract (10 acres) and 1 building, $113.62 valuation, no slaves. {Ref: TL}
COVENHOVEN, JOHN, will probated Jun 13, 1797. {Ref: HW}
COWAN, ALEXANDER, on "a list of insolvents it being for personal property for the road taxes [sic] for 1791" filed by Robert Amoss, tax collector. {Ref: IL 31.12}
COWAN, BOYCE, head of family in 1800 (2nd District). {Ref: CI}
COWAN, ELIZABETH, dau. of Thomas and Sarah, his late wife, b. Feb 26, 1791. {Ref: PR}
COWAN, MARY, dau. of Thomas and Sarah, his late wife, b. in March, 1799. {Ref: PR}. Also see "John Middleton," q.v.
COWAN, SARAH, see "Elizabeth Cowan" and "Mary Cowan," q.v.

COWAN, SUSANNA, m. William Hamby on Aug 14, 1800. {Ref: PR}
COWAN, THOMAS, see "Elizabeth Cowan" and "Mary Cowan," q.v.
COWAN, THOMAS, taxpayer, 1798, Susquehanna Hd., 1 tract (40 acres) and 1 building, $110.25 valuation, no slaves. {Ref: TL}
COWAN, THOMAS, insolvent, Harford Lower and Spesutia Lower Hundreds (listed as a single man), on a tax list returned by George Lyttle on Sep 21, 1791. {Ref: IL 31 20, 31 21}
COWAN, THOMAS, head of family in 1800 (3rd District). {Ref: CI}
COWAN, WILLIAM, insolvent on lists for the county tax and road tax for 1789, 1790, 1791, and 1792, as returned by Thomas Taylor on May 28, 1794, "it being an additional list." {Ref: IL 31.12}
COWAN, WILLIAM ("can't be found"), insolvent on lists due for 1790 and 1791 "fund taxes" in Deer Creek Lower and Susquehanna Hundreds, as returned by Thomas Taylor. {Ref: IL 31 12}
COWEN, LEONARD, m. Mary Fowler on May 15, 1791. {Ref: PR}
COWLEY, THOMAS, insolvent on a list for the road tax due for 1791 in Harford Upper, Harford Lower, and Spesutia Upper as returned by Robert Amos, Jr. on Sep 18, 1793. {Ref: IL 31.18}
COWLEY, THOMAS, head of family in 1800 (1st District). {Ref: CI}
COX, ELIZABETH, see "Mary Ann Cox," q.v.
COX, HERMAN, head of family in 1800 (2nd District). {Ref: CI}. Also see "Peregrine Browning," q.v.
COX, ISRAEL, taxpayer, 1798, Deer Creek Middle Hd., 2 tracts (150 acres) and 1 building, $566.25 valuation, 2 slaves. {Ref: TL}
COX, ISRAEL, treated by Dr. Archer on Oct 9, 1791; also mentioned his wife (no name given). {Ref: JA}
COX, ISRAEL, head of family in 1800 (5th District). {Ref: CI}
COX, JOHN, tract *Restitution* surveyed between 1792 and 1796. {Ref: SB}
COX, JOHN, granted a retailer's permit on June 2, 1797. {Ref: CC}
COX, JOHN, taxpayer, 1798, Bush River Upper & Eden Hd., 1 dwelling house, 3 inferior houses, 2 acres, $400 valuation; 2 tracts (303 acres) in Bush River Upper & Eden Hd., $940.50 valuation, no slaves. {Ref: TL}
COX, JOHN, head of family in 1800 (4th District). {Ref: CI}
COX, JOHN JR., head of family in 1800 (4th District). {Ref: CI}
COX, JOSEPH, subpoenaed to the Grand Jury in August, 1797. {Ref: CC}. Also see "John Monks" and "Mary Ann Cox" and Joseph Cose," q.v.
COX, MARY, insolvent on a list for the county tax due for 1791 in Susquehanna Hd., as returned by Thomas Taylor on Sep 17, 1792. {Ref: IL 31.12}. Also see "Josias W. Dallam," q.v.
COX, MARY ANN, dau. of Joseph and Elizabeth, b. May 7, 1799, bapt. Nov 10, 1800. {Ref: PR}
COX, ROBERT, insolvent on list returned by Robert Carlile for taxes due for the year 1791. {Ref: IL 31 16}

COX, THOMAS, charged for assaulting James Thompson in 1794. {Ref: CD, March Term, 1795}
COX, WILLIAM, taxpayer, 1798, Susquehanna Hd., 1 dwelling house, 3 inferior houses, 2 acres, $275 valuation; 1 tract (87 acres) and 1 building in Susquehanna Hd., $958.50 valuation, 1 slave. {Ref: TL}
COX, WILLIAM, head of family in 1800 (3rd District). {Ref: CI}
COZENS, JOHN, m. Elizabeth Jackson on Feb 7, 1799. {Ref: PR}
CRABISON(?), WILLIAM, head of family in 1800 (3rd District). {Ref: CI}
CRABSON, MOSES, head of family in 1800 (2nd District). {Ref: CI}. Also see "Jacob Lamot," q.v.
CRABSON, REBECCA, m. James Moore (More) on Apr 12, 1798. {Ref: PR}
CRAGUE, SAMUEL, head of family in 1800 (3rd District). {Ref: CI}
CRAIF, DAVID, or THOMAS CHENEY, taxpayer, 1798, 1 tract (80 acres) and 1 building (Thomas Cheney, occupant) in Harford Lower Hd., $320.62 valuation, no slaves. {Ref: TL}
CRAIG, JOHN (Revolutionary War veteran), will probated Jan 20, 1794. {Ref: HW}
CRAIL, THOMAS, see "John Pyle," q.v.
CRANE, DAVID, taxpayer, 1798, Harford Lower Hd., 1 dwelling house, 4 inferior houses, 2 acres, $100.10 valuation; 1 tract (21 acres, 80 perches) in Harford Lower Hd., $406.13 valuation, 1 slave. {Ref: TL}
CRANE, DAVID, served on a Petit Jury in March, 1799 and March, 1800. {Ref: CM}
CRANE, DAVID, m. Susanna Osborne on Mar 10, 1795. {Ref: PR}
CRANE, DAVID, head of family in 1800 (2nd District). {Ref: CI}
CRANE, DAVID JR., served on a Grand Jury in March, 1798. {Ref: CM}
CRANGEL, BARTIS, head of family in 1800 (2nd District). {Ref: CI}
CRASWELL, ROBERT (OF WILLIAM), treated by Dr. Archer on Mar 14, 1791; also mentioned his wife (no name given). {Ref: JA}
CRATON, JAMES, taxpayer, 1798, Bush River Upper & Eden Hd., 1 dwelling house, 7 inferior houses, 2 acres, $550 valuation; 1 tract (28 acres, 80 perches) in Bush River Upper & Eden Hd., $78.75 valuation, 1 slave. {Ref: TL}
CRATON, ROBERT, taxpayer, 1798, Bush River Upper & Eden Hd., 1 dwelling house, 2 inferior houses, 2 acres, $105 valuation; 1 tract (13 acres) in Bush River Upper & Eden Hd., $29.25 valuation, no slaves. {Ref: TL}
CRAWFORD, ALEXANDER, treated by Dr. Archer on May 29, 1792; also mentioned his wife (no name given) and that he lived at Cooptown. {Ref: JA}
CRAWFORD, FRANCES, taxpayer, 1798, Bush River Lower Hd., 1 dwelling house, 1 inferior house, 80 perches of land, $240 valuation, 1 slave. {Ref: TL}
CRAWFORD, FRANCES, head of family in 1800 (Abingdon). {Ref: CI}
CRAWFORD, JAMES, taxpayer, 1798, Deer Creek Lower Hd., no dwelling house listed in this part of the tax schedule, 1 tract (111 acres), $162.28 valuation, 1 slave. {Ref: TL}
CRAWFORD (CRAFORDE), JAMES, head of family in 1800 (5th District). {Ref: CI}

CRAWFORD, JOHN, see "Negro Jacob," q.v.
CRAWFORD, MARGARETT, see "Benjamin Wilmer," q.v.
CRAWFORD, MORDICA, taxpayer, 1798, Deer Creek Lower Hd., 1 dwelling house, 2 inferior houses, 2 acres, $110 valuation; 1 tract (100 acres) in Deer Creek Lower Hd., $168.75 valuation, 1 slave. {Ref: TL}
CRAWFORD, MORDICA, head of family in 1800 (5th District). {Ref: CI}
CRAWFORD, ROBERT, head of family in 1800 (3rd District). {Ref: CI}
CRAWFORD, SEABORN, taxpayer, 1798, Deer Creek Lower Hd., 1 dwelling house, 1 inferior house, 1 acre, $200 valuation, 1 slave. {Ref: TL}
CRAWFORD, SEABORN, head of family in 1800 (5th District). {Ref: CI}
CRAWFORD, SUSANNA, will probated Jan 9, 1797. {Ref: HW}
CRAY, PIERCE, head of family in 1800 (4th District). {Ref: CI}
CRAYTON, EDWARD, son of Patrick and Elizabeth, b. May 6, 1797, bapt. May 20, 1798. {Ref: PR}
CRAYTON, ELIZABETH, dau. of Patrick and Elizabeth, b. Dec 11, 1795, bapt. May 20, 1798. {Ref: PR}
CRAYTON, JOSEPH, son of Patrick and Elizabeth, b. Apr 6, 1789, bapt. May 20, 1798. {Ref: PR}
CRAYTON, PATRICK, see "Edward Crayton" and "Elizabeth Crayton" and "Joseph Crayton," q.v.
CREAGH, PIERSE, treated by Dr. Archer on Jun 12, 1795. {Ref: JA}. Also see "Pierce Cray," q.v.
CREARY, FRANCIS, granted a retailer's permit on July 3, 1797. {Ref: CC}
CREATIN, ANTOINETTA, see "John Cretin," q.v.
CREATIN, CAROLINE, see "John Cretin," q.v.
CREATIN, MATILDA, see "John Cretin," q.v.
CREATON, JANE, insolvent on lists in 1791 due county taxes and road taxes in "Deer Creek Upper, Middle, and Broad Creek Hundreds" as returned by Robert Amos, Jr. {Ref: IL 31.12, 31.22}
CREATON, PATRICK, taxpayer, 1798, Susquehanna Hd., 1 tract (260 acres), $731.25 valuation, no slaves. {Ref: TL}
CREIGH, PIERCE, taxpayer, 1798, Bush River Upper & Eden Hd., 1 dwelling house, 5 inferior houses, 2 acres, $200 valuation; taxpayer, 1798, Bush River Upper & Eden Hd., 1 dwelling house, 2 inferior houses, 1 acre, $200 valuation; taxpayer, 1798, Bush River Upper & Eden Hd., 1 dwelling house, 1 inferior house, 1 acre, $200 valuation; and, 4 tracts (643 acres) in Bush River Upper & Eden Hd., $1446.75 valuation, 3 slaves. {Ref: TL}
CREIGHTON, JAMES ("run"), insolvent on a list of the county tax due William Osborn, sheriff, for 1791, as returned by Edward Prigg on Sep 20, 1791. {Ref: IL 31.17}
CREIGHTON, JOHN, see "James Deaver," q.v.
CRESWELL (CRISWELL), ROBERT, taxpayer, 1798, Susquehanna Hd., 1 tract (152 acres, 40 perches) and 1 building, $780.75 valuation, 1 slave. {Ref: TL}. Also

see "Thomas Ramsey," q.v.

CRESWELL (CRISWELL), ROBERT, taxpayer, 1798, Spesutia Upper Hd., 1 tract (192 acres) and 1 building, $635.62 valuation, no slaves. {Ref: TL}

CRETIN, ANDREW, see "Patrick Cretin," q.v.

CRETIN, JACOB, see "Patrick Cretin," q.v.

CRETIN, JAMES, charged for selling liquors and fined 600 lbs. of tobacco in 1797. {Ref: CD, March Term, 1797}

CRETIN (CREATIN), JOHN, treated by Dr. Archer on May 8, 1796; also mentioned his wife (no name given) and the inoculation of his daughters in 1795: Caroline, Matilda, and Antoinetta Creatin. {Ref: JA}

CRETIN (CREETIN), JOHN, head of family in 1800 (5th District). {Ref: CI}

CRETIN, PATRICK, treated by Dr. Archer on Apr 24, 1799; also mentioned his wife (no name given) and sons Andrew and Jacob. {Ref: JA}

CRETIN, PATRICK, head of family in 1800 (3rd District). {Ref: CI}

CRETIN, PRICILLA, head of family in 1800 (4th District). {Ref: CI}

CRETIN, ROBERT, head of family in 1800 (4th District). {Ref: CI}

CRISSWALL, ROBERT, head of family in 1800 (3rd District). {Ref: CI}

CRISWELL, ISABELLA (widow of William, of Deer Creek Hundred), will probated Sep 22, 1795. {Ref: HW}

CRISWELL, MRS. (widow), treated by Dr. Archer on Aug 20, 1791. {Ref: JA}

CRISWELL, ROBERT, head of family in 1800 (3rd District). {Ref: CI}

CRISWELL, ROBERT SR., treated by Dr. Archer on May 4, 1791. {Ref: JA}. Also see "Robert Crisswall," q.v.

CRISWELL, WILLIAM, see "Isabella Criswell," q.v.

CROCKETT, BENJAMIN, will probated Nov 8, 1796. Also see "William McMath," q.v.

CROMWELL, FRANCES, m. Reason Dorsey on Aug 10, 1797. {Ref: PR}

CROMWELL, JESSE, m. Margaret Paca on Nov 16, 1799. {Ref: PR}. Also see "Samuel Cromwell" and "Andrew Wilson," q.v.

CROMWELL, JOHN H., insolvent on list returned for the road tax due for 1791 by John Bull. {Ref: IL 31.14}

CROMWELL, LETITIA, see "Samuel Cromwell," q.v.

CROMWELL, SAMUEL, son of Jesse and Letitia, b. Dec 27, 1794, bapt. Jan 13, 1799. {Ref: PR}

CROMWELL, VENESA, insolvent on a list in 1792 in Deer Creek Lower Hd., as returned by Benjamin Preston. {Ref: IL 31.03}

CROMWELL, VENETIA, taxpayer, 1798, Deer Creek Lower Hd., no dwelling house listed in this part of the tax schedule, 1 tract (41 acres), $79.20 valuation, no slaves. {Ref: TL}

CROMWELL, VENETICE, head of family in 1800 (5th District). {Ref: CI}

CRONE, JACOB, insolvent on a list for the road tax due for 1791 in Harford Upper, Harford Lower, and Spesutia Upper as returned by Robert Amos, Jr. on

Sep 18, 1793. {Ref: IL 31.18}
CRONE, JACOB'S HEIRS, or JANE JEFFERY, taxpayers, 1798, 1 tract (44 perches, 21 sq. ft.) and 1 building (Jane Jeffery, occupant) in Harford Lower Hd., $56.25 valuation, no slaves. {Ref: TL}
CROOK, ALEXANDER, insolvent on lists for the county tax and road tax due for 1791 in Deer Creek Lower Hd., as returned by Thomas Taylor on Sep 17, 1792 (his name was spelled "Crooks" on one list). {Ref: IL 31.12}
CROOM, ANDREW, head of family in 1800 (4th District). {Ref: CI}
CROSBY, CASSANDRA, see "Richard Crosby," q.v.
CROSBY, RICHARD, son of William and Cassandra, b. Aug 21, 1795, bapt. Oct 11, 1795. {Ref: PR}
CROSBY, TARRENCE, see "Henrietta Wheeler," q.v.
CROSBY, WILLIAM, charged for assaulting John Madden in 1795. {Ref: CD, March and August Terms, 1795}. Also see "Richard Crosby," q.v.
CROSIN, JOHN, taxpayer, 1798, Deer Creek Middle Hd., 1 tract (22 acres) and 1 building, $101.25 valuation, no slaves. {Ref: TL}
CROSS, RANDLE, insolvent, Harford Lower and Spesutia Lower Hundreds (listed as a single man), on a tax list returned by George Lyttle on Sep 21, 1791. {Ref: IL 31.20, 31.21}
CROSS, RANDOLPH, insolvent on a list for the road tax due for 1791 in Harford Upper, Harford Lower, and Spesutia Upper as returned by Robert Amos, Jr. on Sep 18, 1793. {Ref: IL 31.18}
CROSSAN, JOHN, head of family in 1800 (5th District). {Ref: CI}
CROSSMORE, HANNAH, taxpayer, 1798, Gunpowder Upper Hd., 1 dwelling house, 4 inferior houses, 2 acres, $120 valuation; 2 tracts (92 acres) in Gunpowder Upper Hd., $344.25 valuation, no slaves. {Ref: TL}
CROW, MICHAEL, had an account at Hall's Store in March, 1791. {Ref: WH}
CROWNOVER (CROWNOSER?), HANNAH, head of family in 1800 (1st District). {Ref: CI}
CRUISE, RICHARD, taxpayer, 1798, Susquehanna Hd., 1 dwelling house, 3 inferior houses, 2 acres, $150 valuation; 2 tracts (164 acres) in Susquehanna Hd., $369 valuation, 1 slave. {Ref: TL}
CRUISE, RICHARD, head of family in 1800 (2nd District). {Ref: CI}
CRUSEN (CRUSON), RICHARD, subpoenaed to the Grand Jury in August, 1797. {Ref: CC}
CRUSON, MICHAEL, insolvent on a list for the county tax due for 1793 in Susquehanna Hd. as returned to the levy court by Thomas Taylor on May 28, 1794, who noted "put in my hands last fall." {Ref: IL 31.12}
CRUTON(?), JAMES, head of family in 1800 (4th District). {Ref: CI}
CULLEN, WILLIAM, head of family in 1800 (4th District). {Ref: CI}
CULVER, BENJAMIN, treated by Dr. Archer on Dec 24, 1791. {Ref: JA}
CULVER, BENJAMIN, had an account at Hall's Store in October, 1791. {Ref: WH}
CULVER, BENJAMIN, had an account at Hall's Store in July, 1791. {Ref: WH}

CULVER, BENJAMIN, head of family in 1800 (2nd District). {Ref: CI}
CULVER, BENJAMIN, or ACHART SHIDLE, taxpayer, 1798, Susquehanna Hd., 1 tract (200 acres) and 1 building (Achart Shidle, occupant), $472.50, no slaves. {Ref: TL}
CULVER, ELIZABETH, see "Martha Culver," q.v.
CULVER, LEVI, m. Elizabeth Stallings on Jun 1, 1797. {Ref: PR}. Also see "Martha Culver," q.v.
CULVER, MARTHA, dau. of Levi and Elizabeth, b. Dec 2, 1798, bapt. Aug 15, 1799. {Ref: PR}
CULVER, ROBERT, had an account at Hall's Store in October, 1791. {Ref: WH}
CUMINGS, JOHN, see "Henry Green's heirs," q.v.
CUMMINGS, CASSANDRA, head of family in 1800 (3rd District). {Ref: CI}
CUMMINS, ANDREW ("gone"), insolvent on lists due for 1790 and 1791 "fund taxes" and county taxes in Susquehanna Hd., as returned by Thomas Taylor. {Ref: IL 31.12, 31.02}
CUMMINS (CUMINS), JESSE, insolvent on lists returned for the county and road taxes due for 1791 by John Bull in Gunpowder Lower Hd. (name spelled as "Jessees Commings" on one list). {Ref: IL 31.14, 31.15}
CUMMINS, JOHN, will probated May 10, 1800. {Ref: HW}
CUMMINS (CUMMIN), MARK, m. Mary McDole on Aug 7, 1800. {Ref: PR}
CUMMINS, MARCK, head of family in 1800 (2nd District). {Ref: CI}
CUMMINS, PAUL ("gone"), insolvent on lists due for 1790 and 1791 "fund taxes" and county taxes in Susquehanna Hd., as returned by Thomas Taylor. {Ref: IL 31.12, 31.02}
CUMMINS, PHILIP ("gone"), insolvent on lists due for 1790 and 1791 "fund taxes" and county taxes in Susquehanna Hd., as returned by Thomas Taylor. {Ref: IL 31.12, 31.02}
CUMMINS, SAMUEL ("gone"), insolvent on lists due for 1790 and 1791 "fund taxes" and county taxes in Susquehanna Hd., as returned by Thomas Taylor. {Ref: IL 31.12, 31.02}
CUNNING, HUGH, insolvent on a list for the county tax due for 1793 in Susquehanna Hd. as returned to the levy court by Thomas Taylor on May 28, 1794, who noted "put in my hands last fall." {Ref: IL 31.12}
CUNNINGHAM, CHRS., insolvent on a list for the road tax due for 1791 in Harford Upper, Harford Lower, and Spesutia Upper as returned by Robert Amos, Jr. on Sep 18, 1793. {Ref: IL 31.18}
CUNNINGHAM, CRISPIN, see "Francis Cunningham" and "William Barnes" q.v.
CUNNINGHAM, CRISPIN (CRISPINE), served as constable in Susquehanna Hd., 1798. {Ref: CM}
CUNNINGHAM, CRISPIN (CRIPAN), head of family in 1800 (2nd District). {Ref: CI}
CUNNINGHAM, DANIEL, m. Ann Amos on Oct 19, 1797. {Ref: PR}
CUNNINGHAM, FRANCIS, son of Crispin and Rachel, b. Dec 10, 1798. {Ref: PR}
CUNNINGHAM, FRANCIS, head of family in 1800 (2nd District). {Ref: CI}
CUNNINGHAM, GEORGE, taxpayer, 1798, Bush River Lower Hd., 1 dwelling

house, 2 inferior houses, 1 acre, $200 valuation; 2 tracts (92 acres, 120 perches) in Bush River Lower Hd., $260.16 valuation, no slaves. {Ref: TL}. Also see "John Bravat Cunningham," q.v.

CUNNINGHAM, GEORGE, head of family in 1800 (1st District). {Ref: CI}

CUNNINGHAM, JOHN, taxpayer, 1798, Gunpowder Lower Hd., 1 dwelling house, 1 inferior house, 2 acres, $120 valuation; 2 tracts (70 acres) in Gunpowder Lower Hd., $236.25 valuation, no slaves. {Ref: TL}

CUNNINGHAM, JOHN, head of family in 1800 (1st District). {Ref: CI}

CUNNINGHAM, JOHN BRAVAT, son of George and Kezia, b. Sep 21, 1796, bapt. May 14, 1797. {Ref: PR}

CUNNINGHAM, KEZIA, see "John Bravat Cunningham," q.v.

CUNNINGHAM, RACHEL, see "Francis Cunningham," q.v.

CUREY, JAMES, insolvent, Harford Lower and Spesutia Lower Hundreds (listed as a single man), on a tax list returned by George Lyttle on Sep 21, 1791. {Ref: IL 31.20, 31.21}

CUREY (CURREY), SAMUEL, insolvent on lists returned by Robert Carlile and John Guyton (who listed him as a single man) for taxes due for the year 1791. {Ref: IL 31.16, 31.19}

CURLEY, PATRICK, taxpayer, 1798, Deer Creek Upper Hd., 1 tract (127 acres, 40 perches) and 1 building, $250.51 valuation, no slaves. {Ref: TL}

CURLEY, PATRICK, head of family in 1800 (5th District). {Ref: CI}

CURREY, JAMES, insolvent on a list for the road tax due for 1791 in Harford Upper, Harford Lower, and Spesutia Upper as returned by Robert Amos, Jr. on Sep 18, 1793. {Ref: IL 31.18}

CURRY, ELIZA, wife of Israel, b. 1791 in Kent, England, d. Dec 19, 1824, aged 33, bur. in the Rutledge Family Cemetery north of Jarrettsville. {Ref: TI}

CURRY, ELIZABETH, dau. of John and Mary, b. in April, 1795. {Ref: PR}

CURRY, ISRAEL, see "Eliza Curry," q.v.

CURRY, JAMES, taxpayer, 1798, Bush River Upper & Eden Hd., 1 dwelling house, 2 acres, $110 valuation; 3 tracts (147 acres) in Bush River Upper & Eden Hd., $330.75 valuation, no slaves. {Ref: TL}

CURRY, JAMES, insolvent on list returned by Robert Carlile for taxes due for the year 1791. {Ref: IL 31.16}

CURRY, JAMES, m. Nancy Thompson on Jan 14, 1800. {Ref: PR}

CURRY, JAMES, head of family in 1800 (1st District). {Ref: CI}

CURRY, JOHN, see "Elizabeth Curry" and "Thomas Curry" and "Sarah Curry," q.v.

CURRY, JOHN, treated by Dr. Archer on Apr 3, 1791; also mentioned his wife and child (no names given). {Ref: JA}

CURRY, JOHN, head of family in 1800 (3rd District). {Ref: CI}

CURRY, JOHN, head of family in 1800 (4th District). {Ref: CI}

CURRY, MARY, see "Elizabeth Curry" and "Thomas Curry" and "Sarah Curry" and "Samuel McMath," q.c.

CURRY, MOSES, taxpayer, 1798, Susquehanna Hd., 2 tracts (200 acres) and 1 building, $438.75 valuation, no slaves. {Ref: TL}
CURRY, MOSES, head of family in 1800 (2nd District). {Ref: CI}
CURRY, SARAH, dau. of John and Mary, b. Apr 11, 1799. {Ref: PR}
CURRY, SOPHIA, b. Mar 31, 1798, d. May 26, 1869, bur. in Ebenezer Methodist Church Cemetery north of Rutledge. {Ref: TI}
CURRY, THOMAS, son of John and Mary, b. in April, 1796. {Ref: PR}
CURTIS, LESLIE (LESLEY), charged for retailing liquors and assaulting James Allen in 1795. {Ref: CD, March and August Terms, 1795}
CURTIS, LESLIE, charged for assaulting John Cooper in 1794. {Ref: CD, March Term, 1795}
CURTIS, LESLIE, charged for assaulting Asael Hitchcock (of William) in 1797. {Ref: CD, March and August Terms, 1797}
CURTIS, LESLIE, charged for assaulting John Bull in 1797. {Ref: CD, March and August Terms, 1797}
CURY (CENY?), ROBERT, insolvent on list returned by Robert Carlile for taxes due for the year 1791. {Ref: IL 31.16}
DAGG, ANN, see "Elizabeth Dagg" and "Thomas Dagg," q.v.
DAGG, ELIZABETH, dau. of James and Ann, b. Oct 12, 1794, bapt. Sep 17, 1794. {Ref: PR}
DAGG, JAMES, see "Elizabeth Dagg" and "Thomas Dagg," q.v.
DAGG, THOMAS, son of James and Ann, b. Aug 23, 1793, bapt. Sep 17, 1794. {Ref: PR}
DAGS, JAMES, see "Joshua Husband," q.v.
DAILEY, JACOB, head of family in 1800 (4th District). {Ref: CI}
DAILEY, SOLOMON, head of family in 1800 (4th District). {Ref: CI}
DAILEY, WILLIAM, insolvent on list returned for the road tax due for 1791 by John Bull. {Ref: IL 31.14}
DAILY, JOHN, insolvent on lists returned by Robert Carlile and John Guyton (the latter spelled the name as "Dayle") for taxes due for the year 1791. {Ref: IL 31.16, 31.19}
DALE, DELPHA, dau. of John and Mary, b. May 29, 1793, bapt. Oct 6, 1795. {Ref: PR}
DALE, DOCTOR'S HEIRS, insolvents on lists returned for the county and road taxes due for 1791 by John Bull in Gunpowder Lower Hundred. {Ref: IL 31.14, 31.15}
DALE (DAIL), JOHN, mentioned in a survey deposition on May 9, 1799. {Ref: JS}. Also see "Delpha Dale" and "Sarah Dale" and "Mary Dale," q.v.
DALE, MARGARET, see "Mary Dale," q.v.
DALE, MARY, dau. of John and Margaret, his late wife, b. Apr 25, 1784, bapt. Oct 6, 1795. {Ref: PR}. Also see "Delpha Dale" and Sarah Dale," q.v.
DALE, SARAH, dau. of John and Mary, b. Jun 1, 1795, bapt. Oct 6, 1795. {Ref: PR}
DALLAM, ELIZABETH, m. John Jolley on Apr 20, 1797. {Ref: PR}
DALLAM, JOHN, taxpayer, 1798, Spesutia Lower Hd., 1 tract (225 acres) and 1 building, $1389.94 valuation, 5 slaves. {Ref: TL}
DALLAM, JOHN, balance due in November, 1797 at Bush River Store. {Ref: AH}
DALLAM, JOHN, taxpayer, 1798, Deer Creek Lower Hd., 1 dwelling house, 1

inferior house, 2 acres, $200 valuation; 2 tracts (270 acres) in Deer Creek Lower Hd., $749.25 valuation, no slaves. {Ref: TL}

DALLAM, JOHN, head of family in 1800 (2nd District). {Ref: CI}

DALLAM, JOHN, head of family in 1800 (5th District). {Ref: CI}

DALLAM, JOSIAS, head of family in 1800 (2nd District). {Ref: CI}. Also see "John Wilds," q.v.

DALLAM, JOSIAS W., taxpayer, 1798, Spesutia Lower Hd., 1 dwelling house, 12 inferior houses, 2 acres, $490 valuation; taxpayer, Spesutia Lower Hd., 1 dwelling house, 2 inferior houses, 2 acres, $120 valuation; taxpayer, Spesutia Lower Hd., 1 dwelling house, 2 inferior houses, 2 acres, $115 valuation; 8 tracts (1498 acres) and 1 building in Spesutia Lower Hd., and 8 other buildings (occupants: James Hare, Mary Cox, Ephraim Collins, Jacob Collins, Negro Orange, Mrs. Doil, James Oliver, and Negro Jonas) in Spesutia Lower Hd., $12572.89 valuation altogether; number of slaves not indicated; taxpayer, 1 tract (13 acres) and 1 building in Susquehanna Hd. (William Woolsey, occupant), $66.94 valuation, no slaves. {Ref: TL}

DALLAM, JOSIAS WILLIAM, served on a Petit Jury in August, 1798 and August, 1799, and on a Grand Jury in August, 1800. {Ref: CM}. Also see "Sarah Dallam," q.v.

DALLAM, MARGARET, taxpayer, 1798, Deer Creek Lower Hd., 1 dwelling house, 1 inferior house, 120 perches of land, $105 valuation, no slaves. {Ref: TL}

DALLAM, RICHARD, taxpayer, 1798, Gunpowder Lower Hd., 1 dwelling house, 6 inferior houses, 2 acres, $500 valuation; 10 tracts (1140 acres, 80 perches) in Gunpowder Lower Hd., $2025 valuation, 4 slaves. {Ref: TL}

DALLAM, RICHARD, m. Priscilla Paca on Mar 28, 1799. {Ref: PR}

DALLAM, RICHARD, head of family in 1800 (Abingdon). {Ref: CI}

DALLAM, RICHARD B., head of family in 1800 (2nd District). {Ref: CI}

DALLAM, SARAH, wife of Josias W., b. 1748, d. Nov --, 1797, bur. next to her husband in a cemetery now on Aberdeen Proving Grounds. {Ref: TI}

DALLAM, WILLIAM S., taxpayer, 1798, Gunpowder Lower Hd., 1 dwelling house, 1 acre and 40 perches, $200 valuation; 5 tracts (215 acres) in Gunpowder Lower Hd., $1019.81 valuation, 4 slaves; and, taxpayer, 1798, Gunpowder Lower Hd., 1 dwelling house, 2 inferior houses, 2 acres, $120 valuation, no slaves. {Ref: TL}

DALLAM, WILLIAM S. (major), head of family in 1800 (2nd District). {Ref: CI}

DALLAS, CATHARINE REED, dau. of Walter and Catherine, b. Aug 26, 1796. {Ref: PR}

DALLAS, WALTER, see "Catherine Reed Dallas," q.v.

DARAUGH, JOHN, see "Jennet Hutchinson," q.v.

DARLINGTON, JOSEPH, mentioned in a survey deposition on Nov 8, 1799. {Ref: JS}.

DARLINGTON, SUSANNA, see "William Mooberry," q.v.

DARLINGTON, SUSANNA, mentioned in a survey deposition on Jan 29, 1800 as "sworn [that] the place where Joseph Darlington's cabbin formerly stood, it being the place where Wm. Mooberry was sworn at." {Ref: JS}.

DARLINGTON, SUSANNAH, head of family in 1800 (4th District). {Ref: CI}.

DAUGHERTY (DOUGHERTY), JAMES, head of family in 1800 (5th District). {Ref: CI}

DAUGHERTY, JOHN, see "Hugh Caney" and "Henrietta Wheeler," q.v.

DAUGHERTY, JOHN, charged for assaulting ---- Cooper in 1793. {Ref: CD, March and August Terms, 1795}

DAUGHERTY, JOHN, head of family in 1800 (5th District). {Ref: CI}

DAUGHERTY, JOHN (captain), head of family in 1800 (5th District). {Ref: CI}

DAUGHERTY (DOUGHERTY), JOHN, charged for assaulting John Hamby in 1794. {Ref: CD, March and August Terms, 1795}

DAUGHERTY, MICHAEL, head of family in 1800 (3rd District). {Ref: CI}. Also see "Angus Graham," q.v.

DAUGHERTY, SAMUEL, taxpayer, 1798, Spesutia Upper Hd., 1 tract (100 acres) and 1 building, $765 valuation, no slaves. {Ref: TL}

DAVEY, ALEXANDER W. (Baltimore Town), or MICHAEL NIGER, taxpayer, 1798, Deer Creek Lower Hd., 1 dwelling house, 2 inferior houses, 2 acres (Michael Niger, occupant), $300 valuation; 1 tract (105 acres) in Deer Creek Lower Hd. (Michael Niger, occupant), $1770 valuation, no slaves; also, taxpayer, 1 tract (114 acres) in Susquehanna Hd., $342 valuation, no slaves. {Ref: TL}

DAVID, D., licensed practicing attorney in March, 1795. {Ref: CC}

DAVID, DAVIDSON, subpoenaed to the Grand Jury in August, 1797. {Ref: CC}

DAVIDGE, JOHN, d. Jul 15, 1794, bur. in Davidge Family Cemetery near Riverside. {Ref: TI}

DAVIDGE, ONNER H., d. Aug 19, 1791, bur. in Davidge Family Cemetery near Riverside. {Ref: TI}

DAVIDGE, STEWART, d. Jul 28, 1800, bur. in Davidge Family Cemetery near Riverside. {Ref: TI}

DAVIDSON, JAMES, insolvent on lists in 1791 due county taxes and road taxes in "Deer Creek Upper, Middle, and Broad Creek Hundreds" as returned by Robert Amos, Jr. {Ref: IL 31.12, 31.22}

DAVIDSON, JAMES, insolvent on a list in 1792 in Broad Creek Hd., as returned by Benjamin Preston. {Ref: IL 31.03}

DAVIDSON, JOHN, taxpayer, 1798, Spesutia Lower Hd., no dwelling house listed in this part of the tax schedule, 1 tract (88 perches, 42 sq. ft.), $27 valuation, no slaves. {Ref: TL}

DAVIS, AMOS, taxpayer, 1798, Harford Upper Hd., 1 tract (48 acres) and 1 building, $130.50 valuation, no slaves. {Ref: TL}

DAVIS, AMOS, insolvent on a list for county taxes due in 1792 as returned by Benjamin Preston. {Ref: IL 31.00}

DAVIS, AMOSS, insolvent on list returned for the road tax due for 1791 by John Bull. {Ref: IL 31.14}

DAVIS, AMOSS, head of family in 1800 (1st District). {Ref: CI}
DAVID, DAVID, head of family in 1800 (4th District). {Ref: CI}
DAVIS, DAVID SR., taxpayer, 1798, Bush River Upper & Eden Hd., 1 tract (32 acres, 80 perches) and 1 building, $163.13 valuation, no slaves. {Ref: TL}
DAVIS, DAVID JR., taxpayer, 1798, Bush River Upper & Eden Hd., 1 tract (32 acres, 80 perches) and 1 building, $122.34 valuation, no slaves. {Ref: TL}
DAVIS, DOCTOR, see "Samuel Griffith's estate" and "Frances Garrettson" and "Elijah Davis," q.v.
DAVIS, ELIJAH ("charge with property"), insolvent on a list for the road tax due for 1791 in Harford Upper, Harford Lower, and Spesutia Upper as returned by Robert Amos, Jr. on Sep 18, 1793. {Ref: IL 31.18}
DAVIS, ELIJAH (doctor), insolvent, Harford Lower and Spesutia Lower Hundreds (listed as a single man), on a tax list returned by George Lyttle on Sep 21, 1791. {Ref: IL 31.20, 31.21}
DAVIS, ELIJAH (doctor), taxpayer, 1798, Spesutia Lower Hd., 1 dwelling house, 9 inferior houses, 2 acres, $480 valuation; 1 tract (298 acres) in Spesutia Lower Hd., $2621.25 valuation, 6 slaves. {Ref: TL}
DAVIS, ELIJAH (doctor), head of family in 1800 (2nd District). {Ref: CI}
DAVIS, FRANCIS, insolvent, Harford Lower and Spesutia Lower Hundreds, on a tax list returned by George Lyttle on Sep 21, 1791. {Ref: IL 31.20, 31.21}
DAVIS, GEORGE, m. Elizabeth Scott on Aug 13, 1795. {Ref: PR}
DAVIS, ISAAC, taxpayer, 1798, Bush River Upper & Eden Hd., 1 dwelling house, 4 inferior houses, 2 acres, $200 valuation; 1 tract (164 acres, 40 perches) in Bush River Upper & Eden Hd., $144.56 valuation, no slaves. {Ref: TL}
DAVIS, JESSE, head of family in 1800 (4th District). {Ref: CI}
DAVID, JOHN, see "Jesse Jarrett" and "Phebe Davis," q.v.
DAVIS, JOHN, head of family in 1800 (4th District). {Ref: CI}
DAVIS, JOHN, mentioned in a survey deposition on Jan 22, 1800 as "to house John Davis now lives in." {Ref: JS}
DAVIS, JOHN (reverend), taxpayer, 1798, Bush River Upper & Eden Hd., 1 tract (165 acres) and 1 building, $455.63 valuation, 3 slaves. {Ref: TL}
DAVIS, JOHN (reverend), head of family in 1800 (4th District). {Ref: CI}
DAVIS, JOSEPH, taxpayer, 1798, Deer Creek Lower Hd., 1 dwelling house, 1 inferior house, 2 acres, $121 valuation; 3 tracts (114 acres) in Deer Creek Lower Hd., $210.94 valuation, 1 slave. {Ref: TL}
DAVIS, JOSEPH, head of family in 1800 (5th District). {Ref: CI}
DAVIS, LARKIN, b. Aug 25, 1798, d. Feb 5, 1876, bur. in Harford (Old Brick) Baptist Church Cemetery. {Ref: TI}
DAVIS, LUCAS, head of family in 1800 (4th District). {Ref: CI}
DAVIS, MARTHA, b. May 4, 1791, d. May 17, 1855, bur. in Trappe Church Cemetery. {Ref: TI}
DAVIS, PHEBE (mother), wife of Rev. John, b. Nov 23, 1795, d. May 3, 1875, bur. in Darlington Cemetery. {Ref: TI}

DAVIS(?), ROBERT, head of family in 1800 (5th District). {Ref: CI}
DAVIS, SARAH (aunt), b. Feb --, 1796, d. Feb --, 1879, bur. in Darlington Cemetery. {Ref: TI}
DAVIS, SARAH (widow), of Joppa, bur. May 5, 1793, age unknown. {Ref: PR}
DAVIS, THOMAS, taxpayer, 1798, Bush River Upper & Eden Hd., 1 dwelling house, 1 inferior house, 2 acres, $110 valuation; 1 tract (72 acres) in Bush River Upper & Eden Hd., $121.50 valuation, no slaves. {Ref: TL}
DAVIS, THOMAS, head of family in 1800 (4th District). {Ref: CI}
DAVISON, JAMES ("run"), insolvent on a list of the county tax due William Osborn, sheriff, for 1791, as returned by Edward Prigg on Sep 20, 1791. {Ref: IL 31.17}
DAWNEY, JAMES, insolvent on lists returned for the county and road taxes due for 1791 by John Bull in Gunpowder Lower Hundred. {Ref: IL 31.14, 31.15}. Also see "Thomas Dawney" and "William Collins Dawney," q.v.
DAWNEY, SARAH, see "Stephen Chesolm," q.v.
DAWNEY, SOPHIA, see "Thomas Dawney" and "William Collins Dawney," q.v.
DAWNEY, THOMAS, taxpayer, 1798, Gunpowder Lower Hd., 2 tracts (132 acres) and 1 building, $328.50 valuation, no slaves. {Ref: TL}
DAWNEY, THOMAS, son of James and Sophia, b. Mar 21, 1797. {Ref: PR}
DAWNEY, WILLIAM COLLINS, son of James and Sophia, b. Apr 14, 1799. {Ref: PR}
DAWS, EDWARD, m. Ann Grunden on Dec 29, 1793. {Ref: PR}
DAWS, ELISHA, taxpayer, 1798, Deer Creek Lower Hd., 1 dwelling house, 2 inferior houses, 2 acres, $180 valuation; 2 tracts (98 acres) in Deer Creek Lower Hd., $165.38 valuation, no slaves. {Ref: TL}
DAWS, MORDICA, taxpayer, 1798, Gunpowder Upper Hd., 1 tract (28 acres) and 1 building, $159.75 valuation, no slaves. {Ref: TL}
DAWSETT, JONATHAN, head of family in 1800 (Havre de Grace). {Ref: CI}
DAWSON, ELIZABETH, see "William Dawson" and "Mary Dawson," q.v.
DAWSON, ELIZABETH, dau. of William and Mary, bapt. Apr 11, 1796. {Ref: PR}.
DAWSON, ELIZABETH, subpoenaed to the Grand Jury in August, 1797. {Ref: CC}
DAWSON, ISAAC, see "William Dawson," q.v.
DAWSON, JESSE, bur. Feb 7, 1799. {Ref: PR}. Also see "Mary Dawson," q.v.
DAWSON, MARY, dau. of Jesse and Elizabeth, b. Mar 15, 1778, bapt. Mar 20, 1796. {Ref: PR}. Also see "Elizabeth Dawson," q.v.
DAWSON, THOMAS, head of family in 1800 (4th District). {Ref: CI}
DAWSON, WILLIAM, see "Josias Hall" and "Elizabeth Dawson," q.v.
DAWSON, WILLIAM ("poor"), insolvent on a list of the county tax due William Osborn, sheriff, for 1791, as returned by Edward Prigg on Sep 20, 1791. {Ref: IL 31.17}
DAWSON, WILLIAM, son of Isaac and Elizabeth, b. Mar 3, 1771, bapt. Jan 28, 1796. {Ref: PR}
DAWSON, WILLIAM, head of family in 1800 (2nd District). {Ref: CI}
DAY, AGNESS, see "Rebecca Young Day" and Edward Augustus Day" and

"William Young Day," q.v.
DAY, CASSANDRA FULTON, dau. of William Fell and Letitia, b. May 28, 1793. {Ref: PR}
DAY, CHARLOTTE, dau. of Joshua and Sarah, b. Jun 10, 1795, bapt. Jul 17, 1796. {Ref: PR}
DAY, DANIEL, head of family in 1800 (5th District). {Ref: CI}
DAY, DOCTOR, see "John Day," q.v.
DAY, EDWARD, head of family in 1800 (1st District). {Ref: CI}. Also see "Ishmael Day," q.v.
DAY, EDWARD AUGUSTUS, son of John and Agness, b. Sep 3, 1796. {Ref: PR}
DAY, ELISHA, see "Job Barnes," q.v.
DAY, HANNAH, b. Feb 13, 1791, d. May 3, 1869, bur. in Fellowship Cemetery near Harkins. {Ref: TI}
DAY, HANNAH, m. Roger Boyce on Dec 3, 1797. {Ref: PR}
DAY, ELISHA, head of family in 1800 (5th District). {Ref: CI}
DAY, ISHMAEL, son of Edward and Mary, b. Mar 20, 1792. {Ref: PR}
DAY, JAMES H., head of family in 1800 (1st District). {Ref: CI}
DAY, JOHN, see "James Weatherall" and "Rebecca Young Day" and "Young Day" and "Edward Augustus Day" and "William Young Day," q.v.
DAY, JOHN, insolvent on a list in 1792 in Deer Creek Lower Hd., as returned by Benjamin Preston. {Ref: IL 31.03}
DAY, JOHN, son of Dr. Day, bur. in late 1797 or early 1798 (exact date not given), aged 2 years. {Ref: PR}
DAY, JOHN, head of family in 1800 (2nd District). {Ref: CI}
DAY, JOHN, will probated Jan 19, 1791. {Ref: HW}
DAY, JOHN JR., insolvent on a list in 1792 in Deer Creek Lower Hd., as returned by Benjamin Preston. {Ref: IL 31.03}
DAY, JOHN (OF D.), head of family in 1800 (2nd District). {Ref: CI}
DAY, JOSHUA, granted a tavern license in March and August, 1797. {Ref: CC}
DAY, JOSHUA, subpoenaed to the Grand Jury in August, 1797. {Ref: CC}
DAY, JOSHUA, taxpayer, 1798, Harford Upper Hd., 1 dwelling house, 5 inferior houses, 2 acres, $500 valuation; 1 tract (5 acres) in Harford Upper Hd., $45 valuation, 1 slave; taxpayer, 1798, Bush River Lower Hd., 1 dwelling house, 80 perches of land, $180 valuation; 1 tract (60 acres) and 1 building in Harford Upper Hd. (Robert Armstrong, occupant), $157.50 valuation; taxpayer, 1798, 1 building in Bush River Lower Hd. (Susanna Moore, occupant), $45 valuation, no slaves. {Ref: TL}. Also see "Charlotte Day" and "Sianna Day," q.v.
DAY, JOSHUA, head of family in 1800 (1st District). {Ref: CI}
DAY, LETITIA, see "Pamala Day" and "Cassandra Fulton Day," q.v.
DAY, MARY, see "Ishmael Day," q.v.
DAY, MARY ANN, will probated Nov 26, 1796. {Ref: HW}
DAY, MRS., of St. John's Parish, bur. Aug 26, 1796, aged 60. {Ref: PR}
DAY, NICHOLAS, or WILLIAM GROVES, taxpayer, 1798, Gunpowder Lower

Hd., 1 dwelling house, 3 inferior houses, 2 acres (William Groves, occupant), $150 valuation; 1 tract (79 acres) in Gunpowder Lower Hd. (William Groves, occupant), $166.50 valuation, no slaves. {Ref: TL}

DAY, PAMALA, dau. of Wiliam Fell and Letitia, b. in 1791, bapt. Jun 16, 1793. {Ref: PR}

DAY, REBECCA YOUNG, dau. of John and Agness, b. Aug 7, 1794, bapt. Jan 2, 1795 (although record states Jan 2, 1794). {Ref: PR}

DAY, SAMUEL, served as constable in Bush River Lower Hd., 1797-1798. {Ref: CC, CM}

DAY, SAMUEL, served as bailiff for the county court in August, 1798. {Ref: CM}

DAY, SAMUEL, bur. in the fall 1798, aged about 70. {Ref: PR}

DAY, SAMUEL ("old and poor"), insolvent on a list for 1791 in Gunpowder Upper and Bush River Lower Hundreds, as filed by John Bond, Deputy Sheriff, on Sep 20, 1791. {Ref: IL 31.24}

DAY, SARAH, head of family in 1800 (Belle Air). {Ref: CI}. Also see "Charlotte Day" and "Sianna Day," q.v.

DAY, SIANNA, dau. of Joshua and Sarah, b. Sep 5, 1793, bapt. Jul 17, 1796. {Ref: PR}

DAY, WILLIAM, insolvent on lists returned by Robert Carlile and John Guyton for taxes due for the year 1791. {Ref: IL 31.16, 31.19}

DAY, WILLIAM B. (father), b. Mar 3, 1799, d. Feb 23, 1871, bur. in Dublin Methodist Church Cemetery. {Ref: TI}

DAY, WILLIAM FELL, see "Pamala Day" and "Cassandra Fulton Day," q.v.

DAY, WILLIAM YOUNG, son of John and Agness, b. Mar 7, 1798. {Ref: PR}

DAY, YOUNG, child of John and ---- Day, bapt. Jun 8, 1794. {Ref: PR}

DAYLE, JOHN, see "John Daily," q.v.

DEAN, LYDIA, m. John Otley on Mar 22, 1796. {Ref: PR}

DEAN, SAMUEL, head of family in 1800 (3rd District). {Ref: CI}. Also see "John Moores," q.v.

DEARMONT, JOHN, insolvent on list returned for the road tax due for 1791 by John Bull. {Ref: IL 31.14}

DEARMONT, MARY, head of family in 1800 (4th District). {Ref: CI}

DEAVER, ANN, see "George Stolinger," q.v.

DEAVER, AQUILA, see "James Deaver" and "John Rumsey," q.v.

DEAVER, AQUILA, treated by Dr. Archer on Aug 26, 1795; also mentioned his security as James Deaver. {Ref: JA}

DEAVER, AQUILA, insolvent on lists in 1791 due county taxes and road taxes in "Deer Creek Upper, Middle, and Broad Creek Hundreds" as returned by Robert Amos, Jr., but his name was then crossed off both lists. {Ref: IL 31.12, 31.22}

DEAVER (DEAVOUR), AQUILLA, head of family in 1800 (2nd District). {Ref: CI}

DEAVER, DAVID, insolvent on lists for the county tax due for 1791 in Susquehanna Hd., as returned by Thomas Taylor on Sep 17, 1792. {Ref: IL 31.12, 31.02}

DEAVER (DEAVOUR), DAVID, head of family in 1800 (5th District). {Ref: CI}

DEAVER, HANNAH, insolvent on lists in 1791 due county taxes and road taxes in "Deer Creek Upper, Middle, and Broad Creek Hundreds" as returned by Robert Amos, Jr., but her name was then crossed off both lists. {Ref: IL 31.12, 31.22}

DEAVER (DEAVOUR), HANNAH, head of family in 1800 (5th District). {Ref: CI}

DEAVER, HUGH, insolvent on a list for the road tax due for 1791 in Deer Creek Lower Hd., as returned by Thomas Taylor on Sep 17, 1792, but his name was crossed off the list. {Ref: IL 31.12}

DEAVER (DEAVOUR), HUGH, head of family in 1800 (5th District). {Ref: CI}

DEAVER, JAMES, see "Aquila Deaver" and "Benedict Edward Hall" and "John Street" and "Augustin Boyer," q.v.

DEAVER, JAMES, taxpayer, 1798, no dwelling house listed in this part of the tax schedule, no land listed, no Hd. listed (possibly Spesutia Lower Hundred), 1 slave. {Ref: TL}

DEAVER, JAMES, insolvent on a list for the road tax due for 1791 in Harford Upper, Harford Lower, and Spesutia Upper as returned by Robert Amos, Jr. on Sep 18, 1793. {Ref: IL 31.18}

DEAVER, JAMES, treated by Dr. Archer on Jul 20, 1793; also mentioned his wife (no name given). {Ref: JA}

DEAVER, JAMES, tracts *Scheming Defied* and *Benjamin's Neighbour* surveyed in 1795. {Ref: CB, SB}

DEAVER, JAMES, had an account at Hall's Store in May, 1791. {Ref: WH}

DEAVER, JAMES, purchased rye on Oct 18, 1797 at Bush River Store. {Ref: AH}

DEAVER, JAMES (guardian of son Aquila Deaver), taxpayer, 1798, Deer Creek Upper Hd., 1 tract (110 acres) and 1 building, $340.31 valuation, no slaves. {Ref: TL}. In another part of the tax schedule the occupant is listed as John Creighton.

DEAVER (DEAVOR), JAMES, head of family in 1800 (2nd District). {Ref: CI}

DEAVER, JAMES JR., taxpayer, 1798, Deer Creek Upper Hd., 2 tracts (141 acres, 120 perches) and 1 building, $359.16 valuation, no slaves. {Ref: TL}

DEAVER, JAMES (OF RICHARD), tract *Uncle's Grudge* surveyed between 1792 and 1796. {Ref: SB}

DEAVER (DEAVOUR), JAMES (OF RD.), head of family in 1800 (5th District). {Ref: CI}

DEAVER, JOHN, insolvent, Harford Lower and Spesutia Lower Hundreds, on a tax list returned by George Lyttle on Sep 21, 1791. {Ref: IL 31.20, 31.21}

DEAVER, JOHN, insolvent on a list for the road tax due for 1791 in Harford Upper, Harford Lower, and Spesutia Upper as returned by Robert Amos, Jr. on Sep 18, 1793. {Ref: IL 31.18}

DEAVER, MICAJAH, insolvent, Harford Lower and Spesutia Lower Hundreds, on a tax list returned by George Lyttle on Sep 21, 1791. {Ref: IL 31.20, 31.21}

DEAVER, MICAJAH, insolvent on a list for the road tax due for 1791 in Harford Upper, Harford Lower, and Spesutia Upper as returned by Robert Amos, Jr. on Sep 18, 1793. {Ref: IL 31.18}

DEAVER, RICHARD, will probated Mar 8, 1791. {Ref: HW}

DEAVER, RICHARD, taxpayer, 1798, Deer Creek Upper Hd., 2 tracts (100 acres), $253.12 valuation, no slaves. {Ref: TL}
DEAVER, RICHARD, tract *Deaver's Compulsion* surveyed in 1795, and tract *Sarah's Garden* surveyed in 1786 and granted to Thomas Streett in 1796. {Ref: CB}
DEAVER (DEAVOUR), RICHARD, head of family in 1800 (5th District). {Ref: CI}
DEAVER, SARAH, see "Sarah Belinda Stritehoff," q.v.
DEBRULA, GREENBURY, head of family in 1800 (Abingdon). {Ref: CI}
DEBRULA, HANNAH, head of family in 1800 (1st District). {Ref: CI}
DEBRULA, MICAJAH, head of family in 1800 (1st District). {Ref: CI}
DEBRULER, FRANCES, will probated Nov 3, 1792. {Ref: HW}
DEBRULER, GEORGE, m. Arminta Nutterwell (Nutterville?) on Jul 12, 1791. {Ref: PR}
DEBRULER, JACOB, charged for assaulting ---- Harbert in 1793. {Ref: CD, March and August Terms, 1795}
DEBRULER, JAMES, taxpayer, 1798, Gunpowder Lower Hd., 1 dwelling house, 3 inferior houses, 2 acres, $150 valuation; 2 tracts (143 acres) in Gunpowder Lower Hd., $321.75 valuation, 2 slaves. {Ref: TL}
DEBRULER, WILLIAM, taxpayer, 1798, Gunpowder Lower Hd., 1 dwelling house, 1 inferior house, 2 acres, $150 valuation; 2 tracts (130 acres) in Gunpowder Lower Hd., $292.50 valuation, no slaves. {Ref: TL}
DEERAN, THOMAS, son of John and Deborah, b. Sep 12, 1799, bapt. Dec 25, 1799. {Ref: PR}
DEERAN, JOHN, m. Deborah Dormer on Sep 18, 1798. {Ref: PR}
DEERAN, JOHN, head of family in 1800 (1st District). {Ref: CI}
DEETS, FREDERICK, husband of Hannah Poly or Poley, b. 1792, d. Nov 28, 1869, bur. in Bethel Presbyterian Church Cemetery at Madonna. {Ref: BC}
DEETS, HANNAH (neé Poly or Poley), wife of Frederick, b. 1798 in Norristown, Pennsylvania, d. Nov 3, 1866, bur. in Bethel Presbyterian Church Cemetery at Madonna. {Ref: BC}
DEGEON, JOSEPH, m. Margaret Gorril on Sep 21, 1800. {Ref: PR}
DELANEY, JOSHUA, head of family in 1800 (2nd District). {Ref: CI}
DELANY, MARY, m. Laurence Harp on Sep 1, 1796. {Ref: PR}
DELAP, JOSEPH, taxpayer, 1798, Deer Creek Upper Hd., 1 tract (116 acres, 80 perches) and 1 building, $371.35 valuation, no slaves. {Ref: TL}
DELAPORT, BETSEY H., taxpayer, 1798, Gunpowder Upper Hd., 1 dwelling house, 2 inferior houses, 2 acres, $500 valuation; 2 tracts (190 acres) in Gunpowder Upper Hd., $562.50 valuation, 1 slave. {Ref: TL}
DELAPORTE, CLAUDIUS FRANCIS FREDERICK (commonly called Frederick Delaporte), will probated Mar 7, 1797. {Ref: HW}
DELAPORTE, FRANCIS, head of family in 1800 (3rd District). {Ref: CI}
DELAPORTE, ----, see "Negro Guy," q.v.
DELIGRITZ, ALEXIUS, see "Alexius Amedi Raphel," q.v.
DELMAS (DELMASS, DELMOSS), FRANCIS, head of family in 1800 (1st

District). {Ref: CI}. Also see "Monsieur Delmass" and "Monsieur Compagnon" and "Mary H. Delmas," q.v.

DELMAS, MARY H., wife of Francis A., b. 1794, d. Mar 24, 1844, aged 50, bur. in St. Ignatius Catholic Church Cemetery in Hickory. {Ref: TI}

DELMAS, THEODORE, b. Jun 4, 1791, d. Nov 8, 1871, bur. in St. Ignatius Catholic Church Cemetery in Hickory. {Ref: TI}

DELMASS, MONSIEUR, taxpayer, 1798, Bush River Lower Hd., no dwelling house listed in this part of the tax schedule, no land listed, 1 slave; also listed as "Mr. Delmas" by the tax assessor; see "Monsieur Compagnon," q.v.

DEMORSE, JOHN, head of family in 1800 (4th District). {Ref: CI}

DEMORSE, JOHN JR., head of family in 1800 (4th District). {Ref: CI}

DEMOS, JOHN, taxpayer, 1798, Bush River Upper & Eden Hd., 1 dwelling house, 2 inferior houses, 2 acres, $150 valuation; 3 tracts (256 acres) in Bush River Upper & Eden Hd., $576 valuation, no slaves. {Ref: TL}

DEMOSS, JEMIMA, see "Elisha Meads," q.v.

DEMOSS, JOHN JR., see "Jemima Meads," q.v.

DEMPSEY, LUKE, insolvent on lists returned for the county and road taxes due for 1791 by John Bull in Gunpowder Lower Hd. (name spelled as "Densey" on one list). {Ref: IL 31.14, 31.15}

DEMPSEY (DEMSEY), PATRICK, head of family in 1800 (5th District). {Ref: CI}. Also see "Henrietta Wheeler," q.v.

DENBOW, JOHN, served on a Grand Jury in March, 1800. {Ref: CM}

DENBOW, JOHN, taxpayer, 1798, Bush River Upper & Eden Hd., 1 dwelling house, 4 inferior houses, 2 acres, $200 valuation; 2 tracts (90 acres, 80 perches) in Bush River Upper & Eden Hd., $203.63 valuation, no slaves. {Ref: TL}

DENBOW, JOHN, head of family in 1800 (4th District). {Ref: CI}

DENBOW, THOMAS, taxpayer, 1798, Bush River Upper & Eden Hd., 1 dwelling house, 3 inferior houses, 2 acres, $150 valuation; 5 tracts (183 acres) in Bush River Upper & Eden Hd., $308.81 valuation, no slaves. {Ref: TL}

DENBOW, THOMAS, insolvent on lists returned by Robert Carlile and John Guyton (who listed him as a single man, crossed the name off the list, and then wrote the name in again at the end of the same list among the single men) for taxes due for the year 1791. {Ref: IL 31.16, 31.19}

DENBOW, THOMAS, served on a Petit Jury in August, 1798 and August, 1799. {Ref: CM}

DENBOW, THOMAS, head of family in 1800 (4th District). {Ref: CI}

DENNEY, MICHAEL, head of family in 1800 (1st District). {Ref: CI}

DENNEY, JAMES ("poor"), insolvent on a list of the county tax due William Osborn, sheriff, for 1791, as returned by Edward Prigg on Sep 20, 1791. {Ref: IL 31.17}

DENNING, JOHN, insolvent on lists returned for the county and road taxes due for 1791 by John Bull in Gunpowder Lower Hundred. {Ref: IL 31.14, 31.15}

DENNIS(?), THOMAS, head of family in 1800 (3rd District). {Ref: CI}

DENNISON, GIDEON, taxpayer, 1798, Susquehanna Hd., 1 dwelling house, 5 inferior houses, 2 acres, $2000 valuation; 6 tracts (1818 acres) and 10 buildings (occupants: Margaret Evat or Evatt, Sampson G. Hyland, Rulif or Rulife Morgan, and John Hughes, Jr.) in Susquehanna Hd., $5656.50 valuation altogether, 9 slaves. {Ref: TL}

DENNISON, GIDEON, bur. Sep 26, 1799. {Ref: PR}

DENNISON, JERUSHA, head of family in 1800 (2nd District). {Ref: CI}

DENNISON, MATTHEW (MATHER), head of family in 1800 (3rd District). {Ref: CI}. Also see "Arthur Monohon," q.v.

DENNY, JAMES, insolvent on lists in 1791 due county taxes and road taxes in "Deer Creek Upper, Middle, and Broad Creek Hundreds" as returned by Robert Amos, Jr. {Ref: IL 31.12, 31.22}

DENNY, MARGARET, will probated Dec 16, 1791. {Ref: HW}

DENNY, MICHAEL, taxpayer, 1798, Gunpowder Lower Hd., no dwelling house listed in this part of the tax schedule, no land listed, 3 slaves. {Ref: TL}

DENNY, MRS. (widow of Simon), treated by Dr. Archer on Oct 7, 1791. {Ref: JA}

DENNY, SIMON, see "Mrs. Denny," q.v.

DENNY, WALTER, insolvent on lists in 1791 due county taxes and road taxes in "Deer Creek Upper, Middle, and Broad Creek Hundreds" as returned by Robert Amos, Jr. {Ref: IL 31.12, 31.22}

DENZMAN(?), SAMUEL, head of family in 1800 (5th District). {Ref: CI}

DESSAA, JEAN, wrote his will "of Baltimore County, formerly of St. Lucie" on Dec 31, 1792, probated Dec 15, 1797 in Harford County. {Ref: HW}

DEVIN, JOHN, see "Benjamin Rumsey," q.v.

DEVIN, JOHN, insolvent on list returned by Robert Carlile for taxes due for the year 1791. {Ref: IL 31.16}

DEVIN, JOHN, served as constable in Broad Creek Hd., 1799. {Ref: CM}

DEVLIN, JOHN, son of William Devlin and Mary Adamson, b. May 16, 1794, bapt. Nov 22, 1798. {Ref: PR}

DEVLIN, ROBERT STEIN, son of William Devlin and Mary Adamson, b. May 3, 1798, bapt. Nov 22, 1798. {Ref: PR}

DEVLIN (DEVILEN), WILLIAM, head of family in 1800 (2nd District). {Ref: CI}. Also see "William Devlin Smith" and "John Devlin" and "Robert Stein Smith," q.v.

DEVLIN, WILLIAM SMITH, son of William Devlin and Mary Adamson, b. Feb 9, 1796, bapt. Nov 22, 1798. {Ref: PR}

DEVON (DEVOE?), THOMAS, head of family in 1800 (4th District). {Ref: CI}

DEVOE, SARAH, dau. of John and Ann, b. Dec 17, 1796. {Ref: Durham-Devoe Bible}. Also see "Abel A. Durham" and "Sarah Durham," q.v.

DEVOE, WILLIAM, son of John and Ann, b. Sep 15, 1798. {Ref: Durham-Devoe Bible}

DEWBERRY, JOSEPH, insolvent on a list for 1791 in Gunpowder Upper and Bush River Lower Hundreds, as filed by John Bond, Deputy Sheriff, on Sep 20,

1791 (who listed him as a single man). {Ref: IL 31.24}

DEWBERY, JOSEPH, insolvent on list returned for the road tax due for 1791 by John Bull. {Ref: IL 31.14}

DICK, DAVID, insolvent on a list of the county tax due William Osborn, sheriff, for 1791, as returned by Edward Prigg on Sep 20, 1791. {Ref: IL 31.17}

DICK, DAVID, insolvent on lists in 1791 due county taxes and road taxes in "Deer Creek Upper, Middle, and Broad Creek Hundreds" as returned by Robert Amos, Jr. {Ref: IL 31.12, 31.22}

DICK, DAVID, son of David and Mary, b. Oct 13, 1791, bapt. Dec 30, 1795. {Ref: PR}. Also see "Robert Dick" and "Elizabeth Dick," q.v.

DICK, ELIZABETH, dau. of David and Mary, b. Sep 5, 1784, see "Edward Lee" and "David Lee," q.v.

DICK, MARY, see "David Dick" and "Robert Dick" and "Elizabeth Dick," q.v.

DICK, ROBERT, son of David and Mary, b. May 10 or 11, 1786, bapt. Dec 30, 1795. {Ref: PR}

DICKSON, BENJAMIN, see "Samuel Willet," q.v.

DICKSON, HENRY, mentioned in a survey deposition on Nov 13, 1799. {Ref: JS}

DICKSON, HENRY, head of family in 1800 (5th District). {Ref: CI}

DICKSON, JAMES, see "Samuel Willet," q.v.

DICKSON, JOHN, head of family in 1800 (5th District). {Ref: CI}

DICKSON, ROBERT, head of family in 1800 (5th District). {Ref: CI}

DICKSON, THOMAS, head of family in 1800 (4th District). {Ref: CI}

DICKSON, WILLIAM, head of family in 1800 (1st District). {Ref: CI}

DIER, JOHANNA, taxpayer, 1798, Gunpowder Upper Hd., 1 tract (32 acres) and 1 building, $94.50 valuation, no slaves. {Ref: TL}

DIGGS, JAMES, insolvent on lists in 1791 due county taxes and road taxes in "Deer Creek Upper, Middle, and Broad Creek Hundreds" as returned by Robert Amos, Jr., but his name was then crossed off both lists. {Ref: IL 31.12, 31.22}

DINES, MARY, insolvent on lists returned by Robert Carlile and John Guyton (who wrote in her name, crossed it off the list and then wrote "S. Morshell" at the end of the line) for taxes due for the year 1791. {Ref: IL 31.16, 31.19}

DIVEN, JOHN, served as County Court Bailiff in August, 1800. {Ref: CM}

DIVEN, JOHN, head of family in 1800 (1st District). {Ref: CI}

DIVEN (DEVIN), MICHAEL, head of family in 1800 (2nd District). {Ref: CI}. Also see "John Rumsey," q.v.

DIVERS, ANN, dau. of Annanias and Cassandra, b. in February, 1794, bapt. Apr 13, 1794. {Ref: PR}

DIVERS, ANNANIAS, see "Ann Divers" and "Mary Galloway Divers," q.v.

DIVERS, CASSANDRA, see "Ann Divers" and "Mary Galloway Divers," q.v.

DIVERS, MARY, b. 1797, d. May 3, 1875, in her 78th year, bur. in Providence Methodist Cemetery at Upper Crossroads. {Ref: TI}

DIVERS, MARY GALLOWAY, dau. of Annanias and Cassandra, b. May 28,

1795. {Ref: PR}
DIVERS, WILLIAM, head of family in 1800 (3rd District). {Ref: CI}
DIVES, WILLIAM, taxpayer, 1798, Susquehanna Hd., 2 tracts (167 acres) and 1 building, $331.87 valuation, no slaves. {Ref: TL}
DIVIS, WILLIAM, treated by Dr. Archer on Mar 17, 1793; also mentioned his wife and child (no names given). {Ref: JA}
DIXON, MORRIS, insolvent, Harford Lower and Spesutia Lower Hundreds, on a tax list returned by George Lyttle on Sep 21, 1791. {Ref: IL 31.20, 31.21}
DIXON, MORRIS, insolvent on a list for the road tax due for 1791 in Harford Upper, Harford Lower, and Spesutia Upper as returned by Robert Amos, Jr. on Sep 18, 1793. {Ref: IL 31.18}
DIXON, THOMAS, taxpayer, 1798, Deer Creek Upper Hd., 1 tract (140 acres), $315 valuation, no slaves. {Ref: TL}
DIXON, WILLIAM, insolvent on a list for the road tax due for 1791 in Harford Upper, Harford Lower, and Spesutia Upper as returned by Robert Amos, Jr. on Sep 18, 1793. {Ref: IL 31.18}
DOBBINS, JAMES ("dead"), insolvent on a list for 1791 in Gunpowder Upper and Bush River Lower Hundreds, as filed by John Bond, Deputy Sheriff, on Sep 20, 1791. {Ref: IL 31.24}. Also see "Robert Dobbins," q.v.
DOBBINS, ROBERT, son of James and Sarah, b. in the fall of 1788. {Ref: PR}
DOBBINS, SARAH, see "Robert Dobbins," q.v.
DOBBINS, THOMAS, taxpayer, 1798, Broad Creek Hd., 2 tracts (100 acres) and 1 building, $127.50 valuation, no slaves. {Ref: TL}
DOIL, MRS., see "Josias W. Dallam," q.v.
DONAHOO, DANIEL, head of family in 1800 (2nd District). {Ref: CI}
DONAHU, DANIEL, taxpayer, 1798, Susquehanna Hd., 2 tracts (84 acres) and 1 building, $226.13 valuation, no slaves. {Ref: TL}
DONAVAN, EPHRAIM, m. Charlotte Taylor on Mar 28, 1791. {Ref: PR}
DONAVIN, JACOB, insolvent, Harford Lower and Spesutia Lower Hundreds, on a tax list returned by George Lyttle on Sep 21, 1791. {Ref: IL 31.20, 31.21}
DONAVIN, JOHN, insolvent, Harford Lower and Spesutia Lower Hundreds, on a tax list returned by George Lyttle on Sep 21, 1791. {Ref: IL 31.20, 31.21}. Also see "Josias Carvil Hall," q.v.
DONNAVIN, JACOB, insolvent on a list for the road tax due for 1791 in Harford Upper, Harford Lower, and Spesutia Upper as returned by Robert Amos, Jr. on Sep 18, 1793. {Ref: IL 31.18}
DONNAVIN, JOHN, insolvent on a list for the road tax due for 1791 in Harford Upper, Harford Lower, and Spesutia Upper as returned by Robert Amos, Jr. on Sep 18, 1793. {Ref: IL 31.18}
DONNAVIN, MARY, insolvent on a list for the road tax due for 1791 in Harford Upper, Harford Lower, and Spesutia Upper as returned by Robert Amos, Jr. on Sep 18, 1793. {Ref: IL 31.18}

DONNEL, JAMES EZEKIEL, son of Patrick and Margaret, b. Sep 27, 1800. {Ref: PR}
DONNEL, JANE ELINOR, dau. of Patrick and Mary, b. Jul 3, 1795, bapt. Oct 11, 1795. {Ref: PR}
DONNEL, JOHN, son of Patrick and Margaret, b. Mar 23, 1798, bapt. Apr 29, 1798. {Ref: PR}
DONNEL, MARGARET, see "John Donnel" and "James Ezekiel Donnel," q.v.
DONNEL, MARY, see "Unity Donnel" and "Jane Elinor Donnel," q.v.
DONNEL, PATRICK, see "John Donnel" and "Unity Donnel" and "James Ezekiel Donnel" and "Jane Elinor Donnel" and William Ashmore," q.v.
DONNEL, UNITY, dau. of Patrick and Mary, bapt. Oct 23, 1796. {Ref: PR}
DONNELLY, ARCHIBALD, charged with murder in 1797; Andrew Martin and Sarah Martin summoned; no further details. {Ref: CD, August Term, 1797}
DONOVAN, FANNY, see "Paca Smith Donovan," q.v.
DONOVAN, FRANCES, see "Jarrett Donovan," q.v.
DONOVAN, JARRETT, son of John and Frances, b. Jan 11, 1795, bapt. Sep 11, 1796. {Ref: PR}
DONOVAN, JOHN, head of family in 1800 (2nd District). {Ref: CI}. Also see "Paca Smith Donovan" and "Jarrett Donovan," q.v.
DONOVAN, PACA SMITH, son of John and Fanny, b. Jan 21, 1799, bapt. Sep 30, 1799. {Ref: PR}
DOOLEY, WILLIAM, see "William Kitely's heirs," q.v.
DOOLSACUS(?), THOMAS, son of Lewis and Mary, b. Apr 19, 1793. {Ref: PR}
DORAN, EDWARD, taxpayer, 1798, Bush River Upper & Eden Hd., 1 tract (185 acres), $416.25 valuation, no slaves. {Ref: TL}
DORAN, EDWARD, head of family in 1800 (4th District). {Ref: CI}
DORAN, JOHN, see "Margaret Doran," q.v.
DORAN, JOHN, taxpayer, 1798, Bush River Upper & Eden Hd., 2 tracts (76 acres), $42.75 valuation, no slaves. {Ref: TL}
DORAN, JOHN, served on a Petit Jury in March, 1800. {Ref: CM}
DORAN, JOHN, head of family in 1800 (4th District). {Ref: CI}
DORAN, MARGARET (administrators Patrick Doran and John Doran), taxpayers, 1798, Bush River Upper & Eden Hd., 1 dwelling house, 2 inferior houses, 2 acres, $200 valuation; 1 tract (204 acres) in Bush River Upper & Eden Hd., $459 valuation, 4 slaves. {Ref: TL}
DORAN, PATRICK, see "Margaret Doran," q.v.
DORAN, PATRICK, taxpayer, 1798, Deer Creek Upper Hd., 5 tracts (207 acres) and 1 building, $232.87 valuation, no slaves. {Ref: TL}. In another part of the tax schedule the occupant is listed as Edward Blaney.
DORAN, PATRICK, tract *The Castle of Desolation* surveyed in 1790 and granted in 1794. {Ref: CB}
DORAN, PATRICK, subpoenaed to the Grand Jury in August, 1797. {Ref: CC}
DORAN, PATRICK, mentioned in a survey deposition on Sep 26, 1799 and on Jan

21, 1800 as "stone set up in the southside of a marsh, a corner of David West, as told by Pat Doran." {Ref: JS}

DORMER, DEBORAH, m. John Deeran on Sep 18, 1798. {Ref: PR}

DORMER, ELIZABETH, bur. Oct 28, 1796. {Ref: PR}

DORNEY, WILLIAM WOODLAND, b. 1798, d. Dec 10, 1866, aged 68, bur. in Cokesbury Methodist Cemetery in Abingdon. {Ref: TI}

DORSEY, ANN, see "William Henry Dorsey," q.v.

DORSEY, ANN SOPHIA, dau. of Greenberry and Sophia, b. about the year 1780 and bapt. Oct 13, 1799. {Ref: PR}

DORSEY, CHARLOTTE, m. Richard Graves on May 31, 1798. {Ref: PR}

DORSEY, DOROTHY, see "Sarah Hudson," q.v.

DORSEY, EDWARD, see "Henry Dorsey," q.v.

DORSEY, FRISBY, served on a Petit Jury in August, 1800. {Ref: CM}

DORSEY, FRISBY, paid on Dec 30, 1793 for work on the road at Bush River Store. {Ref: AH}

DORSEY, FRISBY, taxpayer, 1798, Spesutia Lower Hd., 1 dwelling house, 6 inferior houses, 2 acres, $195 valuation; 8 tracts (432 acres, 40 perches) in Spesutia Lower Hd., $2479.80 valuation, 7 slaves. {Ref: TL}

DORSEY, FRISBY, had an account at Hall's Store in October, 1791. {Ref: WH}

DORSEY, FRISBY, insolvent on a list for the road tax for 1792, as returned for Robert Amoss, tax collector. {Ref: IL 13.12}

DORSEY, FRISBY, insolvent on a list for the road tax due for 1791 in Harford Upper, Harford Lower, and Spesutia Upper as returned by Robert Amos, Jr. on Sep 18, 1793 (his name was crossed off the list). {Ref: IL 31.18}

DORSEY, FRISBY, warden, 1799, St. George's Episcopal Church. {Ref: PR}

DORSEY, FRISBY, head of family in 1800 (2nd District). {Ref: CI}. Also see "William Henry Dorsey," q.v.

DORSEY, GREENBERRY, will probated Apr 9, 1798. {Ref: HW}. Also see "Ann Sophia Dorsey," q.v.

DORSEY, HENRY, licensed practicing attorney in March, 1795. {Ref: CC}

DORSEY, HENRY, taxpayer, 1798, Spesutia Upper Hd., 1 dwelling house, 4 inferior houses, 1 acre, $200 valuation; 1 tract (319 acres) in Spesutia Upper Hd., $1845 valuation, 6 slaves; taxpayer, 1798, 1 tract (170 acres) in Spesutia Upper Hd., $281.25 valuation, no slaves. {Ref: TL}

DORSEY, HENRY, head of family in 1800 (Belle Air). {Ref: CI}

DORSEY, HENRY (OF EDWARD), m. Elizabeth Smithson on Feb 5, 1794. {Ref: PR}

DORSEY, JAMES, see "Sarah Hudson," q.v.

DORSEY, JAMES H., head of family in 1800 (1st District). {Ref: CI}

DORSEY, JOHN H., taxpayer, 1798, Gunpowder Lower Hd., no dwelling house listed in this part of the tax schedule, 1 tract (150 acres), $506.25 valuation, 6 slaves. {Ref: TL}

DORSEY, JOHN H., head of family in 1800 (Abingdon). {Ref: CI}

DORSEY, JOSHUA, insolvent on list returned by Robert Carlile for taxes due for the year 1791. {Ref: IL 31.16}

DORSEY, MATHEW, head of family in 1800 (1st District). {Ref: CI}

DORSEY, MATTHEW, taxpayer, 1798, no dwelling house listed in this part of the tax schedule, no land listed, no Hd. listed (possibly Gunpowder Lower Hundred), 3 slaves. {Ref: TL}. Also see "James Lee Morgan," q.v.

DORSEY, MATTHEW, had an account at Hall's Store in November, 1791. {Ref: WH}

DORSEY, MATTHEW, insolvent on a list for the road tax due for 1791 in Harford Upper, Harford Lower, and Spesutia Upper as returned by Robert Amos, Jr. on Sep 18, 1793. {Ref: IL 31.18}

DORSEY, REASON, m. Frances Cromwell on Aug 10, 1797. {Ref: PR}

DORSEY, SOPHIA, see "Ann Sophia Dorsey," q.v.

DORSEY, WILLIAM HENRY, son of Frisby and Ann, b. Jul 1, 1799. {Ref: PR}

DOUGHERTY, CATRINE, head of family in 1800 (3rd District). {Ref: CI}

DOUGHERTY, JOHN, insolvent on list returned for the road tax due for 1791 by John Bull. {Ref: IL 31.14}

DOUGHERTY, JOHN, m. Ann Chauncey on Apr 3, 1800. {Ref: PR}

DOUGHERTY, JOHN, head of family in 1800 (2nd District). {Ref: CI}

DOUGHERTY, MICHAEL, see "Angus Graham," q.v.

DOUGHERTY, SAMUEL, head of family in 1800 (3rd District). {Ref: CI}

DOUGHROSE (DOUGHROWN?), JOHN, head of family in 1800 (5th District). {Ref: CI}

DOUGHTY, ANN, dau. of Thomas and Christina, b. May 12, 1792, bapt. Oct 17, 1800. {Ref: PR}

DOUGHTY, CHRISTINA, see "Thomas Doughty" and "Ann Doughty," q.v.

DOUGHTY, THOMAS, son of Thomas and Christina, b. Nov 8, 1781, bapt. Oct 17, 1800. {Ref: PR}. Also see "Ann Doughty," q.v.

DOUGLASS (DUGLESS), JAMES, head of family in 1800 (5th District). {Ref: CI}

DOUGLESS, DANIEL, see "John Taylor (of Charles)," q.v.

DOVE, MARTHA G., b. 1796, d. Feb 25, 1864, aged 68, bur. in a cemetery on Edgewood Arsenal's Aviation Field. {Ref: TI}

DOWNEY, JAMES, head of family in 1800 (1st District). {Ref: CI}

DOWNEY, JAMES, head of family in 1800 (3rd District). {Ref: CI}

DOWNEY, THOMAS, head of family in 1800 (1st District). {Ref: CI}

DOWNING, FRANCIS ("run"), insolvent on a list of the county tax due William Osborn, sheriff, for 1791, as returned by Edward Prigg on Sep 20, 1791. {Ref: IL 31.17}

DOWNING, WILLIAM, treated by Dr. Archer on Aug 25, 1791. {Ref: JA}

DOWNS, HENRY, see "Jesse Jarrett," q.v.

DOWNS, JAMES, insolvent, Harford Lower and Spesutia Lower Hundreds (listed as a single man), on a tax list returned by George Lyttle on Sep 21, 1791. {Ref: IL 31.20, 31.21}

DOWNS, JAMES, insolvent on a list for the road tax due for 1791 in Harford Upper, Harford Lower, and Spesutia Upper as returned by Robert Amos, Jr. on

Sep 18, 1793. {Ref: IL 31.18}
DOWNS, JAMES, head of family in 1800 (1st District). {Ref: CI}
DOYLE, ELIZABETH, m. William Chambers on Nov 7, 1799. {Ref: PR}
DRAPER (DRAPUE?), SIMON, head of family in 1800 (4th District). {Ref: CI}
DREGHORN, JOHN, see "Martha Luckey," q.v.
DREW, ANTHONY, will probated Jul 31, 1794. {Ref: HW}
DREW, GEORGE, insolvent on a list for the road tax due for 1791 in Harford Upper, Harford Lower, and Spesutia Upper as returned by Robert Amos, Jr. on Sep 18, 1793 (his name was crossed off the list). {Ref: IL 31.18}
DREW, GEORGE, insolvent, Harford Lower and Spesutia Lower Hundreds, on a tax list returned by George Lyttle on Sep 21, 1791. {Ref: IL 31.20, 31.21}
DREW, HENRY, insolvent on a list for the road tax due for 1791 in Harford Upper, Harford Lower, and Spesutia Upper as returned by Robert Amos, Jr. on Sep 18, 1793. {Ref: IL 31.18}
DREW, JAMES, insolvent on a list for the road tax due for 1791 in Harford Upper, Harford Lower, and Spesutia Upper as returned by Robert Amos, Jr. on Sep 18, 1793. {Ref: IL 31.18}
DREW, SARAH, had an account at Hall's Store in March, 1791. {Ref: WH}
DREW, SARAH, will probated Sep 6, 1791. {Ref: HW}
DUBNER(?), BENJAMIN, head of family in 1800 (5th District). {Ref: CI}
DUFF, THOMAS, head of family in 1800 (4th District). {Ref: CI}
DULANEY, DANIEL, had an account at Hall's Store in May, 1791. {Ref: WH}
DULANEY, ELIZABETH, m. Thomas Zara(?) on Feb 4, 1798. {Ref: PR}
DULANEY (DULEANEY), JOSHUA, insolvent on a list for the road tax due for 1791 in Harford Upper, Harford Lower, and Spesutia Upper as returned by Robert Amos, Jr. on Sep 18, 1793. {Ref: IL 31.18}. Also see "Benedict Edward Hall," q.v.
DULEY, JAMES, subpoenaed to the Grand Jury in August, 1797. {Ref: CC}
DULEY, JAMES, taxpayer, 1798, Gunpowder Lower Hd., 1 dwelling house, 4 inferior houses, 2 acres, $150 valuation; 1 tract (10 acres) in Gunpowder Lower Hd., $22.50 valuation, 4 slaves. {Ref: TL}. Also see "Negro Dick," q.v.
DULEY, JAMES, head of family in 1800 (1st District). {Ref: CI}
DULEY, WILLIAM, head of family in 1800 (Abingdon). {Ref: CI}
DUN, JOHN, insolvent on a list for the road tax due for 1791 in Harford Upper, Harford Lower, and Spesutia Upper as returned by Robert Amos, Jr. on Sep 18, 1793. {Ref: IL 31.18}
DUNAVIN, DANIEL, insolvent on a list for the road tax due for 1791 in Harford Upper, Harford Lower, and Spesutia Upper as returned by Robert Amos, Jr. on Sep 18, 1793. {Ref: IL 31.18}
DUNBARR, JAMS(?), insolvent on list returned by John Guyton (who listed him as a single man) for taxes due for the year 1791. {Ref: IL 31.19}
DUNCAN, ABEL, insolvent on a list for the road tax due for 1791 in Harford

Upper, Harford Lower, and Spesutia Upper as returned by Robert Amos, Jr. on Sep 18, 1793. {Ref: IL 31.18}

DUNCAN, GEORGE, m. Sarah Evans on Jun 15, 1797. {Ref: PR}

DUNCAN, PETER, insolvent on a list for the road tax due for 1791 in Harford Upper, Harford Lower, and Spesutia Upper as returned by Robert Amos, Jr. on Sep 18, 1793. {Ref: IL 31.18}

DUNGAN, ABLE, insolvent, Harford Lower and Spesutia Lower Hundreds, on a tax list returned by George Lyttle on Sep 21, 1791. {Ref: IL 31.20, 31.21}

DUNGAN, BENJAMIN, see "William Kearn," q.v.

DUNGAN, JESSE, charged for neglecting to keep a bridge over Winter's Run (not keeping his mill race bridge in repair) in 1797. {Ref: CD, March and August Terms, 1797}

DUNGAN, PETER, insolvent, Harford Lower and Spesutia Lower Hundreds (listed as a single man), on a tax list returned by George Lyttle on Sep 21, 1791. {Ref: IL 31.20, 31.21}. Also see "Elisha Tyson," q.v.

DUNGEN, JESSE, head of family in 1800 (1st District). {Ref: CI}

DUNGIN, BENJAMIN, head of family in 1800 (4th District). {Ref: CI}

DUNGIN, PETER, head of family in 1800 (3rd District). {Ref: CI}

DUNLAPP, JOSEPH, head of family in 1800 (4th District). {Ref: CI}

DUNN, DIGGINS, see "John Dunn," q.v.

DUNN, JOHN, insolvent, Harford Lower and Spesutia Lower Hundreds, on a tax list returned by George Lyttle on Sep 21, 1791. {Ref: IL 31.20, 31.21}

DUNN, JOHN, taxpayer, 1798, Spesutia Lower Hd., 1 dwelling house, 43 perches, 38 sq. ft., $118 valuation; 1 tract (225 sq. ft.) in Spesutia Lower Hd., $45 valuation, no slaves. {Ref: TL}

DUNN, JOHN, head of family in 1800 (3rd District). {Ref: CI}

DUNN (DWIN?), JOHN, head of family in 1800 (Havre de Grace). {Ref: CI}

DUNN, John (sadler), treated by Dr. Archer on Apr 28, 1794; also mentioned his son Diggins in 1788. {Ref: JA}

DUNN, MARY, m. Thomas Annis on Sep 7, 1797. {Ref: PR}

DUNNAVAN, D., see "William Judd," q.v.

DUNNIGAN, ANN, wife of Patrick, native of County West Meath, Ireland, b. 1795, d. Oct 19, 1865, aged 70, bur. in St. Ignatius Catholic Church Cemetery in Hickory. {Ref: TI}

DUNNIGAN, PATRICK, husband of Ann Dunnigan, native of County West Meath, Ireland, b. 1796, d. Dec 23, 1863, aged 67, bur. in St. Ignatius Catholic Church Cemetery in Hickory. {Ref: TI}

DUNNING, JOHN, m. Lydia Wilson on Nov 21, 1799. {Ref: PR}

DUNNING, JOHN, head of family in 1800 (Havre de Grace). {Ref: CI}

DUNNINGS, JAMES SKIDMORE, son of John and Lydia, b. Sep 18, 1800. {Ref: PR}

DUNNINGS, LYDIA, see "James Skidmore Dunnings," q.v.

DUNSHEAF, DAVID, insolvent on list returned by Robert Carlile for taxes due for the year 1791. {Ref: IL 31.16}

DUNSHEAF, WILLIAM, insolvent on list returned by Robert Carlile for taxes due for the year 1791. {Ref: IL 31.16}
DUNSHEATH, MARY, m. Jonas Stephenson on Oct 2, 1800. {Ref: PR}
DUNSHEATH, THOMAS, served on a Petit Jury in August, 1797. {Ref: CC}
DUPREY, FERDINAND, charged in 1794 (nature of the case not stated). {Ref: CD, March Term, 1795}. Also see "Joseph Gardener," q.v.
DURBAN, NANCY, see "Moses Taylor," q.v.
DURBIN, DANIEL, insolvent on a list for the road tax due for 1791 in Harford Upper, Harford Lower, and Spesutia Upper as returned by Robert Amos, Jr. on Sep 18, 1793. {Ref: IL 31.18}
DURBIN, FRANCINA, insolvent on list returned for the road tax due for 1791 by John Bull. {Ref: IL 31.14}
DURBIN, SINA (SINAH), will probated Oct 13, 1797. {Ref: HW}
DURBIN, THOMAS ("gone"), insolvent on lists due for 1790 and 1791 "fund taxes" in Deer Creek Lower and Susquehanna Hundreds, as returned by Thomas Taylor. {Ref: IL 31.12, 31.02}
DURHAM, ABEL A., husband of Sarah Devoe, b. Jun 4, 1791, d. Mar 5, 1875, in his 84th year. {Ref: Durham-Devoe Bible}
DURHAM, ANN, bur. Oct 17, 1797, aged about 57. {Ref: PR}
DURHAM, AQUILA (doctor), bur. Sep 4, 1797, aged about 25. {Ref: PR}
DURHAM, AQUILLA, insolvent on list returned for the road tax due for 1791 by John Bull. {Ref: IL 31.14}
DURHAM, CHARLOTTE, taxpayer, 1798, Bush River Lower Hd., no dwelling house listed in this part of the tax schedule, no land listed, 2 slaves. {Ref: TL}
DURHAM, DAVID, taxpayer, 1798, Bush River Upper & Eden Hd., 1 dwelling house, 2 inferior houses, 2 acres, $105 valuation; 3 tracts (134 acres) and 1 building in Bush River Upper & Eden Hd., $369 valuation, no slaves. {Ref: TL}
DURHAM, DAVID, served on a Grand Jury in August, 1798 and August, 1800, and on a Petit Jury in August, 1799. {Ref: CM}
DURHAM, DAVID, head of family in 1800 (4th District). {Ref: CI}
DURHAM, ELIGHA, head of family in 1800 (4th District). {Ref: CI}
DURHAM, ELIJAH, charged for assaulting Thomas Weir in 1794. {Ref: CD, March Term, 1795}
DURHAM, ELIZABETH, head of family in 1800 (1st District). {Ref: CI}
DURHAM, HANNAH ("runaway"), insolvent on a list for 1791 in Gunpowder Upper and Bush River Lower Hundreds, as filed by John Bond, Deputy Sheriff, on Sep 20, 1791. {Ref: IL 31.24}
DURHAM, JOHN, insolvent on list returned for the road tax due for 1791 by John Bull. {Ref: IL 31.14}
DURHAM, JOHN, taxpayer, 1798, Gunpowder Lower Hd., 1 dwelling house, 3 inferior houses, 2 acres, $200 valuation; 2 tracts (246 acres) in Gunpowder Lower Hd., $1107 valuation, 5 slaves. {Ref: TL}
DURHAM, JOHN (OF JOSHUA), insolvent on a list for 1791 in Gunpowder

Upper and Bush River Lower Hundreds, as filed by John Bond, Deputy Sheriff, on Sep 20, 1791 (who listed him as a single man). {Ref: IL 31.24}

DURHAM, JOSHUA, see "John Durham," q.v.

DURHAM, LEE, or HUGH YOUNG, taxpayer, 1798, Bush River Lower Hd., 1 tract (100 acres) and 1 building (Hugh Young, occupant), $765 valuation, no slaves. {Ref: TL}

DURHAM, LLOYD, served on a Petit Jury in August, 1797. {Ref: CC}

DURHAM, LLOYD (LOYD), taxpayer, 1798, Bush River Lower Hd., 1 dwelling house, 2 inferior houses, 1 acre, $240 valuation; 2 tracts (148 acres, 80 perches) in Bush River Lower Hd., $591.19 valuation, no slaves; taxpayer, 1798, 1 dwelling house, 2 inferior houses, 80 perches of land in Bush River Lower Hd., $150 valuation, no slaves. {Ref: TL}. Also see "Thomas Durham," q.v.

DURHAM, SAMUEL (OF SAMUEL), treated by Dr. Archer on Sep 20, 1791. {Ref: JA}

DURHAM, SARAH (neé Devoe), wife of Abel, b. 1796, d. Mar 11, 1866, in her 70th year. {Ref: Durham-Devoe Bible}. Also see "Sarah Devoe," q.v.

DURHAM, THOMAS, m. Rachel Shoudy on Mar 15 or 20, 1791. {Ref: PR}

DURHAM, THOMAS, bur. Feb 13, 1794, aged 66. {Ref: PR}

DURHAM, THOMAS, appeared on list of "recognizances" of the court with Lloyd Durham for his appearance in 1797. {Ref: CD, August Term, 1797}

DURHAM, THOMAS, taxpayer, 1798, Bush River Lower Hd., 1 dwelling house, 4 inferior houses, 1 acre and 80 perches, $180 valuation; 3 tracts (358 acres) in Bush River Lower Hd., $1253.25 valuation, 4 slaves; and, 1 dwelling house, 1 inferior house, 80 perches of land in Bush River Lower Hd., $100.50 valuation, no slaves. {Ref: TL}

DURHAM, THOMAS, head of family in 1800 (1st District). {Ref: CI}

DURHAM, WILLIAM, insolvent on list returned by Robert Carlile for taxes due for the year 1791. {Ref: IL 31.16}. Also see "Mrs. Wilmons," q.v.

DURHAM, WILLIAM, head of family in 1800 (1st District). {Ref: CI}

DURHAM, ZAC., insolvent on a list for the road tax due for 1791 in Harford Upper, Harford Lower, and Spesutia Upper as returned by Robert Amos, Jr. on Sep 18, 1793 (his name was crossed off the list). {Ref: IL 31.18}

DURHAM, ZACARIAH, insolvent, Harford Lower and Spesutia Lower Hundreds (listed as a single man), on a tax list returned by George Lyttle on Sep 21, 1791. {Ref: IL 31.20, 31.21}

DURHAM, ZACHARIA, head of family in 1800 (1st District). {Ref: CI}

DURHAM, ZACHARIAS, m. Lucia Husband on Mar 11, 1792. {Ref: PR}

DUSANS, PETER, insolvent, Harford Lower and Spesutia Lower Hundreds (listed as a single man), on a tax list returned by George Lyttle on Sep 21, 1791. {Ref: IL 31.20, 31.21}

DUTTMAN, JOHN, head of family in 1800 (1st District). {Ref: CI}

DUTTON, JOHN, taxpayer, 1798, Gunpowder Upper Hd., 1 tract (93 acres) and 1 building, $246.94 valuation, no slaves. {Ref: TL}

DUTTON, JOHN, m. Amelia Carman on Jun 26, 1800. {Ref: PR}

DUTTON, JOHN, head of family in 1800 (Havre de Grace). {Ref: CI}
DUTTON, MARY, see "James Armitage," q.v.
DUTTON, MARY, taxpayer, 1798, no dwelling house listed in this part of the tax schedule, no land listed, no Hd. listed (possibly Gunpowder Upper Hundred), 3 slaves. {Ref: TL}
DUTTON, MARY, head of family in 1800 (2nd District). {Ref: CI}
DUTTON, ROBERT, on "a list of insolvents it being for personal property for the road taxs [sic] for 1791" filed by Robert Amoss, tax collector. {Ref: IL 31.12}
DUZAN, ALEXANDER, treated by Dr. Archer on Jul 1, 1791; also mentioned he had moved to Kentucky and his brother John paid his bill in 1793. {Ref: JA}. Also see "John Duzan," q.v.
DUZAN, ALEXANDER, insolvent on a list for the county tax due for 1793 in Harford Upper, Harford Lower, and Spesutia Lower Hundreds returned to the levy court by Thomas Taylor on May 28, 1794. {Ref: IL 31.12}
DUZAN, ALEXANDER, insolvent on a list for the road tax due for 1791 in Harford Upper, Harford Lower, and Spesutia Upper as returned by Robert Amos, Jr. on Sep 18, 1793. {Ref: IL 31.18}
DUZAN, ISAAC, insolvent on a list for the road tax due for 1791 in Harford Upper, Harford Lower, and Spesutia Upper as returned by Robert Amos, Jr. on Sep 18, 1793. {Ref: IL 31.18}
DUZAN, ISAAC, head of family in 1800 (2nd District). {Ref: CI}
DUZAN, JACOB, insolvent on a list for the road tax due for 1791 in Harford Upper, Harford Lower, and Spesutia Upper as returned by Robert Amos, Jr. on Sep 18, 1793. {Ref: IL 31.18}
DUZAN, JOHN, treated by Dr. Archer on May 1, 1791; also mentioned he paid his bill and his brother Alexander's bill in 1793 and moved to Kentucky. {Ref: JA}. Also see "Alexander Duzan," q.v.
DUZAN, PETER, insolvent on a list for the road tax due for 1791 in Harford Upper, Harford Lower, and Spesutia Upper as returned by Robert Amos, Jr. on Sep 18, 1793. {Ref: IL 31.18}
DUZEN, ABRAHAM, insolvent on a list for the road tax due for 1791 in Harford Upper, Harford Lower, and Spesutia Upper as returned by Robert Amos, Jr. on Sep 18, 1793. {Ref: IL 31.18}
DWIN, JOHN, see "John Dunn," q.v.
DYER, JOSEPH (carpenter), will probated Sep 25, 1793. {Ref: HW}
EADY, JAMES, see "James Ady," q.v.
EAGANS, JAMES, treated by Dr. Archer on Aug 13, 1791; also mentioned he was in York County at that time. {Ref: JA}
EAKIN, WILLIAM ("run"), insolvent on a list of the county tax due William Osborn, sheriff, for 1791, as returned by Edward Prigg on Sep 20, 1791. {Ref: IL 31.17}
EASTON, GEORGE, charged for selling liquors as innkeeper in 1793. {Ref: CD, March and August Terms, 1795}

103

EATON, JOHN, head of family in 1800 (4th District). {Ref: CI}
EDEN, JEREMIAH, charged for assaulting William Hollis in 1795. {Ref: CD, March and August Terms, 1795 and 1797}
EDEN, WILLIAM, insolvent on list returned for the road tax due for 1791 by John Bull. {Ref: IL 31.14}
EDEN, WILLIAM (farmer), will probated Aug 19, 1793. {Ref: HW}
EDWARDS, ELIZABETH, see "Jarrett Edwards," q.v.
EDWARDS, JARRETT, son of Thomas and Elizabeth, b. Feb 21, 1797, bapt. Jun 20, 1797. {Ref: PR}
EDWARDS, SIKEY, head of family in 1800 (2nd District). {Ref: CI}
EDWARDS, THOMAS, see "Peter Hoofman (Hoopman)" and "Jarrett Edwards," q.v.
EDWARDS, THOMAS, insolvent on a list for 1791 in Gunpowder Upper and Bush River Lower Hundreds, as filed by John Bond, Deputy Sheriff, on Sep 20, 1791. {Ref: IL 31.24}
EDWARDS, THOMAS, head of family in 1800 (2nd District). {Ref: CI}
EICHELBERGER, WILLIAM, b. 1791, d. Aug 11, 1854, aged 63, bur. in St. Ignatius Catholic Church Cemetery in Hickory. {Ref: TI}
ELIOTT, ANN, insolvent on list returned by Robert Carlile for taxes due for the year 1791. {Ref: IL 31.16}
ELIOTT, JOHN, insolvent on list returned by Robert Carlile for taxes due for the year 1791. {Ref: IL 31.16}
ELLENDER, ELIZABETH, dau. of George and Sarah, b. Jul 9, 1798. {Ref: PR}
ELLENDER, GEORGE, see "Joshua Ellender" and "Nicholas Grimes Ellender" and "Elizabeth Ellender," q.v.
ELLENDER, JOSHUA, aged about 18 months, and SOLOMON ELLENDER, aged about 2 months, bur. Jun 7, 1797. {Ref: PR}. One register listed the names as "Joshua Ellinor" and "Solomon Ellinor."
ELLENDER, JOSHUA, son of George and Sarah, b. Apr 26, 1795. {Ref: PR}
ELLENDER, NICHOLAS GRIMES ("Nicky Ellinder"), son of George and Sarah, b. Apr 20, 1793. {Ref: PR}
ELLENDER, SARAH, see "Joshua Ellender" and "Nicholas Grimes Ellender" and "Elizabeth Ellender," q.v.
ELLENDER, SOLOMON, see "Joshua Ellender," q.v.
ELLENDER, WILLIAM, head of family in 1800 (1st District). {Ref: CI}
ELLETT, ROBERT, head of family in 1800 (3rd District). {Ref: CI}
ELLINDER, NICKY, see "Nicholas Grimes Ellender," q.v.
ELLINOR, JOSHUA, see "Joshua Ellender," q.v.
ELLIOT, MRS. (widow), treated by Dr. Archer on Jun 8, 1795; also mentioned she lived above Trap. {Ref: JA}
ELLIOT, SAMUEL, treated by Dr. Archer on Jan 7, 1791; also mentioned he lived near James Clendennon. {Ref: JA}
ELLIOTT, KAREN, insolvent on lists in 1791 due county taxes and road taxes in

"Deer Creek Upper, Middle, and Broad Creek Hundreds" as returned by Robert Amos, Jr. {Ref: IL 31.12, 31.22}

ELLIOTT, KERIN, taxpayer, 1798, Deer Creek Middle Hd., 1 tract (32 acres, 80 perches) and 1 building, $95.62 valuation, no slaves. {Ref: TL}

ELLIS, ANN, see "Elizabeth Ellis," q.v.

ELLIS, ELIZABETH, dau. of Henry and Ann, b. May 7, 1784, bapt. Jun 6, 1797. {Ref: PR}

ELLIS, HENRY, head of family in 1800 (5th District). {Ref: CI}. Also see "Elizabeth Ellis" and "John Barclay," q.v.

ELLIS, JOHN, taxpayer, 1798, Harford Upper Hd., 1 tract (250 acres) and 1 building, $652.50 valuation, 1 slave. {Ref: TL}

ELLIS, JOHN JR., see "Joseph, William, and John Barnes," q.v.

ELLIS, WILLIAM, or WILLIAM COALE, taxpayer, 1798, 1 tract (44 perches, 21 sq. ft.) in Spesutia Lower Hd. (William Coale, occupant), $111.38, no slaves. {Ref: TL}

ELLISS, JOHN, head of family in 1800 (1st District). {Ref: CI}

ELLITT, EDWARD, tract *Ellitt's Discovery* surveyed between 1792 and 1796. {Ref: SB}

ELLITT, WILLIAM, head of family in 1800 (5th District). {Ref: CI}

ELLOT, DANIEL, son of Thomas and Susan, b. Jul 15, 1793, bapt. Jun 29, 1797. {Ref: PR}

ELLOT, GEORGE, son of Thomas and Susan, b. Mar 17, 1795, bapt. Jun 29, 1797. {Ref: PR}

ELLOT, SUSAN, see "Daniel Ellot" and "George Ellot," q.v.

ELLOT, THOMAS, see "Daniel Ellot" and "George Ellot," q.v.

ELLOT, WILLIAM, head of family in 1800 (5th District). {Ref: CI}

ELY, ANN H. W., b. Jun 26, 1799, d. Mar 26, 1848, aged 48 years and 9 months, bur. in Deer Creek Friends Cemetery in Darlington. {Ref: TI}

ELY, HUGH, taxpayer, 1798, Deer Creek Lower Hd., 1 dwelling house, 2 inferior houses, 2 acres, $160 valuation; 2 tracts (156 acres, 80 perches) and 1 building in Deer Creek Lower Hd., $331.59 valuation, no slaves. {Ref: TL}. In another part of the tax schedule the occupant is listed as Thomas Trego.

ELY, HUGH, will probated Oct 29, 1799. {Ref: HW}

ELY, ISAAC J., b. Aug 25, 1792, d. Jun 6, 1849, bur. in Deer Creek Friends Cemetery in Darlington. {Ref: TI}. Also see "Sarah Ely," q.v.

ELY, JOHN, had an account at Hall's Store in January, 1791. {Ref: WH}

ELY, JOHN, head of family in 1800 (1st District). {Ref: CI}

ELY, JOSEPH, taxpayer, 1798, Deer Creek Lower Hd., 1 tract (89 acres) and 1 building, $240.19 valuation, no slaves. {Ref: TL}

ELY, MAHLON, taxpayer, 1798, Broad Creek Hd., 2 tracts (100 acres) and 1 building, $185.63 valuation, no slaves. {Ref: TL}. In another part of the tax schedule the occupant is listed as Samuel Scarborough.

ELY, SARAH, wife of Isaac, b. Jun 9, 1794, d. Jun 24, 1879, bur. in Deer Creek Friends Cemetery in Darlington. {Ref: TI}

ELY, SARAH, head of family in 1800 (5th District). {Ref: CI}

ELY, THOMAS, taxpayer, 1798, Gunpowder Upper Hd., 1 dwelling house, 5 inferior houses, 2 acres, $230 valuation; 4 tracts (173 acres) in Gunpowder Upper Hd., $583.87 valuation, no slaves. {Ref: TL}

ELY, THOMAS, head of family in 1800 (3rd District). {Ref: CI}

ELY, WILLIAM, taxpayer, 1798, Deer Creek Lower Hd., 1 dwelling house, 2 inferior houses, 2 acres, $101 valuation; 1 tract (100 acres) in Deer Creek Lower Hd., $168.75 valuation, no slaves. {Ref: TL}

ELY, WILLIAM, b. Jan 4, 1799, d. Nov 7, 1852, aged 53 years, 10 months, and 3 days, bur. in Deer Creek Friends Cemetery in Darlington. {Ref: TI}

ELY, WILLIAM, head of family in 1800 (5th District). {Ref: CI}

ENGLAND, ANN, b. 1800, d. Mar 7, 1867, aged 67, bur. in Forest Hill Quaker Cemetery. {Ref: TI}

ENGLAND, CATHARINE, charged for retailing liquors in 1794. {Ref: CD, March and August Terms, 1795}

ENGLAND, GEORGE, taxpayer, 1798, Eden Hd., 1 dwelling house, 3 inferior houses, 2 acres, $150 valuation; 4 tracts (301 acres) in Eden Hd., $622.69 valuation, no slaves. {Ref: TL}

ENGLAND, GEORGE, head of family in 1800 (4th District). {Ref: CI}

ENGLE, HANNAH S., b. Dec 28(?), 1799, d. Apr 8(?), 1885, aged 85 years, 3 months, and 10 days, bur. in Ebenezer Methodist Church Cemetery north of Rutledge. {Ref: TI}

ENGRIM, JOHN, see "John Ingram," q.v.

ENIS, JOHN, insolvent on a list of the county tax due William Osborn, sheriff, for 1791, as returned by Edward Prigg on Sep 20, 1791. {Ref: IL 31.17}

ENLOW, HENRY, mentioned in a survey deposition on Jan 28, 1800 as "to the house where Henry Enlow now lives." {Ref: JS}

ENLOWS, JAMES, taxpayer, 1798, Gunpowder Upper Hd., 1 dwelling house, 3 inferior houses, 2 acres, $150 valuation; 2 tracts (263 acres) in Gunpowder Upper Hd., $591.75 valuation, 1 slave. {Ref: TL}

ENLOWS, JAMES JR., b. 1797, d. Mar 13, 1844, aged 47, bur. in the Enlows Family Graveyard (no longer in existence) near Friendship M. E. Church in Fallston. {Ref: TI}

ENLOWS, TEMPERANCE, b. 1795, d. Jul 12, 1853, aged 58, bur. in the Enlows Family Graveyard (no longer in existence) near Friendship M. E. Church in Fallston. {Ref: TI}

ENOS, JOHN, insolvent on lists in 1791 due county taxes and road taxes in "Deer Creek Upper, Middle, and Broad Creek Hundreds" as returned by Robert Amos, Jr. {Ref: IL 31.12, 31.22}

ENOS, JOHN, insolvent on a list in 1792 in Broad Creek Hd., as returned by Benjamin Preston. {Ref: IL 31.03}

ENSOR, WILLIAM, insolvent on a list for the road tax due for 1791 in Harford Upper, Harford Lower, and Spesutia Upper as returned by Robert Amos, Jr. on

Sep 18, 1793. {Ref: IL 31.18}

ERGOOD, ANNA, wife of Jacob, b. 1793, d. Jul 13, 1863, aged 70, bur. in St. George's Episcopal Church Cemetery at Perryman. {Ref: TI}

ERGOOD, JACOB, b. 1797, d. May 28, 1852, aged 55, bur. in St. George's Episcopal Church Cemetery at Perryman. {Ref: TI}

ERVIN, FRANCIS, head of family in 1800 (4th District). {Ref: CI}

ERVIN (EWIN?), JOSEPH, insolvent on list returned for the road tax due for 1791 by John Bull. {Ref: IL 31.14}

ERVIN, JAMES, insolvent on list returned by Robert Carlile for taxes due for the year 1791. {Ref: IL 31.16}

ERVIN, JAMES, head of family in 1800 (4th District). {Ref: CI}

ERVIN, JOHN, insolvent on lists in 1791 due county taxes and road taxes in "Deer Creek Upper, Middle, and Broad Creek Hundreds" as returned by Robert Amos, Jr. {Ref: IL 31.12, 31.22}

ERVIN, JOHN, head of family in 1800 (2nd District). {Ref: CI}

ERVIN, WILLIAM, head of family in 1800 (4th District). {Ref: CI}

ERWIN, JAMES ("run"), insolvent on a list of the county tax due William Osborn, sheriff, for 1791, as returned by Edward Prigg on Sep 20, 1791. {Ref: IL 31.17}

ERWIN, JAMES, insolvent on a list in 1792 in Broad Creek Hd., as returned by Benjamin Preston. {Ref: IL 31.03}

EVANS, AMOS, see "Elinor Evans" and "Margaret Evans," q.v.

EVANS, AMOS, son of Amos and Sarah, b. Dec 17, 1800. {Ref: St. John's & St. George's Parish Registers, and Jones-Evans Bible}

EVANS, AMOS ("gone" and "can't be found"), insolvent on lists due for 1790 and 1791 "fund taxes" and county taxes in Susquehanna Hd., as returned by Thomas Taylor. {Ref: IL 31.12, 31.02}

EVANS, AMOSS, head of family in 1800 (3rd District). {Ref: CI}

EVANS, CHARLES, b. 1793, d. May 22, 1868, in his 71st year, bur. in Ebenezer Methodist Church Cemetery north of Rutledge. {Ref: TI}

EVANS, ELINOR, dau. of Amos and Sarah, b. May 17, 1792. {Ref: PR}

EVANS, EVAN, see "Henrietta Wheeler," q.v.

EVANS, EVAN, will probated Sep 27, 1791. {Ref: HW}

EVANS (EVENS), EVAN, head of family in 1800 (5th District). {Ref: CI}.

EVANS, JANE, wife of John, b. Jan 25, 1793, d. Mar 23, 1876, bur. in Wesleyan Chapel Methodist Church Cemetery near Aberdeen. {Ref: TI}

EVANS, JOHN, see "Jane Evans" and "James Webster," q.v.

EVANS, JOHN, insolvent on list returned for the road tax due for 1791 by John Bull. {Ref: IL 31.14}.

EVANS, JOHN (cabinetmaker), had an account at Hall's Store in April, 1791. {Ref: WH}

EVANS, JOHN (joiner), will probated Oct 27, 1791. {Ref: HW}

EVANS, MARGARET, dau. of Amos and Sarah, b. Jun 15, 1798. {Ref: PR}

EVANS, RACHEL, b. 1794, d. Mar 10, 1865, in her 71st year, bur. in Ebenezer

Methodist Church Cemetery north of Rutledge. {Ref: TI}
EVANS, SARAH, m. George Duncan on Jun 15, 1797. {Ref: PR}. Also see "Elinor Evans" and "Margaret Evans" and "Amos Evans," q.v.
EVATT, JOHN, taxpayer, 1798, Broad Creek Hd., 1 tract (100 acres) and 1 building (Joseph Carlin, occupant), $168.75 valuation, no slaves; also, taxpayer, Deer Creek Middle Hd., 1 dwelling house, 3 inferior houses, 2 acres, $160 valuation; 1 tract (100 acres) in Deer Creek Middle Hd. (Joseph Carlin, occupant), $150 valuation, no slaves. {Ref: TL}
EVATT (EVAT), MARGARET, taxpayer, 1798, Susquehanna Hd., no dwelling house listed in this part of the tax schedule, no land listed, 1 slave. {Ref: TL}. Also see "Gideon Dennison," q.v.
EVATT, WILLIAM, will probated Mar 20, 1794. {Ref: HW}. Also see "Adlum & Hughes," q.v.
EVENS, WILLIAM, head of family in 1800 (2nd District). {Ref: CI}
EVEREST, BENJAMIN, taxpayer, 1798, Susquehanna Hd., 2 tracts (200 acres) and 2 buildings (Solomon Armstrong, occupant of one of them), $603.74 valuation, 1 slave. {Ref: TL}
EVEREST, HENRY'S HEIRS, taxpayers, 1798, Spesutia Lower Hd., 1 tract (79 acres), $444.37 valuation, no slaves. {Ref: TL}. In another part of the tax schedule the occupant is listed as Jacob Greenfield.
EVEREST, ISAAC, taxpayer, 1798, Gunpowder Upper Hd., 1 tract (70 acres) and 1 building, $281.25 valuation, no slaves. {Ref: TL}
EVEREST, JAMES, taxpayer, 1798, Gunpowder Upper Hd., 1 tract (20 acres) and 1 building, $45 valuation, no slaves. {Ref: TL}. Also see "James Phillips, Sr.," q.v.
EVEREST, JAMES, had an account at Hall's Store in January, 1791. {Ref: WH}
EVEREST, JOSEPH, taxpayer, 1798, Gunpowder Lower Hd., 1 tract (70 acres), $236.25 valuation, 3 slaves. {Ref: TL}. Also see "Elizabeth Maxwell," q.v.
EVEREST, JOSEPH (OF JOSEPH), treated by Dr. Archer on Nov 12, 1796; also mentioned his wife and infant child (no names given). {Ref: JA}
EVEREST, MARY, taxpayer, 1798, Spesutia Lower Hd., 1 dwelling house, 4 inferior houses, 2 acres, $600 valuation; 1 tract (302 acres) in Spesutia Lower Hd., $1208.25 valuation, 4 slaves. {Ref: TL}
EVEREST, RICHARD, had an account at Hall's Store in January, 1791. {Ref: WH}
EVERETT, ANN, bur. Apr 9, 1796. {Ref: PR}
EVERETT, BENJAMIN, head of family in 1800 (2nd District). {Ref: CI}
EVERETT, CHARLOTTE, b. 1798, d. 1859, bur. in Mountain Christian Church Cemetery. {Ref: TI}
EVERETT, CLARA, see "Elizabeth Everett," q.v.
EVERETT (EVERTT), ELIZABETH, dau. of Joseph and Clara, b. Dec 21, 1800. {Ref: PR}
EVERETT, HENRY AUSTIN, bur. Jun 2, 1799. {Ref: PR}
EVERETT, ISAAC, insolvent on list returned by Robert Carlile for taxes due for the year 1791. {Ref: IL 31 16}

EVERETT, ISAAC, head of family in 1800 (3rd District). {Ref: CI}
EVERETT, JAMES, insolvent on list returned by Robert Carlile for taxes due for the year 1791. {Ref: IL 31.16}
EVERETT, JAMES, insolvent on lists in 1791 due county taxes and road taxes in "Deer Creek Upper, Middle, and Broad Creek Hundreds" as returned by Robert Amos, Jr., but his name was then crossed off both lists. {Ref: IL 31.12, 31.22}
EVERETT, JAMES, head of family in 1800 (1st District). {Ref: CI}
EVERETT, JAMES, head of family in 1800 (2nd District). {Ref: CI}
EVERETT, JOHN, head of family in 1800 (1st District). {Ref: CI}
EVERETT, JOHN, head of family in 1800 (3rd District). {Ref: CI}
EVERETT, JOHN, head of family in 1800 (4th District). {Ref: CI}
EVERETT, JOSEPH, head of family in 1800 (2nd District). {Ref: CI}. Also see "Elizabeth Everett," q.v.
EVERETT, MARGARET, m. Isaac Whitaker on Feb 11, 1798. {Ref: PR}
EVERETT, MARY, m. Jacob Michael on Nov 12, 1795. {Ref: PR}
EVERETT, MARY, head of family in 1800 (2nd District). {Ref: CI}
EVERETT, NATHAN, head of family in 1800 (1st District). {Ref: CI}
EVERETT, NATHAN, head of family in 1800 (3rd District). {Ref: CI}
EVERETT, SAMUEL, insolvent on list returned by Robert Carlile for taxes due for the year 1791. {Ref: IL 31.16}
EVERETT, SAMUEL, head of family in 1800 (3rd District). {Ref: CI}
EVERUY(?), JOHN, head of family in 1800 (5th District). {Ref: CI}
EVERIST, JOHN, insolvent on a list for the road tax due for 1791 in Harford Upper, Harford Lower, and Spesutia Upper as returned by Robert Amos, Jr. on Sep 18, 1793. {Ref: IL 31.18}
EVERIST, JOSEPH, treated by Dr. Archer on Sep 16, 1793; also mentioned his wife (no name given) in 1791, and Jacob Greenfield (no relationship stated) in November, 1799. {Ref: JA}
EVERIST, JOSEPH, had an account at Hall's Store in June, 1791. {Ref: WH}
EVERITT, JAMES ("poor"), insolvent on a list of the county tax due William Osborn, sheriff, for 1791, as returned by Edward Prigg on Sep 20, 1791. {Ref: IL 31.17}
EVERITT, THOMAS ("can't be found"), insolvent on lists due for 1790 and 1791 "fund taxes" and county taxes in Susquehanna Hd., as returned by Thomas Taylor. {Ref: IL 31.12, 31.02}
EVERITT, WILLIAM, m. Sarah Cooper on Mar 29, 1795. {Ref: PR}
EVETT, ELIZABETH, m. Andrew Martin on Jul 24, 1799. {Ref: PR}
EVETT, JOHN, licensed retailer in March, 1795 and August, 1797. {Ref: CC}
EVETT, JOHN, head of family in 1800 (5th District). {Ref: CI}
EVETT, MARGARITE, head of family in 1800 (2nd District). {Ref: CI}
EVETT, RICHARD (Baltimore County), insolvent on a list for the road tax due for 1791 in Harford Upper, Harford Lower, and Spesutia Upper as returned by Robert Amos, Jr. on Sep 18, 1793. {Ref: IL 31.18}

EVETT, WILLIAM, head of family in 1800 (2nd District). {Ref: CI}
EVINS, JOHN, insolvent on a list for 1791 in Gunpowder Upper and Bush River Lower Hundreds, as filed by John Bond, Deputy Sheriff, on Sep 20, 1791 (who listed him as a single man). {Ref: IL 31.24}
EVIT, WILLIAM, treated by Dr. Archer on Aug 8, 1792. {Ref: JA}
EWING, JAMES, insolvent on lists of taxes due in 1791 and 1792 in Broad Creek Hd., as returned by Robert Amos, Jr. in 1791 and Benjamin Preston in 1792. {Ref: IL 31.03, 31.12, 31.22}
EWING, JAMES ("run"), insolvent on a list of the county tax due William Osborn, sheriff, for 1791, as returned by Edward Prigg on Sep 20, 1791. {Ref: IL 31.17}
EWING, JOHN, insolvent on a list for 1791 in Gunpowder Upper and Bush River Lower Hundreds, as filed by John Bond, Deputy Sheriff, on Sep 20, 1791 (who listed him as a single man). {Ref: IL 31.24}
EWING, JOHN, taxpayer, 1798, Susquehanna Hd., 1 tract (100 acres) and 1 building, $295.49 valuation, 1 slave. {Ref: TL}
EWING, JOHN, head of family in 1800 (2nd District). {Ref: CI}
EWING, JOSEPH, taxpayer, 1798, Susquehanna Hd., 1 tract (40 acres) and 1 building, $174.38 valuation, no slaves. {Ref: TL}
EWING, JOSEPH, head of family in 1800 (2nd District). {Ref: CI}
EWING, ROBERT ("gone"), insolvent on lists due for 1790 and 1791 "fund taxes" and county taxes in Susquehanna Hd., as returned by Thomas Taylor. {Ref: IL 31.12, 31.02}
EWING, WILLIAM, b. Nov 18, 1795, d. Sep 18, 1871, aged 75 years and 10 months. {Ref: William Ewing Bible}
FAPLIN(?), ANDREW, head of family in 1800 (5th District). {Ref: CI}
FARCHER, DOCTOR, consulted with Dr. Archer in 1792. {Ref: JA}
FARMER, JOHN, son of William and Sarah, b. Nov 22, 1796, bapt. Jun 6, 1797. {Ref: PR}
FARMER, SARAH, see "John Farmer," q.v.
FARMER, WILLIAM, see "John Farmer," q.v.
FASSETT, HENRY, head of family in 1800 (4th District). {Ref: CI}
FAWCET, ELIZABETH, m. William Lester on Nov 19, 1799. {Ref: PR}
FENDLEY, JOHN, see "John Finley," q.v.
FERGUSON, JOHN, b. 1794, d. 1887, bur. in Darlington Cemetery. {Ref: TI}
FERRIE, MONTPHELIER, see "Negro Guy," q.v.
FERRIE, PYRE, see "Negro Guy," q.v.
FIELDS, BILL, see "Sarah Fields," q.v.
FIELDS, SARAH, had an account at Hall's Store in January, 1791, which mentioned her son Bill. {Ref: WH}
FIFE, JOSEPH, head of family in 1800 (5th District). {Ref: CI}
FINDLEY, JAMES, taxpayer, 1798, Bush River Upper & Eden Hd., 1 dwelling house, 2 inferior houses, 2 acres, $250 valuation; 1 tract (162 acres, 120 perches) in Bush River Upper & Eden Hd., $274.50 valuation, no slaves. {Ref: TL}

FINDLEY, JAMES, head of family in 1800 (4th District). {Ref: CI}
FINLEY, JOHN, insolvent on lists returned by Robert Carlile and John Guyton (the latter spelled the name as "John Fendley") for taxes due for the year 1791. {Ref: IL 31.16, 31.19}
FINLEY (FENDLEY), ROBERT, insolvent on lists returned by Robert Carlile and John Guyton (who listed him as a single man) for taxes due for the year 1791. {Ref: IL 31.16, 31.19}
FINNAGAN, HENRY PATRICK, m. Aranea Slemaker on Apr 26, 1792. {Ref: PR}
FINNAGAN, PATRICK, insolvent on a list for 1791 in Gunpowder Upper and Bush River Lower Hundreds, as filed by John Bond, Deputy Sheriff, on Sep 20, 1791. {Ref: IL 31.24}
FINNICUM, BENJAMIN, head of family in 1800 (1st District). {Ref: CI}
FIPPS, JOHN, head of family in 1800 (4th District). {Ref: CI}
FISHER, JAMES, treated by Dr. Archer on Aug 8, 1791. {Ref: JA}
FISHER, JAMES, head of family in 1800 (2nd District). {Ref: CI}
FISHER, JAMES, head of family in 1800 (5th District). {Ref: CI}
FISHER, JAMES, or THOMAS FISHER, taxpayer, 1798, Deer Creek Lower Hd., 1 dwelling house, 2 inferior houses, 2 acres, $101 valuation; 1 tract (218 acres) and 1 building in Deer Creek Lower Hd. (Thomas Fisher, occupant), $413.44 valuation, 3 slaves. {Ref: TL}
FISHER, MARY, insolvent on lists of taxes due in 1791 and 1792 in Broad Creek Hd., as returned by Robert Amos, Jr. in 1791 and Benjamin Preston in 1792. {Ref: IL 31.03, 31.12, 31.22}
FISHER, MARY ("run"), insolvent on a list of the county tax due William Osborn, sheriff, for 1791, as returned by Edward Prigg on Sep 20, 1791. {Ref: IL 31.17}
FISHER, THOMAS, see "James Fisher," q.v.
FISHER, THOMAS, insolvent on a list for the road tax due for 1791 in Deer Creek Lower Hd., but his name was crossed off the list. {Ref: IL 31.12}
FISHER, THOMAS, served as constable in Deer Creek Lower Hd., 1797. {Ref: CC, CM}
FISHER, THOMAS, head of family in 1800 (5th District). {Ref: CI}
FITZGERALD, JAMES, tract *Fitzgerald's Fishery* surveyed in 1798. {Ref: CB}
FITZGERALD, JOHN, will probated Apr 29, 1791. {Ref: HW}
FITZGERALD, SIMON, head of family in 1800 (Belle Air). {Ref: CI}. Also see "John Paul," q.v.
FITZPARTRICK, MICHAEL, insolvent, Harford Lower and Spesutia Lower Hundreds (listed as a single man), on a tax list returned by George Lyttle on Sep 21, 1791. {Ref: IL 31.20, 31.21}
FITZPATRICK, MICHAEL, insolvent on a list for the road tax due for 1791 in Harford Upper, Harford Lower, and Spesutia Upper as returned by Robert Amos, Jr. on Sep 18, 1793. {Ref: IL 31.18}
FLANAGAN, ACHSAH HOLLIDAY, dau. of Edward and Elizabeth, b. Jul 22 or 23, 1792, twin of John Holliday Flanagan. {Ref: PR}
FLANAGAN, CAROL, see "Edward Flanagan," q.v.

FLANAGAN, EDWARD, treated by Dr. Archer on Jul 30, 1792; also mentioned his dau. Sophia in 1787 and his dau. Carol in 1789. {Ref: JA}. Also see "John Holliday Flanagan" and "Achsah Holliday Flanagan," q.v.
FLANAGAN, EDWARD, bur. Apr 25, 1796, aged 45. {Ref: PR}
FLANAGAN, ELIZABETH, see "John B. Onion" and "John Holliday Flanagan" and "Achsah Holliday Flanagan," q.v.
FLANAGAN, JOHN HOLLIDAY, son of Edward and Elizabeth, b. Jul 22 or 23, 1792, twin of Achsah Holliday Flanagan. {Ref: PR}
FLANAGAN, SOPHIA, see "Edward Flanagan," q.v.
FLANNAGAN, EDWARD, insolvent on lists returned by John Guyton and Robert Carlile (the latter spelled the name as "Edward Flannagan" and listed him as a single man, but then crossed the name off the list) for taxes due for the year 1791. {Ref: IL 31.16, 31.19}
FLANNIGAN, ALEXANDER, head of family in 1800 (2nd District). {Ref: CI}
FLATT, JOHN, insolvent on lists in 1791 due county taxes and road taxes in "Deer Creek Upper, Middle, and Broad Creek Hundreds" as returned by Robert Amos, Jr. {Ref: IL 31.12, 31.22}
FLEARTY, JOSHUA, insolvent on list returned by Robert Carlile for taxes due for the year 1791. {Ref: IL 31.16}
FLEEHARTY (FLUHARTY?), JOHN, head of family in 1800 (5th District). {Ref: CI}
FLEEHARTY (FLUHARTY?), THOMAS, head of family in 1800 (4th District). {Ref: CI}
FLEETWOOD, BENJAMIN, or JOHN WILLY (WILLEY), taxpayer, 1798, Susquehanna Hd., 1 tract (2 acres) and 1 building (John Willey, occupant), $13.13 valuation, no slaves. {Ref: TL}
FLETCHER (FLECHER), BEN, insolvent on a list for the road tax due for 1791 in Harford Upper, Harford Lower, and Spesutia Upper as returned by Robert Amos, Jr. on Sep 18, 1793. {Ref: IL 31.18}
FLETCHER, BENJAMIN, taxpayer, 1798, Susquehanna Hd., 1 tract (30 acres) and 1 building, $73.12 valuation, no slaves. {Ref: TL}
FLETCHER (FLITCHER), BENJAMIN, head of family in 1800 (2nd District). {Ref: CI}
FLETCHER, BENNETT, b. Mar 8, 1799, d. Feb 2, 1876, bur. in Wesleyan Chapel Methodist Church Cemetery near Aberdeen. {Ref: TI}
FLETCHER, JOHN, see "Martha Michael Fletcher," q.v.
FLETCHER, MARTHA MICHAEL, wife of John, b. Dec 18, 1798, d. Feb 7, 1885, bur. in Christ Episcopal (Rock Spring) Church Cemetery. {Ref: TI}
FLETCHER, THOMAS C., b. Sep 20, 1796, d. Jan 17, 1847, bur. in Grove Presbyterian Church Cemetery in Aberdeen. {Ref: TI}
FLEURY, PAUL AIME, b. at LaRochelle, France, came to America in June, 1793, attended Cokesbury College in Abingdon, m. Clare Young (1767-1848) on Oct 28, 1794, and d. 1821. Their children were: Samuel Victor Fleury, b. Oct 15, 1795; William Fleury, b. Dec 12, 1796; Robert Fleury, b. Jul 25, 1798; Hennary

Fleury, b. Oct 29, 1800; Benjamin Augustin Fleury, b. Aug 26, 1802; Edwart Fleury, b. Jan 30, 1804; and, Abram Fleury, b. Jul 22, 1808. {Ref: TI, *St. Ignatius, Hickory, and Its Missions*, by Clarence V. Joerndt (1972), pp. 121, 122}

FLINCHAM (FLINCHUM), EDWARD, head of family in 1800 (4th District). {Ref: CI}. Also see "Mary Flincham," q.v.

FLINCHAM, MARY, dau. of Edward and Sarah, b. Nov 17, 1791. {Ref: PR}

FLINCHAM, SARAH, bur. Dec 9, 1792, aged 4 years. {Ref: PR}. Also see "Mary Flincham," q.v.

FLOWERS, JANE, head of family in 1800 (5th District). {Ref: CI}

FOARD, HARRIET, wife of William, b. 1796, d. Mar 16, 1851, in her 55th year, bur. in Union Chapel Methodist Church Cemetery at Wilna. {Ref: TI}

FOARD, JOHN, taxpayer, 1798, Gunpowder Upper Hd., 4 tracts (112 acres) and 1 building, $274.50 valuation, no slaves. {Ref: TL}

FOARD, JOSEPH, insolvent on a list for 1791 in Gunpowder Upper and Bush River Lower Hundreds, as filed by John Bond, Deputy Sheriff, on Sep 20, 1791 (who listed him as a single man). {Ref: IL 31.24}. Also see "Lemuel Howard," q.v.

FOARD, WILLIAM, taxpayer, 1798, Gunpowder Upper Hd., 1 dwelling house, 3 inferior houses, 2 acres, $150 valuation; 1 tract (136 acres) in Gunpowder Upper Hd., $285.75 valuation, no slaves. {Ref: TL}

FOARD, WILLIAM, see "Harriet Foard," q.v.

FOLKNER, JAMES, head of family in 1800 (5th District). {Ref: CI}

FOLKS, WILLIAM, insolvent, Harford Lower and Spesutia Lower Hundreds (listed as a single man), on a tax list returned by George Lyttle on Sep 21, 1791. {Ref: IL 31.20, 31.21}

FOLKS, WILLIAM, insolvent on list returned for the county tax for 1791 by William Osburn in Gunpowder Lower Hd. (which listed him as a single man). {Ref: IL 31.15}

FORD, DAVID, insolvent on lists returned for the county and road taxes due for 1791 by John Bull in Gunpowder Lower Hundred. {Ref: IL 31.14, 31.15}

FORD, GEORGE, insolvent on a list for the county tax due for 1793 in Susquehanna Hd. as returned to the levy court by Thomas Taylor on May 28, 1794, who noted "put in my hands last fall." {Ref: IL 31.12}. Also see "Joseph Ford (of George)," q.v.

FORD, JAMES, insolvent on a list for the road tax due for 1791 in Harford Upper, Harford Lower, and Spesutia Upper as returned by Robert Amos, Jr. on Sep 18, 1793. {Ref: IL 31.18}

FORD, JOHN, insolvent on list returned by Robert Carlile for taxes due for the year 1791. {Ref: IL 31.16}

FORD (FORDE), JOHN, head of family in 1800 (3rd District). {Ref: CI}

FORD (FORDS), JOHN, head of family in 1800 (1st District). {Ref: CI}

FORD, JOSEPH, insolvent on a list for the county tax due for 1793 in Harford Upper, Harford Lower, and Spesutia Lower Hundreds returned to the levy court by Thomas Taylor on May 28, 1794. {Ref: IL 31.12}

FORD, JOSEPH, had an account at Hall's Store in June, 1791, which noted he was

"paid for schooling the 2 Taylors." {Ref: WH}
FORD, JOSEPH, taxpayer, 1798, no dwelling house listed in this part of the tax schedule, no land listed, no Hd. listed (possibly Gunpowder Upper Hd. or Gunpowder Lower Hundred), 2 slaves. {Ref: TL}
FORD, JOSEPH, insolvent on list returned by Robert Carlile for taxes due for the year 1791. {Ref: IL 31.16}
FORD (FORDE), JOSEPH, head of family in 1800 (1st District). {Ref: CI}
FORD, JOSEPH (OF GEORGE), taxpayer, 1798, no dwelling house listed in this part of the tax schedule, no land listed, no Hd. listed (possibly Gunpowder Upper Hd. or Gunpowder Lower Hundred), 5 slaves. {Ref: TL}
FORD, JOSEPH (Cecil County), "executors of Abraham Taylor," insolvent on a list for the road tax due for 1791 in Harford Upper, Harford Lower, and Spesutia Upper as returned by Robert Amos, Jr. on Sep 18, 1793. {Ref: IL 31.18}
FORD (FORDE), JOSHUA, head of family in 1800 (1st District). {Ref: CI}
FORD, MARY, taxpayer, 1798, Susquehanna Hd., no dwelling house listed in this part of the tax schedule, no land listed, 1 slave. {Ref: TL}
FORD, MARY, will probated Feb 8, 1794. {Ref: HW}
FORDE, WILLIAM, head of family in 1800 (3rd District). {Ref: CI}
FORDUN, ISAAC, head of family in 1800 (3rd District). {Ref: CI}
FOREMAN, JOHN, taxpayer, 1798, Spesutia Lower Hd., 1 tract (44 perches), $13.50 valuation, no slaves. {Ref: TL}
FORSYTH, JOHN (Pennsylvania), or SAMUEL WILLETS, taxpayer, 1798, Bush River Upper & Eden Hd., 1 dwelling house, 2 inferior houses, 2 acres (Samuel Willets, occupant), $250 valuation; 3 tracts (500 acres) in Bush River Upper & Eden Hd. (Samuel Willets, occupant), $1488.38 valuation, no slaves. {Ref: TL}
FORSYTHE, SAMUEL, head of family in 1800 (5th District). {Ref: CI}
FORT, ELIZABETH, see "Ellen Fort," q.v.
FORT, ELLEN, dau. of John and Elizabeth Fort, was b. in August, 1798, m. William McComas, d. Dec --, 1859, bur. in Mountain Christian Church Cemetery. {Ref: TI}
FORT, JOHN, see "Ellen Fort," q.v.
FORT, PETER, insolvent on lists of taxes due in 1791 and 1792 in Broad Creek Hd., as returned by Robert Amos, Jr. in 1791 and Benjamin Preston in 1792. {Ref: IL 31.03, 31.12, 31.22}
FORT, PETER ("run"), insolvent on a list of the county tax due William Osborn, sheriff, for 1791, as returned by Edward Prigg on Sep 20, 1791. {Ref: IL 31.17}
FORWOOD, CONSTANT, m. Roger Matthews on Oct 16, 1800. {Ref: PR}
FORWOOD, ELIZABETH, taxpayer, 1798, Harford Upper Hd., 1 tract (180 acres) and 1 building, $315 valuation, no slaves. {Ref: TL}
FORWOOD, ELIZABETH, head of family in 1800 (3rd District). {Ref: CI}
FORWOOD, JACOB, subpoenaed to the Grand Jury in August, 1797. {Ref: CC}
FORWOOD, JACOB, taxpayer, 1798, Harford Lower Hd., 1 tract (20 acres), $155.25 valuation, 5 slaves. {Ref: TL}

FORWOOD, JACOB (esquire), head of family in 1800 (2nd District). {Ref: CI}
FORWOOD, JANE, see "Josiah Matthews," q.v.
FORWOOD, JOHN, served on a Grand Jury in March, 1799. {Ref: CM}
FORWOOD, JOHN, head of family in 1800 (3rd District). {Ref: CI}
FORWOOD, JOHN (esquire), head of family in 1800 (5th District). {Ref: CI}
FORWOOD, JOHN JR., served on a Grand Jury in March, 1800. {Ref: CM}
FORWOOD, JOHN SR., taxpayer, 1798, Spesutia Upper Hd., 1 dwelling house, 3 inferior houses, 1 acre and 80 perches, $350 valuation; 6 tracts (256 acres) in Spesutia Upper Hd., $832.50 valuation, no slaves; also, taxpayer, Spesutia Upper Hd., 1 dwelling house, 1 inferior house, 80 perches of land, $115 valuation, no slaves. {Ref: TL}
FORWOOD, JOHN (OF WILLIAM), taxpayer, 1798, Deer Creek Middle Hd., 1 dwelling house, 7 inferior houses, 2 acres, $300 valuation; 9 tracts (1076 acres) in Deer Creek Middle Hd., and 2 buildings (Samuel Smith and Margaret Brierly, occupants), $2936.51 valuation altogether, 6 slaves. {Ref: TL}
FORWOOD, JOHN (OF WILLIAM), served on a Grand Jury in March, 1798. {Ref: CM}
FORWOOD, LYDIA, see "Charles Coleman," q.v.
FORWOOD, PARKER (doctor), b. May 17, 1797, d. Jan 29, 1866, bur. in Watters Memorial Methodist Church Cemetery on Thomas Run. {Ref: TI}
FORWOOD, SAMUEL, see "Rosannah Shields," q.v.
FORWOOD, SAMUEL, treated by Dr. Archer on Aug 4, 1791; also mentioned his wife (no name given). {Ref: JA}
FORWOOD, SAMUEL, head of family in 1800 (3rd District). {Ref: CI}
FORWOOD, SAMUEL JR., taxpayer, 1798, Spesutia Upper Hd., 1 dwelling house, 20 perches of land, $105 valuation; also, taxpayer, Spesutia Upper Hd., 1 dwelling house, 20 perches of land, $115 valuation, no slaves. {Ref: TL}
FORWOOD, SAMUEL JR., head of family in 1800 (3rd District). {Ref: CI}
FORWOOD, SAMUEL SR., taxpayer, 1798, Spesutia Upper Hd., 1 dwelling house, 4 inferior houses, 1 acre and 80 perches, $385 valuation; 8 tracts (347 acres) in Spesutia Upper Hd., $1941.75 valuation, 2 slaves. {Ref: TL}
FORWOOD, SARAH, wife of William, b. Oct 19, 1796, d. May 17, 1888, aged 91 years, 6 months, and 28 days, bur. in Watters Memorial Methodist Church Cemetery on Thomas Run. {Ref: TI, and William Forwood Bible}
FORWOOD, WILLIAM, see "John Forwood (of William)" and "John Forwood" and "Sarah Forwood," q.v.
FOSTER, BENEDICT, head of family in 1800 (4th District). {Ref: CI}
FOSTER, GEORGE, m. Mary McPhail on Sep 29, 1800. {Ref: PR}
FOSTER, JESSE, taxpayer, 1798, Deer Creek Middle Hd., 1 building, $56.25 valuation, no slaves. {Ref: TL}
FOSTER, JESSE, head of family in 1800 (5th District). {Ref: CI}
FOSTER, JOHN, head of family in 1800 (4th District). {Ref: CI}
FOSTER, MARGARET, will probated Mar 11, 1794. {Ref: HW}

115

FOSTER, MOSES, taxpayer, 1798, Deer Creek Middle Hd., 3 tracts (241 acres) and 1 building, $271.12 valuation, no slaves. {Ref: TL}
FOSTER, MOSES, head of family in 1800 (5th District). {Ref: CI}
FOSTER, RACHEL (mother), b. Dec 14, 1792, d. Sep 17, 184-(?), bur. in Angel Hill Cemetery in Havre de Grace. {Ref: TI}
FOSTER, SAMUEL, will probated Oct 1, 1792. {Ref: HW}
FOSTER, THOMAS, taxpayer, 1798, Deer Creek Middle Hd., 1 dwelling house, 5 inferior houses, 2 acres, $160 valuation; 1 tract (168 acres) in Deer Creek Middle Hd., $146.99 valuation, no slaves. {Ref: TL}
FOWER, WILLIAM, insolvent on a list for the road tax due for 1791 in Harford Upper, Harford Lower, and Spesutia Upper as returned by Robert Amos, Jr. on Sep 18, 1793. {Ref: IL 31.18}
FOWLER, MARY, see "Leonard Cowen," q.v.
FOWLER, PATRICK ("run"), insolvent on lists due for 1790 and 1791 "fund taxes" and county taxes in Susquehanna Hd., as returned by Thomas Taylor. {Ref: IL 31.12, 31.02}
FOWLER, SAMUEL, insolvent on a list for the road tax due for 1791 in Harford Upper, Harford Lower, and Spesutia Upper as returned by Robert Amos, Jr. on Sep 18, 1793. {Ref: IL 31.18}
FOWLER, WILLIAM, purchased flax and a spade on Dec 14, 1797 at Bush River Store. {Ref: AH}
FOWLER, WILLIAM, head of family in 1800 (2nd District). {Ref: CI}
FOX, THOMAS, head of family in 1800 (5th District). {Ref: CI}. Also see "Asaph Warner," q.v.
FOX, WILLIAM, m. Mary Carrol on Aug 15, 1797. {Ref: PR}
FOY, MARY, head of family in 1800 (2nd District). {Ref: CI}
FOY, PALTIS, insolvent, Harford Lower and Spesutia Lower Hundreds, on a tax list returned by George Lyttle on Sep 21, 1791. {Ref: IL 31.20, 31.21}
FOY, PATRICK, head of family in 1800 (3rd District). {Ref: CI}
FOY, POLTES, insolvent on a list for the road tax due for 1791 in Harford Upper, Harford Lower, and Spesutia Upper as returned by Robert Amos, Jr. on Sep 18, 1793. {Ref: IL 31.18}
FRAME, JOHN, insolvent, Harford Lower and Spesutia Lower Hundreds (listed as a single man), on a tax list returned by George Lyttle on Sep 21, 1791. {Ref: IL 31.20, 31.21}
FRAME (FRAM), JOHN, insolvent on a list for the road tax due for 1791 in Harford Upper, Harford Lower, and Spesutia Upper as returned by Robert Amos, Jr. on Sep 18, 1793. {Ref: IL 31.18}
FRANALS (FRANELL), JOHN, see "Thomas Hay," q.v.
FRANCE, JOSHUA, insolvent on list returned by Robert Carlile for taxes due for the year 1791. {Ref: IL 31.16}
FRAZER, JOSEPH, son of Samuel and Penelope, b. Feb 9, 1799. {Ref: PR}
FRAZIER, SAMUEL, head of family in 1800 (4th District). {Ref: CI}. Also see

"Joseph Frazer," q.v.

FREEMAN, THOMAS, head of family in 1800 (3rd District). {Ref: CI}

FRELET LABARBAN(?) & COMPANY, licensed retailers in August, 1797. {Ref: CC}

FRENCH, BENJAMIN, insolvent on lists returned for the county and road taxes due for 1791 by John Bull in Gunpowder Lower Hundred. {Ref: IL 31.14, 31.15}

FRENCH, OTHO (JR.), insolvent on lists returned for the county and road taxes due for 1791 by John Bull in Gunpowder Lower Hundred. {Ref: IL 31.14, 31.15}. His name was listed without the "Jr." on one list.

FRENCH, URITH (EURITH), insolvent on lists returned for the county and road taxes due for 1791 by John Bull in Gunpowder Lower Hundred. {Ref: IL 31.14, 31.15}

FRISBY, THOMAS, head of family in 1800 (2nd District). {Ref: CI}

FRISBY, WILLIAM, taxpayer, 1798, Spesutia Lower Hd., 1 tract (600 acres) and 1 building, $2846.25 valuation, 2 slaves. {Ref: TL}

FRISBY, WILLIAM, head of family in 1800 (2nd District). {Ref: CI}

FULKS, WILLIAM, insolvent on list returned by Robert Carlile for taxes due for the year 1791. {Ref: IL 31.16}

FULLARD, HENRY, taxpayer, 1798, Deer Creek Middle Hd., 3 tracts (330 acres) and 1 building, $607.50 valuation, no slaves. {Ref: TL}

FULLARD, HENRY, head of family in 1800 (5th District). {Ref: CI}

FULLER, ELIZABETH, see "Temperance Fuller," q.v.

FULLER, JAMES, head of family in 1800 (5th District). {Ref: CI}

FULLER, SAMUEL, see "Temperance Fuller," q.v.

FULLER, TEMPERANCE, dau. of Samuel and Elizabeth, b. Jan 16, 1800, bapt. Mar 12, 1800. {Ref: PR}

FULLERTON, JAMES, taxpayer, 1798, Gunpowder Lower Hd., 1 tract (20 perches, 255 sq. ft.), $90 valuation, no slaves. {Ref: TL}. Also see "James Phillips, Sr.," q.v.

FULLERTON, JAMES, charged for assaulting Greenbury Presbury in 1794. {Ref: CD, March Term, 1795}

FULLERTON, JAMES, m. Sarah Bradford on Jan 13, 1791. {Ref: PR}

FULLERTON, MARGARET, see "Archibald Through," q.v.

FULLITON, JAMES, head of family in 1800 (Abingdon). {Ref: CI}

FULLITON, JOHN, head of family in 1800 (5th District). {Ref: CI}

FULTON, J., see "William Wilson (silversmith)," q.v.

FULTON, JAMES, head of family in 1800 (1st District). {Ref: CI}

FULTON, JOHN, taxpayer, 1798, Bush River Lower Hd., 1 dwelling house, 5 inferior houses, 1 acre and 80 perches, $140 valuation; 4 tracts (145 acres) in Bush River Lower Hd., $686.25 valuation, no slaves. {Ref: TL}

FULTON, JOHN, head of family in 1800 (1st District). {Ref: CI}

FULTON, JOSEPH, insolvent on a list for 1791 in Gunpowder Upper and Bush River Lower Hundreds, as filed by John Bond, Deputy Sheriff, on Sep 20, 1791. {Ref: IL 31.24}

FULTON, WILLIAM, served on a Petit Jury in August, 1798. {Ref: CM}
FULTON, WILLIAM, head of family in 1800 (3rd District). {Ref: CI}
FULTZ, WILLIAM, or MICHAEL LAREW, taxpayer, 1798, Deer Creek Upper Hd., 1 tract (730 acres) and 1 building (Michael Larew or Lareu, occupant), $821.25 valuation, no slaves. {Ref: TL}
GAFFORD, ALEY, see "John Hambleton," q.v.
GAFFORD, JOSEPH, taxpayer, 1798, Gunpowder Lower Hd., no dwelling house listed in this part of the tax schedule, no land listed, 2 slaves. {Ref: TL}
GAFFORD, JOSEPH, head of family in 1800 (1st District). {Ref: CI}
GALBRAITH, ALEXANDER, insolvent on lists in 1791 due county taxes and road taxes in "Deer Creek Upper, Middle, and Broad Creek Hundreds" as returned by Robert Amos, Jr. {Ref: IL 31.12, 31.22}
GALLAHER (GALLEHER), PATRICK, see "Nathaniel West, Jr.," q.v.
GALLAWAY, ABSALOM, served on a Petit Jury in March, 1799 and March, 1800. {Ref: CM}
GALLAWAY (GALLIWAY), ABSOLEM, head of family in 1800 (3rd District). {Ref: CI}
GALLION & CALWELL, licensed retailer in March, 1795. {Ref: CC}
GALLION, ALEXANDER, head of family in 1800 (2nd District). {Ref: CI}
GALLION, ELIZA, had an account at Hall's Store in May, 1791. {Ref: WH}
GALLION, ELIZABETH, see "James Gallion," q.v.
GALLION, ELIZABETH, taxpayer, 1798, Spesutia Lower Hd., no dwelling house listed in this part of the tax schedule, no land listed, 1 slave. {Ref: TL}.
GALLION, ELIZABETH, will probated Dec 16, 1799. {Ref: HW}
GALLION, GEORGE, bur. Oct 2, 1796. {Ref: PR}
GALLION, GREGORY ("dead"), insolvent on lists due for 1790 and 1791 "fund taxes" and county taxes in Susquehanna Hd., as returned by Thomas Taylor. {Ref: IL 31.12, 31.02}
GALLION, JACOB, see "John Gallion (of Jacob)," q.v.
GALLION, JAMES, insolvent on a list for the county tax due for 1793 in Harford Upper, Harford Lower, and Spesutia Lower Hundreds returned to the levy court by Thomas Taylor on May 28, 1794. {Ref: IL 31.12}
GALLION, JAMES, head of family in 1800 (2nd District). {Ref: CI}
GALLION, JAMES, or ELIZABETH GALLION, taxpayer, 1798, Spesutia Lower Hd., 1 dwelling house, 3 inferior houses, 2 acres, $130 valuation; 1 tract (127 acres, 120 perches) in Spesutia Lower Hd. (Elizabeth Gallion, occupant), $431.16 valuation, 3 slaves. {Ref: TL}. Also see "Samuel Griffith," q.v.
GALLION, JOHN, see "John Rumsey," q.v.
GALLION, JOHN, taxpayer, 1798, Susquehanna Hd., 1 tract (86 acres) and 1 building, $238.50 valuation, no slaves. {Ref: TL}
GALLION, JOHN, head of family in 1800 (2nd District); two men by this name in this district. {Ref: CI}
GALLION, JOHN (OF C.), head of family in 1800 (2nd District). {Ref: CI}

GALLION, JOHN (OF J.), head of family in 1800 (2nd District). {Ref: CI}
GALLION, JOHN (OF JACOB), taxpayer, 1798, Harford Lower Hd., no dwelling house listed in this part of the tax schedule, no land listed, 2 slaves. {Ref: TL}
GALLION, JOSEPH, insolvent on a list for 1791 in Gunpowder Upper and Bush River Lower Hundreds, as filed by John Bond, Deputy Sheriff, on Sep 20, 1791 (who listed him as a single man). {Ref: IL 31.24}. Also see "Joseph Gallion," q.v.
GALLION, MARY, see "Ruthan Garrison," q.v.
GALLION, RACHEL, head of family in 1800 (2nd District). {Ref: CI}
GALLION, SAMUEL ("poor"), insolvent on lists due for 1790 and 1791 "fund taxes" and county taxes in Susquehanna Hd., as returned by Thomas Taylor. {Ref: IL 31.12, 31.02}
GALLION, SAMUEL, insolvent on a list for the county tax due for 1793 in Susquehanna Hd. as returned to the levy court by Thomas Taylor on May 28, 1794, who noted "put in my hands last fall." {Ref: IL 31.12}
GALLOP, DANIEL, taxpayer, 1798, Spesutia Lower Hd., no dwelling house listed in this part of the tax schedule, no land listed, 1 slave. {Ref: TL}. Also see "Daniel Gallupe," q.v.
GALLOWAY, ABSALOM, see "Elizabeth Galloway," q.v.
GALLOWAY, ABSALOM, taxpayer, 1798, Bush River Lower Hd., 1 dwelling house, 2 inferior houses, 1 acre, $160 valuation; 1 tract (199 acres) in Bush River Lower Hd., $96.60 valuation, no slaves. {Ref: TL}
GALLOWAY, ELIZABETH, dau. of Absalom and Rebecca, b. Oct 23, 1794. {Ref: PR}
GALLOWAY, JOHN, head of family in 1800 (5th District). {Ref: CI}
GALLOWAY, PEGGEY, head of family in 1800 (5th District). {Ref: CI}
GALLOWAY, REBECCA, see "Elizabeth Galloway," q.v.
GALLOWAY, THOMAS SR., insolvent on lists returned by Robert Carlile (who listed the name without the "Sr.) and John Guyton for taxes due for the year 1791. {Ref: IL 31.16, 31.19}
GALLOWAY, THOMAS JR., insolvent on list returned by Robert Carlile for taxes due for the year 1791. {Ref: IL 31.16}
GALLUPE, CHARLES, head of family in 1800 (2nd District). {Ref: CI}. Also see "Charles Gatrop," q.v.
GALLUPE, DANIEL, head of family in 1800 (2nd District). {Ref: CI}. Also see "Daniel Gatrop," q.v.
GALLUPE, GILBERT, head of family in 1800 (2nd District). {Ref: CI}. Also see "Gilbert Gatrop," q.v.
GALLUPE, JOSEPH, head of family in 1800 (2nd District). {Ref: CI}
GALLUPE, THOMAS, head of family in 1800 (2nd District). {Ref: CI}
GALWAY, ABSALOM, served on a Petit Jury in August, 1797. {Ref: CC}
GALWAY, ABSOLEM, subpoenaed to the Grand Jury in August, 1797. {Ref: CC}
GAMBELL, SAMUEL, insolvent on a list for 1791 in Gunpowder Upper and Bush River Lower Hundreds, as filed by John Bond, Deputy Sheriff, on Sep 20, 1791

(who listed him as a single man). {Ref: IL 31.24}

GARDNER (GUARDNER), GEORGE, head of family in 1800 (4th District). {Ref: CI}

GARDENER, JOSEPH, charged for assaulting Ferdinand Duprey in 1794 and 1797. {Ref: CD, March Term, 1795, and March Term, 1797}

GARNER, JOSEPH, taxpayer, 1798, Bush River Upper & Eden Hd., 1 dwelling house, 2 acres, $105 valuation; 1 tract (82 acres) in Bush River Upper & Eden Hd., $92.25 valuation, no slaves. {Ref: TL}

GARRETT, ----, bur. Dec --, 1796. {Ref: PR}

GARRETT, ALEXANDER, bur. ---- 1799. {Ref: PR}. Also see "Mary Garrett," q.v.

GARRETT, AMOS, insolvent, Harford Lower and Spesutia Lower Hundreds, on a tax list returned by George Lyttle on Sep 21, 1791. {Ref: IL 31.20, 31.21}

GARRETT, AMOS, had an account at Hall's Store in February, 1791. {Ref: WH}

GARRETT, AMOSS, head of family in 1800 (1st District). {Ref: CI}

GARRETT (GARROTT), FRANCES, had an account at Hall's Store in January, 1791. {Ref: WH}

GARRETT, HENRY, head of family in 1800 (1st District). {Ref: CI}

GARRETT, JAMES, taxpayer, 1798, Susquehanna Hd., 2 tracts (56? acres), $210.36 valuation, no slaves. {Ref: TL}

GARRETT, JAMES, recognizance with Baker Rigdon and Charles Beaver in £30 to keep Catharine Henderson's baseborn child off the county in 1795. {Ref: CD, August Term, 1795}

GARRETT, JAMES, head of family in 1800 (2nd District). {Ref: CI}

GARRETT, JOHN ("gone"), insolvent on a list for 1791 in Gunpowder Upper and Bush River Lower Hundreds, as filed by John Bond, Deputy Sheriff, on Sep 20, 1791. {Ref: IL 31.24}

GARRETT, MARTHA (MARTH), head of family in 1800 (2nd District). {Ref: CI}. Also see "Mary Garrett," q.v.

GARRETT, MARY, dau. of Alexander and Martha, b. Feb 21, 1796, bapt. Dec 4, 1796. {Ref: PR}

GARRETT, THOMAS (mulatto on Rumsey's Place), treated by Dr. Archer on Aug 15, 1791. {Ref: JA}

GARRETT, WILLIAM, head of family in 1800 (4th District). {Ref: CI}

GARRETTSON (GARRITTSON), CORNELIUS, head of family in 1800 (4th District). {Ref: CI}

GARRETTSON, FRANCES, or DOCTOR DAVIS, taxpayer, 1798, Spesutia Lower Hd., no dwelling house listed in this part of the tax schedule, no land listed, 13 slaves (Doctor Davis, superintendent).

GARRETTSON, FREEBORN, or WILLIAM HOLLEY, taxpayer, 1798, Spesutia Lower Hd., 1 dwelling house, 3 inferior houses, 2 acres, $115 valuation; 7 tracts (277 acres, 40 perches) in Spesutia Lower Hd. (William Holley or Holly, occupant), $1237.50 valuation, no slaves. {Ref: TL}

GARRETTSON, GARRETT, purchased a watch on Sep 20, 1791 at Bush River

Store. {Ref: AH}

GARRETTSON, GARRETT, taxpayer, 1798, Harford Lower Hd., 1 dwelling house, 3 inferior houses, 2 acres, $175 valuation; 1 tract (203 acres) and 1 building, $742.50 valuation, 3 slaves. {Ref: TL}

GARRETTSON, GARRETT (mariner), will probated Feb 5, 1794. {Ref: HW}

GARRETTSON, GEORGE, taxpayer, 1798, Gunpowder Upper Hd., 1 dwelling house, 4 inferior houses, 2 acres, $150 valuation; 1 tract (147 acres) in Gunpowder Upper Hd., $375.75 valuation, 5 slaves. {Ref: TL}

GARRETTSON (GARRITTSON), GEORGE, head of family in 1800 (3rd District). {Ref: CI}

GARRETTSON, JAMES, see "Nancy Garrettson," q.v.

GARRETTSON, JAMES, taxpayer, 1798, Spesutia Lower Hd., 1 dwelling house, 5 inferior houses, 2 acres, $120 valuation; 4 tracts (113 acres), $467.44 valuation, 2 slaves. {Ref: TL}

GARRETTSON, JAMES ("charge twice"), insolvent on a list for the road tax due for 1791 in Harford Upper, Harford Lower, and Spesutia Upper as returned by Robert Amos, Jr. on Sep 18, 1793. {Ref: IL 31.18}

GARRETTSON, JAMES, insolvent, Harford Lower and Spesutia Lower Hundreds (listed as a single man), on a tax list returned by George Lyttle on Sep 21, 1791. {Ref: IL 31.20, 31.21}

GARRETTSON (GARRITTSON), JAMES, head of family in 1800 (2nd District). {Ref: CI}

GARRETTSON (GARRITTSON), JAMES, head of family in 1800 (4th District). {Ref: CI}

GARRETTSON, JOHN'S HEIRS, appeared twice on a list of insolvents for the road tax due for 1791 in Harford Upper, Harford Lower, and Spesutia Upper as returned by Robert Amos, Jr. on Sep 18, 1793. {Ref: IL 31.18}

GARRETTSON (GARRITTSON), JOHN, head of family in 1800 (1st District). {Ref: CI}

GARRETTSON, NANCY, or JAMES GARRETTSON, taxpayer, 1798, Spesutia Lower Hd., 1 tract (50 acres), no buildings listed (James Garrettson, occupant), $225 valuation, no slaves. {Ref: TL}

GARRETTSON, RUTHEN, see "John B. Hall's heirs," q.v.

GARRETTSON, RUTHEN, taxpayer, 1798, Harford Lower Hd., no dwelling house listed in this part of the tax schedule, no land listed, 2 slaves. {Ref: TL}

GARRETTSON, RUTHEN (at B. Neck), treated by Dr. Archer on Jan 6, 1791. {Ref: JA}

GARRETTSON (GARRITSON), RUTHEN, head of family in 1800 (2nd District). {Ref: CI}

GARRETTSON (GARRITSON), SAMUEL, head of family in 1800 (4th District). {Ref: CI}

GARRETTSON, THOMAS, insolvent on list returned by Robert Carlile for taxes due for the year 1791. {Ref: IL 31.16}

GARRISON, CORNELIUS, taxpayer, 1798, Bush River Upper & Eden Hd., no dwelling house listed in this part of the tax schedule, no land listed, 1 slave. {Ref

GARRISON, GARRETT, head of family in 1800 (2nd District). {Ref: CI}
GARRISON, JAMES, taxpayer, 1798, Gunpowder Upper Hd., 1 dwelling house, 4 inferior houses, 2 acres, $150 valuation; 4 tracts (350 acres) in Gunpowder Upper Hd., $1088.44 valuation, 2 slaves. {Ref: TL}
GARRISON, PHILIP, taxpayer, 1798, Bush River Upper & Eden Hd., 1 dwelling house, 5 inferior houses, 2 acres, $300 valuation; 1 tract (184 acres, 120 perches) in Bush River Upper & Eden Hd., $831.37 valuation, no slaves. {Ref: TL}
GARRISON, RUTHAN, m. Mary Gallion on Nov 23, 1797. {Ref: PR}
GASH, HANNAH, insolvent on lists in 1791 due county taxes and road taxes in "Deer Creek Upper, Middle, and Broad Creek Hundreds" as returned by Robert Amos, Jr., but her name was then crossed off both lists. {Ref: IL 31.12, 31.22}
GASH, THOMAS, treated by Dr. Archer on Jan 22, 1791. {Ref: JA}. Also see "James West," q.v.
GASKELL, LARRANCE ("run"), insolvent on a list of the county tax due William Osborn, sheriff, for 1791, as returned by Edward Prigg on Sep 20, 1791. {Ref: IL 31.17}
GASSAWAY, MARY, see "Mary Gazzoway," q.v.
GASSAWAY, NICHOLAS, taxpayer, 1798, Spesutia Lower Hd., no dwelling house listed in this part of the tax schedule, no land listed, 2 slaves. {Ref: TL}
GASWAY, THOMAS, insolvent on list returned for the road tax due for 1791 by John Bull. {Ref: IL 31.14}
GATROP, CHARLES, see "Samuel Hughes" and "Charles Gallupe," q.v.
GATROP, DANIEL, see "Samuel Hughes" and Daniel Gallupe," q.v.
GATROP, GILBERT, see "Samuel Hughes" and "Gilbert Gallupe," q.v.
GATROP, JAMES, see "Samuel Hughes," q.v.
GAUTROPE, JOHN, head of family in 1800 (3rd District). {Ref: CI}
GAWLEY, GRACE, taxpayer, 1798, Bush River Lower Hd., 1 tract (80 perches) and 1 building, $84.38 valuation, no slaves. {Ref: TL}
GAWLEY, WILLIAM, charged for selling liquors in 1790. {Ref: CD, March Term, 1795}
GAY, JNO., licensed retailer in August, 1797. {Ref: CC}
GAZZOWAY, MARY, bur. Nov 22, 1797. {Ref: PR}
GEALE, ----, bur. Feb 2, 1798. {Ref: PR}
GELHAMPTON, ROBERT, insolvent on a list for the county tax due for 1793 in Susquehanna Hd. as returned to the levy court by Thomas Taylor on May 28, 1794, who noted "put in my hands last fall." {Ref: IL 31.12}
GENETT, PETER, head of family in 1800 (4th District). {Ref: CI}
GENNETT, PETER, taxpayer, 1798, Bush River Upper & Eden Hd., 1 dwelling house, 4 inferior houses, 2 acres, $200 valuation; 1 tract (231 acres) in Bush River Upper & Eden Hd., $519.75 valuation, no slaves. {Ref: TL}
GENNEY, THOMAS, head of family in 1800 (5th District). {Ref: CI}
GENTY, LOUIS, taxpayer, 1798, Gunpowder Upper Hd., 1 dwelling house, 2 inferior houses, 2 acres, $400 valuation; 1 tract (150 acres) in Gunpowder

Upper Hd., $309.38 valuation, 4 slaves. {Ref: TL}
GEORGE, SARAH, see "John Branian," q.v.
GIANT, ANN, head of family in 1800 (2nd District). {Ref: CI}. Also see "Ann Jiant," q.v.
GIANT, ISAAC, had an account at Hall's Store in June, 1791. {Ref: WH}
GIBB, JOHN, taxpayer, 1798, Spesutia Upper Hd., 1 dwelling house, 3 inferior houses, 1 acre, $185 valuation; 1 tract (199 acres) in Spesutia Upper Hd., $487.12 valuation, no slaves. {Ref: TL}
GIBB, JOHN, head of family in 1800 (3rd District). {Ref: CI}
GIBSON, ANN, will probated Aug 12, 1794. {Ref: HW}. Also see "William Gibson," q.v.
GIBSON, ARAMINTA ELIZABETH, dau. of Thomas and Elizabeth (Betsy), b. Oct 12, 1792, bapt. Dec 10, 1797. {Ref: PR}
GIBSON, BENJAMIN, head of family in 1800 (3rd District). {Ref: CI}
GIBSON, ELIZABETH (BETSY), taxpayer, 1798, Bush River Lower Hd., 1 dwelling house, 1 inferior house, 80 perches of land, $250 valuation; 1 tract (23 acres, 80 perches) in Bush River Lower Hd., $66.90 valuation, no slaves. In another part of the tax schedule the occupant is listed as Josias Smith. {Ref: TL}. This is the property that Elizabeth (Betsy) Gibson inherited in Bel Air (now known as the Hays House) upon the death of her husband Thomas circa Sep 6, 1796. {Ref: HB 25:42 (1985)}. Also see "Robert Stirling" and "Araminta Elizabeth Gibson" and "Emily Catharine Gibson" and "Thomas Gibson," q.v.
GIBSON, EMILY CATHARINE, dau. of Thomas and Elizabeth (Betsy), b. about Sep 15, 1790, bapt. Dec 10, 1797. {Ref: PR}
GIBSON, JOHN LEE, see "Samuel Hughes" and "John Stump," q.v.
GIBSON, JOHN LEE, charged for neglect of his duty as clerk in 1795. {Ref: CD, March and August Terms, 1795}
GIBSON, JOHN LEE, taxpayer, 1798, Spesutia Lower Hd., 1 dwelling house, 2 inferior houses, 2 acres, $280 valuation; 1 tract (423 acres) in Bush River Lower Hd. (James Jervis, occupant), $1035 valuation, 15 slaves; also, 3 tracts (166 acres) and 1 building in Deer Creek Middle Hd., $996 valuation, no slaves. {Ref: TL}
GIBSON, JOHN LEE, head of family in 1800 (2nd District). {Ref: CI}
GIBSON, THOMAS, purchased property in Bel Air (now known as the Hays House, oldest house still standing in Bel Air built by 1788) on Nov 27, 1794 from Frederick Yeiser who acquired it from Jacob Bull who had acquired it from the original owner Aquila Scott (of James) who founded the town of Bel Air (then called "Scott's Old Fields") circa 1780. {Ref: HB 25:42 (1985)}. Also see "Araminta Elizabeth Gibson" and "Emily Catharine Gibson" and "Elizabeth (Betsy) Gibson" and "Ann Moore," q.v.
GIBSON, WILLIAM, taxpayer, 1798, Deer Creek Upper Hd., 3 tracts (159 acres, 80 perches), $313.45 valuation, no slaves; also, 1 tract (149 acres, 80 perches) in Deer Creek Upper Hd. (James Gladden, occupant), $294.40 valuation, no

slaves. {Ref: TL}

GIBSON, WILLIAM, mentioned in a survey deposition on Jan 14, 1800 as "where formerly stood the dwelling house that Wm. and Ann Gibson formerly lived in" and "all Wm. Gibson's evidence is to be out in one Lott No. 6" and also "to where Wm. Gibson's evidence begins." {Ref: JS}

GIBSON, WILLIAM, head of family in 1800 (4th District). {Ref: CI}

GIBSON, WILLIAM, AND RAMPLEY, JAMES, tract *Every Man's Refuse* surveyed between 1792 and 1796. {Ref: SB}

GILBERT, ----, see "Carlile & Gilbert," q.v.

GILBERT, ABRAM, see "Parker Gilbert," q.v.

GILBERT, BETSY, bur. Nov 6, 1797. {Ref: PR}. Also see "James Gilbert (of Michael)" and "Mary Sophia Hall Gilbert" and "George Thomas Gilbert," q.v.

GILBERT, BILLY, see "James Gilbert (of Michael)," q.v.

GILBERT, CHARLES, taxpayer, 1798, Susquehanna Hd., 1 tract (100 acres) and 1 building, $260.62 valuation, no slaves. {Ref: TL}

GILBERT, CHARLES, head of family in 1800 (2nd District). {Ref: CI}

GILBERT, CHARLES SR., treated by Dr. Archer on Sep 3, 1791. {Ref: JA}

GILBERT, CHARLES, b. 1724, d. 1798, will probated Oct 1, 1798. {Ref: HW}

GILBERT, CHARLES' HEIRS, or WIDOW GILBERT, taxpayers, 1798, Susquehanna Hd., 1 dwelling house, 2 inferior houses, 2 acres (Widow Gilbert, occupant), $200 valuation; 7 tracts (615 acres) in Susquehanna Hd. (Widow Gilbert, occupant), $1417.50 valuation, 7 slaves. {Ref: TL}

GILBERT, CHARLES (OF TAYLOR), will probated Jul 31, 1794. {Ref: HW}

GILBERT, ELIZABETH, m. Skipwith Cole on Jan 22, 1797. {Ref: PR}

GILBERT, ELIZABETH, head of family in 1800 (2nd District). {Ref: CI}

GILBERT, GEORGE THOMAS, son of Michael and Betsy, b. Feb 28, 1797, bapt. Aug 20, 1797. {Ref: PR}

GILBERT, GIDEON, son of Parker and Martha, b. Jun 26, 1798, bapt. Jul 10, 1799. {Ref: PR}

GILBERT, HENRY, b. 1797, d. Mar 23, 1874, aged 77, bur. in Churchville Presbyterian Church Cemetery. {Ref: TI}

GILBERT, JAMES, insolvent, Harford Lower and Spesutia Lower Hundreds (listed as a single man), on a tax list returned by George Lyttle on Sep 21, 1791. {Ref: IL 31.20, 31.21}

GILBERT, JAMES, served as constable in Spesutia Upper Hd., 1797. {Ref: CC, CM}

GILBERT, JAMES, taxpayer, 1798, Spesutia Upper Hd., 1 dwelling house, 2 inferior houses, 80 perches of land, $155 valuation; 1 tract (152 acres) in Spesutia Upper Hd., $297 valuation, no slaves. {Ref: TL}

GILBERT, JAMES, subpoenaed to the Grand Jury in August, 1797. {Ref: CC}

GILBERT, JAMES, head of family in 1800 (3rd District). {Ref: CI}

GILBERT, JAMES (OF MICHAEL), treated by Dr. Archer on Sep 22, 1791; also mentioned children Billy, Betsy, Jimmy, and Johnson. {Ref: JA}

GILBERT, JARVIS, head of family in 1800 (2nd District). {Ref: CI}

GILBERT, JERVIS, taxpayer, 1798, Harford Upper Hd., 1 dwelling house, 1 inferior house, 2 acres, $175 valuation; 1 tract (258 acres) in Harford Upper Hd., $435.38 valuation, no slaves. {Ref: TL}
GILBERT, JERVIS, m. Sophia Cole on Nov 29, 1798. {Ref: PR}
GILBERT, JIMMY, see "James Gilbert (of Michael)," q.v.
GILBERT, JOHANNA, m. Adam Johnson on Aug 17, 1797. {Ref: PR}
GILBERT, JOHN, insolvent on a list for the road tax due for 1791 in Harford Upper, Harford Lower, and Spesutia Upper as returned by Robert Amos, Jr. on Sep 18, 1793. {Ref: IL 31.18}
GILBERT, JOHNSON, see "James Gilbert (of Michael)," q.v.
GILBERT, MARTHA, see "Gideon Gilbert," q.v.
GILBERT, MARTHA, taxpayer, 1798, Susquehanna Hd., no dwelling house listed in this part of the tax schedule, no land listed, 1 slave. {Ref: TL}
GILBERT, MARTHA, bur. Oct 28, 1799. {Ref: PR}
GILBERT, MARTIN, head of family in 1800 (2nd District). {Ref: CI}
GILBERT, MARTIN T., taxpayer, 1798, Susquehanna Hd., 1 tract (100 acres) and 1 building, $225 valuation, no slaves. {Ref: TL}
GILBERT, MARTIN TAYLOR, will probated Oct 16, 1797. {Ref: HW}
GILBERT, MARY, see "Sarah Barnes," q.v.
GILBERT, MARY, taxpayer, 1798, Susquehanna Hd., no dwelling house listed in this part of the tax schedule, no land listed, 4 slaves. {Ref: TL}. Also see "Michael Gilbert," q.v.
GILBERT, MARY, m. Charles McComas on Jun 15, 1800. {Ref: PR}
GILBERT, MARY, head of family in 1800 (2nd District). {Ref: CI}
GILBERT, MARY SOPHIA HALL, dau. of Michael and Betsy, b. Jan 23, 1795, bapt. Jun 19, 1796. {Ref: PR}
GILBERT, MICAH, taxpayer, 1798, Susquehanna Hd., 1 dwelling house, 4 inferior houses, 2 acres, $100.50 valuation; 1 tract (98 acres) in Susquehanna Hd., $165.38 valuation, 4 slaves. {Ref: TL}. Also see "Michael Gilbert (of Micah)," q.v.
GILBERT, MICAH, b. 1797, d. Sep 29, 1855, aged 58, bur. in Churchville Presbyterian Church Cemetery. {Ref: TI}
GILBERT, MICAH, head of family in 1800 (2nd District). {Ref: CI}
GILBERT, MICHAEL, see "Mary Sophia Hall Gilbert" and George Thomas Gilbert," q.v.
GILBERT, MICHAEL, had an account at Hall's Store in June, 1791. {Ref: WH}
GILBERT, MICHAEL, served on a Petit Jury in August, 1797. {Ref: CC}
GILBERT, MICHAEL, subpoenaed to the Grand Jury in August, 1797. {Ref: CC}
GILBERT, MICHAEL, purchased a "cuting box" on Dec 14, 1797 at Bush River Store. {Ref: AH}
GILBERT, MICHAEL, taxpayer, 1798, Harford Upper Hd., 1 dwelling house, 4 inferior houses, 2 acres, $150 valuation; 2 tracts (70 acres) in Harford Upper

Hd., $236.25 valuation, 1 slave; also, 1 tract (150 acres) in Susquehanna Hd. (Mary Gilbert, occupant), $403.31 valuation, no slaves. {Ref: TL}. Also see "Parker Gilbert" and "James Gilbert," q.v.

GILBERT, MICHAEL, served on a Petit Jury in August, 1798 and August, 1799, and was discharged from serving again in August, 1800. {Ref: CM}

GILBERT, MICHAEL, vestryman, 1798, St. George's Episcopal Church. {Ref: PR}

GILBERT, MICHAEL (colonel), head of family in 1800 (1st District). {Ref: CI}

GILBERT, MICHAEL, head of family in 1800 (2nd District). {Ref: CI}

GILBERT, MICHAEL JR., warden, 1796, 1799, St. George's Episcopal Church. {Ref: PR}

GILBERT, MICHAEL (OF MICAH), taxpayer, 1798, Susquehanna Hd., 1 tract (50 acres), $101.25 valuation, and 1 tract (65 acres, 120 perches), $181.69 valuation, no slaves. {Ref: TL}

GILBERT, MICHAEL (OF THOMAS), insolvent on a list for the road tax due for 1791 in Harford Upper, Harford Lower, and Spesutia Upper as returned by Robert Amos, Jr. on Sep 18, 1793. {Ref: IL 31.18}

GILBERT, PARKER, see "Gideon Gilbert," q.v.

GILBERT, PARKER, treated by Dr. Archer on May 2, 1791; also mentioned inoculation of two of his children, Michael and Abram. {Ref: JA}

GILBERT, PARKER, m. Martha McComas on Sep 21 or 22, 1797. {Ref: PR}

GILBERT, PARKER, paid cash on Apr 8, 1794 at Bush River Store. {Ref: AH}

GILBERT, PARKER, taxpayer, 1798, Susquehanna Hd., 1 dwelling house, 4 inferior houses, 2 acres, $150 valuation; 1 tract (94 acres) in Susquehanna Hd., $158.62 valuation, 3 slaves. {Ref: TL}

GILBERT, PARKER, head of family in 1800 (2nd District). {Ref: CI}

GILBERT, PARKER JR., purchased 12 barrels of corn on Dec 14, 1797 at Bush River Store. {Ref: AH}

GILBERT, PARKER JR., taxpayer, 1798, Harford Upper Hd., 1 tract (50 acres), $191.25 valuation, no slaves. {Ref: TL}

GILBERT, PARKER JR., m. Martha Hughes on Oct 2, 1800. {Ref: PR}

GIBERT, PARKER JR., head of family in 1800 (1st District). {Ref: CI}

GILBERT, PHILIP, taxpayer, 1798, Susquehanna Hd., 1 dwelling house, 5 inferior houses, 2 acres, $100.50 valuation; 1 tract (48 acres), $81 valuation, 1 slave. {Ref: TL}

GILBERT, PHILLIP, head of family in 1800 (2nd District). {Ref: CI}

GILBERT, PRISCILLA, m. Richard Mitchell on Feb 15, 1798. {Ref: PR}

GILBERT, SAMUEL, subpoenaed to the Grand Jury in August, 1797. {Ref: CC}

GILBERT, SAMUEL, taxpayer, 1798, Susquehanna Hd., 1 tract (30 acres) and 1 building, $61.88 valuation, no slaves. {Ref: TL}

GILBERT, THOMAS, see "Michael Gilbert," q.v.

GILBERT, WIDOW, see "Charles Gilbert's heirs," q.v.

GILBERT, WILLIAM, head of family in 1800 (2nd District). {Ref: CI}

GILDEA, DANIEL, taxpayer, 1798, Bush River Lower Hd., 1 dwelling house, 2

inferior houses, 1 acre, $150 valuation; 1 tract (1 acre) in Bush River Lower Hd., $22.50 valuation, no slaves. {Ref: TL}
GILDEA (GUILDY), DANIEL, head of family in 1800 (Abingdon). {Ref: CI}
GILES, CHARLES H., b. Sep 15, 1798, d. May 20, 1873, bur. in Christ Episcopal (Rock Spring) Church Cemetery. {Ref: TI}
GILES, ELIZA ANN, dau. of Thomas and Rebecca, b. Dec 23, 1792. {Ref: PR}
GILES, JACOB, see "Negro Valentine," q.v.
GILES, JAMES, on "a list of insolvents it being for personal property for the road taxes [sic] for 1791" filed by Robert Amoss, tax collector. {Ref: IL 31.12}
GILES, JOHANNA, taxpayer, 1798, Susquehanna Hd., 1 dwelling house, 4 inferior houses, 2 acres, $250 valuation; 1 tract (100 acres) in Susquehanna Hd., $258.75 valuation, 2 slaves. {Ref: TL}
GILES, JOHANNAH, head of family in 1800 (2nd District). {Ref: CI}
GILES, REBECCA, see "Eliza Ann Giles" and "Havre de Grace Company," q.v.
GILES, REBECCA, taxpayer, 1798, Spesutia Lower Hd., no dwelling house listed in this part of the tax schedule, no land listed, 1 slave. {Ref: TL}
GILES, REBECCA, head of family in 1800 (2nd District). {Ref: CI}
GILES, RICHARD, insolvent on lists returned by Robert Carlile and John Guyton for taxes due for the year 1791. {Ref: IL 31.16, 31.19}
GILES, THOMAS, see "Eliza Ann Giles" and "Giles Thomas," q.v.
GILES, THOMAS, served on a Grand Jury in August, 1798. {Ref: CM}
GILES, THOMAS, bur. Oct 29, 1798. {Ref: PR}
GILFORD, THOMAS ("run"), insolvent on a list of the county tax due William Osborn, sheriff, for 1791, as returned by Edward Prigg on Sep 20, 1791. {Ref: IL 31.17}
GILHAM, JOSEPH, insolvent on list returned by Robert Carlile for taxes due for the year 1791. {Ref: IL 31.16}
GILHAM, LUKE, head of family in 1800 (1st District). {Ref: CI}
GILHAMPTON, R., see "Josias C. Hall" and "Robert Gelhampton," q.v.
GILLIFORD, THOMAS, insolvent on lists in 1791 due county taxes and road taxes in "Deer Creek Upper, Middle, and Broad Creek Hundreds" as returned by Robert Amos, Jr. {Ref: IL 31.12, 31.22}
GILLIS, JOHN, charged for "resquing" Daniel Lochry (Lockery) in 1797. {Ref: CD, March and August Terms, 1797}
GILLIS, LEVINAH SHARP, see "James Reed Moore," q.v.
GILLISPEY, JOHN, head of family in 1800 (4th District). {Ref: CI}
GILLISPY, CHARLES, tracts *Charley's Struggle* and *First Addition* (adjoining) surveyed in 1798. {Ref: CB}
GILMORE, JOHN, insolvent on a list for the road tax due for 1791 in Harford Upper, Harford Lower, and Spesutia Upper as returned by Robert Amos, Jr. on Sep 18, 1793. {Ref: IL 31.18}
GILMORE, JOHN, treated by Dr. Archer on Oct 9, 1791. {Ref: JA}
GILMORE, JOHN, head of family in 1800 (2nd District). {Ref: CI}

GILMORE, SALLY, treated by Dr. Archer on Oct 23, 1791. {Ref: JA}
GILMORE, SAMUEL, insolvent on a list for the county tax due for 1793 in Susquehanna Hd. as returned to the levy court by Thomas Taylor on May 28, 1794, who noted "put in my hands last fall." {Ref: IL 31.12}
GINKINS, ENOCH, see "Samuel Hughes," q.v.
GIRVIS, JOHN, insolvent on list returned for the road tax due for 1791 by John Bull. {Ref: IL 31.14}
GIST, THOMAS (Baltimore County), tracts *Chestnut Hill* and *Final Settlement* and *Addition to Deer Park* surveyed between 1792 and 1796. {Ref: SB}
GITTINGS, GRIFFITH, see "John Chamberlain," q.v.
GITTINGS, HARRIOTT, see "James Sterrett Gittings," q.v.
GITTINGS, JAMES JR., see "Sall Gittings," q.v.
GITTINGS, JAMES SR. (Baltimore County), taxpayer, 1798, Gunpowder Upper Hd., 1 tract (187 acres), $575.72 valuation, no slaves. {Ref: TL}
GITTINGS, JAMES STERRETT, son of James and Harriott, b. May 22, 1798, bapt. Nov 13 or 15, 1799. {Ref: PR}
GITTINGS, SALL, child of James Jr., bur. in Oct or Nov, 1795 (exact date not given), aged about 3 years. {Ref: PR}
GLADDEN, JACOB, see "Thomas Street," q.v.
GLADDEN, JACOB, served as constable in Deer Creek Middle Hd., 1798-1800. {Ref: CM}
GLADDEN, JACOB, insolvent on lists in 1791 due county taxes and road taxes in "Deer Creek Upper, Middle, and Broad Creek Hundreds" as returned by Robert Amos, Jr. {Ref: IL 31.12, 31.22}
GLADDEN, JACOB, b. 1800, d. Dec 8, 1867, in his 67th year, bur. in Christ Episcopal (Rock Spring) Church Cemetery. {Ref: TI}
GLADDEN, JACOB, head of family in 1800 (4th District). {Ref: CI}
GLADDEN, JAMES, see "William Gibson," q.v.
GLADDEN, JAMES, charged for retailing liquors in 1794 (which was quashed in 1795), for selling liquor by the small in 1795, and again for selling liquors in 1797. {Ref: CD, March and August Terms, 1795, and March Term, 1797}
GLADDEN, JAMES, insolvent on lists in 1791 due county taxes and road taxes in "Deer Creek Upper, Middle, and Broad Creek Hundreds" as returned by Robert Amos, Jr. {Ref: IL 31.12, 31.22}
GLADDEN, JAMES, head of family in 1800 (4th District). {Ref: CI}
GLADDEN, JOHN, see "James Rampley," q.v.
GLADDEN, JOHN, charged for selling liquors by the smalls in 1797. {Ref: CD, March Term, 1797}
GLADDEN, JOHN, head of family in 1800 (4th District). {Ref: CI}.
GLADDEN, MARY, b. Jan 19, 1797, d. Jun 16, 1854, bur. in Harford (Old Brick) Baptist Church Cemetery. {Ref: TI}
GLASHKILL, LAWRENCE, insolvent on lists in 1791 due county taxes and road taxes in "Deer Creek Upper, Middle, and Broad Creek Hundreds" as returned

by Robert Amos, Jr. {Ref: IL 31.12, 31.22}

GLASS, MONSIEUR, taxpayer, 1798, Bush River Upper & Eden Hd., 1 dwelling house, 4 inferior houses, 2 acres, $400 valuation; 1 tract (210 acres) in Gunpowder Lower Hd., $528.75 valuation, 2 slaves. {Ref: TL}

GLASS, RUMFORD, head of family in 1800 (1st District). {Ref: CI}

GLEASON, DENNIS, b. 1799 or 1800 in County Cork, Ireland, d. Jan 16, 1872, aged 72, bur. in St. Mary's Catholic Church Cemetery in Pylesville. {Ref: TI}

GLEEN, JAMES, insolvent on list returned by Robert Carlile for taxes due for the year 1791. {Ref: IL 31.16}

GLENN, DAVID, insolvent on a list for the road tax due for 1791 in Harford Upper, Harford Lower, and Spesutia Upper as returned by Robert Amos, Jr. on Sep 18, 1793. {Ref: IL 31.18}

GLENN, H. B. (M. B.?), d. 1791(?), age not stated, bur. in Bethel Presbyterian Church Cemetery at Madonna. {Ref: BC}

GLENN, JAMES, insolvent on a list for 1791 in Gunpowder Upper and Bush River Lower Hundreds, as filed by John Bond, Deputy Sheriff, on Sep 20, 1791. {Ref: IL 31.24}

GLENN, JOHN, served on a Grand Jury in August, 1800. {Ref: CM}

GLENN (GLAN), JOHN, head of family in 1800 (4th District). {Ref: CI}

GLENN, ROBERT, taxpayer, 1798, Bush River Upper & Eden Hd., 1 dwelling house, 3 inferior houses, 2 acres, $190 valuation; 1 tract (158 acres) in Bush River Upper & Eden Hd., $355.50 valuation, no slaves. {Ref: TL}

GLENN, WILLIAM, taxpayer, 1798, Bush River Upper & Eden Hd., 1 dwelling house, 3 inferior houses, 2 acres, $200 valuation; 1 tract (204 acres) in Bush River Upper & Eden Hd., $459 valuation, 2 slaves. {Ref: TL}

GLENN (GLEN), WILLIAM, head of family in 1800 (4th District). {Ref: CI}

GODDIN, AARON, see "Mary Ann Goddin," q.v.

GODDIN, ELIZABETH, see "Mary Ann Goddin," q.v.

GODDIN, MARY ANN, dau. of Aaron and Elizabeth, bapt. Oct 23, 1796. {Ref: PR}

GODMAN, WILLIAM, m. Deliah (Delilah) White on Jul 22, 1797.

GOODWIN, MARGARETT ("dead"), insolvent on lists due for 1790 and 1791 "fund taxes" and county taxes in and Susquehanna Hd., as returned by Thomas Taylor. {Ref: IL 31.12, 31.02}

GOODWIN, MOSES, insolvent on lists due for 1790 and 1791 "fund taxes" and county taxes in Susquehanna Hd., as returned by Thomas Taylor. {Ref: IL 31.12,31.02} His name was listed as "Moses Goodwin, Baltimore County" on the 1791 list.

GOODWIN, WILLIAM, insolvent on a list for 1791 in Gunpowder Upper and Bush River Lower Hundreds, as filed by John Bond, Deputy Sheriff, on Sep 20, 1791. {Ref: IL 31.24}

GOODWINS, MARGARET, treated by Dr. Archer on Aug 2, 1791; also mentioned a child (no name given). {Ref: JA}

GORDIN, ANN, insolvent on a list of the county tax due William Osborn, sheriff, for 1791, as returned by Edward Prigg on Sep 20, 1791. {Ref: IL 31.17}

GORDON, ARON, insolvent on lists in 1791 due county taxes and road taxes in "Deer Creek Upper, Middle, and Broad Creek Hundreds" as returned by Robert Amos, Jr. {Ref: IL 31.12, 31.22}

GORDON, CHARLES, head of family in 1800 (3rd District). {Ref: CI}. Also see "Thomas Bond (of Thomas)," q.v.

GORDON, JAMES, taxpayer, 1798, Deer Creek Upper Hd., 1 dwelling house, 2 inferior houses, 2 acres, $105 valuation; 2 tracts (183 acres) in Deer Creek Upper Hd., $236.53 valuation, no slaves. {Ref: TL}

GORDON, JAMES, head of family in 1800 (5th District). {Ref: CI}

GORDON, NATHAN, m. Delia Stevenson on Nov 2, 1797. {Ref: PR}

GORDON, WILLIAM, head of family in 1800 (1st District). {Ref: CI}. Also see "William Hall," q.v.

GORDON, WILLIAM JR., head of family in 1800 (1st District). {Ref: CI}

GORRELL (GORREL), ABRAHAM, head of family in 1800 (2nd District). {Ref: CI}. Also see "Abraham Reese," q.v.

GORRELL, JAMES, taxpayer, 1798, Susquehanna Hd., 1 tract (38 acres) and 1 building, $155.62 valuation, no slaves. {Ref: TL}

GORRELL (GORREL), JAMES, head of family in 1800 (2nd District). {Ref: CI}

GORRELL, JOHN, taxpayer, 1798, Susquehanna Hd., 3 tract (171 acres) and 1 building, $486 valuation, 3 slaves. {Ref: TL}

GORRELL (GORREL), JOHN, head of family in 1800 (2nd District). {Ref: CI}

GORRELL, JOHN THOMAS, see "Marth West," q.v.

GORRELL, JOSEPH, will probated Jun 3, 1793. {Ref: HW}

GORRELL (GORRIL), MARGARET, m. Joseph Degeon on Sep 21, 1800. {Ref: PR}

GORRELL, REZIN, see "Martha West," q.v.

GORRELL, THOMAS, insolvent on a list in 1792 in Deer Creek Lower Hd., as returned by Benjamin Preston. {Ref: IL 31.03}

GORRELL, WILLIAM, taxpayer, 1798, Susquehanna Hd., 1 tract (63 acres) and 1 building, $174.37 valuation, no slaves. {Ref: TL}

GORRELL (GORREL), WILLIAM, head of family in 1800 (2nd District). {Ref: CI}

GORSUCH, DIXON (Baltimore County), or JOHN CATHERWOOD, taxpayer, 1798, Deer Creek Upper Hd., 1 tract (288 acres, 80 perches) and 1 building (John Catherwood, occupant), $649.13 valuation, no slaves. {Ref: TL}

GOTT, SAMUEL (Kent County), insolvent on lists returned for the county and road taxes due for 1791 by John Bull in Gunpowder Lower Hd. (name listed without "Kent County" on one list). {Ref: IL 31.14, 31.15}

GOUGH, HARRY, taxpayer, 1798, Bush River Lower Hd., 1 dwelling house, 2 inferior houses, 2 acres, $500 valuation; 2 tracts (548 acres) in Bush River Lower Hd., $2916 valuation, 5 slaves; also, taxpayer, Bush River Lower Hd., 1 dwelling house, 2 inferior houses, 1 acre (James Johnson, occupant), $120 valuation, no slaves. {Ref: TL}

GOUGH, HARRY DORSEY, b. 1800, d. Dec 2, 1867, aged 67, bur. in Christ

Episcopal (Rock Spring) Church Cemetery. {Ref: TI}
GOUGH, HENRY (esquire), head of family in 1800 (3rd District). {Ref: CI}
GOULD, WILLIAM BUDD, served as constable in Susquehanna Hd., 1797. {Ref: CC, CM}
GOVER, ELIZABETH, dau. of Robert and Martha, b. Dec 28, 1798, bapt. Oct 20, 1799. {Ref: PR}
GOVER, ELIZABETH (Mrs.), treated by Dr. Archer on Jun 17, 1791. {Ref: JA}
GOVER, EPHRAIM, see "Robert Gover," q.v.
GOVER, GITTINGS, head of family in 1800 (2nd District). {Ref: CI}
GOVER, MARTHA, see "Elizabeth Gover," q.v.
GOVER, PRISCILLA ("dead"), insolvent on a list for 1791 in Gunpowder Upper and Bush River Lower Hundreds, as filed by John Bond, Deputy Sheriff, on Sep 20, 1791. {Ref: IL 31.24}
GOVER, PRISCILLA, insolvent on list returned for the road tax due for 1791 by John Bull. {Ref: IL 31.14}
GOVER, ROBERT, see "Elizabeth Gover," q.v.
GOVER, ROBERT, taxpayer, 1798, Spesutia Upper Hd., 1 dwelling house, 4 inferior houses, 1 acre and 80 perches of land, $155 valuation; 2 tracts (131 acres, 80 perches) in Spesutia Upper Hd., $465.19 valuation, 5 slaves. {Ref: TL}
GOVER, ROBERT, charged for assaulting Samuel Smith (merchant) in 1794. {Ref: CD, March and August Terms, 1795 and 1797}
GOVER, ROBERT, m. Martha Wheeler on Apr 18, 1787. {Ref: PR}
GOVER, ROBERT (OF E.), head of family in 1800 (3rd District). {Ref: CI}
GOVER, ROBERT (OF EPHRAIM), served on a Petit Jury in August, 1798 and August, 1799 and August, 1800. {Ref: CM}
GOVER, SAMUEL, see "James Mitchell's heirs," q.v.
GOVER, SAMUEL, tract *Gover's Bar* surveyed between 1792 and 1796. {Ref: SB}
GOVER, SAMUEL (Rock Run), taxpayer, 1798, Susquehanna Hd., 1 dwelling house, 1 inferior house, 2 acres (Widow Mahon, occupant), $200 valuation; 1 tract (111 acres) in Susquehanna Hd. (Widow Mahon, occupant) and 2 tracts (400 acres) in Susquehanna Hd., $2459.25 valuation altogether, 3 slaves. {Ref: TL}
GOVER, SAMUEL L., b. 1800, d. Mar --, 1839, aged 39, bur. in Deer Creek Friends Cemetery in Darlington. {Ref: TI}
GOVER, SAMUEL (OF E.), head of family in 1800 (2nd District). {Ref: CI}
GOVER, SAMUEL (OF P.), head of family in 1800 (2nd District). {Ref: CI}
GRACE, ARON, insolvent on a list for the road tax due for 1791 in Harford Upper, Harford Lower, and Spesutia Upper as returned by Robert Amos, Jr. on Sep 18, 1793. {Ref: IL 31.18}
GRACE, BOWYER, m. Mary Brooks on Apr 26, 1798. {Ref: PR}. Also see "James Grace," q.v.
GRACE, JAMES, son of Bowyer and Mary, b. May 19, 1800, bapt. Jul 21, 1800. {Ref: PR}
GRACE, MARY, see "James Grace," q.v.

GRACE, PETER B., insolvent on a list for the county tax due for 1793 in Harford Upper, Harford Lower, and Spesutia Lower Hundreds returned to the levy court by Thomas Taylor on May 28, 1794. {Ref: IL 31 12}

GRAFTON, AQUILA, taxpayer, 1798, Spesutia Upper Hd., 1 dwelling house, 4 inferior houses, 1 acre, $145 valuation; 2 tracts (128 acres) in Spesutia Upper Hd., $360 valuation, no slaves. {Ref: TL}

GRAFTON, AQUILLA, head of family in 1800 (3rd District). {Ref: CI}

GRAFTON, DANIEL, taxpayer, 1798, Spesutia Upper Hd., 1 dwelling house, 2 inferior houses, 1 acre, $110 valuation; 3 tracts (111 acres) in Spesutia Upper Hd., $283.50 valuation, no slaves. {Ref: TL}

GRAFTON, DANIEL(?), head of family in 1800 (3rd District). {Ref: CI}

GRAFTON, DELILA, see "Delila Patterson," q.v.

GRAFTON, MARTIN, b. 1791, d. Sep 18, 1873, in his 82nd year, bur. in Harford (Old Brick) Baptist Church Cemetery. {Ref: TI}

GRAFTON, NATHANIEL, served on a Petit Jury in August, 1797. {Ref: CC}

GRAFTON, NATHANIEL, taxpayer, 1798, Spesutia Upper Hd., 1 dwelling house, 2 inferior houses, 1 acre, $105 valuation; 3 tracts (308 acres) in Spesutia Upper Hd., $866.25 valuation, 1 slave. {Ref: TL}

GRAFTON, NATHANIEL, served on a Grand Jury in August, 1799 and August, 1800. {Ref: CM}

GRAFTON, NATHANIEL, head of family in 1800 (3rd District); two men by this name in this district. {Ref: CI}

GRAFTON, SAMUEL, taxpayer, 1798, Spesutia Upper Hd., 1 tract (120 acres) and 1 building, $433.13 valuation, no slaves. {Ref: TL}

GRAFTON, SAMUEL, head of family in 1800 (3rd District). {Ref: CI}

GRAFTON, WILLIAM, taxpayer, 1798, Spesutia Upper Hd., 1 dwelling house, 5 inferior houses, 1 acre, 80 perches, $205 valuation; 1 tract (187 acres) in Spesutia Upper Hd., $696.38 valuation, no slaves. {Ref: TL}

GRAHAM, ANGUS, taxpayer, 1798, Spesutia Upper Hd., 1 dwelling house, 6 inferior houses, 2 acres, $650 valuation; 3 tracts (858 acres) and 3 buildings in Spesutia Upper Hd. (occupants: Daniel Laughery, Matthew Judd, and Michael Daugherty or Dougherty), $4170.37 valuation altogether, no slaves. {Ref: TL}. This is actually "Angus Greme" (not Graham), a native of France who returned to Harford County after the Revolutionary War and died in 1800.

GRAME, MARY F., head of family in 1800 (3rd District). {Ref: CI}

GRAME, SAMUEL, head of family in 1800 (3rd District). {Ref: CI}

GRANT & HATCHET, see "Hatchet & Grant," q.v.

GRANT, JAMES, head of family in 1800 (5th District). {Ref: CI}

GRAVES, JOHN, taxpayer, 1798, Gunpowder Lower Hd., 1 dwelling house, 3 inferior houses, 2 acres, $200 valuation; 2 tracts (134 acres) in Gunpowder Lower Hd., $376.88 valuation, no slaves. {Ref: TL}

GRAVES, JOHN, head of family in 1800 (1st District). {Ref: CI}

GRAVES, RICHARD, m. Charlotte Dorsey on May 31, 1798. {Ref: PR}
GRAVES, WILLIAM, taxpayer, 1798, Gunpowder Lower Hd., 1 dwelling house, 4 inferior houses, 2 acres, $200 valuation; 3 tracts (350 acres) in Gunpowder Lower Hd., $1575 valuation, no slaves. {Ref: TL}
GRAY, ELIZABETH, see "George Gray" and "John Gray," q.v.
GRAY, GEORGE, son of James and Elizabeth, b. Dec 15, 1797, bapt. Jan 8, 1798. {Ref: PR}
GRAY, JAMES, see "John Gray" and "George Gray," q.v.
GRAY, JAMES, taxpayer, 1798, Gunpowder Upper Hd., 1 tract (102 acres, 40 perches), $316.76 valuation, no slaves. {Ref: TL}
GRAY, JAMES, taxpayer, 1798, Harford Upper Hd., 1 tract (1 acre, 80 perches), $101.25 valuation, no slaves. {Ref: TL}
GRAY, JAMES, head of family in 1800 (2nd District). {Ref: CI}
GRAY, JOHN, taxpayer, 1798, Bush River Upper & Eden Hd., 1 dwelling house, 2 inferior houses, 2 acres, $200 valuation; 1 tract (108 acres) in Bush River Upper & Eden Hd., $182.25 valuation, no slaves. {Ref: TL}
GRAY, JOHN, son of James and Elizabeth, bapt. Mar 20, 1795. {Ref: PR}
GRAYHAM, MRS., bur. Mar 29, 1797, aged about 55. {Ref: PR}
GREEN, ----, child of Harry Green, bur. May 6, 1796, aged 8 months. {Ref: PR}
GREEN, ANN, see "Thomas Wright," q.v.
GREEN, BENJAMIN, taxpayer, 1798, Spesutia Upper Hd., 1 dwelling house, 3 inferior houses, 1 acre and 80 perches of land, $225 valuation; 3 tracts (198 acres, 80 perches) in Spesutia Upper Hd., $704.53 valuation, 3 slaves. {Ref: TL}
GREEN, BENJAMIN, head of family in 1800 (3rd District). {Ref: CI}
GREEN, BENJAMIN JR., served on a Grand Jury in August, 1798 and on a Petit Jury in August, 1799. {Ref: CM}
GREEN, BENJAMIN JR., taxpayer, 1798, Spesutia Upper Hd., no dwelling house listed in this part of the tax schedule, no land listed, 2 slaves. {Ref: TL}
GREEN, BENNIT, treated by Dr. Archer on Mar 27, 1792. {Ref: JA}
GREEN, CASSANDRA, see "Mary Ann Green" and "Thomas Smithson Green," q.v.
GREEN, CLEMENT, wrote his will "of Baltimore County" on Oct 17, 1795, probated Nov 8, 1796 in Harford County. {Ref: HW}. Also see "Hannah Green," q.v.
GREEN, EDWARD, treated by Dr. Archer on Sep 8, 1794. {Ref: JA}
GREEN, ELIZABETH, taxpayer, 1798, Spesutia Upper Hd., no dwelling house listed in this part of the tax schedule, no land listed, 1 slave. {Ref: TL}
GREEN, HANNAH, wife of Clement, b. Jan 21, 1740, d. Feb 26, 1798, aged 58 years, 1 month, and 5 days, bur. in St. Ignatius Catholic Church Cemetery in Hickory. {Ref: TI}
GREEN, HARRY, see "---- Green," q.v.
GREEN, HENRY, will probated May 16, 1797. {Ref: HW}
GREEN, HENRY, taxpayer, 1798, Bush River Lower Hd., 2 tracts (80 acres) and

1 building, $292.50 valuation, no slaves. {Ref: TL}

GREEN, HENRY, head of family in 1800 (3rd District). {Ref: CI}

GREEN, HENRY (OF JOHN), charged for assaulting Joshua Green in 1795. {Ref: CD, March and August Terms, 1795, and March and August, 1797}. The dockets of March And August, 1797 listed his name without "of John" after it.

GREEN, HENRY'S HEIRS, or JOHN CUMINGS, taxpayers, 1798, Spesutia Upper Hd., 2 tracts (162 acres) and 1 building (John Cumings, occupant), $454.50 valuation, no slaves. {Ref: TL}

GREEN, ISAAC, insolvent on a list for the county tax due for 1791 in Susquehanna Hd., as returned by Thomas Taylor on Sep 17, 1792. {Ref: IL 31.12, 31.02}

GREEN, JAMES, insolvent, Harford Lower and Spesutia Lower Hundreds (listed as a single man), on a tax list returned by George Lyttle on Sep 21, 1791. {Ref: IL 31.20, 31.21}

GREEN, JAMES, head of family in 1800 (5th District). {Ref: CI}

GREEN, JOHN, see "Henry Green (of John)" and "Mary Ann Green" and "Thomas Smithson Green," q.v.

GREEN, JOHN, insolvent on lists returned by Robert Carlile and John Guyton (who listed him as single man and then crossed the name off the list) for taxes due for the year 1791. {Ref: IL 31.16, 31.19}

GREEN, JOHN, taxpayer, 1798, Bush River Lower Hd., 1 dwelling house, 3 inferior houses, 1 acre, $110 valuation; 1 tract (99 acres) in Bush River Lower Hd., $222.75 valuation, no slaves. {Ref: TL}

GREEN, JOHN, charged for refusing to aid and assist a constable in 1797. {Ref: CD, March and August Terms. 1797}

GREEN, JONAS ("gone"), insolvent on lists due for 1790 and 1791 "fund taxes" in Deer Creek Lower and Susquehanna Hundreds, as returned by Thomas Taylor. {Ref: IL 31.12}

GREEN, JOSHUA, see "Henry Green (of John)" and "Robert Harris," q.v.

GREEN, JOSHUA, subpoenaed to the Grand Jury in August, 1797. {Ref: CC}

GREEN, JOSHUA, taxpayer, 1798, Bush River Lower Hd., 1 dwelling house, 3 inferior houses, 1 acre, $100.50 valuation; 1 tract (92 acres) in Bush River Lower Hd., $258.75 valuation, no slaves. {Ref: TL}

GREEN, JOSHUA, bur. Mar 31, 1798, aged 18 months. {Ref: PR}

GREEN, JOSHUA, served on a Petit Jury in August, 1799 and August, 1800. {Ref: CM}

GREEN, JOSHUA, head of family in 1800 (3rd District). {Ref: CI}

GREEN, MARY ANN, dau. of John and Cassandra, b. Feb 20, 1794. {Ref: PR}

GREEN, THOMAS, head of family in 1800 (4th District). {Ref: CI}. Also see "Susanna Smithson," q.v.

GREEN, THOMAS SMITHSON, son of John and Cassandra, b. Oct 3, 1795. {Ref: PR}

GREEN, WILLIAM, see "William Smithson," q.v.

GREENE, WILLIAM, head of family in 1800 (3rd District). {Ref: CI}

GREENFIELD, ELIZABETH, see "Jacob Greenfield" and "Polly Greenfield" and "Joseph Greenfield" and Martha Greenfield" and Henry Austin Greenfield," q.v.

GREENFIELD, HENRY AUSTIN, son of Jacob and Elizabeth, b. Oct 30, 1797. {Ref: PR}

GREENFIELD, JACOB, m. Elizabeth Everist on Sep 29, 1791. {Ref: PR}. Also see "Joseph Everist" and "Polly Greenfield" and "Joseph Greenfield" and "Martha Greenfield" and "Henry Austin Greenfield," q.v.

GREENFIELD, JACOB, son of Jacob and Elizabeth, b. Sep 7, 1799. {Ref: PR}

GREENFIELD, JACOB, taxpayer, 1798, Spesutia Lower Hd., 1 dwelling house, 5 inferior houses, 2 acres, $158 valuation; 1 tract (84 acres, 80 perches), $531.56 valuation, 6 slaves. {Ref: TL}. Also see "Henry Everest's heirs," q.v.

GREENFIELD, JACOB, insolvent on a list for the road tax due for 1791 in Harford Upper, Harford Lower, and Spesutia Upper as returned by Robert Amos, Jr. on Sep 18, 1793. {Ref: IL 31.18}

GREENFIELD, JACOB, had an account at Hall's Store in February, 1791; also mentioned in the account of William Williams at Hall's Store in January, 1791. {Ref: WH}

GREENFIELD, JACOB, head of family in 1800 (2nd District). {Ref: CI}

GREENFIELD, JAMES, insolvent, Harford Lower and Spesutia Lower Hundreds, on a tax list returned by George Lyttle on Sep 21, 1791. {Ref: IL 31.20, 31.21}

GREENFIELD, JANE, head of family in 1800 (2nd District). {Ref: CI}

GREENFIELD, JOSEPH, son of Jacob and Elizabeth, b. Jan 1, 1794. {Ref: PR}

GREENFIELD, MARTHA, dau. of Jacob and Elizabeth, b. Oct 6, 1795. {Ref: PR}. Also see "Thomas Waltham," q.v.

GREENFIELD, POLLY (POLY), dau. of Jacob and Elizabeth, b. Sep 3, 1792. {Ref: PR}

GREENFIELD, THOMAS, had an account at Hall's Store in October, 1791. {Ref: WH}

GREENFIELD, THOMAS, insolvent on a list for the road tax due for 1791 in Harford Upper, Harford Lower, and Spesutia Upper as returned by Robert Amos, Jr. on Sep 18, 1793. {Ref: IL 31.18}

GREENLAND, ANN, wife of Elisha Greenland and dau. of John and Elizabeth Osborn, b. Jun 30, 1799, d. Jul 31, 1884, aged 85 years, 1 month, and 1 day, bur. in Calvary Methodist Church Cemetery. {Ref: TI}

GREENLY, GILBERT, son of Samuel and Rachel, b. Mar 3, 1797, bapt. Apr 13, 1800. {Ref: PR}

GREENLY, GREENBERRY, son of James Greenly and Mary Redman, b. Jan 12, 1800, bapt. Apr 13, 1800. {Ref: PR}

GREENLY, JAMES, see "Greenberry Greenly," q.v.

GREENLY, JAMES, m. Mary Redman on Apr 13, 1800. {Ref: PR}

GREENLY (GREENLEY), JAMES, head of family in 1800 (2nd District). {Ref: CI}

GREENLY, RACHEL, see "William Greenly" and "Gilbert Greenly," q.v.

GREENLY, SAMUEL, see "William Greenly" and "Gilbert Greenly," q.v.

GREENLY, SAMUEL, insolvent on a list for the road tax due for 1791 in Harford

Upper, Harford Lower, and Spesutia Upper as returned by Robert Amos, Jr. on Sep 18, 1793. {Ref: IL 31.18}

GREENLY (GREENLEY), SAMUEL, head of family in 1800 (2nd District). {Ref: CI}

GREENLY, THOMAS, m. Mary Howard on Apr 27, 1800. {Ref: PR}

GREENLY (GREENLEY), THOMAS, head of family in 1800 (2nd District). {Ref: CI}

GREENLY, William, son of Samuel and Rachel, b. Mar 18, 1795, bapt. Apr 13, 1800. {Ref: PR}

GREER, AQUILA, taxpayer, 1798, Bush River Lower Hd., 1 dwelling house, 3 inferior houses, 1 acre and 80 perches of land, $180 valuation; 1 tract (86 acres, 80 perches) in Bush River Lower Hd., $291.94 valuation, no slaves. {Ref: TL}

GREER, AQUILLA, head of family in 1800 (3rd District). {Ref: CI}

GREME, ANGUS (captain in the French Army under Lafayette in the American Revolution), b. 1750, d. Jun 11, 1800, bur. in Trappe Church Cemetery. {Ref: TI}. Also see "Angus Graham," q.v.

GREME, CAROLINE M., b. May 1, 1800, d. Aug 13, 1866, bur. in St. Ignatius Catholic Church Cemetery in Hickory. {Ref: TI}

GREME, MARY F., see "Mary F. Grame," q.v.

GREY, DAVID, head of family in 1800 (4th District). {Ref: CI}

GREY, ELIZABETH, see "William Grey," q.v.

GREY, JAMES, insolvent on a list for the road tax due for 1791 in Harford Upper, Harford Lower, and Spesutia Upper as returned by Robert Amos, Jr. on Sep 18, 1793. {Ref: IL 31.18}. Also see "William Grey," q.v.

GREY, JOHN, head of family in 1800 (4th District). {Ref: CI}

GREY, JOSEPH, b. 1794, d. Feb 10, 1877, aged 83 years, bur. in Centre Cemetery at Forest Hill. {Ref: TI}

GREY, WILLIAM, son of James and Elizabeth, b. Apr 4, 1800, bapt. May 11, 1800. {Ref: PR}

GRIFFIN, JOHN, head of family in 1800 (4th District). {Ref: CI}

GRIFFIN, JOHN SR., bur. May 11, 1794, aged 65. {Ref: PR}

GRIFFIN, MARTHA [MARTH], head of family in 1800 (2nd District). {Ref: CI}

GRIFFITH, ALEXANDER, b. 1791, d. Apr 9, 1815, in his 24th year, bur. in St. George's Episcopal Church Cemetery at Perryman. {Ref: TI}

GRIFFITH, ELIZA, dau. of Samuel and Elizabeth, b. May 1, 1799. {Ref: PR}

GRIFFITH, ELIZABETH, see "Lewis Griffith" and "Eliza Griffith" and "Samuel Griffith" and "George Griffith" and "Mary Goldsmith Griffith," q.v.

GRIFFITH, FRANCES, taxpayer, 1798, Spesutia Lower Hd., no dwelling house listed in this part of the tax schedule, no land listed, 6 slaves. {Ref: TL}

GRIFFITH, GEORGE, son of George and Elizabeth, b. Apr 28, 1793, bapt. Nov 8, 1795. {Ref: PR}

GRIFFITH, HANNAH EMILY, b. 1795, d. Jun 16, 1817, aged 22, bur. in St. George's Episcopal Church Cemetery at Perryman. {Ref: TI}

GRIFFITH, JAMES, taxpayer, 1798, Spesutia Lower Hd., 1 dwelling house, 22 perches and 10 sq. ft. of land, $200 valuation, no slaves. {Ref: TL}
GRIFFITH, JOHN, licensed retailer in March, 1795. {Ref: CC}
GRIFFITH, LEVI, head of family in 1800 (2nd District). {Ref: CI}
GRIFFITH, LEWIS, son of Samuel and Elizabeth, b. Mar 24, 1796. {Ref: PR}
GRIFFITH, LEWIS, purchased sundries on Mar 30, 1793 at Bush River Store. {Ref: AH}
GRIFFITH, LEWIS, or JOHN HALL and A. L. SMITH, taxpayers, 1798, Spesutia Lower Hd., no dwelling house listed in this part of the tax schedule, no land listed, 6 slaves. {Ref: TL}
GRIFFITH, LUKE'S HEIRS, or NATHANIEL HUGHES, taxpayers, 1798, Spesutia Lower Hd., 4 tracts (389 acres) and 1 building (Nathaniel Hughes, occupant), $2201.85 valuation, no slaves. {Ref: TL}
GRIFFITH, MARTHA, taxpayer, 1798, Spesutia Lower Hd., 1 dwelling house, 10 inferior houses, 2 acres, $130 valuation; 1 tract (498 acres), $4482 valuation, 5 slaves; also, taxpayer, Susquehanna Hd., 1 dwelling house, 8 inferior houses, 2 acres, $120 valuation; 1 tract (198 acres), $504.90 valuation, no slaves. {Ref: TL}
GRIFFITH, MARY, m. William Perry on Aug 15, 1799. {Ref: PR}
GRIFFITH, MARY GOLDSMITH, dau. of George and Elizabeth, b. Sep 19, 1794, bapt. Nov 8, 1795. {Ref: PR}
GRIFFITH, MRS., see "Negro Amy" and "Negro Fanny," q.v.
GRIFFITH, SAMUEL, see "George Griffith" and "Mary Goldsmith Griffith" and "Lewis Griffith" and "Eliza Griffith," q.v.
GRIFFITH, SAMUEL, insolvent on list returned for the road tax due for 1791 by John Bull. {Ref: IL 31.14}
GRIFFITH, SAMUEL, son of Samuel and Elizabeth, b. Nov 21, 1800. {Ref: PR}
GRIFFITH, SAMUEL, had an account at Hall's Store in April, 1791. {Ref: WH}
GRIFFITH, SAMUEL, vestryman, 1796-1799, St. George's Episcopal Church. {Ref: PR}
GRIFFITH, SAMUEL, will probated Jun 4, 1794. {Ref: HW}
GRIFFITH, SAMUEL (doctor), taxpayer, 1798, Spesutia Lower Hd., 1 dwelling house, 5 inferior houses, 2 acres, $105 valuation; 1 tract (258 acres), $1536.52 valuation, 6 slaves. {Ref: TL}
GRIFFITH, SAMUEL (doctor), head of family in 1800 (2nd District). {Ref: CI}
GRIFFITH, SAMUEL (Virginia), or JAMES GALLION, taxpayer, 1798, Spesutia Lower Hd., 1 dwelling house, 10 inferior houses, 2 acres (James Gallion, occupant), $375 valuation; 3 tracts (584 acres) in Spesutia Lower Hd. (James Gallion, occupant) and 1 building (William Lauder, occupant), $3237.97 valuation altogether, no slaves. {Ref: TL}
GRIFFITH, SAMUEL'S ESTATE, taxpayer, 1798, Spesutia Lower Hd., no dwelling house listed in this part of the tax schedule, no land listed, 1 slave (Doctor Davis, superintendent).
GRIFFITH, SAMUEL JR., purchased a bay horse on Apr 21, 1791 and 91 trees on

Aug 11, 1793 at Bush River Store. {Ref: AH}

GRIFFITH, SARAH, taxpayer, 1798, Spesutia Lower Hd., no dwelling house listed in this part of the tax schedule, no land listed, 6 slaves. {Ref: TL}

GRIMES, ELIZABETH, see "Polly Grimes" and "John N. Grimes," q.v.

GRIMES, JOHN, see "Polly Grimes" and "John N. Grimes," q.v.

GRIMES, JOHN N., son of John and Elizabeth, b. Mar 30, 1798, bapt. Aug 20, 1799. {Ref: PR}

GRIMES, POLLY, dau. of John and Elizabeth, b. Nov 17, 1792. {Ref: PR}

GRINDAL, ELIZA HELEN, dau. of Joseph and Elizabeth Ann, b. Mar 10, 1798. {Ref: PR}

GRINDAL, ELIZABETH ANN, see "Eliza Helen Grindal," q.v.

GRINDAL, JOSEPH, see "Eliza Helen Grindal," q.v.

GRINDALL, JOHN, served on a Petit Jury in March, 1798 and on a Grand Jury in March, 1799 and March, 1800. {Ref: CM}

GRINDALL, JOHN, taxpayer, 1798, Bush River Lower Hd., 1 dwelling house, 1 inferior house, 1 acre, $170 valuation; 4 tracts (243 acres, 80 perches) in Bush River Lower Hd., $718.59 valuation, 5 slaves. {Ref: TL}

GRINDALL, JOHN, head of family in 1800 (3rd District). {Ref: CI}

GRISWOLD, JOSEPH, head of family in 1800 (1st District). {Ref: CI}

GROSS, CATHARINE, consort of Jacob, b. 1793, d. May 18, 1860, aged 67, bur. in Old Salem Evangelical Cemetery near Madonna. {Ref: TI}

GROVER, ROBERT, head of family in 1800 (3rd District). {Ref: CI}

GROVES, ENOCH(?), head of family in 1800 (1st District). {Ref: CI}

GROVES, WILLIAM, see "Nicholas Day," q.v.

GROVES, WILLIAM, taxpayer, 1798, Gunpowder Lower Hd., no dwelling house listed in this part of the tax schedule, no land listed, 1 slave. {Ref: TL}.

GROVES, WILLIAM, will probated Mar 10, 1800. {Ref: HW}

GRUBB(?), THOMAS, head of family in 1800 (5th District). {Ref: CI}

GRUNDEN, ANN, see "Edward Daws," q.v.

GUBBIN, GRACE, head of family in 1800 (3rd District). {Ref: CI}

GUDGON, SUTTON, head of family in 1800 (1st District). {Ref: CI}

GUEST, JOHN, taxpayer, 1798, Spesutia Lower Hd.. 1 tract (1 acre, 16 perches, 84 sq. ft.), $54 valuation, no slaves. {Ref: TL}

GUEST, REBECCA, paid cash on Jul 12, 1797 at Bush River Store. {Ref: AH}

GUILDY, DANIEL, see "Daniel Gildea," q.v.

GUIN, WILLIAM, insolvent on list returned by Robert Carlile for taxes due for the year 1791. {Ref: IL 31 16}

GUIN, WILLIAM, paid for farm work on Jul 28, 1795 at Bush River Store. {Ref: AH}

GUNNION, HUGH, head of family in 1800 (5th District). {Ref: CI}

GUTREE (GUTRIE), JOHN, head of family in 1800 (4th District). {Ref: CI}

GUYBESON, HANNAH, head of family in 1800 (3rd District). {Ref: CI}

GUYTON, ELEANOR, dau. of John and Frances, b. May 9, 1792, bapt. Oct 14, 1792. {Ref: St. John's & St. George's Parish Registers, and John Guyton Bible}

GUYTON, ELIAS, son of John and Frances, b. Sep 17, 1794, d. Sep 13, 1795. {Ref: John Guyton Bible}

GUYTON, ELISHA, son of John and Frances, b. Jul 20, 1796. {Ref: John Guyton Bible}

GUYTON, FRANCES, see "Eleanor Guyton" and Elias Guyton" and "Elisha Guyton" and "John Guyton," q.v.

GUYTON, ISAAC, insolvent on list returned for the road tax due for 1791 by John Bull. {Ref: IL 31.14}

GUYTON (GUITON), ISAAC, insolvent on a list for 1791 in Gunpowder Upper and Bush River Lower Hundreds, as filed by John Bond, Deputy Sheriff, on Sep 20, 1791 (who listed him as a single man). {Ref: IL 31.24}

GUYTON, JAMES, b. 1795, d. Aug 12, 1868, bur. in Harford (Old Brick) Baptist Church Cemetery. {Ref: TI}

GUYTON, JANE, b. 1792, d. Apr 6, 1842, aged 50, bur. in St. Ignatius Catholic Church Cemetery in Hickory. {Ref: TI}

GUYTON, JOHN, see "Eleanor Guyton" and "Elias Guyton" and "Elisha Guyton," q.v.

GUYTON, JOHN, taxpayer, 1798, Bush River Lower Hd., 1 dwelling house, 2 inferior houses, 1 acre, 4 perches and 99 sq. ft. of land, $550 valuation, no slaves. {Ref: TL}

GUYTON, JOHN, licensed ordinary (tavern) in March, 1795 and August, 1797. {Ref: CC}

GUYTON, JOHN, son of John and Frances, b. Oct 2, 1798. {Ref: John Guyton Bible}

GUYTON, JOHN, head of family in 1800 (Belle Air). {Ref: CI}

GUYTON, JOSHUA, see "Josiah Guyton," q.v.

GUYTON, JOSHUA, insolvent on a list for the road tax for 1792, as returned for Robert Amoss, tax collector (Joshua Guyton's name appeared on the same list three times). {Ref: IL 13.12}

GUYTON, JOSHUA, taxpayer, 1798, Bush River Upper & Eden Hd., 1 dwelling house, 2 inferior houses, 2 acres, $105 valuation; 2 tracts (87 acres, 102 perches) in Bush River Upper & Eden Hd., $147.66 valuation, no slaves. {Ref: TL}

GUYTON, JOSHUA, served as constable in Eden Hd., 1797-1800. {Ref: CC, CM}

GUYTON, JOSHUA, head of family in 1800 (4th District). {Ref: CI}

GUYTON, JOSIAH, son of Joshua Guyton and Margaret Mitchell, b. Nov 6, 1800, d. Jul 8, 1880, bur. in Bethel Presbyterian Church Cemetery at Madonna. {Ref: BC}

GWIN, JOHN (Baltimore County), taxpayer, 1798, Bush River Upper & Eden Hd., 1 tract (20 acres), $39.33 valuation, no slaves. {Ref: TL}

HADLEY, JOHN, taxpayer, 1798, Deer Creek Upper Hd., 1 tract (101 acres, 80 perches) and 1 building, $114.19 valuation, no slaves. {Ref: TL}

HADLEY, JOHN, tract *Hadley's Residence* surveyed in 1794. {Ref: CB, SB}

HAGERTY, DANIEL, head of family in 1800 (1st District). {Ref: CI}

HAGERTY (HAGARTY), DANIEL, m. Elizabeth Jones on Mar 17, 1796. {Ref: PR}. Also see "Mary Hagerty" and "Thomas Hagerty," q.v.

139

HAGERTY (HAGARTY), ELIZABETH, see "Mary Hagerty" and "Thomas Hagerty," q.v.

HAGERTY (HAGARTY), MARY, dau. of Daniel and Elizabeth, bapt. Apr 9, 1797. {Ref: PR}

HAGERTY (HAGARTY), THOMAS, son of Daniel and Elizabeth, b. Jun 12, 1799. {Ref: PR}

HAHN, PETER, taxpayer, 1798, Spesutia Lower Hd., 1 tract (132 perches, 63 sq. ft.), $40.50 valuation, no slaves. {Ref: TL}

HAILEY, JOHN, insolvent on list returned for the road tax due for 1791 by John Bull. {Ref: IL 31.14}

HAIR, FRANCIS, taxpayer, 1798, Bush River Upper & Eden Hd., 1 tract (100 acres) and 1 building, $253.12 valuation, no slaves. {Ref: TL}

HAIR, FRANCIS (Baltimore County), taxpayer, 1798, Bush River Upper & Eden Hd., 2 tracts (104 acres), $234 valuation, no slaves. {Ref: TL}

HALEY, GEORGE, charged for assaulting Robert Love in 1797. {Ref: CD, March and August Terms, 1797}. Also see "James Haley" and "John Haley," q.v.

HALEY, JAMES, son of George and Sarah, b. Oct 12, 1798, bapt. Mar 12, 1802. {Ref: PR}

HALEY, JOHN, son of George and Sarah, b. Dec 10, 1800, bapt. Mar 12, 1802. {Ref: PR}

HALEY, SARAH, see "James Haley" and "John Haley" and "James Smith," q.v.

HALL, ADELINE (ADALINE) BERTHIA, dau. of Josias and Martha, b. Apr 19, 1797, bapt. May 26, 1799, d. Feb 9, 1872, bur. in St. George's Episcopal Church Cemetery at Perryman. {Ref: TI, PR}

HALL, ANN, see "William Henry Hall" and "Aquila Hall" and "Edward Carvill Hall," q.v.

HALL, AQUILA, licensed practicing attorney in March, 1795. {Ref: CC}

HALL, AQUILA, purchased 20 barrels of corn on Jan 14, 1793 at Bush River Store. {Ref: AH}. Also see "John Williams," q.v.

HALL, AQUILA ("for F. Holland's heirs"), taxpayer, Deer Creek Middle Hd., 1 tract (200 acres) and 1 building, $225 valuation, no slaves. {Ref: TL}. Also see "John B. Hall's heirs," q.v.

HALL, AQUILA, b. Feb 26, 1791, d. Sep 9, 1870, bur. in St. Mary's Episcopal Church Cemetery. {Ref: TI}

HALL, AQUILA, son of Aquila Hall, Esq., bur. Feb 19, 1793, aged 4 years. {Ref: PR}

HALL, AQUILA, son of Aquila and Ann, b. May 27, 1795. {Ref: PR}. Also see "William Henry Hall" and "Edward Carvill Hall," q.v.

HALL, AQUILA, son of Aquila, Esq., bur. Mar 30, 1797, aged about 2 years. {Ref: PR}

HALL, AQUILA (esquire), tract *Hall's Angle* surveyed between 1792 and 1796. {Ref: SB}

HALL, AQUILA (Baltimore County), taxpayer, 1798, Harford Lower Hd., 1 dwelling house, 7 inferior houses, 2 acres, $130 valuation; 2 tracts (372 acres, 144 perches, 126 sq. ft.) in Harford Lower and Spesutia Lower Hundreds,

$4480.65 valuation, 1 slave. {Ref: TL}. Also see "William Hall," q.v.

HALL, AVARILLA JANE, dau. of Josias and Martha Hall, b. May 18, 1794 (one church register stated 1793), d. Sep 2, 1852, aged 58 years, 3 months, and 14 days [sic], bur. in St. George's Episcopal Church Cemetery at Perryman. {Ref: TI}

HALL, BENEDICT, taxpayer, 1798, Spesutia Lower Hd., no dwelling house listed in this part of the tax schedule, no land listed, 5 slaves. {Ref: TL}

HALL, BENEDICT, head of family in 1800 (Havre de Grace). {Ref: CI}

HALL, BENEDICT (esquire), head of family in 1800 (Havre de Grace). {Ref: CI}

HALL, BENEDICT CHARLES, son of Benedict Edward and Milcah, b. Feb 10, 1797, bapt. Mar 3, 1797. {Ref: PR}

HALL, BENEDICT E., balance due in November, 1797 at Bush River Store. {Ref: AH}

HALL, BENEDICT EDWARD, taxpayer, 1798, Harford Lower Hd., 1 dwelling house, 9 inferior houses, 2 acres, $100 valuation; 17 tracts (2711 acres, 80 perches) in Harford Lower Hd., $12902.23 valuation, 20 slaves; taxpayer, 1 dwelling house (James Deaver, occupant), 2 inferior houses, 2 acres, $100 valuation, and 1 other building (Isaac Whittaker, occupant) in Harford Lower Hundred; taxpayer, Harford Lower Hd., 1 dwelling house (Moses Cannon, occupant), 2 inferior houses, 2 acres, $100 valuation, and 1 other building (John Michael, occupant) in Harford Lower Hundred; taxpayer, Harford Lower Hd., 1 dwelling house, 7 inferior houses, 2 acres, $100 valuation, and 1 other building (Ann Jiant, occupant) in Harford Lower Hundred; taxpayer, 1 building (Joshua Dulaney, occupant) in Harford Lower Hundred; and, taxpayer, 1798, 1 building (Andrew Riddle, occupant) in Harford Lower Hundred; valuation of these latter 5 other buildings: $266.63 altogether. {Ref: TL}. Also see "John Sydney Hall" and "Benedict Charles Hall" and "Frances Susanna Hall," q.v.

HALL, BENEDICT EDWARD, vestryman, 1792, 1794, 1796-1799, St. George's Episcopal Church. {Ref: PR}

HALL, BENEDICT EDWARD (esquire), Associate Justice of the County Court, 1797-1800. {Ref: CC, CM}

HALL, BETSEY (Miss), treated by Dr. Archer on Oct 12, 1791. {Ref: JA}

HALL, BILLY, had an account at Hall's Store in April, 1791. {Ref: WH}

HALL, CARVIL (colonel), head of family in 1800 (2nd District). {Ref: CI}

HALL, CATHARINE (widow of Elihu), treated by Dr. Archer on Jan 8, 1791. {Ref: JA}

HALL, CHARLOTTE JANE, dau. of Nathaniel Ramsay, b. in Baltimore on Jan 3, 1797, m. Henry Hall, d. in Harford County on May 31, 1868, bur. in St. Mary's Episcopal Church Cemetery. {Ref: TI}

HALL, CHRISTOPHER, insolvent on lists for the county tax and road tax due for 1790 and 1791, as returned by Thomas Taylor on May 28, 1794, but his name was crossed off the 1791 road tax list and was included on the 1792 county tax list. {Ref: IL 31.12, 31.03}

HALL, EDWARD, taxpayer, 1798, Spesutia Lower Hd., no dwelling house listed in this part of the tax schedule, no land listed, 4 slaves (John Hall and Thomas Hall, superintendents). {Ref: TL}

HALL, EDWARD ("at Cramburry"), treated by Dr. Archer on Jun 13, 1799; also mentioned that James Hall was his executor in February, 1802. {Ref: JA}

HALL, EDWARD CARVILL, son of Aquila and Ann, b. Nov 23 or 31 [sic], 1797. {Ref: PR}

HALL, ELIHU, see "Catharine Hall" and "Samuel Hall," q.v.

HALL, FRANCES SUSANNA, dau. of Benedict Edward and Milcah, bapt. Nov 11, 1798, bur. Oct 13, 1799. {Ref: PR}

HALL, GEORGE WILLIAM, son of William and Sophia, b. Apr 2, 1798 at Constant Friendship, d. there Jul 26, 1866, bur. in St. Mary's Episcopal Church Cemetery. {Ref: PR, TI}

HALL, HENRY, see "Charlotte Jane Hall," q.v.

HALL, ISABELLA, dau. of Thomas and Isabella, b. Jan 1, 1799. {Ref: PR}. Also see "Sophia Hall" and "Isabella Hall," q.v.

HALL, J. C. (colonel), had an account at Hall's Store in December, 1791. {Ref: WH}

HALL, JACOB, see "Thomas Parry Hill" and "Mary Hall," q.v.

HALL, JACOB, insolvent on a list for 1791 in Gunpowder Upper and Bush River Lower Hundreds, as filed by John Bond, Deputy Sheriff, on Sep 20, 1791. {Ref: IL 31.24}

HALL, JACOB, insolvent on list returned for the road tax due for 1791 by John Bull. {Ref: IL 31.14}

HALL, JACOB, vestryman, 1799, St. George's Episcopal Church. {Ref: PR}

HALL, JACOB (doctor), taxpayer, 1798, Harford Upper Hd., 1 dwelling house, 5 inferior houses, 2 acres, $500 valuation; 1 tract (498 acres) in Harford Upper Hd., $1120.50 valuation, no slaves; also, taxpayer, Bush River Lower Hd., 1 dwelling house, 1 inferior house, 80 perches of land, $450(?) valuation; 1 tract (4 acres), $22.50 valuation, no slaves. {Ref: TL}. In another part of the tax schedule the occupant is listed as Rev. John Allen.

HALL, JACOB (doctor), head of family in 1800 (3rd District). {Ref: CI}

HALL, JAMES, son of James White and Sarah, b. Oct 14, 1798, bapt. Jan 24, 1800. {Ref: PR}

HALL, JAMES, bur. Jan 31, 1800. {Ref: PR}

HALL, JAMES, vestryman, 1791, St. George's Episcopal Church. {Ref: PR}

HALL, JAMES, head of family in 1800 (Havre de Grace). {Ref: CI}

HALL, JAMES W., served on a Petit Jury in August, 1798 and March, 1799. {Ref: CM}

HALL, JAMES WHITE, taxpayer, 1798, Harford Lower Hd., 1 dwelling house, 4 inferior houses, 1 acre and 40 perches of land, $675 valuation; 3 tracts (621 acres, 40 perches) in Harford Lower Hd., $6157.13 valuation, 9 slaves; taxpayer, Harford Lower Hd., 1 dwelling house, 44 perches and 21 sq. ft. of land, $210 valuation; taxpayer, Harford Lower Hd., 1 dwelling house, 5 inferior houses, 2 acres, $135 valuation, no slaves. {Ref: TL}. His name is listed as "James W. Hall" and "James White Hall" in two different parts of these lists. Also see

"Mary Hall" and "James Hall" and "William B. Stokes," q.v.

HALL, JOHN, see "Edward Hall" and "Martha Hall" and "Lewis Griffith," q.v.

HALL, JOHN, taxpayer, 1798, Spesutia Lower Hd., 1 dwelling house, 6 inferior houses, 2 acres, $105 valuation; 7 tracts (558 acres, 70 perches) in Spesutia Lower Hd., $3099.60 valuation, 5 slaves. {Ref: TL}

HALL, JOHN, served on a Petit Jury in March, 1798 and on a Grand Jury in March, 1799 and March, 1800. {Ref: CM}

HALL, JOHN, head of family in 1800 (Havre de Grace). {Ref: CI}

HALL, JOHN (Baltimore County), or BARNEY J. LYNCH, taxpayer, 1798, Gunpowder Upper Hd., 3 tracts (180 acres) and 1 building (Barney J. Lynch, occupant), $697.50 valuation, no slaves. {Ref: TL}

HALL, JOHN (captain), head of family in 1800 (2nd District). {Ref: CI}

HALL, JOHN (esquire), purchased wool on Nov 14, 1797 at Bush River Store. {Ref: AH}

HALL, JOHN ("Forrest"), served on a Petit Jury in March, 1799. {Ref: CM}

HALL, JOHN, WILLIAM, AND NATHANIEL, taxpayers, 1798, Spesutia Lower Hd., no dwelling house listed in this part of the tax schedule, no land listed, 4 slaves. {Ref: TL}

HALL, JOHN B.'S HEIRS, or AQUILA HALL AND RUTHEN GARRETTSON, taxpayers, 1798, Harford Lower Hd., 1 dwelling house (Aquila Hall, occupant), 5 inferior houses, 2 acres, $310 valuation; 1 tract (798 acres) and 4(?) buildings (Ruthen Garrettson and Aquila Hall, occupants) in Harford Lower Hd., $5909.62 valuation, 11 slaves. {Ref: TL}

HALL, JOHN CARVIL CRANBERRY, son of Josias and Martha Hall, b. May 6, 1795, bapt. May 26, 1799, d. Jan 26, 1855, aged 59 years, 8 months, and 20 days, bur. in St. George's Episcopal Church Cemetery at Perryman. {Ref: TI, PR}

HALL, JOHN SYDNEY, son of Benedict Edward and Milcah Hall, b. Oct 15, 1795, bapt. Nov 3, 1795. {Ref: PR}

HALL, JOHN SYDNEY, bur. Sep 3, 1799. {Ref: PR}

HALL, JOSIAS, see "John Carvil Cranberry Hall" and "Adeline Berthia Hall" and "Sophia Stansberry Hall" and "Mary Clarissa Hall" and "Avarilla Jane Hall," q.v.

HALL, JOSIAS, served on a Petit Jury in August, 1799 and was discharged from serving again in August, 1800. {Ref: CM}

HALL, JOSIAS, balance due on Oct 31, 1797 at Bush River Store. {Ref: AH}

HALL, JOSIAS, insolvent on a list for the road tax for 1792, as returned for Robert Amoss, tax collector. {Ref: IL 13.12}

HALL, JOSIAS, taxpayer, 1798, Susquehanna Hd., 1 dwelling house, 8 inferior houses, 2 acres, $800 valuation; 1 tract (566 acres) in Susquehanna Hd., $2547 valuation, 14 slaves; taxpayer, Susquehanna Hd., 1 dwelling house, 2 inferior houses, 44 perches and 21 sq. ft. of land, in Havre de Grace, $350 valuation; taxpayer, Susquehanna Hd., 1 tract (269 acres) and 1 building (John Williams, occupant), $1311.75 valuation, and 3 buildings in Susquehanna Hundred: one at $101.25 valuation (John Williams, carpenter, occupant); one at $39.38 valuation (Henry Winters, occupant); and one at $39.38 valuation (William Dawson, occupant), no slaves. {Ref: TL}

HALL, JOSIAS, vestryman, 1794, 1796, St. George's Episcopal Church. {Ref: PR}

HALL, JOSIAS, head of family in 1800 (2nd District). {Ref: CI}

HALL, JOSIAS CARVEL, purchased plank on Aug 8, 1797 at Bush River Store. {Ref: AH}

HALL, JOSIAS CARVEL, served on a Petit Jury in August, 1798. {Ref: CM}

HALL, JOSIAS CARVIL, vestryman, 1792, 1794, 1797-1798, St. George's Episcopal Church. {Ref: PR}

HALL, JOSIAS CARVIL, taxpayer, 1798, Susquehanna Hd., 1 dwelling house, 6 inferior houses, 2 acres, $600 valuation; 4 tracts (808 acres) in Susquehanna Hd., $4041 valuation, 15 slaves; taxpayer, Susquehanna Hd., 3 buildings (occupants: Philip Bennet, John Donavin or Donovan, and R. Gilhampton or Gelhampton), $112.50 valuation, no slaves. {Ref: TL}

HALL, JOSIAS CARVIL, see "Col. Carvil Hall" and "Col. J. C. Hall," q.v.

HALL, MARTHA, or JOHN HALL, taxpayer, 1798, 1 tract (497 acres) in Spesutia Lower Hd. (John Hall, superintendent), $1118.25 valuation, 1 slave. {Ref: TL}. Written after her name, without further explanation, is "(land in Harford Upper Hundred)". Also see "John Carvil Cranberry Hall" and "Adeline Berthia Hall" and "Josias Stansberry Hall," q.v.

HALL, MARY, see "Thomas Parry Hill," q.v.

HALL, MARY, dau. of James White and Sarah, b. Sep 12, 1796, bapt. May 7, 1797. {Ref: PR}

HALL, MARY, dau. of Dr. Jacob and Mary, b. Oct 3 or 30, 1793. {Ref: PR}

HALL, MARY CLARISSA, dau. of Josias and Martha, b. Oct 8, 1791, d. Oct 14, 1851, aged 60, bur. in St. George's Episcopal Church Cemetery at Perryman. {Ref: TI}

HALL, MILCAH, "Benedict Charles Hall" and "Frances Susanna Hall" and "John Sydney Hall," q.v.

HALL, NATHANIEL, see "John, William, and Nathaniel Hall," q.v.

HALL, PARKER, treated by Dr. Archer on Feb 5, 1792. {Ref: JA}

HALL, PARKER, had an account at Hall's Store in January, 1791. {Ref: WH}

HALL, PARKER, warden, 1793, 1797, St. George's Episcopal Church. {Ref: PR}

HALL, PARKER, head of family in 1800 (2nd District). {Ref: CI}

HALL, POLLY (Miss), insolvent on list returned for the road tax due for 1791 by John Bull. {Ref: IL 31.14}

HALL, SABINA, purchased 10 barrels of corn on Aug 23, 1792 and 11 barrels of rye on Sep 22, 1792 at Bush River Store. {Ref: AH}

HALL, SAMUEL (OF ELIHU), treated by Dr. Archer on Jan 8, 1791. {Ref: JA}

HALL, SARAH, see "Mary Hall" and "James Hall," q.v.

HALL, SARAH, paid on her account by Aquila Hall on Nov 4, 1797 at Bush River Store. {Ref: AH}

HALL, SARAH, m. John Prosser on Feb 12, 1798. {Ref: PR}
HALL, SOPHIA, dau. of Thomas and Isabella, b. Jul 23, 1795. {Ref: PR}. Also see "William Hall" and "George William Hall," q.v.
HALL, SOPHIA STANSBERRY, dau. of Josias and Martha, b. Dec 3, 1799. {Ref: PR}
HALL, THOMAS, see "Sophia Hall" and "Isabella Hall" and "Negro Walton" and "Negro Robert" and "Negro Bill" and "Negro Jacob," q.v.
HALL, THOMAS, taxpayer, 1798, Harford Lower Hd., 1 dwelling house, 14 inferior houses, 2 acres, $1210 valuation; 8 tracts (1445 acres) in Harford Lower Hd., $7055.89 valuation, 17 slaves; also, taxpayer, Harford Lower Hd., 1 dwelling house, 3 inferior houses, 2 acres, $100.50 valuation, no slaves. {Ref: TL}. Also see "Edward Hall" and "William Hall's heirs," q.v.
HALL, THOMAS, balance due in November, 1797 at Bush River Store. {Ref: AH}
HALL, THOMAS, vestryman, 1794, St. George's Episcopal Church. {Ref: PR}
HALL, THOMAS, head of family in 1800 (1st District). {Ref: CI}
HALL, THOMAS PARRY, son of Jacob and Mary, b. Dec 21, 1791, bapt. Nov 30, 1791. {Ref: PR}
HALL, WALTER T., head of family in 1800 (Havre de Grace). {Ref: CI}
HALL, WILLIAM, see "George William Hall," q.v.
HALL, WILLIAM, vestryman, 1791, St. George's Episcopal Church, d. 1792. {Ref: PR}
HALL, WILLIAM, taxpayer, 1798, Bush River Lower Hd., 1 dwelling house, 3 inferior houses, 2 acres, $505 valuation; 9(?) tracts (1103 acres) in Bush River Lower Hd., $4375.13 valuation, 8 slaves; also, taxpayer, 3 buildings (occupants: Mary Saunders, William Gordon, and John Saunders) in Bush River Lower Hd., $185.62 valuation altogether, no slaves. {Ref: TL}. Also see "John, William, and Nathaniel Hall," q.v.
HALL, WILLIAM, served on a Petit Jury in August, 1798. {Ref: CM}
HALL, WILLIAM, had an account at Hall's Store in July, 1791. {Ref: WH}
HALL, WILLIAM, head of family in 1800 (1st District). {Ref: CI}
HALL, WILLIAM (captain), taxpayer, 1798, Gunpowder Lower Hd., 1 tract (3 acres) and 1 building, $29.25 valuation, no slaves. {Ref: TL}
HALL, WILLIAM (OF AQUILA), treated by Dr. Archer on Jun 21, 1791; also mentioned his dau. Sophia. {Ref: JA}
HALL, WILLIAM'S HEIRS, or THOMAS HALL, taxpayers, 1798, Harford Lower Hd., 1 dwelling house, 4 inferior houses, 2 acres, $100.10 valuation; 7 tracts (903 acres) in Spesutia Lower Hd. (Thomas Hall, occupant), $5524.88 valuation, no slaves; also, taxpayers, 1 dwelling house in Harford Lower Hd. (Thomas Hall, occupant), 3 inferior houses, 2 acres, $550 valuation, no slaves. {Ref: TL}
HALL, WILLIAM HENRY, son of Aquila and Ann, b. Nov 11, 1793, bapt. May 22, 1794. {Ref: PR}
HALLCEY(?), WILLIAM, insolvent on a list for 1791 in Gunpowder Upper and Bush River Lower Hundreds, as filed by John Bond, Deputy Sheriff, on Sep 20,

1791. {Ref: IL 31.24}

HAMBLETON & ALLINS, see "Allins & Hambleton," q.v.

HAMBLETON, CATHARINE SALLY, dau. of John and Peggy, b. Mar 10, 1794, bapt. Dec 10, 1797. {Ref: PR}

HAMBLETON, EDWARD, see "John Coleman," q.v.

HAMBLETON, ELIZABETH, see "William Roach," q.v.

HAMBLETON, JAMES, insolvent on lists of taxes due in 1791 and 1792 in Broad Creek Hd., as returned by Robert Amos, Jr. in 1791 and Benjamin Preston in 1792. {Ref: IL 31.03, 31.12, 31.22}

HAMBLETON, JOHN, see "Mary Hambleton" and "Catharine Sally Hambleton," q.v.

HAMBLETON, JOHN, m. Aley Gafford on Jan 26, 1797. {Ref: PR}

HAMBLETON, JOHN, m. Peggy Bond on Jun 17, 1793. {Ref: PR}

HAMBLETON, JOHN, taxpayer, 1798, Susquehanna Hd., 1 tract (100 acres) and 1 building, $225 valuation, 7 slaves. {Ref: TL}

HAMBLETON, JONATHAN, insolvent on lists in 1791 due county taxes and road taxes in "Deer Creek Upper, Middle, and Broad Creek Hundreds" as returned by Robert Amos, Jr., but his name was then crossed off both lists. {Ref: IL 31.12, 31.22}

HAMBLETON, MARGARET (PEGGY), see "Mary Hambleton" and "Catharine Sally Hambleton," q.v.

HAMBLETON, MARY, dau. of John and Margaret, b. May 5, 1796, bapt. May 28, 1796. {Ref: PR}

HAMBLETON, ROBERT, insolvent on a list for the road tax due for 1791 in Deer Creek Lower Hd., as returned by Thomas Taylor on Sep 17, 1792. {Ref: IL 31.12}

HAMBY, JAMES, m. Ann Williams on Jan 12, 1800. {Ref: PR}

HAMBY (AMBY), JOHN, see "Thomas Sheredine" and "John Daugherty" and "John McGahan" and "Joseph Jervis" and "Thomas Jervis," q.v.

HAMBY, WILLIAM, m. Susanna Cowan on Aug 14, 1800. {Ref: PR}

HAMILTON, ALEXANDER, head of family in 1800 (5th District). {Ref: CI}

HAMILTON, EDWARD, head of family in 1800 (3rd District). {Ref: CI}

HAMILTON, ELIZABETH, head of family in 1800 (5th District). {Ref: CI}

HAMILTON, JAMES L., b. 1799, d. Oct 26, 1879, aged 80, bur. in Christ Episcopal (Rock Spring) Church Cemetery. {Ref: TI}

HAMILTON, JOHN, see "Phebe Hamilton," q.v.

HAMILTON, JONATHAN, head of family in 1800 (5th District). {Ref: CI}

HAMILTON, PHEBE, dau. of John and Phebe, b. Mar 13, 1791. {Ref: PR}

HAMME, SARAH, see "James McKelvey Cartwright," q.v.

HANDY, JOHN, head of family in 1800 (3rd District). {Ref: CI}

HANBY, SAMUEL, insolvent on list returned for the road tax due for 1791 by John Bull. {Ref: IL 31.14}

HANBY, SAMUEL, insolvent on a list for county taxes due in 1792 as returned by Benjamin Preston. {Ref: IL 31.00}

HANBY, SAMUEL, head of family in 1800 (3rd District). {Ref: CI}
HANBY, WILLIAM, head of family in 1800 (2nd District). {Ref: CI}
HANDLIN, THOMAS, insolvent on list returned for the road tax due for 1791 by John Bull. {Ref: IL 31.14}
HANDY, JOHN, insolvent on a list for the county tax due for 1793 in Susquehanna Hd. as returned to the levy court by Thomas Taylor on May 28, 1794, who noted "put in my hands last fall." {Ref: IL 31.12}
HANEY, BARNEY, insolvent on a list for the county tax due for 1793 in Susquehanna Hd. as returned to the levy court by Thomas Taylor on May 28, 1794, who noted "put in my hands last fall." {Ref: IL 31.12}
HANEY, BARNEY ("gone"), insolvent on lists due for 1790 and 1791 "fund taxes" and county taxes in Susquehanna Hd., as returned by Thomas Taylor. {Ref: IL 31.12, 31.02}
HANNA, ALEXANDER, see "William Hanna," q.v.
HANNA, ELIZABETH, wife of Robert, b. circa 1795, d. Jan 3, 1838, aged 43(?), bur. in Churchville Presbyterian Church Cemetery. {Ref: TI}
HANNA, JAMES, taxpayer, 1798, Harford Upper Hd., 1 tract (120 acres) and 1 building, $247.50 valuation, 1 slave. {Ref: TL}
HANNA, JOHN, insolvent on list returned for the road tax due for 1791 by John Bull. {Ref: IL 31.14}
HANNA, JOHN, m. Ann Rogers on Mar 22, 1796. {Ref: PR}
HANNA, MARY, treated by Dr. Archer on Jun 16, 1793. {Ref: JA}
HANNA, MARY, m. William Rodgers on Mar 20, 1800. {Ref: PR}
HANNA, ROBERT, see "Elizabeth Hanna," q.v.
HANNA, WILLIAM, treated by Dr. Archer on Mar 25, 1794. {Ref: JA}
HANNA, WILLIAM (Baltimore Town), or ALEXANDER HANNA, taxpayer, 1798, Harford Upper Hd., 2 tracts (286 acres) and 1 building (Alexander Hanna, occupant), $883.12 valuation, no slaves. {Ref: TL}
HANNAH, ALEXANDER, head of family in 1800 (3rd District). {Ref: CI}
HANNAH, EASTER, head of family in 1800 (3rd District). {Ref: CI}
HANNAH, JOHN, head of family in 1800 (1st District). {Ref: CI}
HANNAH, JOHN'S EXECUTORS, insolvent on a list for county taxes due in 1792 as returned by Benjamin Preston. {Ref: IL 31.00}
HANNAH, REBECCA, head of family in 1800 (3rd District). {Ref: CI}
HANNAH, WILLIAM, insolvent on a list for the road tax due for 1791 in Harford Upper, Harford Lower, and Spesutia Upper as returned by Robert Amos, Jr. on Sep 18, 1793. {Ref: IL 31.18}
HANNOWAY, DAVID, licensed retailer in March, 1795. {Ref: CC}
HANSON, AVERILLA, taxpayer, 1798, Harford Lower Hd., 1 dwelling house, 3 inferior houses, 2 acres, $100.10 valuation; 1 tract (448 acres) and 1 building in Harford Lower Hd., $2268 valuation, 3 slaves. {Ref: TL}
HANSON, BENJAMIN, see "Martha H. Webster," q.v.
HANSON, EDWARD, see "Samuel Jackson," q.v.

HANSON, HOLLIS' HEIRS, or JOHN HERBERT, taxpayers, 1798, Susquehanna Hd., 1 dwelling house, 3 inferior houses, 2 acres (John Herbert, occupant), $100.50 valuation; 1 tract (248 acres) in Susquehanna Hd. (John Herbert or Harbert, occupant), $348.75 valuation, no slaves. {Ref: TL}

HANSON, JOHN, warden, 1798, St. George's Episcopal Church. {Ref: PR}

HANSON, JOHN, insolvent, Harford Lower and Spesutia Lower Hundreds, on a tax list returned by George Lyttle on Sep 21, 1791. {Ref: IL 31.20, 31.21}

HANSON, JOHN, d. Feb 5, 1793. {Ref: John Hanson Bible}

HANSON, JOHN, bur. Mar 7, 1799. {Ref: PR}

HANSON, JOHN, will probated Apr 6, 1799. {Ref: HW}

HANSON, JOHN'S HEIRS, or JONAS COURTNEY, taxpayers, 1798, Harford Lower Hd., 1 dwelling house (Jonas Courtney, occupant), 4 inferior houses, 2 acres, $170 valuation; 9 tracts (615 acres, 120 perches) and 1 building (Jonas Courtney, occupant) in Harford Lower Hd., $2739.37 valuation, 3 slaves. {Ref: TL}

HANSON, JOHN'S HEIRS, or JAMES Osborn, taxpayers, 1798, Harford Lower Hd., 1 dwelling house, 3 inferior houses, 2 acres, $100 valuation; 1 tract (90 acres) and 1 building (James Osborn, occupant) in Harford Lower Hd., $742.50 valuation, 3 slaves. {Ref: TL}

HANSON, JOHN'S HEIRS, or JAMES COLE, taxpayers, 1798, Harford Lower Hd., 1 dwelling house, 3 inferior houses, 2 acres, $100 valuation, and 1 building (James Cole, occupant), $78.75 valuation, no slaves. {Ref: TL}

HANSON, JOHN (farmer, Bush River Neck), will probated Feb 16, 1793. {Ref: HW}

HANSON, JOHN (OF BENJAMIN), treated by Dr. Archer on Feb 12, 1791. {Ref: JA}

HANSON, MARTHA, see "Martha H. Webster," q.v.

HANWAY, DAVID, taxpayer, 1798, Bush River Lower Hd., 1 dwelling house, 2 inferior houses, 1 acre and 80 perches of land, $220 valuation; 2 tracts (170 acres) in Bush River Lower Hd., $1153.12 valuation, no slaves. {Ref: TL}

HANWAY, DAVID, head of family in 1800 (4th District). {Ref: CI}

HANWAY, JOHN, taxpayer, 1798, Bush River Upper & Eden Hd., 1 dwelling house, 2 inferior houses, 2 acres, $200 valuation; 1 tract (155 acres, 120 perches) in Bush River Upper & Eden Hd., $350.44 valuation, no slaves. {Ref: TL}

HANWAY, JOHN, head of family in 1800 (4th District). {Ref: CI}

HANWAY, MICHAEL, insolvent on a list for 1791 in Gunpowder Upper and Bush River Lower Hundreds, as filed by John Bond, Deputy Sheriff, on Sep 20, 1791. {Ref: IL 31.24}

HANWAY, THOMAS, b. 1795, d. Jul 27, 1862, in his 67th year, bur. in Grove Presbyterian Church Cemetery in Aberdeen. {Ref: TI}

HARBERT, ----, see "Jacob Debruler," q.v.

HARBERT, JOHN, see "John Herbert" and "Hollis Hanson's heirs," q.v.

HARBERT, JOHN, charged "for dealing with negroes" in 1797. {Ref: CD, March Term, 1797}.

HARBERT, JOHN, licensed retailer in August, 1797. {Ref: CC}

HARBERT, BENJAMIN, taxpayer, 1798, Susquehanna Hd., 1 tract (101 acres and 80 perches) and 1 building, $273.38 valuation, no slaves. {Ref: TL}

HARBERT, RICHARD, insolvent on a list for the road tax due for 1791 in Harford Upper, Harford Lower, and Spesutia Upper as returned by Robert Amos, Jr. on Sep 18, 1793. {Ref: IL 31.18}

HARDGROVE, JOHN, had an account at Hall's Store in August, 1791. {Ref: WH}

HARDGROVE, RICHARD, taxpayer, 1798, Susquehanna Hd., 1 tract (100 acres) and 1 building, $243.74 valuation, no slaves. {Ref: TL}

HARDY, BENEDICT, taxpayer, 1798, Harford Upper Hd., 1 tract (101 acres), no buildings, 3 slaves. {Ref: TL}. Also see "Hugh Young," q.v.

HARDY, BENEDICTT, head of family in 1800 (3rd District). {Ref: CI}

HARE, HENRY, head of family in 1800 (5th District). {Ref: CI}

HARE, JAMES, head of family in 1800 (2nd District). {Ref: CI}. Also see "Josias W. Dallam," q.v.

HARGROVE (HARTGROVE), ----, dau. of Richard, age 16, inoculated by Dr. John Archer in 1791. {Ref: JA}

HARGROVE, FRANCES, see "Susanna Hargrove," q.v.

HARGROVE, JANE, had an account at Hall's Store in December, 1791. {Ref: WH}

HARGROVE, RICHARD, head of family in 1800 (2nd District). {Ref: CI}. Also see "Susanna Hargrove" and "---- Hargrove," q.v.

HARGROVE, SUSANNA, dau. of Richard Hargrove and Rachel Armstrong, b. Apr 23, 1790, bapt. Jul 28, 1796. {Ref: PR}

HARGROVE, THOMAS, appeared on list of "recognizances" of the court for his appearance in 1797. {Ref: CD, August Term, 1797}

HARKINS, AARON, taxpayer, 1798, Bush River Upper & Eden Hd., 1 dwelling house, 2 acres, $105 valuation; 1 tract (101 acres, 120 perches) in Bush River Upper & Eden Hd., $171.28 valuation, no slaves. {Ref: TL}

HARKINS, AARON, head of family in 1800 (4th District). {Ref: CI}

HARKINS, SARAH, b. Feb 6, 1798, d. Jun 1, 1845, aged 45 years and 4 months, bur. in Sharon Quaker Cemetery. {Ref: TI}

HARLAN, DAVID, son of Elisha, b. 1798, d. Dec 30, 1865, aged 67, bur. in Dublin Methodist Church Cemetery. {Ref: TI}

HARLAN, ELISHA, see "David Harlan," q.v.

HARLAN, MARY ANN, consort of James B., b. Oct 30, 1800, d. Feb 3, 1869, "by second marriage M. A. Smith," bur. in St. George's Episcopal Church Cemetery at Perryman. {Ref: TI}

HARLAND, JERIMIAH, head of family in 1800 (5th District). {Ref: CI}

HARLIN, J., see "John Stump," q.v.

HARP, LAURENCE, m. Mary Delany on Sep 1, 1796. {Ref: PR}

HARPER, FRANCIS, insolvent on a list in 1792 in Broad Creek Hd., as returned by Benjamin Preston. {Ref: IL 31.03}

HARPER, FRANCIS ("dead"), insolvent on a list of the county tax due William Osborn, sheriff, for 1791, as returned by Edward Prigg on Sep 20, 1791. {Ref: IL 31.17}
HARPER, JAMES, served as constable in Deer Creek Upper Hd., 1797-1800. {Ref: CC, CM}
HARPER, JAMES, head of family in 1800 (4th District). {Ref: CI}
HARPER, RICHARD, insolvent on a list for 1791 in Gunpowder Upper and Bush River Lower Hundreds, as filed by John Bond, Deputy Sheriff, on Sep 20, 1791 (who listed him as a single man). {Ref: IL 31.24}
HARPER, SAMUEL, taxpayer, 1798, Bush River Upper & Eden Hd., 1 dwelling house, 1 inferior house, 2 acres, $110 valuation; 4 tracts (300 acres) in Bush River Upper & Eden Hd., $337.50 valuation, 1 slave. {Ref: TL}
HARPER, SAMUEL, tracts *The Western Expedition* and *Harper's Residence* and *Cold Rain* surveyed between 1792 and 1796. {Ref: SB}
HARPER, SAMUEL, served as constable in Bush River Upper Hd., 1797-1800. {Ref: CC, CM}
HARPER, SAMUEL, b. 1793, d. Jul 28, 1879, aged 86, bur. in Deer Creek Harmony Presbyterian Church Cemetery near Darlington. {Ref: TI}
HARPER, SAMUEL, head of family in 1800 (4th District). {Ref: CI}
HARPLEY, NATHANIEL, licensed retailer in August, 1797. {Ref: CC}
HARPLY, NATHAN, taxpayer, 1798, Deer Creek Lower Hd., 1 tract (no acreage given), $157.50 valuation, no slaves. {Ref: TL}
HARRIOTT, EPHRAIM, insolvent on a list for the road tax due for 1791 in Harford Upper, Harford Lower, and Spesutia Upper as returned by Robert Amos, Jr. on Sep 18, 1793. {Ref: IL 31.18}
HARRIS, ELIZA, see "Robert Harris," q.v.
HARRIS, ROBERT, treated by Dr. Archer on Jun 15, 1791. {Ref: JA}
HARRIS, ROBERT, charged for assaulting Joshua Green in 1797. {Ref: CD, August Term, 1797}
HARRIS, ROBERT, taxpayer, 1798, Deer Creek Middle Hd., 1 dwelling house, 4 inferior houses, 2 acres, $120 valuation; 1 tract (200 acres) in Deer Creek Middle Hd., $202.50 valuation, 3 slaves. {Ref: TL}
HARRIS, ROBERT, insolvent on a list for the road tax for 1792, as returned for Robert Amoss, tax collector. {Ref: IL 13.12}
HARRIS, ROBERT, head of family in 1800 (5th District). {Ref: CI}
HARRISS, CHARLES, head of family in 1800 (5th District). {Ref: CI}
HARRY, DAVID, taxpayer, 1798, Gunpowder Upper Hd., 1 tract (128 acres) and 1 building, $411.75 valuation, no slaves. {Ref: TL}
HARRY, DAVID, d. on 11th of 8th month, 1800, aged 50 years, 8 months, and 4 days, bur. in Little Falls Quaker Cemetery in Fallston. {Ref: TI}
HARRY, MARY, head of family in 1800 (3rd District). {Ref: CI}
HART, ISABELLA, head of family in 1800 (5th District). {Ref: CI}
HART, JAMES, see "Aquila Massey," q.v.
HART, JOSEPH, see "Robert and Joseph Hart," q.v.

HART, JOSEPH, treated by Dr. Archer on Aug 5, 1792. {Ref: JA}
HART, JOSEPH ("charge twice"), insolvent on a list for the road tax due for 1791 in Harford Upper, Harford Lower, and Spesutia Upper as returned by Robert Amos, Jr. on Sep 18, 1793. {Ref: IL 31.18}
HART, JOSEPH, head of family in 1800 (3rd District). {Ref: CI}
HART, MRS. (widow), treated by Dr. Archer on Jul 18, 1795. {Ref: JA}
HART, ROBERT, taxpayer, 1798, Spesutia Upper Hd., 1 dwelling house, 40 perches of land, $115 valuation; 1 tract (40 acres) in Spesutia Upper Hd., $135 valuation, no slaves. {Ref: TL}
HART, ROBERT AND JOSEPH, taxpayers, 1798, Harford Upper Hd., 1 tract (40 acres), $90 valuation; no buildings, no slaves. {Ref: TL}
HARTLEY, EZEKIEL, son of Thomas and Leah, bapt. in September, 1793. {Ref: PR}
HARTLEY, JONATHAN, taxpayer, 1798, Harford Upper Hd., 1 tract (26 acres) and 1 building, $69.75 valuation, no slaves. {Ref: TL}
HARTLEY, JOSEPH, insolvent on list returned by Robert Carlile for taxes due for the year 1791. {Ref: IL 31.16}
HARTLEY, JOSEPH, insolvent on a list for 1791 in Gunpowder Upper and Bush River Lower Hundreds, as filed by John Bond, Deputy Sheriff, on Sep 20, 1791. {Ref: IL 31.24}
HARTLEY, JOSHUA, m. Ann Bayne on Feb 13, 1798. {Ref: PR}
HARTLEY, LEAH, bur. Sep 10, 1795, aged about 30. {Ref: PR}. Also see "Mary Hartley" and "Ezekiel Hartley" and "Sarah Hartley," q.v.
HARTLEY, MARY, dau. of Thomas and Leah, b. Sep 9, 1792. {Ref: PR}
HARTLEY, SARAH, dau. of Thomas and Leah, b. in 1791. {Ref: PR}
HARTLEY, THOMAS, see "Mary Hartley" and "Ezekiel Hartley" and "Sarah Hartley," q.v.
HARVEY, ARCHIBALD, taxpayer, 1798, Broad Creek Hd., 1 tract (142 acres) and 1 building, $276.90 valuation, no slaves. {Ref: TL}
HARVEY, ARCHIBALD ("gone away"), insolvent on lists in 1791 due county taxes and road taxes in "Deer Creek Upper, Middle, and Broad Creek Hundreds" as returned by Robert Amos, Jr., but his name was then crossed off both lists. {Ref: IL 31.12, 31.22}
HARVEY, ARCHIBALD, tract *Harvey's Discovery* surveyed in 1798, and tract *The Bald Eagle* surveyed in 1799 (resurvey of Harvey's part of *Ohio* tract). {Ref: CB}
HARVEY, ARCHIBALD, head of family in 1800 (5th District). {Ref: CI}
HARVEY, JOHN ("dead"), insolvent on a list for 1791 in Gunpowder Upper and Bush River Lower Hundreds, as filed by John Bond, Deputy Sheriff, on Sep 20, 1791. {Ref: IL 31.24}
HARVEY, JOHN, m. Hannah Johnson on Mar 12, 1799. {Ref: PR}
HARVEY, JOHN, head of family in 1800 (3rd District). {Ref: CI}
HARVEY, JOHN JR., head of family in 1800 (3rd District). {Ref: CI}
HARVEY, WILLIAM, insolvent on list returned by Robert Carlile for taxes due

for the year 1791. {Ref: IL 31.16}
HARWARD, JOHN, see "Letitia Harward," q.v.
HARWARD, LETITIA, dau. of John and Margaret, b. Aug 26, 1799, bapt. Aug 12, 1800. {Ref: PR}
HARWARD, MARGARET, see "Letitia Harward," q.v.
HARWOOD, HENRY, head of family in 1800 (2nd District). {Ref: CI}
HARWOOD, JACOB, taxpayer, 1798, Deer Creek Lower Hd., 1 dwelling house, 1 inferior house, 2 acres, $180 valuation; 1 tract (280 acres) in Deer Creek Lower Hd., $1057.50 valuation, 1 slave. {Ref: TL}
HARWOOD, JOHN, see "John Moores," q.v.
HARWOOD, JOHN, insolvent on a list for the road tax due for 1791 in Harford Upper, Harford Lower, and Spesutia Upper as returned by Robert Amos, Jr. on Sep 18, 1793. {Ref: IL 31.18}
HARWOOD, JOHN, head of family in 1800 (3rd District). {Ref: CI}
HARWOOD, SUSAN, m. Hugh Haughey on Aug 12, 1800. {Ref: PR}
HARWOOD, WALTER, head of family in 1800 (3rd District). {Ref: CI}. Also see "John Love's heirs," q.v.
HATCHESON, WINSON, insolvent, Harford Lower and Spesutia Lower Hundreds (listed as a single man), on a tax list returned by George Lyttle on Sep 21, 1791. {Ref: IL 31.20, 31.21}
HATCHET & GRANT (Baltimore Town), taxpayers, 1798, Bush River Upper & Eden Hd., 1 dwelling house, 1 inferior house, 2 acres, $110 valuation; 1 tract (186 acres, 120 perches), $420.19 valuation, no slaves. {Ref: TL}
HATHHORN, SAMUEL, head of family in 1800 (Belle Air). {Ref: CI}
HAUDUCOEUR, C. P., see "Charles Hautoker," q.v.
HAUGHEY, HUGH, m. Susan Harwood on Aug 12, 1800. {Ref: PR}
HAUGHEY (HOUGHEY), HUGH, head of family in 1800 (3rd District). {Ref: CI}
HAUTOKER, CHARLES, head of family in 1800 (Havre de Grace). {Ref: CI}. This is C. P. Hauducoeur, engineer, who made a map of the upper Chesapeake Bay, Susquehanna River, and the town of Havre de Grace in 1799.
HAVILAND, ESTHER, b. on 15th day of 10th month, 1794, d. on 11th day of 6th month, 1878, aged 83 years, 7 months, and 27 days, bur. in Forest Hill Quaker Cemetery. {Ref: TI}
HAVRE DE GRACE COMPANY, taxpayer, 1798, Harford Lower Hd., 1 dwelling house (Rebecca Giles, occupant), 5 inferior houses, 2 acres, $650 valuation; 3 tracts (750 acres, 42 perches, 87 sq. ft.) and 1 building in Harford Lower Hd., $5385.15 valuation, no slaves; taxpayer, Harford Lower Hd., 1 dwelling house (John Yokely, occupant), 2 acres, $125 valuation, no slaves; taxpayer, Harford Lower Hd., 1 dwelling house (Abraham Steel, occupant), 2 acres, $175 valuation, no slaves; also, taxpayer, 1798, Harford Lower Hd., 1 dwelling house (Mrs. Angle, occupant), 3 inferior houses, 2 acres, $120 valuation, no slaves; taxpayer, 1 tract (200 acres) in Susquehanna Hd., $675 valuation, no

slaves. {Ref: TL}

HAWKINS, CALEB, insolvent on lists in 1791 due county taxes and road taxes in "Deer Creek Upper, Middle, and Broad Creek Hundreds" as returned by Robert Amos, Jr. {Ref: IL 31.12, 31.22}

HAWKINS, CALEB, insolvent on a list in 1792 in Broad Creek Hd., as returned by Benjamin Preston. {Ref: IL 31.03}

HAWKINS, CALIP ("run"), insolvent on a list of the county tax due William Osborn, sheriff, for 1791, as returned by Edward Prigg on Sep 20, 1791. {Ref: IL 31.17}

HAWKINS, CHARLES, served on a Petit Jury in August, 1798 and on a Grand Jury in March, 1800. {Ref: CM}. Also see "Nicholas and Charles Hawkins," q.v.

HAWKINS, JOHN, b. 1800, d. May 15, 1831, aged 31, bur. in St. George's Episcopal Church Cemetery at Perryman. {Ref: TI}

HAWKINS, MATTHEW, b. 1795, d. Feb 17, 1831, aged 36, bur. in St. George's Episcopal Church Cemetery at Perryman. {Ref: TI}

HAWLINS, NICHOLAS, head of family in 1800 (4th District). {Ref: CI}

HAWKINS, NICHOLAS AND CHARLES, taxpayers, 1798, Bush River Upper & Eden Hd., 1 dwelling house, 1 inferior house, 2 acres, $105 valuation; 2 tracts (63 acres) in Bush River Upper & Eden Hd., $141.75 valuation, no slaves. {Ref: TL}

HAWKINS, RICHARD, taxpayer, 1798, Susquehanna Hd., 1 dwelling house, 2 inferior houses, 2 acres, $200 valuation; 2 tracts (143 acres) in Susquehanna Hd., $201.90 valuation, 1 slave. {Ref: TL}

HAWKINS, RICHARD, head of family in 1800 (2nd District). {Ref: CI}

HAWKINS, ROBERT, m. Ann Mitchell on Jul 20, 1797. {Ref: PR}

HAWKINS, ROBERT, taxpayer, 1798, Susquehanna Hd., 1 dwelling house, 2 inferior houses, 2 acres, $120 valuation; 1 tract (56 acres) in Susquehanna Hd., $111.38 valuation, no slaves. {Ref: TL}

HAWKINS, ROBERT, head of family in 1800 (2nd District). {Ref: CI}

HAWKINS, ROBERT JR., taxpayer, 1798, Susquehanna Hd., 1 tract (101 acres), no buildings, 1 slave. {Ref: TL}

HAWKINS, SAMUEL, insolvent on a list in 1792 in Deer Creek Lower Hd., as returned by Benjamin Preston. {Ref: IL 31.03}

HAWKINS, THOMAS, taxpayer, 1798, Broad Creek Hd., 2 tracts (153 acres) and 1 building, $301.22 valuation, no slaves. {Ref: TL}

HAWKINS, THOMAS, insolvent on a list in 1792 in Broad Creek Hd., as returned by Benjamin Preston. {Ref: IL 31.03}

HAWKINS, THOMAS, insolvent on lists in 1791 due county taxes and road taxes in "Deer Creek Upper, Middle, and Broad Creek Hundreds" as returned by Robert Amos, Jr. {Ref: IL 31.12, 31.22}

HAWKINS, THOMAS, head of family in 1800 (5th District). {Ref: CI}

HAWKINS, THOMAS ("saddle"), insolvent on lists in 1791 due county taxes and road taxes in "Deer Creek Upper, Middle, and Broad Creek Hundreds" as returned by Robert Amos, Jr. {Ref: IL 31.12, 31.22}

HAWKINS, THOMAS (sadler), "run," insolvent on a list of the county tax due William Osborn, sheriff, for 1791, as returned by Edward Prigg on Sep 20, 1791. {Ref: IL 31.17}

HAWKINS, WILLIAM, b. Sep 11, 1799, d. Sep 25, 1889, aged 90 years and 14 days, bur. in Smith's Chapel Methodist Church Cemetery in Churchville. {Ref: TI}

HAWKINS, WILLIAM D., taxpayer, 1798, Deer Creek Upper Hd., 1 tract (194 acres) and 1 building, $799.31 valuation, no slaves. {Ref: TL}

HAWKINS, WILLIAM D., head of family in 1800 (4th District). {Ref: CI}

HAWKINS, WILLIAM W., head of family in 1800 (1st District). {Ref: CI}

HAWKS, MICHAEL, had an account at Hall's Store in September, 1791, which noted payment "by bricks at Stony Point." {Ref: WH}

HAY, THOMAS, charged for assaulting John Franals (Franell) in 1797. {Ref: CD, March and August Terms, 1797}

HAY, THOMAS, head of family in 1800 (4th District). {Ref: CI}

HAYES, ARCHER, taxpayer, 1798, Spesutia Upper Hd., 1 dwelling house, 5 inferior houses, 1 acre and 80 perches of land, $200 valuation; 2 tracts (327 acres, 80 perches) in Spesutia Upper Hd., $736.88 valuation, 3 slaves. {Ref: TL}

HAYES, JOHN, taxpayer, 1798, Spesutia Upper Hd., 1 dwelling house, 5 inferior houses, 2 acres, $550 valuation; 5(?) tracts (511 acres) in Spesutia Upper Hd., $2174.63 valuation, 3 slaves. {Ref: TL}. Also see "Alexander Rigdon" and "Archer Hays," q.v.

HAYES, JOHN JR., see "Alexander Rigdon," q.v.

HAYES, JOSEPH, taxpayer, 1798, Harford Upper Hd., 1 tract (143 acres) and 1 building, $345 valuation, no slaves. {Ref: TL}. In another part of the tax schedule the occupant is listed as Roland Rogers.

HAYES, WILLIAM, taxpayer, 1798, Gunpowder Lower Hd., 1 dwelling house, 2 inferior houses, 2 acres, $120 valuation; 1 tract (16 acres) in Gunpowder Lower Hd., $261 valuation, 1 slave. {Ref: TL}

HAYHURST, ANN, insolvent on list returned by Robert Carlile for taxes due for the year 1791. {Ref: IL 31.16}

HAYHURST, ANN, insolvent on a list for 1791 in Gunpowder Upper and Bush River Lower Hundreds, as filed by John Bond, Deputy Sheriff, on Sep 20, 1791. {Ref: IL 31.24}

HAYHURST, JAMES, insolvent on list returned by Robert Carlile for taxes due for the year 1791. {Ref: IL 31.16}

HAYHURST, JAMES, insolvent on a list for 1791 in Gunpowder Upper and Bush River Lower Hundreds, as filed by John Bond, Deputy Sheriff, on Sep 20, 1791. {Ref: IL 31.24}

HAYLEY, DANIEL, insolvent on lists in 1791 due county taxes and road taxes in "Deer Creek Upper, Middle, and Broad Creek Hundreds" as returned by Robert Amos, Jr., but his name was then crossed off both lists. {Ref: IL 31.12, 31.22}

HAYLEY, JOHN SR., insolvent on lists in 1791 due county taxes and road taxes in "Deer Creek Upper, Middle, and Broad Creek Hundreds" as returned by Robert Amos, Jr. {Ref: IL 31.12, 31.22}

HAYLEY, JOSEPH, insolvent on lists in 1791 due county taxes and road taxes in "Deer Creek Upper, Middle, and Broad Creek Hundreds" as returned by Robert Amos, Jr. {Ref: IL 31.12, 31.22}

HAYLEY, MARK, insolvent on lists in 1791 due county taxes and road taxes in "Deer Creek Upper, Middle, and Broad Creek Hundreds" as returned by Robert Amos, Jr. {Ref: IL 31.12, 31.22}

HAYS, ABRAHAM, head of family in 1800 (4th District). {Ref: CI}

HAYS, ARCHER, served on a Petit Jury in August, 1800. {Ref: CM}

HAYS, ARCHER, served on a Petit Jury in March, 1798 and on a Grand Jury in March, 1799. {Ref: CM}

HAYS, ARCHER, head of family in 1800 (3rd District). {Ref: CI}

HAYS, DAVID, insolvent on lists returned by Robert Carlile and John Guyton for taxes due for the year 1791. {Ref: IL 31.16, 31.19}

HAYS, HARRIET B., dau. of John Hays, b. 1795, d. Sep 23, 1872, in her 77th year, bur. in Churchville Presbyterian Church Cemetery. {Ref: TI}

HAYS, JOHN, see "Harriet B. Hays," q.v.

HAYS, JOHN, insolvent on lists in 1791 due county taxes and road taxes in "Deer Creek Upper, Middle, and Broad Creek Hundreds" as returned by Robert Amos, Jr. {Ref: IL 31.12, 31.22}

HAYS, JOHN, head of family in 1800 (3rd District). {Ref: CI}

HAYS, JOHN'S HEIRS, taxpayers, 1798, Gunpowder Lower Hd., 1 dwelling house, 1 inferior house, 2 acres, $100 valuation, no slaves. {Ref: TL}

HAYS, JOSEPH, treated by Dr. Archer on Nov 19, 1796. {Ref: JA}

HAYS, THOMAS, see "James Thornton" and "John Thornton, Jr.," q.v.

HAYS, THOMAS, subpoenaed to the Grand Jury in August, 1797. {Ref: CC}

HAYS, THOMAS, head of family in 1800 (Belle Air). {Ref: CI}.

HAYS, VINCENT, head of family in 1800 (4th District). {Ref: CI}

HAYS, WILLIAM, head of family in 1800 (1st District). {Ref: CI}

HAYS, WILLIAM S. (colonel), b. 1798, d. 1848, aged 50, bur. in the Hays-Jarrett Graveyard. {Ref: TI}

HAYWARD, JOHN BARNEY, bur. Sep 8, 1800. {Ref: PR}

HEALEY, GEORGE, head of family in 1800 (Belle Air). {Ref: CI}

HEALEY, WILLIAM, head of family in 1800 (Abingdon). {Ref: CI}

HEALY, DANIEL, head of family in 1800 (5th District). {Ref: CI}

HEALY, JOSEPH, head of family in 1800 (5th District). {Ref: CI}

HEAP, JOHN, tract *John's Search* surveyed between 1792 and 1796. {Ref: SB}

HEAPS (HEAPE), ARCHIBALD (ARCABD.), mentioned in a survey deposition on Sep 27, 1799. {Ref: JS}

HEAPS, ARTHUR, see "John Norris (tanner)," q.v.

HEAPS, ARTHUR, insolvent on lists in 1791 due county taxes and road taxes in

155

"Deer Creek Upper, Middle, and Broad Creek Hundreds" as returned by Robert Amos, Jr. {Ref: IL 31.12, 31.22}

HEAPS (HEAP), ARTHUR, mentioned in a survey deposition on Sep 26, 1799. {Ref: JS}

HEAPS, ARTHUR, head of family in 1800 (5th District). {Ref: CI}

HEAPS, JOHN, taxpayer, 1798, Deer Creek Upper Hd., 1 tract (96 acres) and 1 building, $108 valuation, no slaves. {Ref: TL}

HEAPS, JOHN, head of family in 1800 (4th District). {Ref: CI}

HEAPS (HEAP), JOHN, mentioned in a survey deposition on Sep 26, 1799. {Ref: JS}

HEAPS (HEEPS), JOHN, insolvent on lists returned by Robert Carlile and John Guyton (who then crossed him off his list) for taxes due for the year 1791. {Ref: IL 31.16, 31.19}

HEAPS, ROBERT, see "John Norris (tanner)" and "Sarah Heaps," q.v.

HEAPS, ROBERT, head of family in 1800 (4th District). {Ref: CI}

HEAPS (HEEPS), ROBERT, insolvent on lists returned by Robert Carlile and John Guyton for taxes due for the year 1791. {Ref: IL 31.16, 31.19}

HEAPS, ROBERT JR., taxpayer, 1798, Deer Creek Upper Hd., 1 tract (91 acres, 80 perches), $128.65 valuation; no buildings, no slaves. {Ref: TL}

HEAPS, SARAH, wife of Robert L., b. 1800, d. Sep 15, 1884, in her 84th year, bur. in Mt. Vernon Methodist Church Cemetery. {Ref: TI}

HEAPS, THOMAS, head of family in 1800 (4th District). {Ref: CI}. Also see "James Akin," q.v.

HEARTLY, WILLIAM, head of family in 1800 (3rd District). {Ref: CI}

HEATH, RICHARD K. (Cecil County), taxpayer, 1798, Spesutia Lower Hd., 1 tract (1 acre, 60 perches, 105 sq. ft.), $67.50 valuation, no slaves. {Ref: TL}

HEATON, JOHN, b. 1794, d. Sep --, 1869, aged 75, bur. in Fellowship Cemetery near Harkins. {Ref: TI}

HEATON, SUSANNA, b. 1794, d. Feb 16, 1859, aged 65, bur. in Fellowship Cemetery near Harkins. {Ref: TI}

HEDERICK, CHARLES (shoemaker at James Moores), treated by Dr. Archer on Nov 10, 1791. {Ref: JA}

HELEMAN, CONRAD, taxpayer, 1798, Spesutia Lower Hd., 1 tract (44 perches, 21 sq. ft.), $13.50 valuation, no slaves. {Ref: TL}

HELMING, RACHEL, b. 1798, d. Feb 18, 1858, bur. in Grove Presbyterian Church Cemetery in Aberdeen. {Ref: TI}

HEMPFIELD, JAMES, noted in James Steele's survey book on Apr 22, 1799 as "this day received of James Hempfield £92, 11s, 8d in full of all accounts" and signed "John Jamison Sqr." {Ref: JS}

HEMPHELL, JOHN ("dead"), insolvent on a list of the county tax due William Osborn, sheriff, for 1791, as returned by Edward Prigg on Sep 20, 1791. {Ref: IL 31.17}

HEMPHILL, JOHN, insolvent on lists of taxes due in 1791 and 1792 in Broad Creek Hd., as returned by Robert Amos, Jr. in 1791 and Benjamin Preston in 1792. {Ref: IL 31.03, 31.12, 31.22}

HENDERSON, ANDREW, insolvent on lists returned by Robert Carlile and John Guyton for taxes due for the year 1791. {Ref: IL 31.16, 31.19}

HENDERSON, ARCHABLE, insolvent on list returned by John Guyton (who listed him as a single man) for taxes due for the year 1791. {Ref: IL 31.19}

HENDERSON, ARCHIBALD, head of family in 1800 (4th District). {Ref: CI}

HENDERSON, BENJAMIN, see "Sarah Henderson," q.v.

HENDERSON, CATHARINE, see "James Garrett," q.v.

HENDERSON, DOCTOR, consulted with Dr. Archer in 1792. {Ref: JA}

HENDERSON, ELIZABETH, head of family in 1800 (2nd District). {Ref: CI}. Also see "Mary Henderson" and "John Henderson" and "Isaac Periman Henderson," q.v.

HENDERSON, FRANCIS, taxpayer, 1798, Bush River Upper & Eden Hd., 1 dwelling house, 2 inferior houses, 2 acres, $120 valuation; 2 tracts (101 acres) in Bush River Upper & Eden Hd., $229.50 valuation, no slaves. {Ref: TL}

HENDERSON, FRANCIS, head of family in 1800 (4th District). {Ref: CI}

HENDERSON, GEORGE, see "James Phillips, Sr.," q.v.

HENDERSON, GEORGE, treated by Dr. Archer on Feb 20, 1791. {Ref: JA}

HENDERSON, GEORGE, taxpayer, 1798, Spesutia Lower Hd., no dwelling house listed in this part of the tax schedule, no land listed, 3 slaves. {Ref: TL}

HENDERSON, GEORGE, m. Charity Cole on Jun 19, 1800. {Ref: PR}

HENDERSON, GEORGE, head of family in 1800 (2nd District). {Ref: CI}

HENDERSON, GILBERT, insolvent on list returned for the road tax due for 1791 by John Bull. {Ref: IL 31.14}

HENDERSON, ISAAC PERIMAN, son of Nathaniel and Elizabeth, b. Oct 8, 1799, bapt. Nov 10, 1799. {Ref: PR}

HENDERSON, JAMES N., b. Mar 30, 1792, d. Jan 24, 1876, aged 83 years, 9 months, and 25 days, bur. in McKendree Cemetery near Black Horse. {Ref: TI}

HENDERSON, JANE (JANET) N., consort of Thomas N., b. 1796 or 1798, d. May 26, 1841, bur. in Bethel Presbyterian Church Cemetery at Madonna. {Ref: BC}

HENDERSON, JOHN, son of Nathaniel and Elizabeth, b. Aug 22, 1797, bapt. Mar 10, 1799. {Ref: PR}

HENDERSON, MARY, dau. of Nathaniel and Elizabeth, b. Sep 2, 1795, bapt. Feb 7, 1796. {Ref: PR}

HENDERSON, NATHANIEL, insolvent on a list for the road tax due for 1791 in Harford Upper, Harford Lower, and Spesutia Upper as returned by Robert Amos, Jr. on Sep 18, 1793 (his name was crossed off the list). {Ref: IL 31.18}. Also see "Sally Henderson" and "Jacob Collins" and "Mary Henderson" and "John Henderson" and "Isaac Periman Henderson," q.v.

HENDERSON, PHILIP (doctor), taxpayer, 1798, Bush River Lower Hd., 1 dwelling house, 7 inferior houses, 2 acres, $340 valuation; 1 tract (498 acres) in Bush River Lower Hd., $3016.26 valuation, 2 slaves. {Ref: TL}

HENDERSON, PHILLIP (doctor), head of family in 1800 (3rd District). {Ref: CI}

157

HENDERSON, SALLY, taxpayer, 1798, Harford Lower Hd., 1 dwelling house, 2 inferior houses, 2 acres, $100.50 valuation; 2 tracts (4 acres) in Harford Lower Hd., $18 valuation, no slaves. {Ref: TL}. In another part of the tax schedule the occupant is listed as Nathaniel Henderson.

HENDERSON, SARAH, b. Aug 2, 1800, d. Sep 2, 1868, aged 68 years and 1 month, bur. in McKendree Cemetery near Black Horse. {Ref: TI}

HENDERSON, SARAH, wife of Benjamin, was b. in 1791, d. 1872, bur. in Mountain Christian Church Cemetery. {Ref: TI}

HENDERSON, THOMAS N., see "Jane (Janet) Henderson," q.v.

HENDON, BENJAMIN, taxpayer, 1798, Gunpowder Upper Hd., 2 tracts (198 acres) and 1 building, $390.37 valuation, 1 slave. {Ref: TL}

HENDON, BENJAMIN, head of family in 1800 (3rd District). {Ref: CI}

HENDRICKS, WILLIAM ("run"), insolvent on a list of the county tax due William Osborn, sheriff, for 1791, as returned by Edward Prigg on Sep 20, 1791. {Ref: IL 31.17}

HENDRICKS, WILLIAM, insolvent on lists in 1791 due county taxes and road taxes in "Deer Creek Upper, Middle, and Broad Creek Hundreds" as returned by Robert Amos, Jr. {Ref: IL 31.12, 31.22}

HENLEY, PATRICK, insolvent on a list for 1791 in Gunpowder Upper and Bush River Lower Hundreds, as filed by John Bond, Deputy Sheriff, on Sep 20, 1791. {Ref: IL 31.24}

HENLIN, THOMAS, insolvent on a list for 1791 in Gunpowder Upper and Bush River Lower Hundreds, as filed by John Bond, Deputy Sheriff, on Sep 20, 1791 (who listed him as a single man). {Ref: IL 31.24}

HENRY, HENRY, head of family in 1800 (1st District). {Ref: CI}. Also see "Henry O'Henry," q.v.

HENRY, ISAAC, tract *Pleasant Hills* surveyed in 1788 and granted in 1798, and tract *Addition to Pleasant Hills* surveyed between 1792 and 1796. {Ref: CB, SB}

HENRY, ISAAC, taxpayer, 1798, Broad Creek Hd., 1 dwelling house, 1 inferior house, 2 acres, $250 valuation; 3 tracts (406 acres) and 1 building in Broad Creek Hd., $1165.31 valuation, no slaves. {Ref: TL}. In another part of the tax schedule the occupant is listed as Jeremiah Benington.

HENRY, ISAAC, head of family in 1800 (5th District). {Ref: CI}

HENRY, ISAAC, AND PERKINS, SOLOMON, tract *Partner's Addition* surveyed between 1792 and 1796. {Ref: SB}

HENRY, JOHN, insolvent on a list in 1792 in Broad Creek Hd., as returned by Benjamin Preston. {Ref: IL 31.03}

HENRY, JOHN ("charge with property"), insolvent on lists in 1791 due county taxes and road taxes in "Deer Creek Upper, Middle, and Broad Creek Hundreds" as returned by Robert Amos, Jr. {Ref: IL 31.12, 31.22}

HENRY, JOHN ("poor"), insolvent on a list of the county tax due William Osborn, sheriff, for 1791, as returned by Edward Prigg on Sep 20, 1791. {Ref: IL 31.17}

HENRY, SAMUEL, head of family in 1800 (4th District). {Ref: CI}

HENRY, WILLIAM, head of family in 1800 (5th District). {Ref: CI}
HENSON, ANN, see "John Henson," q.v.
HENSON, JACOB, see "John Henson," q.v.
HENSON, JOHN, son of Jacob and Ann, bapt. Jul 26, 1795. {Ref: PR}
HENSON, JOHN, head of family in 1800 (2nd District). {Ref: CI}
HEPBURN, REBECCA, wife of Dr. James Hepburn of Williamsport, Pennsylvania, b. 1798, d. Apr 7, 1839, in her 41st year, bur. in Deer Creek Friends Cemetery in Darlington. {Ref: TI}
HERBERT, ANNA, see "Hiram Herbert," q.v.
HERBERT, BENJAMIN, see "Benjamin Harbert" and "Mary Ann Herbert," q.v.
HERBERT, BENJAMIN, head of family in 1800 (2nd District); two men by this name in this district. {Ref: CI}
HERBERT, HIRAM, son of James and Anna, b. Apr 6, 1799. {Ref: PR}
HERBERT, JAMES, head of family in 1800 (2nd District). {Ref: CI}. Also see "Hiram Herbert," q.v.
HERBERT, JAMES B., b. 1794, d. Jul 16, 1830, aged 36, bur. in St. George's Episcopal Church Cemetery at Perryman. {Ref: TI}
HERBERT, JOHN, see "John Harbert" and "Hollis Hanson's heirs," q.v.
HERBERT, JOHN, taxpayer, 1798, Spesutia Upper Hd., 1 dwelling house, 2 inferior houses, 120 perches of land, $510 valuation, no slaves. {Ref: TL}
HERBERT, JOHN, head of family in 1800 (3rd District). {Ref: CI}
HERBERT, MARY, m. Richard Johnson on Oct 23, 1799. {Ref: PR}
HERBERT, MARY ANN, dau. of Benjamin and Sarah, b. Feb 23, 1797. {Ref: PR}
HERBERT, MOSES, head of family in 1800 (3rd District). {Ref: CI}
HERBERT, RICHARD, head of family in 1800 (2nd District). {Ref: CI}
HERBERT, SARAH, see "Mary Ann Herbert," q.v.
HERBERT, WILLIAM P. (doctor), b. 1797, d. Aug 16, 1821, aged 24, bur. in St. George's Episcopal Church Cemetery at Perryman. {Ref: TI}
HERMAN STUMP & COMPANY, taxpayer, 1798, Harford Upper and Harford Lower Hundreds, 4 tracts (121 acres) and 1 building, $4131 valuation, no slaves. {Ref: TL}
HERMITAGE, JAMES, insolvent on list returned by Robert Carlile for taxes due for the year 1791. {Ref: IL 31.16}
HERRING, MARY, m. Isaac Allen on Dec 24, 1800. {Ref: PR}
HERRINGTON (HERINTON), HANNAH, head of family in 1800 (4th District). {Ref: CI}
HEWETT, SAMUEL (captain?), had an account at Hall's Store in December, 1791. {Ref: WH}
HICKS, REBECCA (sister), b. Aug 29, 1800, d. Nov 2, 1862, aged 62 years, 2 months, and 4 days, bur. with the Hendersons in McKendree Cemetery near Black Horse. {Ref: TI}
HIGGINBOTHAM, RALPH, m. Isabella Presbury on Feb 28, 1799. {Ref: PR}
HIGSON, GEORGE'S HEIRS, taxpayers, 1798, 1 tract (44 perches, 21 sq. ft.),

$13.50 valuation, no slaves. {Ref: TL}

HILL, ELIZABETH, taxpayer, 1798, Bush River Upper & Eden Hd., 1 dwelling house, 2 inferior houses, 2 acres, $120 valuation; 1 tract (191 acres) in Bush River Upper & Eden Hd., $370.41 valuation, no slaves. {Ref: TL}

HILL, ELIZABETH, head of family in 1800 (4th District). {Ref: CI}

HILL, GEORGE, see "James Mitchell's heirs," q.v.

HILL, HERMAN, insolvent on a list for the county tax due for 1793 in Harford Upper, Harford Lower, and Spesutia Lower Hundreds returned to the levy court by Thomas Taylor on May 28, 1794. {Ref: IL 31.12}

HILL, HERMAN, had an account at Hall's Store in March, 1791. {Ref: WH}

HILL, JAMES, insolvent on a list for the road tax for 1792, as returned for Robert Amoss, tax collector. {Ref: IL 13.12}

HILL, JAMES, head of family in 1800 (1st District); two men by this name in this district. {Ref: CI}

HILL, JAMES SR., taxpayer, 1798, Gunpowder Lower Hd., 1 dwelling house, 2 inferior houses, 2 acres, $150 valuation; 1 tract (56 acres) in Gunpowder Lower Hd., $126 valuation, no slaves. {Ref: TL}

HILL, JOHN, head of family in 1800 (1st District). {Ref: CI}

HILL, JOHN (OF RICHARD), taxpayer, 1798, Gunpowder Lower Hd., 1 dwelling house, 3 inferior houses, 2 acres, $120 valuation; 2 tracts (148 acres) in Gunpowder Lower Hd., $333 valuation, no slaves. {Ref: TL}

HILL, MOSES, head of family in 1800 (1st District). {Ref: CI}

HILL, RICHARD, head of family in 1800 (4th District). {Ref: CI}. Also see "John Hill," q.v.

HILL, SARAH, insolvent on lists returned for the county and road taxes due for 1791 by John Bull in Gunpowder Lower Hundred. {Ref: IL 31.14, 31.15}

HILL, STEPHEN, insolvent on list returned for the road tax due for 1791 by John Bull. {Ref: IL 31.14}

HILL, THOMAS, taxpayer, 1798, Gunpowder Lower Hd., 2 tracts (60 acres) and 1 building, $292.50 valuation, no slaves. {Ref: TL}

HILL, THOMAS, head of family in 1800 (1st District). {Ref: CI}

HILL, THOMAS (sailor), insolvent on list returned for the county tax for 1791 by William Osburn in Gunpowder Lower Hd. (which listed him as a single man). {Ref: IL 31.15}

HILL, THOMAS JR., head of family in 1800 (1st District). {Ref: CI}

HILTON, ABRAHAM, son of John and Lydia, b. Jun 11, 1793. {Ref: PR}. Also see "Patty Hilton" and "Betsey Hilton" and "John Hilton" and "William Hilton"," q.v.

HILTON, BETSEY, dau. of Abraham and Elizabeth, b. Jun 18, 1795. {Ref: PR}

HILTON, ELIZABETH, see "Patty Hilton" and "Betsey Hilton" and "John Hilton" and "William Hilton," q.v.

HILTON, JOHN, son of Abraham and Elizabeth, b. Oct 13, 1794. {Ref: PR}. Also see "Keturah Hilton," q.v.

HILTON, KETURAH, dau. of John and Lydia, b. Dec 27, 1797, bapt. Mar 10, 1798. {Ref: PR}
HILTON, LYDIA, see "Keturah Hilton," q.v.
HILTON, PATTY, dau. of Abraham and Elizabeth, b. Jan 12 or 13, 1793. {Ref: PR}
HILTON, WILLIAM, son of Abraham and Elizabeth, b. Apr 13, 1798. {Ref: PR}
HINES, LARANCE, head of family in 1800 (4th District). {Ref: CI}
HINES, SAMUEL, head of family in 1800 (1st District). {Ref: CI}
HINKS, THOMAS ("gone" and "dead, no property"), insolvent on lists due for 1790 and 1791 "fund taxes" in Deer Creek Lower and Susquehanna Hundreds, as returned by Thomas Taylor. {Ref: IL 31.12, 31.02}
HIPKINS, CHARLES, insolvent on lists returned for the county and road taxes due for 1791 by John Bull in Gunpowder Lower Hundred. {Ref: IL 31.14, 31.15}
HIPKINS, CHARLES, taxpayer, 1798, Gunpowder Lower Hd., 1 dwelling house, 3 inferior houses, 2 acres, $280 valuation; 1 tract (150 acres) in Gunpowder Lower Hd., $438.75, no slaves. {Ref: TL}
HIPKINS, CHARLES, head of family in 1800 (1st District). {Ref: CI}
HITCHCOCK, ASAEL, see "Daniel Lochry," q.v.
HITCHCOCK, ASAEL, served on a Petit Jury in March, 1798 and on a Grand Jury in March, 1800. {Ref: CM}
HITCHCOCK, ASAEL, taxpayer, 1798, Bush River Upper & Eden Hd., 1 dwelling house, 1 inferior house, 2 acres, $105 valuation; 1 tract (98 acres) in Bush River Upper & Eden Hd., $164.25 valuation, no slaves. {Ref: TL}
HITCHCOCK, ASAEL (ASEL), will probated Jan 3, 1792. {Ref: HW}
HITCHCOCK, ASAEL (ASEL), head of family in 1800 (4th District). {Ref: CI}
HITCHCOCK, ASAEL (ASEL), OF D., head of family in 1800 (4th District). {Ref: CI}
HITCHCOCK, ASAEL (OF WILLIAM), see "Leslie Curtis," q.v.
HITCHCOCK, CHARITY, head of family in 1800 (4th District). {Ref: CI}
HITCHCOCK, ISAAC, head of family in 1800 (4th District). {Ref: CI}. Also see "Abraham Jarrett," q.v.
HITCHCOCK, JESSE, head of family in 1800 (4th District). {Ref: CI}
HITCHCOCK, JOHN, insolvent on list returned by Robert Carlile for taxes due for the year 1791. {Ref: IL 31.16}
HITCHCOCK, JOHN, head of family in 1800 (4th District). {Ref: CI}
HITCHCOCK, JOSIAH, insolvent on list returned by Robert Carlile for taxes due for the year 1791. {Ref: IL 31.16}
HITCHCOCK, JOSIAH, taxpayer, 1798, Bush River Upper & Eden Hd., 1 tract (10 acres), $16.88 valuation; no buildings, no slaves. {Ref: TL}
HITCHCOCK, NATHANIEL, taxpayer, 1798, Bush River Upper & Eden Hd., 1 tract (54 acres, 80 perches) and 1 building, $176.34 valuation, no slaves. {Ref: TL}
HITCHCOCK, RANDLE ("run"), insolvent on a list of the county tax due William Osborn, sheriff, for 1791, as returned by Edward Prigg on Sep 20, 1791. {Ref: IL 31.17}

HITCHCOCK, RANDOLPH, insolvent on lists in 1791 due county taxes and road taxes in "Deer Creek Upper, Middle, and Broad Creek Hundreds" as returned by Robert Amos, Jr. {Ref: IL 31.12, 31.22}

HITCHCOCK, SARAH, taxpayer, 1798, Bush River Upper & Eden Hd., 1 dwelling house, 2 inferior houses, 2 acres, $120 valuation; 1 tract (100 acres) in Bush River Upper & Eden Hd., $168.75 valuation, 3 slaves. {Ref: TL}

HITCHCOCK, WALTER, mentioned in a survey deposition on Nov 13, 1799. {Ref: JS}

HITCHCOCK, WILLIAM, see "Asael Hitchcock," q.v.

HITCHCOCK, WILLIAM, taxpayer, 1798, Bush River Upper & Eden Hd., 1 dwelling house, 2 inferior houses, 2 acres, $105 valuation; 2 tracts (142 acres) in Bush River Upper & Eden Hd., $239.63 valuation, 3 slaves. {Ref: TL}

HITCHCOCK, WILLIAM, head of family in 1800 (4th District). {Ref: CI}

HOBBS, WILLIAM, see "Henry Stump," q.v.

HOBBS, WILLIAM, head of family in 1800 (2nd District). {Ref: CI}

HOBBS, WILLIAM (weaver), treated by Dr. Archer in March, 1791; also mentioned his wife (no name given). {Ref: JA}

HODGKINS, JOSHUA ("run"), insolvent on a list of the county tax due William Osborn, sheriff, for 1791, as returned by Edward Prigg on Sep 20, 1791. {Ref: IL 31.17}

HODKINS, JOSHUA, insolvent on lists in 1791 due county taxes and road taxes in "Deer Creek Upper, Middle, and Broad Creek Hundreds" as returned by Robert Amos, Jr. {Ref: IL 31.12, 31.22}

HOGGINS, WILIAM THOMAS, son of James and Elizabeth, b. Feb 13, 1781. {Ref: PR}

HOGNER, JOHN, taxpayer, 1798, Harford Lower Hd., 1 tract (44 perches, 21 sq. ft.), $22.50 valuation, no slaves. {Ref: TL}

HOKE, JACOB, b. Apr 7, 1799, d. Jan 6, 1874, bur. in St. George's Episcopal Church Cemetery at Perryman. {Ref: TI}

HOLINGSHEAD, TITUS, head of family in 1800 (4th District). {Ref: CI}

HOLKER, JOHN, taxpayer, 1798, Spesutia Lower Hd., 1 tract (3 acres, 48 perches and 252 sq. ft.), $162 valuation, no slaves. {Ref: TL}

HOLLAND, F. (FRANCIS), see "Aquila Hall" and "Robert William Holland," q.v.

HOLLAND, FRANCES, purchased a steer on Oct 23, 1792 at Bush River Store. {Ref: AH}

HOLLAND, FRANCIS (colonel), had an account at Hall's Store in March, 1791. {Ref: WH}

HOLLAND, FRANCIS, licensed practicing attorney in March, 1795. {Ref: CC}

HOLLAND, FRANCIS, bur. Aug 14, 1795. {Ref: PR}

HOLLAND, FRANCIS, vestryman, 1793, 1794, St. George's Episcopal Church. {Ref: PR}

HOLLAND, FRANCIS, will probated Sep 9, 1795. {Ref: HW}

HOLLAND, FRANCIS JR., purchased nails in May, 1797 at Bush River Store. {Ref: AH}

HOLLAND, MRS., see "William Holloway," q.v.

HOLLAND, ROBERT WILLIAM, son of Francis Holland and Hannah Matthews, b. Feb 22, 1793, d. Jun 3, 1866. {Ref: Francis Holland Family Record}
HOLLANDSWORTH, JAMES, insolvent, Harford Lower and Spesutia Lower Hundreds, on a tax list returned by George Lyttle on Sep 21, 1791. {Ref: IL 31.20, 31.21}
HOLLEY, ELIZABETH, dau. of William and Sarah, b. Jun 20 1795, bapt. Nov 8, 1795. {Ref: PR}
HOLLEY, SARAH, see "Elizabeth Holley," q.v.
HOLLEY, WILLIAM, head of family in 1800 (2nd District). {Ref: CI}. Also see "Freeborn Garrettson" and "Elizabeth Holley," q.v.
HOLLINGSWORTH, ABIGAIL, b. on 13th of 12th month, 1796, d. on 17th of 1st month, 1887, bur. in Little Falls Quaker Cemetery in Fallston. {Ref: TI}
HOLLINGSWORTH, ELI, b. on 1st of 9th month, 1793, d. on 20th of 9th month, 1879, bur. in Little Falls Quaker Cemetery in Fallston. {Ref: TI}
HOLLINGSWORTH, ELIZABETH, b. on 17th of 4th month, 1792, d. on 12th of 3rd month, 1861, in her 69th year, bur. in Little Falls Quaker Cemetery in Fallston. {Ref: TI}
HOLLINGSWORTH, JAMES, insolvent on a list for the road tax due for 1791 in Harford Upper, Harford Lower, and Spesutia Upper as returned by Robert Amos, Jr. on Sep 18, 1793. {Ref: IL 31.18}
HOLLINGSWORTH, JESSE, b. on 22nd of 10th month, 1796, d. on 15th of 1st month, 1863, bur. in Little Falls Quaker Cemetery in Fallston. {Ref: TI}
HOLLINGSWORTH, THOMAS, b. on 7th of 8th month, 1791, d. on 7th of 9th month, 1820, aged 29 years and 1 month (no tombstone). {Ref: Little Falls Quaker Cemetery Records}.
HOLLINGSWORTH, Z., licensed practicing attorney in March, 1795. {Ref: CC}
HOLLINGSWORTH, ZEBULON, charged for assaulting James Lytle in 1797. {Ref: CD, March and August Terms, 1797}
HOLLIS, AMOS, see "Benjamin Hollis" and "Chauncey Hollis," q.v.
HOLLIS, AMOS, taxpayer, 1798, Harford Lower Hd., 1 dwelling house, 3 inferior houses, 2 acres, $100.25 valuation; 2 tracts (118? acres) in Harford Lower Hd., $398.25 valuation, 3 slaves. {Ref: TL}
HOLLIS, AMOS, insolvent, Harford Lower and Spesutia Lower Hundreds (listed as a single man), on a tax list returned by George Lyttle on Sep 21, 1791. {Ref: IL 31.20, 31.21}
HOLLIS, AMOS, son of Amos and Elizabeth, bapt. Mar 19, 1795. {Ref: PR}
HOLLIS, AMOS, insolvent on a list for the road tax due for 1791 in Harford Upper, Harford Lower, and Spesutia Upper as returned by Robert Amos, Jr. on Sep 18, 1793. {Ref: IL 31.18}
HOLLIS, AMOSS, head of family in 1800 (2nd District). {Ref: CI}
HOLLIS, BENJAMIN, son of Amos and Elizabeth, b. May 25, 1797, bapt. Apr 8, 1798. {Ref: PR}
HOLLIS (HOLLES), CATHERINE, m. James Cole on Apr 4, 1797. {Ref: PR}
HOLLIS, CHAUNCEY, son of Amos and Elizabeth, b. Mar 29, 1800, bapt. Jun 19,

1800. {Ref: PR}

HOLLIS, CLARK, taxpayer, 1798, Harford Lower Hd., 1 dwelling house, 8 inferior houses, 2 acres, $450 valuation; 2 tracts (173 acres, 120 perches) in Harford Lower Hd., $1139.76 valuation, 3 slaves. {Ref: TL}

HOLLIS, CLARK, head of family in 1800 (2nd District). {Ref: CI}

HOLLIS, ELIZABETH, see "Benjamin Hollis" and "Chauncey Hollis" and "Amos Hollis," q.v.

HOLLIS, JAMES, see "George Budd's heirs," q.v.

HOLLIS, JAMES, head of family in 1800 (2nd District). {Ref: CI}

HOLLIS (HOLLES), JAMES, m. Sarah Osborne on Apr 8, 1798. {Ref: PR}

HOLLIS, JAMES JR., taxpayer, 1798, Harford Lower Hd., no dwelling house listed in this part of the tax schedule, no land listed, 1 slave. {Ref: TL}

HOLLIS, JANE, bur. Apr 1, 1796. {Ref: PR}

HOLLIS, SUSAN ANN, dau. of William Hollis and Mary Combest, b. Feb 13, 1794. {Ref: PR}

HOLLIS, WILLIAM, see "Jeremiah Eden" and "Susan Ann Hollis" and "Joseph Webster," q.v.

HOLLIS, WILLIAM, taxpayer, 1798, Gunpowder Lower Hd., 1 dwelling house, 5 inferior houses, 2 acres, $200 valuation; 4(?) tracts (598 acres) in Gunpowder Lower Hd., $2117.25 valuation, 7 slaves; also, taxpayer, Gunpowder Lower Hd., 1 dwelling house, 40 perches of land, $100.50 valuation, no slaves. {Ref: TL}

HOLLIS, WILLIAM, head of family in 1800 (1st District). {Ref: CI}

HOLLIS, WILLIAM JR., treated by Dr. Archer on Jul 2, 1791; also mentioned his wife and inoculation of six of his family (no names given) in 1789. {Ref: JA}

HOLLOWAY, CHARLES C. SR., b. Feb 25, 1793, d. May 8, 1860, bur. in Wesleyan Chapel Methodist Church Cemetery near Aberdeen. {Ref: TI}

HOLLOWAY, WILLIAM (near Mrs. Holland), treated by Dr. Archer on Apr 13, 1791; also mentioned his wife and child (no names given) in 1787. {Ref: JA}

HOLLOWAY, WILLIAM, insolvent, Harford Lower and Spesutia Lower Hundreds, on a tax list returned by George Lyttle on Sep 21, 1791. {Ref: IL 31.20, 31.21}

HOLLOWAY (HOLLIWAY), WILLIAM, head of family in 1800 (3rd District). {Ref: CI}

HOLMES, JAMES, insolvent on a list for county taxes due in 1792 as returned by Benjamin Preston. {Ref: IL 31.00}. Also see "James Holms," q.v.

HOLMES, JANE, see "Mary Ann Holmes," q.v.

HOLMES, MARY ANN, dau. of William and Jane, b. Dec 4, 1797, bapt. Jan 13, 1799. {Ref: PR}

HOLMES, WILLIAM, m. Jane Cook on Dec 7, 1796. {Ref: PR}. Also see "Mary Ann Holmes," q.v.

HOLMS, JAMES (at Crossroads), treated by Dr. Archer on Jun 9, 1794; also mentioned inoculation of three of his children, Mary, Elizabeth, and Abram. {Ref: JA}

HOMER, TOBIAS, taxpayer, 1798, Gunpowder Upper Hd., 1 tract (10 acres) and

1 building, $22.50 valuation, no slaves. {Ref: TL}

HONORE, JOHN A., taxpayer, 1798, Bush River Upper & Eden Hd., 1 dwelling house, 2 inferior houses, 2 acres, $700 valuation; 4 tracts (509 acres) in Bush River Upper & Eden Hd., $1468.12 valuation, 5 slaves. {Ref: TL}

HONORE, JOHN A., head of family in 1800 (4th District). {Ref: CI}

HOOFMAN, CHRISTIAN, tract *Hay Knife* surveyed between 1792 and 1796. {Ref: SB}

HOOFMAN, CHRISTIAN, subpoenaed to the Grand Jury in August, 1797. {Ref: CC}

HOOFMAN, CHRISTIAN, taxpayer, 1798, Susquehanna Hd., 1 dwelling house, 2 inferior houses, 2 acres, $150 valuation; 1 tract (2 acres, 28 perches, 147 sq. ft.) in Susquehanna Hd., $236.25 valuation, 1 slave; also, taxpayer, Susquehanna Hd., 3 tracts (841 acres) and 1 building in Susquehanna Hd., $2377.26 valuation, no slaves. {Ref: TL}. In another part of the tax schedule the occupant is listed as Erasmus Cannon who lived in a dwelling located in Havre de Grace. Also see "Christian and Peter Hoofman," q.v.

HOOFMAN, CHRISTIAN, head of family in 1800 (2nd District). {Ref: CI}

HOOFMAN, CHRISTIAN AND PETER, taxpayers, 1798, Susquehanna Hd., 4 tracts (520 acres) and 1 building, $1154.25 valuation, no slaves. {Ref: TL}

HOOFMAN, ELIZABETH, head of family in 1800 (2nd District). {Ref: CI}

HOOFMAN, JACOB, insolvent on a list for the road tax due for 1791 in Harford Upper, Harford Lower, and Spesutia Upper as returned by Robert Amos, Jr. on Sep 18, 1793. {Ref: IL 31.18}

HOOFMAN, PETER, insolvent on a list for the road tax due for 1791 in Harford Upper, Harford Lower, and Spesutia Upper as returned by Robert Amos, Jr. on Sep 18, 1793. {Ref: IL 31.18}

HOOFMAN, PETER, head of family in 1800 (2nd District). {Ref: CI}

HOOFMAN (HOOPMAN), PETER, taxpayer, 1798, Spesutia Lower Hd., 1 tract (44 perches, 21 sq. ft.) and 1 building, $135 valuation; also, taxpayer, Susquehanna Hd., 1 building (Thomas Edwards, occupant) and 3 tracts (320 acres) and 1 other building, $929.99 valuation altogether, no slaves. {Ref: TL}. Also see "Christian and Peter Hoofman," q.v.

HOOPER, ABRAHAM, head of family in 1800 (1st District). {Ref: CI}

HOOPER, ISAAC, head of family in 1800 (4th District). {Ref: CI}

HOOPER, JOHN, head of family in 1800 (4th District). {Ref: CI}

HOOPER, JOHN A., taxpayer, 1798, Gunpowder Lower Hd., 2 tracts (83 acres) and 1 building, $389.25 valuation, no slaves. {Ref: TL}

HOOPER, SAMUEL, head of family in 1800 (1st District). {Ref: CI}

HOOPER, WILLIAM, head of family in 1800 (1st District). {Ref: CI}

HOOPES, SILAS, b. 1796, d. Oct 22, 1855, aged 58, bur. in Harford (Old Brick) Baptist Church Cemetery. {Ref: TI}

HOOPMAN, JACOB (reverend), b. Jun 15, 1793, d. May 20, 1856, bur. in Wesleyan Chapel Methodist Church Cemetery near Aberdeen. {Ref: TI}

HOOPMAN, MARY, consort of Peter, b. 1797, d. Jun 7, 1827, aged 30, bur. in

Stump Family Graveyard near Craig's Corner. {Ref: Tl}

HOOPMAN, PETER, see "Peter Hoofman" and "Mary Hoopman," q.v.

HOOPS, ROBERT ("can't be found"), insolvent on lists due for 1790 and 1791 "fund taxes" and county taxes in Susquehanna Hd., as returned by Thomas Taylor. {Ref: IL 31.12, 31.02}

HOPE, AGNES, see "Rebecca Kirkwood," q.v.

HOPE, JAMES, see "Sarah Hope," q.v.

HOPE, JENNETT, see "Richard Hope Kirkwood" and "Robert Kirkwood," q.v.

HOPE, RICHARD, taxpayer, 1798, Bush River Upper & Eden Hd., 1 dwelling house, 2 inferior houses, 2 acres, $300 valuation; 1 tract (219 acres) in Bush River Upper & Eden Hd., $492.75 valuation, no slaves. {Ref: TL}

HOPE, RICHARD, head of family in 1800 (4th District). {Ref: CI}

HOPE, SARAH, first wife of James Hope and dau. of John Nelson and Hannah Hutchins, b. 1796, d. Mar 15, 1855, bur. in Bethel Presbyterian Church Cemetery at Madonna. {Ref: BC}

HOPE, THOMAS, appointed a Judge of Elections in the 4th District on Jul 28, 1800. {Ref: CM}

HOPE, THOMAS, tract *Little Worth* surveyed between 1792 and 1796. {Ref: SB}

HOPE, THOMAS, taxpayer, 1798, Bush River Upper & Eden Hd., 1 dwelling house, 7 inferior houses, 2 acres, $500 valuation; 5 tracts (1082 acres, 120 perches) in Bush River Upper & Eden Hd., $2436.19 valuation, 3 slaves. {Ref: TL}

HOPE, THOMAS, served on a Grand Jury in August, 1798 and August, 1799 and August, 1800. {Ref: CM}

HOPE, THOMAS, head of family in 1800 (4th District). {Ref: CI}

HOPKINS, CHARLES, treated by Dr. Archer on Oct 21, 1793. {Ref: JA}

HOPKINS, CHARLES, taxpayer, 1798, Deer Creek Lower Hd., 1 dwelling house, 2 inferior houses, 2 acres, $140 valuation; 1 tract (109 acres) in Deer Creek Lower Hd., $394.31 valuation, 2 slaves. {Ref: TL}

HOPKINS, CHARLES, head of family in 1800 (5th District). {Ref: CI}

HOPKINS, FRANCES (widow), taxpayer, 1798, Deer Creek Lower Hd., 1 tract (5 acres) and 1 building, $67.50 valuation, no slaves. {Ref: TL}

HOPKINS, GERARD, treated by Dr. Archer on Feb 2, 1791; also mentioned his wife and child (no names given). {Ref: JA}

HOPKINS, GERRARD, taxpayer, 1798, Deer Creek Lower Hd., 1 dwelling house, 3 inferior houses, 2 acres, $150 valuation; 1 tract (257 acres) in Deer Creek Lower Hd., $987.75 valuation, 3 slaves. {Ref: TL}

HOPKINS, GERRARD'S HEIRS (Anne Arundel County), taxpayers, 1798, Spesutia Lower Hd., 1 tract (1 acre, 60 perches, 105 sq. ft.), $67.50 valuation, no slaves. {Ref: TL}

HOPKINS, GERRARD, will probated Dec 9, 1799. {Ref: HW}

HOPKINS, GOVER, head of family in 1800 (2nd District). {Ref: CI}

HOPKINS, J. P., see "Leetta Hopkins," q.v.

HOPKINS, JOHN, taxpayer, 1798, Deer Creek Lower Hd., 1 tract (200 acres), $1125 valuation, no slaves [in another part of the 1798 tax schedule the occupant is listed as John Caldwell]; also, taxpayer, Deer Creek Lower Hd., 1 tract (165 acres) and 1 building, $324.84 valuation, no slaves. {Ref: TL}

HOPKINS, JOHN, head of family in 1800 (5th District). {Ref: CI}

HOPKINS, JOHN (hatter), head of family in 1800 (3rd District). {Ref: CI}

HOPKINS, JOHN (OF G.), head of family in 1800 (5th District). {Ref: CI}

HOPKINS, JOHN W., b. 1799, d. Dec 27, 1873, in his 75th year, bur. in Deer Creek Friends Cemetery in Darlington. {Ref: TI}

HOPKINS, JOSEPH, see "Negro Duke" and "Negro Ben," q.v.

HOPKINS, JOSEPH, will probated Nov 24, 1795. {Ref: HW}

HOPKINS, JOSEPH, taxpayer, 1798, Deer Creek Lower Hd., 1 tract (200 acres) and 1 building, $1147.50 valuation, no slaves. {Ref: TL}. In another part of the tax schedule the occupant is listed as Amos Silvers.

HOPKINS, JOSEPH, head of family in 1800 (5th District). {Ref: CI}

HOPKINS, LEETTA, wife of J. P. Hopkins, b. 1796, d. Dec 4, 1871, in her 76th year, bur. in Rock Run Cemetery at Craig's Corner. {Ref: TI}

HOPKINS, PHILIP, see "Henry Stump," q.v.

HOPKINS, PHILLIP, head of family in 1800 (2nd District). {Ref: CI}

HOPKINS, RACHEL, will probated Jul 17, 1795. {Ref: HW}

HOPKINS, RICHARD, head of family in 1800 (5th District). {Ref: CI}

HOPKINS, SAMUEL, head of family in 1800 (2nd District). {Ref: CI}

HOPKINS, SAMUEL, head of family in 1800 (5th District); two men by this name in this district. {Ref: CI}

HOPKINS, SAMUEL (hatter), taxpayer, 1798, Deer Creek Lower Hd., 1 dwelling house, 4 inferior houses, 2 acres, $300 valuation; 3 tracts (162 acres, 120 perches) in Deer Creek Lower Hd., $598.84 valuation, no slaves. {Ref: TL}. Also see "Abraham Reese," q.v.

HOPKINS, SAMUEL (OF JOSEPH), taxpayer, 1798, Deer Creek Lower Hd., 1 tract (200 acres) and 1 building, $1125 valuation, 1 slave. {Ref: TL}

HOPKINS, WILLIAM, insolvent on a list in 1792 in Deer Creek Lower Hd., as returned by Benjamin Preston. {Ref: IL 31.03}

HOPKINS, WILLIAM, taxpayer, 1798, Deer Creek Lower Hd., 1 dwelling house, 2 acres, $102 valuation; 1 tract (30 acres) in Deer Creek Lower Hd., $101.25 valuation, no slaves. {Ref: TL}

HOPKINS, WILLIAM, head of family in 1800 (5th District). {Ref: CI}

HORN, JOHN, b. May 17, 1796, d. Nov 14, 1870, bur. in Old Salem Evangelical Cemetery near Madonna. {Ref: TI}

HORNE, EASTER, head of family in 1800 (2nd District). {Ref: CI}

HORNER, ----, see "Richard Spence," q.v.

HORNER, CASSANDRA, dau. of Crispin and Elizabeth, b. Jan 24, 1796, bapt. Jan 22, 1797. {Ref: PR}

167

HORNER, CRISPIN, see "Cassandra Horner," q.v.

HORNER, ELIZABETH, see "Cassandra Horner," q.v.

HORNER, JAMES, taxpayer, 1798, Susquehanna Hd., 1 tract (20 acres) and 1 building, $101.25 valuation, no slaves. {Ref: TL}

HORNER, JAMES, head of family in 1800 (2nd District). {Ref: CI}

HORNER, JEAN, will probated Oct 18, 1798. {Ref: HW}

HORNER, NATHAN, m. Delia Carroll on May 2, 1799. {Ref: PR}

HORNER, NICHOLAS, taxpayer, 1798, Gunpowder Lower Hd., 1 dwelling house, 3 inferior houses, 2 acres, $180 valuation; 1 tract (200 acres) in Gunpowder Lower Hd., $472.50, 4 slaves. {Ref: TL}

HORNER, NICHOLAS, served on a Grand Jury in March, 1798 and on a Petit Jury in March, 1799 and March, 1800. {Ref: CM}

HORNER, NICHOLAS, head of family in 1800 (1st District). {Ref: CI}

HORNER, RACHEL (Baltimore Town), taxpayer, 1798, Gunpowder Lower Hd., no dwelling house listed in this part of the tax schedule, no land listed, 2 slaves. {Ref: TL}

HORNER, WILLIAM, tract *William's Chance* surveyed between 1792 and 1796. {Ref: SB}

HORTON, EDWARD ("gone"), insolvent on lists due for 1790 and 1791 "fund taxes" and county taxes in Susquehanna Hd., as returned by Thomas Taylor. {Ref: IL 31.12, 31.02}

HORTON, EDWARD, or JOHN GILMORE, taxpayer, 1798, Susquehanna Hd., 1 tract (125 acres) and 1 building (John Gilmore, occupant), $192.66 valuation, no slaves. {Ref: TL}

HORTON, WILLIAM JR. ("gone"), insolvent on lists due for 1790 and 1791 "fund taxes" and county taxes in Susquehanna Hd., as returned by Thomas Taylor. {Ref: IL 31.12, 31.02}

HOSKINS, ELIZABETH AMOSS, b. 1791, d. in 1st month, 1876, in her 85th year, bur. in Little Falls Quaker Cemetery in Fallston. {Ref: TI}

HOUGHEY, HUGH, see "Hugh Haughey," q.v.

HOUK, MICHAEL, insolvent on a list for the county tax due for 1793 in Susquehanna Hd. as returned to the levy court by Thomas Taylor on May 28, 1794, who noted "put in my hands last fall." {Ref: IL 31.12}

HOUSTON, JOHN, see "Samuel Willet," q.v.

HOUSTON, SARAH, see "Samuel Willet," q.v.

HOW, WILLIAM, see "Jennet Hutchinson," q.v.

HOWARD, AQUILA, aged about 6 years, and Nancy Howard, aged about 7 or 8 years, bur. Jun 22, 1794. {Ref: PR}

HOWARD, BLANCH, bur. Jan 15, 1800, aged about 58. {Ref: PR}

HOWARD, CHARLOTTE, see "Henrietta Jane Howard," q.v.

HOWARD, DORSEY, head of family in 1800 (3rd District). {Ref: CI}

HOWARD, EDWARD AQUILA, m. Charlotte Rumsey on Dec 11, 1798. {Ref: PR}. Also see "Henrietta Jane Howard," q.v.

HOWARD, ELIZABETH, wife of Nathan, b. 1795, d. Jan 19, 1854, aged 59. bur.

in St. George's Episcopal Church Cemetery at Perryman. {Ref: TI}
HOWARD, FRANCES CORBIN, dau. of Thomas Gassaway Howard, b. Nov 13 or 18, 1795. {Ref: PR}
HOWARD, HENRIETTA JANE, dau. of Edward Aquila and Charlotte Howard, b. Oct 25, 1799, bapt. Dec 1, 1799. {Ref: PR}
HOWARD, JOHN, had an account at Hall's Store in January, 1791. {Ref: WH}
HOWARD, JOHN, purchased a hogshead of cider in November, 1797 at Bush River Store. {Ref: AH}
HOWARD, JOHN, head of family in 1800 (1st District). {Ref: CI}
HOWARD, JOHN, head of family in 1800 (2nd District). {Ref: CI}
HOWARD, JOHN (taylor), had an account at Hall's Store in December, 1791. {Ref: WH}
HOWARD, JOHN BEALE, bur. Jul 17, 1799. {Ref: PR}
HOWARD, JOSEPH, b. 1797, d. Sep 9, 1878, bur. in Cokesbury Methodist Cemetery in Abingdon. {Ref: TI}
HOWARD, LEMUEL, taxpayer, 1798, Gunpowder Lower Hd., 1 dwelling house, 1 inferior house, 2 acres, $120 valuation; 1 tract (333 acres) in Gunpowder Lower Hd., $1387.69 valuation, no slaves. {Ref: TL}. In another part of the tax schedule the occupant is listed as Joseph Foard.
HOWARD, LEMUEL (LIMUEL), head of family in 1800 (3rd District). {Ref: CI}
HOWARD, LEONARD, insolvent on a list for the road tax due for 1791 in Harford Upper, Harford Lower, and Spesutia Upper as returned by Robert Amos, Jr. on Sep 18, 1793. {Ref: IL 31.18}
HOWARD, LEONARD, taxpayer, 1798, Spesutia Lower Hd., no dwelling house listed in this part of the tax schedule, no land listed, 1 slave. {Ref: TL}
HOWARD, LEONARD, head of family in 1800 (2nd District). {Ref: CI}
HOWARD, MARTHA SUSANNA, see "Thomas Gassaway Howard," q.v.
HOWARD, MARY, m. Thomas Greenly on Apr 27, 1800. {Ref: PR}
HOWARD, NANCY, see "Aquila Howard," q.v.
HOWARD, NATHAN, see "Elizabeth Howard," q.v.
HOWARD, SARAH, see "James McComas," q.v.
HOWARD, THOMAS G., taxpayer, 1798, Bush River Upper & Eden Hd., 1 dwelling house, 4 inferior houses, 2 acres, $300 valuation; 1 tract (409 acres) in Bush River Upper & Eden Hd., $2300.63 valuation, 3 slaves. {Ref: TL}
HOWARD, THOMAS G., insolvent on list returned by Robert Carlile for taxes due for the year 1791, which noted "2 negros when afsd. to him in Joppa in the year 1786 and taken to Balt. Coty. and afsd. to them to him in the year 1788." {Ref: IL 31.16}
HOWARD, THOMAS G., head of family in 1800 (4th District). {Ref: CI}
HOWARD, THOMAS GASSAWAY, son of Thomas Gassaway and Martha Susanna Howard, b. Dec 2, 1798 [sic], bapt. May 21, 1799, d. Nov 20, 1867, aged 69 years, 11 months, and 18 days, bur. in Christ Episcopal (Rock Spring) Church Cemetery. {Ref: TI, PR}. Also see "Frances Corbin Howard," q.v.

169

HOWE, SUSAN, b. May 1, 1794, d. Jun 18, 1879, bur. in Emory Methodist Church Cemetery at Mill Green. {Ref: TI}

HOWE, THOMAS, b. Sep 2, 1791, d. Mar 5, 1860, bur. in Emory Methodist Church Cemetery at Mill Green. {Ref: TI}

HOWE, WILLIAM, head of family in 1800 (5th District). {Ref: CI}

HOWELL, SAMUEL, insolvent on a list for the county tax due for 1793 in Harford Upper, Harford Lower, and Spesutia Lower Hundreds returned to the levy court by Thomas Taylor on May 28, 1794. {Ref: IL 31.12}

HOWLET, ANDREW, taxpayer, 1798, Broad Creek Hd., 1 dwelling house, 3 inferior houses, 2 acres, $120 valuation; 4 tracts (347 acres, 120 perches) in Broad Creek Hd., $533.99 valuation, no slaves. {Ref: TL}

HOWLET, ANDREW, treated by Dr. Archer on Aug 8, 1794; also mentioned his wife and son John. {Ref: JA}

HOWLETT, ANDREW, head of family in 1800 (5th District). {Ref: CI}

HOWLETT, ELIZA, wife of Matthew, b. Jan 20, 1798. {Ref: Howlett Family Record}

HOWLETT, JAMES, head of family in 1800 (5th District). {Ref: CI}

HOWLETT, JOHN R., b. 1793, d. Feb 7(?), 1818, aged 25, and his is the only stone remaining in an old cemetery across the railroad tracks from Mt. Erin Cemetery in Havre de Grace. {Ref: TI}. Also see "Andrew Howlet," q.v.

HOWLETT, MATTHEW, b. Aug 17, 1791. {Ref: Howlett Family Record}. Also see "Eliza Howlett," q.v.

HOY, JOHN, insolvent on list returned for the county tax for 1791 by William Osburn in Gunpowder Lower Hd. (which listed him as a single man). {Ref: IL 31.15}

HUBBARD, GEORGE, insolvent on a list for the county tax due for 1793 in Susquehanna Hd. as returned to the levy court by Thomas Taylor on May 28, 1794, who noted "put in my hands last fall." {Ref: IL 31.12}

HUBBERT, GEORGE, head of family in 1800 (2nd District). {Ref: CI}

HUDSON, ----, see "William Stinson," q.v.

HUDSON, BENJAMIN, insolvent on a list for 1791 in Gunpowder Upper and Bush River Lower Hundreds, as filed by John Bond, Deputy Sheriff, on Sep 20, 1791 (who listed him as a single man). {Ref: IL 31.24}

HUDSON, BENJAMIN, subpoenaed to the Grand Jury in August, 1797. {Ref: CC}

HUDSON, SARAH, dau. of James and Dorothy, b. Mar 31, 1799, bapt. Sep 12, 1799. {Ref: PR}

HUDSON, THOMAS ("run"), insolvent on a list of the county tax due William Osborn, sheriff, for 1791, as returned by Edward Prigg on Sep 20, 1791. {Ref: IL 31.17}

HUDSON, THOMAS, insolvent on lists in 1791 due county taxes and road taxes in "Deer Creek Upper, Middle, and Broad Creek Hundreds" as returned by Robert Amos, Jr. {Ref: IL 31.12, 31.22}

HUDSON, THOMAS, mentioned in a survey deposition on Nov 7, 1799. {Ref: JS}

HUDSON, WILLIAM, insolvent on lists in 1791 due county taxes and road taxes in "Deer Creek Upper, Middle, and Broad Creek Hundreds" as returned by

Robert Amos, Jr. {Ref: IL 31.12, 31.22}

HUFF, ABRAHAM, taxpayer, 1798, Broad Creek Hd., 1 tract (131 acres) and 1 building, $255.45 valuation, no slaves. {Ref: TL}

HUFF, ABRAHAM, head of family in 1800 (5th District). {Ref: CI}

HUFF, JOHN JR., head of family in 1800 (4th District). {Ref: CI}

HUFF, JOHN SR., head of family in 1800 (4th District). {Ref: CI}

HUGHES & ADLUM, see "Adlum & Hughes," q.v.

HUGHES, ARAM, taxpayer, 1798, Bush River Upper & Eden Hd., 1 dwelling house, 7 inferior houses, 2 acres, $200 valuation; 1 tract (141 acres, 120 perches) in Bush River Upper & Eden Hd., $278.43 valuation, no slaves. {Ref: TL}

HUGHES (HUGHS), ARAM, head of family in 1800 (4th District); two men by this name in this district. {Ref: CI}

HUGHES, BENEDICT, see "Nathan Hughes," q.v.

HUGHES, BENEDICT, son of Nathan Hughes and Elizabeth McClain, b. May 23, 1798. {Ref: PR}

HUGHES, BENEDICT, taxpayer, 1798, Spesutia Lower Hd., no dwelling house listed in this part of the tax schedule, no land listed, 1 slave. {Ref: TL}

HUGHES (HUGHS), BENNEDICT, head of family in 1800 (2nd District). {Ref: CI}

HUGHES, CHARLES, insolvent on list returned by Robert Carlile for taxes due for the year 1791. {Ref: IL 31.16}

HUGHES, CHARLOTTE, see "Polly Hughes" and "John Hall Hughes," q.v.

HUGHES (HUGHS), ELISHA, head of family in 1800 (4th District). {Ref: CI}

HUGHES (HUGHS), ESSOM, head of family in 1800 (4th District). {Ref: CI}

HUGHES, ELIZABETH, see "Emiline Hughes," q.v.

HUGHES, EMILINE, dau. of William and Elizabeth, b. Apr 21, 1799, bapt. May 21, 1799. {Ref: PR}

HUGHES, EVERETT, see "William Perkins" and "James Botts Hughes" and "Everett Scott Hughes" and "John Hall Hughes," q.v.

HUGHES, EVERETT, taxpayer, 1798, Harford Upper Hd., 1 tract (101 acres), no buildings, 1 slave. {Ref: TL}

HUGHES (HUGHS), EVERETT, head of family in 1800 (2nd District). {Ref: CI}

HUGHES, EVERETT SCOTT, son of Everett and Nancy, b. Apr 22, 1798, bapt. Oct 2, 1800. {Ref: PR}

HUGHES, JAMES BOTTS, son of Everett and Nancy, b. Sep 8, 1794, bapt. Oct 2, 1800. {Ref: PR}

HUGHES, JOHN, see "Polly Hughes" and "John Hall Hughes," q.v.

HUGHES, JOHN, insolvent on lists returned for the county and road taxes due for 1791 by John Bull in Gunpowder Lower Hd. (name spelled as "Hughs" on one lists. {Ref: IL 31.14, 31.15}

HUGHES, JOHN, taxpayer, 1798, Deer Creek Upper Hd., 1 tract (75 acres, 40 perches) and 1 building, $190.52 valuation, no slaves. {Ref: TL}

HUGHES, JOHN, taxpayer, 1798, Gunpowder Upper Hd., 1 tract (20 acres) and

1 building, $33.75 valuation, no slaves. {Ref: TL}

HUGHES, JOHN (captain), taxpayer, 1798, Spesutia Lower Hd., 1 tract (1 acre, 16 perches and 84 sq. ft.), $54 valuation, no slaves. {Ref: TL}

HUGHES (HUGHS), JOHN, head of family in 1800 (2nd District). {Ref: CI}

HUGHES, JOHN H., insolvent on a list for the road tax for 1792, as returned for Robert Amoss, tax collector. {Ref: IL 13.12}

HUGHES, JOHN H., served on a Grand Jury in March, 1799. {Ref: CM}

HUGHES (HUGH), JOHN H., head of family in 1800 (2nd District). {Ref: CI}

HUGHES, JOHN HALL, taxpayer, 1798, Susquehanna Hd., 1 dwelling house, 3 inferior houses, 2 acres, $200 valuation; 3 tracts (285 acres) and 1 building in Susquehanna Hd., $877.50 valuation, 8 slaves. {Ref: TL}. In another part of the tax schedule the occupant is listed as Widow Touchstone.

HUGHES, JOHN HALL, son of Everett and Nancy, b. Mar 24, 1796, bapt. Oct 2, 1800. {Ref: PR}

HUGHES, JOHN HALL, son of John and Charlotte, b. May 29, 1800, bapt. Oct 2, 1800. {Ref: PR}

HUGHES, JOHN JR., see "Gideon Dennison," q.v.

HUGHES, MARTHA, m. Parker Gilbert, Jr. on Oct 2, 1800. {Ref: PR}

HUGHES, NAASON, tract *Beautiful Island* surveyed between 1792 and 1796. {Ref: SB}

HUGHES, NANCY, see "James Botts Hughes" and "Everett Scott Hughes" and "John Hall Hughes," q.v.

HUGHES, NASSON, taxpayer, 1798, Bush River Upper & Eden Hd., 1 dwelling house, 3 inferior houses, 2 acres, $150 valuation; 1 tract (141 acres, 120 perches) in Bush River Upper & Eden Hd., $278.43 valuation, no slaves. {Ref: TL}

HUGHES, NATHAN, son of Nathan Hughes and Elizabeth McClain, b. Nov 19, 1800. {Ref: PR}

HUGHES, NATHAN, had an account at Hall's Store in March, 1791. {Ref: WH}

HUGHES, NATHAN, charged for assaulting ---- Cord in 1793. {Ref: CD, March Term, 1795}

HUGHES, NATHAN, had an account at Hall's Store in November, 1791. {Ref: WH}

HUGHES, NATHANIEL, see "Luke Griffith's heirs," q.v.

HUGHES, POLLY, dau. of John and Charlotte, b. May 26, 1798, bapt. Oct 2, 1800. {Ref: PR}

HUGHES, SAMUEL, taxpayer, 1798, Susquehanna Hd., 1 dwelling house, 3 inferior houses, 2 acres, $1500 valuation; 6(?) tracts (1198 acres, 102 perches); $4746.68 valuation included 3 other buildings (occupants: Widow Robertson, Thomas Knight, and Aquila Knight), 2 slaves; taxpayer, Spesutia Lower Hd., 1 dwelling house, 7 inferior houses, 2 acres (John L. Gibson, occupant), $500 valuation; taxpayer, Spesutia Lower Hd., 1 dwelling house, 6 inferior houses, 2 acres (Daniel Gatrop, occupant), $400 valuation; taxpayer, Spesutia Lower Hd., 1 dwelling house, 4 inferior houses, 2 acres (Charles Gatrop, occupant), $170 valuation; taxpayer, Spesutia Lower Hd., 1 dwelling house, 3 inferior houses, 2 acres (James Gatrop, occupant), $200(?) valuation; taxpayer, Spesutia Lower Hd., 1 dwelling house, 5 inferior houses, 2 acres (Gilbert Gatrop, occupant), $125(?) valuation; taxpayer, Spesutia Lower Hd., 1 tract (2144 acres), $24440.63 valuation, plus 2 other buildings (Enoch Ginkins and William McGraw, occupants), $90 valuation, no slaves; taxpayer, 1 tract (1 acre, 60 perches, 105 sq. ft.) in Havre de Grace, $67.50 valuation), no slaves. {Ref: TL}

HUGHES (HUGHS), SAMUEL (colonel), head of family in 1800 (2nd District). {Ref: CI}. Also see "Negro Peter," q.v.

HUGHES, THOMAS, insolvent on list returned by Robert Carlile for taxes due for the year 1791. {Ref: IL 31.16}

HUGHES (HUGHS), WILLIAM, head of family in 1800 (3rd District). {Ref: CI}. Also see "Emiline Hughes," q.v.

HUGHES, ZEANAS, head of family in 1800 (4th District). {Ref: CI}

HUGHES, ZENAS, taxpayer, 1798, Deer Creek Upper Hd., 1 dwelling house, 3 inferior houses, 2 acres, $220 valuation; 1 tract (120 acres, 80 perches) in Deer Creek Upper Hd., $159.19 valuation, no slaves. {Ref: TL}

HUGHSTON (HUSTONE), A. (ALEXDR.), insolvent on lists returned by Robert Carlile and John Guyton for taxes due for the year 1791. {Ref: IL 31.16, 31.19}

HUNNELL, WILLIAM, insolvent on list returned by Robert Carlile for taxes due for the year 1791. {Ref: IL 31.16}

HUNT, BENEDICT, see "Benjamin Jones," q.v.

HUNT, NANCY, subpoenaed to the Grand Jury in August, 1797. {Ref: CC}

HUNTER, WILLIAM, appeared on list of "recognizances" of the court for his appearance in 1797. {Ref: CD, August Term, 1797}

HUNTER, WILLIAM, taxpayer, 1798, Gunpowder Lower Hd., 1 dwelling house, 1 inferior house, 2 acres, $200 valuation, no slaves. {Ref: TL}

HUNTER, WILLIAM, head of family in 1800 (Abingdon). {Ref: CI}

HUSBAND, ELIZABETH, head of family in 1800 (5th District). {Ref: CI}

HUSBAND, HERMAN, b. May 12, 1800, d. Dec 30, 1883, bur. in Deer Creek Friends Cemetery in Darlington. {Ref: TI}

HUSBAND, JOSHUA, taxpayer, 1798, Susquehanna Hd., 1 dwelling house, 2 inferior houses, 2 acres, $200 valuation; 3 tracts (150 acres) in Susquehanna Hd., $990 valuation, no slaves; also, 2 buildings in Susquehanna Hd. (James Dags and William Scotten, occupants), $28.12 valuation, no slaves. {Ref: TL}

HUSBAND, LUCIA, see "Zacharias Husband," q.v.

HUSBAND, MARY, taxpayer, 1798, Susquehanna Hd., 1 dwelling house, 1 acre (William Allen, occupant), $100.50 valuation, no slaves. {Ref: TL}

HUSBAND, RACHEL, taxpayer, 1798, Deer Creek Lower Hd., 1 dwelling house, 3 inferior houses, 2 acres, $250 valuation; 1 tract (167 acres) in Deer Creek Lower Hd., $574.45 valuation, no slaves. {Ref: TL}

HUSBANDS, JOSHUA, treated by Dr. Archer on May 2, 1794; also mentioned his dau. Marian and that his wife was treated on Nov 29, 1793, having been in

labor. {Ref: JA}
HUSBANDS, JOSHUA, head of family in 1800 (3rd District). {Ref: CI}
HUSBANDS, MARIAN, see "Joshua Husbands," q.v.
HUSBANDS, MARY, widow ("gone"), insolvent on lists due for 1790 and 1791 "fund taxes" in Susquehanna Hd., as returned by Thomas Taylor (her name was crossed off the road tax insolvents list for 1791). {Ref: IL 31.12, 31.02}
HUSBANDS, MRS., see "Negro George," q.v.
HUSKINS, THOMAS, head of family in 1800 (4th District). {Ref: CI}
HUSSELTON, JAMES, head of family in 1800 (1st District). {Ref: CI}
HUSSY, NATHAN (wheelwright), treated by Dr. Archer on Oct 5, 1794; also mentioned his wife and child (no names given). {Ref: JA}
HUSTON, JAMES, head of family in 1800 (4th District). {Ref: CI}
HUSTONE, ALEXANDER, see "A. Hughston," q.v.
HUTCHESON, JANE (JANEE), insolvent on lists in 1791 due county taxes and road taxes in "Deer Creek Upper, Middle, and Broad Creek Hundreds" as returned by Robert Amos, Jr. {Ref: IL 31.12, 31.22}
HUTCHESON, VINCENT, insolvent on a list for the road tax due for 1791 in Harford Upper, Harford Lower, and Spesutia Upper as returned by Robert Amos, Jr. on Sep 18, 1793 (his name was crossed off the list). {Ref: IL 31.18}
HUTCHINS, ELIZABETH ANN, see "John Wiley," q.v.
HUTCHINS, HANNAH, see "Sarah Hope," q.v.
HUTCHINS, RICHARD, taxpayer, 1798, Bush River Upper & Eden Hd., 1 dwelling house, 3 inferior houses, 2 acres, $220 valuation; 2 tracts (258 acres) in Bush River Upper & Eden Hd., $725.62 valuation; 3 slaves. {Ref: TL}
HUTCHINS, RICHARD, served on a Grand Jury in March, 1798, on a Petit Jury in March, 1799, and on a Grand Jury in March, 1800. {Ref: CM}
HUTCHINS (HUTCHINGS), RICHARD, head of family in 1800 (4th District). {Ref: CI}
HUTCHINSON, JENNET (executors: James Clark and Archibald McNear, taxpayers), Deer Creek Middle Hd., 1 tract (304 acres) and 1 building, $592.80 valuation, no slaves. {Ref: TL}. One list gave her name as "J. Hutchinson" while another list gave it as "Jennet Hutchinson" and listed the occupants as William How and John Daraugh.
HUTSON, JAMES, insolvent on list returned for the road tax due for 1791 by John Bull. {Ref: IL 31.14}
HUTSON, JAMES, head of family in 1800 (1st District). {Ref: CI}
HUTSON, SAMUEL, head of family in 1800 (3rd District). {Ref: CI}
HUTSON, WILLIAM, head of family in 1800 (4th District). {Ref: CI}
HYLAND, GEORGE S., head of family in 1800 (2nd District). {Ref: CI}
HYLAND, JOHN, head of family in 1800 (3rd District). {Ref: CI}
HYLAND, SAMPSON G., taxpayer, 1798, Susquehanna Hd., 1 tract (101 acres), no buildings, 1 slave. {Ref: TL}. Also see "Gideon Dennison," q.v.
HYNES, JOHN, served as constable in Gunpowder Upper Hd., 1800. {Ref: CM}

INDIAN WILL, see "Corbin Bond," q.v.

INGHAM, ROBERT, m. Lydia Yorke on Apr 20, 1800. {Ref: PR}

INGRAM, JAMES, insolvent on a list for the road tax due for 1791 in Harford Upper, Harford Lower, and Spesutia Upper as returned by Robert Amos, Jr. on Sep 18, 1793. {Ref: IL 31.18}

INGRAM, JOHN, tract *Chinquepine Hill* surveyed between 1792 and 1796. {Ref: SB}

INGRAM, JOHN, insolvent on list returned by Robert Carlile for taxes due for the year 1791. {Ref: IL 31.16}

INGRAM, JOHN, taxpayer, 1798, Deer Creek Upper Hd., 1 dwelling house, 4 inferior houses, 2 acres, $120 valuation; 4 tracts (101 acres) in Deer Creek Upper Hd., $92.25 valuation, no slaves. {Ref: TL}

INGRAM (ENGRIM), JOHN, head of family in 1800 (5th District). {Ref: CI}

INGRAM, LEVIN, insolvent on lists returned for the county and road taxes due for 1791 by John Bull in Gunpowder Lower Hundred. {Ref: IL 31.14, 31.15}

INGRAM, SARAH ("dead"), insolvent on lists due for 1790 and 1791 "fund taxes" and county taxes in Susquehanna Hd., as returned by Thomas Taylor. {Ref: IL 31.12, 31.02}

INLOES, HENRY, head of family in 1800 (4th District). {Ref: CI}. Also see "Jesse Jarrett," q.v.

INLOES, JAMES, head of family in 1800 (3rd District). {Ref: CI}

INLOWS, HENRY, insolvent on list returned by Robert Carlile for taxes due for the year 1791. {Ref: IL 31.16}

IRELAND, JOHN (reverend), see "Josiah Matthews," q.v.

IRELAND, PARSON, see "Johannah Watters," q.v.

IRELAND, REVEREND MR., had an account at Hall's Store in February, 1791. {Ref: WH}

IRONS, RACHEL, insolvent on lists returned for the county and road taxes due for 1791 by John Bull in Gunpowder Lower Hundred. {Ref: IL 31.14, 31.15}

IRONS, WILLIAM, head of family in 1800 (Abingdon). {Ref: CI}

IRWIN, JAMES, see "Samuel Willet," q.v.

IRWIN, WILLIAM, see "Samuel Willet," q.v.

ISAGH, THOMAS, head of family in 1800 (1st District). {Ref: CI}

ISRAEL, ESTHER, see "Andrew McClean," q.v.

JACKSON, EDWARD, son of Samuel and Elizabeth, b. May 24, 1794, bapt. Oct 18, 1795. {Ref: PR}

JACKSON, ELIZABETH, m. John Cozens on Feb 7, 1799. {Ref: PR}. Also see "Edward Jackson" and "James Jackson," q.v.

JACKSON, JAMES, insolvent on lists in 1791 due county taxes and road taxes in "Deer Creek Upper, Middle, and Broad Creek Hundreds" as returned by Robert Amos, Jr. {Ref: IL 31.12, 31.22}

JACKSON, JAMES, son of Samuel and Elizabeth, b. Dec 7, 1792, bapt. Oct 18, 1795. {Ref: PR}

JACKSON, JAMES, insolvent on a list for the road tax due for 1791 in Harford

Upper, Harford Lower, and Spesutia Upper as returned by Robert Amos, Jr. on Sep 18, 1793. {Ref: IL 31.18}

JACKSON, JOHN, granted a tavern license in March, 1797. {Ref: CC}

JACKSON, JOHN, head of family in 1800 (3rd District). {Ref: CI}

JACKSON, SAM, insolvent on a list for the road tax due for 1791 in Harford Upper, Harford Lower, and Spesutia Upper as returned by Robert Amos, Jr. on Sep 18, 1793. {Ref: IL 31.18}

JACKSON, SAMUEL, insolvent on a list for county taxes due in 1792 as returned by Benjamin Preston. {Ref: IL 31.00}. Also see "Edward Jackson" and "James Jackson," q.v.

JACKSON, SAMUEL ("at Dismal"), treated by Dr. Archer on May 14, 1791; also mentioned he was the son-in-law of Edward Hanson. {Ref: JA}

JACOB, SAMUEL, or JOHN KIMBLE, taxpayer, 1798, Spesutia Lower Hd., 1 tract (70 acres) and 1 building (John Kimble, occupant), $289.12 valuation, no slaves. {Ref: TL}

JAMES, ELIAKIM (ELIACHIM), head of family in 1800 (3rd District). {Ref: CI}. Also see "William James," q.v.

JAMES, ELIZABETH, insolvent on list returned by Robert Carlile for taxes due for the year 1791. {Ref: IL 31.16}

JAMES, JACOB, husband of Sarah, b. Feb 27, 1800, d. Sep 19, 1875, aged 75 years, 7 months, and 20 days, bur. in Smith's Chapel Methodist Church Cemetery in Churchville. {Ref: TI}

JAMES, JOHN (yeoman), will probated Jan 31, 1792. {Ref: HW}

JAMES, JOSEPH, head of family in 1800 (3rd District). {Ref: CI}

JAMES McGAW & COMPANY, taxpayer, 1798, Harford Upper Hd., 1 dwelling house, 4 inferior houses, 2 acres, $100.50 valuation; 1(?) tract (594 acres, 80 perches) in Harford Upper Hd., $1675.13 valuation, 1 slave. {Ref: TL}

JAMES, PAMELA, see "William James," q.v.

JAMES, ROBERT, head of family in 1800 (5th District). {Ref: CI}

JAMES, SARAH, see "Jacob James," q.v.

JAMES, SEDGWICK, taxpayer, 1798, Deer Creek Middle Hd., 1 dwelling house, 1 inferior house, 2 acres, $120 valuation; 1 tract (225 acres) in Deer Creek Middle Hd., $438.75 valuation, no slaves. {Ref: TL}

JAMES, SEDWICK, served on a Petit Jury in August, 1798 and August, 1799 and August, 1800. {Ref: CM}

JAMES, SOLOMON, head of family in 1800 (3rd District). {Ref: CI}

JAMES, THOMAS, insolvent on a list for the road tax due for 1791 in Harford Upper, Harford Lower, and Spesutia Upper as returned by Robert Amos, Jr. on Sep 18, 1793. {Ref: IL 31.18}

JAMES, THOMAS, insolvent on lists returned by Robert Carlile and John Guyton for taxes due for the year 1791. {Ref: IL 31.16, 31.19}

JAMES, THOMAS ("poor"), insolvent on lists due for 1790 and 1791 "fund taxes" and county taxes in Susquehanna Hd., as returned by Thomas Taylor. {Ref: IL 31.12, 31.02}

JAMES, WILLIAM, see "William Barnett," q.v.

JAMES, WILLIAM, insolvent on list returned by John Guyton for taxes due for the year 1791. {Ref: IL 31.19}

JAMES, WILLIAM, insolvent on list returned by Robert Carlile for taxes due for the year 1791. {Ref: IL 31.16}

JAMES, WILLIAM, son of Eliakim and Pamela, b. Oct 6, 1798, bapt. May 14, 1799. {Ref: PR}

JAMES, WILLIAM, head of family in 1800 (5th District). {Ref: CI}

JAMESON, ALEXANDER, treated by Dr. Archer on Jul 29, 1799. {Ref: JA}

JAMISON (JAMESON), JOHN, see "James Hempfield," q.v.

JAMISON (JAMSON), RICHARD, head of family in 1800 (5th District). {Ref: CI}. Also see "Hugh Whiteford, Sr.," q.v.

JARRETT, ABRAHAM, tract *Hickory Bottom* surveyed in 1796. {Ref: CB, SB}

JARRETT, ABRAHAM, taxpayer, 1798, Deer Creek Upper Hd., 1 dwelling house, 4 inferior houses, 2 acres, $130 valuation; 1 tract (608 acres) in Deer Creek Upper Hd., $1539 valuation, no slaves. {Ref: TL}. In another part of the tax schedule the occupant is listed as Isaac Hitchcock.

JARRETT, ABRAHAM, tract *Belgrade* surveyed in 1794 (part of original tract *Wild Cat Den* of which *Belgrade* on the Pennsylvania line was resurveyed in 1799). {Ref: CB}

JARRETT, ABRAHAM, head of family in 1800 (Belle Air). {Ref: CI}

JARRETT, BENNET, taxpayer, 1798, Bush River Upper & Eden Hd., 1 dwelling house, 4 inferior houses, 2 acres, $300 valuation; 6 tracts (387 acres) in Bush River Upper & Eden Hd., $870.75 valuation, 2 slaves; also, 3 tracts (281 acres, 120 perches) and 1 building in Deer Creek Upper Hd., $606.94 valuation, no slaves. {Ref: TL}. In another part of the tax schedule the occupants are listed as Samuel Marshal and Alexander Sutherland.

JARRETT, BENNETT, head of family in 1800 (4th District). {Ref: CI}.

JARRETT, BENNETT, see "Jesse Jarrett," q.v.

JARRETT, ELI, will probated Feb 11, 1794. {Ref: HW}

JARRETT, ELISHA, taxpayer, 1798, Bush River Upper & Eden Hd., 1 dwelling house, 3 inferior houses, 2 acres, $300 valuation; 2 tracts (87 acres) in Bush River Upper & Eden Hd., $490.50 valuation, no slaves. {Ref: TL}

JARRETT, JESSE, tracts *Contestable Manor*, *Little Contestable Manor*, *Eserol*, *Pearson's Penn*, and *Contestable Manor Corrected* (on or near the Mason-Dixon Line) surveyed between 1792 and 1797. {Ref: CB, SB}

JARRETT, JESSE, tract *Abraham's Pleasure Corrected* surveyed in 1797, and tract *Pervicacity* surveyed in 1789 (on a milestone of the State Line) and granted to Bennett Jarrett in 1798. {Ref: CB}

JARRETT, JESSE, subpoenaed to the Grand Jury in August, 1797. {Ref: CC}

JARRETT, JESSE, taxpayer, 1798, Bush River Upper & Eden Hd., 1 dwelling house, 7 inferior houses, 2 acres, $560 valuation; 9 tracts (861 acres) in Bush River Upper & Eden Hd., $1395 valuation, 5 slaves; also, 2 tracts (1596 acres) and 5 buildings (occupants: Richard Bond, Daniel Norris, John Davis, Henry Inlowes or Inloes, and Henry Downs) in Deer Creek Upper Hd., $1872 valuation, no slaves. {Ref: TL}

JARRETT, JESSE, involved in a chancery court case against David West in Harford County over a land dispute near the Pennsylvania line in 1799-1800. {Ref: JS}

JARRETT, JESSE (esquire), head of family in 1800 (4th District). {Ref: CI}

JARVIS, ANN, insolvent on lists returned for the county and road taxes due for 1791 by John Bull in Gunpowder Lower Hundred. {Ref: IL 31.14, 31.15}

JARVIS, JAMES, head of family in 1800 (2nd District). {Ref: CI}

JARVIS, JAMES, head of family in 1800 (3rd District). {Ref: CI}

JARVIS, JOHN SR. ("Dd"), insolvent on a list for 1791 in Gunpowder Upper and Bush River Lower Hundreds, as filed by John Bond, Deputy Sheriff, on Sep 20, 1791. {Ref: IL 31.24}

JARVIS, WIDOW, bur. Jun 17, 1798, aged about 65. {Ref: PR}

JAY, JOSEPH, head of family in 1800 (5th District). {Ref: CI}

JAY, SAMUEL, purchased pork on Dec 14, 1797 at Bush River Store. {Ref: AH}

JAY, SAMUEL, head of family in 1800 (Havre de Grace). {Ref: CI}

JAY, SAMUEL C. & COMPANY, licensed retailers in March, 1795 and August, 1797. {Ref: CC}

JAY, STEPHEN, will probated May 10, 1796. {Ref: HW}

JAY, THOMAS, head of family in 1800 (5th District). {Ref: CI}

JEFFERIES, MARY, dau. of Thomas Jefferies and D. Knight, b. May 6, 1794, bapt. Jan 15, 1796. {Ref: PR}

JEFFERIES, THOMAS, see "Mary Jefferies," q.v.

JEFFERSON, JAMES, head of family in 1800 (5th District). {Ref: CI}

JEFFERY, JAMES, non-resident (place of residence not stated), taxpayer, 1798, Spesutia Lower Hd., 1 tract (2 acres, 32 perches, 105 sq. ft.), $108 valuation, no slaves. {Ref: TL}

JEFFERY, JANE, see "Jacob Crone's heirs," q.v.

JEFFERY, ROBERT, see "Adlum & Hughes," q.v.

JEFFERY, THOMAS, taxpayer, 1798, Susquehanna Hd., 1 dwelling house, 4 inferior houses, 2 acres, $110 valuation; 2 tracts (149 acres) in Susquehanna Hd., $335.25 valuation, 5 slaves. {Ref: TL}

JEFFERY, THOMAS, served on a Grand Jury in March, 1798, on a Petit Jury in March, 1799, and on a Grand Jury in March, 1800. {Ref: CM}

JEFFERY, THOMAS, insolvent on a list for the road tax for 1792, as returned for Robert Amoss, tax collector. {Ref: IL 13.12}

JEFFERYS, ELIZABETH, insolvent on a list for the road tax due for 1791 in Harford Upper, Harford Lower, and Spesutia Upper as returned by Robert Amos, Jr. on Sep 18, 1793. {Ref: IL 31.18}

JEFFREY, ALEXANDER, head of family in 1800 (2nd District). {Ref: CI}
JEFFREY, THOMAS, head of family in 1800 (2nd District). {Ref: CI}
JEFFRYES, WILLIAM, head of family in 1800 (4th District). {Ref: CI}
JELLET, MORGAN, head of family in 1800 (1st District). {Ref: CI}
JEMMISON, REBECCA, m. Elijah Small on Feb 21, 1799. {Ref: PR}
JENKINS, ENOCH, head of family in 1800 (2nd District). {Ref: CI}
JENKINS, MICHAEL (Baltimore County), taxpayer, 1798, Gunpowder Upper Hd., 1 tract (216 acres), $668.25 valuation, no slaves. {Ref: TL}
JENKINS, RACHEL (RACHELL), insolvent on lists of taxes due in 1791 and 1792 in Broad Creek Hd., as returned by Robert Amos, Jr. in 1791 and Benjamin Preston in 1792 {Ref: IL 31.03, 31.12, 31.22}
JENKINS, WILLIAM, insolvent on list returned by Robert Carlile for taxes due for the year 1791. {Ref IL 31.16}
JERVIS, JAMES, insolvent on a list for the road tax for 1792, as returned for Robert Amoss, tax collector. {Ref: IL 13.12}. Also see "John Lee Gibson" and "William McClintock," q.v.
JERVIS, JOSEPH, charged for assaulting John Hamby in 1794 and 1797. {Ref: CD, March and August Terms, 1795 and 1797}
JERVIS, THOMAS, charged for assaulting John Hamby in 1794 and 1797. {Ref: CD, March and August Terms, 1795 and 1797}
JEWEL, WILLIAM, insolvent on lists returned for the county and road taxes due for 1791 by John Bull in Gunpowder Lower Hd. (name spelled as "Wm. Jewell" on one list). {Ref: IL 31.14, 31.15}
JEWELL, RICHARD, insolvent on lists in 1791 due county taxes and road taxes in "Deer Creek Upper, Middle, and Broad Creek Hundreds" as returned by Robert Amos, Jr. {Ref: IL 31.12, 31.22}
JEWELLS, AGNES, dau. of Richard and Elizabeth, b. Jan 1, 1788, bapt. Dec 30, 1795. {Ref: PR}
JEWELLS, BLANCHE, dau. of Richard and Elizabeth, b. Jul 3, 1783 (1789?), bapt. Dec 30, 1795. {Ref: PR}
JEWELLS, ELIZABETH, see "William Jewells" and "Sarah Jewells" and "Agnes Jewells" and "George Jewells" and "Blanche Jewells" and "Frances Jewells," q.v.
JEWELLS, FRANCES, dau. of Richard and Elizabeth, b. Mar 26, 1795, bapt. Dec 30, 1795. {Ref: PR}
JEWELLS, GEORGE, son of Richard and Elizabeth, b. Jul 22, 1785, bapt. Dec 30, 1795. {Ref: PR}
JEWELLS, RICHARD, see "William Jewells" and "Sarah Jewells" and "Agnes Jewells" and "George Jewells" and "Blanche Jewells" and "Frances Jewells," q.v.
JEWELLS, SARAH, dau. of Richard and Elizabeth, b. Jun 8, 1790, bapt. Dec 30, 1795. {Ref: PR}
JEWELLS, WILLIAM, son of Richard and Elizabeth, b. Oct 23, 1791, bapt. Dec

30, 1795. {Ref: PR}

JIANT, ANN, see "Benedict Edward Hall," q.v.

JIGORGNE, A., see "Alexius Amedi Raphel," q.v.

JINKINS, RACHEL ("run"), insolvent on a list of the county tax due William Osborn, sheriff, for 1791, as returned by Edward Prigg on Sep 20, 1791. {Ref: IL 31.17}

JINKINS, WILLIAM, insolvent on a list for 1791 in Gunpowder Upper and Bush River Lower Hundreds, as filed by John Bond, Deputy Sheriff, on Sep 20, 1791. {Ref: IL 31.24}

JOHN STUMP & COMPANY, licensed retailers in August, 1797. {Ref: CC}

JOHNS, ANN, head of family in 1800 (1st District). {Ref: CI}

JOHNS, CAROLINE, see "Aquila Massey," q.v.

JOHNS, FRANCIS, see "Sarah Johns," q.v.

JOHNS, HENRY, see "William Prigg Johns" and "Mary Johns," q.v.

JOHNS, HENRY, "struck off - excused" from serving on a Petit Jury in August, 1799. {Ref: CM}

JOHNS, HENRY, taxpayer, 1798, Deer Creek Middle Hd., 1 dwelling house, 4 inferior houses, 2 acres, $120 valuation; 2 tracts (208 acres, 80 perches) in Deer Creek Middle Hd., $334.13 valuation, 2 slaves. {Ref: TL}

JOHNS, HENRY, head of family in 1800 (5th District). {Ref: CI}

JOHNS, MARY, dau. of Henry and Sarah, b. Dec 26, 1796, bapt. Apr 18, 1797. {Ref: PR}

JOHNS, MARY, insolvent on a list for the road tax due for 1791 in Harford Upper, Harford Lower, and Spesutia Upper as returned by Robert Amos, Jr. on Sep 18, 1793. {Ref: IL 31.18}

JOHNS, SARAH, wife of Francis, b. 1794, d. Mar 10, 1853, in her 59th year, bur. in Cokesbury Methodist Cemetery in Abingdon. {Ref: TI}. Also see "William Prigg Johns" and "Mary Johns," q.v.

JOHNS, SKIPWITH, insolvent on a list for the county tax due for 1791 in Susquehanna Hd., as returned by Thomas Taylor on Sep 17, 1792. {Ref: IL 31.12}

JOHNS, WILLIAM PRIGG, son of Henry and Sarah, b. Jun 3, 1794, bapt. Apr 18, 1797. {Ref: PR}

JOHNSON, ADAM, m. Johanna Gilbert on Aug 17, 1797. {Ref: PR}

JOHNSON, ALICE, head of family in 1800 (3rd District). {Ref: CI}

JOHNSON, ALICE (ALCE) AND HANNAH, taxpayers, 1798, Spesutia Upper Hd., 1 dwelling house, 2 inferior houses, 1 acre, $125 valuation; 1 tract (99 acres) in Spesutia Upper Hd., $294.75 valuation, no slaves. {Ref: TL}

JOHNSON, ANN (neé Michael), wife of Barnet, b. Aug 16, 1800, d. Jun 25, 1898, bur. in Christ Episcopal (Rock Spring) Church Cemetery. {Ref: TI, and Barnet Johnson Bible}. Also see "Charles Kinzell," q.v.

JOHNSON, ARCHIBALD, insolvent on a list for the county tax due for 1793 in Harford Upper, Harford Lower, and Spesutia Lower Hundreds returned to the levy court by Thomas Taylor on May 28, 1794. {Ref: IL 31.12}

JOHNSON, ARCHIBALD, insolvent on lists returned for the county and road taxes due for 1791 by John Bull in Gunpowder Lower Hd. (name spelled as "Johnston" on one list). {Ref: IL 31.14, 31.15}

JOHNSON, BARNET, see "Ann Johnson" and "Thomas Johnson (of Barnet)" and Barnett Johnson," q.v.

JOHNSON, BARNET, b. Jan 26, 1796, d. Jan 14, 1862, bur. in Christ Episcopal (Rock Spring) Church Cemetery. {Ref: TI}

JOHNSON, BARNET (OF B.), head of family in 1800 (3rd District). {Ref: CI}

JOHNSON, BARNET (OF BARNET), taxpayer, 1798, Spesutia Upper Hd., 1 dwelling house, 4 inferior houses, 1 acre, $150 valuation; 1 tract (149 acres) in Spesutia Upper Hd., $385.88 valuation, no slaves. {Ref: TL}

JOHNSON, BARNET (OF BARNET), served on a Grand Jury in March, 1798 and March, 1799 and March, 1800. {Ref: CM}

JOHNSON, BARNET (OF JOHN), taxpayer, 1798, Deer Creek Middle Hd., 3 tracts (163 acres) and 1 building, $366.75 valuation, 1 slave. {Ref: TL}

JOHNSON, BARNETT, head of family in 1800 (3rd District). {Ref: CI}

JOHNSON, BERNARD, see "Thomas Johnson, Esq." and "John Thompson," q.v.

JOHNSON, CALEB, taxpayer, 1798, Gunpowder Upper Hd., 1 dwelling house, 3 inferior houses, 2 acres, $250 valuation; 1 tract (191 acres) in Gunpowder Upper Hd., $429.75 valuation, 3 slaves. {Ref: TL}

JOHNSON, CALEB, head of family in 1800 (3rd District). {Ref: CI}

JOHNSON, CAROLINE (aunt), b. 1797, d. Dec 24, 1872, aged 75, bur. next to the Prestons in Christ Episcopal (Rock Spring) Church Cemetery. {Ref: TI}

JOHNSON, CHARLES, insolvent on lists of taxes due in 1791 and 1792 in Broad Creek Hd., as returned by Robert Amos, Jr. in 1791 and Benjamin Preston in 1792. {Ref: IL 31.03, 31.12, 31.22}

JOHNSON, CHARLES ("poor"), insolvent on a list of the county tax due William Osborn, sheriff, for 1791, as returned by Edward Prigg on Sep 20, 1791. {Ref: IL 31.17}

JOHNSON, CHARLES, head of family in 1800 (5th District). {Ref: CI}

JOHNSON, HANNAH, m. John Harvey on Mar 12, 1799. {Ref: PR}. Also see "Alice and Hannah Johnson," q.v.

JOHNSON, HARRIOT, dau. of Joseph and Rebecca, b. May 20, 1796, bapt. Aug 17, 1797. {Ref: PR}

JOHNSON, HESTER, taxpayer, 1798, Spesutia Upper Hd., 1 dwelling house, 5 inferior houses, 1 acre, $200 valuation; 1 tract (99 acres) in Spesutia Upper Hd., $305.16 valuation, 2 slaves. {Ref: TL}

JOHNSON, HESTER, head of family in 1800 (3rd District). {Ref: CI}

JOHNSON, JAMES, see "Harry Gough" and "John Johnson (of James)," q.v.

JOHNSON, JAMES, served on a Grand Jury in August, 1798 and August, 1799, and on a Petit Jury in August, 1800. {Ref: CM}

JOHNSON, JAMES, head of family in 1800 (3rd District). {Ref: CI}

JOHNSON, JESSE BELL, son of John Johnson and Lethe Bell, b. Sep 24, 1796,

bapt. Oct 11, 1796. {Ref: PR}
JOHNSON, JOHN, see "Barnet Johnson (of John)" and "Jesse Bell Johnson," q.v.
JOHNSON, JOHN, licensed ordinary (tavern) in March, 1795 and August, 1797. {Ref: CC}
JOHNSON, JOHN, insolvent on a list for the road tax due for 1791 in Harford Upper, Harford Lower, and Spesutia Upper as returned by Robert Amos, Jr. on Sep 18, 1793. {Ref: IL 31.18}
JOHNSON, JOHN, son of Josiah and Martha, b. Jun 16, 1793, bapt. Dec 15, 1795. {Ref: PR}
JOHNSON, JOHN, head of family in 1800 (4th District). {Ref: CI}
JOHNSON, JOHN (OF JAMES), taxpayer, 1798, Bush River Upper & Eden Hd., 1 dwelling house, 1 inferior house, 2 acres, $105 valuation; 1 tract (258 acres) in Bush River Upper & Eden Hd., $653.60 valuation, no slaves. {Ref: TL}
JOHNSON, JOHN (OF WILLIAM), taxpayer, 1798, Bush River Upper & Eden Hd., 1 dwelling house, 3 inferior houses, 2 acres, $250 valuation; 1 tract (112 acres, 120 perches) in Bush River Upper & Eden Hd., $253.69 valuation, no slaves. {Ref: TL}
JOHNSON, JOHN B., b. 1799, d. Sep 20, 1847, aged 48, bur. in the Johnson Family Cemetery at Upper Crossroads. {Ref: TI}
JOHNSON, JOSEPH, see "Harriot Johnson," q.v.
JOHNSON, JOSEPH, son of Josiah and Martha, b. Oct 10, 1792, bapt. Dec 15, 1795. {Ref: PR}
JOHNSON, JOSEPH, insolvent on a list for the road tax due for 1791 in Harford Upper, Harford Lower, and Spesutia Upper as returned by Robert Amos, Jr. on Sep 18, 1793. {Ref: IL 31.18}
JOHNSON, JOSEPH, head of family in 1800 (2nd District). {Ref: CI}
JOHNSON, JOSHUA, see "James Phillips, Sr.," q.v.
JOHNSON, JOSIAH, served on a Petit Jury in August, 1797. {Ref: CC}. Also see "John Street" and "Joseph Johnson" and "Martha Johnson," q.v.
JOHNSON, JOSIAS, head of family in 1800 (5th District). {Ref: CI}
JOHNSON, MARTHA, see "Joseph Johnson" and "Martha Johnson," q.v.
JOHNSON, MOSES, will probated Dec 13, 1796. {Ref: HW}
JOHNSON, REBECCA, see "Harriot Johnson," q.v.
JOHNSON, RICHARD, m. Mary Herbert on Oct 23, 1799. {Ref: PR}
JOHNSON, ROBERT, served on a Petit Jury in August, 1797, and on a Grand Jury in August, 1798. {Ref: CC, CM}
JOHNSON, THOMAS, see "William Johnson" and "John Coleman," q.v.
JOHNSON, THOMAS, insolvent on a list for the road tax for 1792, as returned for Robert Amoss, tax collector. {Ref: IL 13.12}
JOHNSON, THOMAS, m. Elizabeth Cord on Jun 17, 1792. {Ref: PR}
JOHNSON, THOMAS, m. Elizabeth Taylor on Nov 17, 1796. {Ref: PR}
JOHNSON, THOMAS ("charge twice"), insolvent on lists in 1791 due county taxes and road taxes in "Deer Creek Upper, Middle, and Broad Creek

Hundreds" as returned by Robert Amos, Jr. {Ref: IL 31.12, 31.22}

JOHNSON, THOMAS (esquire), taxpayer, 1798, Spesutia Upper Hd., 1 dwelling house, 2 inferior houses, 1 acre, $185 valuation; 3 tracts (247 acres) in Spesutia Upper Hd., $694.41 valuation, 3 slaves; taxpayer, Spesutia Upper Hd., 1 dwelling house, 3 inferior houses, 1 acre, $125 valuation; 1 tract (149 acres) in Spesutia Upper Hd., $251.15 valuation, no slaves; in another part of the tax schedule the occupant is listed as Bernard Johnson. Also, taxpayer, Broad Creek Hd., 1 dwelling house, 2 inferior houses, 2 acres, $100.30 valuation; 1 tract (144 acres) in Broad Creek Hd., $112.50 valuation, no slaves; in another part of the tax schedule the occupant is listed as Ezekiel Williams. {Ref: TL}.

JOHNSON, THOMAS ("run"), insolvent on a list of the county tax due William Osborn, sheriff, for 1791, as returned by Edward Prigg on Sep 20, 1791. {Ref: IL 31.17}

JOHNSON, THOMAS, head of family in 1800 (3rd District). {Ref: CI}

JOHNSON, THOMAS JR., insolvent on a list in 1792 in Broad Creek Hd., as returned by Benjamin Preston. {Ref: IL 31.03}

JOHNSON, THOMAS JR., insolvent on a list for county taxes due in 1792 as returned by Benjamin Preston. {Ref: IL 31.00}

JOHNSON, THOMAS JR., head of family in 1800 (3rd District). {Ref: CI}

JOHNSON, THOMAS (OF BARNET), taxpayer, 1798, Spesutia Upper Hd., 1 dwelling house, 3 inferior houses, 1 acre, $110 valuation; 1 tract (99 acres) in Spesutia Upper Hd., $222.75 valuation, 1 slave. {Ref: TL}

JOHNSON, THOMAS (OF M.), head of family in 1800 (3rd District). {Ref: CI}

JOHNSON, TOBIAS, head of family in 1800 (2nd District). {Ref: CI}

JOHNSON, WILLIAM, see "John Johnson (of William)" and "Charity Onion," q.v.

JOHNSON, WILLIAM, treated by Dr. Archer on Mar 21, 1798. {Ref: JA}

JOHNSON, WILLIAM, head of family in 1800 (1st District). {Ref: CI}

JOHNSON, WILLIAM, head of family in 1800 (4th District). {Ref: CI}

JOHNSON, WILLIAM (OF THOMAS), treated by Dr. Archer on Feb 4, 1793. {Ref: JA}

JOHNSTON, BERNET (OF THOMAS), treated by Dr. Archer on Jun 13, 1798. {Ref: JA}

JOHNSTON, MARY, will probated Apr 16, 1793. {Ref: HW}

JOHNSTON, THOMAS SR., treated by Dr. Archer on Sep 24, 1791. {Ref: JA}. Also see "Bernet Johnston," q.v.

JOLLY (JOLLEY), EDWARD, taxpayer, 1798, Deer Creek Lower Hd., 4 tracts (946 acres) and 1 building, $1239.75 valuation, 1 slave. {Ref: TL}. In another part of the tax schedule the occupant is listed as Simon Nevel. Also see "John Stump," q.v.

JOLLY (JOLLEY), JOHN, m. Elizabeth Dallam on Apr 20, 1797. {Ref: PR}

JOLLY (JOLLEY), JOHN, taxpayer, 1798, Deer Creek Lower Hd., 2 tracts (150 acres), $294.75 valuation; no buildings, 1 slave. {Ref: TL}

JOLLY (JOLLEY), RICHARD, head of family in 1800 (5th District). {Ref: CI}

JOLLY (JOLLEY), WILLIAM, taxpayer, 1798, Deer Creek Lower Hd., 1 dwelling house, 2 inferior houses, 2 acres, $150 valuation; 2 tracts (150 acres) in Deer Creek Lower Hd., $168.75 valuation, no slaves. {Ref: TL}. In another part of the tax schedule the occupant is listed as Samuel Wallace.

JONES, ----, bur. May 27, 1797. {Ref: PR}. Also see "William Jones, Sr.," q.v.

JONES, AMOS, see "Ann Atkinson" and "Ann Adkinson," q.v.

JONES, AMOS, taxpayer, 1798, Gunpowder Upper Hd., 1 dwelling house, 2 inferior houses, 2 acres, $120 valuation; 1 tract (20 acres) in Gunpowder Upper Hd., $185.62 valuation, no slaves. {Ref: TL}

JONES, AMOS, taxpayer, 1798, Deer Creek Upper Hd., 1 tract (35 acres, 80 perches) and 1 building, $99.84 valuation, no slaves. {Ref: TL}

JONES, AMOSS, head of family in 1800 (3rd District). {Ref: CI}

JONES, ANNE, m. William Mahon on Nov 27, 1800. {Ref: PR}. Also see "Ann Atkinson," q.v.

JONES, AQUILA, taxpayer, 1798, Broad Creek Hd., 2 tracts (213 acres, 80 perches) and 1 building, $297.60 valuation, no slaves. {Ref: TL}

JONES, AQUILA, insolvent on lists in 1791 due county taxes and road taxes in "Deer Creek Upper, Middle, and Broad Creek Hundreds" as returned by Robert Amos, Jr., but his name was then crossed off both lists. {Ref: IL 31.12, 31.22}

JONES, AQUILA, insolvent on lists returned by Robert Carlile and John Guyton (who listed him as a single man) for taxes due for the year 1791. {Ref: IL 31.16, 31.19}

JONES, AQUILLA, head of family in 1800 (5th District). {Ref: CI}

JONES, BENJAMIN, see "Charlotte Jones" and "Rebecca Jones" and "Charles Jones," q.v.

JONES, BENJAMIN, tracts *Jones's Purchase* and *Jones's Surplus* surveyed in 1794, and tract *Third Attempt* surveyed in 1797. {Ref: CB, SB}

JONES, BENJAMIN, served on a Grand Jury in March, 1798. {Ref: CM}

JONES, BENJAMIN, taxpayer, 1798, Deer Creek Middle Hd., 2 tracts (75 acres), $168.75 valuation; no buildings, no slaves. {Ref: TL}

JONES, BENJAMIN, charged for assaulting Benedict Hunt in 1794. {Ref: CD, March Term, 1795}

JONES, BENJAMIN, insolvent on lists in 1791 due county taxes and road taxes in "Deer Creek Upper, Middle, and Broad Creek Hundreds" as returned by Robert Amos, Jr., but his name was then crossed off both lists. {Ref: IL 31.12, 31.22}

JONES, BENJAMIN ("charge twice"), insolvent on lists in 1791 due county taxes and road taxes in "Deer Creek Upper, Middle, and Broad Creek Hundreds" as returned by Robert Amos, Jr. {Ref: IL 31.12, 31.22}

JONES, BENHAMIN, will probated Nov 21, 1794. {Ref: HW}

JONES, BENJAMIN, head of family in 1800 (5th District). {Ref: CI}

JONES, BENJAMIN (York County), taxpayer, 1798, Deer Creek Middle Hd., 1 tract (30 acres), $56.25 valuation, no slaves. {Ref: TL}

JONES, CHARLES, son of Benjamin and Sarah, b. Oct 19, 1771, bapt. Jun 6, 1797. {Ref: PR}

JONES, CHARLES, taxpayer, 1798, Deer Creek Middle Hd., 2 tracts (75 acres) and 1 building, $168.75 valuation, no slaves. {Ref: TL}

JONES, CHARLES, head of family in 1800 (5th District). {Ref: CI}

JONES, CHARLOTTE, dau. of Charles and Mary Ann, b. Dec 20, 1797, bapt. Jun 6, 1797. {Ref: PR}

JONES, ELIZA, see "William Jones, Sr." and "Gilbert Jones," q.v.

JONES, ELIZABETH, charged in 1794 (nature of the case not stated) and in 1795 the court "recognized in £75 with William Jones and William Gibson for the good behaviour of Elizabeth Jones for 1 year." {Ref: CD, March Term, 1795}

JONES, ELIZABETH, m. Daniel Hagerty on Mar 17, 1796. {Ref: PR}

JONES, EWEL (EUEL), head of family in 1800 (Havre de Grace). {Ref: CI}. Also see "John Wood," q.v.

JONES, EZEKIEL, taxpayer, 1798, Deer Creek Upper Hd., 2 tracts (239 acres) and 1 building, $830.53 valuation, no slaves. {Ref: TL}

JONES, EZEKIEL, head of family in 1800 (4th District). {Ref: CI}

JONES, FRANCES, m. Samuel Wilson on Sep 18, 1796. {Ref: PR}

JONES, FRANCES, head of family in 1800 (5th District). {Ref: CI}

JONES, GILBERT, charged in 1795 (nature of the case not stated). {Ref: CD, August Term, 1795}

JONES, GILBERT, taxpayer, 1798, Bush River Lower Hd., 1 dwelling house, 4 inferior houses, 1 acre, $1200 valuation; 1 tract (50 acres) in Bush River Lower Hd., $540 valuation, 3 slaves; also, taxpayer, Bush River Lower Hd., 1 dwelling house, 2 inferior houses, 80 perches of land, $350 valuation, no slaves. {Ref: TL}

JONES, GILBERT, had an account at Hall's Store in March, 1791. {Ref: WH}

JONES, GILBERT, treated by Dr. Archer on Jan 13, 1791; also mentioned his dau. Eliza. {Ref: JA}

JONES, GILBERT, licensed ordinary (tavern) in March, 1795 and August, 1797. {Ref: CC}

JONES, GRIFFITH, insolvent on a list for the county tax due for 1793 in Harford Upper, Harford Lower, and Spesutia Lower Hundreds returned to the levy court by Thomas Taylor on May 28, 1794. {Ref: IL 31.12}

JONES, HANNAH, insolvent on a list for 1791 in Gunpowder Upper and Bush River Lower Hundreds, as filed by John Bond, Deputy Sheriff, on Sep 20, 1791. {Ref: IL 31.24}

JONES, HUGH, insolvent on list returned by Robert Carlile for taxes due for the year 1791. {Ref: IL 31.16}

JONES, HUGH, insolvent on a list for 1791 in Gunpowder Upper and Bush River Lower Hundreds, as filed by John Bond, Deputy Sheriff, on Sep 20, 1791 (who listed him as a single man). {Ref: IL 31.24}

JONES, HUGH, b. Dec 23, 1791, d. Mar 1, 1864, aged 72 years, 2 months, and 8 days [sic], bur. in Dublin Methodist Church Cemetery. {Ref: TI, and Jones-Evans Bible}

JONES, ISAAC, tract *Contestable* surveyed between 1792 and 1796. {Ref: SB}

JONES, ISAAC (OF WILLIAM), tract *Ingram's Neighbour* surveyed in 1794 and tract *Contestable* surveyed between 1792 and 1796. {Ref: CB, SB}

JONES, ISAAC (OF WILLIAM), insolvent on lists in 1791 due county taxes and road taxes in "Deer Creek Upper, Middle, and Broad Creek Hundreds" as returned by Robert Amos, Jr., but his name was then crossed off both lists. {Ref: IL 31.12, 31.22}

JONES, ISAAC (York County), insolvent on lists in 1791 due county taxes and road taxes in "Deer Creek Upper, Middle, and Broad Creek Hundreds" as returned by Robert Amos, Jr. {Ref: IL 31.12, 31.22}

JONES, JAMES, see "Sarah Jones," q.v.

JONES, JAMES, taxpayer, 1798, Spesutia Lower Hd., 1 tract (80 perches) and 1 building, $67.50 valuation, no slaves. {Ref: TL}

JONES, JAMES, m. Mary Stockdale on May 29, 1795. {Ref: PR}

JONES, JAMES, b. Sep 30, 1793, d. Jun 29, 1860, aged 66 years, 8 months, and 29 days, bur. in Dublin Methodist Church Cemetery. {Ref: TI}

JONES, JAMES, head of family in 1800 (2nd District). {Ref: CI}

JONES, JAMES, head of family in 1800 (3rd District). {Ref: CI}

JONES, JAMES (OF A.), head of family in 1800 (5th District). {Ref: CI}

JONES, JINNY, treated by Dr. Archer on Jan 20, 1794; also mentioned "she is now married to Isaac Blake." {Ref: JA}

JONES, JOHN, insolvent on lists of taxes due in 1791 and 1792 in Broad Creek Hd., as returned by Robert Amos, Jr. in 1791 (who listed it as "Jno. Jones, Jess Lewis") and Benjamin Preston in 1792, but all names were then crossed off both lists. {Ref: IL 31.03, 31.12, 31.22}

JONES, JOSEPH, insolvent on lists returned by Robert Carlile and John Guyton for taxes due for the year 1791. {Ref: IL 31.16, 31.19}

JONES, MARY, see "Sarah Ashby Jones," q.v.

JONES, MORGAN, m. Cordelia Baker on Jan 25, 1798. {Ref: PR}

JONES, MORGAN, head of family in 1800 (1st District). {Ref: CI}

JONES, MORGAN JR., head of family in 1800 (1st District). {Ref: CI}

JONES, NICHOLAS, insolvent on a list for 1791 in Gunpowder Upper and Bush River Lower Hundreds, as filed by John Bond, Deputy Sheriff, on Sep 20, 1791 (who listed him as a single man). {Ref: IL 31.24}

JONES, NORTH, head of family in 1800 (4th District). {Ref: CI}

JONES, PRICILLA, head of family in 1800 (5th District). {Ref: CI}

JONES, REBECCA, dau. of Benjamin and Sarah, b. Jun 14, 1776, bapt. Jun 6, 1797. {Ref: PR}

JONES, REUBEN, taxpayer, 1798, Deer Creek Lower Hd., 1 tract (116 acres) and 1 building, $228.38 valuation, no slaves. {Ref: TL}

JONES, REUBEN, head of family in 1800 (5th District). {Ref: CI}

JONES, RICHARD, insolvent on a list for the road tax due for 1791 in Harford Upper, Harford Lower, and Spesutia Upper as returned by Robert Amos, Jr. on Sep 18, 1793. {Ref: IL 31.18}

JONES, ROBERT, see "Sarah Ashby Jones," q.v.

JONES, SARAH, see "Charlotte Jones" and "Rebecca Jones" and "Charles Jones,"

q.v.
JONES, SARAH, taxpayer, 1798, Deer Creek Middle Hd., 2 tracts (75 acres) and 1 building, $168.75 valuation, no slaves. {Ref: TL}
JONES, SARAH, wife of James, b. Dec 1, 1792, d. May 29, 1867, aged 74 years, 5 months, and 28 days, bur. in Dublin Methodist Church Cemetery. {Ref: TI}
JONES, SARAH ASHBY, daugter of Robert and Mary, b. Sep 29, 1794. {Ref: PR}
JONES, SIMON, see "Moses Morris," q.v.
JONES, STEPHEN, taxpayer, 1798, Bush River Lower Hd., 1 dwelling house, 3 inferior houses, 1 acre, 80 perches, $650 valuation; 2 tracts (108 acres, 80 perches) in Bush River Lower Hd., $726.19 valuation, 2 slaves. {Ref: TL}
JONES, STEPHEN, served on a Petit Jury in August, 1797, and on a Grand Jury in March, 1799. {Ref: CC, CM}
JONES, THOMAS, insolvent, Harford Lower and Spesutia Lower Hundreds (listed as a single man), on a tax list returned by George Lyttle on Sep 21, 1791. {Ref: IL 31.20, 31.21}
JONES, THOMAS, charged for selling liquors in 1797 and fined 600 lbs. of tobacco. {Ref: CD, March Term, 1797}
JONES, WILLIAM, see "Isaac Jones" and "William Jones, Sr.," q.v.
JONES, WILLIAM, insolvent on a list for the road tax for 1792, as returned for Robert Amoss, tax collector (Jones' name appeared on the same list twice). {Ref: IL 13.12}
JONES, WILLIAM, head of family in 1800 (3rd District). {Ref: CI}
JONES, WILLIAM, head of family in 1800 (4th District). {Ref: CI}
JONES, WILLIAM SR. (at B. Run), treated by Dr. Archer on May 28, 1798; also mentioned dau. Eliza, son William, and a grandson (no name given) in 1791. {Ref: JA}
JORDAN, ANN, head of family in 1800 (3rd District). {Ref: CI}
JORDAN, KITTY, see "Kitty Patterson," q.v.
JORDON, ROBERT, head of family in 1800 (3rd District). {Ref: CI}
JORDON, THOMAS, head of family in 1800 (5th District). {Ref: CI}
JORDON, WILLIAM, head of family in 1800 (4th District). {Ref: CI}
JORDON(?), WILLIAM, head of family in 1800 (3rd District). {Ref: CI}
JUDD, ANN, m. William Michael on Jul 9, 1797. {Ref: PR}
JUDD, ANNIE, wife of John, b. 1793, d. Feb 14, 1865, in her 72nd year, bur. in St. Ignatius Catholic Church Cemetery in Hickory. {Ref: TI}
JUDD, JOHN, b. 1798, d. Feb 18, 1870, in his 72nd year, bur. in St. Ignatius Catholic Church Cemetery in Hickory. {Ref: TI}
JUDD, JOSHUA, treated by Dr. Archer on Jul 25, 1791; also mentioned he lived on D. Lee's Place. {Ref: JA}
JUDD, MATHEIS, insolvent on a list for county taxes due in 1792 as returned by Benjamin Preston. {Ref: IL 31.00}
JUDD, MATHEW, head of family in 1800 (3rd District). {Ref: CI}
JUDD, MATTHEW, insolvent on list returned for the road tax due for 1791 by John Bull. {Ref: IL 31.14}

JUDD, MATTHEW, see "Angus Graham," q.v.
JUDD, WILLIAM ("charge twice"), insolvent on a list for the road tax due for 1791 in Harford Upper, Harford Lower, and Spesutia Upper as returned by Robert Amos, Jr. on Sep 18, 1793. {Ref: IL 31.18}
JUDD, WILLIAM, treated by Dr. Archer on Jun 1, 1791. {Ref: JA}
JUDD, WILLIAM (near D. Dunnavan's), treated by Dr. Archer in July, 1791; also mentioned his wife (no name given). {Ref: JA}
JUDD, WILLIAM JR., treated by Dr. Archer on Jun 29, 1791. {Ref: JA}
JUEL, MAGDALEN, see "Francis Carty," q.v.
JURDON, WILLIAM, insolvent on list returned by Robert Carlile for taxes due for the year 1791. {Ref: IL 31.16}
KAIN, AQUILA, taxpayer, 1798, Susquehanna Hd., 2 tracts (15 acres) and 1 building, $112.50 valuation, no slaves. {Ref: TL}
KANDLEMEN, JOHN, insolvent on a list for the road tax due for 1791 in Harford Upper, Harford Lower, and Spesutia Upper as returned by Robert Amos, Jr. on Sep 18, 1793. {Ref: IL 31.18}
KANE, JOHN, head of family in 1800 (3rd District). {Ref: CI}
KANE, PATRICK, head of family in 1800 (3rd District). {Ref: CI}
KEAN, JOHN JR., charged for refusing to aid and assist a constable in 1797. {Ref: CD, March and August Terms, 1797}
KEARN (KERNS), WILLIAM, taxpayer, 1798, Gunpowder Upper Hd., 1 dwelling house, 1 inferior building, 2 acres, $300 valuation; 2 tracts (127 acres) in Gunpowder Upper Hd., $353.25 valuation, no slaves. In another part of the tax schedule the occupant is listed as Benjamin Dungan and the owner is listed as William Kerns. {Ref: TL}. Also see "William Cearns," q.v.
KEECH, JOHN R. (reverend), b. Sep 9, 1795, d. Dec 16, 1861, for more than forty years the faithful and beloved rector of St. John's Parish, bur. in Christ Episcopal (Rock Spring) Church Cemetery. {Ref: TI}
KEECH, SUSAN P. SCOTT, wife of Rev. John R., b. Nov 3, 1797, d. Jan 10, 1875, bur. in Christ Episcopal (Rock Spring) Church Cemetery. {Ref: TI}
KEEN, ANN M., wife of James W., b. 1793, d. Feb 15, 1854, in her 61st year, bur. in Rock Run Cemetery at Craig's Corner. {Ref: TI}
KEEN, JAMES W., b. Dec 13, 1800, d. 1880, bur. in Rock Run Cemetery at Craig's Corner. {Ref: TI}
KEEN, REBECCA, see "Rebecca Keen Spencer," q.v.
KEEN, TIMOTHY, see "John Pybus," q.v.
KELL, ALEXA (ALISA?), head of family in 1800 (3rd District). {Ref: CI}.
KELL, ALISANNA, taxpayer, 1798, Gunpowder Upper Hd., 1 dwelling house, 3 inferior buildings, 2 acres, $130 valuation; 2 tracts (128 acres) in Gunpowder Upper Hd., $288 valuation, no slaves. {Ref: TL}
KELLEY, ARTHUR, head of family in 1800 (4th District). {Ref: CI}
KELLEY, HENRY, head of family in 1800 (4th District). {Ref: CI}
KELLEY, JAMES, head of family in 1800 (4th District). {Ref: CI}

KELLEY, JAMES, head of family in 1800 (5th District). {Ref: CI}
KELLEY, THOMAS, head of family in 1800 (3rd District). {Ref: CI}
KELLEY, WANTAL, taxpayer, 1798, Spesutia Lower Hd., 1 tract (44 perches, 21 sq. ft.), $13.50 valuation, no slaves. {Ref: TL}
KELLEY, WILLIAM, head of family in 1800 (1st District). {Ref: CI}
KELLEY, WILLIAM, head of family in 1800 (4th District). {Ref: CI}
KELLY, ALEXANDER, will probated Nov 6, 1794. {Ref: HW}
KELLY, CORNELIUS, b. Dec 25, 1796, d. Oct 15, 1865, bur. in Rock Run Cemetery at Craig's Corner. {Ref: TI}
KELLY, ISAAC, subpoenaed to the Grand Jury in August, 1797. {Ref: CC}
KELLY, JAMES ("can't be found"), insolvent on lists due for 1790, 1791, and 1792 "fund taxes" in Deer Creek Lower and Susquehanna Hundreds, as returned by Thomas Taylor. {Ref: IL 31.12, 31.03}
KELLY, MARY, head of family in 1800 (1st District). {Ref: CI}
KELLY, MICHAEL, charged in 1795 with Benjamin Shipley and Joseph Canear "to keep Mary Sergeant's child off the county." {Ref: CD, March Term, 1795}
KELLY, THOMAS, had an account at Hall's Store in June, 1791. {Ref: WH}. See "Phebe Barton," q.v.
KEMP, HANNAH, of St. John's Parish, bur. Feb 19, 1794, aged 70. {Ref: PR}
KENARD, JOSEPH ("run"), insolvent on a list of the county tax due William Osborn, sheriff, for 1791, as returned by Edward Prigg on Sep 20, 1791. {Ref: IL 31.17}
KENCARTT, JOSEPH, head of family in 1800 (4th District). {Ref: CI}
KENDLEY, RICHARD, taxpayer, 1798, Deer Creek Lower Hd., 1 tract (24 acres, 80 perches) and 1 building, $126 valuation, 2 slaves. {Ref: TL}
KENEDAY, JOHN, head of family in 1800 (4th District). {Ref: CI}
KENEDY, NATHAN, insolvent on a list for the county tax due for 1791 in Susquehanna Hd., as returned by Thomas Taylor on Sep 17, 1792. {Ref: IL 31.12}
KENLEY, DANIEL, treated by Dr. Archer on May 7, 1791; also mentioned Miss Polly Kenley in 1786, and his wife (no name given) treated on Mar 6, 1788 (and subsequently d., as noted in a different handwriting). {Ref: JA}
KENLEY, DANIEL (schoolmaster), treated by Dr. Archer on Jan 3, 1791. {Ref: JA}
KENLY, DANIEL, insolvent on a list for county taxes due in 1792 as returned by Benjamin Preston. {Ref: IL 31.00}
KENLY (KENLEY), RICHARD, head of family in 1800 (5th District). {Ref: CI}
KENLEY (KINGSLEY), SAMUEL, see "William Adair," q.v.
KENLY, SAMUEL, insolvent on a list for the county tax due for 1791 in Susquehanna Hd., as returned by Thomas Taylor on Sep 17, 1792. {Ref: IL 31.12, 31.02}
KENNADY, HANNAH, taxpayer, 1798, Deer Creek Upper Hd., 2 tracts (248 acres, 120 perches) and 1 building, $559.69 valuation, 1 slave. {Ref: TL}. In another part of the tax schedule the occupant is listed as James Lytle.
KENNADY, JAMES, taxpayer, 1798, Harford Upper Hd., 2 tracts (238 acres) and

1 building, $580.50 valuation, no slaves. {Ref: TL}
KENNADY (KENEDAY), JAMES, head of family in 1800 (3rd District). {Ref: CI}
KENNADY, JOHN, charged for assaulting Mary Pyles in 1794. {Ref: CD, March Term, 1795}
KENNADY, JOHN, taxpayer, 1798, Gunpowder Upper Hd., 1 dwelling house, 3 inferior buildings, 2 acres, $130 valuation; 3 tracts (137 acres) in Gunpowder Upper Hd., $319.50 valuation, no slaves. {Ref: TL}
KENNEDY, HOWARD, head of family in 1800 (5th District). {Ref: CI}
KENNARD, ISAAC, see "Thomas Bond," q.v.
KENNARD, JOSEPH, insolvent on lists in 1791 due county taxes and road taxes in "Deer Creek Upper, Middle, and Broad Creek Hundreds" as returned by Robert Amos, Jr. {Ref: IL 31.12, 31.22}
KENNARD, ELIZA, dau. of Matthew and Mary, b. Dec 18, 1796, m. Caleb Pue, d. Sep 7, 1873, aged 76 years, 8 months, and 19 days [sic], bur. in Cokesbury Methodist Cemetery in Abingdon. {Ref: TI}
KENNARD, ISAAC, head of family in 1800 (4th District). {Ref: CI}
KENNARD, MARTHA, dau. of Matthew and Mary, b. Nov 16, 1800, d. Feb 2, 1877, aged 76 years, 2 months, and 19 days, bur. in Cokesbury Methodist Cemetery in Abingdon. {Ref: TI}
KENNARD, MARY, see "Eliza Kennard" and "Martha Kennard," q.v.
KENNARD, MATHEW (MATTHEW), see "John Brown" and "Eliza Kennard" and "Martha Kennard," q.v.
KENNARD, MATHEW (MATTHEW), taxpayer, 1798, no dwelling house listed in this part of the tax schedule, no land listed, no Hd. listed (possibly Spesutia Lower Hundred), 1 slave. {Ref: TL}
KENNARD, MATTHEW, head of family in 1800 (Belle Air). {Ref: CI}
KENNEDY, ANN, consort of James, b. 1748, d. Feb 27, 1798, aged 50, bur. in Churchville Presbyterian Church Cemetery. {Ref: TI}
KENNEDY, ELIHU B., see "Sarah Kennedy," q.v.
KENNEDY, JAMES, see "Ann Kennedy," q.v.
KENNEDY, SARAH, consort of Elihu B., b. Sep 21, 1793, d. Apr 5, 1854, bur. in Churchville Presbyterian Church Cemetery. {Ref: TI}
KENT, JESSE, taxpayer, 1798, Deer Creek Upper Hd., 1 dwelling house, 1 inferior building, 2 acres, $120 valuation; 2 tracts (103 acres) in Deer Creek Upper Hd., $173.81 valuation, no slaves. {Ref: TL}
KENT (KENTT), JESSE, head of family in 1800 (4th District). {Ref: CI}
KENTLEMYRE, JOHN, taxpayer, 1798, Spesutia Lower Hd., 1 dwelling house, 22 perches and 10 sq. ft. of land, $300 valuation; 1 tract (22 perches, 10½ sq. ft.) in Spesutia Lower Hd., $281.25 valuation, no slaves; also, taxpayer, 1 dwelling house, 2 inferior houses, 22 perches and 10 sq. ft. of land in Spesutia Lower Hd., $350 valuation; 1 tract (22 perches, 10½ sq. ft.) in Spesutia Lower Hd., $337.50 valuation, no slaves. {Ref: TL}. In another part of the tax schedule the occupant is listed as John Porter and the taxpayer is John Kentlemyres. Also see

"Nancy Kindle," q.v.

KENTLEMYRE, JOHN, AND B. BARTLEY, taxpayers, 1798, Spesutia Lower Hd., 1 dwelling house, 44 perches and 21 sq. ft. of land, $280 valuation, no slaves. {Ref: TL}

KERENS (KERNS), WILLIAM, head of family in 1800 (4th District). {Ref: CI}. Also see "William Kearn" and "William Cearns," q.v.

KERNAY, HUGH, head of family in 1800 (4th District). {Ref: CI}

KERR, CHARLES, b. 1796, d. Mar 20, 1874 in his 78th year, bur. in St. Ignatius Catholic Church Cemetery in Hickory. {Ref: TI}

KERR, JAMES, tract *Mount Pleasant* (adjoining the State's Mason and Dixon line) surveyed in 1798 and granted in 1802. {Ref: CB}

KERR, JOHN, tract *Hopewell* surveyed in 1794 and granted in 1802. {Ref: CB}

KERR, MARGARET, b. 1793, d. Jul 27, 1850, bur. in Bethel Presbyterian Church Cemetery at Madonna. {Ref: BC}

KERR, ROSE, b. 1800, d. Feb 14, 1874, in her 74th year, bur. in St. Ignatius Catholic Church Cemetery in Hickory. {Ref: TI}

KERRIGAN, MANASSA, taxpayer, 1798, Broad Creek Hd., 1 tract (120 acres) and 1 building, $236.25 valuation, no slaves. {Ref: TL}

KERVEN, HENRY, insolvent, Harford Lower and Spesutia Lower Hundreds, on a tax list returned by George Lyttle on Sep 21, 1791. {Ref: IL 31.20, 31.21}

KERVIN, HENRY, insolvent on a list for the road tax due for 1791 in Harford Upper, Harford Lower, and Spesutia Upper as returned by Robert Amos, Jr. on Sep 18, 1793. {Ref: IL 31.18}

KEY, CHARITY, see "James Wear," q.v.

KEY, PHILIP (St. Mary's County), taxpayer, 1798, Harford Upper Hd., 1 tract (497 acres), $1118.25 valuation, no slaves. {Ref: TL}

KEYS, GEORGE W., head of family in 1800 (Havre de Grace). {Ref: CI}

KEYS, JAMES, insolvent on lists of taxes due in 1791 and 1792 in Broad Creek Hd., as returned by Robert Amos, Jr. in 1791 and Benjamin Preston in 1792. {Ref: IL 31.03, 31.12, 31.22}

KEYS (KEEYS), JAMES, head of family in 1800 (2nd District). {Ref: CI}

KIDD, JAMES, served on a Petit Jury in August, 1797. {Ref: CC}

KIDD, JAMES, taxpayer, 1798, Bush River Upper & Eden Hd., 1 dwelling house, 1 inferior building, 2 acres, $120 valuation; 2 tracts (165 acres) in Bush River Upper & Eden Hd., $278.44 valuation, no slaves. {Ref: TL}

KIDD, JAMES, served on a Grand Jury in August, 1799. {Ref: CM}

KIDD, JAMES, head of family in 1800 (4th District). {Ref: CI}

KIDD, LYDIA S., see "Andrew Turner," q.v.

KILGORE, THOMAS ("run"), insolvent on a list of the county tax due William Osborn, sheriff, for 1791, as returned by Edward Prigg on Sep 20, 1791. {Ref: IL 31.17}

KILGORE, THOMAS, insolvent on lists of taxes due in 1791 and 1792 in Broad Creek Hd., as returned by Robert Amos, Jr. in 1791 (who spelled the name as

"Killgore") and Benjamin Preston in 1792 (who spelled the name as "Gilgore"). {Ref: IL 31.03, 31.12, 31.22}

KILLPATRICK, HUGH, head of family in 1800 (3rd District). {Ref: CI}

KILPATRICK, ----, mentioned in a survey deposition on Jan 14, 1800 as "where Kilpatrick's dwelling house formerly stood." {Ref: JS}

KIMBEL, ELIGHA, head of family in 1800 (2nd District); two men by this name in this district. {Ref: CI}

KIMBEL, JAMES, head of family in 1800 (2nd District). {Ref: CI}

KIMBEL, JOHN, head of family in 1800 (2nd District). {Ref: CI}

KIMBEL, SARAH, head of family in 1800 (2nd District). {Ref: CI}

KIMBEL, STEPHEN, head of family in 1800 (2nd District). {Ref: CI}

KIMBEL, ZACHARIAH, head of family in 1800 (2nd District). {Ref: CI}

KIMBERLEE, JOHN, head of family in 1800 (2nd District). {Ref: CI}

KIMBLE, ANNA, see "Ashbury Kimble" and "George Washington Kimble" and "John Kimble," q.v.

KIMBLE, ASHBURY, son of Stephen and Anna, b. Aug 10, 1800. {Ref: PR}

KIMBLE, ELIJAH, see "James Kimble, Sr.," q.v.

KIMBLE, ELONER, had an account at Hall's Store in August, 1791. {Ref: WH}

KIMBLE, FRANCES, see "Jemima Kimble," q.v.

KIMBLE, GEORGE WASHINGTON, son of Stephen and Anna, b. Oct 8, 1797. {Ref: PR}

KIMBLE, GILES, insolvent on a list for the road tax due for 1791 in Harford Upper, Harford Lower, and Spesutia Upper as returned by Robert Amos, Jr. on Sep 18, 1793. {Ref: IL 31.18}

KIMBLE, GILES' HEIRS, or JOHN KIMBLE, taxpayers, 1798, Spesutia Lower Hd., 1 tract (50 acres) and 1 building (John Kimble, occupant), $241.88 valuation, no slaves. {Ref: TL}

KIMBLE, HANNAH, see "Mary Kimble" and "James Kimble," q.v.

KIMBLE, JAMES, see "William Kimble," q.v.

KIMBLE, JAMES, son of Stephen and Hannah, bapt. Jul 13, 1795. {Ref: PR}

KIMBLE, JAMES, insolvent on a list for the road tax due for 1791 in Harford Upper, Harford Lower, and Spesutia Upper as returned by Robert Amos, Jr. on Sep 18, 1793. {Ref: IL 31.18}

KIMBLE, JAMES JR., served as constable in Harford Lower Hd., 1799 (one list gave his name without the "Jr."). {Ref: CM}

KIMBLE, JAMES SR., taxpayer, 1798, Spesutia Lower Hd., 1 tract (100 acres) and 1 building, $562.50 valuation, no slaves; also, taxpayer, Spesutia Lower Hd., 1 other building, $22.50 valuation, no slaves. {Ref: TL}. In another part of the tax schedule the occupants are listed as Sarah Kimble and Elijah Kimble.

KIMBLE, JEMIMA, dau. of Zachariah and Frances, b. Feb 22, 1800, bapt. Aug 14, 1800. {Ref: PR}

KIMBLE, JOHN, see "William Kimble" and "Giles Kimble's heirs," q.v.

KIMBLE, JOHN, taxpayer, 1798, Spesutia Lower Hd., 1 dwelling house, 3 inferior buildings, 2 acres, $101 valuation; 1 tract (38 acres) in Spesutia Lower Hd., $149.62 valuation, no slaves. {Ref: TL}.

KIMBLE, JOHN, son of Stephen and Anna, b. Feb 27, 1799. {Ref: PR}

KIMBLE, JOHN, insolvent on a list for the road tax due for 1791 in Harford Upper, Harford Lower, and Spesutia Upper as returned by Robert Amos, Jr. on Sep 18, 1793. {Ref: IL 31.18}

KIMBLE, MARGARET, insolvent on a list for the road tax due for 1791 in Harford Upper, Harford Lower, and Spesutia Upper as returned by Robert Amos, Jr. on Sep 18, 1793. {Ref: IL 31.18}

KIMBLE, MARY, dau. of Stephen and Hannah, bapt. Jul 13, 1795. {Ref: PR}

KIMBLE, SARAH, see "James Kimble, Sr.," q.v.

KIMBLE, STEPHEN, see "Ashbury Kimble" and "George Washington Kimble" and "John Kimble" and "Mary Kimble" and "James Kimble" and "William Kimble," q.v.

KIMBLE, STEPHEN, taxpayer, 1798, Spesutia Lower Hd., 1 tract (72 acres) and 1 building, $342.90 valuation, no slaves; also, taxpayer, Spesutia Lower Hd., 1 other building, $22.50 valuation, no slaves. {Ref: TL}. In another part of the tax schedule the occupant is listed as Perry Nowland.

KIMBLE, STEPHEN, had an account at Hall's Store in February, 1791. {Ref: WH}

KIMBLE, STEPHEN, insolvent on a list for the road tax due for 1791 in Harford Upper, Harford Lower, and Spesutia Upper as returned by Robert Amos, Jr. on Sep 18, 1793. {Ref: IL 31.18}

KIMBLE, SUSANNA, insolvent on a list for the road tax due for 1791 in Harford Upper, Harford Lower, and Spesutia Upper as returned by Robert Amos, Jr. on Sep 18, 1793. {Ref: IL 31.18}

KIMBLE, WIDOW, insolvent on a list for the road tax due for 1791 in Harford Upper, Harford Lower, and Spesutia Upper as returned by Robert Amos, Jr. on Sep 18, 1793. {Ref: IL 31.18}

KIMBLE, WILLIAM, charged in 1797 (nature of case not stated), docket mentioned John Kimble, James Kimble and Stephen Kimble. {Ref: CD, March and August Terms, 1797}

KIMBLE, ZACHARIAH, see "Jemima Kimble," q.v.

KIMBLEY, JOHN, charged for selling liquors and fined 600 lbs. of tobacco in 1797. {Ref: CD, March Term, 1797}

KIMBOLY, JOHN, taxpayer, 1798, Spesutia Lower Hd., 1 dwelling house, 2 inferior buildings, 1 acre, $135 valuation, no slaves. {Ref: TL}

KINDLE, NANCY, dau. of John Kindle and Margaret Myers, b. Jun 11, 1797, bapt. Sep 7, 1797. {Ref: PR}. She may actually be the dau. of John Kindlemeyers or Kentlemyers. Additional research will be necessary before drawing conclusions.

KINEART, JOSEPH, taxpayer, 1798, Deer Creek Upper Hd., 1 tract (133 acres, 80 perches) and 1 building, $341.77 valuation, no slaves. {Ref: TL}

KINGIN, THOMAS, taxpayer, 1798, Broad Creek Hd., 1 tract (105 acres) and 1 building, $206.72 valuation, no slaves. {Ref: TL}

KINGSLEY, BARBARA, dau. of Samuel and Barbara, b. Apr 17, 1797. {Ref: PR}

KINGSLEY, SAMUEL, taxpayer, 1798, Spesutia Lower Hd., 1 dwelling house, 88 perches and 42 sq. ft. of land, $140 valuation, no slaves. {Ref: TL}

KINGSLEY, SAMUEL, head of family in 1800 (Havre de Grace). {Ref: CI}

KINLEY, DANIEL, insolvent on list returned for the road tax due for 1791 by John Bull. {Ref: IL 31.14}

KINLEY, LIMUEL, head of family in 1800 (2nd District). {Ref: CI}

KINNAN, SAMUEL, head of family in 1800 (Abingdon). {Ref: CI}

KINNEAR, JOSEPH, head of family in 1800 (4th District). {Ref: CI}

KINZELL, CHARLES, m. Ann Johnson on Feb 8, 1798. {Ref: PR}

KIRK, THOMAS, head of family in 1800 (5th District). {Ref: CI}

KIRKPATRICK, HUGH, insolvent on a list for the road tax due for 1791 in Harford Upper, Harford Lower, and Spesutia Upper as returned by Robert Amos, Jr. on Sep 18, 1793. {Ref: IL 31.18}

KIRKWOOD, JABES, head of family in 1800 (5th District). {Ref: CI}

KIRKWOOD, JOHN, see "Rebecca Kirkwood," q.v.

KIRKWOOD, JOHN, taxpayer, 1798, Bush River Upper & Eden Hd., 1 dwelling house, 1 inferior building, 2 acres, $110 valuation; 1 tract (145 acres, 80 perches) in Bush River Upper & Eden Hd., $327.37 valuation, no slaves. {Ref: TL}

KIRKWOOD, JOHN, head of family in 1800 (4th District). {Ref: CI}

KIRKWOOD, MARY ELIZABETH, see "WIlliam Robinson," q.v.

KIRKWOOD, REBECCA, dau. of John Kirkwood and Agnes Hope, b. Mar 3, 1799, d. Jun 25, 1872 (unm.), bur. in Bethel Presbyterian Church Cemetery at Madonna. {Ref: BC}

KIRKWOOD, RICHARD HOPE, husband of Margaret Cairnes and son of William Kirkwood and Jennett Hope, b. 1799, d. Feb 17, 1887, bur. in Bethel Presbyterian Church Cemetery at Madonna. {Ref: BC}

KIRKWOOD, ROBERT, taxpayer, 1798, Bush River Upper & Eden Hd., 1 dwelling house, 2 inferior buildings, 2 acres, $200 valuation; 1 tract (206 acres) in Bush River Upper & Eden Hd., $463.50 valuation, no slaves. {Ref: TL}

KIRKWOOD, ROBERT, son of William Kirkwood and Jennett Hope, b. 1797, d. Dec 12, 1829 (unm.?), bur. in Bethel Presbyterian Church Cemetery at Madonna. {Ref: BC}

KIRKWOOD, ROBERT, son of Robert Kirkwood and Rebecca Bell, b. 1800, d. Mar 12, 1881 (unm.), bur. in Bethel Presbyterian Church Cemetery at Madonna. {Ref: BC}

KIRKWOOD, ROBERT, head of family in 1800 (4th District). {Ref: CI}

KIRKWOOD, WILLIAM, see "Richard Hope Kirkwood" and "Robert Kirkwood," q.v.

KIRKWOOD, WILLIAM, taxpayer, 1798, Bush River Upper & Eden Hd., 1 tract (259 acres) and 1 building, $684 valuation, no slaves. {Ref: TL}

KIRKWOOD, WILLIAM, head of family in 1800 (4th District). {Ref: CI}
KISKA, JAMES, head of family in 1800 (2nd District). {Ref: CI}
KITELEY, RACHEL, insolvent on list returned for the road tax due for 1791 by John Bull. {Ref: IL 31.14}
KITELY, RACHEL, taxpayer, 1798, Gunpowder Lower Hd., 1 dwelling house, 80 perches of land, $120 valuation, no slaves. {Ref: TL}
KITELY, RACHEL, will probated Dec 21, 1799. {Ref: HW}
KITELY, WILLIAM'S HEIRS, or WILLIAM DOOLEY, taxpayers, 1798, Gunpowder Lower Hd., 1 dwelling house, 1 acre (William Dooley, occupant), $100.50 valuation, no slaves. {Ref: TL}
KNIGHT, ABRAHAM, see "Henrietta Knight," q.v.
KNIGHT, ANN, dau. of Isaac and Tabitha, b. Mar 27, 1796, bapt. Jul 17, 1796. {Ref: PR}. Also see "Margaret Knight" and "Aquila Knight" and "Robert Knight" and "Henrietta Knight," q.v.
KNIGHT, AQUILA, son of Thomas and Ann, b. May 14, 1797. {Ref: PR}. Also see "Peggy Fielding Knight," q.v.
KNIGHT, CHARLOTTE, dau. of William and Sarah, b. Aug 3, 1798, bapt. Nov 24, 1798. {Ref: PR}
KNIGHT, D., see "Mary Jefferies," q.v.
KNIGHT, ELIZABETH, see "Peggy Fielding Knight," q.v.
KNIGHT, HENRIETTA, dau. of Abraham and Ann, b. Oct 15, 1798, bapt. May 5, 1799. {Ref: PR}
KNIGHT, ISAAC, see "Ann Knight" and "Isaac Night," q.v.
KNIGHT, LIGHT, insolvent on a list for the county tax due for 1791 in Susquehanna Hd., as returned by Thomas Taylor on Sep 17, 1792. {Ref: IL 31.12, 31.02}
KNIGHT, MARGARET, dau. of Thomas and Ann, b. Feb 15, 1793. {Ref: PR}
KNIGHT, MICHAEL, son of Thomas and Ann, b. Jun 5, 1795. {Ref: PR}
KNIGHT, PEGGY FIELDING, dau. of Aquila and Elizabeth, b. Nov 15, 1795, bapt. May 25, 1797. {Ref: PR}
KNIGHT, PETER, see "Peter Night," q.v.
KNIGHT, ROBERT, son of Thomas and Ann, b. Oct 5, 1799. {Ref: PR}
KNIGHT, SARAH, see "Charlotte Knight," q.v.
KNIGHT, TABITHA, see "Ann Knight," q.v.
KNIGHT, THOMAS, insolvent on a list for the road tax due for 1791 in Harford Upper, Harford Lower, and Spesutia Upper as returned by Robert Amos, Jr. on Sep 18, 1793. {Ref: IL 31.18}. Also see "Margaret Knight" and "Aquila Knight" and "Robert Knight" and "Burt Whitson," q.v.
KNIGHT, WILLIAM, see "Charlotte Knight," q.v.
KNIGHT, WILLIAM, insolvent on a list for the road tax due for 1791 in Harford Upper, Harford Lower, and Spesutia Upper as returned by Robert Amos, Jr. on Sep 18, 1793. {Ref: IL 31.18}
KNIGHT, WILLIAM, m. Sarah Robison on Oct 1, 1797. {Ref: PR}

KNOCK, DANIEL, insolvent on list returned for the county tax for 1791 by William Osburn in Gunpowder Lower Hd. (which listed him as a single man). {Ref: IL 31.15}

KRUSON, RICHARD, served on a Grand Jury in March, 1798 and on a Petit Jury in March, 1800. {Ref: CM}

KWIGAN(?), THOMAS, head of family in 1800 (5th District). {Ref: CI}

LABARBAN(?), FRELET(?) & COMPANY, licensed retailers in August, 1797. {Ref: CC}

LACEY, THOMAS, insolvent on list returned by Robert Carlile for taxes due for the year 1791. {Ref: IL 31.16}

LACEY, THOMAS, insolvent on a list for 1791 in Gunpowder Upper and Bush River Lower Hundreds, as filed by John Bond, Deputy Sheriff, on Sep 20, 1791. {Ref: IL 31.24}

LACY, PIERCE (tanner), had an account at Hall's Store in September, 1791. {Ref: WH}

LADIBAT DE AILAC, taxpayer, 1798, Spesutia Lower Hd., 1 dwelling house, 6 inferior buildings, 2 acres, $200 valuation; 1 tract (498 acres) in Spesutia Lower Hd., $2342.20 valuation, 1 slave. {Ref: TL}

LAFATONIERE, JOHN J. S., taxpayer, 1798, Gunpowder Upper Hd., 1 dwelling house, 2 inferior buildings, 2 acres, $200 valuation; 3 tracts (95 acres) in Gunpowder Lower Hd., $270 valuation, 4 slaves. {Ref: TL}

LAKE, THOMAS, taxpayer, 1798, Gunpowder Upper Hd., 2 tracts (142 acres) and 1 building, $536.60 valuation, no slaves. {Ref: TL}

LAKE, THOMAS, head of family in 1800 (3rd District). {Ref: CI}

LAMBSDON, THOMAS, head of family in 1800 (3rd District). {Ref: CI}

LAMMOT, HENRY, will probated May 23, 1798. {Ref: HW}

LAMOT, HENRY'S HEIRS, taxpayers, 1798, Spesutia Lower Hd., 1 tract (88 perches, 42 sq. ft.), $29.25 valuation, no slaves. {Ref: TL}

LAMOT, JACOB, or MOSES CRABSON, taxpayer, 1798, Susquehanna Hd., 1 tract (20 acres) and 1 building (Moses Crabson, occupant), $78.75 valuation, no slaves. {Ref: TL}

LANCASTER, BEN JR., insolvent on a list for 1791 in Gunpowder Upper and Bush River Lower Hundreds, as filed by John Bond, Deputy Sheriff, on Sep 20, 1791. {Ref: IL 31.24}

LANCASTER, BENJAMIN, insolvent on a list for 1791 in Gunpowder Upper and Bush River Lower Hundreds, as filed by John Bond, Deputy Sheriff, on Sep 20, 1791 (who listed him as a single man). {Ref: IL 31.24}

LANCASTER, JESSE, taxpayer, 1798, Gunpowder Upper Hd., 1 dwelling house, 4 inferior buildings, 2 acres, $180 valuation; 2 tracts (139 acres) in Gunpowder Upper Hd., $331.31 valuation, no slaves. {Ref: TL}

LANCASTER, JOSEPH, taxpayer, 1798, Gunpowder Upper Hd., 2 tracts (111 acres) and 1 building, $373.50, no slaves. {Ref: TL}

LANDCASTER, B., insolvent on list returned by Robert Carlile for taxes due for the year 1791. {Ref: IL 31.16}

LANKASTER, JESSE, head of family in 1800 (3rd District). {Ref: CI}
LANKESTER, BENJAMIN, head of family in 1800 (3rd District). {Ref: CI}
LANKESTER, JOSEPH, head of family in 1800 (3rd District). {Ref: CI}
LANKISTER, NATHAN, head of family in 1800 (3rd District). {Ref: CI}
LANNAGIN, DENNIS, head of family in 1800 (2nd District). {Ref: CI}
LAREW (LAREU), GEORGE, taxpayer, 1798, Deer Creek Upper Hd., 1 dwelling house, 2 acres, $250 valuation; 1 tract (210 acres) in Deer Creek Upper Hd., $427.50 valuation, no slaves. {Ref: TL}
LAREW (LEREW), GEORGE, head of family in 1800 (4th District). {Ref: CI}
LAREW (LAREU, LEREW), MICHAEL, head of family in 1800 (4th District). {Ref: CI}. Also see "William Fultz," q.v.
LAREW (LARU), MICHAEL, mentioned in a survey deposition on Jan 18, 1800 as "to where Thomas Capens house formerly stood as proved by Michael Laru." {Ref: JS}
LATIMAR, JESSE, head of family in 1800 (4th District). {Ref: CI}
LAUDER, WILLIAM, see "Samuel Griffith," q.v.
LAUGHERY, DANIEL, head of family in 1800 (3rd District). {Ref: CI}. Also see "Angus Graham," q.v.
LAUGHLIN, WILLIAM ("run"), insolvent on lists due for 1790 and 1791 "fund taxes" and county taxes in Susquehanna Hd., as returned by Thomas Taylor. {Ref: IL 31.12, 31.02}
LAURENCE, JOHN ("out back"), insolvent on lists due for 1790 and 1791 "fund taxes" and county taxes in Susquehanna Hd., as returned by Thomas Taylor. {Ref: IL 31.12, 31.02}
LAWRENCE, JOHN, m. Rebecca Yarley on Jul 5, 1795. {Ref: PR}
LAZARUS, MOWHAM(?), head of family in 1800 (5th District). {Ref: CI}
LEE, CHARLES W., taxpayer, 1798, Deer Creek Middle Hd., 1 tract (197 acres) and 2 buildings (Charles McCan or McCann, occupant of one of them), $387.84 valuation, 1 slave. {Ref: TL}
LEE, D., see "Joshua Judd," q.v.
LEE, DAVID, treated by Dr. Archer on Sep 22, 1797; also mentioned son Ralph in 1788. {Ref: JA}
LEE, DAVID, taxpayer, 1798, Gunpowder Upper Hd., 1 dwelling house, 7 inferior buildings, 2 acres, $300 valuation; 4 tracts (191 acres) in Gunpowder Upper Hd., $1283.69 valuation, no slaves. {Ref: TL}
LEE, DAVID, son of John and Martha, b. Sep 13, 1795, bapt. Dec 30, 1795. {Ref: PR}
LEE, DAVID, head of family in 1800 (1st District). {Ref: CI}
LEE, DAVID JR., taxpayer, 1798, Gunpowder Upper Hd., 1 tract (178 acres) and 1 building, $439.88 valuation, no slaves. {Ref: TL}
LEE, DAVID JR., head of family in 1800 (3rd District). {Ref: CI}
LEE, DEBORAH, will probated Aug 19, 1793. {Ref: HW}
LEE, EDWARD, son of John and Martha, b. Sep 23, 1793, bapt. Dec 30, 1795. {Ref: PR}

LEE, EDWARD, head of family in 1800 (5th District). {Ref: CI}
LEE, ELIZABETH, m. James Lee on Feb 25, 1800. {Ref: PR}. Also see "Frances Martha Lee" and "Priscilla Elizabeth Lee" and "Richard Dallam Lee," q.v.
LEE, FRANCES MARTHA, dau. of Parker Hall and Elizabeth, b. Apr 16, 1793, bapt. Sep 17, 1794. {Ref: PR}
LEE, HANNAH, see "Elias Ellicot Amos," q.v.
LEE, JACOB, see "Samuel Lee," q.v.
LEE, JAMES, served on a Petit Jury in March, 1800. {Ref: CM}
LEE, JAMES, taxpayer, 1798, Deer Creek Middle Hd., 1 tract (103 acres) and 1 building, $202.78 valuation, no slaves; in another part of the tax schedule the occupant is listed as Thomas Brown. Also, taxpayer, Deer Creek Lower Hd., 2 tracts (130 acres) and 1 building, $749.25 valuation, no slaves. {Ref: TL}
LEE, JAMES, m. Elizabeth Lee on Feb 25, 1800. {Ref: PR}
LEE, JAMES, head of family in 1800 (5th District). {Ref: CI}
LEE, JAMES (OF J.), head of family in 1800 (3rd District). {Ref: CI}
LEE, JOHN, see "Edward Lee" and "David Lee," q.v.
LEE, JOHN, insolvent on list returned by Robert Carlile for taxes due for the year 1791. {Ref: IL 31.16}. Also see "William Smith," q.v.
LEE, JOHN, insolvent on a list for 1791 in Gunpowder Upper and Bush River Lower Hundreds, as filed by John Bond, Deputy Sheriff, on Sep 20, 1791. {Ref: IL 31.24}
LEE, JOHN, head of family in 1800 (5th District); two men by this name in this district. {Ref: CI}
LEE, JOHN (OF SAMUEL), taxpayer, 1798, Gunpowder Upper Hd., 1 tract (9 acres) and 1 building, $168.75 valuation, no slaves. {Ref: TL}
LEE, JOSIAH, taxpayer, 1798, Deer Creek Middle Hd., 1 dwelling house, 5 inferior buildings, 2 acres, $350 valuation; 4 tracts (134 acres, 80 perches) in Deer Creek Middle Hd., $413.25 valuation, 4 slaves. {Ref: TL}
LEE, JOSIAS, head of family in 1800 (5th District). {Ref: CI}
LEE, LETTISHA C., head of family in 1800 (3rd District). {Ref: CI}
LEE, MARSHALL, m. Rachel Blake on Jan 13, 1799. {Ref: PR}
LEE, MARTHA, see "Edward Lee" and "David Lee," q.v.
LEE, MARTIAL, head of family in 1800 (5th District). {Ref: CI}
LEE, PARKER H., head of family in 1800 (3rd District). {Ref: CI}
LEE, PARKER HALL, taxpayer, 1798, Spesutia Upper Hd., 1 dwelling house, 5 inferior buildings, 1 acre, $200 valuation; 3 tracts (501 acres) in Spesutia Upper Hd., $1775.25 valuation, 8 slaves; also, taxpayer, Spesutia Upper Hd., 1 dwelling house, 3 inferior buildings, 120 perches, $115 valuation, no slaves. {Ref: TL}
LEE, PARKER HALL, served on a Grand Jury in March, 1798 and on a Petit Jury in March, 1800. {Ref: CM}. Also see "Frances Martha Lee" and "Priscilla Elizabeth Lee" and "Richard Dallam Lee," q.v.
LEE, PRESBURY, see "Samuel Lee," q.v.

LEE, PRISCILLA ELIZABETH, dau. of Parker Hall and Elizabeth, b. Jun 5, 1796, bapt. May 14, 1799. {Ref: PR}

LEE, RACHEL (Miss), b. Apr 7, 1796, d. Oct 24, 1881, bur. in Cokesbury Methodist Cemetery in Abingdon. {Ref: TI}

LEE, RALPH, see "David Lee," q.v.

LEE, RICHARD DALLAM, son of Parker Hall and Elizabeth, b. Apr 18, 1799, bapt. May 14, 1799, d. Nov 1, 1841, bur. in Christ Episcopal (Rock Spring) Church Cemetery. {Ref: TI, PR}

LEE, SAMUEL, treated by Dr. Archer on Dec 15, 1791; also mentioned sons Presbury and Jacob. {Ref: JA}

LEE, SAMUEL, taxpayer, 1798, Spesutia Upper Hd., 1 dwelling house, 4 inferior buildings, 1 acre, 80 perches, $475 valuation; 5 tracts (948 acres) in Spesutia Upper Hd., $5070.37 valuation, 8 slaves; also, taxpayer, Spesutia Upper Hd., 1 dwelling house, 80 perches of land, $125 valuation, no slaves. {Ref: TL}. Also see "John Lee (of Samuel)," q.v.

LEE, SAMUEL, insolvent on a list for 1791 in Gunpowder Upper and Bush River Lower Hundreds, as filed by John Bond, Deputy Sheriff, on Sep 20, 1791. {Ref: IL 31.24}

LEE, SAMUEL, insolvent on list returned by Robert Carlile for taxes due for the year 1791. {Ref: IL 31.16}

LEE, SAMUEL, will probated Dec 4, 1798. {Ref: HW}

LEE, SAMUEL, head of family in 1800 (3rd District). {Ref: CI}

LEE, SAMUEL (OF JAMES), head of family in 1800 (3rd District). {Ref: CI}

LEE, SAMUEL W., taxpayer, 1798, Deer Creek Middle Hd., 4 tracts (134 acres, 80 perches) and 1 building, $807 valuation, 3 slaves. {Ref: TL}

LEE, SAMUEL W., served on a Grand Jury in March, 1799. {Ref: CM}

LEE, SAMUEL W., head of family in 1800 (5th District). {Ref: CI}

LEE, SILAS, head of family in 1800 (3rd District). {Ref: CI}

LEE, THOMAS, non-resident (place of residence not stated), taxpayer, 1798, Spesutia Lower Hd., 1 tract (583 acres) and 1 building, $4718.69 valuation, 5 slaves. {Ref: TL}

LEE, WASHINGTON, head of family in 1800 (1st District). {Ref: CI}

LEE, WILLIAM, taxpayer, 1798, Gunpowder Upper Hd., 1 dwelling house, 3 inferior buildings, 2 acres, $110 valuation; 2 tracts (123 acres) in Gunpowder Upper Hd., $299.25 valuation, 1 slave. {Ref: TL}

LEE, WILLIAM, head of family in 1800 (3rd District). {Ref: CI}

LEECH, JAMES, head of family in 1800 (1st District). {Ref: CI}

LEGO (LEGOE), BENEDICT, insolvent on lists returned for the county and road taxes due for 1791 by John Bull in Gunpowder Lower Hundred. {Ref: IL 31.14, 31.15}

LEGOE, SARAH, head of family in 1800 (1st District). {Ref: CI}

LEIGH, MOSES, head of family in 1800 (1st District). {Ref: CI}

LEITLE, WILLIAM ("poor"), insolvent on a list of the county tax due William Osborn, sheriff, for 1791, as returned by Edward Prigg on Sep 20, 1791. {Ref: IL

199

LEMMON, ELIZA (Miss), b. 1797, d. Jan 29, 1886, bur. in Bethel Presbyterian Church Cemetery at Madonna. {Ref: BC}

LEMMON, GEORGE, b. 1795, d. May 29, 1874, bur. in Bethel Presbyterian Church Cemetery at Madonna. {Ref: BC}

LEMMON, GEORGE, taxpayer, 1798, Bush River Upper & Eden Hd., 1 dwelling house, 1 inferior building, 2 acres, $120 valuation; 2 tracts (26 acres) in Bush River Upper & Eden Hd., $117 valuation, 1 slave. {Ref: TL}

LEMMON, GEORGE, head of family in 1800 (4th District). {Ref: CI}

LEMMON, GEORGE ("run"), insolvent on a list of the county tax due William Osborn, sheriff, for 1791, as returned by Edward Prigg on Sep 20, 1791. {Ref: IL 31.17}

LEMOND (LEMONDON), GEORGE, insolvent on lists in 1791 due county taxes and road taxes in "Deer Creek Upper, Middle, and Broad Creek Hundreds" as returned by Robert Amos, Jr. {Ref: IL 31.12, 31.22}

LEMOTT, JACOB, head of family in 1800 (2nd District). {Ref: CI}

LENDRIGAN, DENNIS, see "James Bell," q.v.

LEONARD, EDWARD, insolvent on lists in 1791 due county taxes and road taxes in "Deer Creek Upper, Middle, and Broad Creek Hundreds" as returned by Robert Amos, Jr. {Ref: IL 31.12, 31.22}

LEONARD, EDWARD, taxpayer, 1798, Deer Creek Upper Hd., 1 tract (5 acres) and 1 building, $46.56 valuation, no slaves. {Ref: TL}

LEONARD, EDWARD, head of family in 1800 (4th District). {Ref: CI}

LESHAVER, JOHN (captain), head of family in 1800 (1st District). {Ref: CI}

LESTER, NORRIS, taxpayer, 1798, Spesutia Lower Hd., 1 tract (127 acres) and 1 building, $663.75 valuation, no slaves; taxpayer, 1798, Spesutia Lower Hd., 1 tract (150 acres) and 1 building, $742.50 valuation, no slaves; in another part of the tax schedule the occupant is listed as Thomas Brown. Also, taxpayer, Spesutia Lower Hd., 1 building, $13.50 valuation; in another part of the tax schedule the occupant is listed as a free negro, but no name is given. {Ref: TL}

LESTER, NORRIS, had an account at Hall's Store in December, 1791. {Ref: WH}

LESTER, NORRIS, head of family in 1800 (2nd District). {Ref: CI}

LESTER, WILLIAM, insolvent on a list for the road tax for 1792, as returned for Robert Amoss, tax collector. {Ref: IL 13.12}

LESTER, WILLIAM, licensed retailer in August, 1797. {Ref: CC}

LESTER, WILLIAM, taxpayer, 1798, Bush River Lower Hd., 1 dwelling house, 2 inferior buildings, 60 perches, $300 valuation; 1 tract (100 acres) and 1 building in Bush River Lower Hd., $540 valuation, 2 slaves. {Ref: TL}

LESTER, WILLIAM, m. Elizabeth Fawcet on Nov 19, 1799. {Ref: PR}

LESTER, WILLIAM, head of family in 1800 (Abingdon). {Ref: CI}

LEWIN, JOHN, head of family in 1800 (5th District). {Ref: CI}

LEWIS, ARTHUR, head of family in 1800 (4th District). {Ref: CI}

LEWIS, CLEMENT, insolvent on a list for 1791 in Gunpowder Upper and Bush River Lower Hundreds, as filed by John Bond, Deputy Sheriff, on Sep 20,

1791. {Ref: IL 31.24}

LEWIS, GEORGE, insolvent on list returned for the road tax due for 1791 by John Bull. {Ref: IL 31.14}

LEWIS, GEORGE, insolvent on a list for county taxes due in 1792 as returned by Benjamin Preston. {Ref: IL 31.00}

LEWIS, JAMES, insolvent on lists in 1791 due county taxes and road taxes in "Deer Creek Upper, Middle, and Broad Creek Hundreds" as returned by Robert Amos, Jr., but his name was then crossed off both lists. {Ref: IL 31.12, 31.22}

LEWIS, JESS, see "John Jones," q.v.

LEWIS, JOHN, insolvent on a list for 1791 in Gunpowder Upper and Bush River Lower Hundreds, as filed by John Bond, Deputy Sheriff, on Sep 20, 1791. {Ref: IL 31.24}

LEWIS, JOSEPH, insolvent on a list for 1791 in Gunpowder Upper and Bush River Lower Hundreds, as filed by John Bond, Deputy Sheriff, on Sep 20, 1791. {Ref: IL 31.24}

LEWIS, MARY, head of family in 1800 (Abingdon). {Ref: CI}

LEWIS, NICHOLAS, m. Mary Mackie on Dec 25, 1800. {Ref: PR}

LEWIS, SARAH REBECCA, consort of John Clark Monk, b. Mar 8, 1796, d. Mar 20, 1854, aged 58 years and 12 days, bur. in St. George's Episcopal Church Cemetery at Perryman. {Ref: TI}

LINAM, WILLIAM, m. Sarah Pinix on Dec 17, 1797. {Ref: PR}. Also see "William Lineum," q.v.

LINDSEY, ELIZABETH, taxpayer, 1798, Deer Creek Middle Hd., 1 dwelling house, 4 inferior buildings, 2 acres, $110 valuation; 1 tract (120 acres) in Deer Creek Middle Hd., $182.25 valuation, 1 slave. {Ref: TL}

LINDSEY, ELIZABETH, head of family in 1800 (5th District). {Ref: CI}

LINEUM, WILLIAM, head of family in 1800 (3rd District). {Ref: CI}

LINTON, WILLIAM, purchased beef on Dec 8, 1797 at Bush River Store. {Ref: AH}

LITTEN, JOHN, will probated Apr 9, 1793. {Ref: HW}

LITTLE BLACK GUINEA MAN, see "Corbin Bond," q.v.

LITTLE, JOHN, taxpayer, 1798, Gunpowder Lower Hd., 1 dwelling house, 7 inferior buildings, 2 acres, $300 valuation; 2 tracts (363 acres) in Gunpowder Lower Hd., $1746 valuation, 3 slaves. {Ref: TL}

LITTLE, JOHN, m. Elizabeth Adams on Jul 20, 1794. {Ref: PR}

LIVINGSTON, ----, bur. Jul 20, 1795. {Ref: PR}

LIVINGSTON, JOHN, treated by Dr. Archer on Jan 6, 1791; also mentioned he lived near Slate Ridge Meeting House. {Ref: JA}

LOBDALE, SAMUEL, insolvent on a list for the road tax due for 1791 in Harford Upper, Harford Lower, and Spesutia Upper as returned by Robert Amos, Jr. on Sep 18, 1793. {Ref: IL 31.18}

LOCHARY, JOHN, b. Apr 22, 1798, d. Sep 29, 1850, bur. in St. Ignatius Catholic Church Cemetery in Hickory. {Ref: TI}

LOCHRY (LOCKERY), DANIEL, charged for assaulting Asael Hitchcock in

1797. {Ref: CD, March Term, 1797}. Also see "Michael McElhiney" and "John Gillis," q.v.

LOCKART, BENJAMIN, insolvent on lists in 1791 due county taxes and road taxes in "Deer Creek Upper, Middle, and Broad Creek Hundreds" as returned by Robert Amos, Jr., but his name was then crossed off both lists. {Ref: IL 31.12, 31.22}

LOCKART, SAMUEL, insolvent on lists in 1791 due county taxes and road taxes in "Deer Creek Upper, Middle, and Broad Creek Hundreds" as returned by Robert Amos, Jr., but his name was then crossed off both lists. {Ref: IL 31.12, 31.22}

LOCKHARD, SAMUEL, wrote his will "of Baltimore County" on Oct 30, 1770, probated Apr 17, 1791 in Harford County. {Ref: HW}

LOFLIN, WILLIAM, see "James Mitchell's heirs," q.v.

LOFTON, WILLIAM, head of family in 1800 (2nd District). {Ref: CI}

LOGUE, WILLIAM, see "Henrietta Wheeler," q.v.

LOKART, SAMUEL, insolvent on list returned for the road tax due for 1791 by John Bull. {Ref: IL 31.14}

LOKELEY, JOHN, insolvent on a list for the road tax due for 1791 in Harford Upper, Harford Lower, and Spesutia Upper as returned by Robert Amos, Jr. on Sep 18, 1793. {Ref: IL 31.18}

LONEY, AMOSS (AMOES), head of family in 1800 (2nd District). {Ref: CI}

LONEY, MOSES, treated by Dr. Archer on Apr 22, 1791; mentioned William Loney was his executor in 1804; also mentioned a son (no name given). {Ref: JA}

LONEY, MOSES, licensed retailer in March, 1795. {Ref: CC}

LONEY, MOSES, insolvent on a list for the road tax due for 1791 in Harford Upper, Harford Lower, and Spesutia Upper as returned by Robert Amos, Jr. on Sep 18, 1793. {Ref: IL 31.18}

LONEY, MOSES, had an account at Hall's Store in April, 1791. {Ref: WH}

LONEY, MOSES, insolvent, Harford Lower and Spesutia Lower Hundreds (listed as a single man), on a tax list returned by George Lyttle on Sep 21, 1791. {Ref: IL 31.20, 31.21}

LONEY, WILLIAM, served on a Petit Jury in August, 1798 and on a Grand Jury in August, 1800. {Ref: CM}

LONEY, WILLIAM, taxpayer, 1798, Spesutia Lower Hd., 1 dwelling house, 7 inferior buildings, 2 acres, $225 valuation; 2 tracts (198 acres) in Spesutia Lower Hd., $1181.20 valuation, 7 slaves. {Ref: TL}. Also see "Moses Loney," q.v.

LONEY, WILLIAM, served on a Grand Jury in August, 1799. {Ref: CM}

LONEY, WILLIAM, had an account at Hall's Store in November, 1791. {Ref: WH}

LONEY, WILLIAM, head of family in 1800 (2nd District). {Ref: CI}

LONG, HENRY, husband of Ruth Long, and a soldier in the War of 1812, b. Mar 19, 1795, d. Septeber 4, 1887, bur. in Bethel Presbyterian Church Cemetery at Madonna. {Ref: BC}

LONG, JOHN, head of family in 1800 (4th District). {Ref: CI}

LONG, JOHN JR., head of family in 1800 (4th District). {Ref: CI}

LONG, JOHN JR., taxpayer, 1798, Bush River Upper & Eden Hd., 1 tract (45 acres) and 1 building, $168.75 valuation, no slaves. {Ref: TL}

LONG, JOHN SR., insolvent on list returned by Robert Carlile for taxes due for the year 1791. {Ref: IL 31.16}
LONG, LARK, insolvent on list returned by Robert Carlile for taxes due for the year 1791. {Ref: IL 31.16}
LONG, LUKE, head of family in 1800 (4th District). {Ref: CI}
LONG, NATHANIEL, head of family in 1800 (4th District). {Ref: CI}
LONG, PETER, m. Margarett Carr on Aug 30, 1791. {Ref: PR}
LONG, PETER, insolvent on list returned by Robert Carlile for taxes due for the year 1791. {Ref: IL 31.16}
LONG, PETER, head of family in 1800 (4th District). {Ref: CI}
LONG, RUTH, see "Henry Long," q.v.
LOVE, JACOB, head of family in 1800 (3rd District). {Ref: CI}. Also see "John Love's heirs," q.v.
LOVE, JOHN, served on a Petit Jury in August, 1797. {Ref: CC}
LOVE, JOHN, subpoenaed to the Grand Jury in August, 1797. {Ref: CC}
LOVE, JOHN, served on a Grand Jury in August, 1798 and August, 1799, and on a Petit Jury in August, 1800. {Ref: CM}
LOVE, JOHN, head of family in 1800 (3rd District). {Ref: CI}
LOVE, JOHN, will probated Apr 16, 1793. {Ref: HW}
LOVE, JOHN'S HEIRS, or MARGARET LOVE, taxpayers, 1798, Spesutia Upper Hd., 1 dwelling house, 1 acre (Margaret Love, occupant), $235 valuation; 11 tracts (1005 acres) in Spesutia Upper Hd., $2876.91 valuation (Margaret Love, occupant); taxpayers, Spesutia Upper Hd., 1 dwelling house, 80 perches of land (Jacob Love, occupant), $145 valuation, no slaves; taxpayers, Spesutia Upper Hd., 1 dwelling house, 1 inferior building, 80 perches of land (Walter Harwood, occupant), $120 valuation, no slaves. {Ref: TL}
LOVE, MARGARET (MARGUERITE), head of family in 1800 (3rd District). {Ref: CI}. Also see "John Love's heirs," q.v.
LOVE, ROBERT, see "George Haley," q.v.
LOVE, WILLIAM, head of family in 1800 (3rd District). {Ref: CI}
LOVETT, MARY, subpoenaed to the Grand Jury in August, 1797. {Ref: CC}
LOVETT, WILLIAM, had an account at Hall's Store in August, 1791. {Ref: WH}
LOWERY, JOHN, head of family in 1800 (3rd District). {Ref: CI}
LOWSTATER, JACOB, taxpayer, 1798, Gunpowder Lower Hd., 1 dwelling house, 2 acres, $120 valuation, no slaves. {Ref: TL}
LOWSTATURE, JACOB, head of family in 1800 (Abingdon). {Ref: CI}
LOYD, EDWARD, insolvent on list returned for the road tax due for 1791 by John Bull. {Ref: IL 31.14}
LUCKEY, GEORGE, taxpayer, 1798, Bush River Upper & Eden Hd., 1 dwelling house, 1 inferior building, 2 acres, $150 valuation; 2 tracts (141 acres) in Bush River Upper & Eden Hd., $317.25 valuation, no slaves. {Ref: TL}
LUCKEY, GEORGE (reverend), tracts *Vineyard* and *Heidelburg* surveyed between

1792 and 1796. {Ref: SB}

LUCKEY (LUCKIE), GEORGE, tract *Addition to Bond's Gratuity* surveyed in 1787 and granted in 1797. {Ref: CB}

LUCKEY (LUCKIE), GEORGE (reverend), head of family in 1800 (4th District). {Ref: CI}

LUCKEY, JAMES, see "Martha Luckey," q.v.

LUCKEY, JANE, taxpayer, 1798, no Hd. listed (probably Susquehanna Hundred), 1 slave. {Ref: TL}. Also see "William Luckey's heirs," q.v.

LUCKEY (LUCKIE), JANE, head of family in 1800 (2nd District). {Ref: CI}

LUCKEY, JOSEPH, b. 1791, d. Mar 11, 1867, "at 8 1/2 p.m., supposed to be about 76 years of age from the best information that could be got." {Ref: James Luckey Bible}

LUCKEY, MARTHA, wife of James (veteran of the War of 1812), b. Apr 17, 1795 at Black Horse, m. Dec 13, 1825, d. 1883, in her 88th year, at the residence of her son-in-law John Dreghorn in Toledo, Ohio. {Ref: James Luckey FB, which contained an undated newspaper clipping}

LUCKEY, WILLIAM'S HEIRS, or JANE LUCKEY, taxpayers, 1798, Susquehanna Hd., 1 dwelling house, 1 inferior building, 2 acres (Jane Luckey, occupant), $150 valuation; also, 3 tracts (358 acres) and 1 building in Susquehanna Hd. (Jane Luckey, occupant), $1029.38 valuation, no slaves. {Ref: TL}. In another part of the tax schedule the occupants are listed as Jane Luckey and Benjamin Whitson.

LUCKEY (LUCKY), WILLIAM, had an account at Hall's Store in May, 1791. {Ref: WH}

LUKE, N. W., husband of Henrietta W. Luke, b. 1796, d. Jan 15, 1826, in his 30th year, bur. in St. Ignatius Catholic Church Cemetery in Hickory. {Ref: TI}

LUKINS, BENJAMIN, taxpayer, 1798, Deer Creek Upper Hd., 1 tract (261 acres) and 1 building, $513.84 valuation, no slaves. {Ref: TL}

LUKINS (LEWKINS), BENJAMIN, head of family in 1800 (4th District). {Ref: CI}

LUKINS, MOSES, insolvent on lists in 1791 due county taxes and road taxes in "Deer Creek Upper, Middle, and Broad Creek Hundreds" as returned by Robert Amos, Jr. {Ref: IL 31.12, 31.22}

LUSBY, JOSEPH, insolvent on list returned for the county tax for 1791 by William Osburn in Gunpowder Lower Hd. in Gunpowder Lower Hundred. {Ref: IL 31.15}

LUSBY, JOSEPH, insolvent, Harford Lower and Spesutia Lower Hundreds, on a tax list returned by George Lyttle on Sep 21, 1791. {Ref: IL 31.20, 31.21}

LUSBY, MILCAH, insolvent on a list for 1791 in Gunpowder Upper and Bush River Lower Hundreds, as filed by John Bond, Deputy Sheriff, on Sep 20, 1791. {Ref: IL 31.24}

LUSBY, MILCAH, will probated Oct 28, 1791. {Ref: HW}

LUX, RACHEL RIDGELY, see "James McCormick, Jr.," q.v.

LYNCH, BARNARD, head of family in 1800 (3rd District). {Ref: CI}

LYNCH, BARNEY J., taxpayer, 1798, Gunpowder Upper Hd., no dwelling house listed in this part of the tax schedule, no land listed, 1 slave. {Ref: TL}. Also see

"John Hall," q.v.

LYNCH, ELIZABETH, dau. of John and Sarah, b. about 1793. {Ref: PR}

LYNCH, JAMES, son of John and Sarah, b. in May, 1798. {Ref: PR}

LYNCH, JOHN, see "Thomas Lynch" and "Sarah Lynch" and "James Lynch," q.v.

LYNCH, JOHN, insolvent on a list for the county tax due for 1793 in Susquehanna Hd. as returned to the levy court by Thomas Taylor on May 28, 1794, who noted "put in my hands last fall." {Ref: IL 31.12}

LYNCH, JOHN, head of family in 1800 (2nd District). {Ref: CI}

LYNCH, KIDD, m. Sarah Swarth (Swarts) on Aug 21, 1791. {Ref: PR}

LYNCH, SARAH, see "James Lynch" and "Thomas Lynch" and "Sarah Lynch," q.v.

LYNCH, THOMAS, son of John and Sarah, b. about 1791. {Ref: PR}

LYNCH, WILLIAM, insolvent on lists for the county tax and road tax due for 1791 and 1792 in Deer Creek Lower Hd., as returned by Thomas Taylor on Sep 17, 1792 (his name was spelled "Linch" on one 1791 list). {Ref: IL 31.12, 31.03}

LYON, JOHN, insolvent on list returned by Robert Carlile for taxes due for the year 1791. {Ref: IL 31.16}

LYON, JONATHAN, insolvent on lists returned by Robert Carlile and John Guyton (the latter spelled the name as "Johnathan Lyon") for taxes due for the year 1791. {Ref: IL 31.16, 31.19}

LYON, WALTER, head of family in 1800 (4th District). {Ref: CI}

LYONS, JOHN, head of family in 1800 (5th District). {Ref: CI}

LYTLE, ANN, insolvent on a list for the road tax due for 1791 in Harford Upper, Harford Lower, and Spesutia Upper as returned by Robert Amos, Jr. on Sep 18, 1793 (her name was crossed off the list). {Ref: IL 31.18}

LYTLE, CHARITY, wife of Thomas, b. 1794, d. Aug 2, 1861, aged 67, bur. in McKendree Cemetery near Black Horse. {Ref: TI}

LYTLE, ELIZABETH, see "John Lytle," q.v.

LYTLE, GEORGE, head of family in 1800 (2nd District). {Ref: CI}

LYTLE, JACOB, insolvent on a list for the road tax due for 1791 in Harford Upper, Harford Lower, and Spesutia Upper as returned by Robert Amos, Jr. on Sep 18, 1793 (his name was crossed off the list). {Ref: IL 31.18}

LYTLE, JAMES, see "Zebulon Hollingsworth," q.v.

LYTLE, JAMES, tract *James's Valley* surveyed between 1792 and 1796. {Ref: SB}

LYTLE, JAMES, appointed a Judge of Elections in the 1st District on Jul 28, 1800. {Ref: CM}

LYTLE, JAMES, served on a Petit Jury in March, 1798, on a Grand Jury in March, 1799, and on a Petit Jury in March, 1800. {Ref: CM}

LYTLE, JAMES, head of family in 1800 (1st District). {Ref: CI}

LYTLE, JAMES, head of family in 1800 (5th District). {Ref: CI}

LYTLE, JAMES, or JONATHAN WEST, taxpayer, 1798, Deer Creek Upper Hd., 1 tract (50 acres) and 1 building (Jonathan West, occupant), $87.19 valuation, no slaves. {Ref: TL}. Also see "Hannah Kennady," q.v.

LYTLE, JAMES (Baltimore County), taxpayer, 1798, Bush River Upper & Eden Hd., 1 tract (91 acres), $238.87 valuation, no slaves. {Ref: TL}
LYTLE, JOHN, son of John and Elizabeth, b. Sep 30, 1798, bapt. Mar 31, 1799. {Ref: PR}
LYTLE, JOHN, head of family in 1800 (5th District). {Ref: CI}
LYTLE, THOMAS, see "Charity Lytle," q.v.
LYTLE, WILLIAM, insolvent on lists in 1791 due county taxes and road taxes in "Deer Creek Upper, Middle, and Broad Creek Hundreds" as returned by Robert Amos, Jr. {Ref: IL 31.12, 31.22}. Also see "William Leitle," q.v.
LYTTLE, GEORGE, compiled and returned a list of insolvents in Harford Lower and Spesutia Lower Hundreds in 1792. {Ref: IL 31.20, 31.21}
LYTTLE, JAMES, tract *Benjamin's Neglect* surveyed between 1792 and 1796. {Ref: SB}
LYTTLE, NATHAN, insolvent on list returned for the county tax for 1791 by William Osburn in Gunpowder Lower Hd. in Gunpowder Lower Hundred. {Ref: IL 31.15}
LYTTLE, THOMAS, tract *Agreement* surveyed between 1792 and 1796. {Ref: SB}
MACATEE, GEORGE, b. 1800, d. Jun 12, 1853, in his 53rd year, bur. in St. Ignatius Catholic Church Cemetery in Hickory. {Ref: TI}
MACATEE, IGNATIUS GEORGE, b. Mar 6, 1800, d. Oct 12, 1875, bur. in St. Mary's Catholic Church Cemetery in Pylesville. {Ref: TI}
MACATEE, MARIA, b. 1800, d. Dec 31, 1832, in her 32nd year, bur. in St. Ignatius Catholic Church Cemetery in Hickory. {Ref: TI}
MACKIE, LOSSOM, head of family in 1800 (3rd District). {Ref: CI}
MACKIE, MARY, m. Nicholas Lewis on Dec 25, 1800. {Ref: PR}
MACTON, JOHN, b. May 5, 1791, d. Dec 28, 1820, aged 29 years, 7 months, and 23 days, bur. in Dublin Methodist Church Cemetery. {Ref: TI}
MADDAN, JAMES, head of family in 1800 (4th District). {Ref: CI}
MADDEN, JAMES, taxpayer, 1798, Bush River Upper & Eden Hd., 1 dwelling house, 1 inferior house, 2 acres, $150 valuation; 1 tract (158 acres, 80 perches) in Bush River Upper & Eden Hd., $267.47 valuation, no slaves. {Ref: TL}
MADDEN, JAMES, taxpayer, 1798, Harford Upper Hd., 1 tract (120 acres) and 1 building, $281.25 valuation, no slaves. {Ref: TL}
MADDEN, JOHN, or WILLIAM SHERWOOD, taxpayer, 1798, Harford Upper Hd., 1 tract (100 acres) and 1 building (William Sherwood, occupant), $224.61 valuation, no slaves. {Ref: TL}
MADDEN, JOHN, see "William Crosby" and "John Allen," q.v.
MADDON, JAMES, head of family in 1800 (3rd District). {Ref: CI}
MADDON, JOHN, head of family in 1800 (3rd District). {Ref: CI}
MADDOX, JOHN, head of family in 1800 (1st District). {Ref: CI}
MAGAW, HENRY AMOS, son of Samuel and Jane, b. 1792, d. May 14, 1834, bur. in Churchville Presbyterian Church Cemetery. {Ref: TI}
MAGAW, JANE, wife of Samuel, b. 1793, d. Apr 26, 1865, aged 72, bur. in Churchville Presbyterian Church Cemetery. {Ref: TI}. Also see "Henry Amos

Magaw," q.v.

MAGAW, SAMUEL, see "Henry Amos Magaw" and "Jane Magaw," q.v.

MAGNESS, JAMES, head of family in 1800 (3rd District). {Ref: CI}

MAGNESS (MAGNUS), JESSE, son of Moses and Rachel, b. Apr 29, 1793, bapt. Aug 13, 1795. {Ref: PR}

MAGNESS, JOHN, head of family in 1800 (3rd District). {Ref: CI}

MAGNESS, MOSES, see "Jesse Magness" and "George Walker," q.v.

MAGNESS, MOSES, head of family in 1800 (3rd District). {Ref: CI}.

MAGNESS (MAGNES), MOSES, served on a Petit Jury in August, 1797. {Ref: CC}

MAGNESS, RACHEL, see "Jesse Magness," q.v.

MAGNESS, THOMAS, head of family in 1800 (3rd District). {Ref: CI}

MAGNESS, WILLIAM, head of family in 1800 (3rd District). {Ref: CI}

MAHAN, JAMES, head of family in 1800 (2nd District). {Ref: CI}

MAHAN, JOHN, head of family in 1800 (2nd District). {Ref: CI}

MAHAN, JOHN JR., head of family in 1800 (2nd District). {Ref: CI}

MAHARRY(?), STEPHEN, head of family in 1800 (5th District). {Ref: CI}

MAHON, BENJAMIN, head of family in 1800 (5th District). {Ref: CI}

MAHON, EDWARD, fined £5 for insulting the court, 1795. {Ref: CC, August, 1795}

MAHON, EDWARD, charged for selling liquors in 1794. {Ref: CD, March Term, 1795}

MAHON, ELIZABETH, m. William Smith on Jul 6, 1797. {Ref: PR}

MAHON (MAHAN), ELIZABETH, head of family in 1800 (2nd District). {Ref: CI}

MAHON, JOHN JR., taxpayer, 1798, Susquehanna Hd., 1 tract (100 acres) and 1 building, $238.12 valuation, no slaves. {Ref: TL}

MAHON, JOHN SR., taxpayer, 1798, Susquehanna Hd., 1 tract (60 acres) and 1 building, $83.25 valuation, no slaves. {Ref: TL}

MAHON, WIDOW, see "Samuel Gover (Rock Run)," q.v.

MAHON, WILLIAM, insolvent on lists due for 1790 and 1791 "fund taxes" and county taxes in Susquehanna Hd., as returned by Thomas Taylor (his name was spelled "Mohon" on one list which also noted "no such man"). {Ref: IL 31.12, 31.02}

MAHON, WILLIAM, m. Anne Jones on Nov 27, 1800. {Ref: PR}

MAJOR, JOHN, insolvent on lists of taxes due in 1791 and 1792 in Broad Creek Hd., as returned by Robert Amos, Jr. in 1791 and Benjamin Preston in 1792. {Ref: IL 31.03, 31.12, 31.22}

MAJOR, THOMAS, tract *Major's Venture* surveyed between 1792 and 1796. {Ref: SB}

MAJOR, THOMAS, taxpayer, 1798, Deer Creek Upper Hd., 2 tracts (140 acres, 80 perches) and 1 building, $321.60 valuation, no slaves. {Ref: TL}

MAJOR, THOMAS, head of family in 1800 (5th District). {Ref: CI}

MAJOR, WILLIAM, insolvent on lists of taxes due in 1791 and 1792 in Broad Creek Hd., as returned by Robert Amos, Jr. in 1791 and Benjamin Preston in 1792. {Ref: IL 31.03, 31.12, 31.22}

MAJOR, WILLIAM ("run"), insolvent on a list of the county tax due William Osborn, sheriff, for 1791, as returned by Edward Prigg on Sep 20, 1791. {Ref: IL

31.17}
MALLOTT, JOHN, head of family in 1800 (4th District). {Ref: CI}
MALOY, FRANCIS, head of family in 1800 (4th District). {Ref: CI}
MANTEL, WILLIAM, head of family in 1800 (4th District). {Ref: CI}
MARCH (MARCHE), JOHN, m. Hannah Onion on Jun 5, 1794. {Ref: PR}
MARCHE, JOHN, taxpayer, 1798, Gunpowder Upper Hd., 1 dwelling house, 4 inferior houses, 2 acres, $300 valuation; 2 tracts (506 acres) in Gunpowder Upper Hd., $966.38 valuation, 1 slave. {Ref: TL}
MARPEL, ABEL, head of family in 1800 (Havre de Grace). {Ref: CI}
MARPLE & ADLUM, taxpayers, 1798, Spesutia Lower Hd., 1 dwelling house, 2 inferior houses, 2 acres, $1000 valuation; 1 tract (1 acre, 16 perches and 84 sq. ft.) in Spesutia Lower Hd., $90 valuation, no slaves. {Ref: TL}
MARRY, JAMES, head of family in 1800 (4th District). {Ref: CI}
MARS, SAMUEL, head of family in 1800 (Havre de Grace). {Ref: CI}
MARSH, DAVID, head of family in 1800 (4th District). {Ref: CI}
MARSH, JOHN, head of family in 1800 (2nd District). {Ref: CI}
MARSH, JOHN, head of family in 1800 (3rd District). {Ref: CI}
MARSH, LOYD, insolvent on a list for the road tax due for 1791 in Harford Upper, Harford Lower, and Spesutia Upper as returned by Robert Amos, Jr. on Sep 18, 1793. {Ref: IL 31.18}
MARSH, LOYD, insolvent, Harford Lower and Spesutia Lower Hundreds, on a tax list returned by George Lyttle on Sep 21, 1791. {Ref: IL 31.20, 31.21}
MARSH, WILLIAM, insolvent on list returned for the road tax due for 1791 by John Bull. {Ref: IL 31.14}
MARSH, WILLIAM, insolvent on a list for county taxes due in 1792 as returned by Benjamin Preston. {Ref: IL 31.00}
MARSHAL, SAMUEL, see "Bennet Jarrett," q.v.
MARSHAL, SAMUEL, charged with selling liquors by the smalls (case noted as quashed) in 1797. {Ref: CD, March Term, 1797}
MARSHAL, SAMUEL, taxpayer, 1798, Bush River Upper & Eden Hd., 1 dwelling house, 1 inferior house, 2 acres, $110 valuation; 1 tract (18 acres, 80 perches) in Bush River Upper & Eden Hd., $104.60 valuation, no slaves. {Ref: TL}
MARSHAL, SAMUEL, mentioned in a survey deposition on Jan 17, 1800 as "to a house where Sam. Marshal now lives." {Ref: JS}
MARSHAL, SAMUEL, head of family in 1800 (4th District). {Ref: CI}
MARSHALL, SAMUEL, head of family in 1800 (4th District). {Ref: CI}
MARSHALL, SAMUEL, granted a tavern license in March and August, 1797. {Ref: CC}
MARSHELL, JOHN, insolvent on a list for the road tax due for 1791 in Harford Upper, Harford Lower, and Spesutia Upper as returned by Robert Amos, Jr. on Sep 18, 1793. {Ref: IL 31.18}
MARSTON, DAVID, head of family in 1800 (Abingdon). {Ref: CI}
MARTIN, ----, see "William Morgan's heirs," q.v.
MARTIN, ABRAHAM, see "Mary Martin," q.v.

MARTIN, ANDREW, see "Thomas Martin" and "Jane Martin" and "Archibald Donnelly," q.v.
MARTIN, ANDREW, subpoenaed to the Grand Jury in August, 1797. {Ref: CC}
MARTIN, ANDREW, m. Elizabeth Evett on Jul 24, 1799. {Ref: PR}
MARTIN, ANDREW, head of family in 1800 (1st District). {Ref: CI}
MARTIN, ANDREW, head of family in 1800 (2nd District). {Ref: CI}
MARTIN, EDWARD, had an account at Hall's Store in May, 1791. {Ref: WH}
MARTIN, ELIZABETH, dau. of John and Sarah, b. Sep 20, 1799, bapt. Sep 7, 1800. {Ref: PR}. Also see "Thomas Martin" and "Jane Martin," q.v.
MARTIN, HENRY, head of family in 1800 (3rd District). {Ref: CI}
MARTIN, JAMES, insolvent on a list for the county tax due for 1791 in Susquehanna Hd., as returned by Thomas Taylor on Sep 17, 1792. {Ref: IL 31.12, 31.02}
MARTIN, JANE, dau. of Andrew and Elizabeth, b. Apr 17, 1800 (twin of Thomas). {Ref: PR}
MARTIN, JOHN, see "Elizabeth Martin," q.v.
MARTIN, JOHN, head of family in 1800 (3rd District); two men by this name in this district. {Ref: CI}
MARTIN, MARY, wife of Abraham, b. Nov 3, 1793, d. Feb 17, 1842, aged 49 years, 3 months, and 14 days, bur. in Cokesbury Methodist Cemetery in Abingdon. {Ref: TI}
MARTIN, ROBERT, insolvent on a list for 1791 in Gunpowder Upper and Bush River Lower Hundreds, as filed by John Bond, Deputy Sheriff, on Sep 20, 1791. {Ref: IL 31.24}
MARTIN, SARAH, subpoenaed to the Grand Jury in August, 1797. {Ref: CC}. Also see "Elizabeth Martin" and "Archibald Donnelly," q.v.
MARTIN, THOMAS, son of Andrew and Elizabeth, b. Apr 17, 1800 (twin of Jane). {Ref: PR}
MARTIN, WILLIAM, taxpayer, 1798, Susquehanna Hd., 1 dwelling house, 2 inferior houses, 2 acres, $105 valuation; 3 tracts (26 acres) in Susquehanna Hd., $75.75 valuation, no slaves. {Ref: TL}
MARTIN, WILLIAM, treated by Dr. Archer on Apr 21, 1793. {Ref: JA}
MARTIN, WILLIAM, head of family in 1800 (2nd District). {Ref: CI}
MASALLY, FRANCIS, head of family in 1800 (3rd District). {Ref: CI}
MASH, JOHN, taxpayer, 1798, Gunpowder Upper Hd., 1 tract (104 acres) and 1 building, $279 valuation, no slaves. {Ref: TL}
MASH, THOMAS, taxpayer, 1798, Gunpowder Upper Hd., 1 dwelling house, 5 inferior houses, 2 acres, $250 valuation; 1 tract (298 acres) in Gunpowder Upper Hd., $738 valuation, no slaves. {Ref: TL}
MASON, JOHN, taxpayer, 1798, Gunpowder Upper Hd., 1 dwelling house, 2 inferior houses, 2 acres, $150 valuation; 1 tract (95 acres) in Gunpowder Upper Hd., $213.75 valuation, no slaves. {Ref: TL}
MASON, JOHN, mentioned in a survey deposition on May 24, 1799. {Ref: JS}

MASON (MASSON), JOHN, head of family in 1800 (1st District). {Ref: CI}
MASON (MASSON), PETER, head of family in 1800 (1st District). {Ref: CI}
MASON (MASSON), PETER, head of family in 1800 (4th District). {Ref: CI}
MASSEY, AQUILA, taxpayer, 1798, Deer Creek Lower Hd., 1 dwelling house, 2 inferior houses, 2 acres, $300 valuation; 3 tracts (326 acres) in Deer Creek Lower Hd., $1225.12 valuation, no slaves. {Ref: TL}. In another part of the tax schedule Negro Jacob is listed as an occupant.
MASSEY, AQUILA (silversmith), treated by Dr. Archer on Feb 18, 1796; also mentioned the inoculation of his family in 1795: Caroline Johns, James Massey, and James Hart. {Ref: JA}
MASSEY, AQUILLA, head of family in 1800 (5th District). {Ref: CI}
MASSEY, ISAAC, taxpayer, 1798, Deer Creek Lower Hd., 1 dwelling house, 2 inferior houses, 2 acres, $300 valuation; 1 tract (313 acres) in Deer Creek Lower Hd., $718.87 valuation, no slaves. {Ref: TL}
MASSEY, ISAAC, head of family in 1800 (5th District). {Ref: CI}
MASSEY, JAMES, see "Aquila Massey," q.v.
MASSEY, JOHN W., b. Jul 25, 1796, d. May 31, 1882, bur. in Deer Creek Friends Cemetery in Darlington. {Ref: TI}
MATHER, MICHAEL (Baltimore Town), or SAMUEL SWARTH, taxpayer, 1798, Bush River Lower Hd., 1 dwelling house, 3 inferior houses, 1 acre and 80 perches (Samuel Swarth, occupant), $350 valuation; 3 tracts (187 acres, 80 perches) in Bush River Lower Hd. (Samuel Swarth, occupant), $632.81 valuation, no slaves. {Ref: TL}
MATHER, MICHAEL, head of family in 1800 (1st District). {Ref: CI}
MATHER, THOMAS, b. 1795, d. Feb 1, 1867, in his 72nd year, bur. in Cokesbury Methodist Cemetery in Abingdon. {Ref: TI}
MATHERS, MICH., treated by Dr. Archer on Apr 22, 1791. {Ref: JA}
MATHERS, MRS., bur. Mar 3, 1794, aged 76. {Ref: PR}
MATHEW, FELIX (PHELIX) ANTHONY & CO. [sic], licensed retailers in March, 1795. {Ref: CC}
MATHEWS, BENNET, served on a Petit Jury in March, 1800. {Ref: CM}
MATHEWS, BENNET, taxpayer, 1798, Spesutia Upper Hd., 1 dwelling house, 4 inferior houses, 1 acre, $200 valuation; 1 tract (299 acres) in Spesutia Upper Hd., $1418.63 valuation, 3 slaves. {Ref: TL}
MATHEWS, BENNETT, head of family in 1800 (3rd District). {Ref: CI}
MATHEWS, CARVIL, see "Nancy Mathews" and "Carvil Matthews," q.v.
MATHEWS, CARVIL, taxpayer, 1798, Spesutia Lower Hd., 1 dwelling house, 6 inferior houses, 2 acres, $145 valuation; 1 tract (206 acres) in Spesutia Lower Hd., $785.25 valuation, 7 slaves. {Ref: TL}
MATHEWS, CARVIL, head of family in 1800 (2nd District). {Ref: CI}
MATHEWS, FRANCES, taxpayer, 1798, Spesutia Lower Hd., no dwelling house listed in this part of the tax schedule, no land listed, 1 slave. {Ref: TL}

MATHEWS, JESSE, m. Ann Conn on Aug 1, 1792. {Ref: PR}
MATHEWS, JOHN, see "Thomas Owen," q.v.
MATHEWS, JOSEPH, head of family in 1800 (2nd District). {Ref: CI}
MATHEWS, JOSIAS, taxpayer, 1798, Spesutia Lower Hd., 1 dwelling house, 4 inferior houses, 2 acres, $170 valuation; 1 tract (198 acres) in Spesutia Lower Hd., $880.65 valuation, 3 slaves. {Ref: TL}
MATHEWS, LEVIN, will probated Mar 17, 1795. {Ref: HW}
MATHEWS, MILCAH, will probated Mar 20, 1795. {Ref: HW}
MATHEWS, NANCY (Miss), treated by Dr. Archer on Oct 7, 1795; also mentioned Carvil Mathews (no relationship stated). {Ref: JA}
MATHEWS, PETER FRANCIS, see "Negro Guy," q.v.
MATHEWS, ROGER, served on a Grand Jury in March, 1799 and on a Petit Jury in March, 1800. {Ref: CM}
MATHEWS, ROGER, taxpayer, 1798, Spesutia Lower Hd., 1 dwelling house, 7 inferior houses, 2 acres, $285 valuation; 2 tracts (298 acres) in Spesutia Lower Hd., $1206.90 valuation, 3 slaves. {Ref: TL}
MATHEWS, ROGER, appointed a Judge of Elections in the 2nd District on Jul 28, 1800. {Ref: CM}
MATHEWS, ROGER (major), head of family in 1800 (2nd District). {Ref: CI}
MATTHEWS, ----, bur. Mar 5, 1798. {Ref: PR}
MATTHEWS, ANN, m. Carvil Matthews on Jan 28, 1796. {Ref PR}. Also see "John Carvel Matthews" and "Milcah Lusby Matthews," q.v.
MATTHEWS, CARVIL, m. Ann Matthews on Jan 28, 1796. {Ref: PR}
MATTHEWS, CARVIL, warden, 1793-1794, St. George's Episcopal Church. {Ref: PR}
MATTHEWS, CARVIL, see "John Carvel Matthews" and "Milcah Lusby Matthews" and Ann Matthews" and "Carvil Matthews," q.v.
MATTHEWS, CONSTANCE ELIZA, dau. of Josiah and Jane, b. Jul 6, 1796, bapt. Mar 3, 1797. {Ref: PR}
MATTHEWS, ELIZABETH, m. James Billingslea on Sep 14, 1797. {Ref: PR}
MATTHEWS, HANNAH, see "Robert William Holland," q.v.
MATTHEWS, JACOB FORWOOD, son of Josiah and Jane, b. Aug 20, 1794, bapt. Mar 3, 1797. {Ref: PR}
MATTHEWS, JANE, see "Jacob Forwood Matthews" and "John Matthews" and Constance Eliza Matthews" and "Mary Rebecca Matthews," q.v.
MATTHEWS, JOHN, son of Josiah and Jane, b. Oct 15 or 19, 1792 (both dates were given in two separate registers), bapt. Mar 3, 1797. {Ref: PR}
MATTHEWS, JOHN CARVEL, son of Carvel and Ann, b. Apr 16, 1797, bapt. Jan 7, 1798. {Ref: PR}
MATTHEWS, JOSEPH, see "Mary Rebecca Matthews," q.v.
MATTHEWS, JOSIAH, m. Jane Forwood on Jan 19, 1792 by Rev. John Ireland. {Ref: PR}. Also see "Jacob Forwood Matthews" and "John Matthews" and Constance Eliza Matthews," q.v.

MATTHEWS, LEVIN, treated by Dr. Archer on Jan 14, 1791. {Ref: JA}
MATTHEWS, LEVIN, insolvent on a list for the road tax for 1792, as returned for Robert Amoss, tax collector (Matthew Levins' name appeared on the same list twice). {Ref: IL 13.12}
MATTHEWS, MARY REBECCA, dau. of Joseph and Jane, b. Jun 7 or Jul 6, 1798 (both dates were given in two separate registers), bapt. May 4, 1800. {Ref: PR}
MATTHEWS, MILCAH LUSBY, dau. of Carvil and Ann, b. Feb 28, 1799, bapt. May 4, 1800. {Ref: PR}
MATTHEWS, ROGER, purchased 26 trees on Sep 13, 1797 (1798?) at Bush River Store. {Ref: AH}
MATTHEWS, ROGER, m. Constant Forwood on Oct 16, 1800. {Ref: PR}
MATTHEWS, ROGER, warden, 1796-1797, St. George's Episcopal Church. {Ref: PR}
MATTHEWS, WILLIAM, had an account at Hall's Store in May, 1791. {Ref: WH}
MATTICKS, MARTHA, m. John Mitchell on Sep 6, 1798. {Ref: PR}
MAULSBY, DAVID (carpenter in Belle Air), treated by Dr. Archer on Jul 10, 1794; mentioned son Morris Maulsby in 1787; also spelled the name as "Malsby" and noted "this man has gone to Baltimore County, Va" [sic]. {Ref: JA}
MAULSBY, DAVID, taxpayer, 1798, Gunpowder Upper Hd., 1 tract (137 acres) and 1 building, $320.62 valuation, no slaves. {Ref: TL}
MAULSBY, DAVID (Belle Air), taxpayer, 1798, Bush River Lower Hd., 1 dwelling house, 1 inferior house, 80 perches of land, $215 valuation, no slaves. {Ref: TL}
MAULSBY, DAVID, head of family in 1800 (Belle Air). {Ref: CI}
MAULSBY, DAVID, head of family in 1800 (1st District). {Ref: CI}
MAULSBY, ELIONER (ELEANOR), taxpayer, 1798, Bush River Lower Hd., 1 dwelling house, 2 inferior houses, 80 perches of land, $300 valuation; 5 tracts (211 acres) in Bush River Lower Hd., $474.75 valuation, no slaves. {Ref: TL}. Also see "Maurice Maulsby," q.v.
MAULSBY, MAURICE, m. Eleanor Maulsby on Mar 22, 1792. {Ref: PR}
MAULSBY, MORRIS, head of family in 1800 (1st District). {Ref: CI}. Also see "David Maulsby," q.v.
MAULSBY, WHEELEN (WHEELER?), see "David Ross," q.v.
MAULSBY, WHEELER, head of family in 1800 (3rd District). {Ref: CI}
MAULSBY, WILLIAM, treated by Dr. Archer on Sep 29, 1791. {Ref: JA}
MAXFIELD, MOSES (captain), head of family in 1800 (1st District). {Ref: CI}
MAXFIELD, PARTROK ("run"), insolvent on a list of the county tax due William Osborn, sheriff, for 1791, as returned by Edward Prigg on Sep 20, 1791. {Ref: IL 31.17}
MAXFIELD, WILLIAM, head of family in 1800 (2nd District). {Ref: CI}
MAXWELL, ANN, see "Ann Eliza Maxwell," q.v.
MAXWELL, ANN ELIZA, dau. of Moses and Ann, b. May 12, 1798, bapt. Jul 29, 1798. {Ref: PR}
MAXWELL, ELIZABETH, taxpayer, 1798, Gunpowder Lower Hd., 1 dwelling

house, 2 inferior houses, 2 acres, $130 valuation; 1 tract (198 acres) in Gunpowder Lower Hd., $556.88 valuation, no slaves. {Ref: TL}. In another part of the tax schedule the occupant is listed as Joseph Everest.

MAXWELL, JACOB, will probated Aug 20, 1798. {Ref: HW}

MAXWELL, MARY, see "William Maxwell," q.v.

MAXWELL, MOSES, taxpayer, 1798, Gunpowder Lower Hd., 1 dwelling house, 3 inferior houses, 2 acres, $200 valuation; 3 tracts (826 acres) in Gunpowder Lower Hd., $3342.37 valuation, 7 slaves; also, taxpayer, Gunpowder Lower Hd., 1 dwelling house, 9 inferior houses, 2 acres, $300 valuation, no slaves. {Ref: TL}

MAXWELL, MOSES, m. Sally Charity Bond on Dec 10, 1793. {Ref: PR}

MAXWELL, MOSES, see "Ann Eliza Maxwell" and "Moses Maxfield," q.v.

MAXWELL, PATRICK, insolvent on lists in 1791 due county taxes and road taxes in "Deer Creek Upper, Middle, and Broad Creek Hundreds" as returned by Robert Amos, Jr. {Ref: IL 31.12, 31.22}. Also see "Partrok Maxfield," q.v.

MAXWELL, WILLIAM, taxpayer, 1798, Susquehanna Hd., 1 tract (7 acres, 80 acres) and 1 building, $92.81 valuation, no slaves. {Ref: TL}

MAXWELL, WILLIAM, son of William and Mary, b. Mar 10, 1799. {Ref: William Maxwell Bible}

MAY, ROBERT, head of family in 1800 (5th District). {Ref: CI}

MAY, WILLIAM, head of family in 1800 (5th District). {Ref: CI}

McADOE, JOHN, head of family in 1800 (3rd District). {Ref: CI}

McADOW, JOHN, taxpayer, 1798, Harford Upper Hd., 1 dwelling house, 6 inferior houses, 2 acres, $180 valuation; 1 tract (248 acres) in Harford Upper Hd., $670.50 valuation, 2 slaves. {Ref: TL}

McALLISTER, JAMES, head of family in 1800 (4th District). {Ref: CI}

McALOY, JOHN ("run"), insolvent on lists due for 1790 and 1791 "fund taxes" and county taxes in Susquehanna Hd., as returned by Thomas Taylor. {Ref: IL 31.12, 31.02}

McATEE, ELIZABETH, taxpayer, 1798, Deer Creek Middle Hd., 1 dwelling house, 5 inferior houses, 2 acres, $220 valuation; 2 tracts (285 acres) in Deer Creek Middle Hd., $292.50 valuation, 3 slaves. {Ref: TL}

McATEE (McATTEE), ELIZABETH, head of family in 1800 (5th District). {Ref: CI}

McATEE (McTEE), HENRY, head of family in 1800 (5th District). {Ref: CI}

McATEE, LUCY, b. 1799, d. Feb 11, 1889, aged 90, bur. in St. Ignatius Catholic Church Cemetery in Hickory. {Ref: TI}

McATEER, ----, see "Robert Nesbitt," q.v.

McATTIR, JOHN, head of family in 1800 (3rd District). {Ref: CI}

McBRIDE, WILLIAM ("out back"), insolvent on lists due for 1790 and 1791 "fund taxes" and county taxes in Susquehanna Hd., as returned by Thomas Taylor. {Ref: IL 31.12, 31.02}

McCACKIN, CAPTAIN, treated by Dr. Archer on Jan 24, 1791; also mentioned he was the son-in-law of Thomas Smith. {Ref: JA}

McCALLESTER, JAMES, treated by Dr. Archer on Jul 21, 1795; also mentioned

his security was John McCoy. {Ref: JA}
McCALLY (McCOLLY), EZEKIEL, head of family in 1800 (3rd District). {Ref: CI}
McCAN, CHARLES, see "Charles W. Lee," q.v.
McCANDLESS, JAMES, taxpayer, 1798, Deer Creek Upper Hd., 1 tract (171 acres) and 1 building, $236.50 valuation, no slaves. {Ref: TL}
McCANDLESS (McCANLES), JAMES, tract *Xerxes* surveyed in 1788 (beginning within 3 yards of a branch of Deer Creek to a place in the State's Mason and Dixon Line in Baltimore County, adjoining Alexander Ramsey's land in Harford County) and granted in 1793. {Ref: CB}
McCANDLESS, WILLIAM, treated by Dr. Archer on Mar 30, 1795; also mentioned a child (no name given). {Ref: JA}
McCANDLESS, WILLIAM, taxpayer, 1798, Broad Creek Hd., 1 tract (106 acres), $397.49 valuation, no slaves. {Ref: TL}
McCANDLESS, WILLIAM, head of family in 1800 (3rd District). {Ref: CI}
McCANDLESS, WILLIAM, head of family in 1800 (5th District). {Ref: CI}
McCANN, ARTHEW, insolvent on a list for 1791 in Gunpowder Upper and Bush River Lower Hundreds, as filed by John Bond, Deputy Sheriff, on Sep 20, 1791. {Ref: IL 31.24}
McCANN, ARTHUR, insolvent on list returned by Robert Carlile for taxes due for the year 1791. {Ref: IL 31.16}
McCANN, CHARLES, head of family in 1800 (5th District). {Ref: CI}
McCARLY, JACOB, insolvent on a list for the road tax due for 1791 in Harford Upper, Harford Lower, and Spesutia Upper as returned by Robert Amos, Jr. on Sep 18, 1793. {Ref: IL 31.18}
McCARLY, SARAH, insolvent on a list for the road tax due for 1791 in Harford Upper, Harford Lower, and Spesutia Upper as returned by Robert Amos, Jr. on Sep 18, 1793. {Ref: IL 31.18}
McCARMAN, NANCY, see "Robert Whiteford," q.v.
McCARTY, JACOB, head of family in 1800 (2nd District). {Ref: CI}
McCARTY, JACOB G., taxpayer, 1798, Susquehanna Hd., 1 tract (27 acres) and 1 building, $52.87 valuation, no slaves. {Ref: TL}
McCARTY, SAMUEL, insolvent on a list for county taxes due in 1792 as returned by Benjamin Preston. {Ref: IL 31.00}
McCARTY, SAMUEL, insolvent on list returned for the road tax due for 1791 by John Bull. {Ref: IL 31.14}
McCARY, WILLIAM, insolvent on list returned for the road tax due for 1791 by John Bull. {Ref: IL 31.14}
McCASKEY, ALEXANDER, insolvent on a list for the road tax due for 1791 in Harford Upper, Harford Lower, and Spesutia Upper as returned by Robert Amos, Jr. on Sep 18, 1793. {Ref: IL 31.18}
McCASKEY, BENJAMIN, taxpayer, 1798, Spesutia Lower Hd., 1 tract (44 perches, 21 sq. ft.), $13.50 valuation, no slaves. {Ref: TL}

McCASKEY, CORNELIUS, insolvent on a list for the county tax due for 1793 in Susquehanna Hd. as returned to the levy court by Thomas Taylor on May 28, 1794, who noted "put in my hands last fall." {Ref: IL 31.12}

McCASKEY, CORNELIUS, head of family in 1800 (2nd District). {Ref: CI}

McCASKEY, JAMES, insolvent on a list for 1791 in Gunpowder Upper and Bush River Lower Hundreds, as filed by John Bond, Deputy Sheriff, on Sep 20, 1791. {Ref: IL 31.24}

McCASKEY, PATIENCE, taxpayer, 1798, Harford Upper Hd., 1 tract (89 acres) and 1 building, $195.19 valuation, no slaves. {Ref: TL}

McCASKEY, SARAH, m. Thomas Adlum on Apr 7, 1799. {Ref: PR}

McCASKEY, WILLIAM, licensed retailer in March, 1795 and August, 1797. {Ref: CC}

McCASKEY, WILLIAM, treated by Dr. Archer on Nov 10, 1794. {Ref: JA}

McCASKEY, WILLIAM, subpoenaed to the Grand Jury in August, 1797. {Ref: CC}

McCASKEY, WILLIAM, head of family in 1800 (Havre de Grace). {Ref: CI}

McCAUSLAND, GEORGE, see "Charles Beaver," q.v.

McCAUSLAND, GEORGE, served on a Petit Jury in August, 1800. {Ref: CM}

McCAUSLAND, GEORGE, licensed retailer in March, 1795 and August, 1797. {Ref: CC}

McCAUSLAND, GEORGE, taxpayer, 1798, Deer Creek Middle Hd., 1 tract (120 perches), $51.75 valuation, no slaves. {Ref: TL}.

McCAY, JOHN, see "William McCrackin," q.v.

McCIRK, MICHAEL, head of family in 1800 (4th District). {Ref: CI}

McCLAIN, ELIZABETH, see "Nathan Hughes" and "Benedict Hughes," q.v.

McCLAIN, JOHN ("run"), insolvent on a list of the county tax due William Osborn, sheriff, for 1791, as returned by Edward Prigg on Sep 20, 1791. {Ref: IL 31.17}

McCLAIN, MARY, had an account at Hall's Store in November, 1791. {Ref: WH}

McCLAIN, NANCY, m. Moses Thomas on Dec 29, 1799. {Ref: PR}

McCLASKEY, J., see "James Bell," q.v.

McCLASKEY, JAMES, insolvent on list returned by Robert Carlile for taxes due for the year 1791. {Ref: IL 31.16}

McCLASKEY, JOSEPH, granted a tavern permit on March 29, 1797. {Ref: CC}

McCLASKEY, PATRICK, will probated Aug 10, 1791. {Ref: HW}

McCLAUD(?), JOHN, head of family in 1800 (4th District). {Ref: CI}

McCLAVE, JOHN, insolvent on lists in 1791 due county taxes and road taxes in "Deer Creek Upper, Middle, and Broad Creek Hundreds" as returned by Robert Amos, Jr. {Ref: IL 31 12, 31.22}

McCLAY, WILLIAM, insolvent on a list for 1791 in Gunpowder Upper and Bush River Lower Hundreds, as filed by John Bond, Deputy Sheriff, on Sep 20, 1791 (who listed him as a single man). {Ref: IL 31 24}

McCLEAN, ANDREW, m. Esther Israel on Dec 2, 1800. {Ref: PR}

McCLEARY, WILLIAM, mentioned in a survey deposition on Sep 27, 1799 as "to where Wm. McCleary was sworn [and] same course to a large hickory tree

where said Wm. McCleary was again sworn." {Ref: JS}
McCLINTICK, MATHEW, will probated Apr 1, 1797. {Ref: HW}
McCLENTOCK, MATHEW JR., insolvent on a list for county taxes due in 1792 as returned by Benjamin Preston. {Ref: IL 31.00}
McCLINTOCK, WILLIAM, or JAMES JERVIS, taxpayer, 1798, Harford Upper Hd., 1 tract (10 acres) and 1 building (James Jervis, occupant), $75 valuation, no slaves. {Ref: TL}
McCLULLOUGH, DAVID, insolvent on list returned by Robert Carlile for taxes due for the year 1791. {Ref: IL 31.16}
McCLUNG, JAMES, head of family in 1800 (5th District). {Ref: CI}
McCLUNG, MARY, b. 1796, d. May --, 1851, bur. in Norrisville Methodist Cemetery. {Ref: TI}
McCLUNG, ROBERT, b. 1796, d. Oct 17, 1855, aged 59, bur. in Norrisville Methodist Cemetery. {Ref: TI}
McCLUNG, SAMUEL, served on a Petit Jury in August, 1797. {Ref: CC}
McCLURE, ASENATH ANN, see "Thomas Bay," q.v.
McCLURE, JEMIMA, see "Samuel Street," q.v.
McCLURE, JOHN, insolvent on lists returned by Robert Carlile and John Guyton (the latter spelled the name as "John McCleure") for taxes due for the year 1791. {Ref: IL 31.16, 31.19}
McCOMAS, ----, bur. Nov 16, 1793, aged 19. {Ref: PR}
McCOMAS (McCOMASS), AARON, head of family in 1800 (1st District). {Ref: CI}. Also see "Micah Gilbert McComas," q.v.
McCOMAS, AARON JR., served on a Petit Jury in August, 1797. {Ref: CC}
McCOMAS (McCOMASS), AARON JR., head of family in 1800 (1st District). {Ref: CI}
McCOMAS, ALEXANDER, see "John McComas" and "James Benton McComas" and "Richard McCoy," q.v.
McCOMAS, ALEXANDER, served on a Petit Jury in August, 1797. {Ref: CC}
McCOMAS, ALEXANDER, taxpayer, 1798, Bush River Lower Hd., 1 tract (52 acres, 80 perches) and 1 building, $147.66 valuation, 1 slave. {Ref: TL}.
McCOMAS, ALEXANDER, will probated Apr 8, 1800. {Ref: HW}
McCOMAS (McCOMASS), ALEXANDER, head of family in 1800 (1st District). {Ref: CI}
McCOMAS (McCOMASS), ALEXANDER, head of family in 1800 (4th District). {Ref: CI}
McCOMAS (McCOMASS), ALEXANDER (esquire), head of family in 1800 (1st District). {Ref: CI}
McCOMAS, ALEXANDER (OF ALEXANDER), served on a Petit Jury in March, 1800. {Ref: CM}
McCOMAS, ALEXANDER (OF ALEXANDER), taxpayer, 1798, Harford Upper Hd., 1 tract (8 acres) and 1 building, $40.87 valuation, no slaves. {Ref: TL}. Also see "John McComas (of Alexander)," q.v.
McCOMAS, ALEXANDER (OF AQUILA), taxpayer, 1798, Bush River Upper &

Eden Hd., 1 dwelling house, 1 inferior house, 2 acres, $120 valuation; 1 tract (330 acres, 80 perches) in Bush River Upper & Eden Hd., $743.63 valuation, no slaves. {Ref: TL}

McCOMAS, ALEXANDER (OF AQUILA), served on a Petit Jury in March, 1799 and March, 1800. {Ref: CM}

McCOMAS, ANDREW, head of family in 1800 (3rd District). {Ref: CI}

McCOMAS (McCOMASS), ANN, head of family in 1800 (1st District). {Ref: CI}

McCOMAS (McCOMASS), AQUILA, head of family in 1800 (Abingdon). {Ref: CI}. Also see "Alexander McComas (of Aquila)" and "Alexander McComas," q.v.

McCOMAS, ARON, taxpayer, 1798, Bush River Lower Hd., 1 dwelling house, 1 acre, $100.50 valuation; 1 tract (69 acres) in Bush River Lower Hd., $155.25 valuation, no slaves. {Ref: TL}

McCOMAS, CHARLES, see "Gideon McComas," q.v.

McCOMAS, CHARLES, m. Mary Gilbert on Jun 15, 1800. {Ref: PR}

McCOMAS (McCOMASS), CHARLES, head of family in 1800 (1st District). {Ref: CI}

McCOMAS, DANIEL, see "Sophia Elizabeth McComas" and "Moses Scott McComas" and "James McComas" and "Mary McComas (widow of Daniel)" and "John McComas (of Daniel)" and "James McComas (of Daniel)" and "John McComas," q.v.

McCOMAS, DANIEL, served on a Petit Jury in August, 1798 and March, 1799, and was excused from serving in March, 1800. {Ref: CC, CM}

McCOMAS, DANIEL, bur. Feb 18, 1794, aged 74. {Ref: PR}

McCOMAS, DANIEL, m. Elizabeth Scott on Feb 18, 1796. {Ref: PR}

McCOMAS (McCOMASS), DANIEL, head of family in 1800 (Belle Air). {Ref: CI}

McCOMAS, DANIEL (doctor), taxpayer, 1798, Bush River Lower Hd., 1 dwelling house, 3 inferior houses, 80 perches of land, $210 valuation; 1 tract (2 acres) in Bush River Lower Hd., $22.50 valuation, no slaves. {Ref: TL}

McCOMAS, DEBORAH, see "John McComas," q.v.

McCOMAS, ELIZABETH, b. 1791, d. Apr 8, 1851 in her 60th year, bur. in St. Mary's Episcopal Church Cemetery. {Ref: TI}. Also see "Sophia Elizabeth McComas" and "Moses Scott McComas," q.v.

McCOMAS, ELIZABETH (widow of James), taxpayer, 1798, Bush River Lower Hd., 1 dwelling house, 3 inferior houses, 1 acre, $300 valuation; 1 tract (99 acres) in Bush River Lower Hd., $334.13 valuation, 3 slaves. {Ref: TL}

McCOMAS, ELIZABETH (widow of Moses), taxpayer, 1798, Gunpowder Upper Hd., 1 dwelling house, 6 inferior houses, 2 acres, $150 valuation; 1 tract (94 acres) in Gunpowder Upper Hd., $317.25 valuation, 4 slaves. {Ref: TL}

McCOMAS (McCOMASS), ELIZABETH, head of family in 1800 (1st District); two women by this name in this district. {Ref: CI}

McCOMAS, ELLEN, see "Ellen Fort," q.v.

McCOMAS, FREDERICK, carpenter, "hard drinker" and the father of "Henry G. McComas," q.v.

McCOMAS, GIDEON, son of Charles and Mary, b. Dec 19, 1800. {Ref: PR}
McCOMAS, HANNAH, will probated Sep 23, 1797. {Ref: HW}
McCOMAS, HENRY G., son of Frederick McComas and Susannah Onion, b. Sep 20, 1795, d. 12 Sep 1814, aged 18 years, 11 months, and 22 days; killed at the Battle of North Point. Henry McComas and Daniel Wells were credited with shooting British General Ross and they were killed in return. {Ref: HB 76:47-48 (1998)}
McCOMAS, JAMES, see "Elizabeth McComas (widow of James)," q.v.
McCOMAS, JAMES, m. Sarah Howard on Mar 29, 1794. {Ref: PR}
McCOMAS, JAMES, will probated Mar 5, 1791. {Ref: HW}
McCOMAS (McCOMASS), JAMES, head of family in 1800 (4th District). {Ref: CI}
McCOMASS (McCOMASS), JAMES, head of family in 1800 (5th District). {Ref: CI}
McCOMAS (McCOMASS), JAMES (captain), head of family in 1800 (1st District). {Ref: CI}
McCOMAS, JAMES (OF AQUILA), will probated Mar 11, 1794. {Ref: HW}
McCOMAS, JAMES (OF DANIEL), tract *Timonium* surveyed between 1792 and 1796. {Ref: SB}
McCOMAS, JAMES (OF DANIEL), taxpayer, 1798, Bush River Upper & Eden Hd., 1 dwelling house, 2 inferior houses, 2 acres, $100 valuation; 3 tracts (191 acres) in Bush River Upper & Eden Hd., $341.44 valuation, no slaves. {Ref: TL}
McCOMAS, JAMES (OF JAMES), served on a Petit Jury in August, 1800. {Ref: CM}
McCOMAS, JAMES (OF JAMES), taxpayer, 1798, Bush River Lower Hd., 1 dwelling house, 2 inferior houses, 1 acre, $160 valuation; 1 tract (149 acres) in Bush River Lower Hd., $559.12 valuation, no slaves. {Ref: TL}
McCOMAS, JAMES BENTON, husband of Jemima Beatty and son of Alexander McComas and Susan Amoss, b. 1799, d. 1865, bur. in Bethel Presbyterian Church Cemetery at Madonna. {Ref: BC}
McCOMAS, JOHN, insolvent on a list for the road tax for 1792, as returned for Robert Amoss, tax collector. {Ref: IL 13.12}
McCOMAS, JOHN, subpoenaed to the Grand Jury in August, 1797. {Ref: CC}
McCOMAS (McCOMASS), JOHN, head of family in 1800 (1st District). {Ref: CI}
McCOMAS, JOHN, son of Alexander and Deborah, b. Feb 9, 1793 (1739?), bapt. Aug 21, 1796. {Ref: PR}
McCOMAS (McCOMASS), JOHN (OF A.), head of family in 1800 (1st District). {Ref: CI}
McCOMAS, JOHN (OF ALEXANDER), taxpayer, 1798, Harford Upper Hd., 3 tracts (72 acres) and 1 building, $255.38 valuation, no slaves. {Ref: TL}
McCOMAS, JOHN (OF DANIEL), taxpayer, 1798, Bush River Lower Hd., 1 dwelling house, 5 inferior houses, 1 acre and 80 perches, $300 valuation; 1 tract (228 acres, 80 perches) and 1 building in Bush River Lower Hd., $738.28 valuation, 7 slaves. {Ref: TL}
McCOMAS, JOHN (OF DANIEL), served on a Petit Jury in August, 1798 and August, 1799, and on a Grand Jury in August, 1800. {Ref: CM}

McCOMAS (McCOMASS), JOHN (OF D.), head of family in 1800 (1st District). {Ref: CI}

McCOMAS, JOHN (OF WILLIAM), taxpayer, 1798, Bush River Lower Hd., 1 dwelling house, 4 inferior houses, 1 acre, $110 valuation; 2 tracts (119 acres) in Bush River Lower Hd., $486 valuation, 3 slaves. {Ref: TL}

McCOMAS, MARTHA, see "Micah Gilbert McComas" and "Parker Gilbert," q.v.

McCOMAS, MARY, m. William McComas on Feb 14, 1797. {Ref: PR}. Also see "Gideon McComas," q.v.

McCOMAS (McCOMASS), MARY, head of family in 1800 (1st District). {Ref: CI}

McCOMAS (McCOMASS), MARY, head of family in 1800 (5th District). {Ref: CI}

McCOMAS, MARY (widow of Daniel), taxpayer, 1798, Gunpowder Upper Hd., 1 dwelling house, 4 inferior houses, 2 acres, $200 valuation; 2 tracts (298 acres) in Gunpowder Upper Hd., $1309.50 valuation, no slaves. {Ref: TL}

McCOMAS, MICAH GILBERT, son of Aaron and Martha, b. Nov 18, 1798, bapt. Nov 10, 1799. {Ref: PR}

McCOMAS, MOSES, will probated Nov 4, 1794. {Ref: HW}

McCOMAS (McCOMASS), NICHOLAS, head of family in 1800 (4th District). {Ref: CI}

McCOMAS, MOSES, bur. Mar 24, 1794, aged 53. {Ref: PR}. Also see "Elizabeth McComas (widow of Moses)," q.v.

McCOMAS, MOSES SCOTT, son of Daniel and Elizabeth, b. Dec 5, 1799, bapt. Jul 6, 1800. {Ref: PR}

McCOMAS (McCOMASS), NATHANIEL, head of family in 1800 (1st District). {Ref: CI}

McCOMAS, NICHOLAS D., taxpayer, 1798, Bush River Upper & Eden Hd., 1 dwelling house, 5 inferior houses, 2 acres, $200 valuation; 4 tracts (509 acres, 80 perches) in Bush River Upper & Eden Hd., $1138.50 valuation, 2 slaves. {Ref: TL}

McCOMAS, NICHOLAS D., served on a Petit Jury in August, 1798. {Ref: CM}

McCOMAS, NICHOLAS DAY, m. Elizabeth Onion on Jul 24 or 27, 1794. {Ref: PR}

McCOMAS, SOLOMON, see "William McComas (of Solomon)" and "William McComas," q.v.

McCOMAS, SOPHIA ELIZABETH, dau. of Daniel and Elizabeth, b. Jan 7, 1797, bapt. Oct 28, 1799. {Ref: PR}

McCOMAS, SUSANNAH, see "Henry G. McComas," q.v.

McCOMAS, WILLIAM, see "John McComas (of William)" and "Ellen Fort" and "John Armitage," q.v.

McCOMAS, WILLIAM, charged for selling liquor by the small in 1795. {Ref: CD, August Term, 1795}

McCOMAS, WILLIAM, m. Mary McComas on Feb 14, 1797. {Ref: PR}

McCOMAS (McCOMASS), WILLIAM, head of family in 1800 (Abingdon). {Ref: CI}

McCOMAS, WILLIAM (OF DANIEL), taxpayer, 1798, Gunpowder Lower Hd., 1 dwelling house, 3 inferior houses, 80 perches of land, $400 valuation; 1 tract (148 acres) and 1 building in Gunpowder Lower Hd., $339.75 valuation, no

slaves. {Ref: TL}

McCOMAS, WILLIAM (OF SOLOMON), served on a Grand Jury in August, 1799. {Ref: CM}

McCOMAS, WILLIAM (OF SOLOMON), taxpayer, 1798, Bush River Lower Hd., 1 tract (50 acres) and 1 building, $315 valuation, no slaves. {Ref: TL}

McCOMAS, WILLIAM (OF SOLOMON), served on a Petit Jury in August, 1798. {Ref: CM}

McCOMAS, WILLIAM JR. (OF D.), served as constable in Gunpowder Upper Hd., 1800. {Ref: CM}

McCONKEY, ALEXANDER, insolvent, Harford Lower and Spesutia Lower Hundreds (listed as a single man), on a tax list returned by George Lyttle on Sep 21, 1791. {Ref: IL 31.20, 31.21}

McCONNELL, SAMUEL, insolvent on a list for 1791 in Gunpowder Upper and Bush River Lower Hundreds, as filed by John Bond, Deputy Sheriff, on Sep 20, 1791 (who listed him as a single man). {Ref: IL 31.24}

McCORD, ANN, taxpayer, 1798, Bush River Upper & Eden Hd., 1 tract (106 acres), $178.88 valuation, no slaves. {Ref: TL}

McCORD (McCORDE), ANN, head of family in 1800 (4th District). {Ref: CI}

McCORD, ARTHUR (husband of Ann), will probated Feb 26, 1793. {Ref: HW}

McCORMACK, JOHN, insolvent on list returned for the road tax due for 1791 by John Bull. {Ref: IL 31.14}

McCORMACK, JOHN, insolvent on a list for 1791 in Gunpowder Upper and Bush River Lower Hundreds, as filed by John Bond, Deputy Sheriff, on Sep 20, 1791 (who listed him as a single man). {Ref: IL 31.24}

McCORMICK, GEORGE, head of family in 1800 (4th District). {Ref: CI}

McCORMICK, JAMES JR., an Irish immigrant who lived in Baltimore City, Harford County, and Alexandria, Virginia, m. Rachel Ridgely Lux on Apr 12, 1798, by Rev. Andrew Thomas McCormick. {Ref: James McCormick Bible}. Also see "James Ridgely McCormick" and "John Pleasants McCormick," q.v.

McCORMICK, JAMES RIDGELY, son of James Jr. and Rachel, b. May 2, 1800, d. Oct 14, 1801. {Ref: James McCormick Bible}

McCORMICK, JOHN PLEASANTS, son of James Jr. and Rachel, b. Mar 17, 1799, "a twin" (name of his sibling was not mentioned). {Ref: James McCormick Bible}

McCORMICK, JOHN, THOMAS, AND JAMES, charged in 1794 (nature of the case not stated). {Ref: CD, March Term, 1795}

McCORMICK, RACHEL, see "James McCormick, Jr.," q.v.

McCORMICK, ROBERT, insolvent on a list for the county tax due for 1793 in Harford Upper, Harford Lower, and Spesutia Lower Hundreds returned to the levy court by Thomas Taylor on May 28, 1794. {Ref: IL 31.12}

McCORMICK, SAMUEL, head of family in 1800 (3rd District). {Ref: CI}

McCOWAN, FRANCIS, head of family in 1800 (5th District). {Ref: CI}

McCOWAN, MARGARITE, head of family in 1800 (5th District). {Ref: CI}

McCOWAN, MICHAEL, head of family in 1800 (2nd District). {Ref: CI}

McCOY, ANDREW, insolvent on list returned for the road tax due for 1791 by John Bull. {Ref: IL 31.14}

McCOY, ---- H., wife of David G., b. 1798, d. on 3rd of 6th month, 1866, in her 68th year. {Ref: TI}

McCOY, JOHN, see "James McCallester," q.v.

McCOY, RICHARD, treated by Dr. Archer on Jan 30, 1791; also mentioned he was the stepson of Alexander McComas. {Ref: JA}

McCOY, RICHARD, charged for felony (nature of case not stated) in 1797. {Ref: CD, March Term, 1797}

McCOY, ROBERT, taxpayer, 1798, Deer Creek Lower Hd., 4 tracts (71 acres, 120 perches) and 1 building, $390.38 valuation, no slaves. {Ref: TL}

McCOY, ROBERT, tracts *The Mill Seat* and *McCoy's Chance* surveyed between 1792 and 1796. {Ref: SB}

McCOY, WILLIAM, taxpayer, 1798, Broad Creek Hd., 2 tracts (85 acres, 120 perches) and 1 building, $244.13 valuation, no slaves. {Ref: TL}

McCOY, WILLIAM, insolvent on lists in 1791 due county taxes and road taxes in "Deer Creek Upper, Middle, and Broad Creek Hundreds" as returned by Robert Amos, Jr. {Ref: IL 31.12, 31.22}

McCOY, WILLIAM, b. on 31st of 7th month, 1800, d. on 29th of 9th month, 1875, bur. in Broad Creek Quaker Cemetery. {Ref: TI}

McCRACKEN, CATHERINE, b. 1796, d. 1877, bur. in Churchville Presbyterian Church Cemetery. {Ref: TI}

McCRACKEN, JAMES, charged for assaulting William Morgan (of Ruleph or Ruliff) in 1794 and 1797. {Ref: CD, March and August Terms, 1795 and 1797}

McCRACKEN, JAMES, charged for retailing liquors in 1794 and selling liquors in 1797. {Ref: CD, March and August Terms, 1795, and March Term, 1797}

McCRACKEN, JOHN, see "Marth V. C. McCracken" and "John McCrackin," q.v.

McCRACKEN, MARTHA V. C., dau. of John and Sarah, b. 1793, d. Seotember 11, 1853, in her 60th year, bur. in Churchville Presbyterian Church Cemetery. {Ref: TI}

McCRACKEN, SARAH, see "Martha V. C. McCracken," q.v.

McCRACKIN, JOHN, treated by Dr. Archer on Jan 31, 1791. {Ref: JA}

McCRACKIN, JOHN, head of family in 1800 (5th District). {Ref: CI}

McCRACKIN, WILLIAM, treated by Dr. Archer on Oct 18, 1799; mentioned he was "trans fluis" ["across the water"] at John McCay's. {Ref: JA}

McCRAY, DAVID, insolvent on lists of taxes due in 1791 and 1792 in Broad Creek Hd., as returned by Robert Amos, Jr. and Benjamin Preston in 1792. {Ref: IL 31.03, 31.12, 31.22}

McCRAY, DAVID ("run"), insolvent on a list of the county tax due William Osborn, sheriff, for 1791, as returned by Edward Prigg on Sep 20, 1791. {Ref: IL 31.17}

McCREARY (McCREERY), ARCHIBALD, head of family in 1800 (4th District). {Ref: CI}. Also see "John Watkins," q.v.

McCREARY, BENJAMIN, taxpayer, 1798, Deer Creek Upper Hd., 1 tract (208 acres, 120 perches) and 1 building, $410.98 valuation, no slaves. {Ref: TL}

McCREARY, BENJAMIN, insolvent on lists in 1791 due county taxes and road taxes in "Deer Creek Upper, Middle, and Broad Creek Hundreds" as returned by Robert Amos, Jr., but his name was then crossed off both lists. {Ref: IL 31.12, 31.22}

McCREARY, BENJAMIN, tract *McCreary's Hard Purchase* surveyed in 1787 and granted in 1795. {Ref: CB}

McCREARY (McCREERY), BENJAMIN, head of family in 1800 (4th District). {Ref: Cl}

McCREARY, JANE, dau. of Ralph and Jane, b. Oct 1, 1796, bapt. Jun 29, 1797. {Ref: PR}

McCREARY, RALPH, taxpayer, 1798, Spesutia Upper Hd., 1 dwelling house, 6 inferior houses, 1 acre, $155 valuation; 5 tracts (241 acres) in Spesutia Upper Hd., $542.25 valuation, no slaves. {Ref: TL}. In another part of the tax schedule the occupant is listed as John Barrett. Also see "Jane McCreary," q.v.

McCREARY, ROBERT, see "Alexander Rigdon," q.v.

McCREARY, ROBERT, insolvent on lists in 1791 due county taxes and road taxes in "Deer Creek Upper, Middle, and Broad Creek Hundreds" as returned by Robert Amos, Jr., but his name was then crossed off both lists. {Ref: IL 31.12, 31.22}

McCREARY (McCREERY), ROBERT, head of family in 1800 (4th District). {Ref: Cl}

McCUBBIN, SAMUEL, head of family in 1800 (1st District). {Ref: Cl}

McCULLOCH, DAVID, insolvent on list returned by John Guyton for taxes due for the year 1791. {Ref: IL 31.19}

McCULLOCH, JOHN, see "Hugh Whiteford, Sr.," q.v.

McCULLOCH, ROBERT, head of family in 1800 (4th District). {Ref: Cl}

McCULLOUGH, JOHN, insolvent on lists of taxes due in 1791 and 1792 in Broad Creek Hd., as returned by Robert Amos, Jr. and Benjamin Preston in 1792. {Ref: IL 31.03, 31.12, 31.22}

McCULLOUGH, JOHN, head of family in 1800 (5th District). {Ref: Cl}

McCULLOUGH, LYDIA O., b. 1794, d. Mar 31, 1831, aged 37. {Ref: TI}

McCULLOUGH, ROBERT, head of family in 1800 (5th District). {Ref: Cl}

McDERMOTT, CHRISTOPHER, head of family in 1800 (2nd District). {Ref: Cl}

McDERMOTT, PATRICK, b. Mar 16, 1800, d. Sep 17, 1872, aged 72 years, 6 months, and 1 day, bur. in St. Mary's Catholic Church Cemetery in Pylesville. {Ref: TI}

McDOLE, MARY, m. Mark Cummin on Aug 7, 1800. {Ref: PR}

McDONALD, ANN, see "Andrew Turner" and "Eli Turner," q.v.

McELHINEY, MICHAEL, licensed retailer in March, 1795. {Ref: CC}

McELHINEY, MICHAEL, served on a Petit Jury in August, 1797. {Ref: CC}

McELHINEY, MICHAEL, charged for aiding and assisting Daniel Lochry to make his escape in 1797. {Ref: CD, March Term, 1797}

McELHINEY, MICHAEL, subpoenaed to the Grand Jury in August, 1797. {Ref: CC}

McFADDAN, BENJAMIN, head of family in 1800 (2nd District). {Ref: Cl}

McFADDAN, WILLIAM, head of family in 1800 (3rd District). {Ref: Cl}

McFADDEN, JOHN, tract *The Hunting Ground Resurveyed* surveyed in 1799. {Ref: CB}
McFADDEN, JOHN, head of family in 1800 (5th District). {Ref: CI}
McFADDEN, JOHN JR., head of family in 1800 (5th District). {Ref: CI}
McFADDEN, JOHN JR., insolvent on lists in 1791 due county taxes and road taxes in "Deer Creek Upper, Middle, and Broad Creek Hundreds" as returned by Robert Amos, Jr. {Ref: IL 31.12, 31.22}
McFADDEN, JOHN SR., tract *Niagara* surveyed in 1798 on the north side of Broad Creek. {Ref: CB}
McFADDEN, SAMUEL ("dead"), insolvent on lists due for 1790 and 1791 "fund taxes" and county taxes in Susquehanna Hd., as returned by Thomas Taylor. {Ref: IL 31.12, 31.02}
McFADDIN, JOHN JR., insolvent on a list of the county tax due William Osborn, sheriff, for 1791, as returned by Edward Prigg on Sep 20, 1791. {Ref: IL 31.17}
McFADDON, JOHN JR., taxpayer, 1798, Deer Creek Middle Hd., 1 tract (80 acres) and 1 building, $156 valuation, no slaves. {Ref: TL}
McFADDON, JOHN SR., taxpayer, 1798, Deer Creek Middle Hd., 3 tracts (158 acres, 120 perches) and 1 building, $295.95 valuation, no slaves. {Ref: TL}
McFADDON, WILLIAM, taxpayer, 1798, Harford Upper Hd., 2 tracts (48 acres) and 1 building, $207 valuation, no slaves; 1 tract (15 acres) in Harford Upper Hd., $33.75 valuation, no slaves. {Ref: TL}. In another part of the tax schedule the occupant is listed as Barney Monohon.
McFALLS, CHARLES, insolvent on lists returned by Robert Carlile and John Guyton for taxes due for the year 1791. {Ref: IL 31.16, 31.19}
McFIELD, JANE, head of family in 1800 (2nd District). {Ref: CI}
McGALLON (McGALLA?), GRACE, head of family in 1800 (Abingdon). {Ref: CI}
McGAVIN (McGOVERN?), WILLIAM, head of family in 1800 (3rd District). {Ref: CI}
McGAW, ANN, head of family in 1800 (5th District). {Ref: CI}
McGAW, ISSABELLA, head of family in 1800 (3rd District). {Ref: CI}
McGAW, JAMES ("charge twice"), insolvent on a list for the road tax due for 1791 in Harford Upper, Harford Lower, and Spesutia Upper as returned by Robert Amos, Jr. on Sep 18, 1793. {Ref: IL 31.18}. Also see "James McGaw & Company," q.v.
McGAW, JAMES, subpoenaed to the Grand Jury in August, 1797. {Ref: CC}
McGAW, JAMES, head of family in 1800 (1st District). {Ref: CI}
McGAW, JANE, insolvent on a list for the road tax due for 1791 in Harford Upper, Harford Lower, and Spesutia Upper as returned by Robert Amos, Jr. on Sep 18, 1793. {Ref: IL 31.18}
McGAW, JOHN, taxpayer, 1798, Bush River Upper & Eden Hd., 2 tracts (164 acres, 40 perches) and 1 building, $286.30 valuation, no slaves. {Ref: TL}
McGAW, JOHN, b. Mar 27, 1797, d. Apr 5, 1863, bur. in Grove Presbyterian Church Cemetery in Aberdeen. {Ref: TI}
McGAW, ROBERT, taxpayer, 1798, Harford Upper Hd., no dwelling house listed

in this part of the tax schedule, no land listed, 1 slave. {Ref: TL}
McGAW, ROBERT, head of family in 1800 (1st District). {Ref: CI}
McGAW, SARAH, insolvent, Harford Lower and Spesutia Lower Hundreds, on a tax list returned by George Lyttle on Sep 21, 1791. {Ref: IL 31.20, 31.21}
McGAW, SARAH, insolvent on a list for the road tax due for 1791 in Harford Upper, Harford Lower, and Spesutia Upper as returned by Robert Amos, Jr. on Sep 18, 1793. {Ref: IL 31.18}
McGEAUGH, JAMES, taxpayer, 1798, Deer Creek Upper Hd., 1 tract (126 acres, 120 perches) and 1 building, $249.54 valuation, 1 slave. {Ref: TL}
McGEAUGH, THOMAS, taxpayer, 1798, Deer Creek Upper Hd., 1 tract (126 acres, 120 perches) and 1 building, $249.54 valuation, no slaves. {Ref: TL}
McGEHAN (McGAHAN), JOHN, charged for assaulting John Hamby in 1794 and 1797. {Ref: CD, March and August Terms, 1795, and March Term, 1797}
McGIBBONS (McCUBBINS?), MRS. (widow), treated by Dr. Archer on Nov 13, 1793; also mentioned she lived on Bennet Wheeler's Place. {Ref: JA}
McGILL, JOHN, m. Martha Brazier on Nov 10, 1796. {Ref: PR}
McGILL, MARY, m. William Shidle on Jul 28, 1796. {Ref: PR}
McGOMERY, HAMBURY, see "Hambleton Montgomery," q.v.
McGOMERY, ISAAC, taxpayer, 1798, Harford Upper Hd., 1 tract (60 acres) and 1 building, $129.37 valuation, no slaves. {Ref: TL}
McGONIGALE, DANIEL, head of family in 1800 (3rd District). {Ref: CI}
McGOUGH, BENJAMIN, insolvent on list returned by Robert Carlile for taxes due for the year 1791. {Ref: IL 31.16}
McGOUGH, JAMES, insolvent on lists in 1791 due county taxes and road taxes in "Deer Creek Upper, Middle, and Broad Creek Hundreds" as returned by Robert Amos, Jr. {Ref: IL 31.12, 31.22}
McGOVERN (McGAVIN?), WILLIAM, head of family in 1800 (3rd District). {Ref: CI}
McGOWAN, JAMES, insolvent on lists returned for the county and road taxes due for 1791 by John Bull in Gunpowder Lower Hd. (name spelled as "McGowin" on one list). {Ref: IL 31.14, 31.15}
McGOWAN, JOHN, insolvent on a list for the road tax for 1792, as returned for Robert Amoss, tax collector. {Ref: IL 13.12}. Also see "Catharine Johnson McGowen," q.v.
McGOWEN, CATHARINE JOHNSON, dau. of John and Mary, b. Jun 23, 1792. {Ref: PR}
McGOWEN, MARY, see "Catharine Johnson McGowen," q.v.
McGRAW, EDWARD, head of family in 1800 (2nd District). {Ref: CI}
McGRAW, JAMES, see "James Megrough," q.v.
McGRAW, WILLIAM, see "Samuel Hughes," q.v.
McGREEGOR, JAMES, head of family in 1800 (5th District). {Ref: CI}
McGRIGER, JAMES, taxpayer, 1798, Deer Creek Upper Hd., 1 dwelling house, 6 inferior houses, 2 acres, $200 valuation; 2 tracts (267 acres) in Deer Creek

Upper Hd., $300.38 valuation, no slaves. {Ref: TL}

McGUIRE, BENIDICK, insolvent on list returned by John Guyton (who listed him as a single man) for taxes due for the year 1791. {Ref: IL 31.19}

McINTIRE, JAMES, head of family in 1800 (3rd District). {Ref: CI}

McKEE (McKEY), ANN, head of family in 1800 (1st District). {Ref: CI}. Also see "Elizabeth McKee" and "Jane McKee," q.v.

McKEE, ELIZABETH, dau. of Thomas and Ann, b. Jul 25, 1797, bapt. Sep 16, 1798. {Ref: PR}

McKEE, JANE, dau. of Thomas and Ann, b. May 16, 1800, bapt. Aug 12, 1800. {Ref: PR}

McKEE, THOMAS, granted a retailer's license in March, 1797 and August, 1797. {Ref: CC}

McKEE (McKEY), THOMAS, head of family in 1800 (3rd District). {Ref: CI}. Also see "Elizabeth McKee" and "Jane McKee," q.v.

McKENNEY (McKENNY), JOHN, head of family in 1800 (5th District). {Ref: CI}. Also see "William Mitchell," q.v.

McKINNEY, JOHN, head of family in 1800 (2nd District). {Ref: CI}

McKINNEY, WILLIAM, head of family in 1800 (5th District). {Ref: CI}

McKINSEY, RODRICK, insolvent on a list for 1791 in Gunpowder Upper and Bush River Lower Hundreds, as filed by John Bond, Deputy Sheriff, on Sep 20, 1791. {Ref: IL 31.24}

McKINSEY, WILLIAM, insolvent on lists returned by Robert Carlile and John Guyton (who listed him as a single man and spelled the name as "McKinster") for taxes due for the year 1791. {Ref: IL 31.16, 31.19}

McKISSON, DAVID, see "Stephen Cooper," q.v.

McKISSON, SAMUEL, charged for neglect of his duty as constable in 1795. {Ref: CD, August Term, 1795, and March Term, 1797}

McKISSON, SAMUEL, charged for keeping a ferry without a license in 1797. {Ref: CD, March and August Terms, 1797}

McKISSON, SAMUEL, served as constable in Broad Creek Hd., 1797. {Ref: CC, CM}

McLANE, JOHN, taxpayer, 1798, Deer Creek Upper Hd., 1 tract (211 acres), $237.38 valuation, no slaves. {Ref: TL}

McLANE, MARY, head of family in 1800 (2nd District). {Ref: CI}

McLASKEY, JAMES, head of family in 1800 (3rd District). {Ref: CI}

McLASKEY, JOSEPH, head of family in 1800 (3rd District). {Ref: CI}

McLAUGHLEN, JOHN, see "Zacheus Bond," q.v.

McLAUGHLIN, ABRAHAM STEEL, son of Daniel and Cassandra, b. Nov 13, 1798, bapt. Jul 13, 1799. {Ref: PR}

McLAUGHLIN, ALEXANDER, head of family in 1800 (2nd District). {Ref: CI}

McLAUGHLIN, ANN, see "Erwin Lewis McLaughlin," q.v.

McLAUGHLIN, CASSANDRA, see "Abraham Steel McLaughlin" and "John McLaughlin," q.v.

McLAUGHLIN, CHARLES, m. Margaret Armstrong on Feb 6, 1799. {Ref: PR}

McLAUGHLIN, DANIEL, head of family in 1800 (Havre de Grace). {Ref: CI}. Also see "Abraham Steel McLaughlin" and "John McLaughlin," q.v.

McLAUGHLIN, ERWIN LEWIS, son of Patrick and Ann, b. Nov 27, 1799, bapt. Dec 27, 1799. {Ref: PR}

McLAUGHLIN, JAMES,

McLAUGHLIN, JOHN, son of Daniel and Cassandra, b. Aug 25, 1795, bapt. Jun 12, 1796. {Ref: PR}

McLAUGHLIN, JOHN, insolvent on lists in 1791 due county taxes and road taxes in "Deer Creek Upper, Middle, and Broad Creek Hundreds" as returned by Robert Amos, Jr. {Ref: IL 31.12, 31.22}

McLAUGHLIN, JOHN, head of family in 1800 (2nd District). {Ref: CI}

McLAUGHLIN, JOHN, head of family in 1800 (5th District). {Ref: CI}

McLAUGHLIN, PATRICK, see "Erwin Lewis McLaughlin," q.v.

McLAUGHLIN, PATRICK, served as constable in Susquehanna Hd., 1800. {Ref: CM}

McLAUGHLIN, PATRICK, m. Ann Chandley on Nov 8, 1798. {Ref: PR}

McLAUGHLIN, PATRICK, head of family in 1800 (Havre de Grace). {Ref: CI}

McLAUGHLIN, PATRICK, head of family in 1800 (3rd District). {Ref: CI}

McLAUGHLIN, PATT, subpoenaed to the Grand Jury in August, 1797. {Ref: CC}

McLENNON, JOHN, head of family in 1800 (Abingdon). {Ref: CI}

McLURE, WILLIAM, head of family in 1800 (4th District). {Ref: CI}

McLURE, WILLIAM G., taxpayer, 1798, Bush River Upper & Eden Hd., 1 dwelling house, 2 inferior houses, 2 acres, $150 valuation; 1 tract (51 acres) in Bush River Upper & Eden Hd., $86.60 valuation, no slaves. {Ref: TL}

McMAHAN, BERNARD, charged for assaulting Thomas Simmons in 1795. {Ref: CD, August Term, 1795}

McMANGER (McMANGEN?), HENRY, insolvent on lists for the county tax and road tax due for 1791 and 1792 (which list spelled his name "Henry McNagan") in Deer Creek Lower Hd., as returned by Thomas Taylor on Sep 17, 1792. {Ref: IL 31.12, 31.03}

McMATH, ----, see "Moores & McMath," q.v.

McMATH, MARY, see "Joseph, William, and John Barnes" and "Samuel McMath," q.v.

McMATH, MRS., see "William McMath, " q.v.

McMATH, SAMUEL, see "William McMath," q.v.

McMATH, SAMUEL, m. Mary Curry on Jun 18 or 19, 1792. {Ref: PR}

McMATH, SAMUEL (husband of Mary), will probated Oct 3, 1797. {Ref: HW}

McMATH, WILLIAM, taxpayer, 1798, Spesutia Upper Hd., 1 dwelling house, 4 inferior houses, 80 perches of land, $410 valuation; 4 tracts (208 acres, 80 perches) in Spesutia Upper Hd., $469.12 valuation, 2 slaves; also, taxpayer, Spesutia Upper Hd., 1 dwelling house, 2 inferior houses, 80 perches of land, $110 valuation, no slaves. {Ref: TL}

McMATH, WILLIAM, treated by Dr. Archer on Feb 8, 1795; also mentioned in his account in May, 1803, were Benjamin Crockett, Samuel McMath, John Clark, and Mrs. McMath. {Ref: JA}

McMATH, WILLIAM, m. Sarah Moores on Dec 11, 1792. {Ref: PR}
McMATH, WILLIAM, head of family in 1800 (3rd District). {Ref: CI}
McMURRAIN, ELIZABETH, taxpayer, 1798, Bush River Upper & Eden Hd., 1 tract (58 acres) and 1 building, $185.62 valuation, no slaves. {Ref: TL}
McNABB, ALEE (ALCE?), head of family in 1800 (5th District). {Ref: CI}
McNABB (McNAB), ANN, dau. of Isaac and Jane, b. Mar 13, 1796, bapt. Sep 18, 1796. {Ref: PR}
McNABB, ISAAC, granted a retailer's permit on Aug 1, 1797. {Ref: CC}
McNABB, ISAAC, head of family in 1800 (1st District). {Ref: CI}. Also see "Ann McNabb," q.v.
McNABB, JAMES, insolvent on a list of the county tax due William Osborn, sheriff, for 1791, as returned by Edward Prigg on Sep 20, 1791. {Ref: IL 31.17}
McNABB, JAMES, treated by Dr. Archer on Jan 10, 1792. {Ref: JA}
McNABB, JAMES, insolvent on a list in 1792 in Broad Creek Hd., as returned by Benjamin Preston. {Ref: IL 31.03}
McNABB, JANE, see "Ann McNabb," q.v.
McNABB, JOHN, treated by Dr. Archer on Mar 13, 1791. {Ref: JA}
McNABB, JOHN, taxpayer, 1798, Broad Creek Hd., 1 tract (90 acres) and 1 building, $149.60 valuation, no slaves. {Ref: TL}
McNABB, ROBERT, head of family in 1800 (5th District). {Ref: CI}
McNABB (McNAB), T., see "William Wilson (silversmith)," q.v.
McNAIR (McNARE), ARCHIBALD, charged for selling liquors in 1794 and fined 600 lbs. of tobacco in 1797. {Ref: CD, March and August Terms, 1795, and March Term, 1797}
McNAMARA, JOHN, insolvent on lists in 1791 due county taxes and road taxes in "Deer Creek Upper, Middle, and Broad Creek Hundreds" as returned by Robert Amos, Jr. {Ref: IL 31.12, 31.22}
McNAMARA, JOSEPH (soldier near Broad Creek), treated by Dr. Archer in 1790 and 1791. {Ref: JA}
McNAMARE, JOS., insolvent on a list of the county tax due William Osborn, sheriff, for 1791, as returned by Edward Prigg on Sep 20, 1791. {Ref: IL 31.17}
McNAMEE, JAMES, b. in 1800, d. Aug 7, 1866 in his 66th year, bur. in Wesleyan Chapel Methodist Church Cemetery near Aberdeen. {Ref: TI}
McNEAR, ARCHIBALD, see "Jennet Hutchinson," q.v.
McNULTY, CORNELIUS, head of family in 1800 (4th District). {Ref: CI}
McPHAIL, ANN, m. Joseph Adlum on Nov 8, 1798. {Ref: PR}
McPHAIL, MARY, m. George Foster on Sep 29, 1800. {Ref: PR}
McTEE, HENRY, see "Henry McAtee," q.v.
McVAY, JAMES, head of family in 1800 (5th District). {Ref: CI}
McVAY, JOHN, see "John Rumsey," q.v.
McVAY, JOHN, treated by Dr. Archer on May 28, 1791. {Ref: JA}
McVAY, JOHN, head of family in 1800 (2nd District). {Ref: CI}
MEADS, ELISHA, husband of Jemima Demoss, b. 1795, d. May 13, 1865, bur. in

Bethel Presbyterian Church Cemetery at Madonna. {Ref: BC}

MEADS, JAMES, taxpayer, 1798, Bush River Upper & Eden Hd., 1 dwelling house, 3 inferior houses, 2 acres, $300 valuation; 1 tract (168 acres) in Bush River Upper & Eden Hd., $283.50 valuation, no slaves. {Ref: TL}

MEADS, JAMES, head of family in 1800 (4th District). {Ref: CI}

MEADS, JAMES JR., head of family in 1800 (4th District). {Ref: CI}

MEADS, JEMIMA, wife of Elisha Meads and dau. of John Demoss, Jr., b. Oct 25, 1792, d. Jun 4, 1887, bur. in Bethel Presbyterian Church Cemetery at Madonna. {Ref: BC}

MEAKES, JANE, had an account at Hall's Store in October, 1791. {Ref: WH}

MECHEM, HANNAH, b. on 7th of 2nd month, 1793, d. on 21st of 6th month, 1830, aged 37 years, 4 months, and 14 days, bur. in Little Falls Quaker Cemetery in Fallston. {Ref: TI}

MECHEM, LYDIA G., b. 1795, d. Jan 17, 1885, in her 90th year, bur. in St. Ignatius Catholic Church Cemetery in Hickory. {Ref: TI}

MECHEM, RICHARD (doctor), b. May 29, 1798, d. Jul 16, 1871, bur. in Harford (Old Brick) Baptist Church Cemetery. {Ref: TI, and Abel Alderson Bible}

MEEKS, JENNY, had an account at Hall's Store in February, 1791. {Ref: WH}

MEGROUGH, JAMES, head of family in 1800 (5th District). {Ref: CI}

MEGROUGH, THOMAS, head of family in 1800 (5th District). {Ref: CI}

MELBURN, JAMES, insolvent on a list for the road tax due for 1791 in Harford Upper, Harford Lower, and Spesutia Upper as returned by Robert Amos, Jr. on Sep 18, 1793. {Ref: IL 31.18}

MERRYMAN, NELSON, b. 1795, d. Nov 15, 1879, aged 84, bur. in Fellowship Cemetery near Harkins. {Ref: TI}

MEYERS, MARGARET, see "Nancy Kindle," q.v.

MICHAEL, ANN, see "Ann Johnson" and "Martha Michael," q.v.

MICHAEL, ANN, dau. of William and Ann, b. Aug 15, 1800, bapt. Dec 26, 1800. {Ref: PR}

MICHAEL, ANN, taxpayer, 1798, Spesutia Lower Hd., 1 dwelling house, 3 inferior houses, 2 acres, $105 valuation; 1 tract (298 acres) in Spesutia Lower Hd., $238.13 valuation, 2 slaves. {Ref: TL}

MICHAEL, ANN, head of family in 1800 (2nd District). {Ref: CI}

MICHAEL, BALTSHER, b. in Germany in 1728, d. Feb 14, 1795, bur. in Michael Family Cemetery near Swan Creek in Aberdeen. Marker also erected in his memory in nearby Grove Presbyterian Church Cemetery. {Ref: TI}

MICHAEL, BENNET, taxpayer, 1798, Spesutia Lower Hd., no dwelling house listed in this part of the tax schedule, no land listed, 1 slave. {Ref: TL}

MICHAEL, D., see "Mary Michael," q.v.

MICHAEL, ETHAN, son of Jacob and Mary, b. Oct 20, 1799, d. Sep 10, 1868, in his 69th year, bur. in St. George's Episcopal Church Cemetery at Perryman. {Ref: TI, PR}

MICHAEL, HENRY, b. 1791, d. Jul 4, 1842 in Baltimore, bur. in Grove Presbyterian Church Cemetery in Aberdeen. {Ref: TI}

MICHAEL, HENRY EVERET, son of Jacob and Mary, b. Feb 9, 1798, bapt. Jun 16, 1799. {Ref: PR}
MICHAEL, JACOB, see "Ethan Michael" and "Henry Everet Michael" and "James Phillips, Sr.," q.v.
MICHAEL, JACOB, taxpayer, 1798, Harford Lower Hd., no dwelling house listed in this part of the tax schedule, no land listed, 3 slaves. {Ref: TL}
MICHAEL, JACOB, m. Mary Everett on Nov 12, 1795. {Ref: PR}
MICHAEL, JACOB, head of family in 1800 (2nd District). {Ref: CI}
MICHAEL, JAMES, see "Benjamin Brucebanks' heirs," q.v.
MICHAEL, JAMES, taxpayer, 1798, Spesutia Lower Hd., no dwelling house listed in this part of the tax schedule, no land listed, 1 slave. {Ref: TL}
MICHAEL, JAMES, head of family in 1800 (2nd District). {Ref: CI}
MICHAEL, JOHN, see "Benedict Edward Hall," q.v.
MICHAEL, JOHN, taxpayer, 1798, Spesutia Lower Hd., no dwelling house listed in this part of the tax schedule, no land listed, 2 slaves. {Ref: TL}
MICHAEL, JOHN, head of family in 1800 (2nd District). {Ref: CI}
MICHAEL (MICHEL), JOHN, had an account at Hall's Store in January, 1791. {Ref: WH}
MICHAEL, MARTHA, dau. of William and Ann, b. Dec 18, 1798, bapt. Dec 26, 1800. {Ref: PR}. Also see "Martha Michael Fletcher," q.v.
MICHAEL, MARY, wife of D. Michael, b. 1791, d. Jun 26, 1842, aged 51, bur. in St. George's Episcopal Church Cemetery at Perryman. {Ref: TI}. Also see "Henry Everet Michael" and "Ethan Michael," q.v.
MICHAEL, WILLIAM, see "Ann Michael" and "Martha Michael," q.v.
MICHAEL, WILLIAM, taxpayer, 1798, Spesutia Lower Hd., 1 dwelling house, 44 perches and 21 sq. ft. of land, $100.10 valuation, no slaves. {Ref: TL}
MICHAEL, WILLIAM, m. Ann Judd on Jul 9, 1797. {Ref: PR}
MICHAEL, WILLIAM, head of family in 1800 (2nd District). {Ref: CI}
MIDDLEDITCH, MARGARET, dau. of Michael and Mary, b. Jun 4, 1789, bapt. Sep 17, 1794. {Ref: PR}
MIDDLEDITCH, MARY, see "Margaret Middleditch," q.v.
MIDDLEDITCH (MIDELDITCH), MICHAEL, head of family in 1800 (2nd District). {Ref: CI}. Also see "Margaret Middleditch" and "Henry Stump," q.v.
MIDDLETON, JOHN, m. Mary Cowan on Sep 15, 1793. {Ref: PR}
MIDDLETON (MIDELTON), WILLIAM, head of family in 1800 (1st District). {Ref: CI}. Also see "David Ross," q.v.
MIERS, JOHN, insolvent on a list for the road tax due for 1791 in Harford Upper, Harford Lower, and Spesutia Upper as returned by Robert Amos, Jr. on Sep 18, 1793. {Ref: IL 31.18}
MILBURN, JAMES, insolvent, Harford Lower and Spesutia Lower Hundreds, on a tax list returned by George Lyttle on Sep 21, 1791. {Ref: IL 31.20, 31.21}
MILES, AQUILA, taxpayer, 1798, Bush River Upper & Eden Hd., 1 dwelling house, 3 inferior houses, 2 acres, $145 valuation; 1 tract (83 acres) in Bush

River Upper & Eden Hd., $186.75 valuation, 1 slave. {Ref: TL}

MILES, AQUILA, served on a Petit Jury in August, 1797 and August, 1798 and on a Grand Jury in August, 1799 and August, 1800. {Ref: CC, CM}

MILES, AQUILLA, head of family in 1800 (4th District). {Ref: CI}

MILES, JOSEPH, see "Buchanan & Young," q.v.

MILES, JOSEPH, charged for retailing liquors in 1794. {Ref: CD, March and August Terms, 1795}

MILES, JOSEPH, charged for selling liquors in 1794, for selling liquors by the smalls in 1795, and for selling liquors (also by the smalls) in 1797. {Ref: CD, March and August Terms, 1795 and 1797}

MILES, JOSHUA, taxpayer, 1798, Bush River Upper & Eden Hd., 1 dwelling house, 3 inferior houses, 2 acres, $120 valuation; 1 tract (98 acres) in Bush River Upper & Eden Hd., $220.50 valuation, no slaves. {Ref: TL}

MILES, THOMAS, insolvent on list returned for the road tax due for 1791 by John Bull. {Ref: IL 31.14}

MILES, THOMAS, insolvent on lists in 1791 due county taxes and road taxes in "Deer Creek Upper, Middle, and Broad Creek Hundreds" as returned by Robert Amos, Jr. {Ref: IL 31.12, 31.22}

MILES, THOMAS, insolvent on list returned by Robert Carlile for taxes due for the year 1791. {Ref: IL 31.16}

MILHOOF, JOHN, taxpayer, 1798, Spesutia Lower Hd., 1 dwelling house, 1 inferior house, 44 perches and 21 sq. ft. of land, $420 valuation, no slaves. {Ref: TL}

MILHOOF (MILLHUFF), JOHN, head of family in 1800 (Havre de Grace). {Ref: CI}

MILHOOF (MILLHOOF), MARY, subpoenaed to the Grand Jury in August, 1797. {Ref: CC}

MILLER, HENRY, taxpayer, 1798, Susquehanna Hd., 2 tracts (30 acres) and 1 building, $129.37 valuation, no slaves. {Ref: TL}

MILLER, HENRY ("out back"), insolvent on lists due for 1790 and 1791 "fund taxes" and county taxes in Susquehanna Hd., as returned by Thomas Taylor (his name was crossed off the 1791 road tax list). {Ref: IL 31.12, 31.02}

MILLER, HENRY, head of family in 1800 (2nd District). {Ref: CI}

MILLER, JOSEPH, taxpayer, 1798, Susquehanna Hd., 1 dwelling house, 3 inferior houses, 2 acres, $300 valuation; 2 tracts (325 acres) in Susquehanna Hd., $1642.50 valuation, no slaves. {Ref: TL}

MILLER, JOSEPH, tract *Prospect* surveyed in 1797. {Ref: CB}

MILLER, JOSEPH, head of family in 1800 (3rd District). {Ref: CI}

MILLER, SAMUEL, head of family in 1800 (2nd District). {Ref: CI}. Also see "Stephen Price," q.v.

MILLIGAN, JOHN, see "John Rogers," q.v.

MILLS, MARY, head of family in 1800 (1st District). {Ref: CI}

MILLS, THOMAS, will probated Jan 3, 1791. {Ref: HW}

MINNICK, JACOB, b. Jun 4, 1800, d. Dec 8, 1876, aged 75 years, 6 months, and 4 days, bur. in Christ Episcopal (Rock Spring) Church Cemetery. {Ref: TI}

MITCHELL, ANN, m. Robert Hawkins on Jul 20, 1797. {Ref: PR}

MITCHELL, ANN MARTHA, wife of John, Sr., b. 1800, d. Sep 25, 1824, aged 24, bur. in the Mitchell-Osborn Graveyard on Chapel Road near Aberdeen. {Ref: TI}

MITCHELL, AQUILA, taxpayer, 1798, Susquehanna Hd., 1 dwelling house, 5 inferior houses, 2 acres, $185 valuation; 2 tracts (158 acres) and 1 building in Susquehanna Hd., $591.75 valuation, 1 slave. {Ref: TL}. Also see "Benedict Edward Mitchell," q.v.

MITCHELL (MITCHEL), AQUILLA, head of family in 1800 (2nd District). {Ref: CI}

MITCHELL, BENEDICT EDWARD, son of Aquila and Susanna, b. Jul 3, 1799. {Ref: PR}

MITCHELL (MITCHEL), ELIGHA, head of family in 1800 (3rd District). {Ref: CI}

MITCHELL, ELIJAH, see "John Mitchell," q.v.

MITCHELL, ELIZA, dau. of William and Sarah, b. Oct 13, 1798. {Ref: PR}

MITCHELL (MITCHEL), ELIZABETH, head of family in 1800 (Abingdon). {Ref: CI}

MITCHELL, ELIZABETH SOPHIA, dau. of Richard and Priscilla, b. Dec 4, 1798, bapt. Jun 15, 1800. {Ref: PR}

MITCHELL, ENOCH, insolvent on a list for 1791 in Gunpowder Upper and Bush River Lower Hundreds, as filed by John Bond, Deputy Sheriff, on Sep 20, 1791. {Ref: IL 31.24}

MITCHELL, ENOCK, insolvent on list returned by Robert Carlile for taxes due for the year 1791. {Ref: IL 31.16}

MITCHELL, GABRIEL, taxpayer, 1798, Susquehanna Hd., 1 dwelling house, 3 inferior houses, 2 acres, $100.50 valuation; 3 tracts (211 acres, 120 perches) and 1 building in Susquehanna Hd., $419.20 valuation, 1 slave. {Ref: TL}. In another part of the tax schedule the occupant is listed as Mark Noble.

MITCHELL (MITCHEL), GABRIEL, head of family in 1800 (2nd District). {Ref: CI}

MITCHELL, HANNAH, had an account at Hall's Store in June, 1791. {Ref: WH}

MITCHELL, JAMES' HEIRS, or MARTHA MITCHELL, taxpayers, 1798, Susquehanna Hd., 1 dwelling house, 1 inferior house, 2 acres (Samuel Gover, occupant), $300 valuation; 2 tracts (227 acres), 1 building (Martha Mitchell, occupant), and 1 other building (George Hill, occupant) in Susquehanna Hd., $1291.50 valuation altogether; also, taxpayers, Spesutia Lower Hd., 1 dwelling house, 1 inferior house, 88 perches and 42 sq. ft. of land, $650 valuation; taxpayers, 1 tract (148 acres) in Susquehanna Hd. (Samuel Gover, occupant), $666 valuation; taxpayers, 4 tracts (100 acres) and 1 building (William Loflin, occupant) in Susquehanna Hd., $270 valuation; also, taxpayers, 1 tract (85 acres) and 1 building in Susquehanna Hd., $222.19 valuation; also, taxpayers, 2 tracts (12 acres) in Susquehanna Hd., $20.25 valuation; no slaves. {Ref: TL}

MITCHELL, JOHN SR., see "Ann Martha Mitchell," q.v.

MITCHELL, JOHN, taxpayer, 1798, Harford Upper Hd., 1 dwelling house, 4 inferior houses, 2 acres, $150 valuation; 1 tract (306 acres) and 1 building in

231

Harford Upper Hd., $907.87 valuation, no slaves. {Ref: TL}. In another part of the tax schedule the occupant is listed as Elijah Mitchell.

MITCHELL, JOHN, insolvent on lists in 1791 due county taxes and road taxes in "Deer Creek Upper, Middle, and Broad Creek Hundreds" as returned by Robert Amos, Jr. {Ref: IL 31.12, 31.22}

MITCHELL, JOHN, m. Martha Matticks on Sep 6, 1798. {Ref: PR}

MITCHELL, JOHN, b. May 7, 1799, d. Jan 7, 1891, bur. in Grove Presbyterian Church Cemetery in Aberdeen. {Ref: TI}

MITCHELL, JOHN (millwright), treated by Dr. Archer on May 22, 1793; also mentioned his wife and child (no names given) in 1788, and listed his name as "Jno. Mitchel" in 1793. {Ref: JA}

MITCHELL, JOHN ("charge twice"), insolvent on a list for the road tax due for 1791 in Harford Upper, Harford Lower, and Spesutia Upper as returned by Robert Amos, Jr. on Sep 18, 1793. {Ref: IL 31.18}

MITCHELL (MITCHEL), JOHN, head of family in 1800 (Abingdon). {Ref: CI}

MITCHELL (MITCHEL), JOHN, head of family in 1800 (3rd District). {Ref: CI}

MITCHELL, KENT, will probated Sep 27, 1793. {Ref: HW}

MITCHELL, MARGARET, see "Josiah Guyton," q.v.

MITCHELL, MARTHA, see "James Mitchell's heirs," q.v.

MITCHELL, MARTHA, dau. of William and Sarah, b. Jan 18, 1800. {Ref: PR}

MITCHELL, MARTHA, taxpayer, 1798, Susquehanna Hd., no dwelling house listed in this part of the tax schedule, no land listed, 1 slave. {Ref: TL}

MITCHELL, MARTHA, head of family in 1800 (2nd District). {Ref: CI}

MITCHELL, MICAJAH ("poor"), insolvent on lists due for 1790 and 1791 "fund taxes" and county taxes in Susquehanna Hd., as returned by Thomas Taylor. {Ref: IL 31.12, 31.02}

MITCHELL (MITCHEL), MICAJAH, head of family in 1800 (2nd District). {Ref: CI}

MITCHELL, PARKER, taxpayer, 1798, Susquehanna Hd., 3 tracts (168 acres) and 1 building, $283.50 valuation, 1 slave. {Ref: TL}

MITCHELL (MITCHEL), PARKER, head of family in 1800 (2nd District). {Ref: CI}

MITCHELL, PRISCILLA, see "Elizabeth Sophia Mitchell," q.v.

MITCHELL, RICHARD, see "Elizabeth Sophia Mitchell" and "Thomas Mitchell," q.v.

MITCHELL, RICHARD, taxpayer, 1798, Susquehanna Hd., no dwelling house listed in this part of the tax schedule, no land listed, 1 building, $78.75 valuation, no slaves. {Ref: TL}

MITCHELL, RICHARD, m. Priscilla Gilbert on Feb 15, 1798. {Ref: PR}

MITCHELL (MITCHEL), RICHARD, head of family in 1800 (2nd District). {Ref: CI}

MITCHELL, SARAH, see "Eliza Mitchell" and "Martha Mitchell," q.v.

MITCHELL, SARAH, taxpayer, 1798, Susquehanna Hd., no dwelling house listed in this part of the tax schedule, no land listed, 1 slave. {Ref: TL}

MITCHELL, SARAH, m. William Mitchell on Dec 22, 1796. {Ref: PR}

MITCHELL (MITCHEL), SARAH, head of family in 1800 (2nd District). {Ref: CI}

MITCHELL, SUSANNA, see "Benedict Edward Mitchell," q.v.

MITCHELL, THOMAS, taxpayer, 1798, Susquehanna Hd., 1 dwelling house, 4 inferior houses, 2 acres, $130 valuation; 2 tracts (364 acres) in Susquehanna Hd., $819 valuation, no slaves. {Ref: TL}. In another part of the tax schedule the occupant is listed as Richard Mitchell.

MITCHELL (MITCHEL), THOMAS, head of family in 1800 (2nd District). {Ref: CI}

MITCHELL (MITCHEL), THOMAS JR., head of family in 1800 (2nd District). {Ref: CI}

MITCHELL, THOMAS (OF WILLIAM), taxpayer, 1798, Susquehanna Hd., 3 tracts (50 acres) and 2 buildings, $781.88 valuation; no slaves. {Ref: TL}

MITCHELL, WILLIAM, see "Eliza Mitchell" and "Martha Mitchell" and "Thomas Mitchell (of William)," q.v.

MITCHELL, WILLIAM, served as constable in Susquehanna Hd., 1800. {Ref: CM}

MITCHELL, WILLIAM, taxpayer, 1798, Susquehanna Hd., 1 dwelling house, 2 inferior houses, 2 acres, $130 valuation; 11 tracts (525 acres) in Susquehanna Hd., $1181.25; also, taxpayer, 1 tract (50 acres) and 3 buildings in Susquehanna Hundred: one occupied by Andrew Burns ($157.50 valuation); one occupied by Elisha Bowen ($22.50 valuation); and, one occupied by John McKenny ($67.50 valuation); no slaves listed.

MITCHELL, WILLIAM, paid on Jun 26, 1795 for 2 1/2 days team work and on Sep 25, 1795 for 5 days of team work at Bush River Store. {Ref: AH}

MITCHELL, WILLIAM, m. Sarah Mitchell on Dec 22, 1796. {Ref: PR}

MITCHELL (MITCHEL), WILLIAM, head of family in 1800 (2nd District). {Ref: CI}

MITCHELL (MITCHEL), WILLIAM JR., head of family in 1800 (2nd District). {Ref: CI}

MITCHELL, WILLIAM JR., taxpayer, 1798, Susquehanna Hd., 4 tracts (150 acres) and 1 building, $438.75 valuation, no slaves. {Ref: TL}

MITCHELL, WINSTON, taxpayer, 1798, Susquehanna Hd., 4 tracts (127 acres), $238.12 valuation, no slaves. {Ref: TL}

MITTIGEN, THOMAS, head of family in 1800 (4th District). {Ref: CI}

MOALES (MOLES), NICHOLAS, head of family in 1800 (3rd District). {Ref: CI}. Also see "Thomas Bond (of Bond)," q.v.

MOFFORD, OBEDIAH, charged for selling liquors by the smalls without a license in 1797. {Ref: CD, March and August Terms, 1797}

MOHON, WILLIAM, see "William Mahon," q.v.

MOLTON, JOHN ("dead long ago"), insolvent on lists due for 1790 and 1791 "fund taxes" and county taxes in Susquehanna Hd., as returned by Thomas Taylor. {Ref: IL 31.12, 31.02}

MOLTON, MATHEW, head of family in 1800 (2nd District). {Ref: CI}

MOLTON, MATTHEW, m. Sarah Boyd on Jun 17, 1798. {Ref: PR}. The actual entry was transcribed as "Martha Molton m. Sarah Boyd."

MOLTON, MATTHEW, taxpayer, 1798, Susquehanna Hd., 1 tract (98 acres) and 1 building, $221.62 valuation, no slaves. {Ref: TL}

MONAHON, JOHN ("no such man"), insolvent on lists due for 1790 and 1791 "fund taxes" in Deer Creek Lower and Susquehanna Hundreds, as returned by Thomas Taylor. {Ref: IL 31.12}

MONCRIEF, ARCHIBALD (Baltimore Town), taxpayer, 1798, Spesutia Lower Hd., 1 tract (88 perches, 42 sq. ft.), $27 valuation, no slaves. {Ref: TL}

MONK, ELIZABETH, see "James Brookes Monk," q.v.

MONK, JAMES BROOKES, son of William and Elizabeth, b. Nov 4, 1797, bapt. Feb 4, 1798. {Ref: PR}

MONK, JOHN CLARK, see "Sarah Rebecca Lewis," q.v.

MONK, MR. (merchant in Abingdon), treated by Dr. Archer on Jun 1, 1791. {Ref: JA}

MONK, SARAH REBECCA, see "Sarah Rebecca Lewis," q.v.

MONK, WILLIAM, insolvent on a list for the road tax due for 1791 in Harford Upper, Harford Lower, and Spesutia Upper as returned by Robert Amos, Jr. on Sep 18, 1793. {Ref: IL 31.18}. Also see "James Brookes Monk," q.v.

MONKS, ELICIA, dau. of John and Mary, b. Jan 25, 1795. {Ref: PR}

MONKS, JAMES P., b. 1800, d. Jan 25, 1878, in his 78th year, bur. in Watters Memorial Methodist Church Cemetery on Thomas Run. {Ref: TI}

MONKS, JOHN, see "Louisa Monks" and "Elicia Monks" and "Mary Monks," q.v.

MONKS, JOHN, taxpayer, 1798, Bush River Lower Hd., 1 dwelling house, 9 inferior houses, 2 acres, $700 valuation; 4 tracts (155 acres) in Bush River Lower Hd., $262.54 valuation, no slaves; also, taxpayer, Bush River Lower Hd., 1 dwelling house, $200 valuation; also, taxpayer, Bush River Lower Hd., 1 dwelling house (Joseph Cox, occupant), $170 valuation; also, taxpayer, Bush River Lower Hd., 1 dwelling house and 1 inferior house (John Shields, occupant), $150 valuation; also, taxpayer, Bush River Lower Hd., 1 dwelling house (John Prosser, occupant), $160 valuation; no slaves. {Ref: TL}

MONKS, JOHN, licensed retailer in March, 1795 and August, 1797. {Ref: CC}

MONKS, JOHN, head of family in 1800 (Abingdon). {Ref: CI}

MONKS, JOSHUA(?), head of family in 1800 (1st District). {Ref: CI}

MONKS, LOUISA, dau. of John and Mary, b. Mar 1, 1793. {Ref: PR}

MONKS, MARY, wife of John, d. Oct 14, 1800, aged 35, bur. on Oct 15, 1800 in St. George's Episcopal Church Cemetery at Perryman. {Ref: PR, TI}. Also see "Louisa Monks" and "Elicia Monks," q.v.

MONOHON, ARTHUR, taxpayer, 1798, Harford Upper Hd., 2 tracts (48 acres) and 1 building, $142.88 valuation, no slaves. {Ref: TL}. In another part of the tax schedule the occupant is listed as Matthew Dennison.

MONOHON (MONAHAN), ARTHUR, head of family in 1800 (3rd District). {Ref: CI}

MONOHON, BARNARD, treated by Dr. Archer on Sep 19, 1793. {Ref: JA}

MONOHON (MONAHAN), BARNARD, head of family in 1800 (3rd District).

{Ref: CI}
MONOHON, BARNEY, see "William McFaddon," q.v.

MONOHON (MONAHAN), THOMAS, head of family in 1800 (3rd District). {Ref: CI}

MONTGOMERY, HAMBLETON, insolvent on lists returned by Robert Carlile and John Guyton (who listed him as a single man and spelled the name as "Hambury McGomry") for taxes due for the year 1791. {Ref: IL 31.16, 31.19}

MONTGOMERY, ISAAC, see "Isaac McGomery," q.v.

MONTGOMERY, ISAAC, insolvent on lists returned by Robert Carlile and John Guyton (who listed the name as "Isaac Mtgomry") for taxes due for the year 1791. {Ref: IL 31.16, 31.19}

MONTGOMERY, ISAAC, head of family in 1800 (1st District); two men by this name in this district. {Ref: CI}

MONTGOMERY, JAMES, taxpayer, 1798, Deer Creek Upper Hd., 1 dwelling house, 4 inferior houses, 2 acres, $200 valuation; 2 tracts (173 acres) in Deer Creek Upper Hd., $407.53 valuation, 1 slave. {Ref: TL}. Also see "Mary Montgomery," q.v.

MONTGOMERY, JARRETT, head of family in 1800 (4th District). {Ref: CI}

MONTGOMERY, JOHN, taxpayer, 1798, Broad Creek Hd., 1 dwelling house, 2 inferior houses, 2 acres, $300 valuation; 4 tracts (126 acres) in Broad Creek Hd., $146.25 valuation, no slaves. {Ref: TL}

MONTGOMERY, JOHN, served on a Grand Jury in March, 1798 and March, 1799, and was excused from serving on a Petit Jury in March, 1800. {Ref: CM}

MONTGOMERY, JOHN, licensed practicing attorney in March, 1795. {Ref: CC}

MONTGOMERY, JOHN, taxpayer, 1798, Bush River Lower Hd., 1 dwelling house, 3 inferior houses, 1 acre, $400 valuation; 1 tract (no description) in Bush River Lower Hd., $90 valuation, no slaves. {Ref: TL}

MONTGOMERY, JOHN, head of family in 1800 (Belle Air). {Ref: CI}

MONTGOMERY, JOHN, head of family in 1800 (5th District). {Ref: CI}

MONTGOMERY, JOHN AND WILLIAM, tract *Montgomery's Safety* surveyed between 1792 and 1796. {Ref: SB}

MONTGOMERY, JOHN AND WILLIAM, taxpayers, 1798, Broad Creek Hd., 2 tracts (736 acres), $1656 valuation, no slaves. {Ref: TL}

MONTGOMERY, MARY, wife of James Montgomery and dau. of John Beaty and Nancy Ann Rampley, b. Nov 23, 1800, d. Apr 24, 1872, bur. in Bethel Presbyterian Church Cemetery at Madonna. {Ref: BC}

MONTGOMERY, MICHAEL, taxpayer, 1798, Bush River Upper & Eden Hd., 1 dwelling house, 2 acres, $105 valuation; 4 tracts (118 acres) in Bush River Upper & Eden Hd., $265.50 valuation, no slaves. {Ref: TL}

MONTGOMERY, MICHAEL, head of family in 1800 (4th District). {Ref: CI}

MONTGOMERY, ROBERT, head of family in 1800 (4th District). {Ref: CI}

MONTGOMERY, THOMAS, see "James Barnett, Sr.," q.v.

MONTGOMERY, THOMAS, taxpayer, 1798, Deer Creek Upper Hd., 1 dwelling house, 6 inferior houses, 2 acres, $200 valuation; 6 tracts (286 acres, 80 perches) in Deer Creek Upper Hd., $469.69 valuation, 2 slaves. {Ref: TL}

MONTGOMERY, THOMAS, tracts *Gibraltar* and *Quebec* surveyed between 1792 and 1796. {Ref: SB}

MONTGOMERY, THOMAS, served on a Grand Jury in August, 1798 and August, 1799. {Ref: CM}

MONTGOMERY, THOMAS, insolvent on lists returned by Robert Carlile and John Guyton (who listed the name as "Thos. Mtgomry") for taxes due for the year 1791. {Ref: IL 31.16, 31.19}

MONTGOMERY, THOMAS, head of family in 1800 (5th District). {Ref: CI}

MONTGOMERY, WILLIAM, taxpayer, 1798, Broad Creek Hd., 1 tract (50 acres) and 1 building, $101.25 valuation, no slaves. {Ref: TL}. Also see "John and William Montgomery," q.v.

MONTGOMERY, WILLIAM AND JOHN, tract *Montgomery's Safety* surveyed between 1792 and 1796. {Ref: SB}

MONTGOMERY, WILLIAM B., b. 1799, d. Aug 23, 1839, in his 40th year, bur. in St. Ignatius Catholic Church Cemetery in Hickory. {Ref: TI}

MONTJAR, JAMES, son of William and Mary, b. Dec 9, 1799, bapt. Jan 26, 1800. {Ref: PR}

MONTJAR, MARY, see "William Montjar" and "Peter Montjar" and "Samuel Montjar" and "James Montjar," q.v.

MONTJAR, PETER, son of William and Mary, b. Mar 12, 1793. {Ref: PR}

MONTJAR, SAMUEL, son of William and Mary, b. Sep 12, 1797, bapt. May 27, 1798. {Ref: PR}

MONTJAR, WILLIAM, son of William and Mary, b. Apr 16, 1795, bapt. May 24, 1795. {Ref: PR}. Also see "Peter Montjar" and Samuel Montjar" and "James Montjar" and William Munger," q.v.

MONTPHELIER, MRS., see "Negro Guy," q.v.

MOOBERRY, ELIZABETH, see "John Mooberry," q.v.

MOOBERRY, JOHN, son of William and Elizabeth, b. Sep 15, 1796, bapt. Nov 2, 1797. {Ref: PR}

MOOBERRY, WILLIAM, mentioned in a survey deposition on Nov 8, 1799 and on Jan 18, 1800 as "same day Susanna Darlington showed the place where Wm. Mooberry proved, but not sworn." {Ref: JS}. Also see "John Mooberry," q.v.

MOON (MONE?), DANIEL (doctor), had an account at Hall's Store in July, 1791. {Ref: WH}

MOONY, JAMES (doctor), head of family in 1800 (4th District). {Ref: CI}

MOORE, ANN, licensed ordinary (tavern) in March, 1795, noting "charge Thomas Gibson." {Ref: CC}

MOORE, BENJAMIN P., b. on 6th of 12th month, 1791, d. on 25th of 6th month, 1875, in his 84th year, bur. in Little Falls Quaker Cemetery in Fallston. {Ref: TI}

MOORE, CHARLES, treated by Dr. Archer on Sep 29, 1796. {Ref: JA}

MOORE, EDWARD, treated by Dr. Archer on Jan 22, 1791; also mentioned he lived at Josias Wheeler's. {Ref: JA}

MOORE (MORE), JAMES, m. Rebecca Crabson on Apr 12, 1798. {Ref: PR}

MOORE, JAMES (doctor), charged in 1795 (nature of the case not stated). {Ref: CD. August Term, 1795}

MOORE, JAMES REED (doctor), husband of Levinah Sharp Gillis and son of James Moore and Caroline Slade, b. Jul 12, 1792, d. Sep 5, 1870, bur. in Bethel Presbyterian Church Cemetery at Madonna. {Ref: BC}

MOORE, JASON, taxpayer, 1798, Bush River Lower Hd., 1 dwelling house, 2 inferior houses, 80 perches of land, $500 valuation; 1 tract (22 acres, 80 perches) in Bush River Lower Hd., $126.56 valuation, 1 slave; also, taxpayer, Bush River Lower Hd., 1 dwelling house, 1 inferior house, 80 perches of land, $250 valuation, and 1 dwelling house, 1 acre, $280 valuation, no additional slaves. {Ref: TL}

MOORE, JASSON, head of family in 1800 (3rd District). {Ref: CI}

MOORE, JOHN, insolvent on list returned by Robert Carlile for taxes due for the year 1791. {Ref: IL 31.16}

MOORE, JOHN ("run"), insolvent on a list of the county tax due William Osborn, sheriff, for 1791, as returned by Edward Prigg on Sep 20, 1791. {Ref: IL 31.17}

MOORE, JOHN, m. Mary Scarborough on Aug 3, 1797. {Ref: PR}

MOORE, JOHN, head of family in 1800 (3rd District). {Ref: CI}

MOORE, JOHN, head of family in 1800 (5th District). {Ref: CI}

MOORE, MARGARET, dau. of William and Martha, b. May 8, 1796, bapt. Sep 25, 1796. {Ref: PR}

MOORE, MARTHA, see "Margaret Moore," q.v.

MOORE, MATHEW, head of family in 1800 (2nd District). {Ref: CI}

MOORE, PHILIP, licensed practicing attorney in March, 1795. {Ref: CC}

MOORE, SAMUEL, head of family in 1800 (1st District). {Ref: CI}

MOORE, SUSANNA, see "Joshua Day," q.v.

MOORE, SUSANNA, taxpayer, 1798, Bush River Lower Hd., no dwelling house listed in this part of the tax schedule, no land listed, 1 slave. {Ref: TL}

MOORE, SUSANNA (SUSSANA), head of family in 1800 (Belle Air). {Ref: CI}

MOORE, WILLIAM, see "Margaret Moore" and "William Ashmore," q.v.

MOORE, WILLIAM, insolvent on lists of taxes due in 1791 and 1792 in Broad Creek Hd., as returned by Robert Amos, Jr. in 1791 and Benjamin Preston in 1792. {Ref: IL 31.03, 31.12, 31.22}

MOORE, WILLIAM, charged for selling liquors in 1794. {Ref: CD. March Term, 1795}

MOORE, WILLIAM, head of family in 1800 (5th District). {Ref: CI}

MOORE, WILLIAM (at Slate Ridge), treated by Dr. Archer on Jan 6, 1791. {Ref: JA}

MOORE, WILLIAM (Irish), noted as "run" on an insolvents list of the county tax due William Osborn, sheriff, for 1791, as returned by Edward Prigg on Sep 20, 1791. {Ref: IL 31.17}

MOORES & McMATH, licensed retailers in March, 1795 and August, 1797. {Ref: CC}

MOORES, AQUILA P., b. Oct 26, 1792, d. May 4, 1853, bur. in Christ Episcopal (Rock Spring) Church Cemetery. {Ref: TI}
MOORES, DANIEL, m. Sarah Budd on Jan 1, 1793. {Ref: PR}
MOORES, DOCTOR, consulted with Dr. Archer in 1791. {Ref: JA}
MOORES, ELIZABETH (Miss), b. Sep 11, 1798, d. Oct 29, 1877, bur. in Christ Episcopal (Rock Spring) Church Cemetery. {Ref: TI}
MOORES, JAMES, see "Charles Hederick," q.v.
MOORES, JAMES (tanner), treated by Dr. Archer on Nov 2, 1791. {Ref: JA}
MOORES, JAMES (tanner), will probated Nov 15, 1791. {Ref: HW}
MOORES, JAMES (OF JAMES), treated by Dr. Archer on Dec 20, 1793. {Ref: JA}
MOORES, JOHN, taxpayer, 1798, Spesutia Upper Hd., 1 dwelling house, 8 inferior houses, 2 acres, $200 valuation; 11 tracts (549 acres, 120 perches) and 3 buildings (occupants: Samuel Dean, Esau or Esaw Turk, and John Harwood) in Spesutia Upper Hd., $1973.81 valuation altogether, no slaves. {Ref: TL}
MOORES, JOHN, appointed a Judge of Elections in the 3rd District on Jul 28, 1800. {Ref: CM}
MOORES, JOHN, served on a Petit Jury in March, 1800. {Ref: CM}
MOORES, PARKER, b. 1794, d. 1827, aged 33, bur. in Christ Episcopal (Rock Spring) Church Cemetery. {Ref: TI}
MOORES, SABA H., b. Aug 20, 1762, d. Mar 20, 1795, aged 33 years and 7 months (tombstone inscribed in Latin: *obui martu die 20, 1795, etate an 33 & men 7*), bur. in Christ Episcopal (Rock Spring) Church Cemetery. {Ref: TI}
MOORES, SARAH, see "William McMath," q.v.
MOORES, WILLIAM (Irish), insolvent on lists in 1791 due county taxes and road taxes in "Deer Creek Upper, Middle, and Broad Creek Hundreds" as returned by Robert Amos, Jr. {Ref: IL 31.12, 31.22}
MORATTY, MATTHEW, taxpayer, 1798, Gunpowder Lower Hd., no dwelling house listed in this part of the tax schedule, no land listed, 1 slave. {Ref: TL}
MOREAINS, WILLIAM, insolvent on lists in 1791 due county taxes and road taxes in "Deer Creek Upper, Middle, and Broad Creek Hundreds" as returned by Robert Amos, Jr. {Ref: IL 31.12, 31.22}
MORETON, NATHANIEL, m. Sarah Copeland on Mar 1, 1798. {Ref: PR}
MORFORD, ISAAK (ISAAH?), insolvent on list returned by Robert Carlile for taxes due for the year 1791. {Ref: IL 31.16}
MORGAN, CASSANDRA, taxpayer, 1798, Deer Creek Lower Hd., 1 dwelling house, 2 inferior houses, 2 acres, $300 valuation, 2 slaves. {Ref: TL}
MORGAN, CASSANDRA, head of family in 1800 (5th District). {Ref: CI}
MORGAN, EDWARD, see "Robert Morgan," q.v.
MORGAN, EDWARD, taxpayer, 1798, Deer Creek Lower Hd., 8 tracts (513 acres, 80 perches), $3184.49 valuation, 2 slaves. {Ref: TL}
MORGAN, EDWARD, head of family in 1800 (5th District); two men by this name in this district. {Ref: CI}

MORGAN, HAMILTON, see "Robert Morgan," q.v.

MORGAN, HUGH, taxpayer, 1798, Deer Creek Lower Hd., 1 dwelling house, 2 inferior houses, 2 acres, $300 valuation; 1 tract (100 acres) in Deer Creek Lower Hd., $140.63 valuation, no slaves. {Ref: TL}

MORGAN, HUGH, head of family in 1800 (5th District). {Ref: CI}

MORGAN, JAMES L., head of family in 1800 (5th District). {Ref: CI}

MORGAN, JAMES LEE, or THOMAS CHEW (guardian), taxpayer, 1798, Gunpowder Lower Hd., 1 dwelling house, 3 inferior houses, 2 acres, $180 valuation; 1 tract (498 acres) in Gunpowder Lower Hd., $1800 valuation, no slaves. {Ref: TL}. In another part of the tax schedule the occupant is listed as Matthew Dorsey.

MORGAN, JOHN, see "Dr. John Morgan's heirs," q.v.

MORGAN, JOHN, insolvent on lists of taxes due in 1791 and 1792 in Broad Creek Hd., as returned by Robert Amos, Jr. and Benjamin Preston in 1792. {Ref: IL 31.03}

MORGAN, JOHN, insolvent on a list of the county tax due William Osborn, sheriff, for 1791, as returned by Edward Prigg on Sep 20, 1791. {Ref: IL 31.17}

MORGAN, JOHN'S (DOCTOR) HEIRS, non-residents (place of residence not stated), taxpayers, 1798, Spesutia Lower Hd., 1 tract (1 acre, 60 perches, 105 sq. ft.), $67.50 valuation, no slaves. {Ref: TL}

MORGAN, JULIA ANN, dau. of Robert and Martha, b. Aug 20, 1793, bapt. Dec 30, 1795. {Ref: PR}

MORGAN, LUNNA (SUNNA?), see "Robert Morgan," q.v.

MORGAN, MARGARET, taxpayer, 1798, no dwelling house listed in this part of the tax schedule, no land listed, no hd. listed (possibly Deer Creek Lower Hundred), 1 slave. {Ref: TL}

MORGAN, MARTHA, taxpayer, 1798, no dwelling house listed in this part of the tax schedule, no land listed, no hd. listed (possibly Deer Creek Lower Hundred), 1 slave. {Ref: TL}. Also see "Julia Ann Morgan," q.v.

MORGAN, MARY, taxpayer, 1798, Deer Creek Middle Hd., 4 tracts (245 acres) and 1 building (Samuel Palmer, occupant), $625.22 valuation, no slaves. {Ref: TL}

MORGAN, ROBERT, see "Julia Ann Morgan," q.v.

MORGAN, ROBERT, taxpayer, 1798, Deer Creek Lower Hd., 1 dwelling house, 2 inferior houses, 2 acres, $300 valuation; 2 tracts (319 acres, 40 perches) in Deer Creek Lower Hd., $987.19 valuation, no slaves. {Ref: TL}

MORGAN, ROBERT, served on a Petit Jury in March, 1798 and March, 1799 and March, 1800. {Ref: CM}

MORGAN, ROBERT, treated by Dr. Archer on Mar 21, 1791; also mentioned inoculation of his children Sarah, Hamilton, Lunna (or Sunna), Ed:, and William; also inoculation of negroes Hannah, Phillis, Bill, Betsy, Pliny, Ned, Grace, Hector, Ben, Sin:, Mary. Priss, and Mich. {Ref: JA}

MORGAN, ROBERT (esquire), head of family in 1800 (3rd District). {Ref: CI}

MORGAN, ROBERT (major), taxpayer, 1798, Susquehanna Hd., 1 dwelling house, 2 inferior houses, 2 acres, $300 valuation; 1 tract (171 acres, 120 perches) in Susquehanna Hd., $772.88 valuation, no slaves; also, taxpayer, Deer Creek Middle Hd., 1 dwelling house, 2 inferior houses, 2 acres, $300 valuation; 4 tracts (530 acres, 40 perches) in Deer Creek Middle Hd., $804.52 valuation, 8 slaves. {Ref: TL}

MORGAN, ROBERT (OF RULIFF), head of family in 1800 (2nd District). {Ref: CI}

MORGAN, ROBERT (OF S.), head of family in 1800 (5th District). {Ref: CI}

MORGAN, RULIFF (RULEFF), see "Gideon Dennison" and "William Morgan" and "James McCracken," q.v.

MORGAN, RULIFF (REULIF, RULIFE, RULEPH), taxpayer, 1798, Susquehanna Hd., no dwelling house listed in this part of the tax schedule, no land listed, 2 slaves. {Ref: TL}. His first name was spelled four different ways on three lists.

MORGAN, RULIFF, head of family in 1800 (2nd District). {Ref: CI}

MORGAN, RULOUGH, treated by Dr. Archer on Feb 18, 1791. {Ref: JA}

MORGAN, SAMUEL, insolvent on lists in 1791 due county taxes and road taxes in "Deer Creek Upper, Middle, and Broad Creek Hundreds" as returned by Robert Amos, Jr. {Ref: IL 31.12, 31.22}

MORGAN, SAMUEL ("poor"), insolvent on a list of the county tax due William Osborn, sheriff, for 1791, as returned by Edward Prigg on Sep 20, 1791. {Ref: IL 31.17}

MORGAN, SARAH, taxpayer, 1798, Deer Creek Lower Hd., 1 tract (160 acres), $960 valuation, 1 slave. {Ref: TL}. Also see "Robert Morgan," q.v.

MORGAN, WILLIAM, see "Robert Morgan," q.v.

MORGAN, WILLIAM, tract *Morgan's Gift* surveyed for him in 1795 and granted to Samuel Prigg in 1796. {Ref: CB, SB}

MORGAN, WILLIAM, insolvent on a list for the road tax for 1792, as returned for Robert Amoss, tax collector. {Ref: IL 13.12}

MORGAN, WILLIAM (of Deer Creek), will probated Nov 23, 1795. {Ref: HW}

MORGAN, WILLIAM (potter), insolvent on a list for the road tax due for 1791 in Harford Upper, Harford Lower, and Spesutia Upper as returned by Robert Amos, Jr. on Sep 18, 1793. {Ref: IL 31.18}

MORGAN, WILLIAM H., b. 1795, d. on 13th of 10th month, 1864, in his 69th year, bur. in Little Falls Quaker Cemetery in Fallston. {Ref: TI}

MORGAN, WILLIAM'S HEIRS, taxpayers, 1798, Bush River Lower Hd., 1 tract (4 acres) and 1 building, $112.50 valuation, no slaves. {Ref: TL}. In another part of the tax schedule the occupant is listed as ---- Martin or Martins.

MORGAN, WILLIAM (OF RULEPH or RULIFF), appeared on list of "recognizances" of the court with Ruliff Morgan for his appearance in 1797. {Ref: CD, August Term, 1797}. Also see "James McCracken," q.v.

MORRIS, EDWARD, insolvent on a list for the road tax due for 1791 in Harford Upper, Harford Lower, and Spesutia Upper as returned by Robert Amos, Jr. on Sep 18, 1793. {Ref: IL 31.18}

MORRIS, EDWARD, insolvent, Harford Lower and Spesutia Lower Hundreds, on a tax list returned by George Lyttle on Sep 21, 1791. {Ref: IL 31.20, 31.21}

MORRIS, EDWARD, insolvent on a list for the road tax for 1792, as returned for Robert Amoss, tax collector. {Ref: IL 13.12}

MORRIS, ELIZABETH, charged for a felony (nature of the case not stated) in 1794. {Ref: CD, March and August Terms, 1795}

MORRIS, ELIZABETH, dau. of John and Elizabeth, b. Feb --, 1783, bapt. Oct 24, 1795. {Ref: PR}. Also see "Phebe Morris," q.v.

MORRIS, HANNAH, see "John Morris" and "William Morris" and "Isaac Morris," q.v.

MORRIS, ISAAC, son of William and Hannah, b. Sep 3, 1788, bapt. Mar 18, 1796. {Ref: PR}

MORRIS, ISRAEL, treated by Dr. Archer on Dec 7, 1791; also mentioned dau. Sucky. {Ref: JA}

MORRIS, ISRAEL, taxpayer, 1798, Bush River Lower Hd., 1 dwelling house, 6 inferior houses, 1 acre and 80 perches, $250 valuation; 2 tracts (248 acres, 80 perches) and 2 buildings in Bush River Lower Hd., $2193.75 valuation, no slaves. {Ref: TL}

MORRIS (MORRISS), ISRAEL (ISAREL), head of family in 1800 (3rd District). {Ref: CI}

MORRIS, JOHN, see "Elizabeth Morris" and "Phebe Morris," q.v.

MORRIS, JOHN, taxpayer, 1798, Spesutia Lower Hd., 1 tract (44 perches, 21 sq. ft.) and 1 building, $90 valuation, no slaves. {Ref: TL}

MORRIS, JOHN, name appeared three times on a list of insolvents in Harford Lower and Spesutia Lower Hundreds, as returned by George Lyttle on Sep 21, 1791. {Ref: IL 31.20, 31.21}

MORRIS, JOHN, son of William and Hannah, b. Jul 26, 1795, bapt. Mar 18, 1796. {Ref: PR}

MORRIS, JOHN, insolvent on a list for the road tax due for 1791 in Harford Upper, Harford Lower, and Spesutia Upper as returned by Robert Amos, Jr. on Sep 18, 1793. {Ref: IL 31.18}

MORRIS, JOHN, insolvent on a list for the road tax due for 1791 in Harford Upper, Harford Lower, and Spesutia Upper as returned by Robert Amos, Jr. on Sep 18, 1793. {Ref: IL 31.18}

MORRIS, JOHN, head of family in 1800 (3rd District). {Ref: CI}

MORRIS, MOSES, had an account at Hall's Store in May, 1791. {Ref: WH}

MORRIS, MOSES, charged for assaulting Simon Jones in 1794. {Ref: CD, March and August Terms, 1795}

MORRIS, PHEBE, dau. of John and Elizabeth, b. Jan --, 1780, bapt. Oct 24, 1795. {Ref: PR}

MORRIS, SARAH, bur. May 5, 1799. {Ref: PR}

MORRIS, SUCKY, see "Israel Morris," q.v.

MORRIS, SUSANNAH, had an account at Hall's Store in December, 1791. {Ref: WH}

MORRIS, THOMAS, insolvent on a list for the road tax due for 1791 in Harford Upper, Harford Lower, and Spesutia Upper as returned by Robert Amos, Jr. on

Sep 18, 1793. {Ref: IL 31.18}

MORRIS, THOMAS, insolvent, Harford Lower and Spesutia Lower Hundreds, on a tax list returned by George Lyttle on Sep 21, 1791. {Ref: IL 31.20, 31.21}

MORRIS, WILLIAM ("run"), insolvent on a list of the county tax due William Osborn, sheriff, for 1791, as returned by Edward Prigg on Sep 20, 1791. {Ref: IL 31.17}

MORRIS, WILLIAM, son of William and Hannah, b. Nov 9, 1793, bapt. Mar 18, 1796. {Ref: PR}. Also see "John Morris" and "Isaac Morris," q.v.

MORRISON, AGNUS, insolvent on lists in 1791 due county taxes and road taxes in "Deer Creek Upper, Middle, and Broad Creek Hundreds" as returned by Robert Amos, Jr., but her name was then crossed off both lists. {Ref: IL 31.12, 31.22}

MORRISON, GEORGE SR. (reverend), b. Jan 15, 1797(?), d. Apr 19, 1837, bur. in Bethel Presbyterian Church Cemetery at Madonna. {Ref: BC}

MORRISON, JAMES, served as constable in Gunpowder Upper Hd., 1797-1798. {Ref: CC, CM}

MORRISON, JESSE, head of family in 1800 (4th District). {Ref: CI}

MORRISON, JOHN, head of family in 1800 (1st District). {Ref: CI}

MORRISON, JOSEPH, see "Susanna Smithson," q.v.

MORRISON, MARY, head of family in 1800 (1st District). {Ref: CI}

MORRISON, MATHEW, head of family in 1800 (5th District). {Ref: CI}

MORRISON, MATTHEW, taxpayer, 1798, Deer Creek Middle Hd., 1 tract (130 acres) and 1 building, $146.25 valuation, no slaves. {Ref: TL}

MORRISON, MATTHEW, insolvent on lists in 1791 due county taxes and road taxes in "Deer Creek Upper, Middle, and Broad Creek Hundreds" as returned by Robert Amos, Jr. {Ref: IL 31.12, 31.22}

MORSHELL, S., see "Mary Dines," q.v.

MULHERRIN (MULHERIN), GEORGE, insolvent on lists returned for the county and road taxes due for 1791 by John Bull in Gunpowder Lower Hundred. {Ref: IL 31.14, 31.15}

MULLER, DAVID, head of family in 1800 (4th District). {Ref: CI}

MULLER, WILLIAM, head of family in 1800 (3rd District). {Ref: CI}

MUN, JOHN (York County), insolvent on lists in 1791 due county taxes and road taxes in "Deer Creek Upper, Middle, and Broad Creek Hundreds" as returned by Robert Amos, Jr. {Ref: IL 31.12, 31.22}

MUNGER, WILLIAM, head of family in 1800 (2nd District). {Ref: CI}. Also see "William Montjar," q.v.

MUNN, JOHN, taxpayer, 1798, Deer Creek Middle Hd., 1 tract (47 acres), $91.64 valuation, no slaves. {Ref: TL}

MUNNIKHUYSEN, JOHN A., b. Feb 9, 1800, d. May 18, 1877, bur. in Watters Memorial Methodist Church Cemetery on Thomas Run. {Ref: TI}

MUNROE, REBECCA ANN, m. John Nelson on Sep 23, 1800. {Ref: PR}

MURPHEY, GILBERT, insolvent on a list for 1791 in Gunpowder Upper and Bush River Lower Hundreds, as filed by John Bond, Deputy Sheriff, on Sep 20, 1791 (who listed him as a single man). {Ref: IL 31.24}

MURPHEY, HUGH, insolvent on a list for 1791 in Gunpowder Upper and Bush River Lower Hundreds, as filed by John Bond, Deputy Sheriff, on Sep 20, 1791 (who listed him as a single man). {Ref: IL 31.24}

MURPHEY, PATRICK, insolvent on a list for 1791 in Gunpowder Upper and Bush River Lower Hundreds, as filed by John Bond, Deputy Sheriff, on Sep 20, 1791. {Ref: IL 31.24}

MURPHEY, TIMOTHY, insolvent on a list for the road tax due for 1791 in Harford Upper, Harford Lower, and Spesutia Upper as returned by Robert Amos, Jr. on Sep 18, 1793. {Ref: IL 31.18}

MURPHEY, WILLIAM (listed twice), insolvent on a list for the road tax due for 1791 in Harford Upper, Harford Lower, and Spesutia Upper as returned by Robert Amos, Jr. on Sep 18, 1793. {Ref: IL 31.18}

MURPHY, ELIZABETH, taxpayer, 1798, Deer Creek Upper Hd., 1 tract (171 acres, 80 perches) and 1 building, $257.25 valuation, no slaves. {Ref: TL}

MURPHY, GILBERT, insolvent on list returned for the road tax due for 1791 by John Bull. {Ref: IL 31.14}

MURPHY, HENRY, subpoenaed to the Grand Jury in August, 1797. {Ref: CC}

MURPHY, HENRY, head of family in 1800 (Abingdon). {Ref: CI}

MURPHY, HUGH, insolvent on list returned for the road tax due for 1791 by John Bull. {Ref: IL 31.14}

MURPHY, JAMES, see "Sarah Murphy," q.v.

MURPHY, JAMES, head of family in 1800 (4th District); two men by this name in this district. {Ref: CI}

MURPHY, JOHN, head of family in 1800 (2nd District). {Ref: CI}

MURPHY, JOHN, or FORD ARMSTRONG, taxpayer, 1798, Spesutia Lower Hd., 1 dwelling house, 2 inferior houses, 80 perches of land (Ford Armstrong, occupant), $100.50 valuation, no slaves. {Ref: TL}

MURPHY, SARAH, wife of James, b. 1797, d. Dec 1, 1893, in her 96th year, bur. in St. Ignatius Catholic Church Cemetery in Hickory. {Ref: TI}

MURPHY, TIMOTHY, insolvent, Harford Lower and Spesutia Lower Hundreds, on a tax list returned by George Lyttle on Sep 21, 1791. {Ref: IL 31.20, 31.21}

MURPHY, WILLIAM, insolvent, Harford Lower and Spesutia Lower Hundreds, on a tax list returned by George Lyttle on Sep 21, 1791. {Ref: IL 31.20, 31.21}

MURPHY, WILLIAM, head of family in 1800 (2nd District). {Ref: CI}

MURRAY, ALEXANDER, insolvent on a list in 1792 in Deer Creek Lower Hd., as returned by Benjamin Preston. {Ref: IL 31.03}

MURRAY, ELIZABETH, taxpayer, 1798, Deer Creek Lower Hd., 1 tract (183 acres) and 1 building, $399.66, no slaves. {Ref: TL}

MURRY, ARCHIBALD, insolvent on lists for the county tax and road tax due for 1789, 1790, and 1791, as returned by Thomas Taylor on May 28, 1794. {Ref: IL 31.12}

MURRY, JANE, head of family in 1800 (5th District). {Ref: CI}

MYERS, ANN, tract *Maiden's Alley* surveyed between 1792 and 1796. {Ref: SB}

MYERS, HENRY, tracts *Silvian Plain, The Folly, Mexico Corrected, Pisgah*, and *Declivous* surveyed between 1792 and 1796. {Ref: SB}

MYERS, HENRY, taxpayer, 1798, Deer Creek Upper Hd., 2 tracts (258 acres) and 1 building, $214.87 valuation, no slaves. {Ref: TL}

MYERS, HENRY, taxpayer, 1798, Bush River Upper & Eden Hd., 1 dwelling house, 5 inferior houses, 2 acres, $300 valuation; 9 tracts (487 acres, 120 perches) in Bush River Upper & Eden Hd., $1330.88 valuation, no slaves. {Ref: TL}

MYERS, HENRY, head of family in 1800 (4th District). {Ref: CI}

MYERS, JOHN, insolvent on a list for the county tax due for 1793 in Harford Upper, Harford Lower, and Spesutia Lower Hundreds returned to the levy court by Thomas Taylor on May 28, 1794, but a line was drawn through his name. {Ref: IL 31.12}

MYERS, JOHN K., head of family in 1800 (Havre de Grace). {Ref: CI}

MYRES, JOHN, granted a retailer's permit on Apr 18, 1797. {Ref: CC}

NABB, ELISHA, taxpayer, 1798, no dwelling house listed in this part of the tax schedule, no land listed, no hd. listed (possibly Gunpowder Upper Hundred), 5 slaves. {Ref: TL}

NABB, ELISHA, head of family in 1800 (1st District). {Ref: CI}

NASH, ELIZABETH, head of family in 1800 (1st District). {Ref: CI}

NEAL, JOHN, taxpayer, 1798, Deer Creek Upper Hd., 1 dwelling house, 1 inferior house, 2 acres, $250 valuation; 1 tract (251 acres, 40 perches) in Deer Creek Upper Hd., $354.72 valuation, no slaves. {Ref: TL}

NEAL (NEALL), JOHN, head of family in 1800 (5th District). {Ref: CI}

NEAL, THOMAS (York County), insolvent on lists in 1791 due county taxes and road taxes in "Deer Creek Upper, Middle, and Broad Creek Hundreds" as returned by Robert Amos, Jr. {Ref: IL 31.12, 31.22}

NEEPER, JOHN, or ROBERT WEST, taxpayer, 1798, Deer Creek Lower Hd., 2 tracts (84 acres) and 1 building (Robert West, occupant), $330.74 valuation, no slaves. {Ref: TL}

NEGRO ---- (a free man), see "James Phillips, Sr." and "Norris Lester" and "John S. Webster," q.v.

NEGRO AARON, insolvent on lists for the county tax and road tax due for 1791 and 1792 (on which list his name was crossed off) in Deer Creek Lower Hd., as returned by Thomas Taylor on Sep 17, 1792. {Ref: IL 31.12, 31.03}

NEGRO ABIGAIL (at Capt. Sear's in B. Town), treated by Dr. Archer on Feb 3, 1791. {Ref: JA}

NEGRO AMY, b. about Oct, 1797, dau. of David and Prina, negroes of Mrs. Griffith. {Ref: PR}

NEGRO ANN, see "Negro Walton" and "Negro Robert," q.v.

NEGRO AQUILA, see "Jacob Bull," q.v.

NEGRO BEN, insolvent on list returned for the road tax due for 1791 by John Bull. {Ref: IL 31 14}. Also see "Robert Morgan," q.v.

NEGRO BEN (formerly the property of Joseph Hopkins), charged for a felony (nature of the case not stated) in 1794. {Ref: CD, March and August Terms, 1795}

NEGRO BEN BULL, insolvent on a list for the road tax for 1792, as returned for Robert Amoss, tax collector. {Ref: IL 13.12}

NEGRO BENJAMIN, insolvent on a list for 1791 in Gunpowder Upper and Bush River Lower Hundreds, as filed by John Bond, Deputy Sheriff, on Sep 20, 1791 (who listed him as a single man). {Ref: IL 31.24}

NEGRO BETSY, see "Robert Morgan," q.v.

NEGRO BILL, b. in October, 1795, son of Emanuel and Dina, [on the] estate of Thomas Hall (deceased by 1805). {Ref: PR}. Also see "Robert Morgan" and "Isaac Webster, Jr.," q.v.

NEGRO BILL RODES, see "Negroe Fanny," q.v.

NEGRO CASS, treated by Dr. Archer on Feb 7, 1795; also mentioned she belonged to Robert Bryerly. {Ref: JA}

NEGRO CHARGO, charged for a felony in 1794, but case was quashed in 1795. {Ref: CD, March Term, 1795}

NEGRO CHARLES, insolvent on list returned for the road tax due for 1791 by John Bull. {Ref: IL 31.14}

NEGRO CHARLES, insolvent on a list for 1791 in Gunpowder Upper and Bush River Lower Hundreds, as filed by John Bond, Deputy Sheriff, on Sep 20, 1791. {Ref: IL 31.24}. Also see "William Smithson," q.v.

NEGRO DARBY, see "Aquila Scott," q.v.

NEGRO DAVID, see "Negro Amy," q.v.

NEGRO DAVY, insolvent on a list for the county tax due for 1793 in Harford Upper, Harford Lower, and Spesutia Lower Hundreds returned to the levy court by Thomas Taylor on May 28, 1794. {Ref: IL 31.12}

NEGRO DICK, see "Thomas B. Onion," q.v.

NEGRO DICK, charged in 1795 (nature of the case not stated) and James Duly and Henry Weathral were "recognized in £50 for his good behaviour for 1 year." {Ref: CD, March Term, 1795}

NEGRO DICK, insolvent on list returned for the road tax due for 1791 by John Bull. {Ref: IL 31.14}

NEGRO DICK, charged for assaulting Montphelier Ferrie in 1797. {Ref: CD, August Term, 1797}. Also see "Negro Guy," q.v.

NEGRO DICK RICE, insolvent on a list for the county tax due for 1793 in Harford Upper, Harford Lower, and Spesutia Lower Hundreds returned to the levy court by Thomas Taylor on May 28, 1794, but a line was drawn through his name. {Ref: IL 31.12}

NEGRO DICK SCOTTS, insolvent on a list for 1791 in Gunpowder Upper and Bush River Lower Hundreds, as filed by John Bond, Deputy Sheriff, on Sep 20, 1791. {Ref: IL 31.24}

NEGRO DINA, see "Negro Bill" and "Negro Jacob," q.v.

NEGRO DINAH, treated by Dr. Archer on Feb 7, 1795; also mentioned she belonged to Robert Bryerly. {Ref: JA}

NEGRO DUKE, treated by Dr. Archer on Apr 18, 1796; also mentioned he had been freed by Joseph Hopkins. {Ref: JA}

NEGRO EMANUEL, see "Negro Bill" and "Negro Jacob," q.v.

NEGRO FANNY, b. in December, 1800, dau. of Bill Rodes and Prina, negroes of Mrs. Griffith. {Ref: PR}

NEGRO GEORGE, treated by Dr. Archer on Jan 3, 1791; also mentioned he had been freed by Mrs. Husbands. {Ref: JA}

NEGRO GEORGE, insolvent on lists in 1791 due county taxes and road taxes in "Deer Creek Upper, Middle, and Broad Creek Hundreds" as returned by Robert Amos, Jr. {Ref: IL 31.12, 31.22}

NEGRO GEORGE ("can't be found"), insolvent on lists due for 1790 and 1791 "fund taxes" and road tax in Deer Creek Lower Hd., as returned by Thomas Taylor. {Ref: IL 31.12}

NEGRO GRACE, see "Robert Morgan," q.v.

NEGRO GUINEA, taxpayer, 1798, Bush River Lower Hd., 1 tract (18 acres, 80 perches) and 1 building, $75.38 valuation, no slaves. {Ref: TL}

NEGRO GUY, charged for assaulting Pyre Ferrie in 1797; mentioned Montphelier Ferrie, Peter Francis Mathews (interpreter), ---- Delaporte, Mrs. Montphelier, and Thomas Coffield. {Ref: CD, August Term, 1797}

NEGRO HAGAR, treated by Dr. Archer on Feb 7, 1795; also mentioned he belonged to Robert Bryerly. {Ref: JA}

NEGRO HAMPTON, charged for arson in 1794, found guilty in 1795, and sentenced "to serve and labour fourteen years on the public roads of Baltimore County or in making, repairing, or cleaning the streets or bason of Baltimore Town." {Ref: CD, March Term, 1795}

NEGRO HANNAH, see "Robert Morgan," q.v.

NEGRO HARRY BONDS, insolvent on a list for 1791 in Gunpowder Upper and Bush River Lower Hundreds, as filed by John Bond, Deputy Sheriff, on Sep 20, 1791. {Ref: IL 31.24}

NEGRO HARRY RICHARDSON, insolvent on a list for 1791 in Gunpowder Upper and Bush River Lower Hundreds, as filed by John Bond, Deputy Sheriff, on Sep 20, 1791. {Ref: IL 31.24}

NEGRO HECTOR, see "Robert Morgan," q.v.

NEGRO JACK ("can't be found"), insolvent on lists due for 1790, 1791, and 1792 "fund taxes" and road tax in Deer Creek Lower Hd., as returned by Thomas Taylor. {Ref: IL 31.12, 31.03}

NEGRO JACK PRESTON, insolvent on a list for the road tax for 1792, as returned for Robert Amoss, tax collector. {Ref: IL 13.12}

NEGRO JACOB, see "Aquila Massey," q.v.

NEGRO JACOB (formerly the property of James Rigbie), charged for assaulting John Crawford in 1794. see "Negro Jacob," q.v.

NEGRO JACOB, b. Jun 1, 1799, son of Emanuel and Dina, estate of Thomas Hall, deceased (by 1805). {Ref: PR}

NEGRO JACOB, insolvent on a list for the county tax due for 1791 in Susquehanna Hd., as returned by Thomas Taylor on Sep 17, 1792. {Ref: IL 31.12, 31.02}

NEGRO JAMES, see "James Anderson (a free negro)," q.v.

NEGRO JANE, insolvent on lists for the county tax and road tax for 1790, 1791, and 1792, as returned by Thomas Taylor on May 28, 1794, "it being an additional list." {Ref: IL 31.12}

NEGRO JIM, see "William Smithson," q.v.

NEGRO JOE (the property of Bennet Wheeler in 1794 and formerly of Bennet Wheeler's in 1797), charged for burglary in 1794 and 1797. {Ref: CD, March and August Terms, 1795 and 1797}

NEGRO JONAS, see "Josias W. Dallam," q.v.

NEGRO LONDON, charged for assaulting Mary Talbott in 1794 and found guilty in 1795 and fined. {Ref: CD, March Term, 1795}

NEGRO LONDON, charged for felony (plead not quilty, but found guilty by jury verdict) in 1797. {Ref: CD, March Term, 1797}

NEGRO MARY, insolvent on list returned for the road tax due for 1791 by John Bull. {Ref: IL 31.14}. Also see "Robert Morgan," q.v.

NEGRO MICH, see "Robert Morgan," q.v.

NEGRO NED, see "Robert Morgan," q.v.

NEGRO ORANGE, see "Josias W. Dallam," q.v.

NEGRO PETER (the property of Samuel Wilson), charged for felony (nature of the case not stated) in 1794. {Ref: CD, March and August Terms, 1795}

NEGRO PETER (the property of Col. Samuel Hughes), appeared on list of "recognizances" of the court for his appearance in 1797. {Ref: CD, August Term, 1797}

NEGRO PHILLIS, see "Robert Morgan," q.v.

NEGRO PLINY, see "Robert Morgan," q.v.

NEGRO POMPEY, charged in 1792 (nature of case not stated). {Ref: CD, March Term, 1795}

NEGRO POMPY ("poor"), insolvent on lists due for 1790, 1791, and 1792 "fund taxes" and road tax in Deer Creek Lower Hd., as returned by Thomas Taylor (the 1792 lists spelled his name as "Negro Pomphey"). {Ref: IL 31.12, 31.03}

NEGRO POMPY ("dead"), insolvent on lists due for 1790, 1791, and 1792 "fund taxes" and road tax in Deer Creek Lower Hd., as returned by Thomas Taylor (the 1792 list spelled his name as "Negro Pomphey"). {Ref: IL 31.12, 31.03}

NEGRO PRINA, see "Negro Amy" and "Negro Fanny," q.v.

NEGRO PRISS, see "Robert Morgan," q.v.

NEGRO ROBERT, b. Dec 25, 1800, son of Robert and Ann, estate of Thomas Hall, deceased (by 1805). {Ref: PR}

NEGRO ROBERT ROSS, insolvent on a list for the road tax due for 1791 in Harford Upper, Harford Lower, and Spesutia Upper as returned by Robert Amos, Jr. on Sep 18, 1793. {Ref: IL 31.18}. Also see "Robert Ross (a free negro)," q.v.

NEGRO ROGER, insolvent on lists returned by Robert Carlile and John Guyton (who listed him as a single man) for taxes due for the year 1791. {Ref: IL 31.16, 31.19}

NEGRO SAM, see "Negro Walton," q.v.

NEGRO SAM, treated by Dr. Archer on Aug 2, 1791; also mentioned he had been freed by Skipwith Coale. {Ref: JA}

NEGRO SAM, insolvent on a list for the county tax due for 1793 in Harford Upper, Harford Lower, and Spesutia Lower Hundreds returned to the levy court by Thomas Taylor on May 28, 1794. {Ref: IL 31.12}

NEGRO SIN:, see "Robert Morgan," q.v.

NEGRO SUE, insolvent on lists for the county tax and road tax for 1790, 1791 and 1792, as returned by Thomas Taylor on May 28, 1794, "it being an additional list." {Ref: IL 31.12}

NEGRO TOM, insolvent on list returned for the road tax due for 1791 by John Bull. {Ref: IL 31.14}

NEGRO TOM, charged for burglary in 1797. {Ref: CD, March and August Terms, 1797}

NEGRO TOM ("dead"), insolvent on lists due for 1790, 1791, and 1792 "fund taxes" and road tax in Deer Creek Lower Hd., as returned by Thomas Taylor. {Ref: IL 31.12, 31.03}

NEGRO TOM BULL, insolvent on a list for the road tax for 1792, as returned for Robert Amoss, tax collector. {Ref: IL 13.12}

NEGRO TOWER, insolvent on lists for the county tax and road tax due for 1791 and 1792 in Deer Creek Lower Hd., as returned by Thomas Taylor on Sep 17, 1792. {Ref: IL 31.12, 31.03}

NEGRO VALENTINE, treated by Dr. Archer on Apr 7, 1791; also mentioned he had been freed by Jacob Giles; also mentioned his grandchild (no name given). {Ref: JA}

NEGRO WALTON, b. about fall of 1797, son of Sam and Ann, estate of Thomas Hall, deceased (by 1805). {Ref: PR}

NEGRO WILL ("can't be found"), insolvent on lists due for 1790 and 1791 "fund taxes" and county taxes in Susquehanna Hd., as returned by Thomas Taylor. {Ref: IL 31.12, 31.02}

NEGRO WILL, treated by Dr. Archer in 1792 as noted in John Scarff's account. {Ref: JA}

NEIL, ANN, see "Thomas Sheredine," q.v.

NEILE, FRANCIS (doctor), consulted by Dr. Archer in 1798. {Ref: JA}

NEILL, BENNETT, head of family in 1800 (4th District). {Ref: CI}

NEILL, JOHN, head of family in 1800 (5th District). {Ref: CI}

NEILL, WILLIAM, m. Mary Sheredine on Nov 2, 1797. {Ref: PR}

NEILL, WILLIAM, head of family in 1800 (3rd District). {Ref: CI}

NELSON, AQUILA, see "Garrett Vansicle Nelson" and "Henry Nelson" and "James Phillips, Sr.," q.v.

NELSON, AQUILA, taxpayer, 1798, Harford Lower Hd., no dwelling house listed in this part of the tax schedule, no land listed, 5 slaves. {Ref: TL}

NELSON, AQUILA, had an account at Hall's Store in March, 1791. {Ref: WH}

NELSON, AQUILLA, head of family in 1800 (2nd District). {Ref: CI}
NELSON, CATHARINE, bur. May 23, 1799. {Ref: PR}
NELSON, ELIZABETH, wife of James Nelson and dau. of Joshua Rutledge and Augusta Biddle, b. 1793, d. Aug 22, 1826, bur. in Bethel Presbyterian Church Cemetery at Madonna. {Ref: BC}
NELSON, FRANCES, see "Garrett Vansicle Nelson" and "Henry Nelson," q.v.
NELSON, GARRETT VANSICLE, son of Aquila and Frances, b. about Aug 14, 1796, bapt. Apr 20, 1797, d. Dec 24, 1850, in his 55th year, bur. in St. George's Episcopal Church Cemetery at Perryman. {Ref: TI, PR}
NELSON, HENRY, son of Aquila and Frances, b. Oct 15, 1798, bapt. Apr 21, 1799. {Ref: PR}
NELSON, JAMES, b. Jan 19, 1793, d. Jan 22, 1826, bur. in Bethel Presbyterian Church Cemetery at Madonna. {Ref: BC}. Also see "Elizabeth Nelson," q.v.
NELSON, JOHN, see "Sarah Hope," q.v.
NELSON, JOHN, taxpayer, 1798, Harford Lower Hd., no dwelling house listed in this part of the tax schedule, no land listed, 7 slaves. {Ref: TL}
NELSON, JOHN, m. Rebecca Ann Munroe on Sep 23, 1800. {Ref: PR}
NELSON, JOHN, head of family in 1800 (2nd District). {Ref: CI}
NELSON, JOSEPH, head of family in 1800 (4th District). {Ref: CI}. Also see "Margaret Nelson," q.v.
NELSON, MARGARET, wife of Joseph, Sr., b. Nov 3, 1795, d. Mar 7, 1836, bur. in Bethel Presbyterian Church Cemetery at Madonna. {Ref: BC}
NELSON, REBECCA, see "John Wiley," q.v.
NELSON, ROBERT, taxpayer, 1798, Bush River Upper & Eden Hd., 1 dwelling house, 6 inferior houses, 2 acres, $400 valuation; 5 tracts (466 acres) in Bush River Upper & Eden Hd., $2097 valuation, 3 slaves. {Ref: TL}
NELSON, ROBERT, head of family in 1800 (4th District). {Ref: CI}
NESBETT, ROBERT, appeared on list of "recognizances" of the court on oath of the peace by James Sheridine in 1797. {Ref: CD, August Term, 1797}
NESBETT, ROBERT, taxpayer, 1798, Susquehanna Hd., 1 tract (40 perches), $60.75 valuation, no slaves. {Ref: TL}. In another part of the tax schedule the occupant is listed as ---- McAteer.
NESBETT (NISBETT), ROBERT, head of family in 1800 (Belle Air). {Ref: CI}
NEVELL, THOMAS, insolvent on a list in 1792 in Broad Creek Hd., as returned by Benjamin Preston. {Ref: IL 31.03}
NEVIL, SIMON, insolvent on lists in 1791 due county taxes and road taxes in "Deer Creek Upper, Middle, and Broad Creek Hundreds" as returned by Robert Amos, Jr. {Ref: IL 31.12, 31.22}. Also see "Edward Jolly (Jolley)," q.v.
NEVILL, MOSES, insolvent on a list for the county tax due for 1793 in Susquehanna Hd. as returned to the levy court by Thomas Taylor on May 28, 1794, who noted "put in my hands last fall." {Ref: IL 31.12}
NEVILL, SAMUEL, head of family in 1800 (5th District). {Ref: CI}

NEVILL, THOMAS, insolvent on a list in 1792 in Broad Creek Hd., as returned by Benjamin Preston. {Ref: IL 31.03}
NEVILL, THOMAS ("charge with property"), insolvent on lists in 1791 due county taxes and road taxes in "Deer Creek Upper, Middle, and Broad Creek Hundreds" as returned by Robert Amos, Jr. {Ref: IL 31.12, 31.22}
NEVILLE, ELIZABETH A., b. Jan 18, 1797, d. Dec 8, 1873, bur. in Dublin Methodist Church Cemetery. {Ref: TI}
NEWBERRY, JOSEPH, insolvent on list returned by Robert Carlile for taxes due for the year 1791. {Ref: IL 31.16}
NICHOLAS, JAMES, insolvent on list returned by Robert Carlile for taxes due for the year 1791. {Ref: IL 31.16}
NICHOLSON, JAMES, head of family in 1800 (1st District). {Ref: CI}
NICHOLSON, JOHN (Baltimore Town), insolvent on a list for the road tax due for 1791 in Harford Upper, Harford Lower, and Spesutia Upper as returned by Robert Amos, Jr. on Sep 18, 1793. {Ref: IL 31.18}
NICKLESON, JAMES, treated by Dr. Archer on Feb 14, 1791; also mentioned that he lived near Widow Stinson. {Ref: JA}
NICKOLSON, JOHN, insolvent, Harford Lower and Spesutia Lower Hundreds, on a tax list returned by George Lyttle on Sep 21, 1791. {Ref: IL 31.20, 31.21}
NICOLSON, JOSEPH, head of family in 1800 (2nd District). {Ref: CI}
NIEL, HENRY, insolvent on list returned for the road tax due for 1791 by John Bull. {Ref: IL 31.14}
NIELL, HENRY, insolvent on a list for county taxes due in 1792 as returned by Benjamin Preston. {Ref: IL 31.00}
NIGER (NIGOR), MICHAEL, head of family in 1800 (5th District). {Ref: CI}. Also see "Alexander W. Davey," q.v.
NIGHT, AQUILLA, head of family in 1800 (2nd District). {Ref: CI}
NIGHT, ISAAC, head of family in 1800 (Abingdon). {Ref: CI}
NIGHT, JAMES, head of family in 1800 (2nd District). {Ref: CI}
NIGHT, PETER, m. Sarah Cline on Mar 5, 1798. {Ref: PR}
NIGHT, THOMAS, head of family in 1800 (2nd District). {Ref: CI}
NIGHT, THOMAS, head of family in 1800 (Havre de Grace). {Ref: CI}
NIGHT, WILLIAM, head of family in 1800 (2nd District); two men by this name in this district. {Ref: CI}
NISBETT, ROBERT, see "Robert Nesbett," q.v.
NOBLE (NOBEL), MARK, head of family in 1800 (2nd District). {Ref: CI}. Also see "Gabriel Mitchell," q.v.
NORFOLK, SARAH, wife of John H., b. Dec 23, 1798, d. Nov 15, 1886, bur. in Wesleyan Chapel Methodist Church Cemetery near Aberdeen. {Ref: TI}
NORINTON, FRANCIS, head of family in 1800 (4th District). {Ref: CI}
NORINTON, RACHEL, head of family in 1800 (4th District). {Ref: CI}
NORRINGTON, ISAAC, insolvent on list returned by Robert Carlile for taxes due

for the year 1791. {Ref: IL 31.16}

NORRINGTON, MARTHA, taxpayer, 1798, Bush River Upper & Eden Hd., 1 tract (49 acres) and 1 building, $155.81 valuation, no slaves. {Ref: TL}

NORRINGTON, MARY, insolvent on list returned by Robert Carlile for taxes due for the year 1791. {Ref: IL 31.16}

NORRINGTON, MARY, will probated Apr 17, 1792. {Ref: HW}

NORRIS, ABRAHAM ("dead"), insolvent on a list for 1791 in Gunpowder Upper and Bush River Lower Hundreds, as filed by John Bond, Deputy Sheriff, on Sep 20, 1791. {Ref: IL 31.24}

NORRIS, ABRAHAM, bur. Jun 22, 1794, aged 4 years and 8 months. {Ref: PR}

NORRIS, ALEXANDER, taxpayer, 1798, Bush River Upper & Eden Hd., 1 dwelling house, 2 inferior houses, 2 acres, $120 valuation; 1 tract (28 acres, 120 perches) in Bush River Upper & Eden Hd., $82.12 valuation, no slaves. {Ref: TL}

NORRIS, ALEXANDER, head of family in 1800 (4th District). {Ref: CI}

NORRIS, AQUILA, taxpayer, 1798, Gunpowder Upper Hd., 1 dwelling house, 4 inferior houses, 2 acres, $200 valuation; 2 tracts (123 acres, 80 perches) in Gunpowder Upper Hd., $322.88 valuation, 1 slave. {Ref: TL}

NORRIS, AQUILA, granted a retailer's permit on Jun 13, 1797. {Ref: CC}

NORRIS, AQUILLA, head of family in 1800 (3rd District). {Ref: CI}

NORRIS, ARON, head of family in 1800 (4th District). {Ref: CI}

NORRIS, BENJAMIN, head of family in 1800 (3rd District). {Ref: CI}. Also see "Elizabeth Norris (widow)," q.v.

NORRIS, BENJAMIN B., insolvent on a list for 1791 in Gunpowder Upper and Bush River Lower Hundreds, as filed by John Bond, Deputy Sheriff, on Sep 20, 1791. {Ref: IL 31.24}

NORRIS, COLONEL, see "John Reese (of John)," q.v.

NORRIS, DANIEL, see "Jesse Jarrett" and Susan Norris," q.v.

NORRIS, DANIEL, treated by Dr. Archer on Aug 1, 1796. {Ref: JA}

NORRIS, DANIEL, mentioned in a survey deposition on Jan 21, 1800 as "to a place between the dwelling house and kitchen where Dan. Norris now lives in about 12 foot apart" and also on Jan 28, 1800 as "Daniel Norris sworn to the houses where Wm. Robinson now lives and where said Dan. Norris now lives." {Ref: JS}

NORRIS, DANIEL, head of family in 1800 and "overseer, Harford County, pore" (3rd District). {Ref: CI}

NORRIS, DANIEL, head of family in 1800 (3rd District). {Ref: CI}

NORRIS, DANIEL, head of family in 1800 (4th District). {Ref: CI}

NORRIS, DANIEL T., b. Oct 17, 1793, d. Dec 10, 1873, bur. in Norrisville Methodist Cemetery. {Ref: TI}

NORRIS, DAVID LEE, b. in 1800, d. Nov 4, 1883, in his 83rd year, bur. in Little Falls Quaker Cemetery in Fallston. {Ref: TI}

NORRIS, EDWARD, see "Elizabeth Norris (widow)" and "Ann Pemberton," q.v.

NORRIS, EDWARD, will probated Sep 25, 1793. {Ref: HW}

NORRIS, EDWARD, b. 1799, d. on 25th of 6th month, 1821, aged 22, bur. in Little Falls Quaker Cemetery in Fallston. {Ref: TI}
NORRIS, EDWARD, head of family in 1800 (3rd District). {Ref: CI}
NORRIS, ELIZABETH, see "Jacob Tyson," q.v.
NORRIS, ELIZABETH, head of family in 1800 (1st District). {Ref: CI}
NORRIS, ELIZABETH, head of family in 1800 (3rd District); two women by this name in this district. {Ref: CI}
NORRIS, ELIZABETH (widow of Benjamin), taxpayer, 1798, Bush River Lower Hd., 1 dwelling house, 4 inferior houses, 2 acres, $140 valuation; 1 tract (222 acres) in Bush River Lower Hd., $1057.50 valuation, no slaves. {Ref: TL}
NORRIS, ELIZABETH (widow of Edward), taxpayer, 1798, Gunpowder Upper Hd., 1 dwelling house, 6 inferior houses, 2 acres, $250 valuation; 1 tract (190 acres) in Gunpowder Upper Hd., $461.25 valuation, 1 slave. {Ref: TL}
NORRIS, ELIZABETH (widow of James), taxpayer, 1798, Gunpowder Upper Hd., 2 tracts (110 acres) and 1 building, $264.37 valuation, 2 slaves. {Ref: TL}
NORRIS, ELIZABETH (widow of William), taxpayer, 1798, no dwelling house listed in this part of the tax schedule, no land listed, no hd. listed (possibly Gunpowder Upper Hundred), 1 slave. {Ref: TL}
NORRIS, GEORGE, taxpayer, 1798, Deer Creek Upper Hd., 1 tract (200 acres) and 1 building, $637.50 valuation, no slaves. {Ref: TL}
NORRIS, GEORGE ("charge with property"), insolvent on lists in 1791 due county taxes and road taxes in "Deer Creek Upper, Middle, and Broad Creek Hundreds" as returned by Robert Amos, Jr. {Ref: IL 31.12, 31.22}
NORRIS, GEORGE, head of family in 1800 (4th District). {Ref: CI}
NORRIS, GEORGE C., mentioned in a survey deposition on Jan 17, 1800 as "begun at mile stone where George C. Norris was sworn near the tent meeting house." {Ref: JS}
NORRIS, HANNAH, see "Joseph Scott, Jr.," q.v.
NORRIS, HENRY, head of family in 1800 (1st District). {Ref: CI}
NORRIS, JACOB, served on a Petit Jury in March, 1798 and March, 1799. {Ref: CM}
NORRIS, JACOB, taxpayer, 1798, Bush River Lower Hd., 1 dwelling house, 5 inferior houses, 2 acres, $250 valuation; 4 tracts (390 acres) in Bush River Lower Hd., $2385 valuation, 3 slaves. {Ref: TL}
NORRIS, JACOB, appointed a Judge of Elections in the 3rd District on Jul 28, 1800; later resigned (date not stated). {Ref: CM}
NORRIS, JACOB (captain), head of family in 1800 (3rd District). {Ref: CI}
NORRIS, JACOB (in Belle Aire). treated by Dr. Archer on Mar 28, 1792; also mentioned his wife (no name given) and dau. Sophia. {Ref: JA}
NORRIS, JAMES, see "Elizabeth Norris (widow)," q.v.
NORRIS, JAMES, will probated Nov 22, 1798. {Ref: HW}
NORRIS, JAMES, head of family in 1800 (1st District). {Ref: CI}
NORRIS, JAMES, head of family in 1800 (4th District). {Ref: CI}

NORRIS, JAMES (sadler), insolvent on lists returned by Robert Carlile and John Guyton (who wrote in the name and then crossed it off the list) for taxes due for the year 1791. {Ref: IL 31.16, 31.19}

NORRIS, JOHN, see "William Norris" and "Sophia E. Norris," q.v.

NORRIS, JOHN, insolvent on a list for the road tax for 1792, as returned for Robert Amoss, tax collector. {Ref: IL 13.12}

NORRIS, JOHN, b. Feb 26, 1796, bapt. Oct 17, 1800. {Ref: PR}

NORRIS, JOHN, b. Nov 8, 1791, d. Aug 2, 1864, bur. in Cokesbury Methodist Cemetery in Abingdon. {Ref: TI}

NORRIS, JOHN, head of family in 1800 (1st District). {Ref: CI}

NORRIS, JOHN, head of family in 1800 (3rd District). {Ref: CI}

NORRIS, JOHN, head of family in 1800 (4th District); two men by this name in this district. {Ref: CI}

NORRIS, JOHN (cooper in Harford Town), treated by Dr. Archer on Aug 11, 1791. {Ref: JA}

NORRIS, JOHN (joiner), insolvent on a list for 1791 in Gunpowder Upper and Bush River Lower Hundreds, as filed by John Bond, Deputy Sheriff, on Sep 20, 1791. {Ref: IL 31.24}

NORRIS, JOHN (tanner), taxpayer, 1798, Bush River Lower Hd., 1 dwelling house, 4 inferior houses, 2 acres, $200 valuation; 3 tracts (158 acres) in Bush River Lower Hd., $423 valuation, 1 slave; also, taxpayer, 1 tract (362 acres, 120 perches) and 1 building in Deer Creek Upper Hd., $680.15 valuation, no slaves. {Ref: TL}. In another part of the tax schedule the occupants are listed as Robert and Arthur Heaps.

NORRIS, JOHN (OF JOHN), treated by Dr. Archer on Nov 6, 1792. {Ref: JA}

NORRIS, JONATHAN, see "Vincent Norris," q.v.

NORRIS, JOSEPH, wrote his will "of Baltimore County" on Oct 6, 1772, probated Oct 18, 1795 in Harford County. {Ref: HW}

NORRIS, JOSEPH S., head of family in 1800 (4th District). {Ref: CI}

NORRIS, LUKE(?), head of family in 1800 (3rd District). {Ref: CI}

NORRIS, MARTHA, head of family in 1800 (3rd District). {Ref: CI}

NORRIS, MARY ANN, b. on 4th of 10th month, 1793, d. on 14th of 8th month, 1870 (1869?), bur. in Little Falls Quaker Cemetery in Fallston. {Ref: TI}. Cemetery records state she died in 1869, but tombstone states it was 1870.

NORRIS, MORDICA, head of family in 1800 (4th District). {Ref: CI}

NORRIS, NATHANIEL, insolvent on list returned by Robert Carlile for taxes due for the year 1791. {Ref: IL 31.16}

NORRIS, SAMUEL, see "Philip Albert," q.v.

NORRIS, SOPHIA, see "Jacob Norris," q.v.

NORRIS, SOPHIA E., wife of John, b. Jan 7, 1797, d. Oct 18, 1873, bur. in Cokesbury Methodist Cemetery in Abingdon. {Ref: TI}

NORRIS, SUSAN, wife of Daniel T., b. Mar 7, 1794, d. Dec 16, 1870, bur. in

Norrisville Methodist Cemetery. {Ref: TI}

NORRIS, THOMAS, taxpayer, 1798, Bush River Upper & Eden Hd., 1 dwelling house, 2 acres, $105 valuation; 1 tract (94 acres) in Bush River Upper & Eden Hd., $211.50 valuation, no slaves. {Ref: TL}

NORRIS, THOMAS, insolvent on list returned by Robert Carlile for taxes due for the year 1791. {Ref: IL 31.16}

NORRIS, THOMAS, b. Feb 22, 1800, d. Mar 21, 1800, aged 80 years and 27 days, bur. in McKendree Cemetery near Black Horse. {Ref: TI}

NORRIS, THOMAS JR., head of family in 1800 (4th District). {Ref: CI}

NORRIS, VINCENT, insolvent on list returned by Robert Carlile for taxes due for the year 1791. {Ref: IL 31.16}

NORRIS, VINCENT, or JONATHAN NORRIS, taxpayer, 1798, Deer Creek Upper Hd., 1 tract (200 acres) and 1 building, $525 valuation; no slaves. {Ref: TL}

NORRIS, VINCENT, head of family in 1800 (4th District). {Ref: CI}

NORRIS, WILLIAM, see "Elizabeth Norris (widow)," q.v.

NORRIS, WILLIAM, insolvent on lists in 1791 due county taxes and road taxes in "Deer Creek Upper, Middle, and Broad Creek Hundreds" as returned by Robert Amos, Jr. {Ref: IL 31.12, 31.22}

NORRIS, WILLIAM, taxpayer, 1798, Gunpowder Upper Hd., 1 dwelling house, 3 inferior houses, 2 acres, $150 valuation; 1 tract (98 acres) in Gunpowder Upper Hd., $243 valuation, 1 slave. {Ref: TL}

NORRIS, WILLIAM, served on a Grand Jury in March, 1798. {Ref: CM}

NORRIS, WILLIAM, treated by Dr. Archer on Aug 28, 1792; also mentioned his wife and child (no names given). {Ref: JA}

NORRIS, WILLIAM ("run"), insolvent on a list of the county tax due William Osborn, sheriff, for 1791, as returned by Edward Prigg on Sep 20, 1791. {Ref: IL 31.17}

NORRIS, WILLIAM, head of family in 1800 (1st District). {Ref: CI}

NORRIS, WILLIAM SR., taxpayer, 1798, Bush River Upper & Eden Hd., 1 dwelling house, 5 inferior houses, 2 acres, $200 valuation; 3 tracts (224 acres, 120 perches) in Bush River Upper & Eden Hd., $505.59 valuation, 1 slave. {Ref: TL}

NORRIS, WILLIAM (OF JOHN), served on a Grand Jury in August, 1799 and August, 1800. {Ref: CM}

NORTON, JOHN, head of family in 1800 (1st District). {Ref: CI}

NORTON, STEPHEN, taxpayer, 1798, Deer Creek Lower Hd., 2 tracts (100 acres) and 1 building, $254.25 valuation, no slaves. {Ref: TL}

NORTON, STEPHEN, insolvent on lists in 1791 due county taxes and road taxes in "Deer Creek Upper, Middle, and Broad Creek Hundreds" as returned by Robert Amos, Jr. {Ref: IL 31.12, 31.22}

NORTON, STEPHEN, head of family in 1800 (5th District). {Ref: CI}

NOWELL, THOMAS ("run"), insolvent on a list of the county tax due William Osborn, sheriff, for 1791, as returned by Edward Prigg on Sep 20, 1791. {Ref: IL

31.17}
NOWERY, SAMUEL, head of family in 1800 (5th District). {Ref: CI}.
NOWRY, SAMUEL, charged for assaulting Thomas Coffield in 1797. {Ref: CD, August Term, 1797}
NOWLAND, ----, bur. Oct 9, 1796. {Ref: PR}
NOWLAND, BENJAMIN, served on a Grand Jury in March, 1798. {Ref: CM}
NOWLAND, BENJAMIN, taxpayer, 1798, Gunpowder Lower Hd., 1 dwelling house, 4 inferior houses, 55 perches and 6 sq. ft. of land, $400 valuation, 1 slave. {Ref: TL}
NOWLAND, BENJAMIN, licensed retailer in March, 1795 and August, 1797. {Ref: CC}
NOWLAND, BENJAMIN, granted a tavern permit on May 26, 1797. {Ref: CC}
NOWLAND, BENJAMIN, served on a Petit Jury in March, 1799. {Ref: CM}
NOWLAND, CHARLOTTE, dau. of Peregrine and Rebecca, b. Jan 17, 1798, bapt. Apr 10, 1798. {Ref: PR}
NOWLAND, CHARLOTTE, bur. Sep 12, 1798. {Ref: PR}
NOWLAND, ELIAS, head of family in 1800 (2nd District). {Ref: CI}
NOWLAND, JOHN, head of family in 1800 (2nd District). {Ref: CI}
NOWLAND, PEREGRINE, head of family in 1800 (1st District). {Ref: CI}. Also see "Charlotte Nowland," q.v.
NOWLAND, PERRY, head of family in 1800 (2nd District). {Ref: CI}. Also see "Stephen Kimble," q.v.
NOWLAND, PERRYGRINE, granted a tavern license in August, 1797. {Ref: CC}
NOWLAND, REBECCA, see "Charlotte Nowland," q.v.
NUTTERWELL, ARMINTA, see "George Debruler," q.v.
O'DAIR, WILLIAM, see "Samuel Boots," q.v.
O'DAIR, WILLIAM, appeared on list of "recognizances" of the court with Thomas Coffield to keep the peace with Philip Chamberlain in 1797. {Ref: CD, August Term, 1797}.
O'DAIR, WILLIAM, subpoenaed to the Grand Jury in August, 1797. {Ref: CC}
O'DONNAL, JOHN, head of family in 1800 (3rd District). {Ref: CI}
O'DONNALL, PATRICK, head of family in 1800 (5th District). {Ref: CI}
OLIVER, JAMES, see "Josias W. Dallam," q.v.
OLIVER, JAMES JR., insolvent on a list for the road tax due for 1791 in Harford Upper, Harford Lower, and Spesutia Upper as returned by Robert Amos, Jr. on Sep 18, 1793. {Ref: IL 31.18}
O'HENRY, HENRY, m. Ann Price on Jul 27, 1797. {Ref: PR}. Also see "Henry Henry," q.v.
O'NEAL, FRANCIS (doctor), taxpayer, 1798, Eden Hd., 1 dwelling house, 2 inferior houses, 2 acres, $150 valuation; 5 tracts (264 acres) in Eden Hd., $393.75 valuation, 1 slave. {Ref: TL}
O'NEAL, JOHN, son of John and Mary, b. Mar 27, 1800, bapt. Sep 7, 1800. {Ref: PR}
O'NEAL, MARY, see "John O'Neal" and "Mary O'Neil," q.v.
O'NEIL, JAMES, son of John and Mary, b. Mar 14, 1798, bapt. Jul 13, 1799. {Ref:

O'NEIL, JOHN, see "James O'Neil" and "John O'Neal," q.v.
O'NEIL, MARY, see "James O'Neil" and "John O'Neal," q.v.
O'NEILL, FRANCIS, licensed retailer in March, 1795. {Ref: CC}
O'NEILL, FRANCIS, head of family in 1800 (4th District). {Ref: CI}
O'NEILL, JOHN, subpoenaed to the Grand Jury in August, 1797. {Ref: CC}
O'NEILL, JOHN, head of family in 1800 (Havre de Grace). {Ref: CI}
ONION, CHARITY, taxpayer, 1798, Gunpowder Upper Hd., 2 tracts (298 acres) and 1 building (William Johnson, occupant), $525.37 valuation, 1 slave. {Ref: TL}
ONION, CORBIN, licensed retailer in March, 1795. {Ref: CC}
ONION, ELIZABETH, see "Rebecca Weston Onion" and "Nicholas Day McComas," q.v.
ONION, HANNAH, see "John March (Marche)," q.v.
ONION, JOHN B., served on a Grand Jury in August, 1798. {Ref: CM}
ONION, JOHN B., licensed retailer in March, 1795. {Ref: CC}
ONION, JOHN B. (Annapolis), or ELIZABETH FLANNAGAN (FLANEGAN, FLANIGAN), taxpayer, 1798, Gunpowder Lower Hd., 1 dwelling house, 4 inferior houses, 1 acre (Elizabeth Flanegen, occupant), $505 valuation; 1 tract (298 acres) in Gunpowder Lower Hd. (Elizabeth Flanegin, occupant), no slaves; also, taxpayer, Gunpowder Lower Hd., 1 dwelling house, 2 inferior houses, 80 perches of land, $170 valuation, no slaves; also, taxpayer, Gunpowder Lower Hd., 1 dwelling house, 2 inferior houses, 80 perches of land, $125 valuation, no slaves. {Ref: TL}. Her name was spelled three different ways on two different lists.
ONION, REBECCA WESTON, dau. of William and Elizabeth, b. in 1796 (exact date not given). {Ref: PR}
ONION, STEPHEN, insolvent on a list for 1791 in Gunpowder Upper and Bush River Lower Hundreds, as filed by John Bond, Deputy Sheriff, on Sep 20, 1791. {Ref: IL 31.24}
ONION, STEPHEN, insolvent on list returned by Robert Carlile for taxes due for the year 1791. {Ref: IL 31.16}
ONION, SUSANNAH, see "Henry G. McComas," q.v.
ONION, THOMAS B., taxpayer, 1798, Bush River Lower Hd., 1 dwelling house, 8 inferior houses, 2 acres, $350 valuation; 2 tracts (427 acres) and 2 buildings (Thomas Bryan and Negro Dick, occupants) in Bush River Lower Hd., $3787.88 valuation altogether, 9 slaves. {Ref: TL}
ONION, THOMAS B., head of family in 1800 (3rd District). {Ref: CI}
ONION, WILLIAM, see "Rebecca Weston Onion," q.v.
ONION, ZACHEUS, head of family in 1800 (4th District). {Ref: CI}
ORR, JAMES, taxpayer, 1798, Gunpowder Lower Hd., 1 dwelling house, 5 inferior houses, 2 acres, $350 valuation; 1 tract (4 acres) in Gunpowder Lower Hd., $36 valuation, no slaves. {Ref: TL}
ORR, JAMES, head of family in 1800 (Abingdon). {Ref: CI}

ORR, JOHN, head of family in 1800 (2nd District). {Ref: CI}
ORR, MORDECAI, son of Robert and Ruth, b. May 12, 1795, bapt. Jun 6, 1797. {Ref: PR}
ORR, MORDECAI E., b. 1798, d. Apr 9, 1833, in his 35th year. {Ref: Mordecai Orr Family Record}
ORR, PEREGRINE, head of family in 1800 (1st District). {Ref: CI}
ORR, ROBERT, see "Mordecai Orr" and "Sarah Orr," q.v.
ORR, RUTH, see "Mordecai Orr" and "Sarah Orr," q.v.
ORR, SARAH, dau. of Robert and Ruth, b. Apr 30, 1797, bapt. Jun 6, 1797. {Ref: PR}
ORSBURN, AMOSS, head of family in 1800 (2nd District). {Ref: CI}
ORSBURN, ANN, head of family in 1800 (2nd District). {Ref: CI}
ORSBURN, BENJAMIN, b. 1798, d. 1880, aged 82, bur. in Mountain Christian Church Cemetery. {Ref: TI}
ORSBURN, BENJAMIN, head of family in 1800 (Abingdon). {Ref: CI}
ORSBURN, CYRUS, head of family in 1800 (2nd District). {Ref: CI}
ORSBURN, JOHN, head of family in 1800 (2nd District). {Ref: CI}
ORSBURN, MILDRED, head of family in 1800 (2nd District). {Ref: CI}
ORSE, ROBERT, head of family in 1800 (5th District). {Ref: CI}
OSBORN, ALEXANDER, see "Thomas Brannan, Jr.," q.v.
OSBORN, AMOS, taxpayer, 1798, Susquehanna Hd., 1 tract (44 acres) and 1 building, $154.12 valuation, no slaves; also, osbotaxpayer, 1798, Susquehanna Hd., 2 tracts (95 acres) and 1 building, $261.56 valuation, no slaves. {Ref: TL}. In another part of the tax schedule the occupant is listed as Widow Osborn.
OSBORN, BENJAMIN, taxpayer, 1798, Gunpowder Lower Hd., 1 dwelling house, 4 inferior houses, 2 acres, $200 valuation; 1 tract (171 acres, 80 perches) in Gunpowder Lower Hd., $273.38 valuation, no slaves. {Ref: TL}
OSBORN, CYRUS, see "William Osborn's heirs" and "Henry Warfield's heirs," q.v.
OSBORN, CYRUS, taxpayer, 1798, Harford Lower Hd., 1 dwelling house, 4 inferior houses, 2 acres, $110 valuation; 1 tract (88 acres) in Harford Lower Hd., $544.50 valuation, 1 slave. {Ref: TL}.
OSBORN, CYRUS, will probated Dec 10, 1798. {Ref: HW}
OSBORN, ELIZABETH, see "Ann Greenland," q.v.
OSBORN, GEORGE, b. Apr 15, 1799, d. Oct 31, 1861, bur. in Wesleyan Chapel Methodist Church Cemetery near Aberdeen. {Ref: TI}
OSBORN, HANNAH, b. Dec 24, 1795, d. Oct 19, 1833, bur. next to John Osborn in the Osborn Family Graveyard near Havre de Grace. {Ref: TI}
OSBORN, JAMES, see "John Hanson's heirs" and "John S. Webster," q.v.
OSBORN, JOHN, taxpayer, 1798, Susquehanna Hd., no dwelling house listed in this part of the tax schedule, no land listed, 1 slave. {Ref: TL}
OSBORN, JOHN, b. May 18, 1796, d. ---- (tombstone broken), bur. in Osborn Family Graveyard near Havre de Grace. {Ref: TI}
OSBORN, JOHN, see "Ann Greenland" and "Hannah Osborn," q.v.

OSBORN, MILDRED, see "Mildred Orsburn," q.v.
OSBORN, SUSANNA, taxpayer, 1798, Harford Lower Hd., 1 dwelling house, 6 inferior houses, 2 acres, $280 valuation; 1 tract (274 acres) in Harford Lower Hd., $2466 valuation, 2 slaves. {Ref: TL}
OSBORN, WIDOW, see "Amos Osborn," q.v.
OSBORN, WILLIAM, see "Harry Page Osburn" and "William Osburn" and "Edward Prigg," q.v.
OSBORN, WILLIAM'S HEIRS, or CYRUS OSBORN, taxpayers, 1798, no dwelling house listed, no land listed, no hd. listed (possibly Harford Lower Hundred), 7 slaves (Cyrus Osborn, superintendent). {Ref: TL}
OSBORNE, AMELIA, see "John Hanson Osborne," q.v.
OSBORNE, AMOS, see "John Osborne," q.v.
OSBORNE, ANN, dau. of John and Elizabeth, b. Jun 30, 1799. {Ref: PR}
OSBORNE, ANN, m. Joshua Wood on May 4, 1797. {Ref: PR}
OSBORNE, CYRUS, see "Harriot Osborne" and "Mary Osborne," q.v.
OSBORNE, CYRUS, m. Martha Warfield on Nov 26, 1795. {Ref: PR}
OSBORNE, CYRUS, warden, 1797, St. George's Episcopal Church. {Ref: PR}
OSBORNE, ELIZABETH, see "Ann Osborne" and "James Harvey Osborne" and "John Osborne," q.v.
OSBORNE, HARRIOT, dau. of Cyrus and Martha, b. Dec 7, 1796, bapt. Apr 4, 1797. {Ref: PR}
OSBORNE, JAMES, treated by Dr. Archer in 1790-1791; also mentioned his wife (no name given). {Ref: JA}. Also see "John Hanson Osborne," q.v.
OSBORNE, JAMES HARVEY, son of John and Elizabeth, b. Oct 18, 1795. {Ref: PR}
OSBORNE, JOHN, son of Amos and Elizabeth, b. Nov 9, 1796, bapt. Jun 20, 1797. {Ref: PR}. Also see "Ann Osborne" and "James Harvey Osborne," q.v.
OSBORNE, JOHN HANSON, son of James and Amelia, bapt. Mar 19, 1795. {Ref: PR}
OSBORNE, MARTHA, see "Harriot Osborne" and "Mary Osborne," q.v.
OSBORNE, MARY, dau. of Cyrus and Martha, b. Apr 7, 1799, bapt. Jan 20, 1800. {Ref: PR}
OSBORNE, MARY, bur. Nov 19, 1800. {Ref: PR}
OSBORNE, SARAH, m. James Hollis (Holles) on Apr 8, 1798. {Ref: PR}
OSBORNE, SUSANNA, m. David Crane on Mar 10, 1795. {Ref: PR}
OSBORNE, WILLIAM, bur. Feb 19, 1798. {Ref: PR}
OSBURN, BENJAMIN, insolvent, Harford Lower and Spesutia Lower Hundreds, on a tax list returned by George Lyttle on Sep 21, 1791. {Ref: IL 31.20, 31.21}. Also see "Benjamin Orsburn," q.v.
OSBURN, HARRY PAGE, son of William, b. Apr 1, 1794. {Ref: PR}
OSBURN, WILLIAM, sheriff and tax collector in 1791. {Ref: IL 31.15, 31.17}
OTHASSON, REBECCA, see "John Wright," q.v.
OTLEY, JOHN (JEHU?), m. Lydia Dean on Mar 22, 1796. {Ref: PR}
OTTLEY, JEHUE, head of family in 1800 (3rd District). {Ref: CI}

OWEN, THOMAS, AND JOHN MATHEWS, taxpayers, 1798, Gunpowder Lower Hd., 1 tract (44 perches, 21 sq. ft.), $13.50 valuation, no slaves. {Ref: TL}

PACA, MARGARET, m. Jesse Cromwell on Nov 16, 1799. {Ref: PR}

PACA, PRISCILLA, m. Richard Dallam on Mar 28, 1799. {Ref: PR}

PAIN (PAINE), BEVIS, insolvent on lists of taxes due in 1791 and 1792 in Broad Creek Hd., as returned by Robert Amos, Jr. in 1791 and Benjamin Preston in 1792. {Ref: IL 31.03, 31.12, 31.22}

PAIN, BEVIS ("dead"), insolvent on a list of the county tax due William Osborn, sheriff, for 1791, as returned by Edward Prigg on Sep 20, 1791. {Ref: IL 31.17}

PALMER, MARY ANN, dau. of William and Sarah, b. Apr 30, 1794, bapt. Sep 17, 1794. {Ref: PR}

PALMER, SAMUEL, see "Mary Morgan," q.v.

PALMER, SAMUEL, insolvent on lists of taxes due in 1791 and 1792 in Broad Creek Hd., as returned by Robert Amos, Jr. in 1791 and Benjamin Preston in 1792. {Ref: IL 31.03, 31.12, 31.22}

PALMER, SAMUEL, head of family in 1800 (5th District). {Ref: CI}

PALMER, WILLIAM, head of family in 1800 (5th District). {Ref: CI}

PARINE, JAMES, taxpayer, 1798, Bush River Upper & Eden Hd., 1 dwelling house, 2 acres, $101 valuation; 1 tract (229 acres) in Bush River Upper & Eden Hd., $515.25 valuation, no slaves. {Ref: TL}

PARK, MRS. (widow), treated by Dr. Archer on Jan 6, 1791; also mentioned she lived near John Whiteford in The Barrens. {Ref: JA}

PARKER, ELIZA, b. 1794, d. on 15th of 10th month, 1882, in her 88th year, bur. in Little Falls Quaker Cemetery in Fallston. {Ref: TI}

PARKER, ELIZABETH, dau. of John and Mary, b. Jul 13, 1781, bapt. Jul 17, 1796. {Ref: PR}

PARKER, JOHN, see "Elizabeth Parker" and "Widow Parker," q.v.

PARKER, JOSEPH, head of family in 1800 (5th District). {Ref: CI}. Also see "John Stump," q.v.

PARKER, MARTIN, taxpayer, 1798, Gunpowder Upper Hd., 1 tract (67 acres) and 1 building, $184.50 valuation, no slaves. {Ref: TL}

PARKER, MARTIN, head of family in 1800 (3rd District). {Ref: CI}

PARKER, MARY, see "Elizabeth Parker," q.v.

PARKER, WIDOW, insolvent, Harford Lower and Spesutia Lower Hundreds, on a tax list returned by George Lyttle on Sep 21, 1791. {Ref: IL 31.20, 31.21}

PARKER, WIDOW (OF JOHN), insolvent on a list for the road tax due for 1791 in Harford Upper, Harford Lower, and Spesutia Upper as returned by Robert Amos, Jr. on Sep 18, 1793 (her name was crossed off the list). {Ref: IL 31.18}

PARKER, WILLIAM, taxpayer, 1798, Spesutia Lower Hd., 1 tract (44 perches, 21 sq. ft.) in Bush River Lower Hd., $13.50 valuation, no slaves. {Ref: TL}

PARKS, ANN ("run"), insolvent on a list of the county tax due William Osborn, sheriff, for 1791, as returned by Edward Prigg on Sep 20, 1791. {Ref: IL 31.17}

PARKS, ANN, insolvent on lists in 1791 due county taxes and road taxes in "Deer Creek Upper, Middle, and Broad Creek Hundreds" as returned by Robert Amos, Jr. {Ref: IL 31.12, 31.22}

PARKS, ANN, taxpayer, 1798, Deer Creek Upper Hd., 1 tract (48 acres, 80 perches), $95.44 valuation, no slaves. {Ref: TL}

PARKS, ANN (widow and administratrix of John Parks of York County, Pennsylvania), tract *Ann's Addition* surveyed, no date given, but probably in the 1790's. {Ref CB}

PARKS, JOHN, see "Ann Parks," q.v.

PARKS, RICHARD, charged for a felony in 1794 (nature of the case not stated). {Ref: CD, March and August Terms, 1795}

PARMER, SAMUEL, insolvent on a list of the county tax due William Osborn, sheriff, for 1791, as returned by Edward Prigg on Sep 20, 1791. {Ref: IL 31.17}

PARR, JAMES, insolvent on lists returned by Robert Carlile and John Guyton for taxes due for the year 1791. {Ref: IL 31.16, 31.19}

PARSON, JOHN, insolvent on list returned by Robert Carlile for taxes due for the year 1791. {Ref: IL 31.16}

PARSONS, ABNER, taxpayer, 1798, Gunpowder Upper Hd., 1 tract (42 acres) and 1 building, $198 valuation, no slaves. {Ref: TL}

PARSONS, ABRAHAM, head of family in 1800 (3rd District). {Ref: CI}

PARSONS, ISAAC, taxpayer, 1798, Bush River Upper & Eden Hd., 2 tracts (146 acres) and 1 building, $330.75 valuation, no slaves. {Ref: TL}

PARSONS, ISAAC, head of family in 1800 (4th District). {Ref: CI}

PARSONS, JOHN, head of family in 1800 (3rd District); two men by this name in this district. {Ref: CI}

PARSONS, JOHN JR., charged for staking (stoping?) the public road in 1797. {Ref: CD, March and August Terms, 1797}

PARSONS, JOHN SR. ("old"), insolvent on a list for 1791 in Gunpowder Upper and Bush River Lower Hundreds, as filed by John Bond, Deputy Sheriff, on Sep 20, 1791. {Ref: IL 31.24}

PASQUETT, WILLIAM (reverend), head of family in 1800 (3rd District). {Ref: CI}

PATTEN, BACKLEY, see "John Street," q.v.

PATTERSON, DELILA (neé Grafton), wife of Joshua S., b. Feb 25, 1797, d. Jul 25, 1818, bur. in Bethel Presbyterian Church Cemetery at Madonna. {Ref: BC}

PATTERSON, FRANCES, wife of William P., b. 1792, d. Jan 21, 1860, aged 68, bur. in St. George's Episcopal Church Cemetery at Perryman. {Ref: TI}

PATTERSON, GEORGE, see "George Copeland" and "James Phillips, Sr.," q.v.

PATTERSON, GEORGE, taxpayer, 1798, Harford Lower Hd., 3 tracts (291 acres), $1211.29 valuation, 10 slaves. {Ref: TL}

PATTERSON, GEORGE, served on a Petit Jury in March, 1798 and on a Grand Jury in March, 1800. {Ref: CM}

PATTERSON, GEORGE, purchased a roan horse on Mar 18, 1791 and 144 lbs. of flax on Feb 3, 1794 at Bush River Store. {Ref: AH}

PATTERSON, GEORGE, head of family in 1800 (2nd District). {Ref: CI}
PATTERSON, JESSE, b. Apr 1, 1796. {Ref: Samuel Patterson Bible}. Also see "Kitty Patterson," q.v.
PATTERSON, JOHN'S HEIRS, or WIDOW PATTERSON, taxpayers, 1798, Susquehanna Hd., 1 dwelling house, 4 inferior houses, 2 acres (Widow Patterson, occupant), $400 valuation; 4 tracts (260 acres, 80 perches) in Susquehanna Hd. (Widow Patterson, occupant), $390.75 valuation, 8 slaves. {Ref: TL}
PATTERSON, JOSHUA, see "Delila Patterson," q.v.
PATTERSON, JOSHUA SMITH, b. Feb 24, 1794. {Ref: Samuel Patterson Bible}
PATTERSON, KITTY (neé Jordan), wife of Jesse, b. Sep 13, 1798. {Ref: Samuel Patterson Bible}
PATTERSON, ROBERT, b. Mar 8, 1792. {Ref: Samuel Patterson Bible}
PATTERSON, SAMUEL, charged for assaulting William Osborn in 1795. {Ref: CD, August Term, 1795}
PATTERSON, WIDOW, see "John Patterson's heirs," q.v.
PATTERSON, WILLIAM, taxpayer, 1798, Bush River Upper & Eden Hd., 1 dwelling house, 2 inferior houses, 2 acres, $220 valuation; 1 tract (168 acres) in Bush River Upper & Eden Hd., $283.50 valuation, no slaves. {Ref: TL}
PATTERSON, WILLIAM, head of family in 1800 (4th District). {Ref: CI}
PATTERSON, WILLIAM P., see "Frances Patterson," q.v.
PATTIN, BARTHALEMEW, head of family in 1800 (4th District). {Ref: CI}
PATTON, GEORGE, subpoenaed to the Grand Jury in August, 1797. {Ref: CC}
PATTON (PATTEN), THOMAS, insolvent on lists returned by Robert Carlile and John Guyton for taxes due for the year 1791. {Ref: IL 31.16, 31.19}
PAUL, JOHN, insolvent on a list for 1791 in Gunpowder Upper and Bush River Lower Hundreds, as filed by John Bond, Deputy Sheriff, on Sep 20, 1791 (who listed him as a single man). {Ref: IL 31.24}
PAUL, JOHN, insolvent on list returned by Robert Carlile for taxes due for the year 1791. {Ref: IL 31.16}
PAUL, JOHN (Baltimore County), or SIMON FITZGERALD, taxpayer, 1798, Gunpowder Lower Hd., 1 dwelling house, 2 inferior houses, 2 acres (Simon Fitzgerald, occupant), $130 valuation, no slaves. {Ref: TL}
PAYN, BENJAMIN, head of family in 1800 (4th District). {Ref: CI}
PAYN, ELIZABETH, head of family in 1800 (4th District). {Ref: CI}
PEACOCK, JOHN, insolvent on a list in 1792 in Deer Creek Lower Hd., as returned by Benjamin Preston. {Ref: IL 31.03}
PEACOCK, JOHN, head of family in 1800 (2nd District). {Ref: CI}
PEARCE, JOSHUA, insolvent on lists returned by Robert Carlile and John Guyton for taxes due for the year 1791. {Ref: IL 31.16, 31.19}
PEARSON, RACHEL, see "Rachel Pearson Amoss," q.v.
PEMBERTON, ANN (of Philadelphia), or EDWARD NORRIS, taxpayer, 1798, Bush River Upper & Eden Hd., 1 dwelling house, 4 inferior houses, 2 acres (Edward Norris, occupant), $150 valuation; 1 tract (1165 acres, 120 perches)

in Bush River Upper & Eden Hd. (Edward Norris, occupant), $2622.93 valuation, no slaves. {Ref: TL}

PENIX, JAMES, see "Solomon Perkins" and "James Pinnix," q.v.

PENNINGTON, ELIZA A., wife of William C., b. Oct 5, 1794, d. Oct 22, 1867, aged 73 years and 17 days, bur. in Angel Hill Cemetery in Havre de Grace. {Ref: TI}

PENNINGTON, HANNAH, wife of John M., b. 1799, d. Oct 14, 1882, bur. in Bethel Presbyterian Church Cemetery at Madonna. {Ref: BC}

PENNINGTON, ISAAC, head of family in 1800 (3rd District). {Ref: CI}

PENNINGTON, JOHN, see "Catherine Bishop," q.v.

PENNINGTON, JOHN M., husband of Hannah, b. 1799, d. Aug 24, 1849, bur. in Bethel Presbyterian Church Cemetery at Madonna. {Ref: BC}

PENNINGTON, WILLIAM, b. 1800, d. Nov 8, 1851, aged 51, bur. in Angel Hill Cemetery in Havre de Grace. {Ref: TI}

PENNOCK, JOHN, insolvent on a list for the road tax due for 1791 in Deer Creek Lower Hd., as returned by Thomas Taylor on Sep 17, 1792, but his name was crossed off the list. {Ref: IL 31.12}

PENNY, MARY, appeared on list of "recognizances" of the court with Charles Penny for appearance in 1797. {Ref: CD, August Term, 1797}

PENROSE, HARRIOTT, had an account at Hall's Store in July, 1791. {Ref: WH}

PEOPELS, JAMES, head of family in 1800 (3rd District). {Ref: CI}

PERDUE, MARY, taxpayer, 1798, Gunpowder Upper Hd., 1 tract (98 acres) and 1 building, $265.50 valuation, no slaves. {Ref: TL}

PERDUE, MARY, head of family in 1800 (3rd District). {Ref: CI}

PERDUE, WALTER, bur. Nov 3, 1792, aged about 86. {Ref: PR}

PERDUE, WALTER, will probated Nov 20, 1792. {Ref: HW}

PERKINS (PERKENS), SAMUEL (tanner at Bald Friar), treated by Dr. Archer on Oct 22, 1793. {Ref: JA}

PERKINS, SOLLIMAN, insolvent on a list of the county tax due William Osborn, sheriff, for 1791, as returned by Edward Prigg on Sep 20, 1791. {Ref: IL 31.17}

PERKINS, SOLOMON, tract *The Plough* surveyed between 1792 and 1796. {Ref: SB}

PERKINS, SOLOMON, charged (twice) for selling liquors and fined 600 lbs. of tobacco in 1797, and again charged for selling liquors by the smalls in 1797. {Ref: CD, March and August Terms, 1797}

PERKINS, SOLOMON, insolvent on lists of taxes due in 1791 and 1792 in Broad Creek Hd., as returned by Robert Amos, Jr. in 1791 and Benjamin Preston in 1792. {Ref: IL 31.03, 31.12, 31.22}

PERKINS, SOLOMON ("charge with property"), insolvent on lists in 1791 due county taxes and road taxes in "Deer Creek Upper, Middle, and Broad Creek Hundreds" as returned by Robert Amos, Jr. {Ref: IL 31.12, 31.22}

PERKINS, SOLOMON, head of family in 1800 (5th District). {Ref: CI}

PERKINS, SOLOMON, AND HENRY, ISAAC, tract *Partner's Addition* surveyed between 1792 and 1796. {Ref: SB}

PERKINS, SOLOMON, or JAMES PENIX, taxpayer, 1798, Deer Creek Lower Hd., 1 dwelling house, 1 inferior house, 1 acre (James Penix, occupant), $120 valuation, no slaves. {Ref: TL}

PERKINS, SOLOMON, or ROBERT RAY, taxpayer, 1798, Deer Creek Lower Hd., 1 dwelling house, 1 inferior house, 1 acre, $150 valuation; 8 tracts (412 acres) and 1 building (Robert Ray, occupant) in Deer Creek Lower Hd., $623.25 valuation, 1 slave. {Ref: TL}

PERKINS, WILLIAM (Kentucky), or EVERETT HUGHES, taxpayer, 1798, Susquehanna Hd., 1 tract (100 acres) and 1 building (Everett or Everet Hughes, occupant), $382.50 valuation, no slaves. {Ref: TL}

PERRY, ALICE, see "John Strickland," q.v.

PERRY, JAMES, head of family in 1800 (1st District). {Ref: CI}

PERRY, JOHN, insolvent on lists in 1791 due county taxes and road taxes in "Deer Creek Upper, Middle, and Broad Creek Hundreds" as returned by Robert Amos, Jr. {Ref: IL 31.12, 31.22}

PERRY, MARGARITE, head of family in 1800 (2nd District). {Ref: CI}

PERRY, THOMAS, subpoenaed to the Grand Jury in August, 1797. {Ref: CC}

PERRY, WILLIAM, insolvent on lists in 1791 due county taxes and road taxes in "Deer Creek Upper, Middle, and Broad Creek Hundreds" as returned by Robert Amos, Jr. {Ref: IL 31.12, 31.22}

PERRY, WILLIAM, appeared on list of "recognizances" of the court with John Warham for bastardy case of Mary Griffith in 1797. {Ref: CD, August Term, 1797}

PERRY, WILLIAM, m. Mary Griffith on Aug 15, 1799. {Ref: PR}

PERRY, WILLIAM, head of family in 1800 (2nd District). {Ref: CI}

PERRYMAN, ISAAC, insolvent on a list for the road tax due for 1791 in Harford Upper, Harford Lower, and Spesutia Upper as returned by Robert Amos, Jr. on Sep 18, 1793. {Ref: IL 31.18}

PERRYMAN, ISAAC, or WIDOW PERRYMAN, taxpayer, 1798, Susquehanna Hd., 1 tract (100 acres) and 1 building (Widow Perryman, occupant), $202.50 valuation, no slaves. {Ref: TL}

PERRYMAN, JOHN, charged for assaulting Richard White in 1792. {Ref: CD, March Term, 1795}

PERRYMAN, MARTHA, insolvent on a list for the road tax due for 1791 in Harford Upper, Harford Lower, and Spesutia Upper as returned by Robert Amos, Jr. on Sep 18, 1793. {Ref: IL 31.18}

PERRYMAN (PERYMAN), MARTHA, head of family in 1800 (1st District). {Ref: CI}

PERRYMAN, WIDOW, see "Isaac Perryman," q.v.

PERVEALE, GIDEON, insolvent on a list in 1792 in Deer Creek Lower Hd., as returned by Benjamin Preston. {Ref: IL 31.03}

PETERS, SAMUEL, had an account at Hall's Store in December, 1791. {Ref: WH}

PETTEGREW, WILLIAM (York County), insolvent on lists in 1791 due county taxes and road taxes in "Deer Creek Upper, Middle, and Broad Creek

Hundreds" as returned by Robert Amos, Jr. {Ref: IL 31.12, 31.22}

PHELL, GEORGE, insolvent on list returned for the road tax due for 1791 by John Bull. {Ref: IL 31.14}

PHILLIPS, CORDELIA, b. 1794, d. Jan 24, 1876, aged 82, bur. in St. George's Episcopal Church Cemetery at Perryman. {Ref: T1}

PHILLIPS, JAMES, insolvent, Harford Lower and Spesutia Lower Hundreds (listed as a single man), on a tax list returned by George Lyttle on Sep 21, 1791. {Ref: IL 31.20, 31.21}

PHILLIPS, JAMES (captain), insolvent on a list for the road tax due for 1791 in Harford Upper, Harford Lower, and Spesutia Upper as returned by Robert Amos, Jr. on Sep 18, 1793. {Ref: IL 31.18}. Also see "Capt. James Phillips," q.v.

PHILLIPS, JAMES (captain), or heirs, taxpayers, 1798, 1 tract (44 perches, 21 sq. ft.), $13.50 valuation, no slaves. {Ref: TL}

PHILLIPS, JAMES (captain, Baltimore County), insolvent, Harford Lower and Spesutia Lower Hundreds, on a tax list returned by George Lyttle on Sep 21, 1791. {Ref: IL 31.20, 31.21}

PHILLIPS, JAMES ("charge twice"), insolvent on a list for the road tax due for 1791 in Harford Upper, Harford Lower, and Spesutia Upper as returned by Robert Amos, Jr. on Sep 18, 1793. {Ref: IL 31.18}

PHILLIPS, JAMES, head of family in 1800 (2nd District). {Ref: C1}

PHILLIPS, JAMES SR., subpoenaed to the Grand Jury in August, 1797. {Ref: CC}

PHILLIPS, JAMES SR., taxpayer, 1798, Harford Lower Hd., 1 dwelling house, 7 inferior houses, 2 acres, $650 valuation; 23 tracts (4711 acres, 40 perches) in Harford Lower Hd., $29861.74 valuation, 10 slaves; also, taxpayer, Harford Lower Hd., 1 dwelling house, 3 inferior houses, 2 acres (Aquila Nelson, occupant), $100.50 valuation, and 1 other building (John Revoe, occupant); also, taxpayer, Harford Lower Hd., 1 dwelling house, 3 inferior houses, 2 acres (Benjamin Chancey, occupant), $115 valuation, and 1 other building (Jacob Michael, occupant); also, taxpayer, Harford Lower Hd., 1 dwelling house, 5 inferior houses, 2 acres (Archibald Beaty, occupant), $200 valuation, and 1 other building (Jonas Stevenson, occupant); also, taxpayer, Harford Lower Hd., 1 dwelling house, 4 inferior houses, 2 acres (Henry Vansickle, occupant), $100.10 valuation, and 1 other building (James Everest, occupant); also, taxpayer, Harford Lower Hd., 1 dwelling house, 3 inferior houses, 2 acres (George Henderson, occupant), $100.10 valuation, and 1 other building (a free negro, occupant, name not given); also, taxpayer, Harford Lower Hd., 1 dwelling house, 5 inferior houses, 2 acres (Hutchen Pike, occupant), $100.50 valuation, and 1 other building (Samuel Cannon, occupant); also, taxpayer, Harford Lower Hd., 1 dwelling house, 3 inferior houses, 2 acres (Winston Smith, occupant), $120 valuation, and 1 other building (George Patterson, occupant); also, taxpayer, Harford Lower Hd., 1 dwelling house, 3 inferior houses, 2 acres (Winston Smith, overseer), $100.10 valuation, and 1 other building (Joshua Johnson, occupant); also, taxpayer, Gunpowder Lower Hd.,

1 dwelling house, 1 acre (James Fullerton, occupant), $300 valuation; and, the 5 "other" buildings (listed above), $427.50 valuation altogether. {Ref: TL}

PHILLIPS, JAMES JR., taxpayer, 1798, Harford Lower Hd., 1 dwelling house, 8 inferior houses, 2 acres, $390 valuation; 6 tracts (348 acres) in Harford Lower Hd., $2416.50 valuation, 11 slaves. {Ref: TL}

PHILLIPS, JAMES JR., head of family in 1800 (2nd District). {Ref: CI}

PHILLIPS, JOHN, taxpayer, 1798, Harford Lower Hd., 1 dwelling house, 6 inferior houses, 2 acres, $160 valuation; 1 tract (248 acres) in Harford Lower Hd., $2232 valuation, 4 slaves. {Ref: TL}

PHILLIPS, JOHN, head of family in 1800 (2nd District). {Ref: CI}

PHILLIPS, SARAH, m. Paca Smith on Feb 7, 1799. {Ref: PR}

PHILLIPS, WILLIAM, d. Jul 20, 1791, bur. in a cemetery now on Aberdeen Proving Grounds. {Ref: TI}

PHIPPS, JOHN, son of Nathaniel and Rebecca, b. Jun 7, 1791. {Ref: PR}

PHIPPS, JOSEPH, insolvent on list returned for the road tax due for 1791 by John Bull. {Ref: IL 31.14}

PHIPPS, NATHANIEL, see "John Phipps," q.v.

PHIPPS, REBECCA, see "John Phipps," q.v.

PIERCE, ANDREW, head of family in 1800 (3rd District). {Ref: CI}

PIERCE, PHILLIP, head of family in 1800 (3rd District). {Ref: CI}

PIKE, HUTCHEN, insolvent, Harford Lower and Spesutia Lower Hundreds, on a tax list returned by George Lyttle on Sep 21, 1791. {Ref: IL 31.20, 31.21}. Also see "James Phillips, Sr.," q.v.

PIKE, HUTHING, insolvent on a list for the road tax due for 1791 in Harford Upper, Harford Lower, and Spesutia Upper as returned by Robert Amos, Jr. on Sep 18, 1793. {Ref: IL 31.18}

PIKE, HUTSON, head of family in 1800 (2nd District). {Ref: CI}

PIKE, JOHN, head of family in 1800 (2nd District). {Ref: CI}

PILE, ISAAC, head of family in 1800 (3rd District). {Ref: CI}

PILE, JOHN, head of family in 1800 (3rd District). {Ref: CI}

PILE, RALPH, head of family in 1800 (3rd District). {Ref: CI}

PINIX, SARAH, see "William Linam," q.v.

PINKNEY, ANN, see "Charles Pinkney" and "Caroline Pinkney" and "Charlotte Pinkney," q.v.

PINKNEY, CAROLINE, dau. of William and Ann, b. Sep 14, 1800. {Ref: PR}

PINKNEY, CHARLES, son of William and Ann, b. Feb 4, 1797. {Ref: PR}

PINKNEY, CHARLOTTE, dau. of William and Ann, b. Oct 4, 1798. {Ref: PR}

PINKNEY, WILLIAM, licensed practicing attorney in March, 1795. {Ref: CC}. Also see "Charles Pinkney" and "Caroline Pinkney" and "Charlotte Pinkney," q.v.

PINNIX, JAMES, head of family in 1800 (5th District). {Ref: CI}

PINNIX, JOHN, head of family in 1800 (5th District). {Ref: CI}

PITCOCK, MOSES, taxpayer, 1798, Gunpowder Upper Hd., 1 tract (118 acres)

and 1 building, $317.25 valuation, no slaves. {Ref: TL}
PITCOCK (PITTCOCK), MOSES, head of family in 1800 (1st District). {Ref: CI}
PITT, FRANCIS, treated by Dr. Archer on Dec 7, 1792. {Ref: JA}
PLAXICO, GEORGE, insolvent on lists returned for the county and road taxes due for 1791 by John Bull in Gunpowder Lower Hd. (name spelled as "Plexico" on one list). {Ref: IL 31.14, 31.15}
POCOCK, DANIEL, taxpayer, 1798, Bush River Upper & Eden Hd., 1 dwelling house, 3 inferior houses, 2 acres, $130 valuation; 1 tract (77 acres, 80 perches) in Bush River Upper & Eden Hd., $210.37 valuation, 2 slaves. {Ref: TL}
POCOCK, DANIEL, head of family in 1800 (4th District). {Ref: CI}
POCOCK, DAVID, taxpayer, 1798, Bush River Upper & Eden Hd., 1 dwelling house, 1 inferior house, 2 acres, $200 valuation; 1 tract (109 acres) in Bush River Upper & Eden Hd., $183.94 valuation, no slaves. {Ref: TL}
POCOCK, DAVID, head of family in 1800 (4th District). {Ref: CI}
POCOCK, ELISHA, head of family in 1800 (4th District). {Ref: CI}
POLSON, ASEL (AEEL), head of family in 1800 (4th District). {Ref: CI}
POLY (POLEY), HANNAH, see "Hannah Deets," q.v.
POOLE, RICHARD, head of family in 1800 (2nd District). {Ref: CI}
POOR, NICHOLAS ("poor"), insolvent on lists due for 1790 and 1791 "fund taxes" and county taxes in Susquehanna Hd., as returned by Thomas Taylor. {Ref: IL 31.12, 31.02}
POPE, LOIS K., b. on 22nd of 3rd month, 1795, d. on 5th of 8th month, 1867, bur. in Little Falls Quaker Cemetery in Fallston. {Ref: TI}
PORTER, CATHARINE, see "Sarah Porter" and "Eliza Porter," q.v.
PORTER, DAVID, insolvent on a list in 1792 in Broad Creek Hd., as returned by Benjamin Preston. {Ref: IL 31.03}
PORTER, DAVID, insolvent on lists in 1791 due county taxes and road taxes in "Deer Creek Upper, Middle, and Broad Creek Hundreds" as returned by Robert Amos, Jr. {Ref: IL 31.12, 31.22}
PORTER, DAVID ("run"), insolvent on a list of the county tax due William Osborn, sheriff, for 1791, as returned by Edward Prigg on Sep 20, 1791. {Ref: IL 31.17}
PORTER, ELIZA, dau. of John and Catharine, b. Aug 1, 1793. {Ref: PR}
PORTER, JOHN, see "John Kentlemyre" and "Sarah Porter" and "Eliza Porter," q.v.
PORTER, JOHN (taylor), had an account at Hall's Store in March, 1791. {Ref: WH}
PORTER, JOHN, had an account at Hall's Store in February, 1791. {Ref: WH}
PORTER, JOHN, head of family in 1800 (Havre de Grace). {Ref: CI}
PORTER, ROBERT, see "Sarah Porter," q.v.
PORTER, SARAH, dau. of John and Catharine, b. Jun 11, 1791. {Ref: PR}
PORTER, SARAH, wife of Robert, b. 1793, d. Jan --, 1852, in her 59th year, bur. in Old Jericho Graveyard between Jericho and Franklinville. {Ref: TI}
PORTER, WILLIAM ("charge twice"), insolvent on a list for the road tax due for

1791 in Harford Upper, Harford Lower, and Spesutia Upper as returned by Robert Amos, Jr. on Sep 18, 1793. {Ref: IL 31.18}

POTEET, ELIZABETH, b. 1793, d. Mar 21, 1886, aged 93, bur. in Harford (Old Brick) Baptist Church Cemetery. {Ref: TI}

POTEET, JAMES, taxpayer, 1798, Bush River Upper & Eden Hd., 1 dwelling house, 2 acres, $120 valuation; 1 tract (59 acres, 80 perches) in Bush River Upper & Eden Hd., $100.41 valuation, 1 slave. {Ref: TL}

POTEET, JAMES, served on a Grand Jury in March, 1799 and March, 1800. {Ref: CM}

POTEET, JAMES, head of family in 1800 (4th District). {Ref: CI}

POTEET, JOHN, head of family in 1800 (4th District). {Ref: CI}

POTEET, THOMAS JR., head of family in 1800 (4th District). {Ref: CI}

POTEET, THOMAS JR., taxpayer, 1798, Bush River Upper & Eden Hd., 1 dwelling house, 4 inferior houses, 2 acres, $300 valuation; 3 tracts (172 acres) in Bush River Upper & Eden Hd., $387 valuation, no slaves. {Ref: TL}

POTEET, THOMAS SR., taxpayer, 1798, Bush River Upper & Eden Hd., 1 dwelling house, 2 inferior houses, 2 acres, $175 valuation; 1 tract (463 acres, 80 perches) in Bush River Upper & Eden Hd., $1042.87 valuation, 1 slave. {Ref: TL}

POTHAIN, PETER F., taxpayer, 1798, Gunpowder Upper Hd., 1 dwelling house, 3 inferior houses, 2 acres, $130 valuation; 2 tracts (77 acres) in Gunpowder Upper Hd., $229.50 valuation, 4 slaves. {Ref: TL}

POTHAM (POTHAIN?), PETER, head of family in 1800 (1st District). {Ref: CI}

POTTS, RICHARD, taxpayer, 1798, Spesutia Lower Hd., 1 tract (1 acre, 60 perches, 105 sq. ft.), $67.50 valuation, no slaves. {Ref: TL}

POTTS, RINARD, insolvent, Harford Lower and Spesutia Lower Hundreds, on a tax list returned by George Lyttle on Sep 21, 1791. {Ref: IL 31.20, 31.21}

POTTS, RINORDS, insolvent on a list for the road tax due for 1791 in Harford Upper, Harford Lower, and Spesutia Upper as returned by Robert Amos, Jr. on Sep 18, 1793. {Ref: IL 31.18}

POTTS, SARAH, see "Richard Butler," q.v.

POWELL, AVARILLA, bur. Jan 20, 1800. {Ref: PR}. Also see "Kendel Powell," q.v.

POWELL, DAVIS, b. 1791 (or 1794), d. 1861 (or 1864), in his 70th year, bur. in Little Falls Quaker Cemetery in Fallston. {Ref: TI}

POWELL, KENDEL, son of William and Avarilla, b. Nov 7, 1799, bapt. Jan 20, 1800. {Ref: PR}

POWELL, WILLIAM, see "Kendel Powell," q.v.

PRALL, EDWARD, taxpayer, 1798, Susquehanna Hd., 1 tract (22 acres, 80 perches), $67.50 valuation, no slaves. {Ref: TL}

PRALL, EDWARD, served on a Grand Jury in March, 1798 and on a Petit Jury in August, 1799 and August, 1800. {Ref: CM}

PRATT, FREDERICK, taxpayer, 1798, Spesutia Lower Hd., 1 tract (1 acre, 10 perches, 84 sq. ft.), $54 valuation, no slaves. {Ref: TL}

PRESBURY, GEORGE, see "Mary Presbury," q.v.
PRESBURY, GEORGE, taxpayer, 1798, Gunpowder Lower Hd., 1 dwelling house, 5 inferior houses, 2 acres, $150 valuation; 4 tracts (322 acres) in Gunpowder Lower Hd., $982.12 valuation, 4 slaves. {Ref: TL}
PRESBURY, GEORGE, head of family in 1800 (1st District). {Ref: CI}
PRESBURY, GREENBURY, head of family in 1800 (Abingdon). {Ref: CI}. Also see "James Fullerton," q.v.
PRESBURY, ISABELLA, m. Ralph Higginbotham on Feb 28, 1799. {Ref: PR}
PRESBURY, JAMES, head of family in 1800 (5th District). {Ref: CI}
PRESBURY, MARY, insolvent on lists returned for the county and road taxes due for 1791 by John Bull in Gunpowder Lower Hundred. {Ref: IL 31.14, 31.15}. Her name was listed as "Mary Presbury, widow of Geo." on one list. Also see "William Weatherall," q.v.
PRESBURY, THOMAS P., served on a Petit Jury in August, 1797. {Ref: CC}
PRESBURY, THOMAS P., taxpayer, 1798, Spesutia Upper Hd., 1 dwelling house, 1 acre, $130 valuation; 3 tracts (194 acres) in Spesutia Upper Hd., $607.50 valuation, no slaves. {Ref: TL}
PRESBURY, THOMAS P., head of family in 1800 (3rd District). {Ref: CI}
PRESTON, ALONZA (doctor), b. 1796, d. Mar 26, 1829, aged 33, bur. in Christ Episcopal (Rock Spring) Church Cemetery. {Ref: TI}
PRESTON, BARNARD, head of family in 1800 (3rd District). {Ref: CI}
PRESTON, BARNARD (OF JAMES), treated by Dr. Archer on Sep 6, 1793; also mentioned sons Ralph and Harry. {Ref: JA}
PRESTON, BARNET, served on a Grand Jury in August, 1798. {Ref: CM}
PRESTON, BARNET JR. (OF JAMES), treated by Dr. Archer on Oct 27, 1794. {Ref: JA}
PRESTON, BENJAMIN, treated by Dr. Archer on Oct 15, 1797. {Ref: JA}
PRESTON, BENJAMIN, tax collector, compiled and returned lists for Spesutia Upper Hd. in 1792. {Ref: IL 31.00}
PRESTON, BENJAMIN, taxpayer, 1798, Bush River Lower Hd., 1 dwelling house, 4 inferior houses, 1 acre, $205 valuation; 4 tracts (280 acres) and 1 building in Bush River Lower Hd., $750.37 valuation, 3 slaves. {Ref: TL}
PRESTON, BENJAMIN (colonel), head of family in 1800 (3rd District). {Ref: CI}
PRESTON, BERNARD, see "Henry Ruff, Jr.," q.v.
PRESTON, BERNARD, served on a Petit Jury in August, 1799. {Ref: CM}
PRESTON, BERNARD, taxpayer, 1798, Spesutia Upper Hd., 1 dwelling house, 6 inferior houses, 1 acre, $250 valuation; 4 tracts (490 acres) and 1 building (Thomas Preston, occupant) in Spesutia Upper Hd., $1191.37 valuation, 1 slave. {Ref: TL}
PRESTON, BERNARD'S HEIRS, or HENRY RUFF JR., taxpayers, 1798, Spesutia Upper Hd., 1 dwelling house, 5 inferior houses, 1 acre (Henry Ruff, Jr., occupant), $350 valuation, no slaves. {Ref: TL}
PRESTON, BERNARD (BARNARD), will probated Oct 14, 1794. {Ref: HW}

PRESTON, BERNARD (OF DANIEL), insolvent on a list for 1791 in Gunpowder Upper and Bush River Lower Hundreds, as filed by John Bond, Deputy Sheriff, on Sep 20, 1791. {Ref: IL 31.24}
PRESTON, CORBIN, insolvent on a list for 1791 in Gunpowder Upper and Bush River Lower Hundreds, as filed by John Bond, Deputy Sheriff, on Sep 20, 1791 (who listed him as a single man). {Ref: IL 31.24}
PRESTON, DANIEL, see "Bernard Preston," q.v.
PRESTON, HARRY, see "Barnard Preston (of James)," q.v.
PRESTON, HENRY C., b. 1792, d. Jul 29, 1857, aged 65, bur. in Christ Episcopal (Rock Spring) Church Cemetery. {Ref: TI}
PRESTON, JACK (negro), insolvent on a list for the road tax for 1792, as returned for Robert Amoss, tax collector. {Ref: IL 13.12}
PRESTON, JACOB (doctor), b. 1796, d. Aug 2, 1868, aged 72, bur. in St. George's Episcopal Church Cemetery at Perryman. {Ref: TI}
PRESTON, JAMES, served on a Petit Jury in August, 1797. {Ref: CC}
PRESTON, JAMES, taxpayer, 1798, Spesutia Upper Hd., 1 dwelling house, 3 inferior houses, 1 acre, $155 valuation; 3 tracts (158 acres) and 1 building in Spesutia Upper Hd., $468 valuation, no slaves. {Ref: TL}
PRESTON, JAMES, head of family in 1800 (3rd District). {Ref: CI}
PRESTON, JAMES (OF BERNARD), insolvent on a list for county taxes due in 1792 as returned by Benjamin Preston. {Ref: IL 31.00}
PRESTON, JOHN W., b. 1792, d. Jul 6, 1866, aged 74, bur. in Christ Episcopal (Rock Spring) Church Cemetery. {Ref: TI}
PRESTON, MARY, taxpayer, 1798, Spesutia Upper Hd., no dwelling house listed in this part of the tax schedule, no land listed, 3 slaves. {Ref: TL}
PRESTON, MARY, head of family in 1800 (3rd District). {Ref: CI}
PRESTON, MILLY, see "Benjamin Carroll," q.v.
PRESTON, RALPH, see "Barnard Preston (of James)," q.v.
PRESTON, REBECCA, taxpayer, 1798, Spesutia Upper Hd., 1 dwelling house, 4 inferior houses, 2 acres, $175 valuation; 3 tracts (227 acres, 80 perches) in Spesutia Upper Hd., $812.25 valuation, 1 slave. {Ref: TL}
PRESTON, REBECCA, head of family in 1800 (3rd District). {Ref: CI}
PRESTON, THOMAS, head of family in 1800 (3rd District). {Ref: CI}. Also see "Bernard Preston," q.v.
PRESTON, WILLIAM, head of family in 1800 (3rd District). {Ref: CI}
PREVAIL, ELIZABETH, see "Gideon Prevail," q.v.
PREVAIL, GIDEON (carpenter), treated by Dr. Archer on Jul 14, 1795; also mentioned his wife (no name given), sons John and Samuel, and dau. Elizabeth. see "Gideon Prevail," q.v.
PREVAIL, JOHN, see "Gideon Prevail," q.v.
PREVAIL, SAMUEL, see "Gideon Prevail," q.v.
PREWET, JOHN, taxpayer, 1798, Bush River Upper & Eden Hd., 1 dwelling

house, 1 inferior house, 2 acres, $200 valuation; 2 tracts (116 acres, 80 perches) in Bush River Upper & Eden Hd., $262.13 valuation, no slaves. {Ref: TL}

PREWETT, JOHN, head of family in 1800 (4th District). {Ref: CI}

PRICE, ANN, see "Henry O'Henry," q.v.

PRICE, BENJAMIN, insolvent on lists in 1791 due county taxes and road taxes in "Deer Creek Upper, Middle, and Broad Creek Hundreds" as returned by Robert Amos, Jr. {Ref: IL 31.12, 31.22}

PRICE, BENJAMIN ("run"), insolvent on a list of the county tax due William Osborn, sheriff, for 1791, as returned by Edward Prigg on Sep 20, 1791. {Ref: IL 31.17}

PRICE, CHARLES, son of Robert and Hannah, bapt. Nov 24, 1799. {Ref: PR}

PRICE, EDWARD (at Edward Thompson's), treated by Dr. Archer on Feb 18, 1791; also mentioned his wife (no name given). {Ref: JA}

PRICE, ELIZABETH, insolvent on lists returned by Robert Carlile and John Guyton for taxes due for the year 1791. {Ref: IL 31.16, 31.19}

PRICE, HANNAH, see "Robert Price" and "John Price" and "Joseph Price" and "Charles Price," q.v.

PRICE, JAMES, head of family in 1800 (1st District). {Ref: CI}. Also see "Robert Saunders," q.v.

PRICE, JOHN, son of Robert and Hannah, bapt. Nov 24, 1799. {Ref: PR}

PRICE, JOHN, insolvent on lists returned by Robert Carlile and John Guyton for taxes due for the year 1791. {Ref: IL 31.16, 31.19}

PRICE, JOSEPH, son of Robert and Hannah, bapt. Nov 24, 1799. {Ref: PR}

PRICE, MARY, head of family in 1800 (4th District). {Ref: CI}

PRICE, ROBERT, see "John Price" and "Joseph Price" and "Charles Price," q.v.

PRICE, ROBERT, son of Robert and Hannah, b. in July, 1787, bapt. Nov 24, 1799. {Ref: PR}

PRICE, ROBERT, taxpayer, 1798, Harford Upper Hd., 1 tract (85 acres) and 1 building, $176.24 valuation, no slaves. {Ref: TL}

PRICE, ROBERT, insolvent on a list for the road tax due for 1791 in Harford Upper, Harford Lower, and Spesutia Upper as returned by Robert Amos, Jr. on Sep 18, 1793. {Ref: IL 31.18}

PRICE, ROBERT, insolvent, Harford Lower and Spesutia Lower Hundreds, on a tax list returned by George Lyttle on Sep 21, 1791. {Ref: IL 31.20, 31.21}

PRICE, ROBERT, head of family in 1800 (3rd District). {Ref: CI}

PRICE, STEPHEN, or SAMUEL MILLER, taxpayer, 1798, Susquehanna Hd., 1 tract (17 acres, 80 perches) and 1 building (Samuel Miller, occupant), $74.53 valuation, no slaves. {Ref: TL}

PRICE, VEZEY, insolvent on list returned by Robert Carlile for taxes due for the year 1791. {Ref: IL 31.16}

PRICE, WILLIAM, treated by Dr. Archer on Jul 22, 1791. {Ref: JA}

PRICE, WILLIAM, head of family in 1800 (2nd District). {Ref: CI}

PRICHETT, MARY, bur. Feb 4, 1798. {Ref: PR}

PRICHETT, SARAH, bur. Jul 20, 1800. {Ref: PR}
PRIGG, CARVEL, son of William and Susanna, b. Jul 19, 1796, bapt. Apr 20, 1797. {Ref: PR}
PRIGG, CASSANDRA, m. Richard Brooke on Dec 29, 1795. {Ref: PR}
PRIGG, EDWARD, taxpayer, 1798, Deer Creek Middle Hd., 1 dwelling house, 8 inferior houses, 2 acres, $350 valuation; 3 tracts (150 acres, 80 perches) and 1 building (Nathan Smith, occupant) in Deer Creek Middle Hd., $202.50 valuation, 8 slaves. {Ref: TL}
PRIGG, EDWARD, compiled and returned a list of insolvents due county tax for 1791 on Sep 20, 1791 for William Osborn, sheriff. {Ref: IL 31.17}
PRIGG, EDWARD, head of family in 1800 (5th District). {Ref: CI}
PRIGG, JOHN, see "Joseph Prigg" and "Samuel Prigg," q.v.
PRIGG, JOHN, taxpayer, 1798, Deer Creek Lower Hd., 1 tract (150 acres) and 1 building, $387.74 valuation, 4 slaves. {Ref: TL}
PRIGG, JOHN, insolvent on lists in 1791 due county taxes and road taxes in "Deer Creek Upper, Middle, and Broad Creek Hundreds" as returned by Robert Amos, Jr., but his name was then crossed off both lists. {Ref: IL 31.12, 31.22}
PRIGG, JOHN, head of family in 1800 (5th District). {Ref: CI}
PRIGG, JOS. (Ciscil County), insolvent on a list of the county tax due William Osborn, sheriff, for 1791, as returned by Edward Prigg on Sep 20, 1791. {Ref: IL 31.17}
PRIGG, JOSEPH, insolvent on lists in 1791 due county taxes and road taxes in "Deer Creek Upper, Middle, and Broad Creek Hundreds" as returned by Robert Amos, Jr. {Ref: IL 31.12, 31.22}
PRIGG, JOSEPH, son of John and Mary, b. May 16, 1798, bapt. May 25, 1799. {Ref: PR}
PRIGG, JOSEPH, taxpayer, 1798, Deer Creek Lower Hd., 1 dwelling house, 1 inferior house, 1 acre, $200 valuation; 1 tract (4 acres) in Deer Creek Lower Hd., $27 valuation, 1 slave. {Ref: TL}
PRIGG, JOSEPH, served on a Grand Jury in August, 1798 and August, 1800, and on a Petit Jury in August, 1799. {Ref: CM}
PRIGG, JOSEPH, head of family in 1800 (5th District). {Ref: CI}
PRIGG, MARY, see "Joseph Prigg" and "Samuel Prigg," q.v.
PRIGG, SAMUEL, see "William Morgan," q.v.
PRIGG, SAMUEL, will probated May 7, 1799. {Ref: HW}
PRIGG, SAMUEL, son of John and Mary, b. Dec 29, 1793, bapt. Dec 17, 1795. {Ref: PR}.
PRIGG, SUSANNA, see "Carvel Prigg," q.v.
PRIGG, WILLIAM, see "Carvel Prigg," q.v.
PRIGG, WILLIAM, taxpayer, 1798, Deer Creek Middle Hd., 1 dwelling house, 6 inferior houses, 2 acres, $200 valuation; 2 tracts (271 acres) and 1 building in Deer Creek Middle Hd., $571.95 valuation, 4 slaves. {Ref: TL}
PRIGG, WILLIAM, head of family in 1800 (5th District). {Ref: CI}

PRIGG, WILLIAM JR., head of family in 1800 (5th District). {Ref: CI}

PRIGG, WILLIAM JR., taxpayer, 1798, Deer Creek Lower Hd., 1 dwelling house, 3 inferior houses, 2 acres, $120 valuation; 1 tract (148 acres) in Deer Creek Lower Hd., $532.50 valuation, 2 slaves. {Ref: TL}

PRIGG, WILLIAM JR., insolvent on lists of taxes due in 1791 and 1792 in Broad Creek Hd., as returned by Robert Amos, Jr. and Benjamin Preston in 1792. {Ref: IL 31.03, 31.12, 31.22}

PRIGG, WILLIAM JR., served on a Grand Jury in August, 1798 and on a Petit Jury in August, 1800. {Ref: CM}

PRIGG, WILLIAM SR., tract *Mount Pleasant* surveyed in 1794 on south side of Broad Creek. {Ref: CB, SB}

PRINE, JAMES, head of family in 1800 (4th District). {Ref: CI}

PRINGLE, MARK, insolvent on a list for the road tax due for 1791 in Harford Upper, Harford Lower, and Spesutia Upper as returned by Robert Amos, Jr. on Sep 18, 1793. {Ref: IL 31.18}

PRINGLE, MARK, taxpayer, 1798, Spesutia Lower Hd., 1 tract (3 acres, 137 perches, 22 sq. ft.), $189 valuation, no slaves. {Ref: TL}

PRINGLE, MARK, insolvent on a list for the county tax for 1792 returned by Thomas Taylor on May 28, 1794, "it being an additional list." {Ref: IL 31.12}

PRITCHARD, BENJAMIN, taxpayer, 1798, Susquehanna Hd., 1 tract (80 acres) and 1 building, $189.37 valuation, 1 slave. {Ref: TL}

PRITCHARD, BENJAMIN, head of family in 1800 (2nd District). {Ref: CI}

PRITCHARD, HERMAN, had accounts at Hall's Store in March, 1791, and August, 1791. {Ref: WH}

PRITCHARD, JAMES, will probated Aug 24, 1796. {Ref: HW}

PRITCHARD, JAMES, head of family in 1800 (2nd District). {Ref: CI}

PRITCHARD, JOHN (Baltimore County), or JOHN BULL, taxpayer, 1798, Bush River Lower Hd., 1 dwelling house, 2 inferior houses, 1 acre (John Bull, occupant), $450 valuation, no slaves. {Ref: TL}

PRITCHARD, SAMUEL, insolvent on a list for the county tax due for 1791 in Susquehanna Hd., as returned by Thomas Taylor on Sep 17, 1792. {Ref: IL 31.12, 31.02}

PRITCHARD, SAMUEL, taxpayer, 1798, Susquehanna Hd., 1 tract (98 acres) and 1 building, $194.99 valuation, no slaves. {Ref: TL}

PRITCHARD, STEPHEN, insolvent on a list for the road tax due for 1791 in Harford Upper, Harford Lower, and Spesutia Upper as returned by Robert Amos, Jr. on Sep 18, 1793. {Ref: IL 31.18}

PRITCHARD, THOMAS, insolvent on list returned for the road tax due for 1791 by John Bull. {Ref: IL 31.14}

PRITCHARD, THOMAS, insolvent on a list for county taxes due in 1792 as returned by Benjamin Preston. {Ref: IL 31.00}

PRITCHETT (PRICHETT), ANN, dau. of James and Sarah, bapt. Jun 3, 1798. {Ref: PR}

PRITCHETT, JAMES, son of James and Sarah, bapt. Feb 7, 1796. {Ref: PR}. Also see

"Ann Pritchett," q.v.
PRITCHETT, MARY, dau. of James and Sarah, bapt. Feb 7, 1796. {Ref: PR}
PRITCHETT, SAMUEL, son of James and Sarah, bapt. Feb 7, 1796. {Ref: PR}
PRITCHETT, SARAH, see "Samuel Pritchett" and "James Pritchett" and "Mary Pritchett" and "Ann Pritchett," q.v.
PROCTOR, RICHARD, insolvent on lists in 1791 due county taxes and road taxes in "Deer Creek Upper, Middle, and Broad Creek Hundreds" as returned by Robert Amos, Jr., but his name was then crossed off both lists. {Ref: IL 31.12, 31.22}
PROSSER, JOHN, see "John Monks," q.v.
PROSSER, JOHN, m. Sarah Hall on Feb 12, 1798. {Ref: PR}
PROSSER, JOHN, head of family in 1800 (Abingdon). {Ref: CI}
PRUITT, BENJAMIN F., b. May 25, 1795, d. Dec 19, 1876, aged 81 years, 6 months, and 25 days, bur. in Jarrettsville Cemetery. {Ref: TI}
PUE, CALEB, see "Eliza Kennard," q.v.
PUGMAN, THOMAS ("can't be found"), insolvent on lists due for 1790 and 1791 "fund taxes" and county taxes in Susquehanna Hd., as returned by Thomas Taylor. {Ref: IL 31.12, 31.02}
PYBUS, JOHN, or TIMOTHY KEEN, taxpayer, 1798, Susquehanna Hd., 1 tract (96 acres) and 1 building (Timothy Keen, occupant), $158.63 valuation, no slaves. {Ref: TL}
PYBUS (PYBOS), JOHN, head of family in 1800 (2nd District). {Ref: CI}
PYKE, AQUILA, insolvent on a list for the county tax due for 1793 in Harford Upper, Harford Lower, and Spesutia Lower Hundreds returned to the levy court by Thomas Taylor on May 28, 1794. {Ref: IL 31.12}
PYLE, ANN, b. 1791, d. Jul 30, 1878, in her 87th year, bur. in Deer Creek Methodist Church Cemetery at Chestnut Hill. {Ref: TI}
PYLE, ISAAC, taxpayer, 1798, Spesutia Upper Hd., 1 tract (236 acres) and 1 building, $1163.25 valuation, no slaves. {Ref: TL}. Also see "Isaac Pile," q.v.
PYLE, JOHN, taxpayer Spesutia Upper Hd., 1 tract (235 acres) and 2 buildings (Thomas Crail, occupant of one of them), $1215 valuation, no slaves. {Ref: TL}
PYLE, RALPH, taxpayer, 1798, Spesutia Upper Hd., 1 dwelling house, 1 inferior house, 1 acre, $115 valuation; 1 tract (50 acres) and 1 building (William Quarrells or Quarrell, occupant) in Spesutia Upper Hd., $624.37 valuation, no slaves. {Ref: TL}
PYLES, MARY, see "John Kennady," q.v.
QUARLES, CHARLOTTE, wife of John, b. Jan 12, 1794, d. Feb 1, 1862, bur. in Deer Creek Friends Cemetery in Darlington. {Ref: TI}
QUARRELLS (QUARRELS), JOHN, or ROBERT RIER, taxpayer, 1798, Broad Creek Hd., 1 tract (312 acres) and 1 building (Robert Rier, occupant), $1000.87 valuation, no slaves. {Ref: TL}
QUARRELLS (QUARRELL), WILLIAM, head of family in 1800 (5th District). {Ref: CI}. Also see "Ralph Pyle," q.v.

QUIGLEY, CHARLES, head of family in 1800 (3rd District). {Ref: CI}
QUINLAN, HENRY, b. 1798, d. Jul 27, 1871, in his 73rd year, bur. in St. Ignatius Catholic Church Cemetery in Hickory. {Ref: TI}
QUINLAN, PHILIP, treated by Dr. Archer on Jul 20, 1792. {Ref: JA}
QUINLAN, RUTH (neé Clark), b. Mar 25, 1793, d. Mar 8, 1859, aged 65 years, 11 months, and 11 days, bur. in Christ Episcopal (Rock Spring) Church Cemetery. {Ref: TI}
QUINLEN, BENJAMIN, head of family in 1800 (5th District). {Ref: CI}
QUINLIN, JAMES, taxpayer, 1798, Spesutia Upper Hd., 1 dwelling house, 3 inferior houses, 120 perches, $200 valuation; 2 tracts (218 acres) in Spesutia Upper Hd., $675 valuation, 2 slaves. {Ref: TL}
QUINLIN, JAMES, head of family in 1800 (3rd District). {Ref: CI}
QUINLIN, PHILIP, taxpayer, 1798, Deer Creek Middle Hd., 1 dwelling house, 5 inferior houses, 2 acres, $300 valuation; 3 tracts (301 acres, 80 perches) in Deer Creek Middle Hd., $393.75 valuation, no slaves. {Ref: TL}
RABURGH, ANDREW, insolvent on lists returned for the county and road taxes due for 1791 by John Bull in Gunpowder Lower Hd. (name spelled as "Reaburge" on one list). {Ref: IL 31.14, 31.15}
RADICAN, JAMES, taxpayer, 1798, Deer Creek Middle Hd., 1 tract (30 acres) and 1 building, $78.75 valuation, no slaves. {Ref: TL}. Also see "James Ratikane," q.v.
RAGAN, JAMES, head of family in 1800 (2nd District). {Ref: CI}
RAIN, SAMUEL, taxpayer, 1798, Bush River Upper & Eden Hd., 1 dwelling house, 2 acres, $150 valuation; 1 tract (108 acres) in Bush River Upper & Eden Hd., $243 valuation, no slaves. {Ref: TL}
RAIN (RANE), SAMUEL, head of family in 1800 (4th District). {Ref: CI}
RAINE, SAMUEL, served as constable in Bush River Lower Hd., 1797. {Ref: CC, CM}
RAITT, CHARLES HAMMOND, b. May 8, 1799, d. Aug 28, 1867, aged 68 years, 3 months, and 20 days, bur. in Christ Episcopal (Rock Spring) Church Cemetery. {Ref: TI}
RAMPLEY, ANN, see "Eleanor Turner," q.v.
RAMPLEY, JAMES, taxpayer, 1798, Deer Creek Upper Hd., 1 dwelling house, 1 inferior house, 2 acres, $102 valuation; 2 tracts (380 acres) in Deer Creek Upper Hd. (John Gladdon or Gladden, occupant) and 2 buildings (John Beaty and Edward Berry, occupants), $748.12 valuation altogether, no slaves. {Ref: TL}. A note by the assessor stated "Query whether this is not the same man assessed in B. R. Upper & Eden."
RAMPLEY, JAMES, tract *Addition to Rampley's Venture* surveyed between 1792 and 1796. {Ref: SB}
RAMPLEY, JAMES, mentioned in a survey deposition on Nov 5, 1799 and Jan 14, 1800 as "from Wm. Baker's house where he now lives to where James Rampley's house formerly stood, then called Wells" and also "took James

Rampley's deposition where Kilpatrick's dwelling house formerly stood" and also "into Wm. Barton's field where said Rampley proves he cleared." {Ref: JS}

RAMPLEY, JAMES, head of family in 1800 (4th District). {Ref: CI}

RAMPLEY, JAMES, AND GIBSON, WILLIAM, tract *Every Man's Refuse* surveyed between 1792 and 1796. {Ref: SB}

RAMPLEY, JOHN, taxpayer, 1798, Bush River Upper & Eden Hd., 1 dwelling house, 1 inferior house, 2 acres, $150 valuation; 3 tracts (579 acres) in Bush River Upper & Eden Hd., $977.60 valuation, 1 slave. {Ref: TL}

RAMPLEY, NANCY ANN, see "Mary Montgomery," q.v.

RAMSAY, CUNNINGHAM, see "James Ramsay," q.v.

RAMSAY, ELIZA, see "James Ramsay," q.v.

RAMSAY, JAMES (at Slade Ridge), treated by Dr. Archer on Nov 1, 1796; also mentioned his wife (no name given), son Cunningham, and dau. Eliza. {Ref: JA}

RAMSAY, NATHANIEL, see "Charlotte Jane Hall" and "Nathaniel Ramsey," q.v.

RAMSAY, WILLIAM, treated by Dr. Archer on Mar 4, 1791. {Ref: JA}

RAMSEY, ALEXANDER, see "James McCandless," q.v.

RAMSEY, NATHANIEL (colonel), of Baltimore Town, taxpayer, 1798, Harford Upper Hd., 2 tracts (497 acres) and 1 building, $1140.75 valuation, no slaves. {Ref: TL}

RAMSEY, ROBERT, taxpayer, 1798, Deer Creek Middle Hd., no dwelling house listed in this part of the tax schedule, no land listed, 1 slave. {Ref: TL}

RAMSEY, ROBERT, tract *Ramsey's Search* surveyed in 1799. {Ref: CB}

RAMSEY, ROBERT (Pennsylvania), or HENRY RAMSEY, taxpayer, 1798, Deer Creek Upper Hd., 4 tracts (521 acres) and 1 building (Henry Ramsey, occupant), $1025.72 valuation, no slaves. {Ref: TL}

RAMSEY, THOMAS, taxpayer, 1798, Susquehanna Hd., 1 dwelling house, 4 inferior houses, 2 acres, $275 valuation; 1 tract (309 acres) and 1 building in Susquehanna Hd., $1446.75 valuation, 1 slave. {Ref: TL}. In another part of the tax schedule the occupant is listed as Robert Creswell.

RAMSEY, THOMAS, head of family in 1800 (2nd District). {Ref: CI}

RAMSEY, WILLIAM (colonel), b. Nov 29, 1792, d. Dec 24, 1831, bur. in St. George's Episcopal Church Cemetery at Perryman. {Ref: TI}

RAMSEY, WILLIAM ("no such man"), insolvent on lists due for 1790 and 1791 "fund taxes" and county taxes in Susquehanna Hd., as returned by Thomas Taylor. {Ref: IL 31.12, 31.02}

RAMSLY(?), HENRY AND HANNAH, see "Amelia Jane Sappington," q.v.

RAND, THOMAS, m. Mary Burns on May 5, 1799. {Ref: PR}

RANGE, JOHN JR., head of family in 1800 (4th District). {Ref: CI}

RANKIN, JOHN, insolvent on a list in 1792 in Deer Creek Lower Hd., as returned by Benjamin Preston. {Ref: IL 31.03}

RANKIN, JOHN, insolvent on a list for the county tax due for 1793 in Susquehanna Hd. as returned to the levy court by Thomas Taylor on May 28, 1794, who noted "put in my hands last fall." {Ref: IL 31.12}

RANKIN, SAMUEL (cooper at Stafford Mills), treated by Dr. Archer on Dec 5, 1792. {Ref: JA}

RAPHAEL, STEPHEN, taxpayer, 1798, Gunpowder Lower Hd., 1 dwelling house, 3 inferior houses, 2 acres, $500 valuation; 3 tracts (340 acres) in Gunpowder Lower Hd., $1066.50 valuation, no slaves. {Ref: TL}

RAPHEL, ALEXIUS AMEDI, son of Stephen and Elizabeth Jane Raphel, b. May 23, 1797, bapt. Jun 7, 1797, St. Ignatius Catholic Church in Hickory; sponsors: Alexius de Legritz and A. Jigorgne. {Ref: *St. Ignatius, Hickory, and Its Missions*, by Clarence V. Joerndt (1972), p. 55}

RATIKANE, JAMES, head of family in 1800 (5th District). {Ref: CI}. Also see "James Radican," q.v.

RATTOW, ENOCH, see "Benjamin Whitson" and "Enoch Rittow," q.v.

RAY, GEORGE, son of Robert and Sarah, b. Jun 10, 1799, bapt. Oct 20, 1799. {Ref: PR}. Also see "George Rea," q.v.

RAY, ROBERT, see "George Ray" and "Solomon Perkins," q.v.

RAY, SAMUEL, head of family in 1800 (5th District). {Ref: CI}

RAY, SARAH, see "George Ray," q.v.

REA, BENJAMIN, insolvent on list returned for the road tax due for 1791 by John Bull. {Ref: IL 31.14}

REA, GEORGE ("poor"), insolvent on lists due for 1790 and 1791 "fund taxes" and county taxes in Susquehanna Hd., as returned by Thomas Taylor (his name was spelled "Geo. Ray" on the 1791 road tax list). {Ref: IL 31.12, 31.02}

REARDON, JOHN, taxpayer, 1798, Bush River Lower Hd., 1 dwelling house, 2 inferior houses, 1 acre, $200 valuation, no slaves; also, taxpayer, 1 dwelling house, 80 perches of land in Abingdon, $180 valuation, no slaves. {Ref: TL}

REARDON, JOHN, served on a Grand Jury in March, 1800. {Ref: CM}

REARDON, JOHN, insolvent on list returned for the road tax due for 1791 by John Bull. {Ref: IL 31.14}

REARDON, JOHN, head of family in 1800 (Belle Air). {Ref: CI}

REARDON, JOSIAS (on Bush River Neck), treated by Dr. Archer in 1790-1791. {Ref: JA}

REARDON, PATRICK, head of family in 1800 (3rd District). {Ref: CI}

REARICK, ADAM, husband of Eve H., b. Mar 6, 1799, d. Dec 19, 1863, bur. in Old Salem Evangelical Cemetery near Madonna. {Ref: TI}

REARICK, EVE H., wife of Adam, Sr., b. Mar 13, 1794, d. Jan 18, 1880, bur. in Old Salem Evangelical Cemetery near Madonna. {Ref: TI}

REASIN, SARAH E., wife of William D., b. Sep 29, 1794, d. Mar 5, 1835, bur. in St. George's Episcopal Church Cemetery at Perryman. {Ref: TI}

REASIN, WILLIAM D., b. 1791, d. May 16, 1832, bur. in a cemetery now on Aberdeen Proving Grounds. {Ref: TI}

REASON, JAMES, insolvent, Harford Lower and Spesutia Lower Hundreds (listed as a single man), on a tax list returned by George Lyttle on Sep 21, 1791. {Ref: IL 31.20, 31.21}

REASON, JAMES, insolvent on a list for the road tax due for 1791 in Harford

Upper, Harford Lower, and Spesutia Upper as returned by Robert Amos, Jr. on Sep 18, 1793. {Ref: IL 31.18}

REASON, RICHARD, insolvent on a list for the road tax due for 1791 in Harford Upper, Harford Lower, and Spesutia Upper as returned by Robert Amos, Jr. on Sep 18, 1793. {Ref: IL 31.18}

REASON, RICHARD, insolvent, Harford Lower and Spesutia Lower Hundreds, on a tax list returned by George Lyttle on Sep 21, 1791. {Ref: IL 31.20, 31.21}

REASONS, SARAH, head of family in 1800 (2nd District). {Ref: CI}

REDMAN, MARY, m. James Greenly on Apr 13, 1800. {Ref: PR}. Also see "Greenberry Greenly," q.v.

REECE, ABRAHAM, head of family in 1800 (2nd District). {Ref: CI}

REECE, ALEXANDER, head of family in 1800 (5th District). {Ref: CI}

REECE, JOHN, head of family in 1800 (1st District). {Ref: CI}

REECE, JOHN ("old and poor"), insolvent on a list for 1791 in Gunpowder Upper and Bush River Lower Hundreds, as filed by John Bond, Deputy Sheriff, on Sep 20, 1791. {Ref: IL 31.24}

REECE, WILLIAM, head of family in 1800 (5th District). {Ref: CI}

REECE, WILLIAM JR., head of family in 1800 (5th District). {Ref: CI}

REED, EMANUEL (EMANEL), insolvent on list returned by Robert Carlile for taxes due for the year 1791. {Ref: IL 31.16}

REED, EMANUEL, insolvent on list returned for the county tax for 1791 by William Osburn in Gunpowder Lower Hundred. {Ref: IL 31.15}

REED, REBECCA, see "Thomas Rock," q.v.

REED, THOMAS, insolvent on list returned by Robert Carlile for taxes due for the year 1791. {Ref: IL 31.16}

REED, WILLIAM, taxpayer, 1798, Broad Creek Hd., 1 tract (80 acres, 40 perches), $180.56 valuation, no slaves. {Ref: TL}

REED, WILLIAM, insolvent on lists in 1791 due county taxes and road taxes in "Deer Creek Upper, Middle, and Broad Creek Hundreds" as returned by Robert Amos, Jr. {Ref: IL 31.12, 31.22}

REES, ALEXANDER, son of William and Jane, b. May 12, 1797, bapt. Jun 6, 1797. {Ref: PR}

REES, JANE, dau. of William and Jane, b. May 18, 1795, bapt. Jun 6, 1797. {Ref: PR}. Also see "William Rees" and "Alexander Rees," q.v.

REES, WILLIAM, son of William and Jane, b. Oct 13, 1793, bapt. Jun 6, 1797. {Ref: PR}. Also see "Jane Rees" and "Alexander Rees," q.v.

REESE, ABRAHAM, taxpayer, 1798, Susquehanna Hd., 2 tracts (170 acres) and 3 buildings (Abraham Gorrel or Gorrell, and Samuel Hopkins, occupants of two of them), $667.49 valuation, no slaves. {Ref: TL}

REESE, ALEXANDER, or WILLIAM REESE SR., taxpayer, 1798, Broad Creek Hd., 5 tracts (192 acres, 80 perches) and 1 building (William Reese, Sr., occupant), $432 valuation, no slaves. {Ref: TL}

REESE, DANIEL, insolvent on list returned by Robert Carlile for taxes due for the year 1791. {Ref: IL 31.16}

REESE (REECE), JAMES ("out back"), insolvent on lists due for 1790 and 1791 "fund taxes" and county taxes in Susquehanna Hd., as returned by Thomas Taylor. {Ref: IL 31.12, 31.02}

REESE (REECE), JOHN ("dead"), insolvent on lists due for 1790 and 1791 "fund taxes" and county taxes in and Susquehanna Hd., as returned by Thomas Taylor. {Ref: IL 31.12, 31.02}

REESE, JOHN, insolvent on list returned by Robert Carlile for taxes due for the year 1791. {Ref: IL 31.16}

REESE, JOHN (OF JOHN), now at Col. Norris', treated by Dr. Archer on Jan 5, 1794; also mentioned his wife (no name given). {Ref: JA}

REESE (REECE), JOSEPH ("dead"), insolvent on lists due for 1790 and 1791 "fund taxes" and county taxes in Susquehanna Hd., as returned by Thomas Taylor. {Ref: IL 31.12, 31.02}

REESE, WILLIAM JR., taxpayer, 1798, Broad Creek Hd., 2 tracts (110 acres) and 1 building, $135 valuation, no slaves. {Ref: TL}

REESE, WILLIAM SR., see "Alexander Reese," q.v.

RENSHAW, CASSANDRA, b. 1796, d. Sep 29, 1883, bur. in Bethel Presbyterian Church Cemetery at Madonna. {Ref: BC}

RENSHAW, JAMES, insolvent on list returned by Robert Carlile for taxes due for the year 1791. {Ref: IL 31.16}

RENSHAW, JAMES, insolvent on a list for 1791 in Gunpowder Upper and Bush River Lower Hundreds, as filed by John Bond, Deputy Sheriff, on Sep 20, 1791 (who listed him as a single man). {Ref: IL 31.24}

RENSHAW, JOHN, served on a Petit Jury in August, 1798 and on a Grand Jury in August, 1799. {Ref: CM}

RENSHAW, JOHN, taxpayer, 1798, Bush River Upper & Eden Hd., 1 dwelling house, 3 inferior houses, 2 acres, $110 valuation; 1 tract (98 acres) in Bush River Upper & Eden Hd., $192.94 valuation, no slaves. {Ref: TL}

RENSHAW, JOHN, head of family in 1800 (4th District). {Ref: CI}

RENSHAW, JOSEPH, taxpayer, 1798, Bush River Upper & Eden Hd., 1 dwelling house, 2 inferior houses, 2 acres, $200 valuation; 2 tracts (136 acres) in Bush River Upper & Eden Hd., $306 valuation, 4 slaves. {Ref: TL}

RENSHAW, JOSEPH, head of family in 1800 (4th District). {Ref: CI}

RENSHAW, PHILIP, insolvent on a list for 1791 in Gunpowder Upper and Bush River Lower Hundreds, as filed by John Bond, Deputy Sheriff, on Sep 20, 1791. {Ref: IL 31.24}. Also see "Walter Billingsley, Sr.," q.v.

RENSHAW, PHILLIP, head of family in 1800 (3rd District). {Ref: CI}

RENSHAW, ROBERT, insolvent on lists returned by Robert Carlile and John Guyton for taxes due for the year 1791. {Ref: IL 31.16, 31.19}

RENSHAW, ROBERT, head of family in 1800 (4th District). {Ref: CI}

REVOE, JOHN, see "James Phillips," q.v.

REYLEY, GEORGE, insolvent on a list for 1791 in Gunpowder Upper and Bush River Lower Hundreds, as filed by John Bond, Deputy Sheriff, on Sep 20, 1791. {Ref: IL 31.24}

REYNOLDS, HUGH, see "Hugh Rynolds," q.v.

RIADE(?), MATTHEW, insolvent on a list for the road tax due for 1791 in Harford Upper, Harford Lower, and Spesutia Upper as returned by Robert Amos, Jr. on Sep 18, 1793. {Ref: IL 31.18}

RICE, DAVID, head of family in 1800 (3rd District). {Ref: CI}

RICE, DICK (negro), insolvent on a list for the county tax due for 1793 in Harford Upper, Harford Lower, and Spesutia Lower Hundreds returned to the levy court by Thomas Taylor on May 28, 1794, but a line was drawn through his name. {Ref: IL 31.12}

RICE, JAMES, served on a Petit Jury in August, 1797. {Ref: CC}

RICE, WILLIAM, insolvent on a list for the road tax due for 1791 in Harford Upper, Harford Lower, and Spesutia Upper as returned by Robert Amos, Jr. on Sep 18, 1793. {Ref: IL 31.18}

RICE, WILLIAM, head of family in 1800 (2nd District). {Ref: CI}

RICHARDSON, BENJAMIN, tract *Future Prospect* surveyed between 1792 and 1796. {Ref: SB}

RICHARDSON, BENJAMIN, taxpayer, 1798, Deer Creek Upper Hd., 1 dwelling house, 1 inferior house, 2 acres, $160 valuation; 3 tracts (231 acres) in Deer Creek Upper Hd., $254.41 valuation, no slaves. {Ref: TL}

RICHARDSON, BENJAMIN ("dead"), insolvent on lists in 1791 due county taxes and road taxes in "Deer Creek Upper, Middle, and Broad Creek Hundreds" as returned by Robert Amos, Jr. {Ref: IL 31.12, 31.22}

RICHARDSON, BENJAMIN, served on a Grand Jury in August, 1800. {Ref: CM}

RICHARDSON, BENJAMIN, head of family in 1800 (4th District). {Ref: CI}

RICHARDSON, BENJAMIN AND SAMUEL, licensed retailers in August, 1797. {Ref: CC}

RICHARDSON, HARRY (negro), insolvent on a list for 1791 in Gunpowder Upper and Bush River Lower Hundreds, as filed by John Bond, Deputy Sheriff, on Sep 20, 1791. {Ref: IL 31.24}

RICHARDSON, HENRY, tracts *Falling Branch* and *Addition* surveyed between 1792 and 1796. {Ref: SB}

RICHARDSON, HENRY, taxpayer, 1798, Deer Creek Upper Hd., 5 tracts (440 acres, 40 perches) and 1 building, $1007.82 valuation, 2 slaves. {Ref: TL}

RICHARDSON, HENRY, served on a Petit Jury in March, 1798. {Ref: CM}

RICHARDSON, HENRY, insolvent on a list for the road tax for 1792, as returned for Robert Amoss, tax collector. {Ref: IL 13.12}

RICHARDSON, HENRY (captain), head of family in 1800 (4th District). {Ref: CI}

RICHARDSON, JAMES, insolvent on lists in 1791 due county taxes and road taxes in "Deer Creek Upper, Middle, and Broad Creek Hundreds" as returned by Robert Amos, Jr. {Ref: IL 31.12, 31.22}

RICHARDSON, JAMES, insolvent on a list of the county tax due William Osborn, sheriff, for 1791, as returned by Edward Prigg on Sep 20, 1791. {Ref: IL 31.17}

RICHARDSON, JAMES, insolvent on a list in 1792 in Broad Creek Hd., as returned by Benjamin Preston. {Ref: IL 31.03}

RICHARDSON, JAMES, head of family in 1800 (1st District). {Ref: CI}

RICHARDSON, MARGARET, wife of Vincent, b. 1800, d. Oct 13, 1873, aged 73, bur. in Christ Episcopal (Rock Spring) Church Cemetery. {Ref: TI}

RICHARDSON, MARY, head of family in 1800 (3rd District). {Ref: CI}

RICHARDSON, SAMUEL, taxpayer, 1798, Deer Creek Upper Hd., 1 tract (205 acres) and 1 building in Deer Creek Upper Hd., $403.59 valuation, no slaves. {Ref: TL}

RICHARDSON, SAMUEL, mentioned in a survey deposition on Sep 27, 1799. {Ref: JS}

RICHARDSON, SAMUEL, head of family in 1800 (4th District). {Ref: CI}

RICHARDSON, SAMUEL AND BENJAMIN, licensed retailers in August, 1797. {Ref: CC}

RICHARDSON, SARAH, bur. Aug 21, 1793, aged 8 years. {Ref: PR}

RICHARDSON, THOMAS, served on a Petit Jury in March, 1798 and March, 1799. {Ref: CM}

RICHARDSON, THOMAS, taxpayer, 1798, Gunpowder Upper Hd., 1 dwelling house, 1 inferior house, 2 acres, $106 valuation; 2 tracts (222 acres) in Gunpowder Upper Hd., $598.50 valuation, no slaves. {Ref: TL}

RICHARDSON, THOMAS, head of family in 1800 (3rd District). {Ref: CI}

RICHARDSON, VINCENT, see "Margaret Richardson," q.v.

RICHARDSON, WILLIAM, taxpayer, 1798, Gunpowder Upper Hd., 1 dwelling house, 4 inferior houses, 2 acres, $130 valuation; 5 tracts (448 acres) in Gunpowder Upper Hd., $873.56 valuation, 2 slaves. {Ref: TL}

RICHARDSON, WILLIAM, served on a Grand Jury in August, 1799. {Ref: CM}

RICHARDSON, WILLIAM, insolvent on a list for the road tax for 1792, as returned for Robert Amoss, tax collector. {Ref: IL 13.12}

RICHARSDON, WILLIAM, will probated Dec 24, 1799. {Ref: HW}

RICHARDSON, WILLIAM, head of family in 1800 (3rd District). {Ref: CI}

RICHARDSON, WILLIAM, head of family in 1800 (5th District). {Ref: CI}

RICHMOND, SAMUEL, insolvent on list returned for the road tax due for 1791 by John Bull. {Ref: IL 31.14}

RICHMOND, SAMUEL, insolvent on a list for 1791 in Gunpowder Upper and Bush River Lower Hundreds, as filed by John Bond, Deputy Sheriff, on Sep 20, 1791. {Ref: IL 31.24}

RICKETS, SAMUEL, taxpayer, 1798, Gunpowder Lower Hd., 1 dwelling house, 6 inferior houses, 2 acres, $600 valuation; 1 tract (500 acres) in Gunpowder Lower Hd., $2812.50 valuation, 5 slaves. {Ref: TL}

RICKETTS, EDWARD, insolvent on lists returned for the county and road taxes due for 1791 by John Bull in Gunpowder Lower Hundred. {Ref: IL 31.14, 31.15}

RICKETTS, SAMUEL, head of family in 1800 (1st District). {Ref: CI}
RICKETTS, SAMUEL SR., will probated Jan 2, 1799. {Ref: HW}
RIDAL, ANDREW, insolvent, Harford Lower and Spesutia Lower Hundreds (listed as a single man), on a tax list returned by George Lyttle on Sep 21, 1791. {Ref: IL 31.20, 31.21}
RIDDEL, ANDREW, head of family in 1800 (2nd District). {Ref: CI}
RIDDLE, ANDREW, had an account at Hall's Store in March, 1791. {Ref: WH}
RIDDLE, ANDREW, insolvent on a list for the road tax due for 1791 in Harford Upper, Harford Lower, and Spesutia Upper as returned by Robert Amos, Jr. on Sep 18, 1793. {Ref: IL 31.18}. Also see "Benedict Edward Hall," q.v.
RIDGELY, HENRY (esquire), Chief Justice of the County Court, 1797-1800. {Ref: CC, CM}
RIEBIT(?), JOHN, head of family in 1800 (5th District). {Ref: CI}
RIER, ROBERT, see "John Quarrells," q.v.
RIETENOUR (RICTENOUR?), NICHOLAS' HEIRS, taxpayers, 1798, Spesutia Lower Hd., 1 tract (132 perches, 63 sq. ft.), $40.50 valuation, no slaves. {Ref: TL}
RIGBIE, JAMES, see "Negro Jacob," q.v.
RIGBIE, JAMES, on "a list of insolvents it being for personal property for the road taxs [sic] for 1791" filed by Robert Amoss, tax collector. {Ref: IL 31.12}
RIGBIE, JAMES, tract *Rigbie's Chance* surveyed between 1792 and 1796. {Ref: SB}
RIGBIE, JAMES, will probated Jan 24, 1791. {Ref: HW}
RIGBIE (RIGBY), JAMES, head of family in 1800 (4th District). {Ref: CI}
RIGBIE, JAMES JR., treated by Dr. Archer on Feb 23, 1791. {Ref: JA}
RIGBIE, JAMES JR., insolvent on a list in 1792 in Deer Creek Lower Hd., as returned by Benjamin Preston. {Ref: IL 31.03}
RIGDON, ALEXANDER, see "Elizabeth Rigdon," q.v.
RIGDON, ALEXANDER, tracts *Piney Grove* and *Rigdon's Angle* surveyed between 1792 and 1796, and tract *Trout Run* surveyed in 1798. {Ref: CB, SB}
RIGDON, ALEXANDER, served on a Petit Jury in August, 1797. {Ref: CC}
RIGDON, ALEXANDER, taxpayer, 1798, Deer Creek Upper Hd., 1 dwelling house, 6 inferior houses, 2 acres, $300 valuation; 6 tracts (888 acres, 120 perches) in Deer Creek Upper Hd., $1423.57 valuation, 5 slaves; also, taxpayer, Deer Creek Upper Hd., 3 buildings (occupants: John Hayes, John Hayes, Jr., and Robert McCreary), $90 valuation, no slaves. {Ref: TL}
RIGDON, ALEXANDER, treated by Dr. Archer on Feb 3, 1790 or 1799 (illegible). {Ref: JA}
RIGDON, ALEXANDER, head of family in 1800 (5th District). {Ref: CI}
RIGDON, ALEXANDER, b. Apr 5, 1796, d. Apr 14, 1850, aged 54 years and 9 days, bur. in Cherry Hill (Rock Ridge) Baptist Church Cemetery. {Ref: TI}
RIGDON, ALEXANDER (colonel), tract *Mount Defiance* surveyed between 1792 and 1796. {Ref: SB}
RIGDON, ANN, will probated Oct 3, 1797. {Ref: HW}. Also see "Elizabeth Rigdon," q.v.

RIGDON, BAKER, see "James Garrett," q.v.

RIGDON, BAKER, taxpayer, 1798, Deer Creek Middle Hd., 1 tract (147 acres) and 1 building, $292.50 valuation, no slaves. {Ref: TL}

RIGDON, BAKER, head of family in 1800 (5th District). {Ref: CI}

RIGDON, BENJAMIN, taxpayer, 1798, Deer Creek Upper Hd., 1 dwelling house, 6 inferior houses, 2 acres, $110 valuation; 1 tract (349 acres, 40 perches) in Deer Creek Upper Hd., $567.37 valuation, 2 slaves. {Ref: TL}

RIGDON, BENJAMIN, head of family in 1800 (5th District). {Ref: CI}

RIGDON (RIGDEN), CHARLES, taxpayer, 1798, Susquehanna Hd., 1 dwelling house, 4 inferior houses, 2 acres, $100.10 valuation; 2 tracts (121 acres) in Susquehanna Hd., $1059.75 valuation, no slaves. {Ref: TL}. Also see "Rachel Rigdon" and "Jane Rigdon" and "Henry Rigdon," q.v.

RIGDON, ELIZABETH, dau. of Alexander and Ann, b. Sep 25, 1787, bapt. Jun 29, 1797. {Ref: PR}

RIGDON, HENRY, son of Charles, b. Aug 26, 1799. {Ref: PR}

RIGDON, JANE, dau. of Charles, b. Dec 21, 1796. {Ref: PR}

RIGDON, MARTHA, b. 1791, d. Mar 15, 1865, in her 74th year, bur. in Cherry Hill (Rock Ridge) Baptist Church Cemetery. {Ref: TI}

RIGDON, RACHEL, dau. of Charles, b. Apr 22, 1795. {Ref: PR}

RIGDON, SARAH, m. Thomas Chesholm on Jan 28, 1796. {Ref: PR}

RIGDON, STEPHEN, taxpayer, 1798, Deer Creek Middle Hd., 1 dwelling house, 7 inferior houses, 2 acres, $300 valuation; 3 tracts (645 acres, 80 perches) in Deer Creek Middle Hd., $1255.50 valuation, 5 slaves. {Ref: TL}

RIGDON, STEPHEN, served on a Grand Jury in August, 1798 and August, 1799 and August, 1800. {Ref: CM}

RIGDON, STEPHEN, b. 1791, d. Mar 22, 1865, bur. in Cherry Hill (Rock Ridge) Baptist Church Cemetery. {Ref: TI}

RIGDON, STEPHEN, head of family in 1800 (5th District). {Ref: CI}

RIGDON, WILLIAM, head of family in 1800 (3rd District). {Ref: CI}

RIGHT, BLAYS, head of family in 1800 (4th District). {Ref: CI}

RIGHT, JAMES, head of family in 1800 (1st District). {Ref: CI}

RIGHT, JOHN, head of family in 1800 (4th District). {Ref: CI}

RIGHT, JOHN, head of family in 1800 (5th District). {Ref: CI}

RIGHT, THOMAS, head of family in 1800 (3rd District). {Ref: CI}

RILEY, GEORGE, insolvent on a list for county taxes due in 1792 as returned by Benjamin Preston. {Ref: IL 31.00}

RILEY, JAMES W., b. Apr 10, 1796, d. Mar 11, 1856, bur. in Cokesbury Methodist Cemetery in Abingdon. {Ref: TI}

RILEY, TARRANCE, head of family in 1800 (1st District). {Ref: CI}

RILEY, WILLIAM, b. 1795, d. Aug 15, 1862, in his 67th year, bur. in Ebenezer Methodist Church Cemetery north of Rutledge. {Ref: TI}

RINGOLD, JOHN, insolvent on a list for 1791 in Gunpowder Upper and Bush

River Lower Hundreds, as filed by John Bond, Deputy Sheriff, on Sep 20, 1791. {Ref: IL 31.24}
RITTOW, ENOCH, head of family in 1800 (5th District). {Ref: CI}. Also see "Enoch Rattow," q.v.
ROACH, MARTHA, head of family in 1800 (5th District). {Ref: CI}
ROACH, NATHANIEL, see "William Ashmore," q.v.
ROACH, WILLIAM, m. Elizabeth Hambleton on Jan 27, 1793. {Ref: PR}
ROADS, ANDREW, head of family in 1800 (Havre de Grace). {Ref: CI}
ROADS, MARY ("old and poor"), insolvent on a list for 1791 in Gunpowder Upper and Bush River Lower Hundreds, as filed by John Bond, Deputy Sheriff, on Sep 20, 1791. {Ref: IL 31.24}
ROADS, MARY, head of family in 1800 (3rd District). {Ref: CI}
ROADS, THOMAS, insolvent on a list for 1791 in Gunpowder Upper and Bush River Lower Hundreds, as filed by John Bond, Deputy Sheriff, on Sep 20, 1791. {Ref: IL 31.24}
ROBERSON, ARCHIBALD, head of family in 1800 (3rd District). {Ref: CI}
ROBERSON, JOHN, head of family in 1800 (2nd District). {Ref: CI}
ROBERSON, JOSEPH, head of family in 1800 (2nd District). {Ref: CI}
ROBERSON, JOSEPH, head of family in 1800 (Belle Air). {Ref: CI}
ROBERSON, JOSEPH, head of family in 1800 (4th District); two men by this name in this district. {Ref: CI}
ROBERSON, WILLIAM, head of family in 1800 (1st District). {Ref: CI}
ROBERSON, WILLIAM, head of family in 1800 (3rd District). {Ref: CI}
ROBERSON, WILLIAM, head of family in 1800 (4th District); two men by this name in this district. {Ref: CI}
ROBERTS, ARCHIBALD, AND BARTON, THOMAS, tract *Barton's Chance in the Risen* surveyed between 1792 and 1796. {Ref: SB}
ROBERTS, BILLINGSLEY, served as constable in Gunpowder Lower Hd., 1797. {Ref: CC}
ROBERTS, HENRY, taxpayer, 1798, Bush River Lower Hd., 1 dwelling house, 2 inferior houses, 1 acre, $300 valuation; 1 tract (46 acres, 120 perches) in Bush River Lower Hd., $893.25 valuation, no slaves. {Ref: TL}
ROBERTS (ROBERDS), HENRY, head of family in 1800 (3rd District). {Ref: CI}
ROBERTS, ISAAC, head of family in 1800 (1st District). {Ref: CI}. Also see "Benjamin Rumsey," q.v.
ROBERTS, ISAIAH, served as constable in Gunpowder Hd., 1797 (which listed Billingsley Roberts first and then crossed out "Billingsley" and wrote "Isaiah" over it). {Ref: CM}
ROBERTS, JOHN, insolvent on lists in 1791 due county taxes and road taxes in "Deer Creek Upper, Middle, and Broad Creek Hundreds" as returned by Robert Amos, Jr. {Ref: IL 31.12, 31.22}
ROBERTS, JOHN, head of family in 1800 (1st District). {Ref: CI}
ROBERTS, OWEN, m. Jane Vansick on Jun 3, 1798. {Ref: PR}

283

ROBERTS, PETER JOHN, m. Maria Sanderson on Apr 23, 1792. {Ref: PR}
ROBERTSON, DANIEL (Baltimore Town), taxpayer, 1798, Harford Upper Hd., 1 dwelling house, 2 inferior houses, 2 acres, $200 valuation; 2 tracts (198 acres) in Harford Upper Hd., $594 valuation, no slaves. {Ref: TL}
ROBERTSON, MARY, see "Susanna Robertson," q.v.
ROBERTSON, SUSANNA, dau. of William and Mary, b. Nov 2, 1799, bapt. Nov 10, 1800. {Ref: PR}
ROBERTSON, WILLIAM, see "Susanna Robertson," q.v.
ROBINETT, ELIZABETH, of Joppa, bur. Feb 14, 1796 (age not given). {Ref: PR}
ROBINSON, ABRAHAM, insolvent on a list for the road tax due for 1791 in Harford Upper, Harford Lower, and Spesutia Upper as returned by Robert Amos, Jr. on Sep 18, 1793. {Ref: IL 31.18}
ROBINSON, ARCHIBALD, licensed practicing attorney in March, 1795. {Ref: CC}
ROBINSON, ARCHIBALD, taxpayer, 1798, Gunpowder Upper Hd., 1 dwelling house, 6 inferior houses, 2 acres, $120 valuation; 2 tracts (144 acres, 40 perches) in Gunpowder Upper Hd., $243.43 valuation, 1 slave. {Ref: TL}
ROBINSON, ARCHIBALD, insolvent on a list for the road tax for 1792, as returned for Robert Amoss, tax collector. {Ref: IL 13.12}
ROBINSON, CHARLES, insolvent on a list for the road tax due for 1791 in Harford Upper, Harford Lower, and Spesutia Upper as returned by Robert Amos, Jr. on Sep 18, 1793. {Ref: IL 31.18}
ROBINSON, CHARLES (Baltimore County), taxpayer, 1798, Harford Upper Hd., 1 tract (153 acres) in Harford Upper Hd., $286.88 valuation, no slaves. {Ref: TL}
ROBINSON, DANIEL, insolvent on a list for the road tax for 1792, as returned for Robert Amoss, tax collector. {Ref: IL 13.12}
ROBINSON, ELIZABETH, insolvent on a list for 1791 in Gunpowder Upper and Bush River Lower Hundreds, as filed by John Bond, Deputy Sheriff, on Sep 20, 1791. {Ref: IL 31.24}. Also see "John Bankhead," q.v.
ROBINSON, HUGH, insolvent on a list for 1791 in Gunpowder Upper and Bush River Lower Hundreds, as filed by John Bond, Deputy Sheriff, on Sep 20, 1791 (who listed him as a single man). {Ref: IL 31.24}
ROBINSON, HUGH, insolvent on list returned for the road tax due for 1791 by John Bull. {Ref: IL 31.14}
ROBINSON, JAMES, see "Margaret Robinson" and "Jane Robinson" and "John Robinson," q.v.
ROBINSON, JAMES, charged for assaulting John Cooper in 1794. {Ref: CD, March Term, 1795}
ROBINSON, JAMES, charged for disturbing the peace towards Thomas Ayres in 1794 and ordered to keep the peace in 1795. {Ref: CD, March Term, 1795}
ROBINSON, JANE, dau. of James and Mary, b. Jan 14, 1790, bapt. Sep 18, 1796. {Ref: PR}
ROBINSON, JOHN, son of James and Mary, b. Apr 11, 1787, bapt. Sep 18, 1796. {Ref: PR}
ROBINSON, JOSEPH, see "William Robinson" and "Peregrine Browning," q.v.

ROBINSON, JOSEPH, taxpayer, 1798, Bush River Lower Hd., 1 dwelling house, 2 inferior houses, 80 perches, $750 valuation; 4 tracts (101 acres) in Bush River Lower Hd., $337.50 valuation, no slaves. {Ref: TL}

ROBINSON, JOSEPH, licensed ordinary (tavern) in March, 1795 and August, 1797. {Ref: CC}

ROBINSON, JOSEPH, charged for selling liquors by the gallon and fined £6 in 1797. {Ref: CD, March Term, 1797}

ROBINSON, JOSEPH, charged for disturbing the peace towards Thomas Ayres in 1794 and ordered to keep the peace in 1795. {Ref: CD, March Term, 1795}

ROBINSON, MARGARET, wife of William, b. 1794, d. Feb 1, 1880, in her 86th year, bur. in Union Chapel Methodist Church Cemetery at Wilna. {Ref: TI}

ROBINSON, MARGARET, dau. of James and Mary, b. May 27, 1792, bapt. Sep 18, 1796. {Ref: PR}

ROBINSON, MARGARETT, of St. John's Parish, bur. Aug 1, 1793, aged 60. {Ref: PR}

ROBINSON, MARTHA S., b. 1800, d. Feb 12, 1875, aged 75, bur. in Churchville Presbyterian Church Cemetery. {Ref: TI}

ROBINSON, MARY, see "Margaret Robinson" and "Jane Robinson" and "John Robinson," q.v.

ROBINSON, MARY, charged for disturbing the peace towards Thomas Ayres in 1794 and ordered to keep the peace in 1795. {Ref: CD, March Term, 1795}

ROBINSON, MARY, b. Sep 8, 1797, d. Nov 8, 1886, bur. in Ebenezer Methodist Church Cemetery north of Rutledge. {Ref: TI}

ROBINSON, RICHARD, insolvent on a list for the road tax for 1792, as returned for Robert Amoss, tax collector. {Ref: IL 13.12}

ROBINSON, SAM, insolvent on a list for the road tax due for 1791 in Harford Upper, Harford Lower, and Spesutia Upper as returned by Robert Amos, Jr. on Sep 18, 1793. {Ref: IL 31.18}

ROBINSON, SAMUEL, insolvent, Harford Lower and Spesutia Lower Hundreds (listed as a single man), on a tax list returned by George Lyttle on Sep 21, 1791. {Ref: IL 31.20, 31.21}

ROBINSON, SAMUEL, b. 1797, d. Feb 8, 1858, aged 61, bur. in Churchville Presbyterian Church Cemetery. {Ref: TI}

ROBINSON, WALTER, insolvent on lists of taxes due in 1791 and 1792 in Broad Creek Hd., as returned by Robert Amos, Jr. in 1791 and Benjamin Preston in 1792. {Ref: IL 31.03, 31.12, 31.22}

ROBINSON, WILLIAM, see "Margaret Robinson" and "Daniel Norris," q.v.

ROBINSON, WILLIAM, taxpayer, 1798, Broad Creek Hd., 1 tract (60 acres), $101.25 valuation, no slaves. {Ref: TL}

ROBINSON, WILLIAM, taxpayer, 1798, Bush River Upper & Eden Hd., 1 dwelling house, 2 inferior houses, 2 acres, $150 valuation; 1 tract (88 acres) in Bush River Upper & Eden Hd., $148.50 valuation, no slaves. {Ref: TL}

ROBINSON, WILLIAM, charged for disturbing the peace towards Thomas Ayres in 1794 and ordered to keep the peace in 1795. {Ref: CD, March Term, 1795}

ROBINSON, WILLIAM, insolvent, Harford Lower and Spesutia Lower Hundreds, on a tax list returned by George Lyttle on Sep 21, 1791. {Ref: IL 31.20, 31.21}

ROBINSON, WILLIAM, insolvent on list returned by Robert Carlile for taxes due for the year 1791. {Ref: IL 31.16}

ROBINSON, WILLIAM, insolvent on a list for the road tax due for 1791 in Harford Upper, Harford Lower, and Spesutia Upper as returned by Robert Amos, Jr. on Sep 18, 1793. {Ref: IL 31.18}

ROBINSON, WILLIAM, insolvent on a list for 1791 in Gunpowder Upper and Bush River Lower Hundreds, as filed by John Bond, Deputy Sheriff, on Sep 20, 1791 (who listed him as a single man). {Ref: IL 31.24}

ROBINSON, WILLIAM, mentioned in a survey deposition on Jan 22, 1800 as "to the house Wm. Robinson now lives in." {Ref: JS}

ROBINSON, WILLIAM, son of Joseph Robinson and husband of Mary Elizabeth Kirkwood, b. 1795, d. Oct 1, 1849, bur. in Bethel Presbyterian Church Cemetery at Madonna. {Ref: BC}

ROBISON, MARGARET (widow), treated by Dr. Archer on Jun 21, 1793. {Ref: JA}

ROBISON, SARAH, m. William Knight on Oct 1, 1797. {Ref: PR}

ROBSON, WALTER ("run"), insolvent on a list of the county tax due William Osborn, sheriff, for 1791, as returned by Edward Prigg on Sep 20, 1791. {Ref: IL 31.17}

ROCK, THOMAS, m. Rebecca Reed on May 29, 1791. {Ref: PR}

ROCKHOLD, ELIJAH, b. May 20, 1795, d. Apr 28, 1863, bur. in Ebenezer Methodist Church Cemetery north of Rutledge. {Ref: TI}. Also see "Rachael Rockhold," q.v.

ROCKHOLD, JOHN, served as constable in Bush River Lower Hd., 1797-1800. {Ref: CC, CM}

ROCKHOLD, JOHN, taxpayer, 1798, Bush River Lower Hd., 1 dwelling house, 2 inferior houses, 80 perches, $210 valuation, no slaves. {Ref: TL}

ROCKHOLD, JOHN, charged for neglect of his duty as contable in 1795. {Ref: CD, March and August Terms, 1795 and 1797}

ROCKHOLD, JOHN, insolvent on list returned by Robert Carlile for taxes due for the year 1791. {Ref: IL 31.16}

ROCKHOLD, JOHN, head of family in 1800 (Belle Air). {Ref: CI}

ROCKHOLD, JOHN, head of family in 1800 (4th District). {Ref: CI}

ROCKHOLD, JOHN, JR., head of family in 1800 (Belle Air). {Ref: CI}

ROCKHOLD, LANSLET, head of family in 1800 (4th District). {Ref: CI}

ROCKHOLD, RACHAEL, wife of Elijah, b. May 15, 1792, d. Dec 15, 18--(?), bur. in Ebenezer Methodist Church Cemetery north of Rutledge. {Ref: TI}

ROCKHOLD, THOMAS, insolvent on lists returned by Robert Carlile and John Guyton for taxes due for the year 1791. {Ref: IL 31.16, 31.19}

ROCKWELL, CHARLES, head of family in 1800 (4th District). {Ref: CI}

RODES, BILL (negro), see "Negro Fanny," q.v.

RODGERS, ALEXANDER, served on a Petit Jury in August, 1799. {Ref: CM}

RODGERS, JOSEPH, head of family in 1800 (5th District). {Ref: CI}
RODGERS, THOMAS, treated by Dr. Archer in 1790-1791. {Ref: JA}
RODGERS, WILLIAM, m. Mary Hanna on Mar 20, 1800. {Ref: PR}
RODIEFER, PETER (miller at Cranberry Mill), had an account at Hall's Store in July, 1791. {Ref: WH}
ROGAN, THOMAS, charged (twice) for selling liquors by the smalls in 1797. {Ref: CD, March and August Terms, 1797}
ROGERS, ALEXANDER (esquire), head of family in 1800 (Havre de Grace). {Ref: CI}
ROGERS, ANN, m. John Hanna on Mar 22, 1796. {Ref: PR}
ROGERS, BENJAMIN, insolvent on lists in 1791 due county taxes and road taxes in "Deer Creek Upper, Middle, and Broad Creek Hundreds" as returned by Robert Amos, Jr. {Ref: IL 31.12, 31.22}
ROGERS, BENJAMIN, head of family in 1800 (5th District). {Ref: CI}
ROGERS, ELIZABETH, taxpayer, 1798, Spesutia Lower Hd., 1 dwelling house, 1 inferior house, 44 perches, 21 sq. ft., $450 valuation, no slaves. {Ref: TL}
ROGERS, JOHN, b. 1799, d. Sep 23, 1871, in his 82nd year, bur. in Deer Creek Methodist Church Cemetery at Chestnut Hill. {Ref: TI}
ROGERS, JOHN'S (COLONEL) HEIRS, or JOHN MILLIGAN, taxpayers, 1798, Broad Creek Hd., 1 dwelling house, 2 acres (John Milligan or Milagen, occupant), $200 valuation; 6 tracts (263 acres) in Broad Creek Hd. (John Milligan, occupant), $774 valuation, no slaves. {Ref: TL}
ROGERS, JOSEPH, taxpayer, 1798, Broad Creek Hd., 1 tract (96 acres) and 1 building, $189 valuation, no slaves. {Ref: TL}
ROGERS, RICHARD, head of family in 1800 (1st District). {Ref: CI}
ROGERS, ROLEN, head of family in 1800 (3rd District). {Ref: CI}
ROGERS, ROWLAND, insolvent on a list for the road tax for 1792, as returned for Robert Amoss, tax collector. {Ref: IL 13.12}. Also see "Joseph Hayes," q.v.
ROGERS, SAMUEL, see "Zacheus Bond," q.v.
ROGERS, SAMUEL, insolvent on a list in 1792 in Deer Creek Lower Hd., as returned by Benjamin Preston. {Ref: IL 31.03}
ROGERS, SAMUEL ("gone"), insolvent on lists due for 1790 and 1791 "fund taxes" and road tax in Deer Creek Lower Hd., as returned by Thomas Taylor. {Ref: IL 31.12}
ROGERS, SAMUEL, head of family in 1800 (5th District). {Ref: CI}
ROGERS, SARAH, b. 1791, d. Sep 11, 1868, in her 77th year, bur. in Deer Creek Methodist Church Cemetery at Chestnut Hill. {Ref: TI}
ROGERS (ROGES?), THOMAS, insolvent on a list for the road tax due for 1791 in Harford Upper, Harford Lower, and Spesutia Upper as returned by Robert Amos, Jr. on Sep 18, 1793. {Ref: IL 31.18}
ROGERS, WILLIAM, insolvent on lists in 1791 due county taxes and road taxes in "Deer Creek Upper, Middle, and Broad Creek Hundreds" as returned by Robert Amos, Jr. {Ref: IL 31.12, 31.22}
ROGERS, WILLIAM, head of family in 1800 (3rd District). {Ref: CI}

ROGERS, WILLIAM, head of family in 1800 (5th District). {Ref: CI}
ROOMS, ELIZABETH, head of family in 1800 (5th District). {Ref: CI}
ROOT, CATHARINE, dau. of Samuel and Mary Magdalen, b. Apr 27, 1796, bapt. Sep 11, 1796. {Ref: PR}
ROOT, JOHN, son of Samuel and Mary Magdalen, b. Feb 7, 1794, bapt. Sep 11, 1796. {Ref: PR}
ROOT, MARY MAGDALEN, see "Catharine Root" and "John Root," q.v.
ROOT, SAMUEL, see "Catharine Root" and "John Root," q.v.
ROSE, AQUILLA, head of family in 1800 (3rd District). {Ref: CI}
ROSE, JOSEPH, insolvent on list returned by Robert Carlile for taxes due for the year 1791. {Ref: IL 31.16}
ROSS, DAVID (major), of Kentucky(?), or WILLIAM MIDDLETON, WILLIAM BAKER, AND WHEELEN (WHEELER?) MAULSBY, taxpayers, 1798, Gunpowder Lower Hd., 1 dwelling house, 6 inferior houses, 2 acres, $300 valuation; 4 tracts (1644 acres) in Gunpowder Lower Hd., $9091.68 valuation, 9 slaves; also, taxpayers, Gunpowder Lower Hd., 1 dwelling house, 2 inferior houses, 2 acres, $200 valuation, no additional slaves. {Ref: TL}. The total tax was $42.87 and divided as follows: William Middleton $19.83, William Baker $6.68, and Wheelen (Wheeler?) Maulsby $16.36; yet, none of them were listed as occupants of the land.
ROSS, MARY, see "Richard Ruff," q.v.
ROSS, PETER, m. Arabella Carter on Aug 14, 1800. {Ref: PR}
ROSS, PETER, head of family in 1800 (2nd District). {Ref: CI}
ROSS, PETER, head of family in 1800 (5th District). {Ref: CI}
ROSS, ROBERT (negro), insolvent on a list for the road tax due for 1791 in Harford Upper, Harford Lower, and Spesutia Upper as returned by Robert Amos, Jr. on Sep 18, 1793. {Ref: IL 31.18}
ROSS, ROBERT (a free negro), taxpayer, 1798, Spesutia Lower Hd., 1 tract (40 acres) and 1 building, $253.12 valuation, no slaves. {Ref: TL}
ROUGHCORN, SIMON, see "Simon Ruffcorn," q.v.
ROW (ROWE), CONRAD, head of family in 1800 (Abingdon). {Ref: CI}. Also see "Sarah Row," q.v.
ROW, MARY, see "Sarah Row," q.v.
ROW, SARAH, dau. of Conrad and Mary, b. Feb 14, 1800, bapt. Nov 10, 1800. {Ref: PR}
ROW, WILLIAM, insolvent on list returned by Robert Carlile for taxes due for the year 1791. {Ref: IL 31.16}
ROWAN, ROBERT, insolvent on list returned for the county tax for 1791 by William Osburn in Gunpowder Lower Hd. (which listed him as a single man). {Ref: IL 31.15}
ROWAN, WILLIAM, insolvent on list returned by Robert Carlile for taxes due for the year 1791. {Ref: IL 31.16}
RUCKMAN, THOMAS, insolvent on lists in 1791 due county taxes and road taxes

in "Deer Creek Upper, Middle, and Broad Creek Hundreds" as returned by Robert Amos, Jr. {Ref: IL 31.12, 31.22}

RUFF, ----, bur. Nov 13, 1800. {Ref: PR}

RUFF, DANIEL, taxpayer, 1798, Bush River Lower Hd., 1 dwelling house, 3 inferior houses, 1 acre, 9 perches, $300 valuation; 1 tract (3 acres, 27 perches) in Bush River Lower Hd., $67.50 valuation, no slaves. {Ref: TL}

RUFF, DANIEL, head of family in 1800 (2nd District). {Ref: CI}

RUFF, ELIZABETH, wife of James, b. 1798, d. Mar 6, 1866, in her 68th year, bur. in Watters Memorial Methodist Church Cemetery on Thomas Run. {Ref: TI}

RUFF, HAN, see "Henry Ruff, Sr.," q.v.

RUFF, HENRY, see "James Ruff (of Henry)" and "Henry Ruff, Sr." and "Bernard Preston's heirs," q.v.

RUFF, HENRY, head of family in 1800 (3rd District). {Ref: CI}

RUFF, HENRY JR., head of family in 1800 (3rd District). {Ref: CI}

RUFF, HENRY JR. ("for Bernard Preston's heirs"), taxpayer, 1798, Spesutia Upper Hd., 2 tracts (262 acres), $974.25 valuation, no slaves. {Ref: TL}.

RUFF, HENRY JR., taxpayer, 1798, Spesutia Upper Hd., 2 tracts (92 acres), $207 valuation, 1 slave. {Ref: TL}

RUFF, HENRY SR., taxpayer, 1798, Spesutia Upper Hd., 1 dwelling house, 4 inferior houses, 1 acre, $250 valuation; 2 tracts (267 acres) in Spesutia Upper Hd., $1201.50 valuation, 4 slaves. {Ref: TL}

RUFF, HENRY SR. (farmer), treated by Dr. Archer on Feb 2, 1791 and Mar 26, 1793; also mentioned sons Henry, Richard, and Han [sic] in 1791. {Ref: JA}

RUFF, HENRY'S HEIRS, taxpayers, 1798, Harford Upper Hd., 1 dwelling house, 4 inferior houses, 2 acres, $500 valuation; 2 tracts (56 acres) and 1 building in Harford Upper Hd., $255.37 valuation, no slaves. {Ref: TL}. In another part of the tax schedule the occupant is listed as Widow Ruff.

RUFF, JAMES, b. 1791, d. May 9, 1875, in his 84th year, bur. in Watters Memorial Methodist Church Cemetery on Thomas Run. {Ref: TI}. Also see "Elizabeth Ruff," q.v.

RUFF, JAMES (OF HENRY), treated by Dr. Archer on Mar 4, 1793. {Ref: JA}

RUFF, JOHN, taxpayer, 1798, Harford Lower Hd., 1 dwelling house, 6 inferior houses, 2 acres, $350 valuation; 1 tract (298 acres) in Harford Lower Hd., $1709.77 valuation, 11 slaves. {Ref: TL}

RUFF, JOHN, will probated Feb 19, 1800. {Ref: HW}

RUFF, RICHARD, see "Henry Ruff, Sr.," q.v.

RUFF, RICHARD, subpoenaed to the Grand Jury in August, 1797. {Ref: CC}

RUFF, RICHARD, taxpayer, 1798, Harford Upper Hd., 1 dwelling house, 5 inferior houses, 2 acres, $400 valuation; 5 tracts (806 acres) and 1 building in Harford Upper Hd., $1513.69 valuation, 2 slaves; also, taxpayer, Harford Upper Hd., 1 building (John Bond, occupant), $33.75 valuation, no slaves. {Ref: TL}

RUFF, RICHARD, son of Richard Ruff and Mary Ross, b. Sep 10, 1779, bapt. Sep

16, 1795. {Ref: PR}

RUFF, RICHARD, head of family in 1800 (1st District). {Ref: CI}

RUFF, WIDOW, see "Henry Ruff's heirs," q.v.

RUFFCORN (RUFCORN, ROUGHCORN)), SIMON, insolvent on lists returned by Robert Carlile and John Guyton for taxes due for the year 1791, and on the 1791 road tax list of insolvents filed by Robert Amoss, Jr. in 1793. {Ref: IL 31.16, 31.19}

RUMSEY & TYSON, see "Tyson & Rumsey," q.v.

RUMSEY & VANBIBBER, taxpayer, 1798, Gunpowder Lower Hd., 1 tract (75 acres), $1125 valuation, no slaves. {Ref: TL}

RUMSEY, AMELIA, dau. of Henry and Hannah, b. Apr 14, 1792. {Ref: PR}

RUMSEY, BENJAMIN, taxpayer, 1798, Gunpowder Lower Hd., 1 dwelling house, 3 inferior houses, 2 acres, $500 valuation; 14 tracts (1413 acres, 40 perches) in Gunpowder Lower Hd., $3469.50 valuation, 10 slaves; also, taxpayer, Gunpowder Lower Hd., 1 dwelling house, 2 inferior houses, 1 acre (Isaac Roberts, occupant), $150 valuation, no slaves; also, taxpayer, Gunpowder Lower Hd., 1 dwelling house, 1 inferior house, 1 acre (John Devin, occupant), $150 valuation, no slaves. {Ref: TL}

RUMSEY, BENJAMIN, had an account at Hall's Store in February, 1791. {Ref: WH}

RUMSEY, BENJAMIN, et ux [and wife], tract *Ann's Delight* surveyed between 1792 and 1796. {Ref: SB}

RUMSEY, BENJAMIN (esquire), tract *White's Trail Resurveyed* surveyed between 1792 and 1796. {Ref: SB}

RUMSEY, BENJAMIN (esquire), treated by Dr. Archer on Aug 8, 1797; also mentioned dau. Hannah. {Ref: JA}

RUMSEY, BENJAMIN (colonel), head of family in 1800 (1st District). {Ref: CI}

RUMSEY, BENJAMIN JR., bur. Jan 20, 1799, aged about 24. {Ref: PR}

RUMSEY, CHARLES HENRY, son of Henry and Hannah, b. Aug 14, 1796. {Ref: PR}

RUMSEY, CHARLOTTE, see "Edward Aquila Howard," q.v.

RUMSEY, HANNAH, bur. Apr 24, 1797. {Ref: PR}. Also see "Benjamin Rumsey, Esq." and "Charles Henry Rumsey" and "Amelia Rumsey," q.v.

RUMSEY, HENRY, see "Amelia Rumsey" and "Charles Henry Rumsey," q.v.

RUMSEY, JOHN, taxpayer, 1798, Gunpowder Lower Hd., 1 dwelling house, 6 inferior houses, 2 acres, $400 valuation; 3 tracts (1094 acres) in Gunpowder Lower Hd., $2766.38 valuation, 13 slaves; also, taxpayer, Susquehanna Hd., 1 dwelling house, 4 inferior houses, 2 acres (Joseph Gallion, occupant), $100.10 valuation, no slaves; also, taxpayer, 6 buildings in Susquehanna Hd. (occupants: John Gallion, John McVay, Aquila Deaver, Michael Devin, William Spence, and Abraham Taylor), $112.30 valuation altogether, no slaves. {Ref: TL}

RUMSEY, JOHN, appointed a Judge of Elections in the 1st District on Jul 28, 1800; resignation filed on Dec 31, 1800. {Ref: CM}

RUMSEY, JOHN, tract *Addition to Amos' Delight* surveyed between 1792 and

1796. {Ref: SB}

RUMSEY, JOHN, bur. Jun 30, 1799. {Ref: PR}

RUMSEY, JOHN (esquire), treated by Dr. Archer on Jan 21, 1791; also mentioned his wife and dau. (no names given) in 1789. {Ref: JA}

RUMSEY, JOHN (esquire), head of family in 1800 (1st District). {Ref: CI}

RUSEL, DAVID, insolvent on list returned for the road tax due for 1791 by John Bull. {Ref: IL 31.14}

RUSH, ARNOLD, m. Jane or Janett Conn on Aug 27, 1792. {Ref: PR}

RUSH, ARNOLD, insolvent on a list for 1791 in Gunpowder Upper and Bush River Lower Hundreds, as filed by John Bond, Deputy Sheriff, on Sep 20, 1791 (who listed him as a single man). {Ref: IL 31.24}

RUSSEL, HUGH, head of family in 1800 (4th District). {Ref: CI}

RUSSELL, DANIEL, insolvent on a list for 1791 in Gunpowder Upper and Bush River Lower Hundreds, as filed by John Bond, Deputy Sheriff, on Sep 20, 1791 (who listed him as a single man). {Ref: IL 31.24}

RUTER, RICHARD, insolvent, Harford Lower and Spesutia Lower Hundreds, on a tax list returned by George Lyttle on Sep 21, 1791. {Ref: IL 31.20, 31.21}

RUTH, JACOB, insolvent on lists in 1791 due county taxes and road taxes in "Deer Creek Upper, Middle, and Broad Creek Hundreds" as returned by Robert Amos, Jr. {Ref: IL 31.12, 31.22}

RUTH, JACOB ("poor"), insolvent on a list of the county tax due William Osborn, sheriff, for 1791, as returned by Edward Prigg on Sep 20, 1791. {Ref: IL 31.17}

RUTH, JACOB, head of family in 1800 (4th District). {Ref: CI}

RUTH, JAMES, head of family in 1800 (4th District). {Ref: CI}

RUTH, MOSES, see "Alexander Young," q.v.

RUTH, THOMAS, head of family in 1800 (4th District). {Ref: CI}

RUTLEDGE, ABRAHAM, b. 1799, d. Mar 1, 1868, bur. in North Bend Cemetery. {Ref: TI}

RUTLEDGE, EDWARD, see "Louisa M. Rutledge," q.v.

RUTLEDGE, ELIZABETH, b. 1793, d. Mar 3, 1867, bur. in North Bend Cemetery. {Ref: TI}

RUTLEDGE, JACOB, taxpayer, 1798, Bush River Upper & Eden Hd., 1 dwelling house, 4 inferior houses, 2 acres, $400 valuation; 5 tracts (498 acres) in Bush River Upper & Eden Hd., $1120.50 valuation, 4 slaves. {Ref: TL}

RUTLEDGE, JACOB, served on a Petit Jury in March, 1799 and August, 1800. {Ref: CM}

RUTLEDGE, JACOB, head of family in 1800 (4th District). {Ref: CI}

RUTLEDGE, JOHN, served on a Grand Jury in March, 1798 and August, 1799. {Ref: CM}

RUTLEDGE, JOHN, taxpayer, 1798, Bush River Upper & Eden Hd., 1 dwelling house, 7 inferior houses, 2 acres, $1000 valuation; 2 tracts (558 acres) in Bush River Upper & Eden Hd., $1569.37 valuation, 7 slaves. {Ref: TL}

RUTLEDGE, JOHN, insolvent on a list for the road tax for 1792 for Robert Amoss, tax collector. {Ref: IL 13.12}

RUTLEDGE, JOHN, b. 1753, d. Aug 19, 1800, aged 47, bur. in the Rutledge Family Cemetery north of Jarrettsville. {Ref: TI}
RUTLEDGE, JOSHUA, see "Elizabeth Nelson," q.v.
RUTLEDGE, LOUISA M., wife of Col. Edward Rutledge, b. 1796, d. Sep 24, 1851, in her 55th year, bur. in McKendree Cemetery near Black Horse. {Ref: TI}
RUTLEDGE, RUTH, head of family in 1800 (4th District); two women by this name in this district. {Ref: CI}
RUTLEDGE, SHADRACH, taxpayer, 1798, Bush River Upper & Eden Hd., 1 dwelling house, 5 inferior houses, 2 acres, $300 valuation; 1 tract (145 acres) in Bush River Upper & Eden Hd., $285.19 valuation, no slaves. {Ref: TL}
RUTLEDGE, SHADRACK, head of family in 1800 (4th District). {Ref: CI}
RUTMAN, THOMAS, see "John Scarborough," q.v.
RUTTER, MARY, tract *Hazard* surveyed between 1792 and 1796. {Ref: SB}
RUTTER, RICHARD, insolvent on a list for the road tax due for 1791 in Harford Upper, Harford Lower, and Spesutia Upper as returned by Robert Amos, Jr. on Sep 18, 1793. {Ref: IL 31.18}. Also see "Richard Ruter," q.v.
RUTTER(?), THOMAS, head of family in 1800 (Belle Air). {Ref: CI}
RYAN, WILLIAM, insolvent on a list for 1791 in Gunpowder Upper and Bush River Lower Hundreds, as filed by John Bond, Deputy Sheriff, on Sep 20, 1791 (who listed him as a single man). {Ref: IL 31.24}
RYLEY, GEORGE, insolvent on list returned for the road tax due for 1791 by John Bull. {Ref: IL 31.14}
RYNOLDS, HUGH, insolvent on list returned for the road tax due for 1791 by John Bull. {Ref: IL 31.14}
SADLER, CHRISTIAN, taxpayer, 1798, Deer Creek Upper Hd., 1 tract (195 acres) and 1 building, $292.50 valuation, no slaves. {Ref: TL}
SAMPLE, CUNNINGHAM (esquire), treated by Dr. Archer on Aug 28, 1791 and Aug 7, 1798; also mentioned his wife (no name given) in 1791. {Ref: JA}
SAMPLE, JOHN, tract *Long Fought and Dear Bought* surveyed in 1788 and granted in 1796. {Ref: CB}
SAMPLE, JOHN, tract *Sample's Addition* surveyed in 1794 and granted in 1796. {Ref: CB, SB}
SAMPLE, JOHN (at Slate Ridge), treated by Dr. Archer on Apr 10, 1792. {Ref: JA}
SAMPLE, JOHN (York County), or JONATHAN HAMBLETON, taxpayer, 1798, Broad Creek Hd., 5 tracts (559 acres) and 1 building (Jonathan Hambleton, occupant), $990.30 valuation, no slaves. {Ref: TL}
SAMPLE, WILLIAM, insolvent on lists in 1791 due county taxes and road taxes in "Deer Creek Upper, Middle, and Broad Creek Hundreds" as returned by Robert Amos, Jr. {Ref: IL 31.12, 31.22}
SAMPLE, WILLIAM ("run"), insolvent on a list of the county tax due William Osborn, sheriff, for 1791, as returned by Edward Prigg on Sep 20, 1791. {Ref: IL 31.17}
SAMPSON, RICHARD, head of family in 1800 (3rd District). {Ref: CI}

SAMPSON, THOMAS, insolvent on list returned by Robert Carlile for taxes due for the year 1791. {Ref: IL 31.16}

SAMPSON (SAMSON), THOMAS, head of family in 1800 (1st District). {Ref: CI}

SAMUEL JAY & COMPANY, taxpayers, 1798, Spesutia Lower Hd., 1 dwelling house, 1 inferior house, 44 perches and 21 sq. ft. of land, $650 valuation; 1 tract (44 perches, 21 sq. ft.) in Spesutia Lower Hd., $621.25 valuation, 5 slaves; also, taxpayers, 1 dwelling house, 44 perches and 21 sq. ft. of land in Spesutia Lower Hd., $180 valuation, no slaves. {Ref: TL}

SAMUEL JAY & COMPANY, licensed retailers in March, 1795 and August, 1797. {Ref: CC}

SANDERS, CHARITY, see "Benjamin Vanhorn," q.v.

SANDERS, GREENBERRY, head of family in 1800 (1st District). {Ref: CI}

SANDERS, JOHN, head of family in 1800 (1st District). {Ref: CI}

SANDERS, JOSEPH, head of family in 1800 (Abingdon). {Ref: CI}

SANDERS, MOSES, head of family in 1800 (3rd District). {Ref: CI}

SANDERS, ROBERT, head of family in 1800 (1st District). {Ref: CI}

SANDERS, WILLIAM, head of family in 1800 (1st District). {Ref: CI}

SANDERSON, MARIA, see "Peter John Roberts," q.v.

SANDS, GRIFFEN, had an account at Hall's Store in October, 1791. {Ref: WH}

SANKEY & UNDERHILL, see "Underhill & Sankey," q.v.

SANKEY, GEORGE, head of family in 1800 (4th District). {Ref: CI}. Also see "Thomas Underhill," q.v.

SAPP, PETER, taxpayer, 1798, Spesutia Lower Hd., 1 tract (44 perches, 21 sq. ft.), $13.50 valuation, no slaves. {Ref: TL}

SAPPINGTON, ABIANN, wife of Dr. John K. Sappington and dau. of Gen. John Steel of Philadelphia, b. circa 1795, d. Jun 18, 1850, aged 53 or 55 years, 6 months, and 9 days, bur. in Grove Presbyterian Church Cemetery near Aberdeen. {Ref: TI}

SAPPINGTON, AMELIA JANE, wife of Dr. William Sappington and dau. of Henry and Hannah Ramsly(?), b. Apr 14, 1792, d. Feb 7, 1843, bur. in Blenheim Cemetery at Oakington. {Ref: TI}

SAPPINGTON, DOCTOR, had an account at Hall's Store in January, 1791. {Ref: WH}

SAPPINGTON, DOCTOR, consulted with Dr. Archer between 1787 and 1801. {Ref: JA}

SAPPINGTON, HARRIET, wife of Lemuel, b. Dec 8, 1798, d. Mar 29, 1859, bur. in Christ Episcopal (Rock Spring) Church Cemetery. {Ref: TI}

SAPPINGTON, JOHN K. (doctor), b. Jun 2, 1791, d. Aug 8, 1868, bur. in Grove Presbyterian Church Cemetery in Aberdeen. {Ref: TI}. Also see "Abiann Sappington," q.v.

SAPPINGTON, LEMUAL, see "Harriet Sappington," q.v.

SAPPINGTON, RICHARD (doctor), taxpayer, 1798, Susquehanna Hd., 1 tract (82 acres) and 1 building, $270 acres, no slaves. {Ref: TL}

SAPPINGTON (SAPINGTON), RICHARD (doctor), head of family in 1800 (2nd

District). {Ref: CI}

SAPPINGTON, WILLIAM (doctor), see "Amelia Jane Sappington," q.v.

SARFF, JOHN, see "John Scarff," q.v.

SAUNDERS, JAMES, insolvent on a list for 1791 in Gunpowder Upper and Bush River Lower Hundreds, as filed by John Bond, Deputy Sheriff, on Sep 20, 1791. {Ref: IL 31.24}

SAUNDERS, JOHN, charged for retailing liquors and for selling liquors by the smalls in 1797. {Ref: CD, March and August Terms, 1797}

SAUNDERS, JOHN, son of Joseph and Sarah, b. Mar 27, 1796, bapt. Jun 19, 1796. {Ref: PR}. Also see "William Hall," q.v.

SAUNDERS, JOHN C., b. 1794, d. Feb 20, 1872, aged 78, bur. in Angel Hill Cemetery in Havre de Grace. {Ref: TI}

SAUNDERS, JOSEPH, taxpayer, 1798, Bush River Lower Hd., 1 dwelling house, 2 inferior houses, 1 acre, $180 valuation, no slaves. {Ref: TL}. Also see "John Saunders," q.v.

SAUNDERS, MARY, b. 1796, d. Dec 2, 1880, aged 84, bur. in Angel Hill Cemetery in Havre de Grace. {Ref: TI}. Also see "William Hall," q.v.

SAUNDERS, ROBERT, taxpayer, 1798, Gunpowder Lower Hd., 1 dwelling house, 2 inferior houses, 2 acres, $120 valuation; 1 tract (394 acres) in Gunpowder Lower Hd., $2216.25 valuation, 5 slaves; also, taxpayer, Gunpowder Lower Hd., 1 tract (48 acres) and 1 building (James Price, occupant), $303.75 valuation, no slaves. {Ref: TL}

SAUNDERS, SARAH, see "John Saunders," q.v.

SAUNDERS, THOMAS, taxpayer, 1798, Gunpowder Lower Hd., 1 tract (10 acres) and 1 building, $33.75 valuation, no slaves. {Ref: TL}

SAUNDERS, THOMAS, insolvent on a list for 1791 in Gunpowder Upper and Bush River Lower Hundreds, as filed by John Bond, Deputy Sheriff, on Sep 20, 1791. {Ref: IL 31.24}

SAUNDERS, WILLIAM, see "Thomas Bond (of Thomas)," q.v.

SAVIN, THOMAS, bur. Dec 25, 1798. {Ref: PR}

SAWYER, CHARITY, b. 1798, d. Mar 16, 1882, aged 84, bur. in Mount Carmel Methodist Church Cemetery in Emmorton. {Ref: TI}

SCARBOROUGH, EUCLIDES, head of family in 1800 (5th District). {Ref: CI}

SCARBOROUGH, EUCLIDUS, insolvent on a list in 1792 in Broad Creek Hd., as returned by Benjamin Preston, but his name was then crossed off the list. {Ref: IL 31.03}

SCARBOROUGH, HANNAH, see "Samuel Scarborough" and "William Scarborough," q.v.

SCARBOROUGH, JAMES, see "Samuel Scarborough" and "William Scarborough," q.v.

SCARBOROUGH, JAMES, son of William and Mary, b. May 11, 1794, bapt. Jun 6, 1797. {Ref: PR}

SCARBOROUGH, JAMES, taxpayer, 1798, Deer Creek Middle Hd., 1 tract (45

acres) and 1 building, $112.50 valuation, no slaves. {Ref: TL}
SCARBOROUGH, JAMES, head of family in 1800 (5th District). {Ref: CI}
SCARBOROUGH, JOHN, taxpayer, 1798, Deer Creek Middle Hd., 2 tracts (429 acres) and 2 buildings (Thomas Rutman, occupant of one of them), $920.25 valuation, no slaves. {Ref: TL}
SCARBOROUGH, JOHN, tract *John's Expence* surveyed in 1792 and granted in 1801. {Ref: CB}
SCARBOROUGH, JOHN, head of family in 1800 (5th District). {Ref: CI}
SCARBOROUGH, JOSEPH, see "Mary Scarborough," q.v.
SCARBOROUGH, JOSEPH, taxpayer, 1798, Deer Creek Middle Hd., 3 tracts (75 acres, 120 perches) and 1 building, $225 valuation, no slaves. {Ref: TL}
SCARBOROUGH, JOSEPH, head of family in 1800 (5th District). {Ref: CI}
SCARBOROUGH, MARGARET, see "Thomas Scarborough," q.v.
SCARBOROUGH, MARY, dau. of Joseph and Sarah, b. Sep 25, 1777, bapt. Jun 20, 1797. {Ref: PR}. Also see "James Scarborough," q.v.
SCARBOROUGH, SAMUEL, son of James and Hannah, b. Apr 23, 1793, bapt. Jun 6, 1797. {Ref: PR}. Also see "Mahlon Ely," q.v.
SCARBOROUGH, SARAH, see "Mary Scarborough," q.v.
SCARBOROUGH, THOMAS, see "William Scarborough," q.v.
SCARBOROUGH, THOMAS, son of Thomas and Margaret, b. Jul 13, 1798, bapt. May 14, 1799. {Ref: PR}
SCARBOROUGH, THOMAS, taxpayer, 1798, Deer Creek Middle Hd., 1 tract (72 acres) and 1 building, $202.50 valuation, no slaves. {Ref: TL}
SCARBOROUGH, THOMAS, head of family in 1800 (5th District). {Ref: CI}
SCARBOROUGH, WILLIAM, son of James and Hannah, b. Feb 8, 1796, bapt. Jun 6, 1797. {Ref: PR}
SCARBOROUGH, WILLIAM, served as constable in Deer Creek Middle Hd., 1797. {Ref: CC}
SCARBOROUGH, WILLIAM, taxpayer, 1798, Deer Creek Middle Hd., 1 tract (7 acres) and 1 building, $45.56 valuation, no slaves. {Ref: TL}
SCARBOROUGH, WILLIAM, treated by Dr. Archer on Oct 7, 1799; also mentioned wife (no name given) and son Thomas. {Ref: JA}
SCARBOROUGH, WILLIAM, head of family in 1800 (5th District). {Ref: CI}
SCARBROUGH, JOHN, insolvent on a list for the road tax for 1792, as returned for Robert Amoss, tax collector. {Ref: IL 13.12}
SCARBROUGH, MARY, see "John Moore," q.v.
SCARBROUGH, WILLIAM, served as constable in Deer Creek Middle Hd., 1797-1800. {Ref: CM}
SCARFF, HENRY, taxpayer, 1798, Bush River Upper & Eden Hd., 1 dwelling house, 1 inferior house, 2 acres, $105 valuation; 1 tract (117 acres) in Bush River Upper & Eden Hd., $197.44 valuation, 1 slave. {Ref: TL}
SCARFF, HENRY, head of family in 1800 (4th District). {Ref: CI}

SCARFF, JOHN, see "Negro Will" and "Martha Scarff," q.v.

SCARFF, JOHN, served on a Petit Jury in August, 1797 (which listed the name as "John Sarff") and August, 1799, and on a Grand Jury in August, 1800. {Ref: CM}

SCARFF, JOHN, insolvent on lists returned by Robert Carlile (who listed the name as "John Scarff, Readstone") and John Guyton (who listed the name as "John Scaff") for taxes due for the year 1791, and on the 1791 road tax list of insolvents (which listed the name as "John Scarff, back woods") filed by Robert Amoss, Jr. in 1793. {Ref: IL 31.16, 31.19}

SCARFF, JOHN, head of family in 1800 (4th District). {Ref: CI}

SCARFF, MARTHA, wife of John, b. 1794, d. Aug 13, 1877, in her 83rd year, bur. in Ebenezer Methodist Church Cemetery north of Rutledge. {Ref: TI}

SCARFF, NICHOLAS, insolvent on lists returned by Robert Carlile (who listed the name twice in succession) and John Guyton (who listed him once as a single man and spelled the name as "Nichls. Scaff"). {Ref: IL 31.16, 31.19}

SCARFF, WILLIAM, head of family in 1800 (3rd District). {Ref: CI}

SCIVINGTON, JAMES, taxpayer, 1798, Bush River Upper & Eden Hd., 1 dwelling house, 2 inferior houses, 2 acres, $120 valuation; 2 tracts (158 acres) in Bush River Upper & Eden Hd., $355.50 valuation, no slaves. {Ref: TL}

SCOFIELD, JOHN, insolvent on list returned for the road tax due for 1791 by John Bull. {Ref: IL 31.14}

SCOFIELD, JOHN, insolvent on a list for county taxes due in 1792 as returned by Benjamin Preston. {Ref: IL 31.00}

SCOFIELD, JOHN, head of family in 1800 (5th District). {Ref: CI}

SCOTT, AQUILA, taxpayer, 1798, Bush River Lower Hd., 1 dwelling house, 4 inferior houses, 1 acre, $205 valuation; 3 tracts (229 acres) and 1 building (Negro Darby, occupant) in Bush River Lower Hd., $840.37 valuation, 1 slave. {Ref: TL}

SCOTT, AQUILLA, head of family in 1800 (3rd District). {Ref: CI}

SCOTT, BENJAMIN COLEGATE, son of Nathan and Mary, b. Feb 23, 1794. {Ref: PR}

SCOTT, DANIEL, see "Hugh Caney," q.v.

SCOTT, DANIEL, served on a Petit Jury in March, 1798. {Ref: CM}

SCOTT, DANIEL, m. Margarett Short on Apr 6, 1797. {Ref: PR}

SCOTT, DANIEL, taxpayer, 1798, Bush River Lower Hd., 1 dwelling house, 4 inferior houses, 1 acre, $140 valuation; 5 tracts (99 acres) in Bush River Lower Hd., $479.25 valuation, no slaves. {Ref: TL}

SCOTT, DANIEL, tract *Rural Felicity* surveyed in 1798. {Ref: CB}

SCOTT, DANIEL, head of family in 1800 (3rd District). {Ref: CI}

SCOTT, ELIZABETH, m. George Davis on Aug 13, 1795. {Ref: PR}. Also see "Daniel McComas," q.v.

SCOTT, JAMES, head of family in 1800 (4th District). {Ref: CI}

SCOTT, JOSEPH JR., m. Hannah Norris on Mar 5, 1795. {Ref: PR}

SCOTT, LOUISA M. (neé Boarman), wife of Otho, b. 1799 (or 1800), d. Aug 5,

1840 (or 1841), in her 41st year, bur. in St. Ignatius Catholic Church Cemetery in Hickory. {Ref: TI, *St. Ignatius, Hickory, and Its Missions*, by Clarence V. Joerndt (1972), p. 128}
SCOTT, MARY, see "Benjamin Colegate Scott," q.v.
SCOTT, MORDICA, head of family in 1800 (4th District). {Ref: CI}
SCOTT, NATHAN, see "Benjamin Colegate Scott," q.v.
SCOTT, OTHO, b. Oct 15, 1797, d. Mar 9, 1864, bur. in St. Ignatius Catholic Church Cemetery in Hickory. {Ref: TI}. Also see "Louisa M. Scott," q.v.
SCOTT, ROBERT, insolvent on lists returned for the county and road taxes due for 1791 by John Bull in Gunpowder Lower Hd. (listed as "charged twice" on one list). {Ref: IL 31.14, 31.15}
SCOTT, SARAH, insolvent on lists returned for the county and road taxes due for 1791 by John Bull in Gunpowder Lower Hundred. {Ref: IL 31.14, 31.15}
SCOTT, SUSAN P., see "Susan P. Scott Keech," q.v.
SCOTT, SUSANNA (Mrs.), treated by Dr. Archer in August, 1794. {Ref: JA}
SCOTT, SUSANNA, bur. Nov 7, 1797. {Ref: PR}
SCOTT, SUSANNA, will probated Mar 28, 1798. {Ref: HW}
SCOTTEN (SCOTTON), WILLIAM, head of family in 1800 (2nd District). {Ref: CI}. Also see "Joshua Husband," q.v.
SCOTTS, DICK (negro), insolvent on a list for 1791 in Gunpowder Upper and Bush River Lower Hundreds, as filed by John Bond, Deputy Sheriff, on Sep 20, 1791. {Ref: IL 31.24}
SEAR, ANDREW, see "John Shields," q.v.
SEAR, ANDREW, subpoenaed to the Grand Jury in August, 1797. {Ref: CC}
SEAR, ANDREW, appeared on list of "recognizances" of the court for his appearance in 1797. {Ref: CD, August Term, 1797}.
SEAR, CAPTAIN, see "Negro Abigail," q.v.
SEAR, MARTHA, see "John Shields," q.v.
SEAR, MARTHA, subpoenaed to the Grand Jury in August, 1797. {Ref: CC}
SEAR, MARTHA, head of family in 1800 (2nd District). {Ref: CI}.
SEDGWICK, BEN, insolvent on a list for the road tax due for 1791 in Harford Upper, Harford Lower, and Spesutia Upper as returned by Robert Amos, Jr. on Sep 18, 1793. {Ref: IL 31.18}
SEDGWICK, BENJAMIN, insolvent, Harford Lower and Spesutia Lower Hundreds, on a tax list returned by George Lyttle on Sep 21, 1791. {Ref: IL 31.20, 31.21}
SEDGWICK, BENJAMIN, insolvent on a list for county taxes due in 1792 as returned by Benjamin Preston. {Ref: IL 31.00}
SEDGWICK, BENJAMIN, insolvent on list returned for the road tax due for 1791 by John Bull. {Ref: IL 31.14}
SEDGWICK, BENJAMIN, head of family in 1800 (5th District). {Ref: CI}
SEDGWICK, JAMES, head of family in 1800 (5th District). {Ref: CI}
SERGEANT, MARY, see "Michael Kelly," q.v.
SEVERSON, MARGARET, b. Aug 30, 1794 (1791?), d. Feb 8, 1888 (on same

297

stone as Henry Carver), bur. in Angel Hill Cemetery in Havre de Grace. {Ref TI}
SEWELL, BAZIL, son of John and Elizabeth, b. Feb 26, 1792. {Ref: PR}
SEWELL, ELIZABETH, see "Bazil Sewell," q.v.
SEWELL, JOHN, taxpayer, 1798, Gunpowder Upper Hd., 1 dwelling house, 2 inferior houses, 2 acres, $200 valuation; 2 tracts (400 acres) in Gunpowder Upper Hd., $922.50 valuation, 9 slaves; also, taxpayer, Gunpowder Upper Hd., 1 dwelling house, 3 inferior houses, 2 acres, $110 valuation, no slaves. {Ref: TL}. Also see "Bazil Sewell," q.v.
SHANE, HENRY, head of family in 1800 (4th District). {Ref: CI}
SHANNON, GEORGE, head of family in 1800 (3rd District). {Ref: CI}
SHARP, THOMAS, taxpayer, 1798, Bush River Upper & Eden Hd., 1 dwelling house, 2 inferior houses, 2 acres, $105 valuation; 1 tract (98 acres) in Bush River Upper & Eden Hd., $165.38 valuation, no slaves. {Ref: TL}
SHARP, THOMAS, head of family in 1800 (4th District). {Ref: CI}
SHAVER (SHAVRE), WILLIAM LOUIS, taxpayer, 1798, Gunpowder Lower Hd., 1 dwelling house, 2 inferior houses, 2 acres, $200 valuation; 2 tracts (68 acres) in Gunpowder Lower Hd., $229.50 valuation, 3 slaves. {Ref: TL}.
SHAW, REBECCA, see "William Watt," q.v.
SHAW, ROBERT, taxpayer, 1798, Gunpowder Upper Hd., 1 tract (20 acres) and 1 building, $67.50 valuation, no slaves. {Ref: TL}
SHAW, ROBERT, head of family in 1800 (1st District). {Ref: CI}
SHAY, THOMAS, served as constable in Harford Lower Hd., 1800. {Ref: CM}
SHEAN, HENRY, insolvent on list returned by Robert Carlile for taxes due for the year 1791. {Ref: IL 31.16}
SHECKETT, HENRY, taxpayer, 1798, Spesutia Lower Hd., 1 tract (44 perches, 21 sq. ft.), $13.50 valuation, no slaves. {Ref: TL}
SHEREDINE, DANIEL, insolvent on a list in 1792 in Deer Creek Lower Hd., as returned by Benjamin Preston. {Ref: IL 31.03}
SHEREDINE, MARY, see "Wiliam Neill," q.v.
SHEREDINE, THOMAS, charged for assaulting John Hamby in 1794. {Ref: CD, March and August Terms, 1795}
SHEREDINE, THOMAS, m. Ann Neil on Mar 9, 1797. {Ref: PR}
SHERIDAN, JAMES, head of family in 1800 (3rd District). {Ref: CI}
SHERIDAN, JAMES JR., head of family in 1800 (3rd District). {Ref: CI}
SHERIDAN, THOMAS, head of family in 1800 (3rd District). {Ref: CI}
SHERIDINE, JAMES, see "Robert Nesbett," q.v.
SHERWOOD (SHURWOOD), WILLIAM, head of family in 1800 (3rd District). {Ref: CI}. Also see "John Madden," q.v.
SHEWALL, JOHN, head of family in 1800 (3rd District). {Ref: CI}
SHEWELL, JAMES, head of family in 1800 (3rd District). {Ref: CI}
SHEWELL, THOMAS, head of family in 1800 (4th District). {Ref: CI}
SHIDLE, ACHART, see "Benjamin Culver," q.v.
SHIDLE, WILLIAM, m. Mary McGill on Jul 28, 1796. {Ref: PR}

SHIELDS, ----, see "James Shields," q.v.
SHIELDS, JAMES, son of John and wife ----, bapt. Mar 14, 1798. {Ref: PR}
SHIELDS, JOHN, see "John Monks" and "James Shields," q.v.
SHIELDS, JOHN, charged for beating Martha Sear in 1797; also mentioned Andrew Sear. {Ref: CD, August Term, 1797}
SHIELDS, JOHN, head of family in 1800 (Abingdon). {Ref: CI}
SHIELDS, JOHN, head of family in 1800 (4th District). {Ref: CI}
SHIELDS, PAUL, served as constable in Spesutia Lower Hd., 1797-1800. {Ref: CC, CM}
SHIELDS, ROSANNAH, treated by Dr. Archer on Jan 2, 1791; also mentioned she lived near Samuel Forwood. {Ref: JA}
SHINTON, JOHN, insolvent on list returned for the county tax for 1791 by William Osburn in Gunpowder Lower Hundred. {Ref: IL 31.15}
SHIPLEY, ANN, b. 1800, d. 1872, bur. in St. Mary's Catholic Church Cemetery in Pylesville. {Ref: TI}
SHIPLEY, ANNA, b. Apr 11, 1800, d. Oct 11, 1872, bur. in St. Mary's Catholic Church Cemetery in Pylesville. {Ref: TI}
SHIPLEY, BENJAMIN, see "Michael Kelly," q.v.
SHIPLEY, JOHN R., b. 1798, d. 1885, bur. in St. Mary's Catholic Church Cemetery in Pylesville. {Ref: TI}
SHIRE, WILLIAM, head of family in 1800 (1st District). {Ref: CI}
SHODAY (SHODY), FRANCES, see "Frances Lee Shoday Spencer" and "Charlotte Taylor" and "Sylvester Taylor" and "Otho Taylor" and "Susanna Taylor," q.v.
SHORES, MARY, charged in 1795 (nature of the case not stated). {Ref: CD, August Term, 1795}
SHORES (SHOARS), RICHARD, insolvent on lists returned by Robert Carlile and John Guyton for taxes due for the year 1791. {Ref: IL 31.16, 31.19}
SHORT, MARGARETT, see "Daniel Scott," q.v.
SHOUDY, RACHEL, see "Thomas Durham," q.v.
SHRIVER, CHRISTIAN, head of family in 1800 (2nd District). {Ref: CI}
SHRIVER, JOHN, head of family in 1800 (2nd District). {Ref: CI}
SHRIVER, JOHN, head of family in 1800 (5th District). {Ref: CI}
SIDDLES, JOSEPH, insolvent on a list for the road tax due for 1791 in Harford Upper, Harford Lower, and Spesutia Upper as returned by Robert Amos, Jr. on Sep 18, 1793. {Ref: IL 31.18}
SILVER, DAVID, see "Elizabeth Silver," q.v.
SILVER, ELIZABETH, wife of David, b. Oct 9, 1797, d. Nov 13, 1853, aged 56 years, 1 months and 4 days, bur. in Deer Creek Harmony Presbyterian Church Cemetery near Darlington. {Ref: TI}
SILVERS, AMOS (AMOSS), head of family in 1800 (5th District). {Ref: CI}. Also see "Joseph Hopkins," q.v.
SILVERS, BENJAMIN, treated by Dr. Archer on Oct 24, 1796; also mentioned his

wife (no name given). {Ref: JA}
SILVERS, BENJAMIN, taxpayer, 1798, Susquehanna Hd., 1 tract (300 acres), $1236.37 valuation, no slaves. {Ref: TL}
SILVERS (SYLVERS), BENJAMIN, head of family in 1800 (2nd District). {Ref: CI}
SILVERS (SYLVERS), DAVID, head of family in 1800 (5th District). {Ref: CI}
SIMMONS, JOHN, charged for house breaking in 1795. {Ref: CD, March Term, 1795}
SIMMONS, JOHN, charged for felony (nature of case not stated) in 1797. {Ref: CD, March Term, 1797}
SIMMONS, THOMAS, see "Bernard McMahan" and "Hugh Caney," q.v.
SIMMONS, WILLIAM, head of family in 1800 (1st District). {Ref: CI}
SIMMS, ANDREW, insolvent on list returned by Robert Carlile for taxes due for the year 1791. {Ref: IL 31.16}
SIMMS, RALPH, head of family in 1800 (5th District). {Ref: CI}
SIMONS, WILLIAM, head of family in 1800 (4th District). {Ref: CI}
SINCLAIR, JOHN, see "Leah Sinclair," q.v.
SINCLAIR, LEAH, dau. of John and Margaret, b. Feb 9, 1796, bapt. Sep 11, 1796. {Ref: PR}
SINCLAIR, MARGARET, see "Leah Sinclair," q.v.
SINCLEAR, JAMES, tract *Twice Neglected* surveyed between 1792 and 1796. {Ref: SB}
SINGLETON, JOHN, head of family in 1800 (5th District). {Ref: CI}
SKIVENTON, JAMES, head of family in 1800 (4th District). {Ref: CI}
SLACK, HENY, see "John Slack," q.v.
SLACK, JACOB, treated by Dr. Archer on Sep 13, 1793. {Ref: JA}
SLACK, JOHN, treated by Dr. Archer on Jan 31, 1792; also mentioned a child named Heny (sic) in 1786. {Ref: JA}
SLADE, CAROLINE, see "James Reed Moore," q.v.
SLADE, DIXON, taxpayer, 1798, Bush River Upper & Eden Hd., 1 dwelling house, 4 inferior houses, 2 acres, $200 valuation; 2 tracts (345 acres) in Bush River Upper & Eden Hd., $776.25 valuation, 2 slaves. {Ref: TL}
SLADE, DIXON, head of family in 1800 (4th District). {Ref: CI}
SLADE, EZEAKLE ("run"), insolvent on a list of the county tax due William Osborn, sheriff, for 1791, as returned by Edward Prigg on Sep 20, 1791. {Ref: IL 31.17}
SLADE, EZEKIEL, see "William Slade (of Ezekiel)," q.v.
SLADE, EZEKIEL, taxpayer, 1798, Bush River Upper & Eden Hd., 1 dwelling house, 3 inferior houses, 2 acres, $150 valuation; 3 tracts (192 acres, 80 perches) in Bush River Upper & Eden Hd., $533.53 valuation, 1 slave. {Ref: TL}
SLADE, EZEKIEL, head of family in 1800 (4th District). {Ref: CI}
SLADE, EZEKIL, insolvent on lists in 1791 due county taxes and road taxes in "Deer Creek Upper, Middle, and Broad Creek Hundreds" as returned by Robert Amos, Jr. {Ref: IL 31.12, 31.22}
SLADE, MARY, first wife of Washington M., was b. 1794, d. May 13, 1859 in her 64th year, bur. in St. Mary's Episcopal Church Cemetery. {Ref: TI}

SLADE, MARY, head of family in 1800 (3rd District). {Ref: CI}
SLADE, ROSANNA, b. 1791, d. May 2, 1873, bur. in Bethel Presbyterian Church Cemetery at Madonna. {Ref: BC}
SLADE, WASHINGTON M., b. 1794, d. Dec 12, 1867 in his 73rd year, bur. in St. Mary's Episcopal Church Cemetery. {Ref: TI}. Also see "Mary Slade," q.v.
SLADE, WILLIAM, taxpayer, 1798, Bush River Upper & Eden Hd., 1 dwelling house, 5 inferior houses, 2 acres, $400 valuation; 5 tracts (594 acres, 40 perches) in Bush River Upper & Eden Hd., $1234.12 valuation, no slaves. {Ref: TL}
SLADE, WILLIAM, head of family in 1800 (4th District); two men by this name in this district. {Ref: CI}
SLADE, WILLIAM JR., tract *Disappointment* surveyed between 1792 and 1796. {Ref: SB}
SLADE, WILLIAM (OF EZEKIEL), taxpayer, 1798, Deer Creek Upper Hd., 2 tracts (308 acres, 120 perches) and 1 building, $608.34 valuation, no slaves. {Ref: TL}
SLEMAKER, ARANEA, see "Henry Patrick Finnagan," q.v.
SLEMMONS, JOHN (reverend), treated by Dr. Archer on Apr 9, 1792; also mentioned his wife (no name given). {Ref: JA}
SLOAN, WILLIAM, taxpayer, 1798, Bush River Upper & Eden Hd., 1 dwelling house, 1 inferior house, 2 acres, $120 valuation; 1 tract (141 acres) in Bush River Upper & Eden Hd., $237.94 valuation, no slaves. {Ref: TL}
SLONE, JANE, insolvent on lists in 1791 due county taxes and road taxes in "Deer Creek Upper, Middle, and Broad Creek Hundreds" as returned by Robert Amos, Jr. {Ref: IL 31.12, 31.22}
SLONE, PATRICK ("gone"), insolvent on lists due for 1790 and 1791 "fund taxes" and county taxes in Susquehanna Hd., as returned by Thomas Taylor. {Ref: IL31.12, 31.02}
SLONE, WILLIAM, head of family in 1800 (4th District). {Ref: CI}
SMALL, ELIJAH, m. Rebecca Jemmison on Feb 21, 1799. {Ref: PR}
SMALLWOOD, WILLIAM, head of family in 1800 (1st District). {Ref: CI}
SMITH, ----, charged for keeping a ferry in 1795 (the name Samuel was written in the docket, then crossed out and another first name written over it, but the page is torn and the name is missing). {Ref: CD, August Term, 1795}
SMITH, ALEXANDER, son of William and Margaret, b. Jul 31, 1782, bapt. Nov 22, 1798. {Ref: PR}
SMITH, ALEXANDER, head of family in 1800 (2nd District). {Ref: CI}
SMITH, ALEXANDER LAWSON, taxpayer, 1798, Spesutia Lower Hd., 1 dwelling house, 6 inferior houses, 2 acres, $500 valuation; 2 tracts (293 acres) in Spesutia Lower Hd., $1582.20 valuation, 8 slaves; also, taxpayer, Gunpowder Lower Hd., 1 tract (370 acres) and 1 building, $1248.75 valuation, no slaves. {Ref: TL}. Also see "Lewis Griffith" and "Samuel Griffith Smith" and "Maria Matilda Smith" and "Francinia Frenetta Smith," q.v.
SMITH, ANN, taxpayer, 1798, Spesutia Lower Hd., 1 tract (88 perches, 42 sq. ft.),

$27 valuation, no slaves. {Ref: TL}
SMITH, ANNE, dau. of James and Sarah, b. Aug 20, 1798, bapt. May 14, 1799. {Ref: PR}
SMITH, ANN MONTGOMERY, dau. of William and Margaret, b. Dec 6, 1776, bapt. Jun 4, 1797. {Ref: PR}
SMITH, ARAMINTA, dau. of Henry and Mary, b. circa 1796 (exact date not given). {Ref: PR}
SMITH, BENJAMIN ("gone"), insolvent on lists due for 1790 and 1791 "fund taxes" and county taxes in Susquehanna Hd., as returned by Thomas Taylor. {Ref: IL 31.12, 31.02}
SMITH, CATHERINE (at Freeborn Brown's), dau. of Widow Smith, treated by Dr. Archer on Jun 5, 1792. {Ref: JA}
SMITH, DOCTOR, consulted with Dr. Archer in 1792. {Ref: JA}
SMITH, ELIZABETH, head of family in 1800 (5th District). {Ref: CI}
SMITH, ELIZABETH (widow of Nat.), treated by Dr. Archer on Apr 3, 1791; also mentioned her account was paid by Miss Polly Smith in 1792. {Ref: JA}
SMITH, ELIZABETH G., bur. Jan 30, 1799, aged about 7 months. {Ref: PR}
SMITH, FRANCINIA FRENETTA, dau. of Alexander Lawson and Martha, b. Nov 10, 1797. {Ref: PR}
SMITH, FRANCIS, head of family in 1800 (5th District). {Ref: CI}
SMITH, FRENETTA F., b. 1797 or 1798, d. Feb 10, 1860, aged 62, bur. in St. George's Episcopal Church Cemetery at Perryman. {Ref: TI}
SMITH, HANNAH, taxpayer, 1798, Susquehanna Hd., 1 tract (90 acres) and 1 building, $225 valuation, 2 slaves. {Ref: TL}
SMITH, HARRIETT, b. Dec 30, 1798, d. Aug 24, 1804, bur. in Smith Family Cemetery (Churchville area). {Ref: TI}
SMITH, HENRY, head of family in 1800 (2nd District). {Ref: CI}. Also see "Mary Smith" and "Araminta Smith" and "James Smith," q.v.
SMITH, HUGH, taxpayer, 1798, Deer Creek Lower Hd., 1 tract (156 acres) and 1 building, $1170 valuation, no slaves. {Ref: TL}
SMITH, HUGH, head of family in 1800 (5th District). {Ref: CI}
SMITH, ISABELLA, see "Andrew Stevenson," q.v.
SMITH, JACOB, warden, 1794, St. George's Episcopal Church. {Ref: PR}
SMITH, JACOB G., served on a Grand Jury in March, 1799, and was excused from serving on a Petit Jury in March, 1800. {Ref: CM}
SMITH, JACOB G., taxpayer, 1798, no dwelling house listed in this part of the tax schedule, no land listed, no hd. listed (possibly Spesutia Lower Hundred), 2 slaves. {Ref: TL}
SMITH, JAMES, see "Anne Smith" and "William Smith," q.v.
SMITH, JAMES ("gone"), insolvent on lists due for 1790 and 1791 "fund taxes" in Deer Creek Lower and Susquehanna Hundreds, as returned by Thomas Taylor. {Ref: IL 31.12, 31.02}
SMITH, JAMES, charged for selling liquors in 1794. {Ref: CD, March Term, 1795}

SMITH, JAMES, licensed ordinary (tavern) in March, 1795. {Ref: CC}

SMITH, JAMES, granted a retailer's permit in July, 1797, and a tavern license and a ferry license in August, 1797. {Ref: CC}

SMITH, JAMES, m. Sarah Haley on Sep 21, 1797. {Ref: PR}

SMITH, JAMES, taxpayer, 1798, Susquehanna Hd., 1 dwelling house, 80 perches of land, $150 valuation; 3 tracts (212 acres, 80 perches) and 2 buildings (Henry Smith, occupant of one of them) in Susquehanna Hd., $543.65 valuation, no slaves. {Ref: TL}

SMITH, JAMES, charged for ferrying (keeping a ferry) without a license in 1797. {Ref: CD, March and August Terms, 1797}

SMITH, JAMES, charged for selling liquors by the smalls in 1797. {Ref: CD, March and August Terms, 1797}

SMITH, JAMES, head of family in 1800 (2nd District). {Ref: CI}

SMITH, JAMES, head of family in 1800 (3rd District). {Ref: CI}

SMITH, JAMES (Baltimore County), insolvent on list returned by Robert Carlile for taxes due for the year 1791. {Ref: IL 31.16}

SMITH, JAMES (OF THOMAS), at G. Ferry, treated by Dr. Archer on Sep 9, 1799. {Ref: JA}

SMITH, JOHN ("can't be found"), insolvent on lists due for 1790 and 1791 "fund taxes" and county taxes in Susquehanna Hd., as returned by Thomas Taylor. {Ref: IL 31.12, 31.02}

SMITH, JOHN, insolvent on lists in 1791 due county taxes and road taxes in "Deer Creek Upper, Middle, and Broad Creek Hundreds" as returned by Robert Amos, Jr. {Ref: IL 31.12, 31.22}

SMITH, JOHN, granted a tavern license in March, 1797. {Ref: CC}

SMITH, JOHN, taxpayer, 1798, Susquehanna Hd., 1 dwelling house, 3 inferior houses, 2 acres, $100.50 valuation; 2 tracts (244 acres, 40 perches) in Susquehanna Hd., $457.88 valuation, 1 slave. {Ref: TL}

SMITH, JOHN, taxpayer, 1798, Deer Creek Middle Hd., 1 tract (54 acres) and 1 building, $94.50 valuation, no slaves. {Ref: TL}

SMITH, JOHN, mentioned in a survey deposition on Jan 14, 1800 as "to where formerly stood John Smith's dwelling house near Wild Cat Denn." {Ref: JS}

SMITH, JOHN, head of family in 1800 (2nd District). {Ref: CI}

SMITH, JOHN, head of family in 1800 (5th District); two men by this name in this district. {Ref: CI}

SMITH, JOHN (carpenter), treated by Dr. Archer on Jul 9, 1795. {Ref: JA}

SMITH, JOHN (doctor), appointed a Judge of Elections in the 5th District on Jul 28, 1800. {Ref: CM}

SMITH, JOHN (doctor), taxpayer, 1798, Deer Creek Lower Hd., 1 dwelling house, 2 inferior houses, 2 acres, $160 valuation; 1 tract (200 acres) in Deer Creek Lower Hd., $330 valuation, no slaves. {Ref: TL}

SMITH, JOHN (doctor), head of family in 1800 (5th District). {Ref: CI}

SMITH, JOHN (tanner), taxpayer, 1798, Gunpowder Lower Hd., 1 dwelling house, 2 inferior houses, 2 acres, $450 valuation, 1 slave. {Ref: TL}

SMITH, JOHN (tanner), head of family in 1800 (Abingdon). {Ref: CI}
SMITH, JONATHAN, see "Samuel Smith," q.v.
SMITH, JONATHAN, treated by Dr. Archer on May 10, 1795; also mentioned wife (no name given). {Ref: JA}
SMITH, JONATHAN, head of family in 1800 (2nd District). {Ref: CI}
SMITH, JOSIAH, head of family in 1800 (Belle Air). {Ref: CI}
SMITH, JOSIAS, served on a Grand Jury in March, 1799 and March, 1800. {Ref: CM}. Also see "Elizabeth Gibson," q.v.
SMITH, M. A., see "Mary Ann Harlan," q.v.
SMITH, MARGARET, see "Ann Montgomery Smith" and "Nathaniel Smith" and "Alexander Smith," q.v.
SMITH, MARIA MATILDA, dau. of Alexander Lawson and Martha, b. Jul 1, 1799, d. Sep 14, 1860, aged 61, bur. in St. George's Episcopal Church Cemetery at Perryman. {Ref: PR, TI}
SMITH, MARTHA, see "Samuel Griffith Smith" and "Maria Matilda Smith" and "Francinia Frenetta Smith," q.v.
SMITH, MARY, dau. of Henry and Mary, b. Sep 6, 1794. {Ref: PR}. Also see "Araminta Smith" and "Thomas Gilbert Smith," q.v.
SMITH, MOSES, head of family in 1800 (2nd District). {Ref: CI}
SMITH, NANCY, b. Dec 5, 1793, d. Mar 10, 1873, bur. in Smith Family Cemetery (Churchville area). {Ref: TI}
SMITH, NATHAN, see "Elizabeth Smith (widow)" and "Edward Prigg," q.v.
SMITH, NATHAN, tracts *Clermont* and *Smith's Meadows* surveyed between 1789 and 1795. {Ref: CB, SB}
SMITH, NATHAN, served on a Petit Jury in August, 1798. {Ref: CM}
SMITH, NATHAN, tract *Valenciennes* surveyed between 1792 and 1796. {Ref: CB, SB}
SMITH, NATHAN, taxpayer, 1798, Deer Creek Upper Hd., 2 tracts (230 acres) and 1 building, $879.75 valuation, 2 slaves. {Ref: TL}
SMITH, NATHAN, head of family in 1800 (4th District). {Ref: CI}
SMITH, NATHAN, head of family in 1800 (5th District). {Ref: CI}
SMITH, NATHAN (OF WILLIAM), treated by Dr. Archer on Feb 17, 1795. {Ref: JA}
SMITH, NATHANIEL, son of William and Margaret, b. Apr 9, 1779, bapt. Nov 22, 1798. {Ref: PR}
SMITH, NATHANIEL, insolvent on list returned by Robert Carlile for taxes due for the year 1791. {Ref: IL 31.16}
SMITH, NATHANIEL, head of family in 1800 (2nd District). {Ref: CI}
SMITH, PACA, taxpayer, 1798, Susquehanna Hd., 1 dwelling house, 6 inferior houses, 2 acres, $900 valuation, 1 slave. {Ref: TL}
SMITH, PACA, m. Sarah Phillips on Feb 7, 1799. {Ref: PR}. Also see "Sarah Knight Smith," q.v.
SMITH, PATRICK, head of family in 1800 (5th District). {Ref: CI}

SMITH, PATRICK, or WILLIAM COOLEY, taxpayer, 1798, Deer Creek Upper Hd., 1 tract (270 acres) and 1 building (William Cooley, occupant), $405 valuation, no slaves. {Ref: TL}
SMITH, PATTY (Miss), treated by Dr. Archer on Jul 5, 1791. {Ref: JA}
SMITH, PEGGY, head of family in 1800 (5th District). {Ref: CI}
SMITH, PETER, head of family in 1800 (4th District). {Ref: CI}
SMITH, POLLY, see "Elizabeth Smith (widow)," q.v.
SMITH, RALPH, treated by Dr. Archer on Apr 17, 1790 or 1791. {Ref: JA}
SMITH, ROBERT, insolvent, Harford Lower and Spesutia Lower Hundreds (listed as a single man), on a tax list returned by George Lyttle on Sep 21, 1791. {Ref: IL 31.20, 31.21}
SMITH, ROBERT, insolvent on a list for the road tax due for 1791 in Harford Upper, Harford Lower, and Spesutia Upper as returned by Robert Amos, Jr. on Sep 18, 1793 (his name was crossed off the list). {Ref: IL 31.18}
SMITH, SAMUEL, see "Thomas Gilbert Smith" and "Robert Gover" and "---- Smith" and "William Smith" and "John Forwood (of William)," q.v.
SMITH, SAMUEL, taxpayer, 1798, Harford Upper Hd., 1 dwelling house, 2 inferior houses, 2 acres, $150 valuation; 2 tracts (216 acres) and 1 building (Jonathan Smith, occupant) in Harford Upper Hd., $519.75 valuation, no slaves. {Ref: TL}
SMITH, SAMUEL, insolvent on a list for the road tax for 1792, as returned for Robert Amoss, tax collector. {Ref: IL 13.12}
SMITH, SAMUEL, head of family in 1800 (3rd District). {Ref: CI}
SMITH, SAMUEL, head of family in 1800 (5th District); two men by this name in this district. {Ref: CI}
SMITH, SAMUEL GRIFFITH, dau. of Alexander Lawson and Martha, b. Dec 25, 1794. {Ref: PR}
SMITH, SARAH, see "Anne Smith" and "William Smith," q.v.
SMITH, SUSANNAH (widow of William), will probated Oct 7, 1795. {Ref: HW}
SMITH, THOMAS, see "William Smith (of Thomas)" and "Captain McCackin" and "James Smith (of Thomas)," q.v.
SMITH, THOMAS, will probated Dec 19, 1791. {Ref: HW}
SMITH, THOMAS (at the ferry), treated by Dr. Archer on Jul 20, 1791; also mentioned a child (no name given). {Ref: JA}
SMITH, THOMAS JR. ("out back"), insolvent on lists due for 1790 and 1791 "fund taxes" and county taxes in Susquehanna Hd., as returned by Thomas Taylor. {Ref: IL 31.12, 31.02}
SMITH, THOMAS GILBERT, son of Samuel and Mary, b. Dec 15, 1796, bapt. Jun 6, 1797. {Ref: PR}
SMITH, THOMAS RIGBIE, tract *Dallam's Neglect* surveyed between 1792 and 1796. {Ref: SB}
SMITH, W., insolvent on list returned by Robert Carlile for taxes due for the year 1791. {Ref: IL 31.16}

SMITH, WIDOW, see "Catherine Smith," q.v.

SMITH, WILLIAM, see "Ann Montgomery Smith" and "Nathaniel Smith" and "Alexander Smith" and Susannah Smith" and "Joseph Webster," q.v.

SMITH, WILLIAM, had an account at Hall's Store in January, 1791. {Ref: WH}

SMITH, WILLIAM, served on a Petit Jury in March, 1800. {Ref: CM}

SMITH, WILLIAM, insolvent on lists for the county tax and road tax due for 1791 and 1792 in Deer Creek Lower Hd., as returned by Thomas Taylor on Sep 17, 1792. {Ref: IL 31.12, 31.03}

SMITH, WILLIAM, taxpayer, 1798, Deer Creek Middle Hd., 2 tracts (295 acres) and 2 buildings (John Lee, occupant of one of them), $579.66 valuation, no slaves. {Ref: TL}

SMITH, WILLIAM, insolvent on list returned for the county tax for 1791 by William Osburn in Gunpowder Lower Hd. (which listed him as a single man). {Ref: IL 31.15}

SMITH, WILLIAM, m. Elizabeth Mahon on Jul 6, 1797. {Ref: PR}

SMITH, WILLIAM, son of Samuel Smith and Elizabeth Arnold, b. Oct 1, 1794, bapt. Dec 30, 1795. {Ref: PR}

SMITH, WILLIAM, son of James and Sarah, b. Mar 23, 1800, bapt. Apr 26, 1800. {Ref: PR}

SMITH, WILLIAM, will probated Jun 11, 1796. {Ref: HW}

SMITH, WILLIAM, head of family in 1800 (2nd District); two men by this name in this district. {Ref: CI}

SMITH, WILLIAM, head of family in 1800 (3rd District). {Ref: CI}

SMITH, WILLIAM, head of family in 1800 (5th District). {Ref: CI}

SMITH, WILLIAM (captain), head of family in 1800 (3rd District). {Ref: CI}

SMITH, WILLIAM (captain), taxpayer, 1798, Harford Upper Hd., 3 tracts (100 acres) and 1 building, $270 acres, 1 slave. {Ref: TL}

SMITH, WILLIAM (carpenter), insolvent on a list for the road tax due for 1791 in Harford Upper, Harford Lower, and Spesutia Upper as returned by Robert Amos, Jr. on Sep 18, 1793. {Ref: IL 31.18}

SMITH, WILLIAM (esquire), taxpayer, 1798, Harford Upper Hd., 1 dwelling house, 6 inferior houses, 2 acres, $255 valuation; 1 tract (233 acres) in Harford Upper Hd., $699 valuation, no slaves. {Ref: TL}

SMITH, WILLIAM (esquire), head of family in 1800 (1st District). {Ref: CI}

SMITH, WILLIAM (ship carpenter), insolvent, Harford Lower and Spesutia Lower Hundreds, on a tax list returned by George Lyttle on Sep 21, 1791. {Ref: IL 31.20, 31.21}

SMITH, WILLIAM (OF SAMUEL), served on a Grand Jury in March, 1798. {Ref: CM}

SMITH, WILLIAM (OF THOMAS), taxpayer, 1798, Susquehanna Hd., 2 tracts (75 acres) and 1 building, $275.63 valuation, no slaves. {Ref: TL}

SMITH, WILLIAM (OF WILLIAM), appointed a Judge of Elections in the 1st District on Jul 28, 1800; later resigned (date not stated). {Ref: CM}

SMITH, WILLIAM A., b. Sep 9, 1797, d. Aug 22, 1859, aged 61 years, 11 months,

and 13 days, bur. in Churchville Presbyterian Church Cemetery. {Ref: TI}
SMITH, WILLIAM P., head of family in 1800 (2nd District). {Ref: CI}
SMITH, WINSTON, see "James Phillips, Sr.," q.v.
SMITH, WINSTON, taxpayer, 1798, no dwelling house listed in this part of the tax schedule, no land listed, no hd. listed (possibly Spesutia Lower Hundred), 2 slaves. {Ref: TL}
SMITH, WINSTON, discharged from serving on a Petit Jury in August, 1800. {Ref: CM}
SMITH, WINSTON, head of family in 1800 (2nd District). {Ref: CI}
SMITHSON, ARCHIBALD, charged for assaulting Mary Flynn in 1793. {Ref: CD, March and August Terms, 1795 and 1797}
SMITHSON, ARCHIBALD, charged for assaulting Hugh Young in 1797. {Ref: CD, August Term, 1797}
SMITHSON, ARCHIBALD, charged for refusing to aid and assist a constable in 1797. {Ref: CD, March Term, 1797}
SMITHSON, ARCHIBALD, treated by Dr. Archer on Mar 14, 1799; also mentioned his wife (no name given). {Ref: JA}
SMITHSON, BENJAMIN, head of family in 1800 (3rd District). {Ref: CI}
SMITHSON, D., insolvent on a list returned by Robert Carlile for taxes due for the year 1791. {Ref: IL 31:16}
SMITHSON, DAVID, insolvent on a list returned by John Guyton for taxes due for the year 1791. {Ref: IL 31.19}
SMITHSON, ELIZABETH, see "Henry Dorsey (of Edward)," q.v.
SMITHSON, LUTHER, b. 1794, d. Feb --, 1863, aged 69, bur. in Fellowship Cemetery near Harkins. {Ref: TI}
SMITHSON, NATHANIEL, insolvent on a list for the road tax for 1792, as returned for Robert Amoss, tax collector. {Ref: IL 13.12}
SMITHSON, NATHANIEL, served on a Petit Jury in August, 1797. {Ref: CC}
SMITHSON, NATHANIEL, taxpayer, 1798, Bush River Lower Hd., 1 dwelling house, 6 inferior houses, 1 acre and 80 perches, $210 valuation; 1 tract (198 acres, 80 perches) and 1 building in Bush River Lower Hd., $687.66 valuation, 1 slave. {Ref: TL}
SMITHSON, NATHANIEL, head of family in 1800 (3rd District). {Ref: CI}
SMITHSON, SUSANNA, taxpayer, 1798, Deer Creek Upper Hd., 1 dwelling house, 4 inferior houses, 2 acres, $120 valuation; 4 tracts (1064 acres) and 2 buildings (Thomas Green and Joseph Morrison, occupants) in Deer Creek Upper Hd., $1612.75 valuation, 1 slave. {Ref: TL}
SMITHSON, SUSANNA, head of family in 1800 (4th District). {Ref: CI}
SMITHSON, THOMAS, will probated Oct 27, 1795. {Ref: HW}
SMITHSON, THOMAS SR., bur. Oct 3, 1795, aged 83. {Ref: PR}
SMITHSON, WILLIAM, subpoenaed to the Grand Jury in August, 1797. {Ref: CC}
SMITHSON, WILLIAM, taxpayer, 1798, Bush River Lower Hd., 1 dwelling house, 7 inferior houses, 2 acres, $600 valuation; 3 tracts (688 acres) and 4 buildings (occupants: Negro Charles, William Green, William Smithson, Jr.,

and Negro Jim) in Bush River Lower Hd., $2541.37 valuation altogether, 7 slaves. {Ref: TL}

SMITHSON, WILLIAM (esquire), Associate Justice of the County Court, 1797-1800. {Ref: CC, CM}

SMITHSON, WILLIAM (esquire), head of family in 1800 (3rd District). {Ref: CI}

SMITHSON, WILLIAM JR., see "William Smithson," q.v.

SNODGRASS, WILLIAM, insolvent on lists of taxes due in 1791 and 1792 in Broad Creek Hd., as returned by Robert Amos, Jr. in 1791 (who spelled the name "Snodgrace") and Benjamin Preston in 1792. {Ref: IL 31.03, 31.12, 31.22}

SNODGRASS, WILLIAM ("run"), insolvent on a list of the county tax due William Osborn, sheriff, for 1791, as returned by Edward Prigg on Sep 20, 1791. {Ref: IL 31.17}

SNOWDAY, MATHEW, head of family in 1800 (2nd District). {Ref: CI}

SNOWDY, MATTHEW, taxpayer, 1798, Susquehanna Hd., 1 tract (62 acres) and 1 building, $121.50 valuation, no slaves. {Ref: TL}

SONGSER, JOHN, insolvent on list returned by John Guyton for taxes due for the year 1791. {Ref: IL 31.19}

SPENCE, HENRY, taxpayer, 1798, Susquehanna Hd., 1 tract (40 acres) and 1 building, $101.25 valuation, no slaves. {Ref: TL}

SPENCE, HENRY, head of family in 1800 (2nd District). {Ref: CI}

SPENCE, RICHARD, treated by Dr. Archer on Mar 12, 1791; also mentioned his wife and children (no names given) and that they lived near Horner's Stone House. {Ref: JA}

SPENCE, WILLIAM, head of family in 1800 (2nd District). {Ref: CI}. Also see "John Rumsey," q.v.

SPENCER, ENOCH, will probated May 28, 1799. {Ref: HW}

SPENCER, FRANCES LEE SHODAY, had an account at Hall's Store in December, 1791. {Ref: WH}

SPENCER, HANNAH E., b. 1798, d. on 14th of 2nd month, 1877, in her 79th year, bur. in Little Falls Quaker Cemetery in Fallston. {Ref: TI}

SPENCER, ISAAC, son of Richard and Martha, b. Sep 28, 1799, bapt. Aug 6, 1800. {Ref: PR}

SPENCER, JAMES, head of family in 1800 (2nd District). {Ref: CI}

SPENCER, JOHN W., b. Dec 25, 1793, d. Jan 18, 1855, bur. in Rock Run Cemetery at Craig's Corner. {Ref: TI}. Also see "Rebecca Keen Spencer," q.v.

SPENCER, MAHLON, taxpayer, 1798, Gunpowder Upper Hd., 1 dwelling house, 8 inferior houses, 2 acres, $230 valuation; 4 tracts (208 acres) in Gunpowder Upper Hd., $479.25 valuation, no slaves. {Ref: TL}

SPENCER, MALON, head of family in 1800 (3rd District). {Ref: CI}

SPENCER, MARTHA, see "Isaac Spencer," q.v.

SPENCER, REBECCA KEEN, wife of John W., b. Jan 28, 1796, d. Aug 4, 1873, bur. in Rock Run Cemetery at Craig's Corner. {Ref: TI}

SPENCER, RICHARD, see "Isaac Spencer," q.v.
SPENCER, RICHARD, taxpayer, 1798, Susquehanna Hd., 1 tract (80 acres) and 1 building, $206.25 valuation, no slaves. {Ref: TL}
SPENCER, RICHARD, insolvent on a list for the road tax due for 1791 in Harford Upper, Harford Lower, and Spesutia Upper as returned by Robert Amos, Jr. on Sep 18, 1793. {Ref: IL 31.18}
SPENCER, RICHARD, head of family in 1800 (1st District). {Ref: CI}
SPENCER, RICHARD, head of family in 1800 (2nd District). {Ref: CI}
SPENCER, SARAH, head of family in 1800 (3rd District). {Ref: CI}
SPICER, JOHN, head of family in 1800 (1st District). {Ref: CI}
ST. CLAIR, JAMES, granted a retailer's permit on Jun 12, 1797. {Ref: CC}
ST. CLAIR, JAMES, taxpayer, 1798, Bush River Upper & Eden Hd., 1 dwelling house, 4 inferior houses, 2 acres, $200 valuation; 3 tracts (418 acres, 120 perches) in Bush River Upper & Eden Hd., $1035 valuation, 1 slave. {Ref: TL}
ST. CLAIR, JAMES, head of family in 1800 (4th District). {Ref: CI}
ST. CLAIR, JAMES JR., head of family in 1800 (4th District). {Ref: CI}
ST. CLAIR, JAMES JR., taxpayer, 1798, Bush River Upper & Eden Hd., 1 dwelling house, 3 inferior houses, 2 acres, $135 valuation; 2 tracts (163 acres) in Bush River Upper & Eden Hd., $458.44 valuation, no slaves. {Ref: TL}
ST. CLAIR, JOHN, taxpayer, 1798, Deer Creek Upper Hd., 1 tract (139 acres, 40 perches) and 1 building, $355.80 valuation, no slaves. {Ref: TL}
ST. CLAIR, JOHN, served on a Grand Jury in March, 1799 and on a Petit Jury in March, 1800. {Ref: CM}
ST. CLAIR, JOHN, m. Temperance West on Dec 19, 1799. {Ref: PR}
ST. CLAIR, JOHN, head of family in 1800 (4th District). {Ref: CI}
ST. CLAIR (ST. CLAIRE), JOHN, head of family in 1800 (2nd District). {Ref: CI}
ST. CLAIR, MARTHA, taxpayer, 1798, Bush River Upper & Eden Hd., 1 dwelling house, 1 inferior house, 2 acres, $150 valuation; 2 tracts (105 acres) in Bush River Upper & Eden Hd., $236.25 valuation, no slaves. {Ref: TL}
ST. CLAIR, MARTHA, head of family in 1800 (4th District). {Ref: CI}
ST. CLAIR, THOMAS, head of family in 1800 (4th District). {Ref: CI}
ST. CLAIR, WILLIAM, taxpayer, 1798, Bush River Upper & Eden Hd., 1 dwelling house, 2 inferior houses, 2 acres, $300 valuation; 2 tracts (160 acres) in Bush River Upper & Eden Hd., $360 valuation, 1 slave. {Ref: TL}
ST. CLAIR, WILLIAM, head of family in 1800 (4th District). {Ref: CI}
STAFFORD, J. W., b. Aug --, 1798, d. May --, 1870, bur. in Mountain Christian Church Cemetery. {Ref: TI}
STALLINGS, ELIZABETH, m. Levi Culver on Jun 1, 1797. {Ref: PR}. Also see "Anna Kitty Dunn Tomkins," q.v.
STALLINGS, REBECCA, see "William Stallings" and "Samuel Stallings," q.v.
STALLINGS, SAMUEL, son of William and Rebecca, b. about Jul 1, 1795, bapt. May 27, 1798. {Ref: PR}

STALLINGS, WILLIAM, son of William and Rebecca, b. in August, 1796, bapt. May 27, 1798. {Ref: PR}. Also see "Samuel Stallings," q.v.

STALLINS, JACOB, insolvent on a list for the road tax due for 1791 in Harford Upper, Harford Lower, and Spesutia Upper as returned by Robert Amos, Jr. on Sep 18, 1793, but his name was crossed off the list. {Ref: IL 31.18}

STALLIONS, JACOB, head of family in 1800 (1st District). {Ref: CI}

STALLIONS, REBECCA, head of family in 1800 (1st District). {Ref: CI}

STALLIONS (STALLINS), RICHARD, served as constable in Harford Upper Hd., 1797. {Ref: CC, CM}

STANDIFORD, ANN, insolvent on a list for 1791 in Gunpowder Upper and Bush River Lower Hundreds, as filed by John Bond, Deputy Sheriff, on Sep 20, 1791. {Ref: IL 31.24}

STANDIFORD, ANN, insolvent on list returned by Robert Carlile for taxes due for the year 1791. {Ref: IL 31.16}

STANDIFORD, ANN, will probated May 9, 1797. {Ref: HW}

STANDIFORD, BENJAMIN, head of family in 1800 (4th District). {Ref: CI}

STANDIFORD, DAVID, taxpayer, 1798, Gunpowder Upper Hd., 1 tract (26 acres) and 1 building, $100.13 valuation, no slaves. {Ref: TL}

STANDIFORD (STANDEFORDE), DAVID, head of family in 1800 (1st District). {Ref: CI}

STANDIFORD, EDMOND, taxpayer, 1798, Bush River Upper & Eden Hd., 1 dwelling house, 1 inferior house, 2 acres, $105 valuation; 1 tract (83 acres) in Bush River Upper & Eden Hd., $93.38 valuation, no slaves. {Ref: TL}

STANDIFORD (STANDEFORD), EDMUND, head of family in 1800 (4th District). {Ref: CI}

STANDIFORD, LLOYD, see "Mary Standiford," q.v.

STANDIFORD, MARY, widow of Lloyd Standiford, b. 1791, d. Dec --, 1863, in her 72nd year, bur. in Christ Episcopal (Rock Spring) Church Cemetery. {Ref: TI}

STANDIFORD (STANDEFORD), RICHARD, head of family in 1800 (3rd District). {Ref: CI}

STANDIFORD, SAMUEL, insolvent on list returned by Robert Carlile for taxes due for the year 1791. {Ref: IL 31.16}

STANIFORD, SALLY, wife of John, was b. in 1796, d. 1861, aged 65, bur. in Mountain Christian Church Cemetery. {Ref: TI}

STANDIFORD, WILLIAM, will probated Jan 7, 1794. {Ref: HW}

STANLEY, MARGARITE, head of family in 1800 (1st District). {Ref: CI}

STANSBURY, ABRAHAM, see "James Edward Stansbury," q.v.

STANSBURY, ELIJAH, served on a Petit Jury in March, 1799. {Ref: CM}

STANSBURY, ELIJAH, taxpayer, 1798, Deer Creek Upper Hd., 1 dwelling house, 6 inferior houses, 2 acres, $160 valuation; 2 tracts (231 acres) in Deer Creek Upper Hd., $415.65 valuation, 3 slaves. {Ref: TL}

STANSBURY (STANDSBURY), ELIGHA, head of family in 1800 (4th District). {Ref: CI}

STANSBURY, ELIZABETH, see "James Edward Stansbury," q.v.
STANSBURY, JAMES EDWARD, son of Abraham and Elizabeth, b. Feb 26, 1799, bapt. Sep 25, 1799. {Ref: PR}
STEARNS, JOHN L., b. Jan --, 1798, d. May 1, 1867, bur. in North Bend Cemetery. {Ref: TI}
STEEL, ABRAHAM, head of family in 1800 (2nd District). {Ref: CI}. Also see "Havre de Grace Company," q.v.
STEEL, CASSANDRA, dau. of John and Mary, b. Jul 4, 1797, bapt. Jul 28, 1799. {Ref: PR}
STEEL (STEELL), ELIZABETH, head of family in 1800 (5th District). {Ref: CI}
STEEL (STEELL), JAMES, head of family in 1800 (5th District). {Ref: CI}
STEEL, JAMES, appointed a Judge of Elections in the 5th District on Jul 28, 1800. {Ref: CM}
STEEL, JOHN, see "Cassandra Steel," q.v.
STEEL, JOHN, had accounts at Hall's Store in January, 1791, and August, 1791. {Ref: WH}
STEEL, JOHN, head of family in 1800 (2nd District). {Ref: CI}
STEEL, JOHN HENDERSON, son of Joseph and Margaret, b. Jul 13, 1798, bapt. Oct 27, 1800. {Ref: PR}
STEEL, JOSEPH, see "Pinchen Steel" and "John Henderson Steel," q.v.
STEEL, MARGARET, see "Pinchen Steel" and "John Henderson Steel," q.v.
STEEL, MARY, see "Cassandra Steel," q.v.
STEEL, PEGGY, taxpayer, 1798, Broad Creek Hd., 3 tracts (243 acres) and 2 buildings (Charles Bevin or Beven was the occupant of one of them), $465.95 valuation, no slaves. {Ref: TL}
STEEL, PINCHEN, child of Joseph and Margaret, b. Oct 21, 1795, bapt. Jun 12, 1796. {Ref: PR}
STEELE, JOHN, see "Abiann Sappington," q.v.
STEPHENSON, GEORGE, head of family in 1800 (2nd District). {Ref: CI}
STEPHENSON, HANNAH, wife of William B., b. 1800, d. Jun --, 1880, bur. in Rock Run Cemetery at Craig's Corner. {Ref: TI}
STEPHENSON, HETTY, wife of Rev. William, b. 1800, d. Aug 3, 1854, in her 54th year, bur. in the Parker Family Graveyard near Craig's Corner. {Ref: TI}
STEPHENSON, JAMES, head of family in 1800 (2nd District). {Ref: CI}
STEPHENSON, JOHN, head of family in 1800 (2nd District). {Ref: CI}
STEPHENSON, JONAS, m. Mary Dunsheath on Oct 2, 1800. {Ref: PR}
STEPHENSON, MARY A. (Miss), b. 1799, d. Oct 3, 1811, in her 12th year, bur. in the Parker Family Graveyard near Craig's Corner. {Ref: TI}
STEPHENSON, SUSANNAH, head of family in 1800 (5th District). {Ref: CI}
STEPHENSON, THOMAS (cooper), treated by Dr. Archer on Jul 26, 1797. {Ref: JA}
STEPHENSON, WILLIAM, head of family in 1800 (2nd District). {Ref: CI}. Also see "Hetty Stephenson," q.v.
STERRETT, ALEXANDER, insolvent on a list for 1791 in Gunpowder Upper and Bush River Lower Hundreds, as filed by John Bond, Deputy Sheriff, on Sep 20,

1791 (who listed him as a single man). {Ref: IL 31.24}

STERRETT, ALEXANDER, insolvent on list returned by Robert Carlile for taxes due for the year 1791. {Ref: IL 31.16}

STEVENS, JOHN, insolvent on list returned by Robert Carlile for taxes due for the year 1791. {Ref: IL 31.16}

STEVENSON, ANDREW, m. Isabella Smith on Nov 30, 1793. {Ref: PR}

STEVENSON, ANN, insolvent on a list for the road tax due for 1791 in Harford Upper, Harford Lower, and Spesutia Upper as returned by Robert Amos, Jr. on Sep 18, 1793. {Ref: IL 31.18}

STEVENSON, ANN, treated by Dr. Archer on Dec 17, 1792. {Ref: JA}

STEVENSON, DELIA, m. Nathan Gordon on Nov 2, 1797. {Ref: PR}

STEVENSON, GEORGE, taxpayer, 1798, Susquehanna Hd., 1 tract (120 acres) and 1 building, $427.50 valuation, no slaves. {Ref: TL}

STEVENSON, GEORGE, insolvent on a list for the county tax due for 1791 in Susquehanna Hd., as returned by Thomas Taylor on Sep 17, 1792. {Ref: IL 31.12, 31.02}

STEVENSON, HENRY (doctor), of Baltimore Town, taxpayer, 1798, Spesutia Lower Hd., 1 dwelling house, 4 inferior houses, 2 acres, $100.10 valuation; 1 tract (582 acres) and 1 building in Spesutia Lower Hd., $3953.20 valuation, no slaves. {Ref: TL}

STEVENSON, HENRY (doctor, Baltimore Town), insolvent on a list for the road tax due for 1791 in Harford Upper, Harford Lower, and Spesutia Upper as returned by Robert Amos, Jr. on Sep 18, 1793. {Ref: IL 31.18}. Also see "Dr. Henry Stevenson's heirs," q.v.

STEVENSON, HENRY'S (DOCTOR) HEIRS, insolvents on a list for the road tax due for 1791 in Harford Upper, Harford Lower, and Spesutia Upper as returned by Robert Amos, Jr. on Sep 18, 1793. {Ref: IL 31.18}

STEVENSON, JAMES, taxpayer, 1798, Susquehanna Hd., 1 dwelling house, 1 inferior house, 2 acres, $100 valuation; 2 tracts (260 acres, 16 perches) in Susquehanna Hd., $780.30 valuation, 3 slaves. {Ref: TL}

STEVENSON, JONAS, insolvent on a list for the road tax due for 1791 in Harford Upper, Harford Lower, and Spesutia Upper as returned by Robert Amos, Jr. on Sep 18, 1793. {Ref: IL 31.18}. Also see "James Phillips, Sr.," q.v.

STEVENSON, RACHEL, taxpayer, 1798, Susquehanna Hd., 1 tract (163 acres) and 1 building, $488.99 valuation, 1 slave. {Ref: TL}

STEVENSON, RACHEL (widow), treated by Dr. Archer on Apr 2, 1794. {Ref: JA}

STEVENSON, REBECCA, bur. Nov 13, 1798. {Ref: PR}

STEVENSON, WILLIAM, taxpayer, 1798, Susquehanna Hd., 1 tract (108 acres) and 1 building, $443.25 valuation, 1 slave. {Ref: TL}

STEWARD, SAMUEL, head of family in 1800 (1st District). {Ref: CI}

STEWART, ALEXANDER, insolvent on lists returned by Robert Carlile and John Guyton (the latter listed the name as "Alexdr. Steward") for taxes due for the year 1791. {Ref: IL 31.16, 31.19}

STEWART, ELIZABETH, taxpayer, 1798, Susquehanna Hd., 1 tract (200 acres) and 2 buildings, $517.50 valuation, 2 slaves. {Ref: TL}
STEWART, JOHN, insolvent on list returned for the road tax due for 1791 by John Bull. {Ref: IL 31.14}
STEWART, JOHN, insolvent on lists of taxes due in 1791 and 1792 in Broad Creek Hd., as returned by Robert Amos, Jr. in 1791 and Benjamin Preston in 1792. {Ref: IL 31.03, 31.12, 31.22}
STEWART, MARY, see "David Sweeney," q.v.
STEWART, MITCHELL, insolvent on a list for the road tax due for 1791 in Harford Upper, Harford Lower, and Spesutia Upper as returned by Robert Amos, Jr. on Sep 18, 1793. {Ref: IL 31.18}
STILES, EDWARD, head of family in 1800 (Havre de Grace). {Ref: CI}
STILES, ELIZA (widow), treated by Dr. Archer on Jun 26, 1791. {Ref: JA}
STINSON, ANDREW, head of family in 1800 (3rd District). {Ref: CI}
STINSON, JAMES, mentioned in a survey deposition on Jan 14, 1800 as "to where formerly stood James Stinson's dwelling house near *Wild Cat Denn*." {Ref: JS}
STINSON, WIDOW, see "James Nickleson," q.v.
STINSON, WILLIAM, mentioned in a survey deposition on Jan 29, 1800 as "Wm. Stinson's house where Hudson formerly lived or the place where said Stinson's house formerly stood." {Ref: JS}
STIRLING, ANN (neé Sutton), wife of Robert, b. May 1, 1800, d. Mar 30, 1845, bur. in Bethel Presbyterian Church Cemetery at Madonna. {Ref: BC}
STIRLING, JAMES, see "Robert Stirling," q.v.
STIRLING, ROBERT, husband of Ann Sutton and son of James Stirling (b. 1751 and came to America from Scotland in 1774) and Elizabeth Gibson, b. Apr 20, 1800, d. Sep 30, 1875, bur. in Bethel Presbyterian Church Cemetery at Madonna. {Ref: BC}
STOCKDALE, JOHN, taxpayer, 1798, Bush River Lower Hd., 1 dwelling house, 1 inferior house, 1 acre, $150 valuation; 1 tract (130 acres) in Bush River Lower Hd., $483.75 valuation, no slaves. {Ref: TL}
STOCKDALE, JOHN, head of family in 1800 (3rd District). {Ref: CI}
STOCKDALE, MARY, m. James Jones on May 29, 1795. {Ref: PR}
STOCKSDALE, THOMAS, m. Sarah Baxter on Dec 18, 1797. {Ref: PR}
STOFER, JACOB, head of family in 1800 (4th District). {Ref: CI}
STOKES (STOAKES), DAVID, head of family in 1800 (5th District). {Ref: CI}
STOKES, ELEANOR ROGER, b. 1783, d. Aug 7, 1791, in her 8th year, bur. in St. George's Episcopal Church Cemetery at Perryman. {Ref: TI}
STOKES, JOSEPH, taxpayer, 1798, Deer Creek Middle Hd., 1 dwelling house, 5 inferior houses, 2 acres, $200 valuation; 1 tract (85 acres) in Deer Creek Upper Hd., $122.50 valuation, no slaves. {Ref: TL}
STOKES (STOAKES), JOSEPH, head of family in 1800 (5th District). {Ref: CI}
STOKES, WILLIAM, head of family in 1800 (2nd District). {Ref: CI}

STOKES, WILLIAM B., or JAMES THOMPSON, taxpayer, 1798, Spesutia Lower Hd., 1 dwelling house, 1 inferior house, 105 perches and 213 sq. ft. of land (James Thompson, occupant), $3000 valuation; 2 tracts (111 acres, 80 perches) in Spesutia Lower Hd. (James W. Hall, occupant), $3582.70, 1 slave. {Ref: TL}

STOKESBERRY, WILLIAM ("dead"), insolvent on a list for 1791 in Gunpowder Upper and Bush River Lower Hundreds, as filed by John Bond, Deputy Sheriff, on Sep 20, 1791. {Ref: IL 31.24}

STOLINGER, GEORGE, m. Ann Deaver on Jan 23, 1800. {Ref: PR}. Also see "George Strolenger," q.v.

STONELY, JAMES, insolvent on list returned for the road tax due for 1791 by John Bull. {Ref: IL 31.14}

STONELY, JAMES, insolvent on a list for county taxes due in 1792 as returned by Benjamin Preston. {Ref: IL 31.00}

STREET, DAVID, taxpayer, 1798, Bush River Upper & Eden Hd., 1 dwelling house, 4 inferior houses, 2 acres, $200 valuation; 4 tracts (314 acres, 40 perches) in Bush River Upper & Eden Hd., $530.29 valuation, 2 slaves. {Ref: TL}

STREET, DAVID, head of family in 1800 (4th District). {Ref: CI}

STREET, J., see "John Streett," q.v.

STREET, JEMIMA, head of family in 1800 (4th District). {Ref: CI}. Also see "John Bay," q.v.

STREET, JOHN, tract *Archy's Denn* surveyed between 1792 and 1796. {Ref: SB}

STREET, JOHN, subpoenaed to the Grand Jury in August, 1797. {Ref: CC}

STREET, JOHN, served on a Petit Jury in March, 1798. {Ref: CM}

STREET, JOHN, taxpayer, 1798, Deer Creek Upper Hd., 1 dwelling house, 7 inferior houses, 2 acres, $350 valuation; 1 tract (836 acres) in Deer Creek Upper Hd., $1459.13 valuation, 6 slaves; also, taxpayer, Deer Creek Upper Hd., 1 building (Backley Patten, occupant), $28.12 valuation; also, taxpayer, Deer Creek Upper Hd., 2 tracts (199 acres) and 1 building (James Deaver, occupant), $761.18 valuation, no slaves; also, taxpayer, Deer Creek Middle Hd., 1 dwelling house, 4 inferior houses, 2 acres (Josiah Johnson, occupant), $120 valuation, no slaves; also, taxpayer, 2 tracts (227 acres) in Deer Creek Middle Hd. (Josiah Johnson, occupant), $375.75 valuation, no slaves. {Ref: TL}

STREET, ROGERS, see "Thomas Street, Sr.," q.v.

STREET, ROGERS, taxpayer, 1798, Deer Creek Upper Hd., no dwelling house listed in this part of the tax schedule, no land listed, 1 slave. {Ref: TL}

STREET, ROGERS (captain), head of family in 1800 (4th District). {Ref: CI}

STREET, SAMUEL, husband of Isabel Bay and son of Thomas Street and Jemima McClure, b. 1800, d. May 20, 1881, bur. in Bethel Presbyterian Church Cemetery at Madonna. {Ref: BC}

STREET, THOMAS, see "Samuel Street," q.v.

STREET, THOMAS, tracts *Pleasant Hills Corrected, Reviction, Sarah's Garden,* and *Rock Ridge* surveyed between 1792 and 1796. {Ref: SB}

STREET, THOMAS, head of family in 1800 (4th District). {Ref: CI}
STREET, THOMAS JR., head of family in 1800 (4th District). {Ref: CI}
STREET, THOMAS JR., taxpayer, 1798, Bush River Upper & Eden Hd., 1 dwelling house, 1 inferior house, 2 acres, $250 valuation; 1 tract (337 acres, 80 perches) in Bush River Upper & Eden Hd., $569.53 valuation, no slaves. {Ref: TL}
STREET, THOMAS SR., taxpayer, 1798, Bush River Upper & Eden Hd., 1 dwelling house, 5 inferior houses, 2 acres, $400 valuation; 5 tracts (1385 acres, 40 perches) in Bush River Upper & Eden Hd., $2041.73 valuation, 3 slaves; also, taxpayer, Deer Creek Upper Hd., 1 building (Rogers Street, occupant), and 2 tracts (116 acres, 80 perches) and 1 building (Jacob Gladdon, occupant), $180 valuation altogether. {Ref: TL}
STREET, WILLIAM, head of family in 1800 (4th District). {Ref: CI}
STREETT, ABRAHAM J. (doctor), b. Jun 6, 1799, d. Nov 9, 1867, aged 68 years, 5 months, and 3 days, bur. in Holy Cross Church Cemetery at The Rocks. {Ref: TI}
STREETT, GLENN, b. 1795, d. Mar 26, 1835, aged 40, bur. in Christ Episcopal (Rock Spring) Church Cemetery. {Ref: TI}
STREETT, ISABELLA, see "Isabella Butler," q.v.
STREETT, JOHN, son of Col. J. Streett, b. 1797, d. Apr 29, 1873, aged 76, bur. in Christ Episcopal (Rock Spring) Church Cemetery. {Ref: TI}
STREETT, JOHN (esquire), head of family in 1800 (5th District). {Ref: CI}
STREETT, MARY A., wife of William, b. Sep 23, 1799, d. Nov 17, 1874, aged 76 years, 1 month, and 24 days, bur. in St. Mary's Catholic Church Cemetery in Pylesville. {Ref: TI}
STREETT, NANCY, b. Nov 2, 1800, d. Nov 8, 1852, bur. in Christ Episcopal (Rock Spring) Church Cemetery. {Ref: TI}
STREETT, SARAH, see "James Watt" and "William Watt," q.v.
STREETT, THOMAS, tract *Reviction* surveyed in 1796 and granted in 1797, and tract *Sarah's Garden Resurveyed* surveyed in 1797 and granted in 1798. {Ref: CB}. Also see "Richard Deaver," q.v.
STREETT, WILLIAM, husband of Mary A., b. Dec 6, 1795, d. Mar 6, 1860, aged 64 years and 3 months, bur. in St. Mary's Catholic Church Cemetery in Pylesville. {Ref: TI}
STRICKER, JOHN, m. Catharine Wilson on Mar 30, 1797. {Ref: PR}
STRICKLAND (STRIKLAND), HENRY, insolvent on list returned for the county tax for 1791 by William Osburn in Gunpowder Lower Hundred. {Ref: IL 31.15}
STRICKLAND, JOHN, m. Alice Perry on Jun 30, 1793. {Ref: PR}
STRICKLAND, JOHN, insolvent on list returned for the county tax for 1791 by William Osburn in Gunpowder Lower Hundred. {Ref: IL 31.15}
STRICKLAND, JOHN, head of family in 1800 (1st District). {Ref: CI}
STRITEHOFF, SARAH BELINDA (neé Deaver), wife of John, b. Feb 17, 1798, d. Aug 23, 1877, bur. in Bethel Presbyterian Church Cemetery at Madonna. {Ref:

STROBLE, CASSANDRA, taxpayer, 1798, Bush River Upper & Eden Hd., 1 tract (103 acres) and 1 building, $202.50 valuation, no slaves. {Ref: TL}
STROLENGER, GEORGE, head of family in 1800 (2nd District). {Ref: CI}
STROLENGER, GEORGE JR., head of family in 1800 (2nd District). {Ref: CI}
STRONG, ELIZABETH, head of family in 1800 (1st District). {Ref: CI}
STRONG, JOSEPH, head of family in 1800 (1st District). {Ref: CI}
STRONG, NATHANIEL, insolvent on lists returned for the county and road taxes due for 1791 by John Bull in Gunpowder Lower Hd. (listed as "Nathan Strong" on one listed). {Ref: IL 31.14, 31.15}
STRONG, THOMAS, taxpayer, 1798, Gunpowder Lower Hd., 1 dwelling house, 3 inferior houses, 2 acres, $150 valuation; 1 tract (198 acres), $668.25 valuation, 6 slaves. {Ref: TL}
STROUD, JOHN, head of family in 1800 (4th District). {Ref: CI}
STROUD, MARY, see "William Stroud," q.v.
STROUD, RACHEL, insolvent on list returned for the road tax due for 1791 by John Bull. {Ref: IL 31.14}
STROUD (STROWD), RACHEL, insolvent on a list for county taxes due in 1792 as returned by Benjamin Preston. {Ref: IL 31.00}
STROUD, THOMAS, see "William Stroud," q.v.
STROUD, THOMAS, insolvent on list returned for the road tax due for 1791 by John Bull. {Ref: IL 31.14}
STROUD, THOMAS, head of family in 1800 (5th District). {Ref: CI}
STROUD (STROWD), THOMAS, insolvent on a list for county taxes due in 1792 as returned by Benjamin Preston. {Ref: IL 31.00}
STROUD, WILLIAM, son of Thomas and Mary, b. Jun 29, 1797, bapt. Jun 29, 1797. {Ref: PR}
STUART, JOHN, taxpayer, 1798, Bush River Upper & Eden Hd., 1 tract (74 acres, 80 perches), $125.72 valuation, no slaves. {Ref: TL}
STUMP, ----, see "Wilson & Stump," q.v.
STUMP, HANNAH C., see "Hannah C. Williams," q.v.
STUMP, HENRY (judge), of Perry Point and Baltimore, b. Dec 28, 1795, d. Nov 29, 1865, bur. in Stump Family Graveyard near Craig's Corner. {Ref: TI}
STUMP, HENRY, taxpayer, 1798, Susquehanna Hd., 1 dwelling house, 1 inferior house, 2 acres, $300 valuation; 8 tracts (457 acres, 40 perches) in Susquehanna Hd., $1533.94 valuation, and 4 buildings (occupants: Philip Hopkins, John Warham or Wareham, William Hobbs, and Michael Middleditch), $70.88 valuation, 6 slaves. {Ref: TL}
STUMP, HENRY, head of family in 1800 (2nd District). {Ref: CI}
STUMP, HENRY, head of family in 1800 (5th District). {Ref: CI}
STUMP, HENRY JR., taxpayer, 1798, Deer Creek Lower Hd., 1 dwelling house, 3 inferior houses, 2 acres, $150 valuation; 2 tracts (178 acres) in Deer Creek Lower Hd., $835 valuation, no slaves. {Ref: TL}

STUMP, HERMAN, charged for not keeping a sufficient bridge over his mill race in 1797. {Ref: CD, August Term, 1797}
STUMP, HERMAN, purchased pork on Dec 8, 1797 at Bush River Store. {Ref: AH}
STUMP, HERMAN, taxpayer, 1798, Harford Upper Hd., 1 dwelling house, 9 inferior houses, 2 acres, $650 valuation, no slaves. {Ref: TL}.
STUMP, HERMAN, b. at Stafford on Aug 13, 1798, d. Mar 13, 1881, bur. in Stump Family Graveyard near Craig's Corner. {Ref: TI}
STUMP, HERMAN, head of family in 1800 (1st District). {Ref: CI}
STUMP, HERMAN (HARMAN) & COMPANY, licensed retailers in March, 1795 and August, 1797. {Ref: CC}
STUMP, JOHN, taxpayer, 1798, Deer Creek Lower Hd., 1 dwelling house, 2 inferior houses, 1 acre, $800 valuation; 3 tracts (606 acres) in Deer Creek Lower Hd., $8882.24 valuation, no slaves; also, taxpayer, Deer Creek Lower Hd., 1 dwelling house, 1 inferior house, 40 perches of land (J. Harlin, occupant), $150 valuation; also, taxpayer, 1 tract (706 acres) in Spesutia Lower Hd., $8339.62 valuation, no slaves; also, taxpayer, Deer Creek Lower Hd., 1 dwelling house, 1 inferior house, 80 perches of land (Joseph Parker, occupant), $250 valuation; also, taxpayer, 1 tract (236 acres) and 1 building (John Carter, occupant) in Susquehanna Hd., $4657.50 valuation, no slaves; also, taxpayer, Deer Creek Lower Hd., 1 dwelling house, 40 perches of land (Isaac Towson, occupant), $170 valuation, no slaves; also, taxpayer, Deer Creek Lower Hd., 1 dwelling house, 3 inferior houses, 1 acre (Edward Jolly, occupant), $150 valuation, no slaves; and, taxpayer, 1798, Spesutia Lower Hd., 1 dwelling house, 4 inferior houses, 2 acres (J. L. Gibson, occupant), $250 valuation, no slaves. {Ref: TL}
STUMP, JOHN, insolvent on a list for the road tax for 1792, as returned for Robert Amoss, tax collector. {Ref: IL 13.12}
STUMP, JOHN, head of family in 1800 (5th District). {Ref: CI}
STUMP, JOHN JR., treated by Dr. Archer on Jan 9, 1792; also mentioned his wife and child (no names given). {Ref: JA}
STUMP, JOHN SR., wrote his will "of Cecil County" in 1794, probated Mar 17, 1797 in Harford County. {Ref: HW}
STUMP, JOHN & COMPANY, licensed retailers in August, 1797. {Ref: CC}
STUMP, JOHN WILSON, b. Feb 23, 1792, d. Oct 21, 1862, bur. in Stump Family Graveyard near Craig's Corner. {Ref: TI}. Also see "Sarah Biays Stump," q.v.
STUMP, SAMUEL C., b. 1792, d. May 13, 1854, in his 62nd year, bur. in Stump Family Graveyard near Craig's Corner. {Ref: TI}
STUMP, SARAH BIAYS, wife of John W., b. Oct 26, 1797, d. May 19, 1876, bur. in Stump Family Graveyard near Craig's Corner. {Ref: TI}
STUMP, THOMAS C., b. Feb 8, 1794, d. Feb 12, 1858 or 1859, bur. in Stump Family Graveyard near Craig's Corner. {Ref: TI}
STUMP, WILLIAM, taxpayer, 1798, Deer Creek Lower Hd., 1 dwelling house, 1

inferior house, 2 acres, $250 valuation; 2 tracts (330 acres) in Deer Creek Lower Hd., $1377.37 valuation, 1 slave; also, taxpayer, Deer Creek Lower Hd., 1 dwelling house, 2 inferior houses, 2 acres (James Vissage, occupant), $215 valuation, no slaves. {Ref: TL}

STUMP, WILLIAM, head of family in 1800 (5th District). {Ref: CI}

STUMP, WILLIAM HERMAN, b. 1797, d. Jun 21, 1880, aged 83, bur. in St. George's Episcopal Church Cemetery at Perryman. {Ref: TI}

SUDER, NICHOLAS, taxpayer, 1798, Spesutia Lower Hd., 1 tract (44 perches, 21 sq. ft.) and 1 building, $101.25 valuation, no slaves. {Ref: TL}. Also see "James Brindley," q.v.

SUDER, WILLIAM, head of family in 1800 (2nd District). {Ref: CI}

SUPHER(?), SAMUEL, had an account at Hall's Store in January, 1791. {Ref: WH}

SUTER, ANN, dau. of Nicholas and Mary, b. Jan 27, 1796, bapt. Jul 13, 1799. {Ref: PR}

SUTER, GABRIEL, son of Nicholas and Mary, b. Mar 22, 1798, bapt. Jul 13, 1799. {Ref: PR}

SUTER, JACOB, son of Nicholas and Mary, b. Jul 25, 1791, bapt. Jul 13, 1799, d. Jul 12, 1840, in his 49th year, bur. in St. George's Episcopal Church Cemetery at Perryman. {Ref: TI, PR}

SUTER, MARY, dau. of Nicholas and Mary, b. Aug 19, 1793, bapt. Jul 13, 1799. {Ref: PR}. Also see "Jacob Suter" and "Ann Suter" and "Gabriel Suter" and "Nicholas Suter," q.v.

SUTER, NICHOLAS, see "Nicholas Suder" and "Jacob Suter" and "Mary Suter" and "Ann Suter" and "Gabriel Suter," q.v.

SUTER, NICHOLAS, son of Nicholas and Mary, b. May 3, 1800, bapt. Sep 7, 1800. {Ref: PR}

SUTER (SUITOR), NICHOLAS, head of family in 1800 (Havre de Grace). {Ref: CI}

SUTHERLAND, ALEXANDER, see "Bennet Jarrett," q.v.

SUTHERLAND, ALEXANDER, mentioned in a survey deposition on Jan 17, 1800 as "Lotts 9, 10, 11 & 12 is Alexr. Sutherland's place." {Ref: JS}

SUTHERLAND (SUTHERLIN), ALEXANDER, head of family in 1800 (4th District). {Ref: CI}.

SUTHERLAND, ISABELLA, b. 1791, d. Mar 25, 1873, aged 82, bur. in Christ Episcopal (Rock Spring) Church Cemetery. {Ref: TI}

SUTHERTHWAITS, JOHN, charged for selling liquors in 1797. {Ref: CD, March Term, 1797}

SUTTON, ANN, see "Ann Stirling" and "Robert Stirling," q.v.

SUTTON, JONATHAN, insolvent on a list for the road tax due for 1791 in Harford Upper, Harford Lower, and Spesutia Upper as returned by Robert Amos, Jr. on Sep 18, 1793. {Ref: IL 31 18}. Also see "Sally Sutton," q.v.

SUTTON, MARGARET, m. Nicholas York on Dec 20, 1798. {Ref: PR}

SUTTON, MARTHA, consort of Samuel, b. Apr 29, 1794, d. Jun 10, 1824, aged 30 years, 1 month, and 11 days, bur. in St. George's Episcopal Church

Cemetery at Perryman. {Ref: Tl}

SUTTON, OSWIN, insolvent, Harford Lower and Spesutia Lower Hundreds, on a tax list returned by George Lyttle on Sep 21, 1791. {Ref: IL 31.20, 31.21}

SUTTON, OSWIN, insolvent on a list for the road tax due for 1791 in Harford Upper, Harford Lower, and Spesutia Upper as returned by Robert Amos, Jr. on Sep 18, 1793. {Ref: IL 31.18}

SUTTON, REBECCA, head of family in 1800 (1st District). {Ref: Cl}

SUTTON, RUBEN, head of family in 1800 (3rd District). {Ref: Cl}

SUTTON, RUBIN, insolvent, Harford Lower and Spesutia Lower Hundreds, on a tax list returned by George Lyttle on Sep 21, 1791. {Ref: IL 31.20, 31.21}

SUTTON, RUBIN, insolvent on a list for the road tax due for 1791 in Harford Upper, Harford Lower, and Spesutia Upper as returned by Robert Amos, Jr. on Sep 18, 1793 (his name was crossed off the list). {Ref: IL 31.18}

SUTTON, RUBIN, insolvent on list returned for the county tax for 1791 by William Osburn in Gunpowder Lower Hd. (which listed him as a single man). {Ref: IL 31.15}

SUTTON, SALLY, dau. of Jonathan and Sally, b. Jan 2, 1799. {Ref: PR}

SUTTON, SAMUEL, see "Susan Sutton" and Martha Sutton," q.v.

SUTTON, SAMUEL, insolvent, Harford Lower and Spesutia Lower Hundreds, on a tax list returned by George Lyttle on Sep 21, 1791. {Ref: IL 31.20, 31.21}

SUTTON, SAMUEL, insolvent on a list for the road tax due for 1791 in Harford Upper, Harford Lower, and Spesutia Upper as returned by Robert Amos, Jr. on Sep 18, 1793 (his name was crossed off the list). {Ref: IL 31.18}

SUTTON, SAMUEL, will probated Aug 13, 1793. {Ref: HW}

SUTTON, SAMUEL, b. 1795, d. Mar 8, 1878, aged 83, bur. in St. George's Episcopal Church Cemetery at Perryman. {Ref: Tl}.

SUTTON, SUSAN, wife of Samuel, b. 1792, d. Jun 2, 1879, aged 87, bur. in St. George's Episcopal Church Cemetery at Perryman. {Ref: Tl}

SWAIN, NATHAN, head of family in 1800 (2nd District). {Ref: Cl}

SWAINE, ELIZABETH, m. Amos Cord on Jan 23, 1798. {Ref: PR}

SWAN, CATHERINE, taxpayer, 1798, Bush River Upper & Eden Hd., 1 dwelling house, 1 inferior house, 2 acres, $105 valuation; 1 tract (122 acres) in Bush River Upper & Eden Hd., $274.50 valuation, no slaves. {Ref: TL}

SWAN, CATHERINE AND JACOB, tract *Swan's Delight* surveyed between 1792 and 1796. {Ref: SB}

SWAN (SWANN), CATRINE, head of family in 1800 (4th District). {Ref: Cl}

SWAN, FRED, insolvent on list returned by Robert Carlile for taxes due for the year 1791. {Ref: IL 31.16}

SWAN, FREDERICK, will probated May 13, 1793 (1794?). {Ref: HW}

SWAN, JACOB AND CATHERINE, tract *Swan's Delight* surveyed between 1792 and 1796. {Ref: SB}

SWAN (SWANN), JACOB, head of family in 1800 (4th District). {Ref: Cl}

SWARTH (SWARTS), SARAH, see "Kidd Lynch," q.v.

SWARTS, SAMUEL, head of family in 1800 (1st District). {Ref: CI}. Also see "Michael Mather," q.v.
SWEENEY, DAVID, charged for killing a deer in 1794. {Ref: CD, March and August Terms, 1795}
SWEENEY, DAVID, served as constable in Broad Creek Hd., 1798-1799. {Ref: CM}
SWEENEY, DAVID, insolvent on lists of taxes due in 1791 and 1792 in Broad Creek Hd., as returned by Robert Amos, Jr. in 1791 and Benjamin Preston in 1792. {Ref: IL 31.03, 31.12, 31.22}
SWEENEY, DAVID, charged for assaulting Mary Stewart in 1792. {Ref: CD, March and August Terms, 1795, and March Term, 1797}
SWEENEY, DAVID, charged for killing a deer in 1796. {Ref: CD, March and August Terms, 1797}
SWEENEY, DAVID, head of family in 1800 (5th District). {Ref: CI}
SWEENEY (SWENEY), MATHEW (schoolmaster), treated by Dr. Archer on Jul 18, 1792. {Ref: JA}. Also see "James Wells," q.v.
SWEENEY, PATRICK, b. in 1800 in Dunlow, County Donegal, Ireland, d. Dec 17, 1895, aged 95, bur. in St. Mary's Catholic Church Cemetery in Pylesville. {Ref: TI}
SWEENEY, SARAH, insolvent on lists of taxes due in 1791 and 1792 in Broad Creek Hd., as returned by and Robert Amos, Jr. in 1791 and Benjamin Preston in 1792. {Ref: IL 31.03, 31.12, 31.22}
SWEENEY, SARAH ("run"), insolvent on a list of the county tax due William Osborn, sheriff, for 1791, as returned by Edward Prigg on Sep 20, 1791. {Ref: IL 31.17}
SWIFT, DAVID, head of family in 1800 (1st District). {Ref: CI}
SYLVERS, DAVID, see "David Silvers," q.v.
SYMINGTON, JOHN, b. Dec 23, 1796 in Delaware, entered West Point in 1813, commissioned 1815, colonel of Ordnance, U. S. Army, d. Apr 4, 1864 in this parish [Trappe Church, formerly St. James]. {Ref: Inscription on side at entrance to the church}. Also see *Maryland Genealogical Society Bulletin*, Vol. 4, No. 1 (February, 1963).
SYNG, CHARLES' HEIRS, taxpayers, 1798, Spesutia Lower Hd., 1 tract (1 acre, 60 perches, 105 sq. ft.), $67.50 valuation, no slaves. {Ref: TL}
TALBOTT, EDMOND, will probated Dec 8, 1794. {Ref: HW}
TALBOTT, MARY, see "Negro London," q.v.
TANNER, PIERCE, head of family in 1800 (Abingdon). {Ref: CI}
TARBOUT, JAMES, head of family in 1800 (5th District). {Ref: CI}
TATE, DAVID, taxpayer, 1798, Bush River Upper & Eden Hd., 1 dwelling house, 3 inferior houses, 2 acres, $200 valuation; 2 tracts (269 acres, 80 perches) in Bush River Upper & Eden Hd., $606.38 valuation, 1 slave. {Ref: TL}
TATE, DAVID, head of family in 1800 (4th District). {Ref: CI}
TAYLOR, ABRAHAM, head of family in 1800 (2nd District). {Ref: CI}. Also see "John Rumsey" and "Isbel Taylor," q.v.
TAYLOR, AQUILA, had an account at Hall's Store in December, 1791. {Ref: WH}
TAYLOR, AQUILA ("lower countys"), insolvent on lists due for 1790 and 1791 "fund taxes" and county taxes in Susquehanna Hd., as returned by Thomas

Taylor. {Ref: IL 31.12, 31.02}
TAYLOR, ASA, or WILLIAM BENNET, taxpayer, 1798, Susquehanna Hd., 1 tract (50 acres) and 1 building (William Bennet, occupant), $119.25 valuation, no slaves. {Ref: TL}
TAYLOR, ASHBERRY (ASHBURY), see "Charlotte Taylor" and "Sylvester Taylor" and "Otho Taylor" and "Susanna Taylor," q.v.
TAYLOR, ASHBERRY, subpoenaed to the Grand Jury in August, 1797. {Ref: CC}
TAYLOR, ASHBERRY, taxpayer, 1798, Spesutia Lower Hd., 1 dwelling house, 5 inferior houses, 2 acres, $145 valuation; 2 tracts (98 acres) in Spesutia Lower Hd., $551.25 valuation, 2 slaves. {Ref: TL}
TAYLOR, ASHBERRY, served as constable in Harford Lower Hd., 1797-1798. {Ref: CC, CM}
TAYLOR, ASHBURY, head of family in 1800 (2nd District). {Ref: CI}
TAYLOR, CHARLES, head of family in 1800 (3rd District). {Ref: CI}
TAYLOR, CHARLOTTE, dau. of Ashbury Taylor and Frances Shody, b. Oct 26, 1799. {Ref: PR}. Also see "Eprhaim Donovan," q.v.
TAYLOR, CORBIN, b. Jun 1, 1794, d. Feb 10, 1837, aged 42 years, 8 months, and 9 days, bur. in the Heaps Cemetery in northern Harford County. {Ref: TI}
TAYLOR, EDWARD, head of family in 1800 (2nd District). {Ref: CI}
TAYLOR, ELIZABETH, see "Thomas Johnson," q.v.
TAYLOR, GEORGE, taxpayer, 1798, Gunpowder Lower Hd., 1 dwelling house, 1 inferior house, 80 perches, $200 valuation, no slaves. {Ref: TL}
TAYLOR, GEORGE, head of family in 1800 (Abingdon). {Ref: CI}
TAYLOR, HANNAH, bur. Jun 11, 1795, aged 25. {Ref: PR}
TAYLOR, ISBEL (widow of Abraham), insolvent on a list for the road tax due for 1791 in Harford Upper, Harford Lower, and Spesutia Upper as returned by Robert Amos, Jr. on Sep 18, 1793. {Ref: IL 31.18}
TAYLOR, JAMES, see "William Taylor," q.v.
TAYLOR, JAMES, insolvent on a list for the road tax due for 1791 in Harford Upper, Harford Lower, and Spesutia Upper as returned by Robert Amos, Jr. on Sep 18, 1793. {Ref: IL 31.18}
TAYLOR, JAMES, insolvent on list returned by Robert Carlile for taxes due for the year 1791. {Ref: IL 31.16}
TAYLOR, JAMES, m. Sarah Aitken on Feb 6, 1800. {Ref: PR}
TAYLOR, JAMES, head of family in 1800 (1st District). {Ref: CI}
TAYLOR, JAMES, head of family in 1800 (2nd District). {Ref: CI}
TAYLOR, JAMES (OF STEPHEN), taxpayer, 1798, Spesutia Lower Hd., 1 dwelling house, 4 inferior houses, 2 acres, $112 valuation; 2 tracts (128 acres) in Spesutia Lower Hd., $504 valuation, 1 slave. {Ref: TL}
TAYLOR, JANE, taxpayer, 1798, Susquehanna Hd., 1 tract (30 acres, 120 perches) and 1 building, $108.56 valuation, no slaves. {Ref: TL}
TAYLOR, JANE, had an account at Hall's Store in October, 1791. {Ref: WH}
TAYLOR, JANE, head of family in 1800 (2nd District). {Ref: CI}

TAYLOR, JESSE, see "William Taylor," q.v.

TAYLOR, JESSE ("charge twice"), insolvent on a list for the road tax due for 1791 in Harford Upper, Harford Lower, and Spesutia Upper as returned by Robert Amos, Jr. on Sep 18, 1793. {Ref: IL 31.18}

TAYLOR, JESSE, taxpayer, 1798, Gunpowder Lower Hd., 1 dwelling house, 4 inferior houses, 2 acres, $160 valuation; 1 tract (115 acres) in Gunpowder Lower Hd., $337.50 valuation, 1 slave. {Ref: TL}

TAYLOR, JESSE, insolvent on a list for the road tax due for 1791 in Harford Upper, Harford Lower, and Spesutia Upper as returned by Robert Amos, Jr. on Sep 18, 1793. {Ref: IL 31.18}

TAYLOR, JESSE, head of family in 1800 (1st District). {Ref: CI}

TAYLOR, JOHN, see "Thomas Taylor" and "Thomas Taylor (of John)," q.v.

TAYLOR, JOHN, licensed retailer in March, 1795. {Ref: CC}

TAYLOR, JOHN, taxpayer, 1798, Deer Creek Upper Hd., 1 tract (107 acres) and 1 building, $272.85 valuation, no slaves. {Ref: TL}

TAYLOR, JOHN, insolvent on a list of the county tax due William Osborn, sheriff, for 1791, as returned by Edward Prigg on Sep 20, 1791. {Ref: IL 31.17}

TAYLOR, JOHN, insolvent on lists in 1791 due county taxes and road taxes in "Deer Creek Upper, Middle, and Broad Creek Hundreds" as returned by Robert Amos, Jr. {Ref: IL 31.12, 31.22}

TAYLOR, JOHN, head of family in 1800 (3rd District). {Ref: CI}

TAYLOR, JOHN, head of family in 1800 (4th District). {Ref: CI}

TAYLOR, JOHN (esquire), treated by Dr. Archer on Mar 7, 1791; also mentioned his wife (no name given). {Ref: JA}

TAYLOR, JOHN SR., insolvent on a list for 1791 in Gunpowder Upper and Bush River Lower Hundreds, as filed by John Bond, Deputy Sheriff, on Sep 20, 1791. {Ref: IL 31.24}

TAYLOR, JOHN (OF CHARLES), charged for assaulting Daniel Dougless in 1790. {Ref: CD, March Term, 1795}

TAYLOR, JOHN WILSON, head of family in 1800 (2nd District). {Ref: CI}. This is most likely "John Wilson (taylor)," q.v.

TAYLOR, MARY, see "William Taylor," q.v.

TAYLOR, MATHEW (captain), insolvent, Harford Lower and Spesutia Lower Hundreds, on a tax list returned by George Lyttle on Sep 21, 1791. {Ref: IL 31.20, 31.21}

TAYLOR, MATTHEW (captain), insolvent on a list for the road tax due for 1791 in Harford Upper, Harford Lower, and Spesutia Upper as returned by Robert Amos, Jr. on Sep 18, 1793. {Ref: IL 31.18}

TAYLOR, MOSES, m. Nancy Durban on Dec 27, 1792. {Ref: PR}

TAYLOR, NANCY, b. Feb 16, 1798, d. Oct 18, 1879, aged 81 years, 8 months, and 2 days, bur. in the Heaps Cemetery in northern Harford County. {Ref: TI}

TAYLOR, OTHO, son of Ashbury Taylor and Frances Shody, b. Jul 2, 1796. {Ref: PR}

TAYLOR, RACHAEL, had an account at Hall's Store in May, 1791. {Ref: WH}
TAYLOR, RACHEL, insolvent on list returned for the county tax for 1791 by William Osburn in Gunpowder Lower Hundred. {Ref: IL 31.15}
TAYLOR, RICHARD, taxpayer, 1798, Harford Upper Hd., 1 tract (162 acres) and 1 building, $403.88 valuation, no slaves. {Ref: TL}
TAYLOR, RICHARD, m. Eleanor Courtney on Dec 25, 1800. {Ref: PR}
TAYLOR, RICHARD, head of family in 1800 (2nd District). {Ref: CI}
TAYLOR, ROBERT, had an account at Hall's Store in February, 1791. {Ref: WH}
TAYLOR, ROBERT, insolvent on a list for the road tax due for 1791 in Harford Upper, Harford Lower, and Spesutia Upper as returned by Robert Amos, Jr. on Sep 18, 1793 (his name was crossed off the list). {Ref: IL 31.18}
TAYLOR, ROBERT, taxpayer, 1798, Spesutia Lower Hd., 1 dwelling house, 2 inferior houses, 2 acres, $100.50 valuation; 1 tract (68 acres) in Spesutia Lower Hd., $267.75 valuation, 1 slave. {Ref: TL}
TAYLOR, ROBERT, charged in 1794 (nature of the case not stated). {Ref: CD, March Term, 1795}
TAYLOR, ROBERT, head of family in 1800 (2nd District). {Ref: CI}
TAYLOR, SARAH, insolvent on list returned for the road tax due for 1791 by John Bull. {Ref: IL 31.14}
TAYLOR, STEPHEN, insolvent on a list for the road tax due for 1791 in Harford Upper, Harford Lower, and Spesutia Upper as returned by Robert Amos, Jr. on Sep 18, 1793. {Ref: IL 31.18}. Also see "James Taylor (of Stephen)," q.v.
TAYLOR, SUSANNA, dau. of Ashbury Taylor and Frances Shody, b. Mar 18, 1795. {Ref: PR}
TAYLOR, SYLVESTER, son of Ashbury Taylor and Frances Shody, b. Jan 24, 1798. {Ref: PR}
TAYLOR, THOMAS, see "Thomas Waltham's heirs," q.v.
TAYLOR, THOMAS, tax collector, compiled and returned lists between 1790-1794. {Ref: IL 31.12, 31.02}
TAYLOR, THOMAS, licensed retailer in March, 1795. {Ref: CC}
TAYLOR, THOMAS, head of family in 1800 (3rd District). {Ref: CI}
TAYLOR, THOMAS, head of family in 1800 (Belle Air). {Ref: CI}
TAYLOR, THOMAS (taylor), insolvent on list returned by Robert Carlile for taxes due for the year 1791. {Ref: IL 31.16}
TAYLOR, THOMAS (ship carpenter), taxpayer, 1798, Bush River Lower Hd., 1 dwelling house, 4 inferior houses, 1 acre, $120 valuation; 1 tract (111 acres) in Bush River Lower Hd., $255.66 valuation, 3 slaves. {Ref: TL}
TAYLOR, THOMAS (ship carpenter), treated by Dr. Archer on Mar 2, 1791; also mentioned his wife and child (no names given) and that they lived near Old Fields. {Ref: JA}
TAYLOR, THOMAS, AND WALTHAM, THOMAS, charged for retailing liquors in 1795. {Ref: CD, August Term, 1795}
TAYLOR, THOMAS (OF JOHN), served on a Petit Jury in August, 1799 and

August, 1800. {Ref: CM}
TAYLOR, THOMAS (OF JOHN), treated by Dr. Archer on Jul 25, 1791. {Ref: JA}
TAYLOR, THOMAS (OF JOHN), taxpayer, 1798, Bush River Lower Hd., 1 dwelling house, 3 inferior houses, 80 perches of land, $510 valuation, no slaves. {Ref: TL}
TAYLOR, WALTER ("out back"), insolvent on lists due for 1790 and 1791 "fund taxes" and county taxes in Susquehanna Hd., as returned by Thomas Taylor. {Ref: IL 31.12, 31.02}
TAYLOR, WILLIAM ("run"), insolvent on a list of the county tax due William Osborn, sheriff, for 1791, as returned by Edward Prigg on Sep 20, 1791. {Ref: IL 31.17}
TAYLOR, WILLIAM, insolvent on a list in 1792 in Broad Creek Hd., as returned by Benjamin Preston. {Ref: IL 31.03}
TAYLOR, WILLIAM, insolvent on lists of taxes due in 1791 and 1792 in Broad Creek Hd., as returned by Robert Amos, Jr. in 1791 and Benjamin Preston in 1792. {Ref: IL 31.03, 31.12, 31.22}
TAYLOR, WILLIAM ("charge with property"), insolvent on lists in 1791 due county taxes and road taxes in "Deer Creek Upper, Middle, and Broad Creek Hundreds" as returned by Robert Amos, Jr. {Ref: IL 31.12, 31.22}
TAYLOR, WILLIAM, son of Jesse and Mary, b. Mar 10, 1799, bapt. Sep 12, 1799. {Ref: PR}
TAYLOR, WILLIAM, son of James Taylor and Sarah Aitken, b. Jul 22, 1799, bapt. Feb 6, 1800. {Ref: PR}
TAYLOR, WILLIAM, head of family in 1800 (3rd District). {Ref: CI}
TAYLOR, WILLIAM, head of family in 1800 (4th District). {Ref: CI}
TAYLOR, WILLIAM, head of family in 1800 (5th District). {Ref: CI}
TAYOL(?), JAMES, head of family in 1800 (2nd District). {Ref: CI}
TAYSON, MARY, head of family in 1800 (4th District). {Ref: CI}
TEMPLETON, SUSANNA, m. John Burke on May 25, 1797. {Ref: PR}
TEREL, JOHN, head of family in 1800 (2nd District). {Ref: CI}
TERME & AUZE, licensed retailers in August, 1797. {Ref: CC}
TERRELL, JOHN (New Jersey), or SAMUEL FOWLER, taxpayer, 1798, Spesutia Lower Hd., 1 dwelling house, 2 inferior houses, 2 acres (Samuel Fowler, occupant), $140 valuation; 1 tract (1408 acres) in Spesutia Lower Hd. (Samuel Fowler, occupant), $6300 valuation, no slaves. {Ref: TL}
TEW, NATHANIEL, insolvent on a list for the road tax due for 1791 in Harford Upper, Harford Lower, and Spesutia Upper as returned by Robert Amos, Jr. on Sep 18, 1793. {Ref: IL 31.18}
THATCHER, JOHN & COMPANY, licensed retailers in March, 1795. {Ref: CC}
THOMAS, A. J., see "Mary S. Thomas," q.v.
THOMAS, BETTY, taxpayer, 1798, Spesutia Upper Hd., 1 dwelling house, 3 inferior houses, 1 acre, $115 valuation; 3 tracts (314 acres, 80 perches) in Spesutia Upper Hd., $575.72 valuation, no slaves. {Ref: TL}

THOMAS, CATH., see "Philip Thomas, " q.v.
THOMAS, CHIL., see "Philip Thomas," q.v.
THOMAS, ELIZABETH, head of family in 1800 (3rd District). {Ref. CI}
THOMAS, EVAN W., taxpayer, 1798, Susquehanna Hd., 1 dwelling house, 1 inferior house, 2 acres, $600 valuation; 5 tracts (686 acres) and 1 building in Susquehanna Hd., $2387.25 valuation, 12 slaves. {Ref. TL}
THOMAS, EVEN, head of family in 1800 (2nd District). {Ref. CI}
THOMAS, GILES, treated by Dr. Archer on Dec 9, 1794. {Ref. JA}
THOMAS, HERMAN, b. 1798, d. Jun 14, 1858, aged 60, bur. in Cokesbury Methodist Cemetery in Abingdon. {Ref. TI}
THOMAS, JAMES, head of family in 1800 (3rd District). {Ref. CI}. Also see "Mary Thomas," q.v.
THOMAS, JOHN, insolvent on a list in 1792 in Broad Creek Hd., as returned by Benjamin Preston. {Ref. IL 31.03}
THOMAS, JOHN, name appeared twice as an insolvent on a list returned for the county tax for 1791 by William Osburn in Gunpowder Lower Hundred. {Ref. IL 31.15}
THOMAS, JOHN, insolvent on lists returned by Robert Carlile and John Guyton for taxes due for the year 1791. {Ref. IL 31.16, 31.19}
THOMAS, JOHN ("run"), insolvent on a list of the county tax due William Osborn, sheriff, for 1791, as returned by Edward Prigg on Sep 20, 1791. {Ref. IL 31.17}
THOMAS, JOHN, tract *Golden Hill* surveyed between 1792 and 1796. {Ref. SB}
THOMAS, JOHN, will probated Jun 27, 1797. {Ref. HW}
THOMAS, JOHN, head of family in 1800 (1st District). {Ref. CI}
THOMAS, JOSEPH, m. Hannah Carty on Oct 29, 1799. {Ref. PR}
THOMAS, JOSEPH, head of family in 1800 (2nd District). {Ref. CI}
THOMAS, MARY, taxpayer, 1798, Spesutia Upper Hd., 1 tracts (263 acres) and 1 building, $732.37 valuation, no slaves. {Ref. TL}
THOMAS, MARY, wife of James, b. 1794, d. Dec --, 1877, in her 84th year, bur. in Deer Creek Methodist Church Cemetery at Chestnut Hill. {Ref. TI}
THOMAS, MARY, head of family in 1800 (3rd District). {Ref. CI}
THOMAS, MARY S., wife of A. J., b. 1797, d. Sep 20, 1826, aged 29, bur. in St. George's Episcopal Church Cemetery at Perryman. {Ref. TI}
THOMAS, MOSES, m. Nancy McClain on Dec 29, 1799. {Ref. PR}
THOMAS, MOSES, head of family in 1800 (2nd District). {Ref. CI}
THOMAS, PHILIP, treated by Dr. Archer on Sep 22, 1799; also mentioned his wife (no name given) and children "Chil:" and "Cath." {Ref. JA}
THOMAS, RICHARD, treated by Dr. Archer on Aug 10, 1794. {Ref. JA}
THOMAS, RICHARD S., non-resident (place of residence not stated), or JOHN H. BARNEY, taxpayer, 1798, Susquehanna Hd., 1 dwelling house, 6 inferior houses, 2 acres (John H. Barney, occupant), $4000 valuation; 3 tracts (13 acres) in Susquehanna Hd. (John H. Barney, occupant), $67.50 valuation, no slaves.

{Ref: TL}
THOMAS, SARAH, head of family in 1800 (1st District). {Ref: CI}
THOMAS, WILLIAM, head of family in 1800 (2nd District). {Ref: CI}
THOMPSON, ALEXANDER, taxpayer, 1798, Bush River Upper & Eden Hd., 1 dwelling house, 8 inferior houses, 2 acres, $395 valuation; 4 tracts (288 acres, 80 perches) in Bush River Upper & Eden Hd., $649.12 valuation, no slaves. {Ref: TL}
THOMPSON, ALEXANDER, head of family in 1800 (4th District). {Ref: CI}
THOMPSON, ANDREW, head of family in 1800 (3rd District). {Ref: CI}
THOMPSON, AQUILA, see "James Thompson," q.v.
THOMPSON, AQUILA, taxpayer, 1798, Bush River Upper & Eden Hd., 1 dwelling house, 4 inferior houses, 2 acres, $300 valuation. 2 tracts (375 acres, 120 perches) in Bush River Upper & Eden Hd., $845.44 valuation, no slaves. {Ref: TL}
THOMPSON, AQUILLA, head of family in 1800 (3rd District). {Ref: CI}
THOMPSON, AQUILLA, head of family in 1800 (4th District). {Ref: CI}
THOMPSON, DANIEL, taxpayer, 1798, Bush River Upper & Eden Hd., 1 dwelling house, 1 inferior house, 2 acres, $105 valuation; 2 tracts (150 acres) in Bush River Upper & Eden Hd., $253.13 valuation, no slaves. {Ref: TL}
THOMPSON, DANIEL, head of family in 1800 (4th District). {Ref: CI}
THOMPSON, DAVID, see "Mrs. Thompson," q.v.
THOMPSON, DAVID, insolvent on a list for the road tax due for 1791 in Harford Upper, Harford Lower, and Spesutia Upper as returned by Robert Amos, Jr. on Sep 18, 1793. {Ref: IL 31.18}.
THOMPSON, DAVID, will probated Feb 24, 1791. {Ref: HW}
THOMPSON, ELIZABETH, dau. of James and Hannah, b. Oct 16, 1795, bapt. Aug 9, 1796. {Ref: PR}
THOMPSON, HANNAH, see "Elizabeth Thompson" and "James Thompson," q.v.
THOMPSON, INGREE (captain), at Otter Point, treated by Dr. Archer between 1787 and 1790; mentioned his wife and child (no names given) in 1790; also mentioned his sister-in-law (no name given) was treated on Mar 2, 1795. {Ref: JA}
THOMPSON, JAMES, see "Thomas Cox" and "Elizabeth Thompson" and "William B. Stokes," q.v.
THOMPSON, JAMES, bur. in Harford (Old Brick) Baptist Church Cemetery; either d. Aug 3, 1866, aged 72, or d. Aug 3, 1786, aged 52 (tombstone inscription unclear).
THOMPSON, JAMES, insolvent on list returned for the road tax due for 1791 by John Bull. {Ref: IL 31.14}
THOMPSON, JAMES, granted a tavern and ferry permit in Havre de Grace on July 9, 1797. {Ref: CC}
THOMPSON, JAMES, son of James and Hannah, b. Jul 24, 1793, bapt. Aug 9, 1796. {Ref: PR}
THOMPSON, JAMES, served on a Petit Jury in August, 1797. {Ref: CC}
THOMPSON, JAMES, subpoenaed to the Grand Jury in August, 1797. {Ref: CC}

THOMPSON, JAMES, taxpayer, 1798, Spesutia Lower Hd., 1 dwelling house, 1 inferior house, 44 perches and 21 sq. ft. of land, $320 valuation, 3 slaves. {Ref: TL}

THOMPSON, JAMES, taxpayer, 1798, Susquehanna Hd., 1 tract (87 acres, 80 perches) and 1 building, $230.63 valuation, no slaves. {Ref: TL}. A note by the assessor stated "Query whether this is not the same James Thompson assessed in Spesutia Lower."

THOMPSON, JAMES, taxpayer, 1798, Bush River Upper & Eden Hd., 1 dwelling house, 4 inferior houses, 2 acres, $175 valuation; 1 tract (48 acres) in Bush River Upper & Eden Hd., $108 valuation, no slaves. {Ref: TL}

THOMPSON, JAMES, head of family in 1800 (Havre de Grace). {Ref: CI}

THOMPSON, JAMES, head of family in 1800 (4th District). {Ref: CI}

THOMPSON, JAMES (OF A.), head of family in 1800 (4th District). {Ref: CI}

THOMPSON, JAMES (OF AQUILA), served on a Petit Jury in August, 1798 and August, 1800, and on a Grand Jury in August, 1799. {Ref: CM}

THOMPSON, JASON, husband of Sophia, b. 1797, d. Mar 25, 1881, bur. in Bethel Presbyterian Church Cemetery at Madonna. {Ref: BC}

THOMPSON, JOHN, treated by Dr. Archer on Aug 23, 1791; also mentioned a John Thompson, ferryman, treated on Jul 19, 1790. {Ref: JA}

THOMPSON, JOHN, charged for perjury in 1794, assaulting Bernard Johnson, and "turning a road" in 1795. {Ref: CD, March and August Terms, 1795}

THOMPSON, JOHN, insolvent on a list for the road tax due for 1791 in Harford Upper, Harford Lower, and Spesutia Upper as returned by Robert Amos, Jr. on Sep 18, 1793. {Ref: IL 31.18}

THOMPSON, JOHN, insolvent on list returned by Robert Carlile for taxes due for the year 1791. {Ref: IL 31.16}

THOMPSON, JOHN, insolvent on list returned by John Guyton (who listed him as a single man) for taxes due for the year 1791. {Ref: IL 31.19}

THOMPSON (TOMPSON), JOHN, head of family in 1800 (4th District). {Ref: CI}

THOMPSON, JOSHUA, insolvent on list returned by Robert Carlile for taxes due for the year 1791. {Ref: IL 31.16}

THOMPSON, JOSHUA, head of family in 1800 (4th District). {Ref: CI}

THOMPSON, MAHLON (MALON), head of family in 1800 (2nd District). {Ref: CI}. Also see "Daniel Bowley," q.v.

THOMPSON, MRS. (widow of David), treated by Dr. Archer on Mar 5, 1791; also mentioned "gone to the western country." {Ref: JA}

THOMPSON, NANCY, m. James Curry on Jan 14, 1800. {Ref: PR}

THOMPSON, SARAH, charged for selling liquors and fined 600 lbs. of tobacco in 1797. {Ref: CD, March Term, 1797}

THOMPSON, SARAH, taxpayer, 1798, Spesutia Lower Hd., no dwelling house listed in this part of the tax schedule, no land listed, 2 slaves. {Ref: TL}

THOMPSON, SARAH, head of family in 1800 (2nd District). {Ref: CI}

THOMPSON, SARAH RUCKMAND, b. 1800, d. on 5th of 11th month, 1886, in her 86th year, bur. in Broad Creek Quaker Cemetery. {Ref: TI}

THOMPSON, SOPHIA, wife of Jason, b. Mar 12, 1794, d. Jan 22, 1880, bur. in Bethel Presbyterian Church Cemetery at Madonna. {Ref: BC}. Also see "Jason Thompson," q.v.

THOMPSON, SUSAN J., b. Nov 16, 1792, d. Mar 18, 1867, bur. in St. George's Episcopal Church Cemetery at Perryman. {Ref: TI}

THOMPSON, THOMAS, served as constable in Bush River Lower Hd., 1798-1800. {Ref: CM}

THOMPSON, THOMAS, insolvent on a list for 1791 in Gunpowder Upper and Bush River Lower Hundreds, as filed by John Bond, Deputy Sheriff, on Sep 20, 1791. {Ref: IL 31.24}

THOMPSON, THOMAS, taxpayer, 1798, Bush River Upper & Eden Hd., 1 dwelling house, 3 inferior houses, 2 acres, $150 valuation; 5 tracts (120 acres, 80 perches) in Bush River Upper & Eden Hd., $203.34 valuation, no slaves. {Ref: TL}

THOMPSON, THOMAS, insolvent on a list in 1792 in Broad Creek Hd., as returned by Benjamin Preston. {Ref: IL 31.03}

THOMPSON (THOMSON), THOMAS, head of family in 1800 (4th District). {Ref: CI}

THOMPSON, THOMAS A., insolvent on a list for 1791 in Gunpowder Upper and Bush River Lower Hundreds, as filed by John Bond, Deputy Sheriff, on Sep 20, 1791. {Ref: IL 31.24}

THOMPSON, THOMAS A., insolvent on list returned by Robert Carlile for taxes due for the year 1791. {Ref: IL 31.16}

THOMPSON, WILLIAM, b. 1791, d. Jul 20, 1845, aged 54, bur. in Cokesbury Methodist Cemetery in Abingdon. {Ref: TI}

THOMPSON, WILLIAM, head of family in 1800 (2nd District). {Ref: CI}

THORN, JOHN ("can't be found"), insolvent on a list for 1791 in Gunpowder Upper and Bush River Lower Hundreds, as filed by John Bond, Deputy Sheriff, on Sep 20, 1791. {Ref: IL 31.24}

THORN, JOHN, head of family in 1800 (3rd District). {Ref: CI}

THORNTON, JAMES, charged for assaulting Thomas Hays in 1797; mentioned John Thornton, Sr. {Ref: CD, August Term, 1797}. Also see "John Thornton," q.v.

THORNTON, JOHN, treated by Dr. Archer on Aug 26, 1794; mentioned his wife and child (no names given). {Ref: JA}

THORNTON, JOHN, appeared on list of "recognizances" of the court with James Thornton for his appearance in 1797. {Ref: CD, August Term, 1797}

THORNTON, JOHN JR., charged for assaulting Thomas Hays in 1797; mentioned John Thornton, Sr. {Ref: CD, August Term, 1797}

THORNTON, JOHN SR., see "John Thornton, Jr." and "James Thornton," q.v.

THRAP, ROBERT, insolvent on list returned by Robert Carlile for taxes due for the year 1791. {Ref: IL 31.16}

THRAP, WILLIAM, insolvent on list returned by Robert Carlile for taxes due for the year 1791. {Ref: IL 31.16}

THROUGH, ARCHIBALD, charged for selling liquors in 1794. {Ref: CD, March and August Terms, 1795 and 1797}

THROUGH, ARCHIBALD, charged for assaulting Margaret Fullerton in 1797. {Ref: CD, August Term, 1797}

TIMMONS, EDWARD, head of family in 1800 (1st District). {Ref: CI}

TIMMONS, THOMAS, insolvent on list returned for the county tax for 1791 by William Osburn in Gunpowder Lower Hd. (which listed him as a single man). {Ref: IL 31.15}

TIMMONS, THOMAS, taxpayer, 1798, Gunpowder Lower Hd., 1 dwelling house, 4 inferior houses, 2 acres, $150 valuation; 1 tract (134 acres) in Gunpowder Lower Hd., $301.50 valuation, no slaves. {Ref: TL}

TIMMONS, THOMAS, head of family in 1800 (1st District). {Ref: CI}

TIPTON, JABEZ ("out back"), insolvent on lists due for 1790 and 1791 "fund taxes" and county taxes in Susquehanna Hd., as returned by Thomas Taylor. {Ref: IL 31.12, 31.02}

TIPTON, JOHN ("out back"), insolvent on lists due for 1790 and 1791 "fund taxes" and county taxes in Susquehanna Hd., as returned by Thomas Taylor. {Ref: IL 31.12, 31.02}

TODD, PATRICK, head of family in 1800 (4th District). {Ref: CI}

TOLINGER, GEORGE, insolvent on a list for the county tax due for 1793 in Susquehanna Hd. as returned to the levy court by Thomas Taylor on May 28, 1794, who noted "put in my hands last fall." {Ref: IL 31.12}

TOLLEY, EDWARD C., insolvent on a list for the road tax due for 1791 in Harford Upper, Harford Lower, and Spesutia Upper as returned by Robert Amos, Jr. on Sep 18, 1793 (his name was crossed off the list). {Ref: IL 31.18}

TOLLEY, EDWARD C., on "a list of insolvents it being for personal property for the road taxs [sic] for 1791" filed by Robert Amoss, tax collector. {Ref: IL 31.12}

TOLLEY, ELIZABETH, bur. Dec 2, 1800, aged about 14. {Ref: PR}

TOLLEY, MARTHA, had an account at Hall's Store in November, 1791. {Ref: WH}

TOLLINGER, GEORGE, treated by Dr. Archer on Aug 11, 1791. {Ref: JA}

TOMKINS, ANNA KITTY DUNN, dau. of Thomas Tomkins and Elizabeth Stallings, b. Oct 27, 1793, bapt. Jun 1, 1797. {Ref: PR}

TOMKINS, THOMAS, see "Anna Kitty Dunn Tomkins," q.v.

TORNE(?), PETER, head of family in 1800 (5th District). {Ref: CI}

TOUCHSTONE (TUCHSTONE), BENJAMIN, head of family in 1800 (5th District). {Ref: CI}. Also see "John Touchstone" and "Nancy Touchstone," q.v.

TOUCHSTONE, ESTHER, see "John Touchstone" and "Nancy Touchstone," q.v.

TOUCHSTONE (TUCHSTONE), HENRY, head of family in 1800 (2nd District); two men by this name in this district. {Ref: CI}

TOUCHSTONE, JOHN, son of Benjamin and Esther, b. Oct 29, 1792. {Ref: PR}

TOUCHSTONE, NANCY, dau. of Benjamin and Esther, b. Dec 11, 1797. {Ref: PR}

TOUCHSTONE, RICHARD, m. Sarah Touchstone on Jan 7, 1800. {Ref: PR}

TOUCHSTONE (TUCHSTONE), SARAH, head of family in 1800 (2nd District).

{Ref: CI}. Also see "Richard Touchstone," q.v.

TOUCHSTONE, WIDOW, see "John Hall Hughes," q.v.

TOWLAND, BENJAMIN, taxpayer, 1798, Bush River Upper & Eden Hd., 1 dwelling house, 1 inferior house, 2 acres, $110 valuation; 5 tracts (270 acres, 80 perches) in Bush River Upper & Eden Hd., $304.31 valuation, no slaves. {Ref: TL}

TOWLAND, BENJAMIN, head of family in 1800 (4th District). {Ref: CI}

TOWNSLEY, JOHN, taxpayer, 1798, Harford Upper Hd., 1 tract (1 acre) and 1 building, $94.50 valuation, no slaves. {Ref: TL}

TOWNSLEY, JOHN, head of family in 1800 (3rd District). {Ref: CI}

TOWSEN, JOHN, head of family in 1800 (2nd District). {Ref: CI}

TOWSON, ISAAC, head of family in 1800 (5th District). {Ref: CI}. Also see "John Stump," q.v.

TRAGO, JOHN, head of family in 1800 (1st District). {Ref: CI}

TRAPNELL, JAMES, insolvent on a list for the road tax for 1792, as returned for Robert Amoss, tax collector. {Ref: IL 13.12}

TRAPNELL, JAMES, taxpayer, 1798, Gunpowder Upper Hd., 1 dwelling house, 9 inferior houses, 2 acres, $500 valuation; 2 tracts (538 acres) in Gunpowder Upper Hd., $1555.87 valuation, 5 slaves. {Ref: TL}

TRAPNELL, JAMES, served on a Petit Jury in March, 1798 and on a Grand Jury in March, 1799 and August, 1800. {Ref: CM}

TRAPNELL, JAMES, head of family in 1800 (3rd District). {Ref: CI}

TRAVIS, JOHN, insolvent on list returned by Robert Carlile for taxes due for the year 1791. {Ref: IL 31.16}

TRAVIS, JOHN C., head of family in 1800 (1st District). {Ref: CI}

TREADWAY (TREADAWAY), ANN, dau. of Thomas and Christiana, b. May 12, 1792. {Ref: PR}

TREADWAY (TREADAWAY, TREDWAY), AQUILA, son of Thomas and Christiana, b. Apr 8, 1789, bapt. Aug 14, 1800. {Ref: PR}

TREADWAY, CRISPEN, head of family in 1800 (4th District). {Ref: CI}

TREADWAY, CHRISTIANA, see "Elizabeth Treadway" and "Aquila Treadway" and "John Norris Treadway" and "Ann Treadway," q.v.

TREADWAY (TREDWAY), CHRISTINA, dau. of Thomas and Christina, b. May 27, 1782, bapt. Oct 17, 1800. {Ref: PR}. Also see "Edward Treadway" and "Sarah Treadway" and "Mary Treadway," q.v.

TREADWAY, DANIEL, head of family in 1800 (4th District). {Ref: CI}

TREADWAY (TREDWAY), DANIEL, taxpayer, 1798, Bush River Upper & Eden Hd., 1 dwelling house, 2 inferior houses, 2 acres, $150 valuation; 2 tracts (250 acres) in Bush River Upper & Eden Hd., $492.19 valuation, no slaves. {Ref: TL}

TREADWAY (TREDWAY), DANIEL JR., insolvent on list returned by Robert Carlile for taxes due for the year 1791. {Ref: IL 31.16}

TREADWAY (TREDWAY), EDWARD, son of Thomas and Christina, b. Dec 15, 1783, bapt. Oct 17, 1800. {Ref: PR}

TREADWAY (TREDWAY), EDWARD, taxpayer, 1798, Bush River Lower Hd., 1 tract (134 acres) and 1 building, $502.87 valuation, no slaves. {Ref: TL}
TREADWAY (TREDWAY), EDWARD, head of family in 1800 (1st District). {Ref: CI}
TREADWAY (TREADAWAY, TREDWAY), ELIZABETH, dau. of Thomas and Christiana, b. about 1782, bapt. Aug 14, 1800. {Ref: PR}
TREADWAY, JOHN, head of family in 1800 (4th District). {Ref: CI}
TREADWAY (TREADAWAY), JOHN NORRIS, son of Thomas and Christiana, b. Feb 26, 1796. {Ref: PR}
TREADWAY (TREDWAY), MARY, dau. of Thomas and Christina, b. May 27, 1782, bapt. Oct 17, 1800. {Ref: PR}
TREADWAY (TREDWAY), SARAH, dau. of Thomas and Christina, b. Novembe 26, 1776, bapt. Oct 17, 1800. {Ref: PR}
TREADWAY (TREDWAY), THOMAS, mentioned in a survey deposition on Jan 22, 1800 as "to the houses [sic] where Thos. Tredway formerly lived." {Ref: JS}
TREADWAY (TREDWAY), THOMAS, head of family in 1800 (1st District). {Ref: CI}.
TREADWAY (TREDWAY), THOMAS, see "Edward Treadway" and "Sarah Treadway" and "Christina Treadway" and "Mary Treadway" and "Elizabeth Treadway" and "Aquila Treadway" and "John Norris Treadway" and "Ann Treadway," q.v.
TREADWELL, ELIZABETH, wife of James, b. 1793, d. Jul 6, 1859, aged 66, bur. in St. Ignatius Catholic Church Cemetery in Hickory. {Ref: TI}
TREADWELL, JAMES, husband of Elizabeth, b. 1792, d. Feb 15, 1858, aged 66, bur. in St. Ignatius Catholic Church Cemetery in Hickory. {Ref: TI}
TREDEAN(?), WILLIAM, head of family in 1800 (3rd District). {Ref: CI}
TREGO, THOMAS, see "Hugh Ely," q.v.
TRIMBLE, ISAAC, insolvent on lists returned by Robert Carlile and John Guyton for taxes due for the year 1791. {Ref: IL 31.16, 31.19}
TRISLER, VALENTINE, served as constable in Susquehanna Hd., 1797. {Ref: CC,CM}
TRISLER, VALENTINE, head of family in 1800 (Havre de Grace). {Ref: CI}
TROUTMAN, JOHN(?), head of family in 1800 (5th District). {Ref: CI}
TRUELOCK, DANIEL, licensed retailer in August, 1797. {Ref: CC}
TRUELOCK, DANIEL (Baltimore Town), or NATHANIEL McCOMAS, taxpayer, 1798, Bush River Lower Hd., 1 dwelling house, 2 inferior houses, 40 perches of land (Nathaniel McComas, occupant), $220 valuation, no slaves. {Ref: TL}
TRUELOVE, ANN, head of family in 1800 (2nd District). {Ref: CI}
TRUMPH, ABRAHAM, taxpayer, 1798, Spesutia Lower Hd., 1 tract (44 perches, 21 sq. ft.), $13.50 valuation, no slaves. {Ref: TL}
TRUSS, CATHERINE, dau. of William and Mary, b. Dec 22, 1799, bapt. Apr 26, 1801. {Ref: PR}. Also see "William Truss," q.v.
TRUSS, HARRIOTT, dau. of William and Mary, b. May 11, 1796, bapt. Apr 26,

1801. {Ref: PR}

TRUSS, WILLIAM, see "Harriott Truss" and "Catherine Truss," q.v.

TRUSS, WILLIAM, son of William and Catherine, b. Apr 9, 1790, bapt. Apr 26, 1800. {Ref: PR}

TRUSS, WILLIAM, head of family in 1800 (1st District). {Ref: CI}

TUCKER, HENRY, taxpayer, 1798, Gunpowder Lower Hd., 2 tracts (76 acres) and 1 building, $227.25 valuation, no slaves. {Ref: TL}

TUCKER, HENRY, head of family in 1800 (1st District). {Ref: CI}

TUCKER, RACHAEL, b. 1794, d. on 10th day of 2nd month, 1879, in her 85th year, bur. in Forest Hill Quaker Cemetery. {Ref: TI}

TUCKER, WILLIAM, head of family in 1800 (1st District). {Ref: CI}

TUDOR, JOSHUA, insolvent on a list for the road tax due for 1791 in Harford Upper, Harford Lower, and Spesutia Upper as returned by Robert Amos, Jr. on Sep 18, 1793. {Ref: IL 31.18}

TURK, CATHARINE, see "George Turk," q.v.

TURK, ESAU, see "John Moores" and "George Turk," q.v.

TURK, ESAU (ESAW), insolvent on a list for 1791 in Gunpowder Upper and Bush River Lower Hundreds, as filed by John Bond, Deputy Sheriff, on Sep 20, 1791. {Ref: IL 31.24}

TURK, ESAU (EASAW), head of family in 1800 (3rd District). {Ref: CI}

TURK, GEORGE, son of Esau and Catharine, b. Sep 15, 1793. {Ref: PR}

TURNER, ABEL, head of family in 1800 (4th District). {Ref: CI}

TURNER, ANDREW, see "Eli Turner," q.v.

TURNER, ANDREW, taxpayer, 1798, Bush River Upper & Eden Hd., 1 dwelling house, 6 inferior houses, 2 acres, $300 valuation; 2 tracts (384 acres, 80 perches) in Bush River Upper & Eden Hd., $865.13 valuation, 1 slave. {Ref: TL}

TURNER, ANDREW, served on a Petit Jury in August, 1799. {Ref: CM}

TURNER, ANDREW, husband of Lydia S. Kidd and son of Col. Andrew Turner and Ann McDonald, b. Sep 17, 1797, d. Nov --, 1850, bur. in Bethel Presbyterian Church Cemetery at Madonna. {Ref: BC}

TURNER, ANDREW (captain), head of family in 1800 (4th District). {Ref: CI}

TURNER, ANN, see "John Turner," q.v.

TURNER, ARABELLA, see "Thomas Bay," q.v.

TURNER, DANIEL, insolvent on lists returned by Robert Carlile and John Guyton for taxes due for the year 1791. {Ref: IL 31.16, 31.19}

TURNER, DANIEL, taxpayer, 1798, Harford Upper Hd., 1 tract (110 acres) and 1 building, $275.62 valuation, no slaves. {Ref: TL}

TURNER, DANIEL, head of family in 1800 (3rd District). {Ref: CI}

TURNER, ELEANOR (ELLENORA), wife of Eli Turner and dau. of John Beatty and Ann Rampley, b. 1796, d. Mar 1, 1855, bur. in Bethel Presbyterian Church Cemetery at Madonna. {Ref: BC}

TURNER, ELI, husband of Eleanor Beatty and son of Col. Andrew Turner and

Ann McDonald, b. 1794, d. Sep 28, 1863, bur. in Bethel Presbyterian Church Cemetery at Madonna. {Ref: BC}

TURNER, JAMES, see "Sarah Turner," q.v.

TURNER, JOHN, son of Noble and Ann, b. Mar 31, 1798, bapt. Nov 11, 1798. {Ref: PR}

TURNER, MARGARET, dau. of Thomas and Martha Turner, b. 1791, d. Oct 29, 1858, bur. in Bethel Presbyterian Church Cemetery at Madonna. {Ref: BC}

TURNER, MARTHA, taxpayer, 1798, Bush River Upper & Eden Hd., 1 dwelling house, 3 inferior houses, 2 acres, $230 valuation; 1 tract (199 acres, 80 perches) in Bush River Upper & Eden Hd., $448.87 valuation, no slaves. {Ref: TL}. Also see "Margaret Turner," q.v.

TURNER, NOBLE, see "John Turner," q.v.

TURNER, SAMUEL, insolvent on lists returned by Robert Carlile and John Guyton for taxes due for the year 1791. {Ref: IL 31.16, 31.19}

TURNER, SAMUEL, head of family in 1800 (4th District). {Ref: CI}

TURNER, SAMUEL (OF THOMAS), insolvent on lists returned by Robert Carlile and John Guyton for taxes due for the year 1791. {Ref: IL 31.16, 31.19}

TURNER, SARAH, wife of Capt. James Turner (1783-1861) and dau. of Capt. James Calder and Margaret Bagnet, b. May 24, 1796, d. May 11, 1874, bur. in Bethel Presbyterian Church Cemetery at Madonna. {Ref: BC}

TURNER, THOMAS, see "Margaret Turner," q.v.

TURNER, THOMAS, taxpayer, 1798, Gunpowder Upper Hd., 1 dwelling house, 3 inferior houses, 2 acres, $250 valuation; 3 tracts (141 acres) in Gunpowder Upper Hd., $393.19 valuation, no slaves. {Ref: TL}

TURNER, THOMAS, insolvent on list returned for the road tax due for 1791 by John Bull. {Ref: IL 31.14}

TURNER, THOMAS, licensed ordinary (tavern) in March, 1795 and August, 1797. {Ref: CC}

TURNER, THOMAS, head of family in 1800 (1st District). {Ref: CI}

TURNPAUGH, JOHN, head of family in 1800 (3rd District). {Ref: CI}

TUSKEY, SAMUEL, insolvent on a list for the road tax due for 1791 in Harford Upper, Harford Lower, and Spesutia Upper as returned by Robert Amos, Jr. on Sep 18, 1793 (his name was crossed off the list). {Ref: IL 31.18}

TYDER, JOSHUA, insolvent, Harford Lower and Spesutia Lower Hundreds, on a tax list returned by George Lyttle on Sep 21, 1791. {Ref: IL 31.20, 31.21}

TYSON & RUMSEY, taxpayers, 1798, Gunpowder Lower Hd., 1 tract (no description), $168.75 valuation, no slaves. {Ref: TL}

TYSON, DANIEL, insolvent on a list for 1791 in Gunpowder Upper and Bush River Lower Hundreds, as filed by John Bond, Deputy Sheriff, on Sep 20, 1791. {Ref: IL 31.24}

TYSON, ELISHA (Baltimore Town), or PETER DUNGAN, taxpayer, 1798, Gunpowder Upper Hd., 1 dwelling house, 4 inferior houses, 2 acres (Peter Dungan, occupant), $600 valuation; 4 tracts (310 acres) in Gunpowder Upper

Hd. (Peter Dungan, occupant), $1656 valuation, no slaves. {Ref: TL}

TYSON, JACOB (Baltimore County), or ELIZABETH NORRIS, taxpayer, 1798, Gunpowder Upper Hd., 1 dwelling house, 1 inferior house, 2 acres (Elizabeth Norris, occupant), $200 valuation; 3 tracts (239 acres) in Gunpowder Upper Hd. (Elizabeth Norris, occupant), $554.63 valuation, no slaves. {Ref: TL}

UNDERHILL & SANKEY, licensed retailers in August, 1797. {Ref: CC}

UNDERHILL, THOMAS (Cecil County), or GEORGE SANKEY, taxpayer, 1798, Bush River Upper & Eden Hd., 1 dwelling house, 1 inferior house, 2 acres, $200 valuation; 1 tract (83 acres) in Bush River Upper & Eden Hd. (George Sankey, occupant), $1433.43 valuation, no slaves. {Ref: TL}

VANBIBBER & RUMSEY, see "Rumsey & Vanbibber," q.v.

VANCE, ANDREW, taxpayer, 1798, Bush River Upper & Eden Hd., 1 dwelling house, 2 inferior houses, 2 acres, $150 valuation; 1 tract (84 acres) in Bush River Upper & Eden Hd., $189 valuation, no slaves. {Ref: TL}

VANCE, ANDREW, head of family in 1800 (4th District). {Ref: CI}

VANCE, ANN, dau. of Samuel and Elizabeth, b. Jan 24, 1788, bapt. Aug 13, 1795. {Ref: PR}

VANCE, ELIZABETH, see "Ann Vance" and "Sarah Vance," q.v.

VANCE, JOHN, taxpayer, 1798, Bush River Upper & Eden Hd., 1 tract (98 acres), $220.50 valuation, no slaves. {Ref: TL}

VANCE, JOHN, head of family in 1800 (4th District). {Ref: CI}

VANCE, SAMUEL, see "Ann Vance" and "Sarah Vance," q.v.

VANCE, SAMUEL, insolvent on a list for 1791 in Gunpowder Upper and Bush River Lower Hundreds, as filed by John Bond, Deputy Sheriff, on Sep 20, 1791 (who listed him as a single man). {Ref: IL 31.24}

VANCE, SAMUEL, insolvent on list returned for the road tax due for 1791 by John Bull. {Ref: IL 31.14}

VANCE, SAMUEL, m. Mary Walters on Oct 9, 1798. {Ref: PR}

VANCE, SARAH, dau. of Samuel and Elizabeth, b. Sep 27, 1791, bapt. Aug 13, 1795. {Ref: PR}

VANCLIEF, ELIZABETH, insolvent on lists for the county tax and road tax due for 1791 and 1792 in Deer Creek Lower Hd., as returned by Thomas Taylor on Sep 17, 1792. {Ref: IL 31.12, 31.03}

VANCLIEF, ELIZABETH, insolvent on a list in 1792 in Deer Creek Lower Hd., as returned by Benjamin Preston. {Ref: IL 31.03}

VANCLIEF, MARY, insolvent on a list for county taxes due in 1792 as returned by Benjamin Preston. {Ref: IL 31.00}

VANCLIEF, MARY, insolvent on list returned for the road tax due for 1791 by John Bull. {Ref: IL 31.14}

VANDEGRIFF, GEORGE, taxpayer, 1798, Susquehanna Hd., 1 dwelling house, 4 inferior houses, 2 acres, $175 valuation; 1 tract (26 acres) in Susquehanna Hd., $117 valuation, no slaves. {Ref: TL}

VANDEGRIFT, GEORGE, treated by Dr. Archer on Sep 11, 1793; also mentioned his wife and child (no names given). {Ref: JA}

VANDEGRIFT, GEORGE, head of family in 1800 (3rd District). {Ref: CI}

VANDERGRAFT, GEORGE, had an account at Hall's Store in March, 1791. {Ref: WH}

VANHORN, BENJAMIN, m. Charity Sanders on Feb 15, 1791. {Ref: PR}

VANHORN, GABRIEL P., insolvent on a list for the road tax due for 1791 in Harford Upper, Harford Lower, and Spesutia Upper as returned by Robert Amos, Jr. on Sep 18, 1793. {Ref: IL 31.18}

VANHORN, ISAAC, b. 1797, d. Nov 17, 1887, in his 90th year, bur. in Harford (Old Brick) Baptist Church Cemetery. {Ref: TI}

VANHORN, MARTHA, insolvent on list returned for the county tax for 1791 by William Osburn in Gunpowder Lower Hundred. {Ref: IL 31.15}

VANHORN, MARTHA, head of family in 1800 (1st District). {Ref: CI}

VANHORN, PETER, taxpayer, 1798, Gunpowder Lower Hd., 1 tract (47 acres) and 1 building, $128.25 valuation, no slaves. {Ref: TL}

VANHORNE, PETER, head of family in 1800 (1st District). {Ref: CI}

VANSANT, JOHN, head of family in 1800 (1st District). {Ref: CI}

VANSICK, JANE, m. Owen Roberts on Jun 3, 1798. {Ref: PR}

VANSICKLE (VANSICLE), ELIZABETH, dau. of Henry and Elizabeth, b. Nov 12, 1792, bapt. Mar 2, 1797. {Ref: PR}

VANSICKLE, HENRY, see "James Phillips, Sr." and "Elizabeth Vansickle," q.v.

VANSICKLE, HENRY, taxpayer, 1798, Harford Lower Hd., 1 dwelling house, 3 inferior houses, 2 acres, $100.50 valuation; 3 tracts (622 acres) and 1 building in Harford Lower Hd., $3463.54 valuation, 9 slaves; also, taxpayer, Gunpowder Lower Hd., 1 dwelling house, 3 inferior houses, 2 acres, $130 valuation, no slaves. {Ref: TL}

VANSICKLE, HENRY, served on a Grand Jury in March, 1798. {Ref: CM}

VANSICKLE (VANSICKEL), HENRY, head of family in 1800 (2nd District). {Ref: CI}

VARNEY, JAMES, treated by Dr. Archer on Dec 21, 1793; also mentioned his wife and child (no names given). {Ref: JA}

VARNEY, JAMES, served on a Grand Jury in March, 1799 and August, 1800. {Ref: CM}

VARNEY, JAMES, taxpayer, 1798, Bush River Upper & Eden Hd., 1 dwelling house, 3 inferior houses, 2 acres, $150 valuation; 1 tract (149 acres, 80 perches) in Bush River Upper & Eden Hd., $252.28 valuation, no slaves. {Ref: TL}

VARNEY, JAMES, appointed a Judge of Elections in the 4th District on Jul 28, 1800. {Ref: CM}

VARNEY, JAMES, head of family in 1800 (4th District). {Ref: CI}

VEACHWORTH, SALLY, see "William Veachworth," q.v.

VEACHWORTH, WILLIAM, treated by Dr. Archer on Jul 24, 1795; also mentioned his wife (no name given) and dau. Sally. {Ref: JA}

VINCENT, SAMUEL, had an account at Hall's Store in May, 1791. {Ref: WH}

VISSAGE, JAMES, head of family in 1800 (5th District). {Ref: CI}. Also see

"William Stump," q.v.

VISSAGE, JOHN, insolvent on lists in 1791 due county taxes and road taxes in "Deer Creek Upper, Middle, and Broad Creek Hundreds" as returned by Robert Amos, Jr. {Ref: IL 31.12, 31.22}

VOGAN, ISAAC, insolvent on lists in 1791 due county taxes and road taxes in "Deer Creek Upper, Middle, and Broad Creek Hundreds" as returned by Robert Amos, Jr. {Ref: IL 31.12, 31.22}

VOGIN, GEORGE ("run"), insolvent on a list of the county tax due William Osborn, sheriff, for 1791, as returned by Edward Prigg on Sep 20, 1791. {Ref: IL 31.17}

WADLOW, ELIZABETH, b. Apr 18, 1800, d. Jan 9, 1898, bur. in Christ Episcopal (Rock Spring) Church Cemetery. {Ref: TI}

WADSWORTH, JAMES, head of family in 1800 (4th District). {Ref: CI}

WADSWORTH, THOMAS, head of family in 1800 (4th District). {Ref: CI}

WAKELAND (WAKELEN), JOHN, head of family in 1800 (3rd District). {Ref: CI}. Also see "Walter Billingsley, Sr.," q.v.

WAKES, ELIHU, taxpayer, 1798, Gunpowder Upper Hd., 1 tract (26 acres) and 1 building, $114.75 valuation, no slaves. {Ref: TL}

WALDRON, PHEBY, head of family in 1800 (3rd District). {Ref: CI}

WALDRON, RICHARD, will probated May 2, 1797. {Ref: HW}

WALKER, ANDREW, head of family in 1800 (4th District). {Ref: CI}

WALKER, BILLY, had an account at Hall's Store in February, 1791. {Ref: WH}

WALKER, GEORGE, taxpayer, 1798, Susquehanna Hd., 1 dwelling house, 4 inferior houses, 2 acres, $140 valuation; 2 tracts (210 acres) in Susquehanna Hd., $569.99 valuation, 1 slave; also, taxpayer, Harford Upper Hd., 1 tract (117 acres) and 1 building (Moses Magnes or Magness, occupant), $353.25 valuation, no slaves. {Ref: TL}

WALKER, JOHN, had an account at Hall's Store in October, 1791. {Ref: WH}

WALKER, JOHN JR., had an account at Hall's Store in January, 1791. {Ref: WH}

WALLACE, EDWARD, see "Samuel Wallace, et al.," q.v.

WALKER, GEORGE, head of family in 1800 (2nd District). {Ref: CI}

WALLACE, JAMES, see "Samuel Wallace, et al.," q.v.

WALLACE, JAMES ("gone"), insolvent on lists due for 1790 and 1791 "fund taxes" and county taxes in Susquehanna Hd., as returned by Thomas Taylor. {Ref: IL 31.12, 31.02}

WALLACE, JAMES, head of family in 1800 (Belle Air). {Ref: CI}

WALLACE, RANDALL, head of family in 1800 (5th District). {Ref: CI}

WALLACE, SAMUEL, head of family in 1800 (5th District). {Ref: CI}. Also see "William Jolly" and "Samuel Wallis," q.v.

WALLACE, SAMUEL JR., taxpayer, 1798, Deer Creek Lower Hd., no dwelling house listed in this part of the tax schedule, no land listed, 1 slave. {Ref: TL}

WALLACE, SAMUEL, JAMES, AND EDWARD, appeared collectively on lists of insolvents for 1790, 1791, and 1792 "fund taxes" and road tax in Deer Creek

Lower Hd., as returned by Thomas Taylor. {Ref: IL 31.12, 31.03}
WALLACE, SARAH, head of family in 1800 (5th District). {Ref: CI}
WALLACE, THOMAS ("gone"), insolvent on lists due for 1790 and 1791 "fund taxes" and road tax in Deer Creek Lower Hd., as returned by Thomas Taylor. {Ref: IL 31.12}
WALLINGSFORD, JAMES, had an account at Hall's Store in August, 1791. {Ref: WH}
WALLINGSFORD, JOHN, insolvent on list returned for the county tax for 1791 by William Osburn in Gunpowder Lower Hd. (which listed him as a single man). {Ref: IL 31.15}
WALLIS, SAMUEL, taxpayer, 1798, Deer Creek Lower Hd., 1 dwelling house, 5 inferior houses, 2 acres, $460 valuation; 1 tract (298 acres) in Deer Creek Lower Hd., $1158.75 valuation, no slaves. {Ref: TL}
WALSH, WILLIAM, served on a Petit Jury in March, 1799. {Ref: CM}
WALTER, NICHOLAS, taxpayer, 1798, Spesutia Lower Hd., 1 tract (44 perches, 21 sq. ft.), $13.50 valuation, no slaves. {Ref: TL}
WALTER, PETER, taxpayer, 1798, Spesutia Lower Hd., 1 tract (44 perches, 21 sq. ft.), $13.50 valuation, no slaves. {Ref: TL}
WALTERS, MARY, see "Samuel Vance," q.v.
WALTHAM, CLEMENT, head of family in 1800 (Abingdon). {Ref: CI}
WALTHAM, ELIZABETH, insolvent on list returned for the county tax for 1791 by William Osburn in Gunpowder Lower Hundred. {Ref: IL 31.15}
WALTHAM, THOMAS, taxpayer, 1798, Gunpowder Lower Hd., no dwelling house listed in this part of the tax schedule, no land listed, 3 slaves. {Ref: TL}
WALTHAM, THOMAS, m. Martha Greenfield on May 21, 1795. {Ref: PR}
WALTHAM, THOMAS, licensed retailer in March, 1795. {Ref: CC}
WALTHAM, THOMAS, b. 1798, d. Mar 11, 1845, aged 47 years, bur. in a cemetery on Edgewood Arsenal's Aviation Field. {Ref: TI}
WALTHAM, THOMAS, head of family in 1800 (1st District). {Ref: CI}
WALTHAM, THOMAS, AND TAYLOR, THOMAS, charged for retailing liquors in 1795. {Ref: CD, August Term, 1795}
WALTHAM, THOMAS' HEIRS, or THOMAS TAYLOR, taxpayers, 1798, Bush River Lower Hd., no dwelling house listed in this part of the tax schedule, no land listed, 1 slave (Thomas Taylor, superintendent).
WANE (WANA), JOHN, of Joppa, bur. Deember 16, 1792, aged 50. {Ref: PR}
WANN, JOHN, head of family in 1800 (3rd District). {Ref: CI}
WANN, WILLIAM, b. Mar 16, 1791, d. Jan 19, 1885, bur. in Mount Tabor Methodist Cemetery at Gibson. {Ref: TI}
WARD, ANN, taxpayer, 1798, Bush River Upper & Eden Hd., 1 dwelling house, 5 inferior houses, 2 acres, $150 valuation; 1 tract (178 acres) in Bush River Upper & Eden Hd., $400.50 valuation, 3 slaves. {Ref: TL}
WARD, ANN, will probated Feb 11, 1800. {Ref: HW}
WARD, CASSANDRA, taxpayer, 1798, Deer Creek Lower Hd., 2 tracts (80 acres)

and 1 building, $204 valuation, 1 slave. {Ref: TL}

WARD (WARDE), CASSANDRA, head of family in 1800 (5th District). {Ref: CI}

WARD, CHARLES, b. Jan 19, 1791, d. Aug 15, 1865, bur. in Dublin Methodist Church Cemetery. {Ref: TI}

WARD, EDWARD, will probated May 27, 1791. {Ref: HW}

WARD, JAMES, will probated Nov 12, 1793. {Ref: HW}

WARD, JAMES, b. Feb 4, 1793, d. Jan 29, 1822, aged 28 years, 11 months, and 25 days, bur. in Dublin Methodist Church Cemetery. {Ref: TI}

WARD, JOHN, taxpayer, 1798, Deer Creek Upper Hd., 2 tracts (314 acres, 40 perches) and 1 building, $618.69 valuation, 1 slave. {Ref: TL}

WARD, JOHN, taxpayer, 1798, Susquehanna Hd., 1 tract (50 acres) and 1 building, $81.56 valuation, no slaves. {Ref: TL}

WARD, JOHN, tracts *Rocky Points* and *Patty's Delight* surveyed between 1792 and 1796. {Ref: SB}

WARD, JOHN, head of family in 1800 (2nd District). {Ref: CI}

WARD, JOHN, head of family in 1800 (4th District). {Ref: CI}

WARD, JOHN JR., taxpayer, 1798, Deer Creek Upper Hd., 1 tract (120 acres), $236.25 valuation, no slaves. {Ref: TL}

WARD, JOHN JR., tract *Addition to Ward's Intent* surveyed in 1793. {Ref: CB, SB}

WARD, JOHN (OF JOHN), tract *Ward's Intent* surveyed in 1797. {Ref: CB}

WARD, JOSEPH, see "Martha Ward," q.v.

WARD, MARTHA, wife of Joseph, b. Mar 19, 1792, d. Apr 14, 1871, aged 79 years and 26 days, bur. in Deer Creek Methodist Church Cemetery at Chestnut Hill. {Ref: TI}

WARD, MARY, head of family in 1800 (2nd District). {Ref: CI}

WARD, RICHARD, taxpayer, 1798, Deer Creek Lower Hd., 1 tract (178 acres) and 1 building, $459 valuation, no slaves. {Ref: TL}

WARD, RICHARD, head of family in 1800 (5th District). {Ref: CI}

WARD, RUBIN, insolvent on list returned by Robert Carlile for taxes due for the year 1791. {Ref: IL 31.16}

WARE, JOHN, taxpayer, 1798, Bush River Upper & Eden Hd., 1 dwelling house, 3 inferior houses, 2 acres, $175 valuation; 1 tract (76 acres) in Bush River Upper & Eden Hd., $171 valuation, no slaves. {Ref: TL}

WARE, JOHN, head of family in 1800 (4th District). {Ref: CI}

WARE, THOMAS, head of family in 1800 (4th District). {Ref: CI}

WARE, THOMAS, taxpayer, 1798, Bush River Upper & Eden Hd., 1 dwelling house, 4 inferior houses, 2 acres, $105 valuation; 1 tract (259 acres, 40 perches) in Bush River Upper & Eden Hd., $583.31 valuation, no slaves. {Ref: TL}

WAREHAM, HENRY, son of John and Rachel, b. Aug 19, 1798, bapt. Jul 13, 1799. {Ref: PR}

WAREHAM, JOHN, son of John and Rachel, b. Sep 11 (14?), 1795, bapt. Jul 13, 1799, d. Jun 9, 1870, bur. in Angel Hill Cemetery in Havre de Grace. {Ref: TI, PR}

WAREHAM, JOHN, head of family in 1800 (2nd District). {Ref: CI}
WAREHAM, JOHN, head of family in 1800 (Havre de Grace). {Ref: CI}
WAREHAM, JOHN ("charge twice"), insolvent on a list for the road tax due for 1791 in Harford Upper, Harford Lower, and Spesutia Upper as returned by Robert Amos, Jr. on Sep 18, 1793. {Ref: IL 31.18}.
WAREHAM (WARHAM), JOHN, see "Margaret Wareham" and "Henry Wareham" and "Henry Stump" and "William Perry," q.v.
WAREHAM (WARHAM), JOHN, insolvent, Harford Lower and Spesutia Lower Hundreds (listed as a single man), on a tax list returned by George Lyttle on Sep 21, 1791. {Ref: IL 31.20, 31.21}
WAREHAM (WARHAM), JOHN, taxpayer, 1798, Spesutia Lower Hd., 1 dwelling house, 1 inferior house, 44 perches and 21 sq. ft. of land, $550 valuation, no slaves. {Ref: TL}
WAREHAM (WARHAM), JOHN (sadler), had an account at Hall's Store in December, 1791. {Ref: WH}
WAREHAM (WOREHAM), JOHN, insolvent on a list for the road tax due for 1791 in Harford Upper, Harford Lower, and Spesutia Upper as returned by Robert Amos, Jr. on Sep 18, 1793. {Ref: IL 31.18}
WAREHAM, MARGARET, dau. of John and Rachel, b. Sep 19, 1793, bapt. Jul 13, 1799. {Ref: PR}
WAREHAM, RACHEL, see "Margaret Wareham" and "John Wareham" and "Henry Wareham"," q.v.
WARFIELD, HENRY'S HEIRS, or CYRUS OSBORN, taxpayers, 1798, Harford Lower Hd., 1 dwelling house, 2 acres, $100.10 valuation; 2 tracts (84 acres) in Harford Lower Hd. (Cyrus Osborn, occupant), $283.50 valuation, 2 slaves. {Ref: TL}
WARFIELD, MARTHA, m. Cyrus Osborne on Nov 26, 1795. {Ref: PR}
WARNER, ASAPH, taxpayer, 1798, Deer Creek Middle Hd., 1 dwelling house, 2 inferior houses, 2 acres, $101 valuation; 3 tracts (109 acres) in Deer Creek Middle Hd. (Thomas Fox, occupant), $122.63 valuation, no slaves; also, taxpayer, Spesutia Lower Hd., 1 dwelling house, 44 perches and 21 sq. ft. of land, $350 valuation, no slaves. {Ref: TL}
WARNER, ASAPH, head of family in 1800 (Havre de Grace). {Ref: CI}
WARNER, CROSDEL, taxpayer, 1798, Deer Creek Lower Hd., 1 dwelling house, 3 inferior houses, 2 acres, $120 valuation; 1 tract (148 acres) in Deer Creek Lower Hd., $247.50 valuation, no slaves. {Ref: TL}
WARNER, CROSDEL, taxpayer, 1798, Gunpowder Upper Hd., 1 tract (51 acres, 120 perches) and 1 building, $239.63 valuation, no slaves. {Ref: TL}
WARNER, CUDDY, treated by Dr. Archer on Oct 11, 1799; also mentioned his wife and infant (no names given). {Ref: JA}
WARNER, CUTHBERT (Baltimore Town), or JOSEPH WIGGINS, taxpayer, 1798, Deer Creek Lower Hd., 1 dwelling house, 2 acres (Joseph Wiggins, occupant), $340 valuation; 1 tract (80 acres) in Deer Creek Lower Hd. (Joseph

Wiggins, occupant), $135 valuation, no slaves. {Ref: TL}
WARNER, CUTHBERT, insolvent on a list in 1792 in Deer Creek Lower Hd., as returned by Benjamin Preston. {Ref: IL 31.03}
WARNER, H. E., see "Sarah Warner," q.v.
WARNER, JOSEPH, taxpayer, 1798, Deer Creek Lower Hd., 1 tract (150 acres) and 1 building, $343.13 valuation, no slaves. {Ref: TL}
WARNER, SARAH, wife of H.(?) E., b. 1793(?), d. Apr 11, 1869(?), aged 72(?), bur. in William Watters Methodist Church Cemetery near Jarrettsville. {Ref: TI}
WARNICH, PHILLIP, head of family in 1800 (5th District). {Ref: CI}
WARNOCK, PHILIP, treated by Dr. Archer on May 12, 1795. {Ref: JA}
WARRICK, ELIZABETH, taxpayer, 1798, Bush River Upper & Eden Hd., 1 tract (75 acres, 120 perches) and 1 building, $216.37 valuation, no slaves. {Ref: TL}
WARRICK, ELIZABETH, head of family in 1800 (4th District). {Ref: CI}
WARRIN, BAILEY, head of family in 1800 (1st District). {Ref: CI}
WARTS, CASPER, taxpayer, 1798, Spesutia Lower Hd., 1 tract (44 perches, 21 sq. ft.), $13.50 valuation, no slaves. {Ref: TL}
WASKEY, CHRISTIAN, taxpayer, 1798, Gunpowder Lower Hd., 1 dwelling house, 2 inferior houses, 2 acres, $200 valuation; 1 tract (1 acre) in Gunpowder Lower Hd., $9 valuation, no slaves. {Ref: TL}
WASKEY, CHRISTIAN, head of family in 1800 (Abingdon). {Ref: CI}
WATERS, ELIZABETH, see "Thomas Birkhead," q.v.
WATERS, GODFREY, taxpayer, 1798, Harford Upper Hd., 1 tract (100 acres) and 1 building, $309.28 valuation, 1 slave. {Ref: TL}
WATERS, GODFREY, served on a Petit Jury in March, 1798. {Ref: CM}
WATERS, GODFREY (OF HENRY), treated by Dr. Archer on Jul 24, 1791. {Ref: JA}
WATERS, HENRY, see "Godfrey Waters," q.v.
WATERS, HENRY, taxpayer, 1798, Spesutia Upper Hd., 1 dwelling house, 7 inferior houses, 2 acres, $295 valuation; 1 tract (148 acres) in Spesutia Upper Hd., $767.25 valuation, 3 slaves. {Ref: TL}
WATERS, HENRY, m. Grace Wilson on Feb 21, 1792. {Ref: PR}
WATERS, HENRY JR., served on a Petit Jury in March, 1798. {Ref: CM}
WATERS, SALLY, see "Walter Waters," q.v.
WATERS, STEPHEN, taxpayer, 1798, Bush River Upper & Eden Hd., 1 dwelling house, 5 inferior houses, 2 acres, $300 valuation; 6 tracts (681 acres) in Gunpowder Lower Hd., $1566 valuation, 6 slaves. {Ref: TL}
WATERS, WALTER, taxpayer, 1798, Harford Upper Hd., 1 dwelling house, 4 inferior houses, 2 acres, $120 valuation; 1 tract (214 acres) in Harford Upper Hd., $301.12 valuation, no slaves. {Ref: TL}
WATERS, WALTER, treated by Dr. Archer on Dec 5, 1792; also mentioned his dau. Sally in 1788. {Ref: JA}
WATERS, WILLIAM, taxpayer, 1798, Bush River Lower Hd., 1 tract (50 acres), $56.25 valuation, no slaves. {Ref: TL}

WATKINS, ELIZABETH, insolvent on lists in 1791 due county taxes and road taxes in "Deer Creek Upper, Middle, and Broad Creek Hundreds" as returned by Robert Amos, Jr. {Ref: IL 31.12, 31.22}

WATKINS, JAMES, insolvent, Harford Lower and Spesutia Lower Hundreds, on a tax list returned by George Lyttle on Sep 21, 1791. {Ref: IL 31.20, 31.21}

WATKINS, JAMES, taxpayer, 1798, Spesutia Lower Hd., 1 tract (44 perches, 21 sq. ft.) and 1 building, $101.25 valuation, no slaves. {Ref: TL}

WATKINS, JAMES, head of family in 1800 (Havre de Grace). {Ref: CI}

WATKINS, JOHN, taxpayer, 1798, Deer Creek Upper Hd., 1 tract (261 acres, 120 perches) and 2 buildings (Archibald McCreary, occupant of one of them), $666 valuation, no slaves. {Ref: TL}

WATKINS, JOHN, insolvent on lists in 1791 due county taxes and road taxes in "Deer Creek Upper, Middle, and Broad Creek Hundreds" as returned by Robert Amos, Jr. {Ref: IL 31.12, 31.22}

WATKINS, JOHN, tract *John's First Chance* surveyed in 1787 and granted in 1793. {Ref: CB}

WATKINS, JOHN, head of family in 1800 (2nd District). {Ref: CI}

WATKINS, JOHN, head of family in 1800 (4th District). {Ref: CI}

WATSON, ARCHIBALD, head of family in 1800 (4th District). {Ref: CI}

WATSON, CHARLES, insolvent on a list for 1791 in Gunpowder Upper and Bush River Lower Hundreds, as filed by John Bond, Deputy Sheriff, on Sep 20, 1791 (who listed him as a single man). {Ref: IL 31.24}

WATSON, CHARLES, insolvent on list returned by Robert Carlile for taxes due for the year 1791. {Ref: IL 31.16}

WATSON, JAMES, insolvent on list returned by John Guyton for taxes due for the year 1791. {Ref: IL 31.19}

WATSON, JAMES, mentioned in a survey deposition on May 9, 1799. {Ref: JS}

WATSON, JAMES, head of family in 1800 (3rd District). {Ref: CI}

WATSON, JANE, head of family in 1800 (4th District). {Ref: CI}

WATSON, WILLIAM, head of family in 1800 (5th District). {Ref: CI}

WATT, JAMES, husband of Mary Amos and son of Robert Watt and Sarah Streett, b. Sep 25, 1791 or 1792, d. Jul 17, 1866, bur. in Bethel Presbyterian Church Cemetery at Madonna. {Ref: BC}. Also see "Martha Watt," q.v.

WATT, JOSEPH, insolvent on lists in 1791 due county taxes and road taxes in "Deer Creek Upper, Middle, and Broad Creek Hundreds" as returned by Robert Amos, Jr. {Ref: IL 31.12, 31.22}

WATT, JOSEPH, insolvent on list returned by Robert Carlile for taxes due for the year 1791. {Ref: IL 31.16}

WATT, JOSEPH ("run"), insolvent on a list of the county tax due William Osborn, sheriff, for 1791, as returned by Edward Prigg on Sep 20, 1791. {Ref: IL 31.17}

WATT, MARTHA, b. 1795, and child (unnamed), wife and son of James Watt, d. Oct 25, 1824, she in her 29th year, bur. in Christ Episcopal (Rock Spring)

Church Cemetery. {Ref: TI}

WATT, ROBERT, taxpayer, 1798, Bush River Upper & Eden Hd., 1 dwelling house, 3 inferior houses, 2 acres, $150 valuation; 1 tract (108 acres, 80 perches) in Bush River Upper & Eden Hd., $183.90 valuation, no slaves. {Ref: TL}. Also see "James Watt" and "William Watt," q.v.

WATT, WILLIAM, husband of Rebecca Shaw and son of Robert Watt and Sarah Streett, b. 1798, d. Apr 30, 1839, bur. in Bethel Presbyterian Church Cemetery at Madonna. {Ref: BC}

WATTERS(?), CROSDEL, head of family in 1800 (3rd District). {Ref: CI}

WATTERS, DANIEL R., son of Henry and Grace, b. Nov 30, 1792, d. Aug 10, 1857, bur. in Watters Memorial Methodist Church Cemetery on Thomas Run. {Ref: TI}. Also see "Sarah P. Watters," q.v.

WATTERS, GODFREY, see "Susan Watters" and "Margaret Watters" and "Godfrey Waters," q.v.

WATTERS, GODFREY, served on a Petit Jury in August, 1800. {Ref: CM}

WATTERS, GODFREY, head of family in 1800 (1st District). {Ref: CI}

WATTERS, GRACE, wife of Henry, Jr., d. Apr 4, 1796, aged 27, bur. in Watters Memorial Methodist Church Cemetery on Thomas Run. {Ref: TI}. Alsos see "Daniel R. Watters," q.v.

WATTERS, HENRY, see "Daniel R. Watters" and "Grace Watters" and "John W. Watters" and "Mary Watters" and "Henry Waters," q.v.

WATTERS, HENRY, head of family in 1800 (3rd District). {Ref: CI}

WATTERS, HENRY JR., served on a Grand Jury in March, 1800. {Ref: CM}

WATTERS, HENRY JR., head of family in 1800 (1st District). {Ref: CI}

WATTERS, JOHANNA, insolvent on lists due for 1790 and 1791 "fund taxes" and county taxes in Susquehanna Hd., as returned by Thomas Taylor. Her name was listed as "Johannh. Watters, exempt by Parson Ireland" on one 1791 list and as "Johannah Walters" on another. {Ref: IL 31.12, 31.02}

WATTERS, JOHN, head of family in 1800 (3rd District). {Ref: CI}

WATTERS, JOHN W., son of Henry, Jr., d. Feb 17, 1796, aged 17 months, bur. in Watters Memorial Methodist Church Cemetery on Thomas Run. {Ref: TI}

WATTERS, MARGARET, dau. of Godfrey and Martha, b. 1792, d. Nov 3, 1829, in her 37th year, bur. in Watters Memorial Methodist Church Cemetery on Thomas Run. {Ref: TI}

WATTERS, MARTHA, see "Susan Watters" and "Margaret Watters," q.v.

WATTERS, MARY, wife of Henry G., b. 1796, d. 1871, bur. in Watters Memorial Methodist Church Cemetery on Thomas Run. {Ref: TI}

WATTERS, MARY, wife of Walter, b. Mar 15, 1799, d. May 21, 1871, bur. in William Watters Methodist Church Cemetery near Jarrettsville. {Ref: TI}

WATTERS, NICHOLAS, head of family in 1800 (3rd District). {Ref: CI}

WATTERS, SARAH P., wife of Daniel R., b. Sep 30, 1792, d. Aug 16, 1875, bur. in Watters Memorial Methodist Church Cemetery on Thomas Run. {Ref: TI}

WATTERS, STEPHEN, head of family in 1800 (1st District). {Ref: CI}
WATTERS, SUSAN, dau. of Godfrey and Martha, b. 1794, d. Sep 29, 1842, in her 48th year, bur. in Watters Memorial Methodist Church Cemetery on Thomas Run. {Ref: TI}
WATTERS, THOMAS, insolvent on a list for the road tax due for 1791 in Harford Upper, Harford Lower, and Spesutia Upper as returned by Robert Amos, Jr. on Sep 18, 1793. {Ref: IL 31.18}
WATTERS, WALTER, see "Mary Watters," q.v.
WATTERS, WILLIAM, head of family in 1800 (1st District). {Ref: CI}
WATTERS, WILLIAM, head of family in 1800 (3rd District); three men by this name in this district. {Ref: CI}
WATTS, ROBERT, head of family in 1800 (4th District). {Ref: CI}
WAY, DAVID, head of family in 1800 (3rd District). {Ref: CI}
WAY, ELIZABETH, dau. of John and Sarah, bapt. Apr 20, 1797. {Ref: PR}
WAY, JAMES, son of John and Sarah, bapt. Apr 20, 1797. {Ref: PR}
WAY, JOB, head of family in 1800 (4th District). {Ref: CI}
WAY, JOHN, head of family in 1800 (2nd District). {Ref: CI}. Also see "Elizabeth Way" and "James Way" and "Leveridge Way," q.v.
WAY, LEVERIDGE, son of John and Sarah, bapt. Apr 20, 1797. {Ref: PR}
WAY, SARAH, see "Elizabeth Way" and "James Way" and "Leveridge Way," q.v.
WEAR, JAMES, m. Charity Key on Sep 11, 1791. {Ref: PR}
WEATHERALL, ELIZABETH, see "Elizabeth Wetherill," q.v.
WEATHERALL, HENRY, taxpayer, 1798, Gunpowder Lower Hd., 1 dwelling house, 4 inferior houses, 2 acres, $300 valuation; 4 tracts (269 acres) in Gunpowder Lower Hd., $526.50 valuation, 4 slaves. {Ref: TL}
WEATHERALL, HENRY, served on a Grand Jury in August, 1798 and August, 1799. {Ref: CM}
WEATHERALL (WEATHERAL), HENRY, head of family in 1800 (1st District). {Ref: CI}
WEATHERALL, JAMES, taxpayer, 1798, Gunpowder Lower Hd., 1 dwelling house, 5 inferior houses, 2 acres, $500 valuation; 4 tracts (533 acres) in Gunpowder Lower Hd., $1199.25 valuation, 8 slaves. {Ref: TL}
WEATHERALL (WEATHERAL), JAMES, head of family in 1800 (1st District). {Ref: CI}
WEATHERALL, JAMES ("for John Day's heirs"), taxpayer, 1798, Gunpowder Lower Hd., 1 dwelling house, 5 inferior houses, 2 acres, $300 valuation; 3 tracts (595 acres) in Gunpowder Lower Hd., $4016.25 valuation, no slaves. {Ref: TL}
WEATHERALL, SAMUEL, see "Elizabeth Wetherill," q.v.
WEATHERALL, WILLIAM, m. Mary Presbury on Sep 21 or 22, 1797. {Ref: PR}
WEATHERINGTON, JOSEPH, head of family in 1800 (5th District). {Ref: CI}
WEATHRAL, HENRY, see "Negro Dick," q.v.
WEAVER, JASPER, insolvent on lists returned by Robert Carlile and John Guyton (who listed him as a single man) for taxes due for the year 1791. {Ref: IL 31.16, 31.19}

343

WEBB, ELIZABETH, dau. of George and Margaret, b. Sep 28, 1799, bapt. Dec 27, 1799. {Ref: PR}

WEBB, GEORGE, m. Margaret Baughman on Nov 8, 1798. {Ref: PR}. Also see "Elizabeth Webb," q.v.

WEBB, GEORGE, head of family in 1800 (Havre de Grace). {Ref: CI}

WEBB, JOHN, taxpayer, 1798, Deer Creek Upper Hd., 2 tracts (238 acres, 120 perches) and 1 building, $470.40 valuation, no slaves. {Ref: TL}

WEBB, JOHN, insolvent on lists in 1791 due county taxes and road taxes in "Deer Creek Upper, Middle, and Broad Creek Hundreds" as returned by Robert Amos, Jr. {Ref: IL 31.12, 31.22}

WEBB, JOHN, head of family in 1800 (5th District). {Ref: CI}

WEBB, MARGARET, see "Elizabeth Webb," q.v.

WEBB, RICHARD, b. Jul 9, 1798, bapt. Jul 12, 1798 (name of parents not indicated). {Ref: PR}

WEBB, RICHARD, bur. Jul 12, 1798. {Ref: PR}

WEBB, SAMUEL, taxpayer, 1798, Deer Creek Middle Hd., no dwelling house listed in this part of the tax schedule, no land listed, 1 slave. {Ref: TL}

WEBB, SAMUEL, head of family in 1800 (4th District). {Ref: CI}

WEBB, SAMUEL, head of family in 1800 (5th District). {Ref: CI}

WEBSTER, CAROLINE, dau. of Joseph and Martha, b. Apr 23, 1798, bapt. Oct 21, 1798. {Ref: PR}

WEBSTER, CHAUNCEY, son of Joseph and Martha, bapt. Mar 19, 1795. {Ref: PR}

WEBSTER, GEORGE, see "Richard Webster," q.v.

WEBSTER, HANNAH, will probated May 8, 1795. {Ref: HW}

WEBSTER, HENRY, son of Richard and Phebe Webster, b. Mar 16, 1793, d. Oct 22, 1872, bur. in Calvary Methodist Church Cemetery. {Ref: TI}

WEBSTER, ISAAC, balance due on Nov 13, 1797 at Bush River Store. {Ref: AH}

WEBSTER, ISAAC, will probated Sep 30, 1799. {Ref: HW}

WEBSTER, ISAAC, head of family in 1800 (1st District). {Ref: CI}

WEBSTER, ISAAC JR., insolvent on a list for 1791 in Gunpowder Upper and Bush River Lower Hundreds, as filed by John Bond, Deputy Sheriff, on Sep 20, 1791. {Ref: IL 31.24}

WEBSTER, ISAAC JR., insolvent on list returned for the road tax due for 1791 by John Bull. {Ref: IL 31.14}

WEBSTER, ISAAC JR., taxpayer, 1798, Spesutia Lower Hd., 1 dwelling house, 1 inferior house, 1 acre, $105 valuation; 1 tract (no description given) in Spesutia Lower Hd., $67.50 valuation, no slaves. {Ref: TL}

WEBSTER, ISAAC JR., license retailer in August, 1797. {Ref: CC}

WEBSTER, ISAAC JR., charged "for dealing with Negro Bill" in 1797. {Ref: CD, March and August Terms, 1797}

WEBSTER, ISAAC SR., taxpayer, 1798, Harford Upper Hd., 1 dwelling house, 3 inferior houses, 2 acres, $650 valuation; 3 tracts (488 acres) and 3 buildings in Harford Upper Hd., $2070 valuation, no slaves. {Ref: TL}

WEBSTER, ISAAC LEE, taxpayer, 1798, Harford Upper Hd., 1 dwelling house, 6 inferior houses, 2 acres, $500 valuation; 8 tracts (736 acres, 120 perches) in Harford Upper Hd., $1968.75 valuation, no slaves. {Ref: TL}. In another part of the tax schedule the occupant is listed as John Wilson.

WEBSTER, JAMES, will probated Jan 26, 1793. {Ref: HW}

WEBSTER, JAMES (Baltimore County), or JOHN EVANS, taxpayer, 1798, Harford Upper Hd., 1 tract (200 acres) and 1 building (John Evans, occupant), $386.25 valuation, no slaves. {Ref: TL}. In another part of the tax schedule the occupant is listed as John Evans (plaisterer).

WEBSTER, JAMES (Baltimore County), insolvent on a list for the road tax due for 1791 in Harford Upper, Harford Lower, and Spesutia Upper as returned by Robert Amos, Jr. on Sep 18, 1793. {Ref: IL 31.18}

WEBSTER, JOHN, see "Michael Webster," q.v.

WEBSTER, JOHN, head of family in 1800 (3rd District). {Ref: CI}

WEBSTER, JOHN (OF RICHARD), taxpayer, 1798, Harford Upper Hd., 1 tract (60 acres) and 1 building, $118.12 valuation, no slaves. {Ref: TL}

WEBSTER, JOHN A., see "Rachel Biays," q.v.

WEBSTER, JOHN LEE (of Spesutia), will probated Aug 19, 1795. {Ref: HW}

WEBSTER, JOHN S., taxpayer, 1798, Spesutia Lower Hd., 1 dwelling house, 13 inferior houses, 2 acres, $1100 valuation; 1 tract (845 acres) in Spesutia Lower Hd., $8006.63 valuation, 3 slaves; also, taxpayer, Harford Lower Hd., 1 dwelling house, 4 inferior houses, 2 acres (James Osborn, occupant), $400 valuation; also, taxpayer, 3 tracts (121 acres, 80 perches) and 1 building in Spesutia Lower Hd., $672.86 valuation; in another part of the tax schedule the occupant is listed as a free negro, but no name is given. Also, taxpayer, 1 tract (53 acres) in Harford Lower Hd. (James Osborn, occupant), $327.94 valuation, no slaves. {Ref: TL}

WEBSTER, JOHN S., head of family in 1800 (2nd District). {Ref: CI}

WEBSTER, JOSEPH, see "Sarah Webster" and "Caroline Webster" and "Chauncey Webster," q.v.

WEBSTER, JOSEPH, taxpayer, 1798, Harford Lower Hd., 1 dwelling house, 4 inferior houses, 120 perches of land, $500 valuation; 1 tract (2 acres, 80 perches) in Harford Lower Hd., $101.25 valuation, 2 slaves. {Ref: TL}

WEBSTER, JOSEPH, licensed retailer in March, 1795 and August, 1797. {Ref: CC}

WEBSTER, JOSEPH, appeared on list of "recognizances" of the court for "mishaving" to William Smith, Esq., in the execution of his office as Justice of the Peace and on oath of the peace by William Hollis. {Ref: CD, August Term, 1797}

WEBSTER, JOSEPH, bur. Mar 9, 1800. {Ref: PR}

WEBSTER, MARTHA, bur. Jan 13, 1800. {Ref: PR}. Also see "Caroline Webster" and "Chauncey Webster," q.v.

WEBSTER, MARTHA H., wife of Henry Webster and dau. of Benjamin and Martha Hanson, b. 1795, d. Jan 31, 1850, in her 55th year, bur. in Calvary

Methodist Church Cemetery. {Ref: TI}
WEBSTER, MARY, see "Sarah Webster," q.v.
WEBSTER, MARY, head of family in 1800 (1st District); two women by this name in this district. {Ref: CI}
WEBSTER, MARY (widow), taxpayer, 1798, Harford Upper Hd., 1 tract (250 acres) and 1 building, $486.74 valuation, no slaves. {Ref: TL}
WEBSTER, MICHAEL, insolvent on a list for the road tax due for 1791 in Harford Upper, Harford Lower, and Spesutia Upper as returned by Robert Amos, Jr. on Sep 18, 1793. {Ref: IL 31 18}
WEBSTER, MICHAEL, head of family in 1800 (1st District). {Ref: CI}
WEBSTER, MICHAEL (OF JOHN), insolvent on list returned for the county tax for 1791 by William Osburn in Gunpowder Lower Hundred. {Ref: IL 31.15}
WEBSTER, PEGGY (Miss), had an account at Hall's Store in October, 1791. {Ref: WH}
WEBSTER, PHEBE, see "Henry Webster," q.v.
WEBSTER, RACHEL, see "Rachel Biays," q.v.
WEBSTER, RICHARD, see "Henry Webster" and "Samuel Webster (of Richard)" and "John Webster (of Richard)," q.v.
WEBSTER, RICHARD, treated by Dr. Archer in March, 1792; also mentioned his sons William, George, and Samuel. {Ref: JA}
WEBSTER, RICHARD, taxpayer, 1798, Harford Upper Hd., 1 dwelling house, 4 inferior houses, 2 acres, $250 valuation; 2 tracts (360 acres) in Harford Upper Hd., $1282.50 valuation, no slaves. {Ref: TL}
WEBSTER, RICHARD, head of family in 1800 (3rd District). {Ref: CI}
WEBSTER, RICHARD JR., head of family in 1800 (3rd District). {Ref: CI}
WEBSTER, SAMUEL, see "Richard Webster," q.v.
WEBSTER, SAMUEL, insolvent on a list for the road tax for 1792, as returned for Robert Amoss, tax collector. {Ref: IL 13.12}
WEBSTER, SAMUEL, b. 1791 or 1792, d. Dec 21, 1862, in his 71st year, bur. in Calvary Methodist Church Cemetery. {Ref: TI}
WEBSTER, SAMUEL, head of family in 1800 (3rd District). {Ref: CI}
WEBSTER, SAMUEL, SR., head of family in 1800 (1st District). {Ref: CI}
WEBSTER, SAMUEL (tanner), taxpayer, 1798, Harford Upper Hd., 1 dwelling house, 3 inferior houses, 2 acres, $250 valuation; 3 tracts (308 acres) in Harford Upper Hd., $693 valuation, no slaves. {Ref: TL}
WEBSTER, SAMUEL (OF RICHARD), taxpayer, 1798, Harford Upper Hd., 1 tract (370 acres) and 1 building, $855 valuation, no slaves. {Ref: TL}
WEBSTER, SAMUEL (OF SAMUEL), insolvent on a list for the road tax due for 1791 in Harford Upper, Harford Lower, and Spesutia Upper as returned by Robert Amos, Jr. on Sep 18, 1793. {Ref: IL 31.18}
WEBSTER, SARAH, dau. of Joseph and Mary, b. Dec 26, 1796, bapt. Apr 4, 1797. {Ref: PR}
WEBSTER, WILLIAM, see "Richard Webster," q.v.

WEEKS, ANN, see "Sarah Weeks," q.v.
WEEKS, CATHARINE, dau. of Daniel and Mary, b. Nov 6, 1796. {Ref: PR}
WEEKS, DANIEL, son of Daniel and Mary, b. Jun 13, 1792. {Ref: PR}. Also see "John Weeks" and "Catharine Weeks" and "Ezekiel Weeks," q.v.
WEEKS, DANIEL, taxpayer, 1798, Harford Upper Hd., 1 tract (65 acres) and 1 building, $227.81 valuation, no slaves. {Ref: TL}
WEEKS (WEEKES), DANIEL, head of family in 1800 (1st District). {Ref: CI}
WEEKS, EZEKIEL, son of Daniel and Mary, b. Mar 17, 1799. {Ref: PR}
WEEKS, EZEKIEL, head of family in 1800 (3rd District). {Ref: CI}
WEEKS, JOHN, see "Sarah Weeks," q.v.
WEEKS, JOHN, son of Daniel and Mary, b. Sep 2, 1794. {Ref: PR}
WEEKS, JOHN, taxpayer, 1798, Broad Creek Hd., 1 tract (75 acres) and 1 building, $146.25 valuation, no slaves. {Ref: TL}
WEEKS (WEEKES), JOHN, head of family in 1800 (5th District). {Ref: CI}
WEEKS, MARY, see "Daniel Weeks" and "Catharine Weeks" and "John Weeks" and "Ezekiel Weeks," q.v.
WEEKS, SARAH, dau. of John and Ann, b. Aug 9, 1791. {Ref: PR}
WEILY, NATHIN, "twist chd" (meaning "twice charged"), insolvent on a list of the county tax due William Osborn, sheriff, for 1791, as returned by Edward Prigg on Sep 20, 1791. {Ref: IL 31.17}
WEIR, THOMAS, see "Elijah Durham," q.v.
WELCH, WILLIAM, taxpayer, 1798, Spesutia Upper Hd., 1 dwelling house, 3 inferior houses, 80 perches of land, $105 valuation; 1 tract (123 acres) and 1 building in Spesutia Upper Hd., $499.50 valuation, 1 slave. {Ref: TL}
WELCH, WILLIAM (captain), head of family in 1800 (3rd District). {Ref: CI}
WELLS, BENJAMIN, son of James and Ruth, b. Jul 16, 1797, bapt. Apr 29, 1798. {Ref: PR}
WELLS, DANIEL, see "Henry G. McComas," q.v.
WELLS, ELIZABETH, bur. Dec 10, 1799. {Ref: PR}
WELLS, JAMES, treated by Dr. Archer on Jan 10, 1791; also mentioned he lived at B. Friar [Bald Friar, a Susquehanna River crossing] near M. Sweney's Mill. {Ref: JA}. Also see "Benjamin Wells," q.v.
WELLS, JANE, taxpayer, 1798, Deer Creek Lower Hd., no dwelling house listed in this part of the tax schedule, no land listed, 1 slave. {Ref: TL}
WELLS, RICHARD, insolvent on lists for the county tax and road tax due for 1791 and 1792 (listed twice in 1792) in Deer Creek Lower Hd., as returned by Thomas Taylor on Sep 17, 1792. {Ref: IL 31.12, 31.03}
WELLS, RUTH, see "Benjamin Wells," q.v.
WELLS, WILLIAM, taxpayer, 1798, Broad Creek Hd., no dwelling house listed in this part of the tax schedule, no land listed, 1 slave. {Ref: TL}
WELLS, WILLIAM, served as constable in Deer Creek Lower Hd., 1798-1800. {Ref: CM}
WELLS, WILLIAM, insolvent on a list for the road tax for 1792, as returned for

Robert Amoss, tax collector. {Ref: IL 13.12}

WELLS, WILLIAM, head of family in 1800 (5th District). {Ref. CI}

WELLS, WILLIAM JR., or WILLIAM WELLS SR., taxpayer, 1798, Broad Creek Hd., 1 tract (100 acres) and building (William Wells, Sr., occupant), $195 valuation, no slaves. {Ref: TL}

WELLS, ZENAS, head of family in 1800 (1st District). {Ref: CI}

WELSH, WILLIAM, licensed ordinary (tavern) in March, 1795. {Ref: CC}

WEST, ABEL, head of family in 1800 (4th Dis'rict). {Ref: CI}. Also see "David West," q.v.

WEST, ANN, bur. Oct 20, 1799. {Ref: PR}

WEST, ANN, head of family in 1800 (2nd District). {Ref: CI}

WEST, BENJAMIN, see "David West," q.v.

WEST, DAVID, taxpayer, 1798, Deer Creek Upper Hd., 1 tract (115 acres, 80 perches) and 1 building, $168.75 valuation, no slaves. {Ref: TL}

WEST, DAVID, tracts *Armstrong's Misfortune*, *Manyfold's Refuse*, and *Jarrett's Disappointment* surveyed between 1792 and 1795. {Ref: CB, SB}

WEST, DAVID, charged in 1794 (nature of case not stated) with many people summoned to testify, including Abel West and Benjamin West. {Ref: CD, March Term, 1795}

WEST, DAVID, involved in a chancery court case against Jesse Jarrett regarding a land dispute in 1799. {Ref: JS}

WEST, DAVID, tracts *The Conclusion* surveyed in 1799, *The Buckskin* surveyed in 1799, *Misfortune* (at a milestone on the State Line) surveyed in 1799, and *The Buckskin Corrected* (partially lying in Pennsylvania) surveyed in 1800. {Ref: CB}

WEST, DAVID, head of family in 1800 (4th District). {Ref: CI}

WEST, EANUS, insolvent on list returned for the road tax due for 1791 by John Bull. {Ref: IL 31.14}

WEST, ELIZABETH, see "Hannah West" and "Washington West" and "Thomas West," q.v.

WEST, ENOCH, insolvent on lists for the county tax and road tax due for 1791 in Susquehanna Hd., as returned by Thomas Taylor on Sep 17, 1792. {Ref: IL 31.12, 31.02}

WEST, ENOS, insolvent on list returned by Robert Carlile for taxes due for the year 1791. {Ref: IL 31.16}

WEST, HANNAH, dau. of Thomas and Elizabeth, b. Feb 26, 1799. {Ref: PR}. Also see "Thomas West," q.v.

WEST, ISAAC, see "Thomas West," q.v.

WEST, JAMES, treated by Dr. Archer on Jun 7, 1791; also mentioned his wife (no name given) and that they lived near T. Gash. {Ref: JA}

WEST, JOHN ("run away"), insolvent on lists due for 1790, 1791, and 1792 "fund taxes" and road tax in Deer Creek Lower Hd., as returned by Thomas Taylor. {Ref: IL 31.12, 31.03}

WEST, JOHN, insolvent on lists returned by Robert Carlile and John Guyton for taxes due for the year 1791. {Ref: IL 31.16, 31.19}

WEST, JONATHAN, insolvent on list returned for the road tax due for 1791 by John Bull. {Ref: IL 31.14}. Also see "James Lytle," q.v.

WEST, JOSEPH, insolvent on lists in 1791 due county taxes and road taxes in "Deer Creek Upper, Middle, and Broad Creek Hundreds" as returned by Robert Amos, Jr. {Ref: IL 31.12, 31.22}

WEST, JOSEPH, bur. May 25, 1799. {Ref: PR}

WEST, JOSEPH, will probated Dec 4, 1798. {Ref: HW}

WEST, LUKE, head of family in 1800 (3rd District). {Ref: CI}

WEST, MARTHA, wife of Rezin Gorrell, b. Jun 11, 1792. {Ref: John Thomas Gorrell Bible}

WEST, MICHAEL, insolvent on a list for 1791 in Gunpowder Upper and Bush River Lower Hundreds, as filed by John Bond, Deputy Sheriff, on Sep 20, 1791. {Ref: IL 31.24}

WEST, NATHANIEL, taxpayer, 1798, Spesutia Upper Hd., 2 tracts (188 acres) and 1 building in Spesutia Upper Hd., $513 valuation, no slaves. {Ref: TL}

WEST, NATHANIEL, insolvent on a list for the road tax for 1792, as returned for Robert Amoss, tax collector. {Ref: IL 13.12}

WEST, NATHANIEL, head of family in 1800 (3rd District). {Ref: CI}

WEST, NATHANIEL JR., charged for assaulting Patrick Gallaher (Galleher) in 1794. {Ref: CD, March and August Terms, 1795}

WEST, ROBERT, see "John Neeper," q.v.

WEST, ROBERT, insolvent on a list in 1792 in Broad Creek Hd., as returned by Benjamin Preston. {Ref: IL 31.03}

WEST, ROBERT ("run"), insolvent on a list of the county tax due William Osborn, sheriff, for 1791, as returned by Edward Prigg on Sep 20, 1791. {Ref: IL 31.17}

WEST, ROBERT, head of family in 1800 (5th District). {Ref: CI}

WEST, TEMPERANCE, m. John St. Clair on Dec 19, 1799. {Ref: PR}

WEST, THOMAS, see "Hannah West" and "Washington West," q.v.

WEST, THOMAS, taxpayer, 1798, Bush River Upper & Eden Hd., 1 dwelling house, 4 inferior houses, 2 acres, $175 valuation; 4 tracts (348 acres) in Bush River Upper & Eden Hd., $783 valuation, no slaves. {Ref: TL}

WEST, THOMAS, tract *West's Addition* surveyed in 1795. {Ref: CB}

WEST, THOMAS, head of family in 1800 (2nd District). {Ref: CI}

WEST, THOMAS, head of family in 1800 (4th District). {Ref: CI}

WEST, THOMAS SR., head of family in 1800 (2nd District). {Ref: CI}

WEST, THOMAS, ISAAC, HANNAH, AND ELIZABETH, charged in 1795 (nature of the case not stated). {Ref: CD, August Term, 1795}

WEST, WASHINGTON, son of Thomas and Elizabeth, b. Dec 15, 1799. {Ref: PR}

WESTON, JOHN, tract *Jay's Treaty* surveyed between 1792 and 1796. {Ref: SB}

WESTON, JOHN, served as foreman on a Grand Jury in August, 1799, and as a Grand Jury member in August, 1800. {Ref: CM}

WESTON, JOHN, taxpayer, 1798, Gunpowder Upper Hd., 1 dwelling house, 5 inferior houses, 2 acres, $500 valuation; 7 tracts (613 acres) in Gunpowder Upper Hd., $1491.75 valuation, 9 slaves. {Ref: TL}

WESTON (WESTERN), JOHN (esquire), head of family in 1800 (1st District). {Ref: CI}

WESTON, THOMAS, insolvent on list returned by John Guyton for taxes due for the year 1791. {Ref: IL 31.19}

WETHERALL, JAMES (of Abingdon), will probated Aug 24, 1797. {Ref: HW}

WETHERILL, ELIZABETH (wife of Samuel), b. 1800, d. Jul 23, 1880, aged 80 years, --(?) months, and 11 days, bur. in William Watters Methodist Church Cemetery near Jarrettsville. {Ref: TI}

WHEELER, BENJAMIN, taxpayer, 1798, Spesutia Upper Hd., 1 dwelling house, 7 inferior houses, 2 acres, $390 valuation; 12 tracts (918 acres) in Spesutia Upper Hd., $4215.37 valuation, 10 slaves. {Ref: TL}

WHEELER, BENJAMIN, head of family in 1800 (3rd District); two men by this name in this district. {Ref: CI}

WHEELER, BENJAMIN JR., taxpayer, 1798, no dwelling house listed in this part of the tax schedule, no land listed, no hd. listed (possibly Spesutia Upper Hundred), 1 slave. {Ref: TL}

WHEELER, BENNET, taxpayer, 1798, Spesutia Upper Hd., 1 dwelling house, 3 inferior houses, 1 acre, $132 valuation; 4 tracts (729 acres) in Spesutia Upper Hd., $2100.37 valuation, 3 slaves. {Ref: TL}. Also see "Mrs. McGibbons" and "Negro Joe," q.v.

WHEELER, BENNETT, insolvent on a list for the road tax for 1792, as returned for Robert Amoss, tax collector. {Ref: IL 13.12}

WHEELER, BENNETT, head of family in 1800 (3rd District). {Ref: CI}

WHEELER, BENNIT (OF IGNATIUS), treated by Dr. Archer on Dec 24, 1791. {Ref: JA}

WHEELER, GEORGE, b. 1794, d. Dcember 3, 1839, aged 45, bur. in St. Ignatius Catholic Church Cemetery in Hickory. {Ref: TI}

WHEELER, HENRIETTA, wife of Joseph A., b. 1799, d. Jan 25, 1858, in her 59th year, bur. in St. Ignatius Catholic Church Cemetery in Hickory. {Ref: TI}

WHEELER, HENRIETTA, taxpayer, 1798, Deer Creek Middle Hd., 1 dwelling house, 9 inferior houses, 2 acres, $750 valuation; 3 tracts (1925 acres, 40 perches) and 5 buildings in Deer Creek Middle Hd. (occupants: Tarrence Crosby, George Carlin, Evan Evans, and Edward Cain), $4317.64 valuation, 25 slaves; also, taxpayer, Deer Creek Upper Hd., 1 dwelling house, 4 inferior houses, 2 acres, $120 valuation; also, taxpayer, Deer Creek Upper Hd., 1 tract (1158 acres) and 3 buildings (occupants: Thomas Butler, Patrick Demsey, and William Logue), $2817.90 valuation; and, taxpayer, 1798, Broad Creek Hd., 2 tracts (190 acres) and 1 building (John Daugherty, occupant), $320.63 valuation, no slaves. {Ref: TL}

WHEELER, HENRIETTA, head of family in 1800 (5th District). {Ref: CI}

WHEELER, IGNATIUS, see "Bennit Wheeler (of Ignatius)" and "Mrs. Wheeler,"

q.v.
WHEELER, IGNATIUS, b. 1791, d. 1866, bur. in St. Mary's Catholic Church Cemetery in Pylesville. {Ref: TI}.
WHEELER, IGNATIUS (colonel), will probated Aug 13, 1793. {Ref: HW}
WHEELER, JACOB, insolvent on list returned by Robert Carlile for taxes due for the year 1791. {Ref: IL 31.16}
WHEELER, JOSEPH, taxpayer, 1798, Spesutia Upper Hd., 1 dwelling house, 3 inferior houses, 1 acre, $325 valuation; 5 tracts (1581 acres, 80 perches) in Spesutia Upper Hd., $3558.38 valuation, 5 slaves. {Ref: TL}
WHEELER, JOSEPH, insolvent on a list for the road tax for 1792, as returned for Robert Amoss, tax collector. {Ref: IL 13.12}
WHEELER, JOSEPH, head of family in 1800 (3rd District). {Ref: CI}
WHEELER, JOSIAH, will probated Feb 7, 1791. {Ref: HW}
WHEELER, JOSIAS, see "Edward Moore," q.v.
WHEELER, MARGARET A., husband of Henrietta Wheeler, b. 1794, d. May 5, 1860, in his 66th year, bur. in St. Ignatius Catholic Church Cemetery in Hickory. {Ref: TI}
WHEELER, MARGRET, insolvent on a list for the road tax due for 1791 in Harford Upper, Harford Lower, and Spesutia Upper as returned by Robert Amos, Jr. on Sep 18, 1793. {Ref: IL 31.18}
WHEELER, MARTHA, m. Robert Gover on Apr 18, 1787. {Ref: PR}
WHEELER, MRS., of Ignatius [sic], treated by Dr. Archer on Jul 31, 1794. {Ref: JA}
WHEELER, THOMAS, tract *The Mill Seat* surveyed between 1792 and 1796. {Ref: SB}
WHEELER, THOMAS, taxpayer, 1798, Spesutia Upper Hd., 1 dwelling house, 6 inferior houses, 1 acre, $280 valuation; 3 tracts (435 acres) in Spesutia Upper Hd., $1552.50 valuation, 4 slaves. {Ref: TL}
WHEELER, THOMAS, head of family in 1800 (3rd District). {Ref: CI}
WHITAKER, HANNAH, wife of Howard, b. Mar 10, 1799, d. Jul 28, 1875, aged 77 years, 4 months, and 18 days, bur. in William Watters Methodist Church Cemetery near Jarrettsville. {Ref: TI}
WHITAKER, HEZEKIAH, insolvent on a list for the road tax due for 1791 in Harford Upper, Harford Lower, and Spesutia Upper as returned by Robert Amos, Jr. on Sep 18, 1793. {Ref: IL 31.18}
WHITAKER, HEZEKIAH, insolvent on a list for the county tax due for 1793 in Harford Upper, Harford Lower, and Spesutia Lower Hundreds returned to the levy court by Thomas Taylor on May 28, 1794. {Ref: IL 31.12}
WHITAKER, HOWARD, see "Hannah Whitaker," q.v.
WHITAKER, ISAAC, m. Margaret Everett on Feb 11, 1798. {Ref: PR}
WHITAKER, ISAAC, head of family in 1800 (1st District). {Ref: CI}
WHITAKER, ISAAC, head of family in 1800 (4th District). {Ref: CI}
WHITAKER, JOHN S., head of family in 1800 (3rd District). {Ref: CI}
WHITAKER, JOSHUA, head of family in 1800 (3rd District). {Ref: CI}

WHITAKER, PLATT, head of family in 1800 (Havre de Grace). {Ref: CI}
WHITE, ABRAHAM, served on a Grand Jury in August, 1800. {Ref: CM}
WHITE, ABRAHAM, head of family in 1800 (4th District). {Ref: CI}
WHITE, AGNES, taxpayer, 1798, Gunpowder Lower Hd., 1 tract (116 acres) and 1 building, $317.25 valuation, no slaves. {Ref: TL}
WHITE, CASSANDRA, dau. of Robert and Mary Ann, b. Mar 17, 1800, bapt. Jul 20, 1800. {Ref: PR}
WHITE, DELIAH (DELILAH), see "William Godman," q.v.
WHITE, HUGH, tract *Hugh's Adventure* surveyed in 1799 and granted in 1805. {Ref: CB}
WHITE, JAMES, head of family in 1800 (1st District). {Ref: CI}
WHITE, JONATHAN, insolvent, Harford Lower and Spesutia Lower Hundreds, on a tax list returned by George Lyttle on Sep 21, 1791. {Ref: IL 31.20, 31.21}
WHITE, JONATHAN, insolvent on a list for the road tax due for 1791 in Harford Upper, Harford Lower, and Spesutia Upper as returned by Robert Amos, Jr. on Sep 18, 1793. {Ref: IL 31.18}
WHITE, MARY ANN, see "Robert White" and "Cassandra White," q.v.
WHITE, RICHARD, see "John Perryman," q.v.
WHITE, ROBERT, see "Cassandra White," q.v.
WHITE, ROBERT, son of Robert and Mary Ann, b. Dec 10, 1798, bapt. Decembe 26, 1798. {Ref: PR}
WHITE, ROBERT, head of family in 1800 (5th District). {Ref: CI}
WHITE, STEPHEN, head of family in 1800 (1st District). {Ref: CI}
WHITE, WILLIAM, head of family in 1800 (1st District). {Ref: CI}
WHITEFORD, ANN, head of family in 1800 (3rd District). {Ref: CI}
WHITEFORD, ANNA, will probated Nov 17, 1795. {Ref: HW}
WHITEFORD, DAVID, insolvent on list returned by Robert Carlile for taxes due for the year 1791. {Ref: IL 31.16}
WHITEFORD, DAVID, insolvent on list returned by Robert Carlile for taxes due for the year 1791. {Ref: IL 31.16}
WHITEFORD, HUGH, tracts *Hugh's Adventure* and *Whiteford's Gift* surveyed between 1792 and 1796. {Ref: SB}
WHITEFORD, HUGH, head of family in 1800 (5th District). {Ref: CI}
WHITEFORD, HUGH (tanner), appointed a Judge of Elections in the 5th District on Jul 28, 1800. {Ref: CM}
WHITEFORD, HUGH (tanner), taxpayer, 1798, Broad Creek Hd., 1 dwelling house, 3 inferior houses, 2 acres, $200 valuation; 3 tracts (277 acres, 80 perches) and 1 building (Benjamin Amos, occupant) in Broad Creek Hd., $433.12 valuation, 3 slaves. {Ref: TL}
WHITEFORD, HUGH JR., head of family in 1800 (5th District). {Ref: CI}
WHITEFORD, HUGH SR., taxpayer, 1798, Deer Creek Middle Hd., 1 dwelling house, 3 inferior houses, 2 acres, $220 valuation; 2 tracts (578 acres, 80 perches) in Deer Creek Middle Hd., $1208.47 valuation, 2 slaves; also,

taxpayer, 1 tract (536 acres) and 2 buildings in Deer Creek Middle Hd. (John McCulloch and Richard Jamison or Jammison, occupants), $1206 valuation, no slaves. {Ref: TL}

WHITEFORD, HUGH (OF HUGH), treated by Dr. Archer on Aug 3, 1793. {Ref: JA}

WHITEFORD (WHITEFORDE), JAMES, head of family in 1800 (4th District). {Ref: CI}

WHITEFORD, JOHN, taxpayer, 1798, Deer Creek Upper Hd., 2 tracts (320 acres) and 1 building, $810 valuation, no slaves. {Ref: TL}. Also see "Mrs. Park," q.v.

WHITEFORD, JOHN, insolvent on list returned by Robert Carlile for taxes due for the year 1791. {Ref: IL 31.16}

WHITEFORD, JOHN, head of family in 1800 (5th District). {Ref: CI}

WHITEFORD, MICHAEL, tract *Michael's Beginning* surveyed in 1800. {Ref: CB}

WHITEFORD, ROBERT, m. Nancy Carman (McCarman?) on Feb 2, 1796. {Ref: PR}

WHITEFORD, SAMUEL, b. May 27, 1796, d. Apr 25, 1849, bur. in Cokesbury Methodist Cemetery in Abingdon. {Ref: TI}

WHITEFORD, WILLIAM, taxpayer, 1798, Deer Creek Middle Hd., 1 dwelling house, 4 inferior houses, 2 acres, $490 valuation; 1 tract (290 acres, 120 perches) in Deer Creek Middle Hd., $562.50 valuation, 1 slave. {Ref: TL}

WHITEFORD, WILLIAM, tract *Trigon* surveyed between 1792 and 1796. {Ref: SB}

WHITEFORD, WILLIAM, head of family in 1800 (5th District). {Ref: CI}

WHITELOCK, WILLIAM ("gone"), insolvent on lists due for 1790 and 1791 "fund taxes" and county taxes in and Susquehanna Hd., as returned by Thomas Taylor. {Ref: IL 31.12, 31.02}

WHITSON, BENJAMIN, see "William Luckey's heirs," q.v.

WHITSON, BENJAMIN, taxpayer, 1798, Harford Upper Hd., 1 tract (17 acres, 80 perches) and 1 building (Enoch Rattow, occupant), $125.62 valuation, no slaves. {Ref: TL}

WHITSON, BENJAMIN, licensed retailer in August, 1797. {Ref: CC}

WHITSON, BENJAMIN, served as constable in Harford Upper Hd., 1798-1800. {Ref: CM}

WHITSON, BENJAMIN, head of family in 1800 (2nd District). {Ref: CI}

WHITSON, BURT, b. Jan 3, 1793, d. Aug 27, 1875, aged 82 years, 7 months, 3 weeks and 3 days. {Ref: Thomas Knight Bible}

WHITSON (WHISSON), DAVID, head of family in 1800 (5th District). {Ref: CI}

WHITSON, MARGARET, b. on 5th of 1st month, 1793, d. on 20th of 2nd month, 1854, aged 61 years, 1 month, and 15 days, bur. in Little Falls Quaker Cemetery in Fallston. {Ref: TI}

WHITSON (WHISSON), SAMUEL, head of family in 1800 (5th District); two men by this name in this district {Ref: CI}

WHITSON, SARAH, taxpayer, 1798, Gunpowder Upper Hd., 1 tract (92 acres) and 1 building, $297 valuation, no slaves. {Ref: TL}

WHITSON, SARAH, head of family in 1800 (3rd District). {Ref: CI}

WHITTAKER, ABRAHAM, taxpayer, 1798, Bush River Upper & Eden Hd., 1 tract (105 acres) and 1 building, $292.50 valuation, no slaves. {Ref: TL}

WHITTAKER, ISAAC, taxpayer, 1798, Spesutia Lower Hd., no dwelling house listed in this part of the tax schedule, no land listed, 2 slaves. {Ref: TL}. Also see "Benedict Edward Hall," q.v.

WHITTAKER, JOHN, bur. Aug 13, 1797, aged 4 years. {Ref: PR}

WHITTAKER, JOHN S., taxpayer, 1798, Bush River Lower Hd., 1 dwelling house, 5 inferior houses, 2 acres, $500 valuation; 5 tracts (618 acres) in Bush River Lower Hd., $2209.50 valuation, 1 slave; also, taxpayer, Bush River Lower Hd., 1 dwelling house, 3 inferior houses, 80 perches of land (Joseph Aston, occupant), $135 valuation, no slaves. {Ref: TL}

WHITTAKER, JOSHUA, taxpayer, 1798, Bush River Lower Hd., 1 dwelling house, 4 inferior houses, 1 acre and 80 perches, $305 valuation; 4 tracts (704 acres, 80 perches) in Bush River Lower Hd., $2433.94 valuation, 4 slaves. {Ref: TL}

WHITTAKER, PLATT, taxpayer, 1798, Susquehanna Hd., 1 tract (53 acres), $238.50 valuation, no slaves. {Ref: TL}

WIGFIELD, WILLIAM, insolvent on list returned for the county tax for 1791 by William Osburn in Gunpowder Lower Hd. (which listed him as a single man). {Ref: IL 31.15}

WIGGIN, RASEL E., head of family in 1800 (3rd District). {Ref: CI}

WIGGINS, JOSEPH, see "Cuthbert Warner," q.v.

WIGGINS, JOSEPH, taxpayer, 1798, Deer Creek Lower Hd., 2 tracts (107 acres, 80 perches), $427.12 valuation, no slaves. {Ref: TL}

WIGGINS, JOSEPH, head of family in 1800 (5th District). {Ref: CI}

WILDS, JOHN, treated by Dr. Archer on Sep 16, 1791; also mentioned he lived on Jos. Dallam's place. {Ref: JA}

WILES, JOHN, insolvent on a list for the county tax due for 1793 in Harford Upper, Harford Lower, and Spesutia Lower Hundreds returned to the levy court by Thomas Taylor on May 28, 1794. {Ref: IL 31.12}

WILEY, DAVID, taxpayer, 1798, Deer Creek Upper Hd., 1 dwelling house, 2 acres, $200 valuation; 1 tract (212 acres) in Deer Creek Upper Hd., $450.74 valuation, no slaves. {Ref: TL}

WILEY, DAVID, mentioned in a survey deposition on Jan 28, 1800. {Ref: JS}

WILEY, DAVID, head of family in 1800 (4th District). {Ref: CI}

WILEY, HUGH, insolvent on list returned by Robert Carlile for taxes due for the year 1791. {Ref: IL 31.16}

WILEY, HUGH, insolvent on a list for 1791 in Gunpowder Upper and Bush River Lower Hundreds, as filed by John Bond, Deputy Sheriff, on Sep 20, 1791. {Ref: IL 31.24}

WILEY, JOHN (captain), husband of Elizabeth Ann Hutchins and son of Matthew Wiley and Rebecca Nelson, and a soldier in the War of 1812, b. 1791, d. Jan 17, 1868, bur. in Bethel Presbyterian Church Cemetery at Madonna. {Ref: BC}

WILEY, MATHEW, see "John Wiley," q.v.

WILEY, MATHEW, tracts *Wolf Range*, *Hollows and Hills*, and *Rocky Point*

Enlarged surveyed between 1792 and 1797. {Ref: CB, SB}

WILEY, MATHEW, head of family in 1800 (4th District). {Ref: CI}

WILEY, MATTHEW, taxpayer, 1798, Bush River Upper & Eden Hd., 1 dwelling house, 1 inferior house, 2 acres, $110 valuation; 6 tracts (823 acres, 120 perches) in Bush River Upper & Eden Hd., $1913.20 valuation, 2 slaves. {Ref: TL}

WILEY, MATTHEW, insolvent on lists in 1791 due county taxes and road taxes in "Deer Creek Upper, Middle, and Broad Creek Hundreds" as returned by Robert Amos, Jr. {Ref: IL 31.12, 31.22}

WILEY, MATTHEW, b. 1798, d. Jan 27, 1879, aged 81, bur. in Norrisville Methodist Cemetery. {Ref: TI}

WILEY, NATHANIEL, see "Nathin Weily," q.v.

WILEY, NATHANIEL ("charge twice"), insolvent on lists in 1791 due county taxes and road taxes in "Deer Creek Upper, Middle, and Broad Creek Hundreds" as returned by Robert Amos, Jr. {Ref: IL 31.12, 31.22}

WILEY, NATHANIEL, taxpayer, 1798, Broad Creek Hd., 1 tract (100 acres) and 1 building, $217.50 valuation, no slaves. {Ref: TL}

WILEY, NATHANIEL, head of family in 1800 (5th District). {Ref: CI}

WILEY, WILLIAM, insolvent on a list for the county tax due for 1793 in Susquehanna Hd. as returned to the levy court by Thomas Taylor on May 28, 1794, who noted "put in my hands last fall." {Ref: IL 31.12}

WILGESS, JAMES, head of family in 1800 (4th District). {Ref: CI}

WILLET, PETER, see "Samuel Willet," q.v.

WILLET, SAMUEL, treated by Dr. Archer on Mar 1, 1795; also mentioned inoculation of his wife (no name given) and eight of their family: William Irwin, James Irwin, Sarah Houston, Peter Willet, Thomas Willet, John Houston, James Dickson, Benjamin Dickson, and Cassey Willey. {Ref: JA}. Also see "John Forsyth," q.v.

WILLET (WILLIT), SAMUEL, head of family in 1800 (4th District). {Ref: CI}

WILLET, THOMAS, see "Samuel Willet," q.v.

WILLEY, CASSEY, see "Samuel Willet," q.v.

WILLEY, JOHN, see "Benjamin Fleetwood," q.v.

WILLGESS, ANN, b. 1798, d. Feb 19, 1877, in her 79th year, bur. in McKendree Cemetery near Black Horse. {Ref: TI}

WILLIAMS, ANN, m. James Hamby on Jan 12, 1800. {Ref: PR}

WILLIAMS, EPHIRIM, head of family in 1800 (5th District). {Ref: CI}

WILLIAMS, EZEKIEL, head of family in 1800 (5th District). {Ref: CI}. Also see "Thomas Johnson, Esq.," q.v.

WILLIAMS, HANNAH C. (neé Stump), wife of James W., b. Jul 20, 1796. {Ref: Williams-Neilson Bible}

WILLIAMS, JAMES W., b. Oct 8, 1792. {Ref: Williams-Neilson Bible}. Also see "Hannah C. Williams," q.v.

WILLIAMS, JEREMIAH, insolvent on a list for 1791 in Gunpowder Upper and

Bush River Lower Hundreds, as filed by John Bond, Deputy Sheriff, on Sep 20, 1791 (who listed him as a single man). {Ref: IL 31.24}

WILLIAMS, JEREMIAH, insolvent on list returned by Robert Carlile for taxes due for the year 1791. {Ref: IL 31.16}

WILLIAMS, JOHN SR., taxpayer, 1798, Spesutia Lower Hd., 1 dwelling house, 1 inferior house, 44 perches and 21 sq. ft. of land, $280 valuation, no slaves. {Ref: TL}. Also see "Josias Hall," q.v.

WILLIAMS, JOHN, m. Rosanna Costen on Jun 2, 1791. {Ref: Williams-Nielson Bible}

WILLIAMS, JOHN, insolvent on a list for the road tax due for 1791 in Harford Upper, Harford Lower, and Spesutia Upper as returned by Robert Amos, Jr. on Sep 18, 1793. {Ref: IL 31.18}

WILLIAMS, JOHN, had an account at Hall's Store in December, 1791. {Ref: WH}

WILLIAMS, JOHN, insolvent on lists for county taxes due in 1792 as returned by Benjamin Preston. {Ref: IL 31.00}

WILLIAMS, JOHN, insolvent on a list due for 1791 road taxes in Susquehanna Hd., as returned by Thomas Taylor. {Ref: IL 31.02}

WILLIAMS, JOHN, insolvent, Harford Lower and Spesutia Lower Hundreds, on a tax list returned by George Lyttle on Sep 21, 1791. {Ref: IL 31.20, 31.21}

WILLIAMS, JOHN, paid Aquila Hall at Bush River Store in November, 1797 "for rent of house from January last past to January 1." {Ref: AH}

WILLIAMS, JOHN, head of family in 1800 (2nd District); three men by this name in this district. {Ref: CI}

WILLIAMS, MORRISS, head of family in 1800 (2nd District). {Ref: CI}

WILLIAMS, PETER, served as constable in Deer Creek Upper Hd., 1797. {Ref: CC, CM}

WILLIAMS, PETER, mentioned in a survey in 1799. {Ref: JS}

WILLIAMS, PETER, head of family in 1800 (4th District). {Ref: CI}

WILLIAMS, WILLIAM, taxpayer, 1798, Spesutia Lower Hd., 1 dwelling house, 44 perches and 21 sq. ft. of land, $110 valuation, no slaves. {Ref: TL}

WILLIAMS, WILLIAM, taxpayer, 1798, Broad Creek Hd., 2 tracts (86 acres) and 1 building, $83.84 valuation, no slaves. {Ref: TL}

WILLIAMS, WILLIAM, had an account at Hall's Store in January, 1791, which mentioned Jacob Greenfield. {Ref: WH}

WILLIAMS, WILLIAM, head of family in 1800 (Havre de Grace). {Ref: CI}

WILLIAMS, WILLIAM, head of family in 1800 (5th District). {Ref: CI}

WILLIAMSON, MERCY, b. 1799, d. 1867, bur. in Broad Creek Quaker Cemetery. {Ref: TI}

WILLS, SARAH, see "Joseph Clayton," q.v.

WILLSON, ANDREW, see "Andrew Wilson," q.v.

WILMER, BENJAMIN, m. Margarett Crawford on May 29, 1800. {Ref: PR}

WILMER, BENJAMIN, head of family in 1800 (Abingdon). {Ref: CI}

WILMER, CATHERINE, bur. Jan 7, 1800. {Ref: PR}

WILMER, GODFREY, head of family in 1800 (5th District). {Ref: CI}

WILMER (WILLMORE), GODFREY, insolvent on lists in 1791 due county taxes and road taxes in "Deer Creek Upper, Middle, and Broad Creek Hundreds" as returned by Robert Amos, Jr. {Ref: IL 31.12, 31.22}
WILMER, HENRY LAMBERT, son of William and Kitty, b. Mar 30, 1798, bapt. Jul 28, 1798. {Ref: PR}
WILMER, JAMES J. (reverend), head of family in 1800 (1st District). {Ref: CI}
WILMER, KITTY, see "Henry Lambert Wilmer," q.v.
WILMER, LAMBERT, taxpayer, 1798, Gunpowder Lower Hd., 1 dwelling house, 5 inferior houses, 2 acres, $400 valuation; 1 tract (198 acres) in Gunpowder Lower Hd., $941.63 valuation, 7 slaves. {Ref: TL}
WILMER, WILLIAM, see "Henry Lambert Wilmer," q.v.
WILMER, WILLIAM, granted a ferry license in August, 1797. {Ref: CC}
WILMER, WILLIAM (Baltimore Town), taxpayer, 1798, Harford Upper Hd., no dwelling house listed in this part of the tax schedule, no land listed, 1 slave. {Ref: TL}.
WILMER, WILLIAM, head of family in 1800 (1st District). {Ref: CI}
WILMONS, MRS. (Baltimore Town), or WILLIAM DURHAM, taxpayer, 1798, Gunpowder Upper Hd., 1 tract (2 acres) and 1 building (William Durham, occupant), $45 valuation, no slaves. {Ref: TL}
WILMOTT, RICHARD, bur. May 28, 1797. {Ref: PR}
WILMOTT, RICHARD, will probated Jun 13, 1797. {Ref: HW}
WILMOTT, SAMUEL, insolvent on list returned for the road tax due for 1791 by John Bull. {Ref: IL 31.14}
WILSON & STUMP, licensed retailers in March, 1795. {Ref: CC}
WILSON, ANDREW, taxpayer, 1798, Spesutia Lower Hd., 1 dwelling house, 44 perches and 21 sq. ft. of land, $450 valuation; 1 tract (44 perches, 21 sq. ft.) in Spesutia Lower Hd., $22.50 valuation, no slaves; also, taxpayer, Spesutia Lower Hd., 1 dwelling house, 1 inferior house, 44 perches and 21 sq. ft. of land (Jesse Cromwel or Cromwell, occupant), $130 valuation, no slaves. {Ref: TL}
WILSON, ANDREW, insolvent on lists returned by Robert Carlile and John Guyton (who listed him as a single man and spelled the name as "Andw. Willson") for taxes due for the year 1791. {Ref: IL 31.16, 31.19}
WILSON, ANDREW, head of family in 1800 (Havre de Grace). {Ref: CI}
WILSON, ARCHIBALD, taxpayer, 1798, Deer Creek Upper Hd., 1 dwelling house, 1 inferior house, 2 acres, $120 valuation; 1 tract (262 acres, 80 perches) in Deer Creek Upper Hd., $455.63 valuation, no slaves. {Ref: TL}
WILSON, ARCHIBALD, head of family in 1800 (5th District). {Ref: CI}
WILSON, BENJAMIN K. (Baltimore County), taxpayer, 1798, Gunpowder Upper Hd., 1 dwelling house, 3 inferior houses, 2 acres, $400 valuation; 2 tracts (481 acres, 40 perches) in Gunpowder Upper Hd., $2327.60 valuation, 7 slaves. {Ref: TL}
WILSON, CATHARINE, m. John Stricker on Mar 30, 1797. {Ref: PR}
WILSON, CHRISTOPHER, see "Mary Wilson" q.v.

WILSON, CHRISTOPHER, treated by Dr. Archer on Feb 5, 1791; also mentioned his wife (no name given). {Ref: JA}
WILSON, CHRISTOPHER, taxpayer, 1798, Deer Creek Lower Hd., 1 dwelling house, 2 inferior houses, 2 acres, $180 valuation; 2 tracts (242 acres) in Deer Creek Lower Hd., $1294.87 valuation, no slaves. {Ref: TL}
WILSON, CHRISTOPHER, b. Feb 25, 1792, d. Mar 23, 1876, bur. in Stump Family Graveyard near Craig's Corner. {Ref: TI}
WILSON, CHRISTOPHER, head of family in 1800 (5th District). {Ref: CI}
WILSON, ELIZABETH, b. Jul 10, 1797, d. Jul 15, 1829, aged 32 years and 5 days, bur. in Wilson Family Cemetery near Glenville. {Ref: TI}
WILSON, FANNY, see "James Wilson," q.v.
WILSON, FRANCES, see "Samuel Wilson," q.v.
WILSON, GEORGE H., b. 1792, d. Apr 28, 1834, bur. in Wilson Family Cemetery near Glenville. {Ref: TI}
WILSON, GRACE, see "Henry Waters," q.v.
WILSON, HENRY (Baltimore County), son of Kid Wilson, taxpayer, 1798, Gunpowder Upper Hd., 1 tract (120 acres), $540 valuation, no slaves. {Ref: TL}
WILSON, HUMPHREY, taxpayer, 1798, Bush River Lower Hd., 1 dwelling house, 2 inferior houses, 1 acre, $105 valuation; 2 tracts (90 acres) in Bush River Lower Hd., $258.75 valuation, no slaves. {Ref: TL}
WILSON, HUMPHREY, head of family in 1800 (3rd District). {Ref: CI}
WILSON, ISAAC, taxpayer, 1798, Susquehanna Hd., 1 dwelling house, 5 inferior houses, 2 acres, $200 valuation; 1 tract (30 acres) in Susquehanna Hd., $562.50 valuation, no slaves. {Ref: TL}
WILSON, JAMES, see "John Wilson" and "William Wilson," q.v.
WILSON, JAMES, son of Samuel and Fanny, b. Mar 26, 1797, bapt. Jun 9, 1797. {Ref: PR}
WILSON, JAMES ("can't be found"), insolvent on lists due for 1790 and 1791 "fund taxes" (and crossed off the 1791 road tax list) in Deer Creek Lower and Susquehanna Hundreds, as returned by Thomas Taylor. {Ref: IL 31.12}
WILSON, JAMES, head of family in 1800 (5th District). {Ref: CI}
WILSON, JOHN, see "William Wilson (of John)" and "Robert Wilson" and "Isaac Lee Webster," q.v.
WILSON, JOHN, licensed retailer in March, 1795. {Ref: CC}
WILSON, JOHN, tract *Octagon* surveyed between 1792 and 1796. {Ref: SB}
WILSON, JOHN, served as constable in Susquehanna Hd., 1798-1800. {Ref: CM}
WILSON, JOHN, insolvent on a list for the road tax for 1792, as returned for Robert Amoss, tax collector. {Ref: IL 13.12}
WILSON, JOHN, will probated Jun 11, 1793. {Ref: HW}
WILSON, JOHN, m. Norry Brady on Apr 20, 1797. {Ref: PR}
WILSON, JOHN, head of family in 1800 (3rd District); two men by this name in this district. {Ref: CI}
WILSON, JOHN (miller), insolvent on list returned by Robert Carlile for taxes due

for the year 1791, which noted "charge twice wth. one half of this property." {Ref: IL 31.16}

WILSON, JOHN (taylor), taxpayer, 1798, Susquehanna Hd., 1 tract (80 acres) and 1 building, $236.25 valuation, no slaves. {Ref: TL}

WILSON, JOHN (taylor), head of family in 1800 (2nd District). {Ref: CI}

WILSON, JOHN (weaver), treated by Dr. Archer on Jun 3, 1792; also mentioned that he lived near Bald Friar. {Ref: JA}

WILSON, JOHN (OF JAMES), insolvent on list returned for the county tax for 1791 by William Osburn in Gunpowder Lower Hundred. {Ref: IL 31.15}

WILSON, JOHN (OF JOSEPH), taxpayer, 1798, Susquehanna Hd., 2 tracts (142 acres, 120 perches), $481.78 valuation, no slaves. {Ref: TL}

WILSON, JOSEPH, charged for neglecting his duty as overseer of the public roads in 1794. {Ref: CD, March and August Terms, 1795}

WILSON, JOSEPH, taxpayer, 1798, Deer Creek Lower Hd., 1 dwelling house, 4 inferior houses, 2 acres, $300 valuation; 3 tracts (200 acres) and 1 building in Deer Creek Lower Hd., $618.75 valuation, no slaves. {Ref: TL}

WILSON, JOSEPH, head of family in 1800 (5th District). {Ref: CI}

WILSON, JOSIAS, b. Oct 22, 1794, d. Jul 26, 1870, bur. in St. Ignatius Catholic Church Cemetery in Hickory. {Ref: TI}

WILSON, KID, see "Henry Wilson," q.v.

WILSON, LYDIA, m. John Dunning on Nov 21, 1799. {Ref: PR}

WILSON, MARGARET, taxpayer, 1798, Gunpowder Upper Hd., 1 tract (126 acres) and 1 building, $306 valuation, no slaves. {Ref: TL}

WILSON, MARTHA (Miss), treated by Dr. Archer on Jul 29, 1793. {Ref: JA}

WILSON, MARTHA, taxpayer, 1798, Deer Creek Lower Hd., 1 tract (50 acres) and 1 building, $225 valuation, no slaves. {Ref: TL}

WILSON, MARY, b. 1793, d. Dec 5, 1868, bur. next to Christopher Wilson in Stump Family Graveyard near Craig's Corner. {Ref: TI}

WILSON, MARY GOVER, see "Mary Gover Wilson Bouldin," q.v.

WILSON, MICHAEL, insolvent on list returned by Robert Carlile for taxes due for the year 1791. {Ref: IL 31.16}

WILSON, MICHAEL, insolvent on a list for 1791 in Gunpowder Upper and Bush River Lower Hundreds, as filed by John Bond, Deputy Sheriff, on Sep 20, 1791 (who listed him as a single man). {Ref: IL 31.24}

WILSON, PEGGEY, head of family in 1800 (3rd District). {Ref: CI}

WILSON, PETER, insolvent on lists for the county tax and road tax due for 1791 in Deer Creek Lower Hd., as returned by Thomas Taylor on Sep 17, 1792. {Ref: IL 31.12}

WILSON, PETER, taxpayer, 1798, Deer Creek Lower Hd., 1 dwelling house, 5 inferior houses, 2 acres, $270 valuation; 1 tract (150 acres) in Deer Creek Lower Hd., $253.13 valuation, no slaves. {Ref: TL}

WILSON, PETER, head of family in 1800 (5th District). {Ref: CI}

WILSON, RACHEL, will probated Jun 11, 1793. {Ref: HW}

WILSON, RACHEL, b. Aug 15, 1795, d. Mar 10, 1883, bur. in Mount Carmel Methodist Church Cemetery in Emmorton. {Ref: TI}

WILSON, ROBERT, insolvent on a list in 1792 in Broad Creek Hd., as returned by Benjamin Preston. {Ref: IL 31.03}

WILSON, ROBERT, insolvent on lists in 1791 due county taxes and road taxes in "Deer Creek Upper, Middle, and Broad Creek Hundreds" as returned by Robert Amos, Jr. {Ref: IL 31.12, 31.22}

WILSON, ROBERT, insolvent on a list in 1792 in Broad Creek Hd., as returned by Benjamin Preston. {Ref: IL 31.03}

WILSON, ROBERT, "twist chargd" (meaning "twice charged"), insolvent on a list of the county tax due William Osborn, sheriff, for 1791, as returned by Edward Prigg on Sep 20, 1791. {Ref: IL 31.17}

WILSON, ROBERT ("run"), insolvent on a list of the county tax due William Osborn, sheriff, for 1791, as returned by Edward Prigg on Sep 20, 1791. {Ref: IL 31.17}

WILSON, ROBERT (OF JOHN), insolvent on lists in 1791 due county taxes and road taxes in "Deer Creek Upper, Middle, and Broad Creek Hundreds" as returned by Robert Amos, Jr. {Ref: IL 31.12, 31.22}

WILSON, SAMUEL, see "James Wilson" and "William Wilson (of Samuel)" and "Negro Peter," q.v.

WILSON, SAMUEL, taxpayer, 1798, Susquehanna Hd., 1 dwelling house, 6 inferior houses, 2 acres, $290 valuation; 2 tracts (546 acres) and 1 building (William Wilson, of Samuel, occupant), $2159.24 valuation, 7 slaves. {Ref: TL}

WILSON, SAMUEL, m. Frances Jones on Sep 18, 1796. {Ref: PR}

WILSON, SAMUEL, son of Samuel and Frances, b. Nov 9, 1798, bapt. Janaury 26, 1800. {Ref: PR}

WILSON, SAMUEL, insolvent on list returned by Robert Carlile for taxes due for the year 1791. {Ref: IL 31.16}

WILSON, SAMUEL, head of family in 1800 (2nd District). {Ref: CI}

WILSON, SAMUEL, head of family in 1800 (3rd District). {Ref: CI}

WILSON, SAMUEL JR., head of family in 1800 (1st District). {Ref: CI}

WILSON, SAMUEL E., b. 1797, d. Jul 21, 1856, aged 59, bur. in St. George's Episcopal Church Cemetery at Perryman. {Ref: TI}

WILSON, SARAH, taxpayer, 1798, Susquehanna Hd., 1 dwelling house, 4 inferior houses, 2 acres (William Wilson, of John, occupant), $180 valuation; 1 tract (298 acres) in Susquehanna Hd., $670.50 valuation, 1 slave. {Ref: TL}. The tax assessor listed her as "Sarah Wilson (of William)" on one list, but on another list gave her name simply as "Sarah Wilson."

WILSON, SARAH (widow of Thomas), taxpayer, 1798, Deer Creek Lower Hd., 1 dwelling house, 2 inferior houses, 2 acres, $110 valuation; 2 tracts (196 acres) in Deer Creek Lower Hd., $1089 valuation, no slaves. {Ref: TL}

WILSON, THOMAS, see "Sarah Wilson," q.v.

WILSON, WILLIAM, see "Sarah Wilson" and "Samuel Wilson," q.v.

WILSON, WILLIAM, bur. Feb 20, 1794, aged 3 years. {Ref: PR}
WILSON, WILLIAM, insolvent on lists in 1791 due county taxes and road taxes in "Deer Creek Upper, Middle, and Broad Creek Hundreds" as returned by Robert Amos, Jr. {Ref: IL 31.12, 31.22}
WILSON, WILLIAM, taxpayer, 1798, Bush River Lower Hd., 1 dwelling house, 5 inferior houses, 2 acres, $475 valuation; 2 tracts (598 acres, 40 perches) in Bush River Lower Hd., $2101.62 valuation, 9 slaves. {Ref: TL}
WILSON, WILLIAM, head of family in 1800 (1st District). {Ref: CI}
WILSON, WILLIAM (silversmith), treated by Dr. Archer on Sep 13, 1791; also mentioned a child (no name was given). {Ref: JA}
WILSON, WILLIAM (silversmith), taxpayer, 1798, Harford Upper Hd., 1 dwelling house, 2 inferior houses, 2 acres, $200 valuation; 5 tracts (398 acres) and 3 buildings (occupants: James Byard, T. McNab, and J. Fulton) in Harford Upper Hd., $1790.24 valuation, 1 slave. {Ref: TL}
WILSON, WILLIAM JR., head of family in 1800 (3rd District). {Ref: CI}
WILSON, WILLIAM (OF B.), head of family in 1800 (1st District). {Ref: CI}
WILSON, WILLIAM (OF G.), head of family in 1800 (1st District). {Ref: CI}
WILSON, WILSON (OF J.), head of family in 1800 (3rd District). {Ref: CI}
WILSON, WILLIAM (OF JAMES), served on a Grand Jury in March, 1800. {Ref: CM}
WILSON, WILLIAM (OF JAMES), served on a Grand Jury in March, 1798 and on a Petit Jury in March, 1799 {Ref: CM}
WILSON, WILLIAM (OF JOHN), treated by Dr. Archer on Jan 27, 1792; also mentioned a child (no name given). {Ref: JA}
WILSON, WILLIAM (OF S.), head of family in 1800 (1st District). {Ref: CI}
WILSON, WILLIAM (OF SAMUEL), taxpayer, 1798, no dwelling house listed in this part of the tax schedule, no land listed, 3 slaves. {Ref: TL}
WINE, THOMAS JR., insolvent on list returned by Robert Carlile for taxes due for the year 1791. {Ref: IL 31.16}
WINEMAN, JOHN, will probated Oct 13, 1795. {Ref: HW}
WINSTANLY, MARGARET, taxpayer, 1798, Gunpowder Lower Hd., no dwelling house listed in this part of the tax schedule, no land listed, 4 slaves. {Ref: TL}
WINTERS, HENRY, head of family in 1800 (2nd District). {Ref: CI}. Also see "Josias Hall," q.v.
WOOD, ANN, head of family in 1800 (2nd District). {Ref: CI}. Also see "John Wood" and "Matilda Wood," q.v.
WOOD, ELIZABETH, m. Edward Bean on May 23, 1797. {Ref: PR}
WOOD, ISAAC, head of family in 1800 (2nd District). {Ref: CI}
WOOD, JAMES, subpoenaed to the Grand Jury in August, 1797. {Ref: CC}
WOOD, JAMES, head of family in 1800 (Havre de Grace). {Ref: CI}
WOOD, JOHN, see "Amos Barnes" and "Joshua and John Wood," q.v.
WOOD, JOHN, insolvent on list returned by Robert Carlile for taxes due for the

year 1791. {Ref: IL 31.16}.

WOOD, JOHN, licensed ferry operator in March, 1795. {Ref: CC}

WOOD, JOHN, insolvent on a list for 1791 in Gunpowder Upper and Bush River Lower Hundreds, as filed by John Bond, Deputy Sheriff, on Sep 20, 1791 (who listed him as a single man). {Ref: IL 31.24}

WOOD, JOHN, licensed ordinary (tavern) in March, 1795. {Ref: CC}

WOOD, JOHN, charged for keeping a ferry without a license in 1795. {Ref: CD, August Term, 1795}

WOOD, JOHN, son of Joshua and Ann, b. Mar 17, 1798, bapt. Jul 1, 1798. {Ref: PR}

WOOD, JOHN, or AQUILA BAILEY, taxpayer, 1798, Susquehanna Hd., 1 tract (96 acres) and 1 building (Aquila Bailey, occupant), $182.25 valuation, no slaves. {Ref: TL}

WOOD, JOHN, or EWEL JONES, taxpayer, 1798, Spesutia Lower Hd., 1 dwelling house, 44 perches and 21 sq. ft. of land, $100.10 valuation, no slaves. {Ref: TL}

WOOD, JOSHUA, see "John Wood" and "Matilda Wood," q.v.

WOOD, JOSHUA, taxpayer, 1798, Spesutia Lower Hd., 1 dwelling house, 2 inferior houses, 2 acres, $100 valuation; 1 tract (128 acres) in Spesutia Lower Hd., $604.80 valuation, no slaves. {Ref: TL}

WOOD, JOSHUA, served on a Petit Jury in August, 1800. {Ref: CM}

WOOD, JOSHUA, m. Ann Osborne on May 4, 1797. {Ref: PR}

WOOD, JOSHUA, head of family in 1800 (2nd District). {Ref: CI}

WOOD, JOSHUA AND JOHN, granted a retailer's permit on Apr 25, 1797. {Ref: CC}

WOOD, MATILDA, dau. of Joshua and Ann, b. Jun 23, 1799, bapt. Sep 29, 1799. {Ref: PR}

WOOD, SUSANNA, head of family in 1800 (2nd District). {Ref: CI}

WOODLAND, JAMES, m. Sarah Collins on Dec 25, 1792. {Ref: PR}

WOODLAND, JOHN H., b. 1795, d. 1858, aged 63, bur. in Mountain Christian Church Cemetery. {Ref: TI}

WOODLAND, JONATHAN, insolvent on list returned for the county tax for 1791 by William Osburn in Gunpowder Lower Hundred. {Ref: IL 31.15}

WOOLEN, RACHEL, head of family in 1800 (1st District). {Ref: CI}

WOOLEY, JOHN, head of family in 1800 (2nd District). {Ref: CI}

WOOLLY (WOOLLEY), JOHN ("dead"), insolvent on lists due for 1790 and 1791 "fund taxes" and county taxes in Susquehanna Hd., as returned by Thomas Taylor. {Ref: IL 31.12, 31.02}

WOOLSEY, JOSEPH, insolvent on a list for the road tax for 1792, as returned for Robert Amoss, tax collector (Woolsey's name appeared on the same list twice). {Ref: IL 13.12}

WOOLSEY, JOSEPH, taxpayer, 1798, Spesutia Upper Hd., 1 dwelling house, 3 inferior houses, 1 acre, $215 valuation; 3 tracts (108 acres) in Spesutia Upper Hd., $316.13 valuation, no slaves. {Ref: TL}

WOOLSEY, JOSEPH, will probated Jan 28, 1800. {Ref: HW}

WOOLSEY, WILLIAM, head of family in 1800 (2nd District). {Ref: CI}. Also see "Josias W. Dallam," q.v.

WOOLSEY, SARAH, head of family in 1800 (3rd District). {Ref: CI}

WORSLEY, GEORGE, head of family in 1800 (3rd District). {Ref: CI}

WORTHINGTON, CHARLES, taxpayer, 1798, Deer Creek Lower Hd., 1 dwelling house, 5 inferior houses, 2 acres, $300 valuation; 2 tracts (370 acres) in Deer Creek Lower Hd., $1336.50 valuation, 3 slaves. {Ref: TL}

WORTHINGTON, ESTHER, insolvent on a list for the county tax due for 1793 in Susquehanna Hd. as returned to the levy court by Thomas Taylor on May 28, 1794, who noted "put in my hands last fall." {Ref: IL 31.12}

WORTHINGTON, JOHN, tract *Drunkard's Harbour* surveyed between 1792 and 1796. {Ref: SB}

WORTHINGTON, JOHN, taxpayer, 1798, Deer Creek Lower Hd., 1 dwelling house, 5 inferior houses, 2 acres, $615 valuation; 2 tracts (450 acres) in Deer Creek Lower Hd., $1987.12 valuation, 2 slaves. {Ref: TL}

WORTHINGTON, JOHN, head of family in 1800 (5th District). {Ref: CI}

WRIGHT, ANN, see "Harry Wright," q.v.

WRIGHT, CALEB (father), b. Sep 22, 1799, d. May 29, 1880, aged 80 years, 8 months, and 28 days, bur. in Ayres Chapel Methodist Protestant Cemetery at Dry Branch. {Ref: TI}

WRIGHT, HARRY, son of Thomas and Ann, bur. May 14, 1796, aged 3 years. {Ref: PR}

WRIGHT, JAMES, see "William Wright," q.v.

WRIGHT, JOHN, insolvent on lists in 1791 due county taxes and road taxes in "Deer Creek Upper, Middle, and Broad Creek Hundreds" as returned by Robert Amos, Jr. {Ref: IL 31.12, 31.22}

WRIGHT, JOHN, taxpayer, 1798, Bush River Upper & Eden Hd., 1 dwelling house, 1 inferior house, 2 acres, $105 valuation; 1 tract (238 acres) in Bush River Upper & Eden Hd., $401.63 valuation, 2 slaves. {Ref: TL}

WRIGHT, JOHN, taxpayer, 1798, Deer Creek Middle Hd., 1 tract (124 acres, 80 perches) and 1 building, $93.37 valuation, no slaves. {Ref: TL}

WRIGHT, JOHN, m. Rebecca Othasson (Otherson) on Aug 21, 1791. {Ref: PR}

WRIGHT, JOHN, tract *Wright's View* surveyed in 1787 and granted in 1795. {Ref: CB}

WRIGHT, REBECCA, of Joppa, bur. Nov 3, 1793, aged 35. {Ref: PR}

WRIGHT, RUTH, see "William Wright," q.v.

WRIGHT, THOMAS, see "Harry Wright," q.v.

WRIGHT, THOMAS, m. Ann Green on Mar 17, 1791. {Ref: PR}

WRIGHT, THOMAS, taxpayer, 1798, Spesutia Upper Hd., 2 tracts (163 acres) and 1 building, $407.25 valuation, 1 slave. {Ref: TL}

WRIGHT, WILLIAM, son of James and Ruth, b. Oct 1, 1799, bapt. Jan 20, 1800. {Ref: PR}

WYANT, PETER, taxpayer, 1798, Spesutia Lower Hd., 1 tract (88 perches, 42 sq. ft.), $27 valuation, no slaves. {Ref: TL}

YARLEY, RALPH, m. Ruth Barton on Dec 24, 1795. {Ref: PR}

YARLEY, REBECCA, see "John Lawrence," q.v.

YARNALL, ELIZABETH, b. 1791, d. Feb 8, 1860, aged 69, bur. in Angel Hill Cemetery in Havre de Grace. {Ref: TI}
YARNEL, STEPHEN, taxpayer, 1798, Spesutia Lower Hd., 1 dwelling house, 1 inferior house, 44 perches and 21 sq. ft. of land, $250 valuation, no slaves. {Ref: TL}
YARNELL, STEPHEN, head of family in 1800 (Havre de Grace). {Ref: CI}
YATES, ANN, head of family in 1800 (1st District). {Ref: CI}
YEALDIN, JOHN ("run"), insolvent on a list of the county tax due William Osborn, sheriff, for 1791, as returned by Edward Prigg on Sep 20, 1791. {Ref: IL 31.17}
YELDON, JOHN, insolvent on lists in 1791 due county taxes and road taxes in "Deer Creek Upper, Middle, and Broad Creek Hundreds" as returned by Robert Amos, Jr. {Ref: IL 31.12, 31.22}
YELLET (JELLET?), MORGAN, head of family in 1800 (1st District). {Ref: CI}
YELLETT, JOHN, head of family in 1800 (3rd District). {Ref: CI}
YELLOTT, JOHN, taxpayer, 1798, Bush River Lower Hd., 1 dwelling house, 9 inferior houses, 2 acres, $400 valuation; 1 tract (778 acres) and 1 building in Bush River Lower Hd., $3686.63 valuation, 2 slaves. {Ref: TL}
YOAKUM (YOCOM), CHARLES, head of family in 1800 (3rd District). {Ref: CI}. Also see "James Bell," q.v.
YOKELY, JACKSON, son of John and Sarah, b. Oct 11, 1795. {Ref: PR}
YOKELY, JOHN, head of family in 1800 (Havre de Grace). {Ref: CI}. Also see "Jackson Yokely" and "Havre de Grace Company," q.v.
YOKELY, SARAH, see "Jackson Yokely," q.v.
YORK, EDWARD, will probated Apr 16, 1793. {Ref: HW}
YORK, GEORGE, taxpayer, 1798, Gunpowder Lower Hd., 1 dwelling house, 3 inferior houses, 2 acres, $200 valuation; 4 tracts (258 acres, 80 perches) in Gunpowder Lower Hd., $609.47 valuation, 2 slaves. {Ref: TL}
YORK, GEORGE, head of family in 1800 (1st District). {Ref: CI}
YORK, JAMES, taxpayer, 1798, Gunpowder Lower Hd., no dwelling house listed in this part of the tax schedule, no land listed, 4 slaves. {Ref: TL}
YORK, JAMES, insolvent on list returned for the county tax for 1791 by William Osburn in Gunpowder Lower Hundred. {Ref: IL 31.15}
YORK, JOHN, insolvent on list returned for the county tax for 1791 by William Osburn in Gunpowder Lower Hundred. {Ref: IL 31.15}
YORK (YORKE), LYDIA, m. Robert Ingham on Apr 20, 1800. {Ref: PR}
YORK, NICHOLAS, m. Margaret Sutton on Dec 20, 1798. {Ref: PR}
YORK, NICHOLAS, head of family in 1800 (1st District). {Ref: CI}
YORK, SARAH, head of family in 1800 (1st District). {Ref: CI}
YORK, WILLIAM, taxpayer, 1798, Gunpowder Lower Hd., 1 tract (140 acres) and 1 building, $348.75 valuation, no slaves. {Ref: TL}
YORK, WILLIAM, head of family in 1800 (1st District). {Ref: CI}
YOUNG & BUCHANAN, see "Buchanan & Young," q.v.

YOUNG, ALEXANDER ("for Moses Ruth's heirs"), insolvent on a list for the road tax due for 1791 in Harford Upper, Harford Lower, and Spesutia Upper as returned by Robert Amos, Jr. on Sep 18, 1793. {Ref: IL 31.18}

YOUNG, ALEXANDER, taxpayer, 1798, Harford Upper Hd., 1 tract (188 acres) and 1 building, $356.62 valuation, 1 slave. {Ref: TL}

YOUNG, ALEXANDER, head of family in 1800 (3rd District). {Ref: CI}

YOUNG, CLARE, see "Paul Aimé Fleury," q.v.

YOUNG, GEORGE, licensed ordinary (tavern) in March, 1795 and August, 1797. {Ref: CC}

YOUNG, GEORGE, charged in 1795 with selling liquors. {Ref: CD, August Term, 1795}

YOUNG, GEORGE, insolvent on a list for 1791 in Gunpowder Upper and Bush River Lower Hundreds, as filed by John Bond, Deputy Sheriff, on Sep 20, 1791. {Ref: IL 31.24}

YOUNG, GEORGE, head of family in 1800 (Abingdon). {Ref: CI}

YOUNG, HUGH, see "Archibald Smithson" and Lee Durham," q.v.

YOUNG, HUGH, taxpayer, 1798, Spesutia Upper Hd., 1 dwelling house, 3 inferior houses, 1 acre, $150 valuation; 1 tract (188 acres) and 1 building (Benedict Hardy, occupant) in Harford Upper Hd., $337.50 valuation, 3 slaves. {Ref: TL}

YOUNG, HUGH, head of family in 1800 (3rd District). {Ref: CI}

YOUNG, MARGARET, m. James Brewer on Aug 31, 1797. {Ref: PR}

YOUNG, MR. (Philadelphia), insolvent on list returned by Robert Carlile for taxes due for the year 1791. {Ref: IL 31.16}

YOUNG, SAMUEL'S HEIRS, insolvents on list returned by Robert Carlile for taxes due for the year 1791. {Ref: IL 31.16}

YOUNG, THOMAS, insolvent on list returned by John Guyton for taxes due for the year 1791. {Ref: IL 31.19}

YOUNG, WILLIAM ("run"), insolvent on a list of the county tax due William Osborn, sheriff, for 1791, as returned by Edward Prigg on Sep 20, 1791. {Ref: IL 31.17}

YOUNG, WILLIAM, insolvent on lists in 1791 due county taxes and road taxes in "Deer Creek Upper, Middle, and Broad Creek Hundreds" as returned by Robert Amos, Jr. {Ref: IL 31.12, 31.22}

YOUNG, WILLIAM, insolvent on a list in 1792 in Broad Creek Hd., as returned by Benjamin Preston. {Ref: IL 31.03}

YOUR, FREDERICK, taxpayer, 1798, Spesutia Lower Hd., 1 tract (44 perches, 21 sq. ft.), $13.50 valuation, no slaves. {Ref: TL}

ZARA(?), THOMAS, m. Elizabeth Dulaney on Feb 4, 1798. {Ref: PR}

ZIMMERMAN, ISAAC, b. Nov 3, 1798, d. Nov 22, 1864, aged 66 years and 19 days, bur. in Cokesbury Methodist Cemetery in Abingdon. {Ref: TI}

Other Heritage Books by Henry C. Peden, Jr. :

A Closer Look at St. John's Parish Registers [Baltimore County, Maryland], 1701–1801

A Collection of Maryland Church Records

A Guide to Genealogical Research in Maryland: 5th Edition, Revised and Enlarged

Abstracts of the Ledgers and Accounts of the Bush Store and Rock Run Store, 1759–1771

Abstracts of the Orphans Court Proceedings of Harford County, 1778–1800

Abstracts of Wills, Harford County, Maryland, 1800–1805

Baltimore City [Maryland] Deaths and Burials, 1834–1840

Baltimore County, Maryland, Overseers of Roads, 1693–1793

Bastardy Cases in Baltimore County, Maryland, 1673–1783

Bastardy Cases in Harford County, Maryland, 1774–1844

Bible and Family Records of Harford County, Maryland Families: Volume V

Children of Harford County: Indentures and Guardianships, 1801–1830

Colonial Delaware Soldiers and Sailors, 1638–1776

Colonial Families of the Eastern Shore of Md.: Vols. 5, 6, 7, 8, 9, 11, 12, 13, 14, and 16

Colonial Maryland Soldiers and Sailors, 1634–1734

Dr. John Archer's First Medical Ledger, 1767–1769, Annotated Abstracts

Early Anglican Records of Cecil County

Early Harford Countians, Individuals Living in Harford Co., Md. in Its Formative Years Volume 1: A to K, Volume 2: L to Z, and Volume 3: Supplement

Harford County Taxpayers in 1870, 1872 and 1883

Harford County, Maryland Divorce Cases, 1827–1912: An Annotated Index

Heirs and Legatees of Harford County, Maryland, 1774–1802

Heirs and Legatees of Harford County, Maryland, 1802–1846

Inhabitants of Baltimore County, Maryland, 1763–1774

Inhabitants of Cecil County, Maryland, 1649–1774

Inhabitants of Harford County, Maryland, 1791–1800

Inhabitants of Kent County, Maryland, 1637–1787

Joseph A. Pennington & Co., Havre De Grace, Maryland Funeral Home Records: Volume II, 1877–1882, 1893–1900

Maryland Bible Records, Volume 1: Baltimore and Harford Counties

Maryland Bible Records, Volume 2: Baltimore and Harford Counties

Maryland Bible Records, Volume 3: Carroll County

Maryland Bible Records, Volume 4: Eastern Shore

Maryland Deponents, 1634–1799

Maryland Deponents: Volume 3, 1634–1776

Maryland Public Service Records, 1775–1783: A Compendium of Men and Women of Maryland Who Rendered Aid in Support of the American Cause against Great Britain during the Revolutionary War

Marylanders to Carolina: Migration of Marylanders to North Carolina and South Carolina prior to 1800

Marylanders to Kentucky, 1775–1825
Methodist Records of Baltimore City, Maryland: Volume 1, 1799–1829
Methodist Records of Baltimore City, Maryland: Volume 2, 1830–1839
Methodist Records of Baltimore City, Maryland: Volume 3, 1840–1850 (East City Station)
More Maryland Deponents, 1716–1799
More Marylanders to Carolina: Migration of Marylanders to North Carolina and South Carolina prior to 1800
More Marylanders to Kentucky, 1778–1828
Outpensioners of Harford County, Maryland, 1856–1896
Presbyterian Records of Baltimore City, Maryland, 1765–1840
Quaker Records of Baltimore and Harford Counties, Maryland, 1801–1825
Quaker Records of Northern Maryland, 1716–1800
Quaker Records of Southern Maryland, 1658–1800
Revolutionary Patriots of Anne Arundel County, Maryland
Revolutionary Patriots of Baltimore Town and Baltimore County, 1775–1783
Revolutionary Patriots of Calvert and St. Mary's Counties, Maryland, 1775–1783
Revolutionary Patriots of Caroline County, Maryland, 1775–1783
Revolutionary Patriots of Cecil County, Maryland
Revolutionary Patriots of Charles County, Maryland, 1775–1783
Revolutionary Patriots of Delaware, 1775–1783
Revolutionary Patriots of Dorchester County, Maryland, 1775–1783
Revolutionary Patriots of Frederick County, Maryland, 1775–1783
Revolutionary Patriots of Harford County, Maryland, 1775–1783
Revolutionary Patriots of Kent and Queen Anne's Counties
Revolutionary Patriots of Lancaster County, Pennsylvania
Revolutionary Patriots of Maryland, 1775–1783: A Supplement
Revolutionary Patriots of Maryland, 1775–1783: Second Supplement
Revolutionary Patriots of Montgomery County, Maryland, 1776–1783
Revolutionary Patriots of Prince George's County, Maryland, 1775–1783
Revolutionary Patriots of Talbot County, Maryland, 1775–1783
Revolutionary Patriots of Worcester and Somerset Counties, Maryland, 1775–1783
Revolutionary Patriots of Washington County, Maryland, 1776–1783
St. George's (Old Spesutia) Parish, Harford County, Maryland: Church and Cemetery Records, 1820–1920
St. John's and St. George's Parish Registers, 1696–1851
Survey Field Book of David and William Clark in Harford County, Maryland, 1770–1812
The Crenshaws of Kentucky, 1800–1995
The Delaware Militia in the War of 1812
Union Chapel United Methodist Church Cemetery Tombstone Inscriptions, Wilna, Harford County, Maryland

www.ingramcontent.com/pod-product-compliance
Lightning Source LLC
Chambersburg PA
CBHW050330230426
43663CB00010B/1803